CRISIS OF SOCIALISM—
Notes in Defence of a Commitment—Vol. 2

WHAT WAS BUILT AND WHAT FAILED IN THE SOVIET UNION

CRISIS OF SOCIALISM—
Notes in Defence of a Commitment—Vol. 2

WHAT WAS BUILT AND WHAT FAILED IN THE SOVIET UNION

Randhir Singh

What was Built and What Failed in the Soviet Union
Randhir Singh

First Published, 2011

Published by
AAKAR BOOKS
28 E Pocket IV, Mayur Vihar Phase I, Delhi 110 091
Phone : 011 2279 5505 Telefax : 011 2279 5641
info@aakarbooks.com; www.aakarbooks.com

Printed at
Mudrak, 30 A Patparganj, Delhi 110 091

To the memory of

CHE GUEVARA

AND

COUNTLESS KNOWN AND UNKNOWN

MARTYRS

OF THE

COMMUNIST MOVEMENT

Contents

Publisher's Note

Professor Randhir Singh's *Crisis of Socialism—Notes in Defence of a Commitment* (Royal size xiii+1087 pages) was originally published by Ajanta Books International in 2006. A response to the collapse of the Soviet Union's 'actually existing socialism' and dealing with the basic issues of the why and how of this collapse, its implications and where it leaves the question of socialism in our time, the book has been hailed as a pioneering work—'one of the most important, if not *the* most important book we have ever read', 'a key to all that is going on in our world today', 'if there were a required reading list for the U.S. left, this should be on it', and so on—and there has been a persistent demand for its argument to be available in a form easier to handle and access. Therefore, with the consent of the author and in consultation with him, we at Aakar Books have decided to publish it as a thematically reorganised 6-volume edition : Volume I (chapters 2 and 3, titled **Of Marxism and Socialism** — available in the author's **Marxism, Socialism, Indian Politics—A View from the Left**, published by us); Volume II (Prologue chapters 1, 4, 5, 6, 7, 8, 9, 11, 12, 13 and Epilogue, titled **What Was Built and What Failed in the Soviet Union**); Volume III (chapters 10, 14, 15, 16, 17, titled **The World after the Collapse of the Soviet Union**); Volume IV (chapters 18 and 19, titled **The Right Lesson and the Wrong Conclusion**); Volume V (chapter 20, titled **Contemporary Ecological Crisis—A Marxist View**); Volume VI (chapter 21 and 22, titled **Struggle for Socialism—Some Issues**).

—K.K. Saxena

In Lieu of a Biodata*

There is a certain inevitability about it. Sooner or later someone was bound to ask me, again, for my biodata.

A 'biodata', now, has been a source of perennial embarrassment for me. For I simply don't have any—I have no credentials at all so far as scholarship in the academy goes. I have only a life to speak of, lived somewhat differently, and on a generous interpretation, maybe a little more meaningfully too. Here, very sketchily, then, is some of the more public part of the story, for whatever it is worth.

Childhood, they say, is important, always and in many ways. For me it was a rather unhappy childhood, very bleak and altogether lonely. I literally lived and survived on books, which partly explains my lifelong love for and involvement with them. This childhood, possibly, also left me with a certain sensitivity for the reality of suffering in the human condition of our time.

Over this childhood loomed large the heroic figure of Bhagat Singh. A morning is still vividly etched on my mind, the morning after he and his comrades were hanged. I was detained, briefly, while passing in front of the Lahore Central Jail on my way to the Borstal primary school in the neighbourhood. The army and the police, a surging sea of humanity, tears in each eye and the

* An 'autobiographical note' written in response to a request for biodata for a felicitation volume (1988).

proud faces, portraits, of the martyrs everywhere—and the defiant unending cry of '*Inquilab zindabad*'.... That morning was born a dream which, I believe, in some form or the other, has always stayed with me. Years later I was to spend a few months, among the happiest in my life, in the 'Terrorist Ward' of this very prison with some of the surviving comrades of Bhagat Singh—Kishori Lal and others—who had in the meantime joined the Communist Party.

Thus I grew up. And in due course, on the eve of the Second World War, I again came to Lahore, this time for my studies at a college there. My father, a remarkable man in his own mixed sort of way—a brilliant physician and surgeon, profoundly religious and puritanical, with a rather deadly combination of Gandhi and Lenin in his head—sensing the turbulence inside me, his only son, had advised: 'Do anything out there but don't join some illegal organisation'. Predictably, this was the first thing I did on reaching Lahore. Even as I was searching for it, the Communist Party found me. When my father admonished me that I had shown scant regard for the family, I wrote back: 'I have found my real family'. The Communist Party meant this and very much more in those days, to many of us at least. Besides, there was a certain pride in being a Communist. I still remember from those times two lines from the poet C. Day Lewis. A question and an answer, they went something like this:

> Why do we on seeing a Red feel small?
> For he is future walking to meet us—

Fifty years later, badly buffeted, some of this pride yet remains. Incidentally, this is also how I came to Marxism—beginning with whatever Marxism was then available with the Comintern and permitted or possible in our country under the British rule.

Followed years of hectic activity in the students' movement and in the underground with the Communist Party, including entire vacations spent with workers in factories away from Lahore or with peasants in their villages.

We were good students, among the best in the University. I duly qualified for admission to the Medical College. But it was clear that the demands of ever-increasing political work would be impossible to reconcile with those of a study in medicine. I decided to shift to a 'soft' discipline. I was advised that Political Science was, possibly, the easiest subject to get your master's degree in. That, perhaps, is one reason why I could never take it seriously. Later I was to discover that it is also, possibly, the poorest among the social sciences. And if I may suggest, one important reason for its poverty as a social scientific enterprise is its near-universal ignorance of or hostility towards Marxism as social science; though, in recent years, it has not been averse to recognising Marxism as 'political thought'.

Be that as it may, in a couple of years even the pursuit of Political Science had to be given up for full-time work with the Communist Party—on the party wage of, I think, rupees twenty or twenty-five per month. For most of the next five years and more, till after the Partition, I moved around the villages and towns of Punjab, organising people and persuading them to move through their struggle for freedom towards a social revolution in this country, which I believe still needs to be made.

Soon enough I landed in prison, charged with opposition to 'the war effort' of the British Government in India. (Incidentally, it was 'the people's war' period!) Released, after nearly a year's imprisonment, I was for some time put under the usual restrictions on movement, meetings, etc. I filled up the time with a stint on the editorial staff of the Party's Punjabi weekly, *Jang-i-Azadi*. I also started work on a biography of the still active legendary revolutionary, Baba Gurmukh Singh, a fragment of which was later published as *Ghadar Heroes: A Forgotten Story of the Punjab Revolutionaries of 1914-1915* (1945). My professor at the University—he was none other than Dr. J.N. Khosla—who was rather fond of me, insisted that I use this opportunity to at least finish my studies. The Party gave me the required leave for a couple of months, and my professor provided me with the necessary certificate of attendance at classes—which partly overlapped the period I was in prison! I duly took the examination—and was soon back in the villages. (The degree, a first-class-first, was to come in very handy later in my life, at Delhi.)

Came the great popular struggles, the near-revolutionary upsurge of the mid-1940s, the haggling and compromising presided over by Imperialism, the consequent riots, the Partition, and more riots—and Indian independence. A faith had been kept *and* betrayed. Those were glorious yet ignominy-laden years, the years at once of victory and defeat for the Indian people. More specifically, it was the final success, however ambiguous, of a Gandhi and bourgeois-led politics, and a definitive failure, only temporary we thought, of our Communist politics, which included that last adventurist flourish with B.T.R. as well as the heroic struggle in Telengana. One lived, shared and fought through it all—and survived. Some of this experience, intensely personal as well as political and collective, found expression in a small collection of poems in Punjabi—*Rahan Di Dhoor* (1950). In one of these, I recorded:

> A caravan has reached the destination,
> And yet lost its way—

I never wrote poetry again—don't ask me why. Only very recently I have learnt that early in 1951 itself, a distinguished critic had, in a review, hailed my book as a truly significant piece of work. A contemporary scholar even considers it to be the best poetry of that period, though, as he told me, he had difficulty in locating its author!

It would appear that, as in scholarship, so in poetry, and may be in much else besides, I am a genuine 'might have been'.

I came to Delhi sometime after the Partition, having lived with death the previous few months and on the way. Uprooted, a refugee, everything around me, including my politics in a shambles, I sought a new foothold in life—only temporarily, I had then thought, mistakenly. I started teaching at what was then known as Camp College, an institution set up by the Punjab University at Delhi for refugee students and teachers. Even as I began to enjoy my new vocation, the Party, passing through a series of crises, both internal and external, finally opted for 'peaceful', 'parliamentary' ways. And so it came to pass, with other tangible and not-so-tangible factors contributing, that, over a period of time—during which I still edited from Delhi its theoretical monthly in Punjabi, *Sada Jug* (till removed, charged with 'individualism' and 'intellectual arrogance' for refusing to publish a BTR criticism of Mao Tse-tung), and translated *Communist Manifesto* and some more Marx into Punjabi—I just opted out of the Party. [Later, soon after its formation, I was to spend a few years in the Communist Party (Marxist)]. For me the comforting rationalisation was that in our society, after 'revolution-making', teaching perhaps holds the maximum possibilities for a non-alienated life. Here, if you want, but only if you *want*, earning your living can be at the same time living your life. So teaching it was to be for me for the rest of my life. Soon I moved from Camp College to Delhi College, where I was to teach for nearly two decades; then, after a brief stint at Jawaharlal Nehru University, in 1972 I joined Delhi University, rather late in life, as Professor of Political Theory.

Thus it is that having spent some of the best years of my life elsewhere, away from the academy, and the rest only teaching, scholarship has simply passed me by. Hence, as I said in the beginning, 'biodata' has been a perennial embarrassment —for I never managed to acquire one as a scholar. I have no research degrees and no publications except some odd entirely casual exercises, including the book, *Reason, Revolution and Political Theory*, which was an ad hoc response to a provocation in the classroom when my students wanted me to explain and defend an observation I had made. I have had no string of scholars working 'under' me, no fellowships, no research projects, no study or other academic leaves, no 'seminaring', national or international, nothing—not even a visit abroad that has come to certify any sort of achievement or standing as a scholar these days!

Recently, the Indian Council of Social Science Research, perhaps wanting to be helpful, more than once extended me invitations involving 'a foreign visit' each time. Having somehow missed or evaded every such opportunity or activity in the past, I thought, I would make a virtue of it—and declined. Besides, it seemed a bit too late in life for me to now get started on this. Perhaps I also wanted to make certain that there is at least one professor in this country who has not been abroad!

Incidentally, the Council have also very generously offered me a National Fellowship which I have accepted. So I may yet end up as a scholar, though, I am not too sure. For the subject on which I have chosen to write a brief monograph is rather away from what have been my major concerns as a teacher—Western Political Thought, Contemporary Political Theory, Marxism. My subject is so obviously *political*, not 'scholarly'; I seek an understanding of Indian politics which may, it is hoped, help towards 'a more effective people's intervention in what is happening in our country'. What is more, contrary to the current fashions in the world of Marxian scholarship, where 'orthodoxy' is almost a dirty word, and a comfortable and comforting 'post-Marxism' is abroad, I visualise my work as an exercise in Marxist orthodoxy!

If I have, most of the time, done none of the things that scholars are normally supposed to do, I have been, most of the time, busy with what they are normally supposed to keep away from. Which is as well, for life has been such fun this way. I have thus functioned, in the profession and in the university, more as a militant on the Left—even when revising the syllabi in Political Science whenever or wherever I got the opportunity to do so, or putting in a rather noisy plea on behalf of Political Theory in general and Marxism in particular on the campuses of Indian universities. As a militant, the aim was always *hegemony* and not factional or mere economic or organisational gains.

Over the years, teaching and related work apart, I have, along with many others of course, spent a great deal of time helping build up the teachers' movement, fighting for democratic rights and reforms in the university (with the vice-chancellors and against them), carrying on socialist education among workers, students and teachers, including school-teachers, running Marx Clubs and putting together Socialist Groups (one such effort, incidentally, went into the making of the Communist Party (Marxist) on Delhi University campus), writing and publishing pamphlets and bulletins, editing and producing, distributing or circulating journals like *Enquiry*, *Socialist Digest*, *The Marxist Review*, *Monthly Review*, *Science and Society* and *New Left Review*, campaigning on issues like Vietnam and Czechoslovakia, collecting signatures for Iranian students and others, mobilising and marching for all sorts of popular causes, associating with almost any radical initiative on the campus and every revolutionary venture off it, an association which on occasions, quite understandably, even ended in a love–hate relationship, —and so on. That is how it has been for the most part over nearly forty long years.

But if scholarship has passed me by, I have not done too badly as a teacher. At least that is what my students, colleagues, and many others tell me. And I am inclined to believe them; maybe because I very much want to. I have taught in the departments of History, Political Science, and occasionally Philosophy. Students have come to my classes from other disciplines and other universities, from Economics and Sociology, Law and Literature, Mathematics, even Chemistry and Physics. (Perhaps Commerce and Business Management alone have been missing!) And they have given me abundantly of their love and affection, and thoughtful appreciation. This has been compensation enough for whatever I may have missed out on not being a scholar. It was compensation enough especially during periods of bitter conflict and controversy which, inevitably, have been a persistent feature of my long career as a teacher. It is the students who first spoke of 'a legend in Delhi University'. And it is, above all, to them that I trace the real source of an observation Bertell Ollman has made, though it is also expressive of his own characteristic generosity. After his recent visit to Delhi and Jawaharlal Nehru Universities, he writes: 'If I wasn't already over 50, I would probably say something like: when I grow up I want to be a Professor like Randhir Singh.' Yes, teaching has been compensation enough.

At one of the farewell meetings at Delhi University, they questioned me on the subject of my teaching. I responded that, given the 'functional rationality' governing the organised structures of teaching and research, so that scholarly writing is increasingly addressed not to problems or publics but to peers and to prestige and preferment in the needlessly bureaucratised academic professions, and given the growing, and often mindless, specialisation in the social sciences (including Political

Science) which is resulting in a situation where fewer and fewer people are hearing more and more about less and less—given all this, a certain lack of conventional academic scholarship can even be an advantage in that it may help one see the social reality as a whole, see the wood and not just the trees, and thus address, as teacher or scholar (or activist), the real problems of society.

Incidentally, I also told them, my students and colleagues, that, for one speaking up for Marxism, my knowledge of Economics is shockingly poor and that I have always regretted it. But this lack, perhaps, has made me that much more sensitive to the humanist, philosophical, and above all political dimensions of Marxism. Of course, I added that 'politics as revolution' is central to Marxism, at least to Marxism as Karl Marx practised it. 'Marx was before all else a revolutionist', as Engels put it.

These are, however, somewhat peripheral considerations. I had gone on to suggest that its strictly academic aspects apart, my teaching could be viewed as a form of 'robinhooding' which, even as it functions within the system, yet seeks to stretch it to its limits. Of course, this 'robinhooding', this functioning as a radical or a Marxist inside the classroom, has its problems and its risks too. The most important problem is that it needs to have a certain quality about it which, above all, demands a genuine and acknowledged familiarity with the mainstream scholarship in the concerned field or discipline, one's reservations about it notwithstanding. Lacking this, it can easily degenerate into vulgar propaganda or empty moral rhetoric. As a student coming from the discipline of English literature, in a complementary reference, once said: 'One needs to have that rare combination of idealism and intelligence.' As for the risks, the most important ones concern the security of job and the denial of promotion. I must admit that I have been rather lucky in this regard. It is true that whenever interviewed, the selection committees invariably turned me down. Yet appointments came, by invitation, including the professorship in 1972, when, incidentally, seeing everyone making a beeline for Jawaharlal Nehru University, I chose instead to opt for the University of Delhi.

'Robinhooding' has its minor risks also. For me it has meant another continuous struggle from the day I started teaching. At the very outset they asked for an undertaking 'not to teach subversion'. Later, they stopped you, again and again, from teaching, or teaching a particular course. For long years, they would let me teach only Plato and not Marx—so that you learn to teach Marx via Plato, which is not only possible but is in some ways far more effective also, for obvious reasons. They can organise harassment and humiliation for you in diverse ways, with the lumpen elements in the academic community thrown in.... One has struggled against all this and *them* all along, and with a reasonable measure of success. My only regret is for the students and teachers who, now and then, had to suffer for their association with me.

There are problems and there are risks. And for better credibility here one must learn to say 'no' to at least some of the innumerable benefits, the cooptive attractions the system has to offer even to a radical teacher, though this 'no' is only of symbolic value. But the most important thing is to be aware of the limitations, even ambiguities, inherent in the very nature of 'robinhooding' as an academic exercise. And for this reason one needs to be very modest about what one is doing or achieving here.

What is more, in so far as it is an exercise *within* the system, it is always in danger of itself becoming a form of cooption into it. In fact, the more you succeed in what you are doing, the more you are also, in an important sense, lending legitimacy to the system as a whole. Such is the dialectics implicit in this mode or style of teaching. That is why its quality is of decisive importance. Even so, how effective it is in its own modest manner, and how it contributes to any qualitative departures in the system, will be determined by other, larger social forces at work in the historical process in this country. We can only recognise and try to help these in whatever way we can.

I will only add that what goes on within the discipline of Political Science or its classrooms, or, for that matter, within the universities and the social science institutes of this country, is only of marginal relevance to the problems and prospects of the Indian people's struggle for a better future. But this is where we work—teachers, students, scholars, all others. And it is axiomatic, for most of us, that we make our efforts where we work, or we shall make no effort at all.

Preface to the Original Edition

This is a book which ought to have been published more than a decade back when its argument was first delivered as a series of lectures in memory of my friend and political associate Professor Moin Shakir at Marathwada University, Aurangabad, in February 1991. The writing naturally bears its mark but the delay has taken nothing away from the validity or relevance of my argument.

I had spoken from detailed notes and was supposed to produce a written version of these lectures. Associated with the communist movement for more than half a century, and mindful of Moin Shakir's concerns, I proceeded to write them down as a militant's response to what had happened in the Soviet Union, addressed to fellow militants in the movement and radicals at large. Part of what I wrote was published from time to time in the following years. The opening section was published in 1992 itself – in *Economic and Political Weekly* – entitled 'Crisis of Socialism – Notes in Defence of a Commitment'. This piece of writing, conveying something of my 'journey through communism' since 1939, was much noticed and appreciated at home and abroad and was reproduced and translated in many places, including an Urdu journal in Pakistan. Victor G. Kiernan, the distinguished historian, called it a 'splendid article'. Paul Sweezy and Harry Magdoff were equally appreciative. Sweezy noticed its appeal for readers of *Monthly Review* – 'many of whom (perhaps too many!) have been through similar experiences in their own lives' – and wrote to me: 'I read the piece with great interest and found it both eloquent and moving. Different as our experiences have been during the last half century, there is still much we have in common in reacting to the collapse of the revolutionary experiment in which and for which we had such high hopes'. This article soon came to be viewed as a document of the times. I have included it here as a *Prologue* to the book.

I had begun writing this draft but could not, or did not, complete it for reasons as diverse as my diffidence or lack of discipline when it comes to writing things down, more pressing or welcome academic engagements or political work, bouts of personal ill-health and, not the least, the hassles and harassments of ordinary middle class existence in the corrupt, communalised and mafiaised polity that much of India is today. The most important reason, however, was my awareness that scholars far more competent than me were writing on the subject, making it unnecessary for me to carry out the essentially secondary exercise of putting on paper what I had said at Aurangabad. And I was not wrong. We have since, for example, Istvan Meszaros' magisterial *Beyond Capital – Towards a Theory of Transition,* which has been rightly assessed as 'the definitive Marxian synthesis for the present moment, the phase of what Meszaros calls capital's *structural crisis*'. I have myself found it most useful for my argument in several places while completing these notes.

I however kept speaking on the subject or its sub-themes, discussing them with radical groups, at universities and other formal and informal gatherings; and pressure kept mounting, as much from the old-generation friends of socialism as from the new crop of young activists, that I put down my argument, such as it is, in writing. A National Fellowship at the Institute of Advanced Study, Shimla, finally persuaded me to take the plunge. But for this fellowship I would have made no progress at all with the completion of these notes. But the unexplained termination of this fellowship proved equally disruptive and delayed the completion of even this first draft by a few years. The writing is therefore obviously flawed in many ways. It bears the mark of being written, or completed, in bits, over a long period of time. That its sub-themes were the subject of separate treatment or lectures at different times or places has also contributed to uneven writing and to repetition in parts of the book. The format of Notes, with its need to provide the context of and complete the specific point being made has also added to the problem of repetition. I had expected my student and friend Arvind N. Das to take care of all this, edit and put this draft in proper shape for publication. But his premature death ruled this out. I thought of doing the needful myself, but somehow this has not been possible. In the meantime, the publication of some parts in the weekly *Mainstream* had created a constituency for what I have to say. The desirability of a better organised, more rigorously argued, and linguistically felicitous book notwithstanding, there was a growing demand that these notes be published, as they are – in their present rough form, even without references or footnotes – without any further delay. S. Balwant at the Ajanta Books International having agreed to do so, I, for myself, can only seek reader's indulgence, ask her or him to bear with the many inadequacies of this publication. What is important or really matters is its basic argument.

Occasional use of my earlier writings, particularly *Reason, Revolution and Political Theory* apart, these notes are based on my necessarily limited reading, rather what I remembered of it. I have borrowed freely from other scholars, taken their analyses as my own, used their arguments, at times in their own words, and not hesitated to quote them at length for the simple reason that they had expressed the idea or the argument better than I could have done. My debts are far too many to be acknowledged. Those familiar with the literature will easily recognise them. For me it is enough to rationalise it all by saying that these are scholars who are, so to speak, more or less on my side of the barricades.

There is one debt, however, which I would still like to explicitly acknowledge – to *Monthly Review*. It is the journal I have felt most comfortable with, intellectually and politically, over the past 50 odd years, and my debt here is writ large over several important parts of this book. For Marxist theory and sustained revolutionary commitment, there has been indeed nothing else like *Monthly Review*. Its authentic Marxist analysis of developments across the globe, easily accessible yet sophisticated in the best sense of the word, its unwavering commitment to the cause of socialism and principled support to revolutionary struggles everywhere, have educated, encouraged and inspired socialists and radicals throughout the world. Paul Sweezy and Harry Magdoff have been a constant source of enlightenment and inspiration. For me personally, Paul Sweezy was and remains a model of what a Marxist intellectual should be in our times. In recent years I have much benefited from the wide-ranging work of Ellen Meiksins Wood and John Bellamy Foster's writings in the field of ecology.

The original impulse for this writing lay in my long-time interest in understanding why and how things had gone wrong with socialism in the Soviet Union. As the crisis in Soviet society deepened in the 1980s, the subject became a matter of still more serious concern. Sometime before 'the earthquake of 1989', in my Preface to Bertell Ollman's Indian publication, *Marxism: A Uncommon Introduction*, referring to Macpherson's view that 'the utility of Marxism as a means of understanding the world is increasing over time', I had added: '"the world" includes.... not only the advanced capitalist countries or India and the so-called Third World, but the world of "actually existing socialism" also, with its troublous past, continuing problems and the truly historical predicament today'. The predicament soon ended in the ignominious collapse of Soviet socialism and then of the Soviet Union itself. But no viable Marxist explanation of what had happened was forthcoming from within the country's communist movement – a situation that still persists; even the later, more informed or updated 'official' efforts are a string of eclectic propositions: 'serious mistakes'; 'wrong notions of the role of the Party and the state'; 'the failure to effect timely changes in the economy and its management'; the failure to 'deepen socialist democracy'; 'the erosion of ideological consciousness'; etc. In this situation, as the enemies' explanation – 'socialism has failed', 'Marxism is dead', etc. – held sway, there was a demand on me to share my understanding of what had happened. The opportunity to put my ideas together for the purpose came in the form of the invitation to deliver the Moin Shakir Memorial Lectures at the Marathwada University. As originally written or rather loosely expanded or updated in many places, these lectures – my 1991 response to the inter-related set of issues involved in the collapse of the Soviet Union – constitute the core of these notes, now being published as a book.

This response is obviously not an academic exercise, a work of scholarship or historical research, and it makes no claims, absolutely none, to originality. As the sub-title indicates, my response has a strong personal dimension to it. But this does not make it merely a declaration of faith. On the contrary, what is presented here is a serious argument in behalf of the continuing validity and relevance of socialism as a historically necessary, superior-to-capitalism, social order, and the need for the common people everywhere to struggle for it. Even as each chapter stands by itself, different chapters well hold together in support of this argument. The text apart, evidence in support of my argument is there, scattered all around us, only if we are willing to see; a little reason and ability to interconnect is all that is needed.

Not an academic exercise, these are notes of a militant in the movement, 'a small "C" communist', to borrow that most helpful self-description from E.P. Thompson. And the argument is addressed to fellow militants in what is left of the communist movement, to 'social democrats' who still remain socialist, to the new crop of radicals, in the social movements or outside them, struggling to find their bearings in a world now almost universally dominated by capitalism, and to all those on the Left who share my concern with the present and future of socialism. Even others may find it of interest for their present and future too is now involved in the present and future of socialism in a way that was never the case before. If anything, these notes are an exercise in theory, a plea to parties and activists on the Left for a return to the basics. Theory, it may be added, does not directly yield a political programme which is the task of political parties or activists on the ground. But it serves to provide a basic understanding of things, a perspective or sense of direction, most necessary for the success of any popular struggle. A struggling people will not get very far without some substantial knowledge of the structures they need to overthrow for their emancipation and a sense of direction in their struggle.

[The format of Notes has enabled me to deal with a wide range of issues in this regard, many of them raised with me by the concerned activists or friends on the Left. (The chapter on Marxism, for example, in its overall thrust and detail, is very much a response to an express request from two such friends, most eminent in the fields of literature and people's theatre in Punjab). The way the original lectures were planned and delivered, there is little direct reference to India, but relevance to India is more than implicit in the argument throughout these Notes. The language (English), I know, is a handicap in reaching out to a larger readership, especially at the level of activists on the ground. I hope translation will help out as has already happened with some already published parts of these Notes.]

I have already regretted the repetition that marks these Notes and offered an explanation, not justification, for it; though even a justification is not to be entirely ruled out. Gunter Grass has said: 'In politics you have to repeat and repeat, like a parrot, ideas you know to be correct and proven as such, which is exhausting – you constantly hear the echo of your own voice, and end up sounding like a parrot even to yourself. But this is evidently part of the job, if one is to find any listeners at all in a world so full of different voices', or, I may add, when the noisy voice of those currently dominant in society seeks to drown all other voices and wants us to forget what was said earlier and has been proved to be true, or forbids what needs to be said or repeated anew today.

If my experience with the sophisticates of the academy or bourgeois ideology, or plain anti-socialist propagandists, is any guide, 'crudeness and simplification' is a charge sure to be brought against my argument. I will not here argue or complain over it, but borrow from Marcuse to suggest that, at times, crudeness and simplification also help to make the truth of an idea more visible. And truth of the socialist idea is my main concern in these Notes.

During the heady, rebel days in the late sixties, students of Paris used to ask of everyone who would address them to first tell them: 'where do you speak from?' For every speaker, and for that matter every writer, inescapably speaks or writes from a particular philosophical-political standpoint and owes it to his audience or readers to publicly state it. It is only fair to acknowledge that I have written from the standpoint of Marxism, rather Marxism as I understand it. For I have no pretensions to scholarship in Marxism. I picked up some on the way and have found it useful not only in my politics or profession as a teacher but in living my life as well. This last is not just a formal statement. Knowing Marx does make a difference to what sense you make of life, how you understand, live and act in the world. 'Indeed, I must confess that Karl Marx made a man of me', is how George Bernard Shaw once put it. Marx, therefore, is important to me and, I believe, he is important to all of us, today more so than ever before, if for no other reason than this: the world we are living in is a capitalist world, more capitalist than ever before after the Soviet collapse, and Marx more than any other human being, then or now, devoted his life to explaining the reality of this world and his achievement here remains unrivalled. In one sense, this is what this book is about.

I know that the way I have been speaking or writing about Marx, about capitalism, socialism, and such other things, in recent years, not a few have thought of me as someone woefully out of sync with our post-modern, neo-liberal or globalised times, a 'dinosaur', as it were, from another age. Many will think the same of this book and will be similarly dismissive about its argument. This is nothing to be surprised at or complain about, only something that even the best among us have to endure. Paul Sweezy and Harry Magdoff had the distinction of being referred to as 'paleolithic sectarian survivals' in the aftermath of the Soviet collapse because they continued to argue and speak up for socialism. Recently we have had the example of the Nobel Laureate Gunter Grass and the world famous sociologist Pierre Bourdieu. Holding that neoliberalism is 'simply a return to the methods of nineteenth-century Manchester liberalism', 'a strange revolution that restores the past but presents itself as progressive, transforming regression itself into a form of progress', they have said: 'It does this so well that those who oppose it are made to appear regressive themselves. This is something we have both endured: we are readily treated as old-fashioned, "has-beens", "throwbacks"... "dinosaurs".' Grass and Bourdieu have nevertheless insisted that one must continue to speak up.

So have Paul Sweezy and Harry Magdoff, all along. Some years back, apropos post-Soviet capitalist triumphalism, they had written: 'Capitalism's victory settles nothing. In its global form, it encompasses ever more people and intensifies their exploitation and oppression. History shows that there have been alternatives in the past, and reason tells us that there will be others in the future.... It is of the greatest importance to keep the radical tradition alive and vigorous, ready to undergrid and give direction to the revolutionary struggles that lie ahead'. This is how I too had conceived this writing in 1991. Since then, the euphoria over 'capitalism's victory' long over, the struggles that lay ahead are already on the agenda of the peoples everywhere. This is where I locate whatever relevance this book has.

I would like to thank the Institute for Development and Communication, Chandigarh and its Director Dr. Pramod Kumar, for providing the facilities to complete and put together the manuscript of this book and getting the book itself into shape for the printer and publisher at Delhi. I can never be too thankful to Ashwini Kumar for the hard work he personally put into all this. I am grateful to my wife, Mohinder Kaur, for bearing with me as I struggled with this writing in Delhi, Shimla and Chandigarh. Not exactly thanks but something more is due to Priyaleen, Shimareet, Meenakshi Gopinath and Bertell Ollman who, each in her or his own way, sustained me in writing these Notes. The responsibility for the argument, of course, remains mine.

Randhir Singh

March 2004

Introduction

Friends have insisted that this volume needs an introduction of its own. Currently not in a position to write one, I am reproducing a few passages from the original book which will serve the purpose:

...Socialism, as Marx visualised it, is a negation of capitalism, its transcendence in the strict sense of Marxian dialectic. It is a new society different from and beyond the bourgeois society, operating according to radically different principles. In its material or economic structural basis, with the dissolution of private property and supersession of the *capitalist* market, it is 'a society of free and associated producers', 'whose social relations are subordinated to their own collective control', making them masters of their own lives and destiny; it will have put an end to that separation of the direct producers from the conditions of production which is one of the basic characteristics of capitalism. This is the essential meaning of replacing the private with 'social ownership of the means of production'—social not in a formal sense or juridically ordained but, as Marx had insisted, 'in its *real* configuration'. Unlike capitalism, which treats people as a means for the expansion, 'the self-expression', of capital—the root cause of its manifold contradictions and evils—socialism, according to Marx, is 'an association of free men, working with the means of production held in common, and expending their... labour power in full self-awareness', 'a society of civilised cooperators' in Lenin's words, for whom the means of production, indeed all human and natural resources, are simply the means for satisfying genuine human needs, for shaping an ever better and fuller life for themselves. With social ownership of the means of production and the accompanying allocation of resources by 'conscious plan', instead of by 'the blind forces' of the market as under capitalism, it becomes possible to move towards greater equality and the eventual elimination of classes, of state as coercive public power, and of invidious distinctions between manual and mental labour and between city and country. In its ultimate outcome it will also mean replacement of all money and commodity relations by direct human relations and the ending of 'the enslaving subordination of the individual to the division of labour', thus ensuring 'the all round development of the individual' and, the way we have noticed earlier, a non-alienated, 'truly rich' human life for all. As Marx himself put it: 'In place of the old bourgeois society, with its classes and class antagonisms, we shall have an association in which the free development of each is the condition for the free development of all'.

Such briefly was Marx's view of socialism—a view born of a masterful socio-historical analysis and lit up, as everything with Marx always was, by the touch of a certain *Traum* (*Dream*) that he carried with him throughout his life. A vision, it was yet rooted in real life; profoundly insightful of the present, it was remarkably prophetic about possibilities of the future, the promise as well as the threat it holds, both of which have today already become compellingly real, confronting humanity with possibly the most momentous choice of its long history: 'socialism or barbarism'. And it is this view of the situation that helps us understand how socialism was also a programme of struggle for Marx who was always disdainful of ideas and thoughts not carried into praxis...

The construction of socialism, or communist society proper, itself constitutes a long period of transition. That is how Marx visualised it... But, as we have already noticed, Marx simply refused to speculate about the economic or political organisation of this society of the future. If there is little in Marx or Engels about its economic structure beyond some very general propositions, there is even less about its political arrangements. But there is one issue concerning the politics of this transition which Marx touched upon when he spoke of the 'dictatorship of the proletariat' that needs to be considered, however briefly. It is necessary to do so, not only because of the intrinsic importance of the issue, or because there is a great deal of unnecessary confusion over it among friends and foes of socialism, but above all because whatever the problems with the 'administrative command economy', Soviet central planning or Soviet economy as a whole, properly understood, that is not in isolation from economic-structural or class issues, a decisively important source of Soviet crisis and cause of the ultimate collapse of socialism in the Soviet Union lay, not in the realm of its economy, but here in the realm of its politics, its failure to practice the 'dictatorship of the proletariat' as Marx and Engels, and following them Lenin himself visualised it.

The book on 'the State' originally planned by Marx—as the sequel to *Capital,* it was supposed to develop the political implications of Marx's global theory—never came to be written; it is an important missing dimension of his unfinished theoretical project. Marx did stipulate a *political form* (the proletarian state) under which the transition from the old to the new society was to be accomplished, a transitional state—'the political form of social emancipation', 'the Communal form of political organisation'—which was not a state in the conventional sense and destined to ultimately wither away. But the stipulation was not even sketched, let alone fully worked out. Amidst the scattered reference to the political problems of a transitional socialist society and a few general observations on the Paris Commune, what stands out is Marx's concept of the 'dictatorship of the proletariat', its untheorised status a source of much confusion and abuse among friends and foes of socialism.

Marx recognised that 'every provisional state set up after a revolution requires a dictatorship and an energetic dictatorship at that'; a proposition well testified to by the historical experience of the successful bourgeois revolutions of the past—in England in the seventeenth century (Cromwell), and in America (Washington) and France (Robespierre's Jacobins) in the eighteenth—as well as by the successful (e.g. the Bolsheviks in Russia) or failed (e.g. Social Democracy in Germany) revolutions of the twentieth century... It is important to note that Marx saw this proletarian rule as the establishment of democracy. As the *Manifesto* put it: '...the first step in the revolution of the working class is to raise the proletariat to the position of ruling class, to win the battle of democracy'.

Viewing capitalism and communism as two distinct societies, each existing in its own right, Marx saw the emerging socialist polity as a transitional period between capitalism and communism in which classes would necessarily persist for a long time, classlessness being a feature not of socialism but of the higher stage of communism. Therefore this period will be characterised by contradictions and conflicts, by class struggle in diverse spheres as its motive force right upto the achievement of a classless and stateless society. In Marx's social theory, any government in a class society, regardless of its specific form—be it democratic or any other—is essentially a dictatorship of the ruling class over the ruled classes. And this is how he visualised the 'dictatorial' state during this transitional period. For Marx, it was to be a regime which, while dictatorial towards the old exploiting classes would be the broadest kind of democracy for the workers and the people in general, much more democratic than the most liberal of bourgeois democracies, extending to the working people all those civil rights and political freedoms through whose exercise alone they could transform themselves into new human beings capable of building a new society. It is in *this* specific context that he spoke of the 'dictatorship of the proletariat'. He wrote: 'Between capitalist and communist society lies the period of the revolutionary transformation of the one into the other. There corresponds to this also a political transition period in which the state can be nothing but the revolutionary dictatorship of the proletariat'.

What needs to be understood is that this was a statement about the essential *social content*, the class character of public or political power in a transitional socialist society—just as, for Marx, even the most democratically organised bourgeois state, in this sense, is yet a 'dictatorship of the bourgeoisie'. 'Dictatorship' here is not something opposed to democracy as the conventional view has it. Laski, for example, recognised this in his own way, when apropos this concept he wrote: '...neither for Marx nor for Engels was it an anti-thesis of democracy; for them, its anti-thesis was the "dictatorship of the bourgeoisie" which, as they believed, obtained in every country, even when concealed by formally democratic political institutions, so long as the ownership of the means of production remained in middle class (*sic*) hands'.

In other words, Marx's was not a statement about form of government, its institutional structure or organisation, its parties or politics, or for that matter any specific 'dictatorial' policies to be pursued. Marx had in fact warned against confusing the 'state' with the 'government machine'. As the absolute political power of the proletariat, exercised by it as a class for self-emancipation and emancipation of the people in general, the 'dictatorship of the proletariat' had no implications at all of a totalitarian dictatorship of a party, group, or individual, such as it ultimately came to be in the Soviet Union and elsewhere in the regimes of 'actually existing socialism'. In fact, it was visualised as so devoid of repression or domination in relation to 'the immediate producers' and the overwhelming majority of the people, that it was to be, in Engels' celebrated phrase, 'no longer a state in the proper sense of the term'; as 'a *state*', according to Marx and Engels, it was to begin to wither away as soon as it was established.

Nevertheless, 'dictatorship of the proletariat', has remained one of the most misunderstood and mispracticed concepts in Marxism. Marx never elaborated upon it, perhaps he never found it necessary to do so. In any case he never had the time to do so. As we have already noticed, his proposed work on 'the State' never came to be written and much of what he said or wrote on the state, politics, party, democracy, etc. never came to be theorised by him. But he was always deeply suspicious of state power. He opposed 'setting the state "free"... as in Russia', and wrote: 'Freedom consists in converting the state from an organ superimposed upon society into one completely subordinate to it, and even today forms of the state are more or less free to the extent that they restrict the "freedom of the state".' I don't need to enter into any detailed discussion of this subject here. For my purpose it would suffice to draw attention to one *decisive* expression of Marx's view of the 'dictatorship of the proletariat' in his brief comment on the Paris Commune of 1871. He regards the Parisian Communards—Marx's 'heaven-stormers'—as the pioneers of such 'dictatorship'. Marx saw the Paris Commune, despite its limitations or inadequacies and short duration, as a workers' state in action, an example of the *rule* (or 'dictatorship') of the proletariat. Describing it as a self-liberating 'working-class government', he assessed it as 'the political form at last discovered under which to work out the economic emancipation of Labour'. Marx noticed the extraordinary advance in *democracy* which Commune represented both as a form of government and in the measures it carried out. Commune, wrote Marx, 'supplied the Republic with the basis of really democratic institutions', though he recognised, especially in view of the brief duration of the Commune, that its measures 'could but betoken the tendency of a government of the people by the people'.

The Commune, elected in a general election, destroyed the old military-bureaucratic bourgeois state apparatus, suppressed parliamentarism, and substituted it by people more directly governing themselves with binding mandates (*mandat imperatif*) on delegates to representative bodies; it 'got rid of the standing army and the police', replacing one with people at arms and turning the other into a responsible, 'at all times revocable agent of the Commune'; it abolished bureaucracy and put in its place an elected civil service, all its officials—administrative, judicial, educational and any other—to be elected on the basis of universal suffrage and subject to recall at any time at the demand of the electorate, their salaries at par with the wages of the working people; it divested the police and clergy of their political influence, and so on. Its view of national organisation, which Commune had no time to develop, involved decentralised democratic structures so that, in Marx's words, 'the unity of the nation was... to become a reality by the destruction of the State power which claimed to be the embodiment of that unity, independent of, and superior to, the nation itself, from which it was but a parasitic excrescence'.

Crucially important in the measures of the Commune, which covered the Commune members themselves, was the concern for effective safeguards or barriers against corruption, place-hunting, coercion or arrogance of the state officials and their own deputies, making difficult, if not impossible, the emergence of any privileged bureaucratic elite. As if half-aware of the bureaucratic threat that could arise in the future, Marx and Engels were at great pains to underline the measures that the Commune had undertaken to guarantee a socialist revolution against the recrudescence of bureaucratic power. Even as Marx praised the Communards for their 'Revolution against the *state* itself', and welcomed the 'amputation' of the 'merely repressive organs of the old governmental power' (the army and the police) and the return of the state's 'legitimate functions' to the democratically elected and modestly compensated, responsible agents of society, he wrote: "Nothing could be more foreign to the spirit of the Commune than to supersede universal suffrage by hierarchic investiture'. There was no room here for any *nomenklatura* or bureaucratic rule which became the dominant feature of government and politics in the erstwhile Soviet Union. The Parisian workers sought to make impossible *ex ante* the rise of a special caste (bureaucratic or any other) standing above and opposed to the people that was later the source of so-called 'deviations' and 'distortions' and so much else that went so grievously wrong in the Soviet Union. Severely critical of the 'statist superstition' of the German Social Democrats, it was precisely this significance of the Commune that Engels underlined when he approvingly wrote of the measures taken by it 'against transformation of the state and the organs of the state from servants of society into masters of society—an inevitable transformation in all previous states'. For Marx and Engels, the Paris Commune was and remained the model of a 'dictatorship of the proletariat' as they had visualised it. Two decades after the Commune arose and was soon drowned in blood by a most ruthless bourgeois counter-revolution, in a sharp rejoinder to the rather shallow critics of their concept, Engels wrote: 'Of late, the social-democratic philistine has once more been filled with the wholesome terror at the words: Dictatorship of the Proletariat. Well and good, gentlemen, do you want to know what this dictatorship looks like? Look at the Paris Commune. That was the Dictatorship of the Proletariat.' It needs to be specifically noted that Marx not only saw the extraordinarily democratic Paris Commune as the model of 'the dictatorship of the proletariat', a 'thoroughly expansive' political form for a socialist transition, but, insofar as class struggle continues throughout the *transitional* period, Marx also viewed it as affording 'the rational medium in which that class struggle can run through its different phases in the most rational and humane way.'

It will not be out of place to mention that Lenin understood 'dictatorship of the proletariat' exactly as Marx and Engels did. He argued for it in his *State and Revolution* and sought to practice it—'Soviets' being its new historical form—in the immediate aftermath of the revolution he led in Russia; though it all withered away and perished too early and too fast. The how and why of it we shall explore later. The fact to be immediately noticed is that 'dictatorship of the proletariat' soon become 'the great absence' in the historical experiment of 'building socialism' in the Soviet Union. This is what R. Khasbulatov, himself a servant become master, and a latter-day accomplice in the final decay, degeneration and collapse of the Soviet experiment, in an earlier, honest moment wrote: 'If the Soviets had really become the organs of power, if the regime of the dictatorship of the proletariat and peasantry had really been organised, Stalinism would never have existed... The paradox of socialism consists in the fact that the concept itself of the proletarian dictatorship was discredited without ever being applied in the USSR'. That this observation betrays rank ignorance of Lenin and the early Soviet history only shows up the kind of leadership Stalinism ultimately spawned in the Soviet Union.

★

I would like to conclude this rather scrappy account of how Marx and Engels thought about socialism, the values and ideals which, according to them, socialism embodied, with a brief discussion of an implication of this account for what was built and has now collapsed as socialism in the Soviet Union. The implication is that if such indeed was socialism as visualised in classical Marxism, such its economic and political values and ethical-aesthetic ideals, then it can be legitimately argued that what was built in the Soviet Union was not socialism; and this has raised an issue that needs to be noticed and taken care of, before I proceed with my discussion of more substantive themes.

That what was built in the Soviet Union, or later imposed or more or less copied in East Europe, was not socialism as Karl Marx or the classical Marxist tradition had visualised it, was common knowledge for a pretty long time, except in official communist circles; it had compelled even its friendly critics, willing to give it every benefit of doubt, to speak of it as only 'actually existing socialism', though 'formerly existing socialism' would be, perhaps, more appropriate now. Scholars had argued about it previously and now any number are busy pointing out that it 'ran counter to what socialism has meant to all shades of socialist thought', that it was indeed not socialism at all. We are informed that it was 'not socialism as historically understood, for example, by Marx, involving a democratically controlled economy and a state subordinate to society', that it was 'very far from socialism—a form of society where the associated producers are the masters of the process of production, a society based on the largest economic, social, and political democracy, a commonwealth liberated from all class, ethnic, and gender exploitation and oppression', that it was 'at best an authoritarian welfare state', or something 'closer to what Marx dismisses as "crude communism"', and so on.

The failure of 'actually existing socialism', really a non-socialism according to these critics, has therefore, most naturally, given rise to a response which needs to be taken note of, for it is widely shared on the Left including knowledgeable scholars and even activists, who would still defend and speak up for socialism. It has been argued that since the 'socialism' in question had little or no relation to the real thing, the socialism of Karl Marx, but was only propagated and sought to be legitimised as such by the powers that be, the question of failure of socialism simply does not arise; to talk either of failure or 'crisis' of socialism is, strictly speaking, irrelevant. Far too many on the Left, especially Marxologists among them, have been opting for this response. We are told that 'socialism has not failed because it has not been tried', that socialism 'was not tried—or rather, socialism as the attempt by the majority to establish democratic control of economic life was not tried, only control of society by the State bureaucracy was', that 'what never even existed cannot be said to have failed', that 'one cannot die before being born', that 'Communism is not dead, it is not yet born—the same applies to socialism', that to speak of failure 'is a grotesque misrepresentation of facts, because socialism was not even started... not even the first steps were taken', that 'only what has lived can die, that socialism therefore could never die in the East', and so on. And if this response is deemed a sufficient answer to the 'enemies' of socialism who incessantly speak of its 'failure' or 'crisis', its 'friends', the 'official' communists and others, who have complained of 'dismantling' of socialism in the erstwhile Soviet Union and Eastern Europe, are told that it is not possible to dismantle something which does not exist. And that is that.

It is significant that the overwhelming majority of theoretical contributions sustaining this position have been made in the developed capitalist countries, which, however, is not to deny that such argumentation has its validity, it certainly has an empirical basis and theoretical coherence. Nevertheless, for socialists it is a very weak response. Whatever its attraction as an easily scored propaganda point for the academically inclined, it cannot be acceptable to those who take their socialism seriously or are actively involved with the movement, because of the theoretical as well as practical implications of this response. Since 'socialism' in the Soviet Union was not really socialism—an ideal still to be realised—and since it had nothing to do with genuine Marxism, the implications are that its record or failure poses no particular problems for socialists, least of all for those of Marxist persuasion, that the collapse in the Soviet Union does not in any way compromise the socialist cause and therefore there is no need or obligation on the part of such believers in genuine socialism to undertake a rigorously critical reappraisal of this truly agonising historical experience. They only need, as so often in the past, to differentiate themselves and take their distance from this 'fraudulent' socialism and proclaim that, despite everything, real or true socialism is alive and well and as destined to triumph as ever—an argument or political position which, bypassing all the difficult demands of the objective situation and revolutionary praxis, generally ends up either constructing 'visions' of 'true socialism' and appealing in its name, or persuading people of the historical necessity, indeed inevitability, of socialism.

The validity of this argument, such as it is, does not save it from being an argument of utter political poverty. If ever there was an argument that preaches only to the already persuaded, this is it. Those who have experienced or rather suffered this 'socialism', far from getting converted now, will not find even consolation in being informed that it was not socialism at all, certainly not real socialism—they have already turned, for the time being at least, to Yeltsins and their ilk in their midst, to the magic of the capitalist market and authoritarianism of its 'democratic politics', while those in opposition would rather be damned than speak again of socialism, 'real' or any other. For others, elsewhere, this argument amounts to a self-defeating denial of a historic experiment carried out in the name of socialism, simply because it did not take place strictly according to the book. An evasion of the real and difficult issues raised by the failure of this experiment, it is a politically impotent response, and plain bad tactics for those genuinely committed to the cause of socialism. It is wholly unrealistic to believe that the damage done to the idea of socialism by what has happened in the erstwhile Soviet Union can be wished away by abstract theoretical exercises or faithful assertions on behalf of real socialism, its inevitability or invincibility.

It would simply not do for Marxists or serious socialists to disclaim any association with or responsibility either for the October Revolution or the state and socialism which issued from it. The current appellation, usage and vocabulary of socialism, as of Marxism as revolutionary theory and practice, is so deeply embedded in this historical context that the attempts to change or bypass it, to escape its contemporary historical predicament through its denial or abstract exercises in Marxism or socialism, are not only sterile, they could even be harmful to the struggle for socialism in the coming years. The October Revolution and most other revolutions which followed in *its* wake were genuine socialist revolutions with deep roots in an international movement going back to mid-nineteenth century and they were won with the support of tens of millions of people, won and defended by the heroism and sacrifice, dedication and ingenuity of millions of communist or socialist men and women the world over. Parties which led the revolutionary struggles successfully, by and large did so under the banner of Marxism and their leaders were for the most part seasoned Marxists whose mission in life was to overthrow an unjust and exploitative system and to replace it with one based on the principles of socialism as expounded by Marx and Engels and their followers in the late nineteenth and early twentieth centuries. And these leaders, Lenin onwards, appealed to Marx, sought to organise support for their new regimes on the basis that they were Marxists, and at the subjective level, no matter how mistaken, believed that, in a difficult and unexpected situation, they acted in furtherance of the socialist cause as they understood it; and for the most part, at least till recently, their political credentials were accepted by a powerful, even if somewhat stagnant international movement. These leaders had every intention of creating a new social system along the lines suggested, though never elaborated, by Marx in the nineteenth century. And the concerned regimes, again under Marxist inspiration, regardless of the nature of what ultimately came to be built, were explicitly committed to building socialist societies, which was well expressed in their initial and at least some of the later achievements, in economic development as well as in matters of job security, education and healthcare, of social security in general and a cultured life for all. Whatever their success or failure in implementing the classical Marxist or socialist programme, their effort certainly implicated, in some degree, any politics that chooses public ownership and planning as a means and popular welfare as a goal. They certainly came to provide an alternative model of development with impressive achievements to its credit and several features of great appeal to the masses of impoverished and exploited people in what has come to be described as the third world. It is through the October Revolution and the establishment of a state of the Soviets that the crucially important message of Marxism and militant revolutionary struggle reached the vast masses of these poor people in the periphery of the global capitalist system. And like so many others the world over, they identified the countries of 'actually existing socialism' as socialist and Marxist. It is as such that these countries were admired and condemned, vigorously defended and viciously attacked, for seventy odd years in case of the Soviet Union. These years had witnessed a global spread of communist movement and socialist ideas, producing organisations, parties, and individuals by their tens of millions all over the world who identified with the Soviet Union—they looked to it as supporters, as forgiving or gullible friends, as apologists—and did so as socialists or communists. Many of them supported it as Marxists, just as not a few criticised and opposed it, even died for their opposition, as Marxists (which, incidentally, means that not all Marxists and *a fortiori* not all socialists are answerable for the terrible Soviet deformation of the socialist idea). This support and opposition in the name of Marxism implicates the Marxist doctrine in what has happened in the Soviet Union in a manner that no one who cares for Marxism or socialism can afford to ignore. To deny or refuse to see all this—the authentic revolutionary socialist origins and Marxist associations of the Soviet Union, its complex and turbulent, at times heroic history in pursuit of the socialist idea, its professed aims and ambitions, the not inconsiderable initial success and some at least of later achievements, its place in the world socialist movement over these seventy odd years, etc. and the implications of it all for the future of socialism, for the struggle for socialism that continues—is not only falsification of history, it is also bad socialist politics. However we assess it, the Soviet experience is part of our heritage as socialists. We cannot simply deny or disown it, or cast it away so easily. If it is a dream gone sour, it was yet our dream.

The assessments of course vary and the debate will continue for long. There are those, the old 'faithfuls', who till the end believed that what obtained in the Soviet Union was indeed socialism, albeit with some 'deviations' and 'distortions'. To many others it embodied, in however distorted a form, a genuine and at least partially successful effort to build a socialist society, which had a great deal to be said for it and was worth defending. As a somewhat sympathetic summing up we have Isaac Deutscher's suggestive epigram: 'Socialism in a backward country is backward socialism', though it must not be interpreted too literally. Not a few have seen it, with Stefan Heym, as 'pioneering socialism', humankind's first experiment with socialism as society of the future. That it was some kind of capitalism is a mistaken view, but there is no denying that in terms of the classical socialist tradition, it was anything but socialism. Certainly, it was not our model—not so, at least for a pretty long time. But as the argument goes on about what was built as socialism in the Soviet Union, there is no escaping the fact that its spectacularly ignominious overnight collapse will haunt any socialist project in the world for decades to come and continue to demand that we understand what has happened and come to terms with it, for our own sake and even more to be able to explain to the skeptical why and how the society we continue to struggle for will be different from the recently demised 'socialism'...

Surely it does not help to be told that the October Revolution was premature, or that it was no socialist revolution, or that the socialism just demised was just a non-socialism and no more. Nor should critical reflection content itself with simply denouncing its evident denial of democracy, bureaucratic degeneration and loss of ideals, or with the making of better visions of the socialism of the future. It will also not do to explain the failure in the Soviet Union as the fault of evil men, blaming it all on Stalin in the first place and secondarily on a corrupted *nomenklatura*, with due roles assigned to Khrushchevs, Brezhnevs and Gorbachevs of the Soviet Communist Party. And certainly it is neither desirable nor possible to pass by the experience of 'historical communism', as it has been called, as something without significance to those who would today seek to construct a socialist alternative to capitalism. What is needed is a properly serious Marxist analysis of what went wrong; its absence can only harm the socialist cause—not only will the much-needed lessons remain unlearnt, the interpretations of the enemies of socialism will go uncontested and gain acceptability. In fact, the socialist left will have no credibility unless it comes to terms with what has happened, with honesty and clarity, and above all, courage this demands. It has to be a ruthlessly critical analysis of why socialist revolutions of our times have ended the way they have, in new forms of class society, or a 'socialism' that has collapsed so ignominiously, an analysis which does not avoid difficult or painful issues by idealistically defining them out of socialism.

There has to be an honest appraisal not only of errors, which generally do have a certain qualified admissibility, but also crimes committed in the name of socialism, which can never be condoned. The distinction is important. Errors, it has been pointed out, 'are misjudgements in the service of our agreed-upon program, unnecessary compromises or pompous refusals to compromise, faulty estimates of our progress and the enemy's weakness, passive acceptance of capitalist ways of doing things in the hope that they could be domesticated to socialist ends'. Crimes, on the other hand, 'are violations of socialist democracy, socialist legality, revolutionary humaneness, and that fierce honesty which is basic to the commitment to liberate and mobilise the collective intelligence of all the oppressed. Crimes are the debasement of Marxism to apologetics, the use of force to settle disagreements within the revolution, the covering up of corruption'. There is, of course, truth in the claim that the criminal episodes of Soviet history are not socialism but distortions of socialism. But it is well to remember that not socialism but *distortions* of socialism, they are yet distortions *of* socialism, which compels us to think of what in our theory and practice made socialism vulnerable to crimes.

Only a bold confrontation with history in Marxist fashion, a willingness to 'think as Marx would have thought in (our) place' can enable us to make fresh beginnings in our struggle and be equal to the tasks of the day: to defend the gains of more than 150 years' struggle for socialism, acknowledge the reality of the current defeat in a responsible, self-critical manner, evaluate the reasons for it, draw the necessary lessons and regroup and prepare for the next wave of revolutionary upsurge, which may be sooner than most people, friends and foes of socialism, think. It is an agenda for years and even decades and yet an agenda for here and now.*

* I may here also draw attention to the volume *Struggle for Socialism–Some Issues*, where the first issue discussed deals with the need for a balanced assessment of the failed Soviet experiment—'What was built and what failed as socialism in the Soviet Union'—which does not 'throw any baby out with the bathwater.'

PROLOGUE *

The theoretical conclusions of the Communists are in no way based on the ideas and principles that have been invented or discovered by this or that would be universal reformer.

They merely express, in general terms, actual relations springing from an existing class struggle, from a historical movement going on under our very eyes.

Communist Manifesto

Socialism is young.....
The road is long and in part unknown....
To build communism, a new man must be created simultaneously with the material base.

Che Guevara

It is only when people get to the point of seeing that the price of contradictions is yet more intolerable than the price of ending them that they acquire the nerve to go all the way through to a consistent socialist politics.....
Once you have decided for revolutionary socialism, not because it is quicker or more exciting, but because no other way is possible, then you can even experience defeat, temporary defeat, such as a socialist of my generation has known, without any loss of commitment.

Raymond Williams

These are tragic, indeed traumatic times for those who still take their socialism seriously....

* First published in 1992

A long time ago, even as the modern socialist tradition, inspired above all by Marxism, had just established itself, someone as little suspect of sympathy for any sort of socialism as Ludwig Von Mises described it as the 'most powerful reform movement that history has ever known, the first ideological trend not limited to a section of mankind but supported by people of all races, nations, religions and civilizations'. More recently, even as *The Times* too noticed the truly global reach of the ideas of Karl Marx – 'there is no country in which at this moment someone is not discussing Marx's ideas', etc. – Peter Laslett, very far from being a Marxist, pointed out that the teachings of Marx 'have proved more successful than any other set of doctrines which the West has brought forth, swifter and more final in its conquest of the world than ever Christianity was'. In the meantime, even so hostile a critic as Leopold Schwarzschild seemed to sum it all up when he wrote: 'If a name had to be found for the age in which we live, we might safely call it the Marxian era'. And now!....

Many of us had known, even from afar and without ever visiting there, for nearly four decades if not more, that it was bad, in fact pretty bad, in the countries of 'the socialist world' as it was called. We had come to recognize these regimes as, at best, aberrant or deformed versions of socialism as Karl Marx and the classical Marxist tradition had visualized it. Taking our distance, as disappointed but still friendly critics, always hopeful of a change for the better, we had learnt to speak of them, in Rudolf Bahro's more truthful though somewhat ambiguous expression, as countries of 'actually existing socialism', whose crisis, as expressed in domestic and foreign policies, was increasingly seen by us as a negative factor in the development of world revolutionary process, in many ways more decisive for the future of socialism than 'the general crisis of capitalism' that Marxists conventionally, though quite rightly, focused upon. Yes, it was pretty bad there, but it is only fair to confess that even the most knowledgeable amongst us did not know it was *that* bad! For now even the 'actually existing' has ceased to exist in the Soviet Union and Eastern Europe and is in real crisis elsewhere. As we move into the last decade of the twentieth century, the wreckage around us is already sufficiently comprehensive not only to eliminate the so-called 'Marxist-Leninist' model of socialism as an alternative to capitalism, it has compromised the very idea of socialism, in every one of its forms, Marxist or non-Marxist, be it Trotskyism or Maoism, or reform-Communism, or social democracy, or even whatever anti-Communist socialism is still around in India and elsewhere. The deluge of disenchantment has in fact put a question mark not only on the possibility of any escape from capitalism but on the validity of Marxism itself as the theory and practice of the struggle for human emancipation in our times. As I look back upon my more than fifty years of hopeful involvement with the 'idea of communism', and as today the memory of the heroic struggles of generations of communists and common people for a cause recedes and the reality of broken illusions, wasted lives and bloody sacrifices behind a shattered political model grows on you, one begins to doubt, if only for a while, whether hope will ever again create 'from its own wreck the thing it contemplates'! One almost instinctively turns, once again, to Goethe's injunction, so apt for our troublous times: 'One must from time to time repeat what one believes in, proclaim what one agrees with and what one condemns'.

For me it all began in 1939....

Global capitalism, as imperialism or its fascist variant, driven by the logic of its contradictions, was inexorably moving towards yet another world war, in the process seeking desperately to destroy, as it had sought all along, the barely two-decades old Soviet Union, still struggling to survive and 'build socialism', no matter how one qualified this pioneering effort, then or now. In India, the struggle for freedom was poised to enter its most critical phase and, despite a certain well-justified distrust of its leadership, there was a hopeful turbulence in the atmosphere around us. For me, personally, Bhagat Singh's had been a compelling presence since childhood, and now there was the immediate inspiration of the still-fresh saga of the struggle in Spain – the International Brigades, the finest of writers, poets and artists, across the continents, taking sides and committing themselves to political action against 'war and fascism', their manifestos speaking the language of 'the revolutionary cause', 'proletarian revolution' and 'the destruction of capitalism', 'the establishment of a workers' government', and so on. And most important of all that fired our radical imagination in that age, that which held together and gave its essential meaning to our idealism, was the continuing reality of Lenin's revolution in Russia – John Reed's *Ten Days That Shook The World* – and its cause now embodied in the Soviet Union; yes, the fabled and forbidden 'land of the Soviets', so distant and yet always so near, the centre of a world-wide fraternity of revolutionaries and the bearer of the promise of *other* possibilities for the oppressed and exploited everywhere, indeed, at last, of a full and truly rich life for the entire humankind. One almost inevitably moved left, to revolutionary socialism which was then gathering unto itself, in Punjab and elsewhere in the country, virtually all the streams of modern India's revolutionary tradition – the legendary survivors of Kartar Singh Sarabha's Ghadarite uprising, old revolutionaries in exile or jails of India and the Andamans, comrades of Bhagat Singh and the battle-scarred fighters from different strands of 'revolutionary terrorism', leaders and activists of the militant peasant and working class movements, left-wing socialists and congressmen, radical young students, poets, artists and intellectuals, and many more. This is how I recorded it in an autobiographical note some years ago:

> And in due course, on the eve of the Second World War, I again came to Lahore, this time for my studies at a college there. My father, a remarkable man in his own mixed sort of way – a brilliant physician and surgeon, profoundly religious and puritanical, with a rather deadly combination of Gandhi and Lenin in his head – sensing the turbulence inside me, his only son, had advised: 'Do anything out there, but don't join some illegal organisation'. Predictably, this was the first thing I did on reaching Lahore. Even as I was searching for it, the Communist Party found me. When my father admonished me that I had shown scant regard for the family, I wrote back: 'I have found my real family'. The Communist Party meant this and very much more in those days, to many of us at least. Besides, there was a certain pride in being a Communist. I still remember from those early years two lines from the poet

> C. Day Lewis. A question and an answer, they went something like this:
>
> Why do we on seeing a Red feel small?
> For he is future walking to meet us.
>
> Fifty years later, badly buffeted, some of this pride yet remains. Incidentally, this is also how I came to Marxism – beginning with whatever Marxism was then available with the Comintern and permitted or possible in our country under the British rule.

In fact, we had very little of Marx and Engels, or for that matter Lenin, available to us in those days, and a governmental ban on libraries at Lahore in this regard took care of much of even this little. 'Party literature' apart, Palme Dutt's *India Today* and Stalinist 'summing up' of Leninism in *History of the Communist Party of the Soviet Union (Bolshevik) – Short Course*, in illegally printed or cyclostyled editions, were the staple of our education in Marxism. Sympathetic writing on Soviet Union was not easy to reach either; though later, with Hitler's invasion and the heroic Soviet resistance to Fascism as the war progressed, a great deal more of the Soviet Union became available. There was the monumental work of Sidney and Beatrice Webb, *Soviet Communism: A New Civilisation* – 'In all social history, there has been no such a colossal and so exciting an experiment', they had written. And we noticed that within two years they had withdrawn the interrogation mark they had put against the title in the first edition, published in 1935. The Fabian bias of the Webbs notwithstanding – a certain identification of socialism with statification – their exceptionally well argued and documented writing was at once a recognition of and a tribute to the truly astonishing achievement of the Soviet people and communists in building what they had built – built, I may add, with Stalin and despite Stalin. This achievement retains its rich significance for all socialist experiments of the future. Webbs apart, there was Dean of Canterbury's *The Socialist Sixth of the World*, Joshua Kunitz's *Dawn Over Samarkand*, reports by Nehru and Tagore and so much else on the Soviet Union that we mostly avidly imbibed. So many with impeccable credentials had visited there and assured us with Lincoln Steffens: 'I have been over into the future and it works'. 'A land where utopia was becoming reality', Andre Gide had said – that he later turned a bitter critic was, for us, part of a different story. I can still recall the argument which Eugene Vargas' *Two Systems* had, in its own way, endorsed; namely, that given the massive release of people's creativity which socialism ensures as against its pitiful expression under capitalism (or for that matter under all class-divided societies of the past), it is only a question of time before socialism established its superiority and ultimately triumphed over capitalism. A little later we had that 'strange and frightening story' as *Newsweek* called it, *The Great Conspiracy Against Russia* by Sayers and Kahn – a book which should be compulsory reading for every socialist even today. We learnt, yet again, how bourgeoisie conspired and how it lied when it came to the Soviet Union and Socialism! Voracious readers, we devoured all this and despite all the odds, the illegal or semi-legal conditions of life and work, grew ever more firm in our solidarity with the Soviet Union as the first effective breach in the global capitalist system, and in our revolutionary commitment to the cause of freedom and socialism in India. At the time, nothing, literally nothing appeared impossible to us. As the distinguished historian, V.G. Kiernan, my teacher and comrade of those years recently wrote to me: 'Yes, those were exciting days we lived through when the dear old Party seemed to be soaring towards heaven'. We indeed lived and functioned in 'the actuality of the revolution' as Lukacs once phrased it.

Today it all seems to be so very long ago. Not that the ideal has not held – the ideal of socialism as the historically necessary negation of capitalism, a free, cooperative and democratic society based on a social, *genuinely* social, ownership of the means of production. It has. Through more than five decades, at Lahore or in Delhi, inside the Party or outside, in one form or another, a certain involvement with the socialist cause has always been there: the early activity in the students' movement, years of full-time open or secret work with the Communist Party, including a stint in jail, writing, editing and translating for the party; or later, after the partition, as a teacher, occasionally as a party member, but always as an ordinary activist, often with an understandable love-hate relationship with the diverse currents or formations of the Communist Left, and so on. Through it all I have held on to the ideal of socialism and to whatever little Marxism I came to acquire, finding it useful, beyond politics, not only in my work as a teacher but in living my life as well.

But if the ideal has held, it is also true that today the vision is somewhat blurred, due not so much to the passage of time as to the developments of these past few years which, in their totality, indeed constitute an unprecedented 'crisis of socialism' that demands an explanation, an honest coming to terms with it.

Before I attempt such an exercise, it is necessary to make a point which is often obscured in the current euphoria or despair over what has happened. The era that began in 1917 may in one sense be seen as having ended. But it needs to be recognized that when the balance sheet of this era is finally drawn up it will not be as one-sided as on-the-spur-of-the-moment assessments, improvised by the enemies and often meekly accepted by the much-demoralised friends. This era had its dark chapters. But this era was also a saga of struggle and sacrifice by people unparalleled in history, and its achievements are a revolutionary inheritance that will always inspire the poor and the oppressed everywhere in their struggle for a better life. More specifically, I would like to affirm that the 'crisis of socialism' we are witnessing, though diversely damaging in its consequences, takes nothing away from the historic significance of the world's first socialist revolution or from the achievements of either the pioneering experiment in the erstwhile Soviet Union or the world communist movement – the achievements of 'historical communism' as it is being described in certain epitaph-like pronouncements these days.

The October Revolution, a truly electrifying moment in history, by its revolutionary breaching of the world imperialist system, not only heralded the necessary beginning of the new epoch of transition from capitalism to communism – a fact fully vindicated by the historical experience since then – it also achieved the immediate demolition of 'the prison house' that was Czarist Russia, ending age-old oppressions and freeing vast masses of human beings, peoples and nationalities, within its extensive frontiers. Local variations apart, even when led or supported by the Red Army, the changes in Eastern Europe at the end of the Second World War had similar liberating consequences for the common people in these countries.

This historical truth should not be too difficult to recognise or accept. But the pervasiveness of the crisis, the disillusionment and despair accompanying the collapse of the communist regimes in Soviet Union and Eastern Europe, makes it equally necessary to point out that these post-revolutionary societies have had real achievements to their credit in the period following the initial revolutionary transformations, particularly noteworthy if account is taken of the conditions they had to a greater or lesser degree inherited and the circumstances in which they survived and achieved what they did – economic, social, cultural and political backwardness, massive illiteracy, war, civil war and counter-revolution, continuous imperialist intervention in one form or another and, in most cases, a long tradition of centralized authoritarian rule, often imposed from outside, etc. etc. The record is far, very far, from being only negative as the hostile critics are busy making out today. In the Soviet Union, for example, it is not merely that its prodigies of industrialization in the thirties constitute an incontrovertible argument for the capacity of a planned economy to achieve growth – in a single decade it turned the country into the world's second industrial power and created the powerful Soviet state that survived years of capitalist hostility and encirclement and could take on the full might of world fascism and defeat it, an argument well confirmed by the spectacular performance of the Soviets during the years of reconstruction immediately following the Second World War when, with more than 20 million dead and its lands ravaged and economy wrecked by war, rejecting all imperialist aid, through its own planned, self-reliant effort, the country was rebuilt into the world's other super-power. Still more significant have been the other successes of the first experiment in building socialism: the establishment of the right to work and social security for the working people; the equitable distribution of scarcity and reallocation of resources so as to reduce the economic disparities among different, unevenly developed regions; the rapid elimination of the conditions of extreme poverty and the development of social consumption in health, education and cultural life; the breaching of some at least of the traditional forms of sexism and securing unprecedented participation of women in social occupations and political life; the remarkable initial responses to such difficult and complex issues as national oppression or the protection of nature; and, especially in the early years, the extraordinary flowering of human creativity in every sphere and mass participation of workers and peasants in public life, through their Soviets and otherwise, etc., etc. Even though there were retreats later on, tragic distortions and reversals in many areas, including the catastrophically rapid decay of Soviet democracy, the Soviet Union assured for vast masses of its ordinary citizens a life of material security and moral and aesthetic culture far superior to what even the countries of advanced capitalism have to offer to their common people. In Eastern Europe too, under the communist regimes, there were parallel achievements in economic, social and cultural spheres. These achievements even today have a great deal of explosive potential for the revolutionary process of the future in these countries.

The impact of Soviet Union and the movements associated with or inspired by it has been no less powerful and profound outside of its borders. And this does not refer only to their decisive contribution to the defeat of Fascism. It is no doubt true that while the communist movement attracted to itself some of the finest minds in the first world – writers, poets, artists, scientists and others – it was generally less influential than 'social democracy' as the latter had come to be. Despite its powerful presence in Italy and France, communism could not shift politics effectively in a socialist direction anywhere in Western Europe, though its heroic role in the resistance movements of occupied Europe gained for it extraordinary prestige and popularity which was eventually frittered away, partly because of the Soviet connection. But there is no denying world communism's immense *civilizing influence* on capitalism in the first world, in curbing its structurally inherent predatory logic at home and abroad. The very existence and survival of Soviet Union over these years, together with the communist, socialist or labour movements it inspired or supported, was a most important factor, of course among many others, in persuading the ruling classes in the West not only to cede ground to anticolonial liberation movements, especially after the Second World War, but also to make concessions to their own people, to establish and enlarge the elementary democratic rights in capitalist societies. It has been pointed out that social welfare provisions were often at their most generous in the West European states bordering the former Soviet bloc; those instituted at a time when the prestige of the Soviet Union was at its highest in the early post-war period, are even spoken of as 'the fruits of 1945'.

Far more significant in the short as well as the long run, perhaps, is the continuing impact of the October Revolution on a world scale, which the erstwhile Soviet Union, in its own much distorted manner, reinforced. Though the immediately following European revolution was betrayed, suppressed or aborted in different countries, the Russian Revolution survived to be a source of constant inspiration for the anti-capitalist revolutionary movements everywhere. What is more, it ignited the world-wide anti-colonial liberation struggles in the periphery and semi-periphery of the global capitalist system. This way well turn out to be its crowning achievement in history. The pioneering exploits of the Bolsheviks, the seizure of power by the workers, gave hope and courage to millions of downtrodden throughout the world. The salvoes from the battleship *Avrora*, heralding a 'Workers' and Peasants' Government' in Russia, sent out the message of Marxism to the oppressed and exploited in the remotest corners of the earth, and with it came the Leninist summons to militant revolutionary politics, which have since moved vast masses of people to resist and rebel and become effective actors in political life, to make their own more or less successful revolutions in China, Cuba, Vietnam, and elsewhere. It needs to be noted that not all these subsequent revolutions were sponsored from above, and, no matter what happens now or in future, together with the Russian Revolution, they remain the landmarks they have been in the saga of humankind's long struggle for freedom and a better life. The Soviet Union, just as it aided the radical causes and the communist movements abroad, also provided help to people's liberation struggles and a certain support and protection when they emerged as revolutionary regimes. That, increasingly, this aid or help, support and protection, was born not of any consideration for world revolutionary process but of mixed compulsions of own history, ideological legitimacy, or 'national interest' and even *realpolitik*, or plain superpower politics, should not be allowed to obscure the signal Soviet contribution to the anti-colonial liberation in the Third World. If the world revolutionary interests came to be subordinated to the interests of Soviet foreign policy, yet the very existence of that policy often acted as a check on the power and expansion of western imperialism. Certainly, the sweep of post-war decolonization owed much to the challenge and competition resulting from the need for the western colonial powers to contend with a powerful and prestigious global rival.

Indeed, without 'historical communism' as it has been called, this world of ours would have been a far more inhuman and hopeless place. Beyond its historically specific achievements mentioned above, to which could be added many more, is a somewhat intangible aspect of the social reality around us today, a general illumination, as it were, that bathes all the failed or successful particularities of our age. You have to take only one quick look around to recognize the living presence of 'historical communism' in the enhanced awareness of humankind the world over concerning issues of human dignity, of justice and injustice, of equality, oppression and exploitation, in the voice and hope the poor and oppressed have come to acquire in our times, in the quality and spread of their struggles for a better life and, above all, in their confidence, despite all the retreats and reverses, that they can fight and win their emancipation....

I am aware of the complexities of the historical processes subsumed in the sketchy account above, aware of the need to make qualifications as also to take notice of the terrible, often needless, price paid for some of the achievements. But as E.H. Carr had written: 'The danger is not that we shall draw a veil over the enormous blots on the record of the Revolution, over the cost in human suffering, over the crimes committed in its name. The danger is that we shall be tempted to forget altogether, and to pass over in silence, its immense achievements'. Carr's warning still holds. And today, when the latter temptation seems to have swamped about everything, the point I am immediately wanting to make is the simple one: there is a great deal to be said, even today, even in this hour of 'defeat', for Lenin's Revolution, for the Soviet Union that was, and for the world communist movement – they have another record which holds promise of other possibilities that may yet be. With the spiritual forces set free by it, the hope and inspiration it remains for the struggling poor and oppressed everywhere, the October Revolution of 1917, a *defining* event in history, may yet come to be more universally assessed the way Goethe assessed the French Revolution. After the defeat of the German forces at Valmy, Goethe had said to officers in bivouac: 'From this place and from today there issues a new epoch in the history of the world, and you can say you were present at its birth'.

But the point made, the fact of 'defeat' retains its overwhelming reality. It may be too early or rash to speak of the termination of the historical process that began in 1917, but *the* issue today is the 'crisis of socialism', dramatically highlighted by the collapse in Soviet Union and Eastern Europe and the stampede backward into the world capitalist system. And this evokes memories of another kind, they come rushing in a welter, filtered through time.

Even as I left home and took the road to life and politics with Marxism, among the very first books I read was one then recently published by a professor of Economics at Lahore, Brij Narain, titled *Marxism Is Dead*. Later I was to learn that periodic pronouncements of this sort are the historic destiny of the doctrine of Karl Marx. One that claimed more than the usual attention and was constantly thrown at us was that symposium by six penitents with communist pasts, *The God That Failed* (as if God ever does anything else but fail, at least most of the time). However, I must confess that never before did such a pronouncement sound so convincing as it does today. And the memories, in their rush, travel over that other territory – the territory of doubt and disillusionment over these fifty long years: the dubious aspects of Stalin's pact with Hitler; the sudden switch to 'Peoples War' – 'who lives if Russia dies' – whose ambiguities overnight reduced us from heroes in the freedom struggle to its 'traitors'; the dissolution of the Communist International and the post-war surrender of revolution in Greece and the revolutionary possibilities in Italy and France; the embarrassments of Zhadanov's cultural pronouncements, Stalin's foray into linguistics, and the Lysenko affair; the breaking away of Tito's Yugoslavia; the purges of 1945-52 in the Soviet Union and the trials, purges and executions in Eastern Europe, reminiscent of the Moscow trials, purges and executions of 1934-39, in which perished, as we now fully know, among millions of other 'enemies of the people', more than a million communists, including almost the entire leadership of the Red Army and 1108 of the 1966 delegates present, together with 98 of 139 Central Committee members elected, at the 17th congress of CPSU (B) held in 1934 – 'the entire flower of the revolution had been butchered', as E.P. Thompson put it later, decimating whatever was left of the 'Party of Lenin'. (Incidentally, this Congress, held in 1934 and known as the 'Congress of Victors', was hailed by Stalin himself for its 'colossal achievements', for 'the decisive results achieved by socialism in all branches of economic and cultural life', for laying 'an unshakeable foundation of a socialist economic system in our country', etc., etc.).

It is not that we had no idea earlier of this dark chapter of Soviet history. But we believed Stalin entirely – persuaded as much by the weight of evidence made available on the left in support of the trials as by our knowledge of the then rapidly deteriorating international situation (threat of fascism, betrayal at Munich, collapse of the Spanish Republic, the slide towards another world war increasingly sought to be turned into a war against the Soviet Union, etc.). We were in fact all the time learning, without entirely believing though, something of the barbarism, ruthlessness and terror behind some of the Soviet achievements; if ideals had indeed moved millions of Russian people and communists to heroic endeavour, their actual practice had also caused these people and communists untold pain and suffering. Socialism was acquiring, above all in its lack of democratic freedoms, its arbitrary and cruel exercise of political power, an ugly and inhuman face. This was certainly a contributory factor in the working people of advanced capitalist countries turning away from this socialism, though it retained its attraction for the backward, poverty-stricken countries of the Third World where an increasing number of people saw in it the promise of rapid economic development and a better life. For us, however, it was socialism as we believed it to be, and socialism by definition has a human face. Its ugliness in Soviet Russia, whatever part of it we were then willing to see, was credibly attributed to its historical origins – hadn't Marx argued against utopianism and written of the 'inevitable defects' in 'the first phase of communist society' as it emerged from the old capitalist society? In any case our official Marxism was content to explain it all, really explain it away most of the time, as so many 'mistakes' or 'distortions', as unfortunate 'deviations' from 'socialist norms'.... Such 'explanation' was not difficult to accept because we knew, and we were daily reminded of it by irrefutable, ever accumulating, new evidence, how wholly unscrupulous the bourgeoisie was in its hostility to socialism, how it lied and conspired against the Soviet Union. The lies and conspiracies of the bourgeoisie indeed stood between us and the truth. For the rest, we were young and youth has its resilience, an optimism or buoyancy that sees and shines through even the most darkened vistas of the future; our idealism, our faith and commitment, well made up for our ignorance, our lack of information and understanding. Besides, despite everything, Marxism for us was a morality that simply would not countenance ethical justification for crime and cruelties in revolutionary politics, a morality which was daily reinforced by the integrity, the dedication and self-sacrifice of any number of communists immediately around us and in the world communist movement. It was one such, Julius Fucik, our comrade, who had written those *Notes from the Gallows*.....

And then, as we thus survived in our revolutionary

commitment and faith in the Soviet Union, confirming our worst fears, came Khrushchev's report at the 20th Party Congress, to be followed in regular succession, after the earlier rumblings in East Germany, by Hungary (1956), Czechoslovakia (1968) and Poland (1980), interspersed with the American-backed brutal massacre of over one million communists in Indonesia, liquidating the largest communist party in the non-socialist world, and the near total silence of the entire communist world over it, the violent breach between Soviet Union and China and further splits within 'the socialist world' and the communist movement, the armed conflicts between countries professing socialism amidst widespread charges that some were taking 'the capitalist road', the military misadventure in Afghanistan, and so on, accompanied all the while by authentic news about the stagnation of Soviet economy and society and the continuing degeneration of the Communist Party and its leadership, the rulers of Soviet Union – the public bestowal of Soviet honours on Suharto, the butcher of Indonesia or the likes of Marcos being as good a symbol as any of this degeneration... Such are the memories of doubt and disillusionment over the years. And now, finally, no longer the memories but the harsh contemporary reality, the earthquake of 1989-90 and its tremors at Tiananmen Square, the ignominious collapse of Eastern Europe and then of the Soviet Union itself! 'Defeat of socialism', 'triumph of capitalism', the enemies exult and proclaim. And, once again, 'Marxism is dead'.

'Upturned Utopia' is how Norberto Bobbio has described the recent developments in the Soviet Union and Eastern Europe, and to convey the full tragic meaning of the metaphor, he points out that it was 'the first utopia that tried to enter into history', for it was sought to be raised on a real, material basis. Utopias have been with us for a very long time. Religion, for example, has invariably promised a heaven, up there, to its votaries, especially those who have little or nothing down here on this earth – only its details have varied with the varying historical and even geographical contexts of different religions. And there have been the secular versions too, like *Island of the Sun* in antiquity, or those of Thomas More and Utopian Socialists in our times. But all such utopias, religious or secular, were imaginary, like Plato's in *The Republic* which was, as Glaucon put it to Socrates, true only 'in our words'. These utopias indeed played a socially important ideological role in human affairs, but they did so primarily by virtue of their real significance which lay not so much in the imagined ideal they projected as in the implicit critique they carried of the inadequacies of contemporary society. But the utopia now 'upturned' was different – it had dared to move from the realm of 'words' to that of 'things', and seemed to have succeeded, almost, in giving a real expression to the ideal. And even if, for the moment, we must speak in the past tense, it is well to remember what an ideal it was! Even as it claimed the allegiance of any number of master spirits of our time – a Neruda or Picasso, Joliot-Curie or Einstein, Aragon or Hikmet, Brecht or Faiz, to mention only a few from more recent years – it had also the power to move, more than any other ideal in history, millions below, Fanon's 'wretched of the earth', to heroic action in behalf of freedom and dignity of all on this earth. It had behind it, as Gandhiji once said, 'the purest sacrifice of countless men and women who (had) given up their all for its sake'; they had indeed risked everything they held dear, cheerfully braving the hazards of life-long revolutionary struggles, the prison and exile, torture and death in the extermination camps. It was the inspiration of Bhagat Singh when he chose to 'mount the gallows boldly and with a smile', and of Che Guevara when death surprised him in the jungles of Bolivia. Gabriel Peri, on the eve of his execution by the fascists had spoken of it as 'singing tomorrows' of humankind.

'Upturned Utopia' is an understandable description of what has happened, but as a metaphor it has its limitations too. Taken literally, it can be quite misleading. Not only because it is certainly too early to speak of these matters in the past tense, but far more because it simply was no utopia. As 'actually existing socialism', its problems, contradictions and dilemmas, its very nature, were for long a subject of angry or anxious, friendly or hostile discussion among socialists and Marxists of the world. Trotsky onward, and including Mao Tse-tung's critique and Bettelheim's multi-volume *Class Struggles in the USSR*, there is a whole corpus of authentic socialist criticism of what was being built in these post-revolutionary societies. While most hoped, rather wishfully it is obvious now, for a turn from 'actual' to 'real' socialism, and none even remotely anticipated the present ignoble denouement, the analytic comment was uncompromisingly sharp and the forebodings clearly expressed. More than a decade back, for example, Paul Swezy wrote of the very real possibility that the Soviet Society may have reached 'a dead end... with no visible signs of a way out'. And as long ago as 1949, in an explicit statement of his commitment to socialism – 'Why Socialism?' – Einstein had, in his own straightforward manner, thus focused on one of the most crucial issues: 'Nonetheless, it is necessary to remember that a planned economy is not yet socialism. A planned economy as such may be accompanied by the complete enslavement of the individual. The achievement of socialism requires the solution of some extremely difficult socio-political problems: How is it possible, in view of the far-reaching centralization of political and economic power, to prevent bureaucracy from becoming all powerful and over-weaning? How can the rights of the individuals be protected and therewith a democratic counterweight to the power of bureaucracy be assured?' Later, equally specifically, the Marxist economist, Lange, wrote, 'The real danger of socialism is that of a bureaucratization of economic life'. And we had the characteristically pungent and perceptive observation of Kalecki: 'Here in Poland we have successfully abolished capitalism; all we have to do now is to abolish feudalism' – he had thus drawn our attention to the formation of neo-feudal structures of power and exploitation in the post-revolutionary societies, which involved not only the denial of political equality, the socialist sharing of power and freedoms, but also a politically coercive appropriation of surplus from the direct producers, very much akin to the feudal mode of production.

There was plenty of such criticism, and obviously, for these socialist critics there was no utopia in the Soviet Union or elsewhere. It is true, however, that these critics, though socialists or Marxists, were strictly speaking 'outsiders' for official Marxism and the mainstream communist parties, and they were treated as such. It is the 'insiders', those who belonged, who really mattered, and for them it was indeed an utopia realized – they saw or heard or spoke no evil!

But now it has become impossible not to see or hear or speak. And much as I would have liked to avoid it, a nagging question persists, especially for the period after the Khrushchev Report of 1956. What of the hordes of these 'insiders', scholars, academics and writers of all sorts, members of friendship societies or peace, solidarity and sundry other international organizations, leaders and functionaries of the communist parties, and so many others, who visited there year after year, often several times in a year, and yet saw and heard nothing – nothing not merely of the terrible costs of forced collectivization, the deaths of millions of ordinary Soviet citizens and communists as 'internal enemies', the Terror, the Gulag and the labour camps, the purges and executions of the past, or of the growing chauvinism, national and ethnic antagonisms, gender or minority oppression, drunkenness and religiosity, even racism and anti-Semitism, but more specifically and to the point, nothing of the almost mafia-like degeneration of the Communist Party, producing and putting in power Khrushchevs, Brezhnevs, Gorbachevs and Yeltsins, or the self-serving abuse of their monopoly of power by the new rulers to secure a most corrupt and vulgarly luxurious living for themselves – no different from and in many ways worse and more obscene than what Engels spoke of as 'the senseless luxury and extravagance of the present ruling class and its political representatives' in capitalist society. They saw and heard nothing of the yawning chasm that had come to exist between the rulers and the ruled, the total alienation of the people from the powers that be, their indifference, hostility or contempt for the new rulers, the communist leadership, which, denied other avenues, found an eloquent expression in the politically explosive humour of popular jokes. Remember the one about Khrushchev's vulgar flaunting of his material acquisitions before his old mother who, impressed, yet has other memories, remains worried, and fearfully asks: 'But son, what if the Bolsheviks come back?' Or the one where a tired and disgusted citizen leaves his never ending queue in anger to go and kill Brezhnev, only to return, soon, disappointed, for 'the queue there is much longer', etc., etc.

Scholars, perhaps, one can understand – and I am not here speaking of the far too many hangers-on or racketeers in the academic business and the business of left politics as well. Their mundane interests apart, compulsions of official Marxism or 'party loyalty', together with the dominant methodological orientations and the 'functional rationality' that has come to govern the organized academic disciplines and research, may well have prevented these scholars from seeking the reality behind the appearances; they simply chose to be 'scholars' first and Communists or Marxists only a long time afterwards. But what about others, above all the leaders and functionaries of the fraternal communist parties and allied organizations, whom Lenin once likened to *inspectors* visiting Soviet Union for a check-up on what was being done? How come they failed to see what a poet, who was a communist too, saw so early and so clearly, namely, the awesome alienation of the people from their rulers. This is what Bertolt Brecht wrote, way back in 1953, when the first rumblings of the coming earthquake were heard and a workers' uprising was suppressed in Berlin:

> After the uprising of the 17th June
> The Secretary of the Writers' Union
> Had leaflets distributed in the Stalinallee
> Stating that the people
> Had forfeited the confidence of the government
> And could win it back only
> By redoubled efforts. Would it not be easier
> In that case for the government
> To dissolve the people
> And elect another?

The communist rulers in Berlin, however, did the next best thing – they went on to build the Wall!

Whatever the motivations or extenuating circumstances, this stubborn refusal to see or hear or speak, when it was their revolutionary duty to see, hear and speak, constitutes an act of historic complicity on the part of these leaders and functionaries that is crying out for atonement, which must visibly express itself, above all, in a return to communist norms of personal conduct and a better, revolutionary practice of Marxism. One can only hope that they have the necessary honesty and courage, for the sake of their comrades in the ranks and the cause they hold dear. One does not have to be a repentent communist to thus come to terms with our past.

1

Collapse of the Soviet Union—The Initial Impact

Ours has been described as 'an age of revolution'. The phrase did not merely signify the extraordinary range and depth of social awakening and mass mobilisation, massive popular upheavals, the dissolution of vast colonial empires and so much more in our times, it also carried a more specific reference to the dominant character of the historical changes in the 20th century. For even as the old world of global capitalism and bourgeois society in its liberal version collapsed in 1914 and for the next forty years, capitalism, impelled by its contradictions, stumbled from one crisis and catastrophe to another (the most prominent being the Great Depression and yet another World War), the most significant outcome was the emergence of a possible, socialist, alternative to capitalism.

With the overturning of the old order in Russia in 1917 and the establishment of communist power, one-sixth of the world broke away from the global capitalist social order. The inspiration and a certain support thus provided, the overturning continued and in due course revolution spread in one country after another. It spread to East Europe in the wake of the Red Army during the last phase of the Second World War. Next came the Chinese Revolution to be followed by a dozen or so, more or less successful, post-World War II revolutions – in Korea, Indo-China, Cuba, Portugal's former African colonies, the Horn of Africa, and later still in Southern Yemen, Nicaragua and elsewhere. Approximately a third of the world's land surface and population went through revolutions involving profound socio-structural changes, constituting a whole new 'Second World', more or less detached from the global capitalist orbit. This vast historical process was positively inspired by Marxism. Most of these revolutions were fought for and triumphed under the banner of Marxism, and the rest (with the notable exception of that entirely different kind of upheaval, the Iranian revolution) espoused Marxism (or Marxism-Leninism) soon after the conquest of power. They proclaimed socialism and communism as their proximate and ultimate goals. Even otherwise, since Marxism has always argued that the successor to capitalism will be socialism, it was almost natural that the post-revolutionary regimes chose to call themselves socialist (though, given the overall role and position of the Communist Parties, they were often spoken of as communist regimes). These regimes did indeed seek to build socialism, or given their low levels of development, move towards building a socialist society in their respective countries. It appeared that Marx's vision of creating a new society, a more humane economic and social order that must replace capitalism, was on the way to realisation.

The developments elsewhere in the capitalist world, its so-called First and Third Worlds, lent credibility to this hope. The First World of industrially advanced capitalism certainly witnessed an unprecedented post-War boom but its exhaustion in the early 1970s was marked by a spectacular escalation of class struggle in several countries of the West – the Portuguese and Spanish revolutions of 1974–76 and the accompanying strike wave which brought workers and soldiers together into the streets under revolutionary banners, the French students rebellion and the general strike of May-June 1968, the upheaval unleashed by the Italian 'hot autumn' of 1969, the struggles which brought down the 1970–74 Heath Government in Britain, and so on. While its working class did not share in this radicalisation, the United States had its share of popular struggles – the mass opposition to the Vietnam war, the upsurge for civil rights in the South and the series of insurrectionary developments in the northern ghettoes. Above and beyond these struggles in the West, was the overarching fact of the post-boom stagnation of the capitalist economy which showed no signs of abating and in its diverse consequences was contributing to the growing disenchantment with the system. But far more significant were the happenings in the Third World, the periphery and semi-periphery of global capitalism. Under the long-term impact of the October Revolution and signally facilitated by the presence and prestige of the Soviet Union, the post-Second World War period witnessed a prolonged, worldwide process of decolonisation, which shook the global capitalist system, yet again. And winning their political freedom from imperialist domination, the newly-liberated countries of the Third World increasingly saw their future, often with Soviet inspiration and support, as some kind of non-capitalist or socialist development. Even when they faltered or failed, given the presence of the Soviet Union, capitalism as a world system, continued to feel threatened and insecure.

To any dispassionate observer of the world scene during this period, the concept of the 'general crisis of capitalism' regardless of its simplistic, even vulgar, Soviet interpretations, had a great deal to be said for it. There was a growing anti-capitalist sentiment, a worldwide questioning of the capitalist social order on not only economic but even more on social, moral and cultural grounds. The idea of socialism as a successor to capitalism had caught the imagination of the vast masses of the common people the world over. If to the skeptic or the more cautious the kind of society that would dominate the future was still uncertain, it certainly appeared more uncertain for capitalism than socialism. The ideologues of capitalism were openly apprehensive about it. Socialists, including those critical of Soviet socialism and aware of its growing crisis, could with good reason argue and believe that, however painfully, socialism had already arrived as a historically ordained, that is necessary and possible, future for humankind. Till this other day, 'an age of revolution' indeed seemed so apt a description of our times, a deservedly optimistic assessment of the 20th century.

And then, as if mocking all such historical optimism, we had another explosive upsurge, revolutions of another kind, which in a seeming reversal of the historical process of our times, overturned one communist regime after another in Eastern Europe and then in the Soviet Union itself. The destruction of the infamous Berlin Wall signalled more a 'triumph of capitalism' than of democracy and the triumphant capitalism moved fast to repossess the territories lost to it through the socialist revolutions of the 20th century. The century itself, in this ironic turn of events, seemed to be ending a mere witness to Hegel's aphorism, 'history is a slaughter house', and in doing so putting a question-mark over socialism itself as the emancipatory project for our times. The future seemed to have decided in favour of capitalism and there were no alternatives, not any longer. Not only socialism, even radicalism in the traditional sense of the term was now passé. Effective opposition, where permitted or possible, could at most take the form of mild, meliorative reforms.

II

Triggered off by 'the Gorbachev phenomenon', but essentially born of and fuelled by the long-festering contradictions of the 'socialism' that was built, this new upsurge, described by some as 'the greatest transformation in the world economic and political scene since the end of World War II', swept through the entire socialist world*, undermining, damaging and destroying the inherited economic, political and ideological structures in one country of 'actually existing socialism' after another, pushing these countries, once again, into a new, entirely uncharted territory, forcing the remaining communist or associated regimes to negotiate their own terms of adjustment

---

* The term 'socialist' is used here and in what follows (except where the context or qualification indicates otherwise) in the sense explained by Deutscher: 'We all speak... colloquially about the USSR and the associated and disassociated states as "socialist countries", and we are entitled to do so as long as we intend merely to oppose their regimes to the capitalist states, to indicate their post-capitalist character, or to refer to the socialist origins and intentions of their governments and policies'.

and survival within the global capitalist system, and leaving the entire communist movement stranded in the midst of an unprecedented crisis.

If the communist regimes in Eastern Europe, established at the end of the Second World War, seemingly stable even where imposed from above, simply disintegrated or were swept out of existence in a matter of days in, on the whole, remarkably peaceful popular revolts, leaving these countries willy-nilly busy finding a subservient place for themselves within the global capitalist social order, that in the Soviet Union, born of the October Revolution and in position for more than seventy years, collapsed, and the union came apart, in a matter of a few years, to give way to lumpen capitalism and authoritarianism of a new kind. These countries had all missed the moment of genuine socialism (which more than anything else has to be democratic). While sane socialist voices have not altogether disappeared and elements of socialist radicalism still survive, it will be long, may be very long, before the people of these erstwhile 'socialist' countries find their way back to socialism as it was originally meant to be. Elsewhere in the 'socialist world', in China, North Korea, Vietnam or Cuba, all sites of more or less recent indigenous revolutionary movements with a certain social as well as nationalist basis of their own and owing little to the Red Army, the communist regimes, more exposed and vulnerable to the offensive of global capitalism than ever before, are desperately adjusting, often succumbing, to the new situation, to the pressure to open up their economies to global capitalism, opt for the market and its incentives, reform their economic structures, and take other measures that will enable them to find their niches in the global capitalist market. The most important among the surviving communist regimes, China, had been already for more than a decade, travelling the road to 'a market economy'. Somewhat shaken initially by Tiananmen Square, it continues to survive, but in the name of building 'socialism with Chinese characteristics', persists with what has been described as 'market-Stalinism', its future open to the dangerous consequences of both 'market' and 'Stalinism'; even if it somehow manages to evade them, unless the present course is reversed, what is likely to be built in China will be anything but socialism as Marxism or the classical socialist tradition has understood it. Cuba alone stands out, so far, for its heroic effort at 'rectification' in order to defend the gains of its revolution and survive as a socialist country. The states of so-called 'socialist orientation' in Africa, their backwardness and vulnerability reinforced with the Soviet departure from the scene, are being pushed or sucked back into the world capitalist system as its traditional peripheries even as other countries of the region are threatened with the prospects of further peripheralisation within the same global economy. And the communist movement, long tied up with the 'socialist world', even otherwise in retreat for quite some time, now further defeated, demoralised and disoriented, faces the deepest-ever crisis of its history, compelling it to undertake, on pain of extinction, a painful reappraisal of its theory and practice over these seventy long years.

Momentous as its consequences have been for the countries and movements involved immediately or directly, the disintegration of the Soviet Union and the socialist bloc is a continuing disaster for the vast mass of humanity in the Third World. (Though, one may notice that of all the Third World regions, the radical movements in Latin America are perhaps least damaged by the Soviet collapse. Apart from Cuba, the ex-Soviet Union did not invest heavily in this area and the movements here always had a somewhat greater indigenous strength and independence.) The struggling peoples in country after country in Asia, Africa and Latin America had subsisted for decades on end on the socialist dream. Now, not only has the dream disintegrated but the Soviet collapse leaves them confronting the most basic question of their post-colonial existence. In a historical perspective, issues concerning socialism apart, the Soviet collapse is now also the case of a poor, economically backward country, breaking out of global capitalism, getting sucked back into it at the end of seventy-odd years and thus raising anew the question: what does a Third World country do in a situation of global domination of capitalism? Some 'nationalist' hiccups notwithstanding, the post-colonial bourgeoisie or ruling elites seem to have made their choice and, in a characteristic act of 'secession', gone over for the joys of junior partnerships in a global capitalist economy. But how about the common people? For them the choice now may well be: socialism or peripheralisation within the global capitalist system. In any case, with the Soviet collapse and the renewed offensive of global capitalism, the revolutionary struggles in the Third World, as they confront the above-mentioned question and the options available, face new and unprecedented special problems which, apart from matters of theory or political strategy and tactics, include vastly increased dangers of direct military intervention or prolonged 'low intensity warfare' by imperialism. Needless to add, the task of any pro-people 'national reconstruction' has now become vastly more difficult and tortuous than ever before.

The collapse in East Europe and Soviet Union is of course economically beneficial to the advanced industrial countries of the First World. As the countries in the East go on to construct their third-rate capitalisms, they also turn into satellite zones for exploitation by western capitalism, and western capitalism can also use their highly skilled but low-cost labour force, all the more vulnerable for lack of significant countervailing left or trade union presence, to weaken the organisation of the working class in the west and undercut its social conquests. The virtual disappearance of the socialist challenge leaves western capitalism in a much stronger position to depress social benefits and economic conditions of the working classes at home. In that sense if the working people in the East are the worst sufferers, those in the West are going to feel the negative effects of the collapse of Soviet Union every bit as much. But far more significant than any economic benefits are the ideological-political gains of capitalism centred in the countries of the First World – and what happens here has its resonance worldwide. It is not just socialism which has collapsed with the collapse of the Soviet Union, but literally every tendency which emphasises the necessity of some form of intervention by a conscious agency for the improvement of the human condition. Even as socialism is being banalised by ex-socialists into a species of welfare-capitalism, this is no longer acceptable to capitalism in its newly acquired post-Cold War aggressiveness. As right-wing convictions are spreading leftward, they are displacing even milder form of neo-Keynesianism, indeed any kind of social welfarism or planning. The collapse of the Soviet Union and the allied communist movements, combined with the collapse of traditional social democracy and associated labour movements in Western Europe, have given unbridled licence to the ideologues of the Right; everywhere market economy and liberal-democratic rhetoric seem to be defeating socialism and socialist or socialistic ideas. It needs to be understood that all this, the *defeat* of socialism as a political force in Europe and the *triumph* of the most brutal kind of capitalism, the disorganisation of labour movements and the rise of right-wing politics across Europe, are parts of a single process: the Cold War did not just fade away; it was *won* by one side, *lost* by the other. And most grievously damaged by this loss has been the cause of socialism, not only in the West but everywhere. Capitalism is not only globally dominant as never before, now 'there is no alternative' to it either, as a Margaret Thatcher has proclaimed.

Indeed, so comprehensively disastrous for socialism has the Soviet collapse been that the previous existence of the Soviet Union itself is being interpreted as only an episode in the history of contemporary capitalism. The current triumphalism of the enemies expressed in the jocular invitations to consider the longest route from capitalism to capitalism and similar conundrums apart, we have the more substantial argument of a friend, Eric Hobsbawm. Pointing out that the institutions of liberal democracy virtually disappeared from all but a fringe of Europe in the two decades following 1922 as Fascism and its satellite authoritarian movements or regimes arose in one country after another, he has argued that but for the Red Army, the immense sacrifices of the USSR and its peoples, Western liberal capitalism would probably have succumbed to this threat and the contemporary Western world (outside of an isolated USA) would now consist of a set of variations of authoritarian and fascist regimes rather than a set of variations of liberal ones.

He concludes: 'Perhaps history, in its irony, will decide that the most lasting achievement of the October Revolution was to make the "developed world" once again safe for "bourgeois democracy"'! Hobsbawm however immediately adds: 'But that is of course to assume that it will remains safe....'

It is well to remember, as history of our times has shown again and again, that Right-wing authoritarianism or fascism is a tendency naturally inherent within contemporary capitalist societies. While Stalinism indeed finally failed to build anything resembling socialism and whatever was built has come unglued out of its anti-socialist deformations, especially suppression of democracy, capitalism yet remains impaled on its own contradictions and in crisis, and therefore open to fascist or similar authoritarian options for its continued survival.

III

The collapse in Eastern Europe and even more in the Soviet Union was a surprise for foes and friends alike. Once the surprise was over, the reactions to what had happened, on the Right as on the Left, have been along expected lines.

The Right everywhere, most vocally in the West, with inevitable echoes in the East, has been jubilant – the ancient spectre, 'spectre of communism' as Marx put it, which had haunted the capitalist world for almost a century and a half, has been finally laid. Convinced, like most on the Left, that what existed in these countries was socialism, and one based on the teachings of Karl Marx, its failure is seen as a debacle of not only socialism – declared 'dead on arrival' – but of Marxism as well. More than winning the Cold War, it is the final victory in the global civil war started by the Bolsheviks in 1917, which at the same time effectively establishes the superiority of the market economy and liberal democratic form of social organisation. The turn to market and free enterprise in Eastern Europe and Soviet Union, as in China, Vietnam and elsewhere, means not the crisis of a type of movement, regime or economy but its very end, certainly the beginning of the end, the ultimate elimination of any kind of socialist alternative to capitalism – henceforth it would be all plain liberal-free market sailing. The authoritarian connotations imparted to socialism in its Soviet or Stalinist version having made it that much easier for the capitalist ideologues to obscure socialism's essential connotations of anti-capitalism, they have gone to town associating capitalism with democracy and socialist equality with undemocracy. Capitalism is not only immune to criticism on democratic grounds, it is itself a democratic social order. And it speaks volumes for capitalism's ideological domination today that the very vocabulary of socialism, with its progressive, liberating associations, has been appropriated, literally plundered, for capitalist purposes – 'radical reform' now is a change in the direction of privatisation and greater marketisation, and 'revolution' a synonym for a no holds-barred plunge into capitalism! It is thus that the Right of various hues, the world over, has been having a field day celebrating 'the triumph of capitalism' – 'we have won', 'communism is finished, we can do what we like' – and even proclaiming, through its Fukuyamas, 'the end of history' itself. It is not the first time, though, that servants or apologists of a ruling system have proclaimed that history has come to an end with the victory of their masters.

In the midst of this Right-wing cacophony, we have also heard another voice that deserves to be noticed, that of Galbraith, who has, in his own characteristic manner, more than once insisted that 'the Right is wrong'. Galbraith has ridiculed the Right for its 'primitive ideology' which poses a stark choice between capitalism and socialism. Even as he takes note of the ugly, inhuman face of early capitalism, with its intolerable inequalities of income and power, economic crises, human alienation, and so on, he points out the significant achievements of what he calls 'early socialism': its abolition of feudal oppressions, building up of a modern industrial state, providing of exemplary social security to the people, and so on. The crux of Galbraith's argument is: 'Capitalism in its original or pristine form could not have survived. But under pressure it did adapt. Socialism in its original form and for its first tasks did succeed. But it failed to adapt.' He contrasts the 'reframed and socially more responsible capitalist state' which has adapted to the imperatives of Trade Unions, Keynesianism, managerial revolution, social welfare, etc., with the 'inflexible and sterile socialist state' which has failed to adapt to the complexity and diversity of 'the new world of consumer society' – its centralised planning and command system have simply failed to cope with it. Socialism too must adapt, he insists, and 'the only evident remedy is to move towards the market'. He informs the Right that what Eastern Europe, the Soviet Union, or for that matter China see as the alternative is not 'traditional capitalism'. 'Were this the alternative,' he says, 'they would not want to change.' The alternative they see and seek, according to Galbraith, is 'the modern socially concerned state with a large mellowing and stabilizing role by government'.

Galbraith's is a persuasive argument; in its positive thrust it has been in fact a regular feature of the rich trajectory of his thought over the decades. It is a tribute to his discerning and robust liberal commitment. But as an expression of faith in a 'socially concerned state' in a market-based capitalist society, it is seriously flawed in its essential content and many details. I shall revert to this issue briefly later in these notes. Immediately I am only concerned to note this other voice, a voice of sanity as it were, coming from the otherwise euphoric centre of global capitalism.

It needs to be noted, however, that the original Right-wing euphoria has much abated with the passage of time – the capitalist triumph remains incomplete, old problems are back and new anxieties have emerged. Fukuyama himself, who had announced 'the end of history' in 1989 and claimed that the collapse in the East signalled the conclusive bankruptcy of all alternatives to liberal-democratic capitalism, has been distinctly less triumphalist and more cautious in his later articulations on the subject; and these have included an interesting, rather insightful, admission that liberal democracies, in their ultimate success, *sans* historically relevant conflicts or challenge, might well find their citizens regress into an affluent animality!

IV

On the Left, the reaction, understandably more varied and complex, has been again along predictable lines.

The collapse of 'a system which nurtured and sustained the hopes of generation after generation of socialists throughout the world (is) a dreadful event from the point of view of socialists everywhere' – this is how Ralph Miliband put it at the very outset. It has been seen as a tragedy and a defeat not only for the 'faithfuls' among them but for the critics too, who had criticised in the hope of a change for the better and had never even remotely visualised this change for the worst. It is a defeat not because the regimes in Eastern Europe and Soviet Union were models of the society the socialists want, but because they and the political movements influenced by them were the focus of the first worldwide challenge to capitalist power, capitalist exploitation, capitalist morality and culture. And however flawed or deformed their 'actually existing socialism', it was yet the symbol of a possibility, the possibility of escape from that essentially predatory system, capitalism. Socialists who had no illusions about the Soviet Union nevertheless viewed it as a strategically significant entity. As G.A. Cohen has underlined it:

> The Soviet Union needed to be there as a defective model so that, with one eye on it, we could construct a better one. It created a non-capitalist space in which to think about socialism.

There were others, socialists again, who had an entirely negative assessment of the Soviet Union for the future of socialism. But even they have not escaped the demoralising impact of its collapse, an impact well-expressed by Ronald Aronson:

> No longer believing that a reformed communism might fulfil Marxism's promise, I had become sure that its very existence blocked political energies in the West as well as the East, and eagerly anticipated that the end of this 'sustaining menace' would release enormous emancipatory forces everywhere. But the opposite happened: the end of Communism instead became part of a stunning defeat of those social forces, ideas, structures, projects and even values, which for two centuries have been identified with the Left....
>
> The very immobility and ponderousness of the Soviet Union counted for something positive in our collective psychic space,

> allowing us to keep hope alive that a successful socialism might still emerge. It provided a backdrop against which such alternatives could be thought about and discussed, including, for some, the hope that some other versions of Marxism remained viable....

Thus, the pain and anguish, or the dejection over the collapse of Soviet Union has more than involved its erstwhile critics on the Left too. Many indeed would share the early response of Cohen as the Soviet tragedy unfolded itself – a response distinguished for its exceptional sensitivity. While, like so many others, Cohen too had a pretty adverse assessment of the Soviet Union's claim to be a socialist society, he deplored the disappearance of both 'the Sovietness and the unionhood' of the Soviet Union, was saddened by 'what I perceive to be the impending final abandonment of the Bolshevik experiment' and regretted the impact of the termination of the experiment on how socialism is assessed. But, adding that his dejection goes beyond such matters of political calculation, this is how Cohen put it on the eve of the final break-up of the Soviet Union:

> The answer is that, although I have long since sustained little hope that things in the Soviet Union might get substantially better, in a socialist sense, there is, in certain domains, and people are prone to overlook this, a vast difference between nourishing little hope and giving up all hope. The small hope that I kept was, as it were, an immense thing, since so much was at stake. And now that residual hope has to be foresworn. So a feeling of loss is not surprising.
>
> And there is also another perhaps less rational motive here. It is true that I was heavily critical of the Soviet Union, but the angry little boy who pummels his father's chest will not be glad if the old man collapses. As long as the Soviet Union seemed safe, it felt safe for one to be anti-Soviet. Now that it begins, disobligingly, to crumble, I feel impotently protective towards it.

V

The loss of a viable alternative to capitalism, however inadequate it might have been, has induced a widespread pessimism where any kind of programmatic commitment to socialism, indeed the very idea or hope of socialism has come to be abandoned. The Soviet collapse has resulted in a general retreat from socialism on the Left. It is now 'an old and failed social order', 'an impossible dream', in any case of no relevance in the practical politics of today or tomorrow. A good, almost typical, example here is the much-noticed shift in the thinking of the eminent Marxist historian, Eric Hobsbawm, a long-time socialist and a former member of the now defunct Communist Party of Great Britain. Hobsbawm's definitive phrase, 'the short twentieth century, 1914–1991', underlines the historically significant presence and demise of the Soviet experiment in socialism, and while explaining its failures he has been equally explicit about its achievements. (Incidentally, he suggests that among other factors, the post-War 'Golden Age' of capitalism would have been impossible without the emergence of mixed economies in the advanced capitalist countries and that this development was partially due to the Soviet example of state intervention in the economy.) Flashes of old understanding and commitment still shine through Hobsbawm's recent writing when he points out that 'the collapse of one part of the world revealed the malaise of the rest' and urges us 'to consider, once again, the built-in defects of capitalism', or speaks of 'the world crisis' which is 'not only general in an economic sense, but equally general in politics' and is accompanied by social and moral crises, or insists that 'maximum growth does not mean maximum well-being' and agrees that 'unlocking market forces as a solution to mass unemployment' is today 'a monument to human folly' or, hoping for 'a better, more just and more viable world', warns of 'the price' of a failure here, 'that is to say, the alternative to a changed society is darkness', etc., etc., Thus, Hobsbawm surely seems unwilling to entirely chuck the future of socialism and hop a ride on the new world order. But then he is equally unwilling to argue *for* socialism, not any longer. When he urges 'Labour intellectuals' 'to talk about the publicly unspeakable', it is not socialism he is thinking of. Instead his concern now is with such things as making 'the case for redistributive taxation to achieve public purpose and relieve the growth of poverty' – and this when Hobsbawm himself recognises how, under the present conditions, 'the policies that worked so well in the golden mid-century decades of cohabitation between regulated capitalism and social democracy broke down and cannot be restored'. If there is a certain hopefulness, however vague or vacuous, about his proposition, 'the only completely certain generalization about history is that, so long as there is a human race, it will go on', the limits to this hopefulness are severely set by Hobsbawm's more precise, programmatic statement:

> Except for a few paleolithic sectarian survivals, everyone agrees that the future of the European Left lies in Centre-Left governments finding a viable mix of private and public interests.

Hobsbawm has thus moved fast and far, Rightwards, to finally settle for social democracy which is left with hardly any credibility these days. It is indeed a trivialisation of history to thus circumscribe the contemporary options of the European Left (and by implication of the Left elsewhere). It is equally a refusal to see, odd theoretical nods in that direction notwithstanding, the stark reality of contemporary capitalism, its contradictions all the sharper in its hour of triumph and threatening an ecological disaster which will soon make impossible any kind of 'going on' for the human race on our planet.

Admitting to being 'paleolithics', but all the same in 'very good company' – 'outside of Europe there are literally millions of paleolithics by Eric's definition, and even in Europe there are quite a few of them' – Sweezy and Magdoff have observed:

> Here we must pose a question that Hobsbawm's analysis clearly implies but that he seems not to recognize and certainly fails to make explicit: What happened to the conditions that made possible the golden decades of cohabitation between regulated capitalism and social democracy? Why did they break down? Are they likely to return in the foreseeable future? If not, what chance is there that the European Left, or any other Left for that matter, will ever again be able to enjoy the luxury of cohabitation with capitalism, whether regulated or unregulated? This is the question that all non-paleolithics must sooner or later face up to.

One may well pose another question too: What relevance does Hobsbawm's prescription have to the situation of overwhelming majority of humankind living outside of Europe, the millions upon millions of impoverished and hungry people in the backward, worst-exploited zones of the capitalist world, in Asia, Africa and Latin America, now facing the prospect of only further peripheralisation under the recharged domination of global capitalism?

VI

Soviet Union apart, the idea of socialism had, historically, found its most significant organised expression in social democracy in the West and the worldwide communist movement. In decline for quite sometime now, both have been, directly or otherwise, hit hard by the Soviet collapse. Long involved in softening the contradictions of capitalist society and ensuring its smooth functioning, the submission of social democracy to capitalism is now virtually complete. And the collapse in the Soviet Union has finally exposed the long-festering bankruptcy of 'historical communism' as it has been called. The degeneration and decline of these two movements is an important factor in the contemporary retreat from socialism on the Left, making the search for any new society a truly unfashionable affair in the West and even more difficult and problematic a task elsewhere. Socialism as an ideal, the promise of a just and humane society, has receded as never before in its long history.

Social democracy is a concept with a very shifting meaning. Having lost not only its original connotation of the times of Marx and Engels, but also the one it acquired after the Bolshevik Revolution, it is virtually a misnomer now. Even between the two World Wars, that is, after the break-up of the Second International, social democrats were committed, at least in theory, to the transfer of power to the working people and the social ownership of the means of production, in other words, to the abolition of the capitalist system. They still felt compelled to proclaim their faith in a different social order. Only, as against Lenin and Communists or revolutionary socialists, they claimed that this could be achieved gradually and peacefully, democratically as they put it, within existing institutions.

But things changed rapidly and totally after the Second World War. After a more or less brief period of ritualistic lip-service, all pretence to socialism was dropped. The resilience and vitality of post-War capitalism (nearly thirty years of unprecedented expansion which enabled it to make concessions to the working class as also prosecute the Cold War effectively) and the disappointments, dissensions and defeats on the Left (the failure of Soviet socialism to reform itself, communist–socialist divide, dissipation of the hopes generated by the spasm of 1968, etc.) were among the important factors that contributed to the ever more pronounced integration of social democratic parties and governments into the fabric of capitalist society. With the post-War boom giving way to economic stagnation in the early 1970s, the foundations of the so-called 'historical compromise' that had sustained mutual concessions between capital and labour, simply crumbled. The capitalist class would no longer countenance any such compromise. Instead it chose to dismantle the welfare state. While the social democratic Left, continuing to move towards the centre, was opting for yet more class collaboration, the radicalised Right opted for open class war, backing its electoral and other victories with a new ideological offensive on behalf of capitalism: a renewed affirmation of the virtues of the market and the superiority of 'free enterprise' and competition, and glorification of socially indifferent 'possessive' individualism. With the Soviet collapse, the capitalist offensive, economic, political and ideological, has become all the more open and aggressive, even brutal, leaving little scope for social democratic reformism. For a long time, social democrats had become the reforming managers of capitalist society, but now such 'reformism' has become not merely problematic but near-impossible. Capitalism, simultaneously triumphant in the Cold War and stagnant economically, will not allow and cannot afford any 'reformist social welfare'. Social democracy, even as we had come to know it in recent times, has finally collapsed. Only the working class in the West has yet to see this collapse not as a further demise of socialism but as the impossibility of changing capitalism progressively by reformism instead of fundamentally by revolutionary class struggle.

The other significant organised expression of the idea of socialism has been the worldwide communist movement, born proximately or ultimately of the October Revolution. It has tremendous achievements to its credit, including several successful revolutions (in China and elsewhere) and an extraordinarily rich worldwide legacy of popular struggles, of heroism and sacrifice. But it too had tended to decay and decline over the recent decades. The factors that contributed to the reformist degeneration of social democracy were at work here too. Additionally, dogmatism in matters of theory – via mostly the 'official Marxism' emanating from Moscow – and a pseudo-internationalism – in effect a voluntary subservience that subordinated communist politics to the requirements of the foreign policy or *raison d'etat* of the Soviet Union – had a serious disabling consequence for the Communist Parties, disorienting them in their national politics and undermining their capacity for coping with the complex and constantly changing realities of the world around them, for independent thought and action as parties of revolutionary Marxism that they claimed to be.

Despite occasional doubts or reservations and the somewhat more persistent criticism of 'revisionism' of the post-Stalin era, Soviet Union (along with the 'socialist camp') was a reference point for most leaders and cadres of the Communist Parties. Such developments as Khrushchev's report at the Twentieth Party Congress, or the Soviet–Chinese split, were cause enough for anxiety, but the dynamics of Gorbachev's *glasnost* – which revealed as never before the *other* face of the Soviet Union, disfigured by illegality and injustices, crimes and oppressions, purges, executions and gulags, and degeneration of Communist leadership – dealt a heavy blow to the most sacrosanct underpinnings of this reference point or identity, leaving the Communist leaders and cadres bewildered and demoralised. And when along with the *glasnost* came *perestroika* which ended up in the collapse of Soviet socialism and disintegration of the Soviet Union and the 'socialist camp', it was an absolute disaster for the Communist Parties. Decades of reformist practice had already taken its toll. Now in one country after another, including East Europe, they have either gone defunct or dropping even the pretence of being Communists, formally lapsed into social democracy. Even the label 'communist' has been rapidly abandoned along with the earlier formal commitment to at least some sort of socialism. Henceforth, even as an ideal, it has to be capitalism, albeit 'capitalism with a human face', where 'human' itself is defined in a minimal, vulgar materialist sense. Not only is 'communism' now an obsolete theory, so is every variant of reformist socialism as well. The communist movement as we had known it over these seventy-odd years has more or less collapsed.

Of course, there still remain on the Left Communist Parties which have refused to surrender their name or identity, 'the old faithfuls' which always unquestioningly accepted the claims of the collapsed regimes to be truly socialist; occasional reservations about a Khrushchev or a Brezhnev only made them all the more nostalgic about the Stalin era (a nostalgia shared by most ultra-Left Communist formations who easily combine it with an equally dogmatic attachment to Mao and Maoism). They have indeed been having a really anxious time. Having travelled, full of hope, anxiety and finally fear, the entire distance with Gorbachev, his promise of 'socialist renewal', his *perestroika* and *glasnost*, often believing the one and doubting the other, they have been simply overtaken by the events. Thus overwhelmed, there is incomprehension and an acute sense of betrayal. But given their ideological conditioning and the inherited modes of inquiry, they have found it difficult to produce a viable *Marxist* understanding of this final collapse and its horrendous immediate aftermath – break-up of the states, national chauvinisms and xenophobia, ethnic cauldrons and civil wars, fundamentalist reactions and revivals, anti-Semitism and atavistic regressions of all kinds – which understanding is necessary for rectification of these old Communist Parties, if they would survive as radical political formations and not end up as mere orphans of 'actually existing socialism'. But instead of such rectification, so far they have been content to make, at best, mild critical nods in the direction of Stalin, complain of 'serious mistakes', 'distortions and misapplications' in the practice of socialism, blame it all mostly on Gorbachev and US imperialism. Pressed for more, there is an eclectic listing of 'evils' – 'violation of Leninist norms of inner-party democracy', 'growth of bureaucratism', 'ideological erosion', 'the corrupting influence of opportunists', and so on – or catch all phrases like 'the deviations from revolutionary theory and practice', but no *explanation*, even as they continue to pay their cliché-ridden obeisance to the doctrine of Karl Marx (to which, incidentally, historical materialist explanation is central) or proclaim, at regular intervals, the 'invincibility' of 'the science of Marxism-Leninism', and having done that carry on with their reformist political practices, aligning their politics to 'realistic policies', jumping from doctrine to 'reality' without the slightest moral or epistemological scruples. Needless to say, this way, there is, if any, certainly no socialist future for them.

That socialist aspirations have lost their traditional moorings in the social democratic and communist parties which were historically the two main institutional embodiments of the socialist project in our times, that the former having long lost any interest in transcending capitalist social relations and marginalised those within who sought to re-establish socialist ideals and practices, have finally definitely divested themselves of even the pretence of any commitment whatsoever to socialism, and the latter, under the impact of the current crisis, rather than move in the direction of revival of socialism, have in most cases, both in the East and the West, dramatically or otherwise, collapsed, often all the way, even formally, into contemporary social democracy, is a major factor behind the retreat from socialism we are witnessing all around us.

VII

So far as an effective struggle against capitalism or any socialist project is concerned, contemporary social democratic and communist movements or parties, the two major institutional expressions of socialist politics, had gone sclerotic long before the Soviet collapse or the current crisis of socialism, losing out to bourgeois politics primarily due to 'economism', their reformist misinterpretation and practice of 'class politics'. (It is significant that almost all the popular movements of the last three decades, all of them potential allies in the struggle for socialism – youth rebellion of 1968, women's liberation, the ecological movement, the struggle for democratic rights and so on – have grown outside these traditional parties of the Left, often in the face of their suspicion and hostility.) But now a more or less explicit disavowal of socialism and its values is accompanied by an open theoretical surrender to capitalism and its ideology. It is not merely that in throwing away the dirty bath water of 'actually existing socialism', its anti-democratic, repressive political regime and system of bureaucratically centralised planning, they have thrown out the baby too, namely, the idea of moving beyond capitalism towards a free, democratic, socially just society built on the basis of a genuine social ownership of the means of production and democratically planned economy. It is also that in their so-called 'reconciliation with reality' – 'there is no alternative' – even as they are abandoning the time-honoured socialist values that generations of Socialists and Communists have fought and suffered for – human freedom, social democracy, economic justice, social equality, fraternity and solidarity – they are opting for not just the values of bourgeois democracy – which whatever the limitations are indeed valuable – but also the much clichéd values of predatory capitalism – 'market economy', 'free competition', 'free enterprise', monetarism, culture of the market, etc. etc.

The retreat from socialism and from the politics of struggle for it, accommodation to the capitalist system and an overall loss of character as fighting formations of the working people they were supposed to be, has naturally led to an organisational crisis in these parties of the Left, all the more serious in those with more radical or revolutionary pretensions – a crisis of identity leading to dramatic splits or disintegration in some cases and stagnation and slow decline in most others. An erosion of popular support has been accompanied by the loss of involved or active membership. While many have stayed on for sheer habit and inertia or old times sake, or are content, under slogans of 'realism' or 'practical politics', to seek minor amelioration of oppressions within the existing social order, others have moved away to more viable bourgeois platforms for their reformist politics or for the spoils of new partnerships.

Some, grown tired and indifferent, all passions spent, have dropped out, adding to the growing numbers of cynical ex-Socialists or ex-Communists. And there are yet others who have left in anguish because history did them dirty, leaving a residue of despair and confusion even among many who struggled for decades with courage, imagination and sacrifice for a better world that is not yet.

Taking a longer view of the development of the organised socialist movement of modern times, a thought is inescapable. Emerging in the 19th century Europe, largely Marxist in inspiration and committed to socialism as Marx saw it, Social Democracy simultaneously grew and degenerated (with the exception of the Bolsheviks in Russia) along the reformist path to finally collapse with the War in 1914, when abandoning its declared socialist principles and commitments, its different parties lined up behind their respective national bourgeoisies to become accomplices in their imperialist adventure. It needs to be noticed that not one of these parties of the Second International ever recovered its socialist commitment. They continued to degenerate along the reformist path to reach the present denouement, when even the best of them can hope or dream of nothing better than 'capitalism with a human face', a face that capitalism itself is now refusing to put on. The failure of Social Democracy was only underlined by the success of the October Revolution, following which came another, now worldwide, wave of parties of socialism, the Communist Parties, wholly Marxist in inspiration and committed to a revolutionary struggle for socialism. They struggled and grew, won revolutions and lost them. However, their chequered history has not saved them too from sliding down the reformist path to reach, with the collapse in the Soviet Union, more or less the same denouement as Social Democracy. It is quite likely that history repeats itself as yet another tragedy and the now lost or disoriented parties of the Third International too never ever recover their lost commitment to socialism.

Capitalism survives, but life cannot be denied. The causes which gave rise to the first two waves on behalf of socialism not only remain, they are in many ways more imperative now than ever in the past. Only the historically blind or shortsighted will rule out a third wave of socialism. And it may come sooner than most people think. For today, more than ever before, we are face to face with the alternatives, 'socialism or barbarism' as Rosa Luxemburg, the Marxist Revolutionary, formulated it years ago.

VIII

The collapse in the Soviet Union is not just the collapse of a system; the debacle has been interpreted as in effect the liquidation of a collage of ideas and of praxis inspired by those ideas. The retreat from socialism we have noticed is only a part of this larger debacle which has involved the loss of any and every theory, including Marxism, which could provide a mobilising vision for a social order other than capitalism, leaving behind a vacuum where all sorts of facile syllogisms thrive and which now resounds with the clichéd-wisdom and commonplaces of Right-wing ideologies. It is a theoretical defeat which, expressed more explicitly and vocally among the intellectual and academic Left in the West, has found its resonance in every other part of the world. The quick and final unravelling of the first and now recognisably 'false' start on the road to socialism has been indeed so debilitating as to result in what can only be described as 'a devastation of the mind' on the Left, the magnitude of which is still awesomely difficult to assess.

While the opponents have reached back to question Marxism, and with it any kind of radical or revolutionary politics for human emancipation, it is not difficult to find socialists busy questioning the authenticity of the October Revolution and its aspirations. It is not merely that 'those of us who believed that the October Revolution was the gate to the future of world history have been shown to be wrong', as Eric Hobsbawm has put it, or that the era 'in which world history was about the October Revolution' has definitively ended, the October Revolution and its sequel is seen not as a process which degenerated in stages but as 'a regression *ab origine*, or a pile of rubble'. The view is common that the origins of the failure of socialism in Russia lay precisely in a premature attempt to break away from the model of capitalist civilisation, and, therefore, a return to the canons of capitalist social and economic system now taking place is only a necessary and legitimate historical process – a necessity asserting itself in history. Arguments abound with such vulgar Hegelianism that seeks to dress up the actual outcome in the garb of historical necessity.

In the recoil from general notions of human emancipation, particularly socialism, or Marxism which inspired it, all large schemes of social reform or renewal, however necessary, or cautious and qualified, have come to attract suspicion, hostility and denunciation. This was always an intrinsic part of conservative or liberal-conservative thought; now it has also become part of the thinking of a substantial part of the intellectual Left, loudly proclaimed by people who once were committed to progressive politics or even Marxism. The very notion of socialism as a comprehensive reorganisation of the social order has come under fire. Any such 'meta-saga' as Jean-Francois Lyotard – one-time Marxist radical, now a high priest of the much fancied 'post-modernism' – has contemptuously called it, is a dangerous illusion. And this is being touted everywhere when the most lethal of the 'meta-sagas', *the* 'meta-saga' of our times, capitalism, is very much on, now more comprehensively than ever before! 'Deideologisation' accompanying the current triumph of capitalism has served to make capitalism virtually invisible. Now it is only 'one world', 'the world market' and 'a new world order'; yes, 'globalisation', and with it 'the end of geography', including 'the territorialised nation-state of proven inadequacy', only the 'global village' and revitalised micro-histories. With the collapse of politics understood in the sense of a collectivist project, the accent now has to be on partial, localised, fragmented, specific goals, on small-scale movements, as against universal, dangerously illusionary, 'totalising' projects or perspectives.

A 'new realism' is abroad which rejects the very notion of a comprehensive reorganisation of society on socialist lines as an unrealistic and even a dangerous utopia – and many on the Left are happy proclaiming their loss of faith. The very terms capitalism, socialism, classless society are suspect, anti-diluvian concepts which only dinosaurs, as it were, use these days – 'paleolithic sectarians', Hobsbawm has called them. 'Socialism has become stale', echoes Zillah Eisenstein. If you must, speak now in the vocabulary of 'democracy'. And many are indeed doing so. There is a swelling literature on citizenship, 'rule-of-law' and 'law-abiding state', multi-party politics, democratic and constitutional reforms, the virtues of civil society and so on, where socialism is replaced with social citizenship and the enhancement of 'social rights' within capitalism is viewed as the highest (feasible) emancipatory aspiration and, of course, the superiority of the market is taken as axiomatic. The seemingly 'sensible and intelligent' retreat from socialism leads to an almost unthinking, fashion-driven rush in the direction of a non-planning or minimally planning, private property-based market society. Those not willing to thus travel the whole distance dignify their destination with that rather ambiguous term, 'market socialism'. Much of what now passes for socialist thought with the 'new realists' is indistinguishable from run-of-the-mill liberalism.

The 'new realists', most of them at least, are knowledgeable enough to recognise that the 'socialism' which has just suffered demise had little affinity with the real thing, with socialism of Karl Marx. But they know now that the latter just won't work and one must take a practical view of things. We are also told that capitalism that Marx wrote about and condemned is simply not there, not any more. We have moved far beyond it, and for the better, into post-capitalism. In any case, call it what you like, the reality of this dispensation, a society inescapably based on private property and the market, has to be accepted as permanent. The only thing practical is to try for its more humane management. It is indeed symptomatic of the shift in the whole spectrum of debate on the Left that loyalty to the Keynesian welfare state has come to be seen as an increasingly revolutionary position, and many on the farther Left have staked out this ground as their own. Socialism, if you must still use the term, must be defined in terms of a series of remedies to specific problems within the confines of capitalism – though one is always free to hold on to a vague hope of a more equitable society.

It has been for long a commonplace in social thinking that appeal to 'realism' is often a cover for abandonment of principles. This is certainly the case with contemporary 'new realism', the new faith on the Left. Far from being an accurate reading of the new situation and its possibilities, or even remotely adequate response to the theoretical needs of the present moment, in its abandonment of socialist principles, 'new realism' represents acceptance of a defeat, the Left intellectuals' capitulation to the ideological and political offensive of capitalism.

IX

There is one aspect of this intellectual capitulation on the Left which needs to be specifically noticed. As Gramsci had pointed out, the essence of ruling class hegemony is to ensure willing acceptance of capitalism's domination in society. And traditionally it has been the obligation of intellectuals to offer a critique of capitalism, to help people see through the existing social order and to sustain their hope for a future worthy of humankind – an obligation, reasonably well discharged on the Left, till recently. Today, along with a renewed idealisation of capitalism and hosanna cries to its market, with so many, not only in Russia and East Europe but everywhere, in the West and the East, looking to capitalism for paradigms of economic and political success, capitalist hegemony in society has been sought to be further secured with the argument that 'there is no alternative' and that the alternatives tried or proposed are far worse or simply quixotic or utopian. The instilling of such acceptance and resignation in society on behalf of capitalism is indeed a great triumph for capitalism. And it is precisely at this movement, when a critique of capitalism was most needed, so many on the Left appear to have abdicated the traditional role of the intellectual as a critic of capitalism. Instead, turned 'realists', or 'modernisers' as more recent jargon has it, many of them are even busy conceptualising away the very concept of capitalism in favour of the currently fashionable concepts of 'civil society', 'identity', 'difference', 'pluralism', etc., concepts which obscure the *reality* of capitalism, the 'totalising logic' of its inner drives to competitive accumulation and thus the overall coercive power of capital and the market in a capitalist society.

Ellen Meiksins Wood, a most perceptive analyst of the contemporary ideological scene in the capitalist world, writes:

> The critique of capitalism is out of fashion – and here there is a curious convergence, a kind of unholy alliance, between capitalist triumphalism and socialist pessimism. The triumph of the Right is mirrored on the Left by a sharp contraction of socialist aspirations. Left intellectuals, if they are not actually embracing capitalism as the best of all possible worlds, have little hope for anything more than a bit more space within the interstices of capitalism; and they look forward, at best, to only the most local and particular resistances. And there is another curious effect of all this. Capitalism is becoming so universal, so much taken for granted, that it is becoming invisible.
>
> Now clearly we have plenty to be pessimistic about. Recent and current events have given us plenty of cause. But there is something curious about the way many of us are reacting to all this. If capitalism has indeed triumphed, you might think that what we need now more than ever is a *critique* of capitalism. Why is this the right moment to embrace modes of thought which seem to deny the very possibility not only of surpassing capitalism but even of critically understanding it?...
>
> I really do think we are in an unprecedented situation now, something we have not seen in the whole history of capitalism. What we are experiencing is not just a deficit of *action*, or the absence of the necessary instrumentalities and organisation of struggle (though those are certainly thin on the ground). It is not only that we do not know how to *act* against capitalism but that we are forgetting even how to *think* against it.

That intellectuals have so largely sold out their critical responsibilities is one of the great moral disasters of our time; which, conversely, also helps us define the courage of those who have stood firmly by their commitment as intellectuals.

X

The retreat from socialism has inevitably meant a retreat from Marxism. In fact, in its entire history, no specific development has more single-handedly opened the floodgates of attack on

Marxism, its analytic categories and political project than the collapse of the degenerate and deformed regimes in the Soviet Union and East Europe which claimed to have successfully built socialism and to be on the road to communism. This world historic event, whose substantive origins lay in a series of developments in the post-Lenin Soviet Union, coupled with the stagnation, retreat or even defeats of the international revolutionary movement in recent years, has negatively conditioned, in its process and combination, so much of what is happening around and within Marxist theory today. 'Actually existing socialism' was born of revolutions primarily led by Marxists, had proclaimed Marxism as its official ideology and in its own way represented the first major and seemingly successful revolutionary wave against capitalism. It should not be difficult to understand, therefore, that its collapse is seen as defeat of Marxism itself by its opponents. In their anti-communist perspective which refuses to make any distinction at all between theory and practice, Marxism is proclaimed to be finally dead and best forgotten. Marxism bashing is currently more popular in the academies of the capitalist world than ever before, now that, as the mainstream media tell us, it has been bashed in the streets of Moscow or Prague. And Marxism bashers include not only the predictable conservatives but also trendy intellectuals of all sorts who are busy finding methodological and epistemological reasons to discredit and finally dispose of the entire Marxist enterprise of critical social theory.

Marxism has, of course, been regularly denounced and declared 'dead' or 'failed' over the last hundred years, not only by its opponents but often also by adherents gone penitent. Periodic pronouncements of this sort have been the historic destiny of the doctrine of Karl Marx. In recent times, during the Cold War era, as mentioned in the Prologue, a whole generation of former Marxists denounced the 'God that failed'; many others, like Sidney Hook, had already declared it more or less dead by the 1940s. The 1950s saw the intellectuals in France proclaiming the end of history and with it also the obsolescence of Marxism. Across the Atlantic, in the United States, the 1950s and 1960s witnessed the emergence of heady discourses on the 'end of ideology', 'post-industrial society', etc., which made their own declarations about the end of Marxism. In the post-1960s, as the failure of 1968 produced a renewed conservative assault on Marxism, it also led many disillusioned adherents to turn on Marxism itself and, typically, we had a Jean-Francois Lyotard declaring that the era of totalising theories of history and grand narratives of emancipation was over. The chequered history of the socialist movement during this period, its successes far outweighed by retreats and failures – the 'dissipation' of European reformism in both its social democratic and Eurocommunist variants, the failure of the new Left in the historic upheaval of 1968, the decline of revolutionary struggles and regimes in the Third World, the growing crisis of 'actually existing socialism' and the general 'exhaustion' of the global communist movement – indeed provided a certain credibility to such funereal pronouncements on Marxism, especially in a context of the unprecedented success of capitalism in its post-War boom. But Marxism was seen to have not only survived but retained its intellectual and moral authority on the Left, and even among many critics. However, the events of 1989 and 1991 are now widely believed to have delivered a definitive death blow to Marxism. It is not only that the great world-historic project of struggle and transformation identified with the name of Karl Marx has ended, with it has crashed too an entire world view which inspired and sustained it. As the enemies pronounce Marxism to be finally dead and done with, even friends seem compelled to agree. As Aranson has argued: 'Marxism is over, and we are on our own'.

XI

If the attack from without has become more virulent than ever before, regularly proclaiming the failure, disintegration and final demise of Marxism, transforming it virtually into a term of ridicule and opprobrium, within the costs of Stalinist legacy are being exacted in ways that are as complex as they are often unanticipated in Marxist theory. The repudiation of 'official Marxism', as it came to be described, has opened cracks in doors that have widened to explicit assaults on even basic principles of Marxist theory. There is a state of deep ideological confusion, disarray, and perplexity. Even those who are not yet ready to give away the whole Marxist heritage and plunge into the current chaos of academic and political obscurantism, are trying to retreat in good order. With others it has become almost a rout.

An interesting case here are the Left intellectuals who, still wanting to be socialists of some kind or the other, in turning away from classical Marxism have sought self-serving refuge in what can only be described as pre-Marxian socialism, very much akin to what Marx at the end of the *Communist Manifesto* castigated as 'true socialism'. In a manner reminiscent of the Frankfurt School of Marxists of the 1930s, those theorists whose search for humanistic socialism in the face of Stalinism led backward to Hegel and Kant, or others who similarly turned to the writings of the young Marx, they are resuscitating versions of utopianism (which Marx always frowned upon), often presenting it as 'post-Marxism' or 'post-modern socialism'. Far too many on the Left are today busy, in the name of rehabilitating the 'idea' of socialism, completing or perfecting its vision, putting into it every conceivable value they can think of or they think the Soviet system in its dark days lacked – often painting the darkness thick for their visionary light to shine the brighter!

This modern variant of 'true socialism' has its socialist aspirations but it explicitly abandons any historical grounding for them in favour of a moral appeal on behalf of socialism. It indeed prides itself on a rejection of what it describes as Marxist 'economism' or 'class reductionism' and in doing so virtually excises class or class struggle from its socialist project. Instead it would construct the socialist movement by moral and political means which are treated as essentially autonomous from any social-material basis or, more specifically, economic-class conditions. The moral element is certainly the driving force behind any socialist project, but with the new 'true socialism', the morally grounded appeal for socialism in effect absolves the socialists of any need to seek or formulate the new social-material or economic-class conditions under which capitalist rule can and has to be challenged. Socialism stands reduced to a 'vision' as it was before Karl Marx.

As distinct from *this* regression to pre-Marxist 'true socialism', another, presently dominant intellectual tendency on the Left, however, seeks to 'reconstruct' or 'modernise' Marxism, to 'go beyond' Marx in order to improve and update his supposedly antiquated methods and theories – a tendency that easily merges into the 'theoreticist deluge' of academic, analytical or exegetical, exercises that have characterised Marxist studies in recent years and are collectively spoken of as 'post-Marxism'. (The tag 'post-Marxist', it has been suggested, has a nicer ring to ears than the alternative 'ex-Marxist', it evokes the idea of forward movement, of 'an upto-the-minute thinker', rather than, as does the latter, of a change of colours if not of renegacy itself.) Earlier 'making sense of Marx,' or more recently 'reconstructing Marxism' in the face of what is seen as 'a crisis.... even the end of Marxism', such politically safe exercises may have generated new insights along the way but, as a whole, they represent an infinite regression in theory rather than a new synthesis of understanding, a theoretically more adequate Marxism, 'a reconstructed Marxism.... far sounder than any of its ancestors', as one such exercise has claimed for itself. The regression has in fact involved a rejection of the Marxist tradition altogether, even its basic principled positions; and in a backward-looking combination or rehash of old theories and ideologies, it has adapted Marxism to the ruling class ideas, not only to liberalism, individualism, or positivism but even to the market, its idols, rituals and dogmas. There is 'an aspect of black humour', writes Suchting, about contemporary exercises at 'modernising' or 'reconstructing' Marxism:

> Marxism is reconstructed in something like the way in which those monks approached their work of 'reconstruction' by penning, as the *Communist Manifesto* says, 'silly lives of Catholic Saints over the manuscripts on which the classical works of ancient heathendom had been written'!

Many of the intellectuals involved in these exercises in 'post-' or 'neo-' Marxism as it is called, were once Marxist scholars and even politically engaged people. Obviously, scholars alright, their Marxism or political commitment was only skin deep. As has been well pointed out, in their demoralised or fashionable shift Rightward, away from the classical to one or the other form of hyphenated Marxism, they have simply lost their frame of reference and in tune with the now dominant intellectual fashions, not hesitated to adopt ideas or analyses totally alien or antagonistic to Marxism and peddle the most stupid platitudes of 'post-modernity'. Marxists still, they have gone around proclaiming new paradigms capriciously or declaring ideas obsolete because they were written in the last century or because they seem to go against the trend of the moment. In trying to make up for 'the failure of orthodox Marxism', to replace its outmoded concepts or theories, so many have only dredged up a mélange of conceptual or theoretical banalities from all sorts of bourgeois orthodoxies of the present and the past: individualism (methodological, economic or political), theories of freedom of the market and economic equilibrium, consumer sovereignty, rational choice or preferences, distributive justice or equity, formal democracy, rule of law, freedom of expression, political pluralism, and so on. A 'realist' retreat from Marxism, when it is not a reversion to pre-Marxian socialism, has often been a reversion to neo-liberal orthodoxies in economics and politics. Discarding the world-historic aims of Marxism, gutting its holistic perspective and the emphasis on the structural basis of radical change, socialism itself is put in quotation marks and shrunk down to merely a humane economics, a programme of social-democratic econometrics to give capitalism a human face. 'Post'- or 'neo'- Marxism, in turning away from Marxist revolutionary politics, has only created a metaphysics of post-politics. Hyphenated Marxism in its most important expression, indeed turns out to be 'a half-way house between the radical past and a final reconciliation with orthodox neo-classical economics, mainstream pluralist politics and micro sociology'.

XII

The ideological retreat on the Left has been, as hinted above, both facilitated and conditioned by the overall philosophical context of 'post-modernism' as the cultural logic of late capitalism, which beyond the crisis of socialism or Marxism, reflects a phase of the more basic, epochal crisis of our times.

If the Right has proclaimed the 'end of history' or the final triumph of capitalism, many on the Left, unsettled by the movement's weakness or disarray, have also come to concede that an epoch has indeed ended, that we are living in a 'post-modern' age, that the 'Enlightenment project' is dead, that all the old verities and ideologies have lost their relevance, that old principles of rationality or ethical judgment no longer apply, and so on. In trying to be 'with it', quite a few have indeed queued up to renounce any lingering attachment to such old hat notions as truth, reason, critique, ideology or false consciousness. These are all said to be mistaken, rendered obsolete by the passage to a post-modern outlook that acknowledges the collapse of any hopes once vested in Marxism or any other similarly delusive 'meta-narrative' creeds. As grand narratives, totalising knowledge and even conceptions of causality are rejected for 'post-modern' fragmentation, difference, contingency and 'the politics of identity', the very notion of capitalism as a systemic unity, of its structural logic, becomes impossible to entertain. The 'post-modern' thought simply cannot accommodate the idea of capitalism, let alone subject the capitalist system to critique. The only option that survives the 'post-modern' nihilism is acceptance of what is and, therefore, also a submission to it. And what is, of course, is capitalism – capitalism, the universal reality and the market an inevitable natural law. To opt for anything else, for socialism, is to opt for a delusion. History is indeed over.

Surprised and somewhat scared by the turn of events a Derrida may, rather late in the day for him, nod feebly in the direction of Marx – 'upon rereading the *Manifesto* and a few other great works of Marx, I said to myself that I knew of few texts in the philosophical tradition, perhaps none, whose lesson seemed more urgent *today*', and even recall Benjamin's reference to the 'weak messianic power' we need to preserve and sustain during dark ages. Others of that ilk too may so shift and turn. But with its obscurantist celebration of all kinds of intellectually fashionable skepticism, agnosticism and cynicism, post-modernism is incapable of summoning any kind of power to understand and act in the dark age that a capitalism living beyond its historical time portends. 'Post-modernism' is a philosophy of status quo-serving political impotence wherein even the theoretical possibility of meaningful generalisation is rejected in favour of petty empiricism, and the painstaking search for truth about an objectively existing social reality has been abandoned for a comfortable subjectivism; wherein pursuit of knowledge has given way to academic word games and the faddish followers of Foucault and Derrida talk subtle abstractions about language, knowledge and power but are silent about the grim concreteness of people's powerlessness or about how to empower them to stand up and resist; wherein power itself is seen bounded not so much by the structures of historically determined political economy or class relations and struggles but by discursive exercises; wherein along with a denial of the intelligibility of the world, absolute relativism in matters of knowledge or ethics has emerged as a new orthodoxy; wherein social reality itself is dissolved into a discourse, exploitation is only a set of words or a state of mind and imperialism merely an unpleasant ideological construct. Such is the philosophical or intellectual freight accompanying human descent into the so-called 'post-modern world', which is yet as ancient a world as capitalism ever was.

'Post' is a buzz-word these days. Scholarship abounds with writings that are 'post-this-and-post-that'. To be post-something is in fact the current fashion, especially for those who are ex-something. Thus we are post-modern, post-enlightenment, post-scientific, post-industrial, post-structuralist, even post-liberal and post-western, and, as we must be, post-Marxist, indeed post-everything including capitalism – but 'post-capitalist' notwithstanding, it is capitalism forever!

XIII

Yes, there have been massive retreats and desertions on the Left. But in the midst of it all, at the other end of the Left spectrum, there yet remain the 'heretics' who have refused to retreat or surrender, who still remain committed to socialism and to Marxism of Karl Marx, who continue to believe in the necessity of revolutionary politics, of social revolution and the possibility of achieving an egalitarian, cooperative and democratic (ultimately classless) society which, making a planned, rational use of available resources ensures for all its members immediately a more decent, equitable and humane social existence than it ever lies in the power of capitalism to achieve, and ultimately an all-sided, genuinely rich human development for all as visualised by Karl Marx. Firm as they are in their socialist commitment, they are also fully aware of the enormity of what has happened. They know that life and struggle cannot go on just as before; but they also know that it has to go on. The number of such men and women, though small, is not inconsiderable. And their number is bound to grow as people, in the East and the West – in the First World of advanced capitalism as much as in its peripheries and semi-peripheries in the Third World and the vanished Second World as well – catch up with the ugly, rapacious reality of the currently triumphant capitalism. In fact they have already begun to do so and are increasingly moving into action against it.

As the Soviet Union passes into history, a heavy price is being exacted for the dependence, and often the identification, of the socialist cause with the grossly deformed Soviet experiment in socialism. There is nothing surprising in the Soviet collapse turning into a major defeat for the socialist idea. And insofar as no idea can for long hold out against reality, this defeat means a difficult time for Marxist theory, all the more difficult because Marxist theory, while it has been eminently successful (especially when compared to bourgeois social science) in analysing the large-scale historical structures and processes of capitalism, even though it did not mean anticipating particular futures, has been by and large incapable of providing similar analysis or understanding when this future took the shape of 'socialism' in post-revolutionary societies in the Soviet Union and elsewhere. For many Marxists, the failure here included even the use of Marxism to defend or justify the ugliness, the cruelty and barbarities and worse, that came to disfigure what was built there as socialism. It is no use therefore to assert, once again – as has been customarily done in times of crisis in the past – the 'invincibility' of 'the science of Marxism' (or the science of Marxism-Leninism plus, at times, 'Mao Tse-tung Thought' too). If Marxism, with or without these hyphenations was indeed *that* kind of science, then surely socialism would not have been in *this* kind of mess today. Such ideological rhetoric, however comforting when in distress, only betokens a dogmatism which treats Marxism 'as a hermetically sealed fortress to be defended against the enemies'. Far from being 'a guide to action', as it was intended to be, Marxism becomes theoretically sterile, helpless against new ideas and challenges and incapable of that combination of principle and flexibility which is necessary for any socialist advance, now or at any other time. But in rejecting dogmatism we must not lapse into 'realism' or 'pragmatism' that abandons principles in the name of flexibility. Socialism *has* suffered a defeat, what has happened was unexpected. But the experience of defeat must not be generalised into the impossibility of the struggle, nor the confrontation with the unexpected that has happened into an abandonment of historical materialism which alone can help us understand and cope with it. The defeat does not have to become a rout, nor disappointment lead to a panicky depression. There is no reason at all for Marxists to either don sack cloth and ashes, or, surrendering to the pull of conventional thinking or current fashions, prune or abandon Marxism to jump on bandwagons labelled 'neo'- or 'post'-, etc. That is not the way out of the current crisis but buying into it and its logic of disintegration. The need instead is to recognise and affirm that Marxism as a 'critique' and as the pre-eminent theory of human emancipation in our times, is not exhausted with the exhaustion of 'actually existing socialism'. History is certainly at a specific crossroads, but it has neither ended as proclaimed from the pulpits of the ideological Right, nor is it afflicted with a post-modernist unintelligibility and therefore to be jettisoned as the currently fashioned theoretical texts are making out. Classical Marxism still has sufficient resources to provide theoretical and political guidance through the contemporary world of late capitalism. In fact the relevance of Marxism, its philosophical premises, analytical method and ethical commitment are most certainly going to increase over time as the unhindered logic of the currently triumphant global capitalism reveals itself, which may not be very long. Though it is necessary to add that in many matters we have indeed to begin again, and the process of recovery of socialism in historical terms will be long and bitter.

The task is certainly not a retreat into the idealism of setting forth blueprints for a future socialism, for, if not perfect, a better socialism than what 'actually existing socialism' was. Whatever marginal usefulness such exercises may have, socialist renewal will not be substantially forwarded by constructing abstract models of socialist society, attractive as such models may be in their detailed features. To engage in such exercises, especially at this time, is really to mock what is sound and viable in Marxist social science. Social systems do not come into being because someone has a good idea, by the automatic operations of principles. Nor do they collapse because of lack of them. Either way, the crucial dimensions of material basis and human agency are decisive.

The real task therefore lies elsewhere. As the struggle for socialism goes on, or is resumed, in the historically specific conditions of different countries or regions of the world, the task in its general formulation remains as Marx stated it at the very beginning of his vocation as a communist:

> It is not our task to build up the future in advance and to settle all problems for all time; our task is uncompromising critical evaluation of everything that exists, uncompromising in the sense that our criticism will not shrink either from its own conclusions or from conflict with the powers that be....

This indeed is the challenge confronting Marxists today – an 'uncompromising critical evaluation of *everything* that exists' and this, in the present context means, above all, the failed effort that was Soviet socialism and the seeming triumph of capitalism today. As a *Marxist* evaluation it must seek to take us behind the immediate appearances to the reality of things, the epochal historical processes of our times.

XIV

The collapse of the Soviet Union, disastrous as it has been for socialism, also provides an opportunity for renewal of socialism. The identification of the socialist cause with the deformed Soviet experiment, helpful in some ways, had over the years, for reasons already noticed, also become an obstacle to the effective prosecution of this cause. To the extent that the left has been, consciously or otherwise, positively and at times even negatively, dependent or parasitic on 'actually existing socialism' – here benefiting the most, the Communists have also been the worst sufferers – the events of 1989-91 represent a moment of liberation, and an occasion not to abandon but to recover and renew the authentic Marxist tradition. The Socialists, or the Communists no more need to carry the burden of a deformed and degenerated socialism; they are no longer answerable for its ugliness and cruelties. The burden of a Marxist explanation of what has happened is still theirs, but this in its own way can also serve as a vantage point to consider afresh the problems of the struggle for socialism, including the construction of any new socialism. In this strictly Marxist sense, all Socialists including Communists are indeed, once again, 'on their own'.

The road ahead is indeed an uncharted territory, there are no easy solutions or ready-made answers, not any more. But the new situation also leaves us all, Socialists and Communists, *free* after a long time, for a better, bolder practice of Marxism, for a confident, truly innovative, non-sectarian Left politics in the tradition of revolutionary Marxism – in other words, free 'to think and act as Marx would have done in our place'. As Engels had insisted, 'it was only in that sense that the word Marxist had any *raison d'etre*'. As we do so we may also draw strength from what the same Engels once wrote. It is the end of the letter which he wrote to his comrade Sorge, the day after Marx died:

> Local lights and lesser minds, if not the humbugs, will now have a free hand. The final victory is certain, but circuitous paths, temporary and local errors – things which even now are so

> unavoidable – will become more common than ever. Well, we must see it through. What else are we here for? And we are not near losing courage yet.

Yes, not yet. For even as the first worldwide wave of popular movements seeking an escape from capitalism is disintegrating, the causes that gave rise to it not only remain but are more powerfully effective and urgent today than ever before. Not only will history continue, the 'age of revolution' too is not over.

2

History's Trick on the Doctrine of Karl Marx–I

In August 1989, in a passing reference to the developing situation in the world of 'actually existing socialism', particularly in East Europe and the Soviet Union, I had written of its 'truly historical predicament'. The predicament was there right from the beginning as the Soviet Union set out on the road to socialism – and in a way it is still with us in the third world – as a consequence of the 'trick' which history seems to have played with the doctrine of Karl Marx.

The doctrine of Karl Marx is no determinist philosophy. There is no 'historicism' or 'historical inevitability' in Marx, nor any evolutionist metaphysics either. No doubt there are passages in Marx which, torn out of their immediate context, or the context of Marx's overall theory and practice, are amenable to such misrepresentation. But this remains a misrepresentation. Again, the *scientific* logic of Marx's critique of capitalism does have a certain necessitarian optimism about the future of socialism which also led to a certain undervaluation, not of the factor of will, but of the power of bourgeois ideology and social conditioning and, therefore, of the ideological-cultural struggle needed to create and sustain the will for socialism. But this critique does not have any determinist implications. The critics have, however, continued to speak of 'determinism' in Marx, of 'the orthodox Marxist metaphor of a determining economic base and a derivative superstructural realm', of 'historicism', 'historical inevitability', 'stages of history', etc. in Marxism. For obviously non-scholarly reasons, they have preferred to ignore not only the general thrust of Marx's argument, but the far more important and frequent passages in Marx which question and contradict such misinterpretations, as also Marx's emphasis on the liberating quality of human praxis and own lifelong revolutionary activism. Critics apart, such determinist and associated scientistic or economistic interpretations have been a regular tendency in Marxism itself, though, it must be added, not without protest from within Marxism. The tendency appeared early, compelling Marx to make his much misinterpreted statement: 'all I know is that I am no "Marxist"'. Later it surfaced as the dominant feature of the reformist mode of thinking in the Second International – Kautsky viewing socialism as 'something inevitable', so decreed by 'irresistible natural necessity', and Plekhanov declaring 'the victory of our program is as inevitable as tomorrow's sunrise' – to be questioned and rejected by Lenin and those who followed him in the authentic, revolutionary tradition of Marxism. In more recent years we have the eminent examples of Raymond Williams and E.P. Thompson dissociating themselves from such vulgar Marxism – now a noticeable feature of 'Soviet Marxism' – with Thompson specifically asking us to relearn, what Marx and Engels understood well, that it is not history or any economic basis, but *men* who do it all, that 'man is human by virtue of his culture' and 'history is the record of his struggle truly to apprehend his own social existence....' This dissociation from economist or determinist Marxism, however, never implied an abandonment of the basic premises of historical materialism, a denigration of the material and reification of the ideal which opts for the currently fashionable 'culturist' position – a position which incidentally was sought to be foisted on E.P. Thompson but was rightly dismissed by him as an 'invention' constructed 'from some sloppy and impressionistic' understanding of his work.

II

Marx's theoretical work, particularly his major discoveries concerning the dynamics of socio-historical processes and of capitalism in particular, involving an enormous shift in social scientific thinking, indeed opened up the continent of social sciences. It should not be difficult to understand that awareness of the path-breaking nature of his own work, combined with the science-intoxicated ethos and idiom of his time, found Marx, on occasion, expressing himself in the strong language of 'laws' or 'inevitability' or 'necessity'. (In our skeptical times, people are chary, not the scientists so much as those who philosophise about their work, of using the word 'law' even for what was previously, or still is, legitimately spoken of as 'laws of nature'; 'probabilities' is the maximum they would allow). Thus Marx spoke of 'the economic law of motion of modern society', 'the absolute general law of capitalist accumulation', 'the natural laws of capitalist production' which are 'self-assertive tendencies working with iron necessity', or, in another translation, 'It is a question of these laws themselves, of these tendencies working with iron necessity towards inevitable results', or, again, of 'law of the tendency of the rate of profit to fall', etc. etc. (Incidentally, even this brief reference shows that translation matters which once led Engels to write of 'How not to translate Marx').

A superficial reading which deliberately or otherwise, fastens on to 'law' and chooses to ignore the word 'tendency' in these propositions can easily see and cite them as evidence of 'determinism' in Marx, suggestive of men being governed by economic or historical necessities beyond their control. But to do so is to miss out on their correct understanding, for they are anything but determinist propositions.

Marx and Engels were from the very beginning concerned to emphasise the peculiar character of social laws by calling special attention to the distinction between their theoretical statement in abstract or pure form, and their working out in reality, to their character as 'approximations' or as 'tendencies', even when they are described as 'working and asserting themselves with iron necessity'. In *Capital* (Volume I) Marx posited a somewhat 'pure' or 'abstract' bourgeois mode of production – taking England as its classical ground – for the purpose of analysing its basic law of motion, but he knew that in history there are no 'pure' modes and that the real-life existence of the bourgeois mode of production would always affect and modify the working of what he had discovered as its 'laws of motion' (a problem he sought to tackle in volumes II and III of *Capital*, later put together from his notes by Engels). Marx wrote: 'In (describing) the theory it is assumed that the laws of the capitalist mode of production develop in pure form. In reality there is always an approximation'. Again, 'the general law asserts itself through the whole of capitalist production as the predominant tendency, but in a way which is always very complicated and approximate, as a never ascertainable average of perpetual fluctuations'. Years later, in 1895, in a letter to Conrad Schmidt, Engels told him: 'And of economic laws in general – none of them has any reality except as approximation, tendency, average, and not as immediate reality. This is partly due to the fact that their action clashes with the simultaneous action of other laws, but partly to their own nature as concepts'.

History deals with men who are endowed with wills, who constantly choose and decide, and act. Consequently the working of the law inevitably results in counteracting factors which compensate for each other, cancel each other out, and eventuate in corresponding fluctuations. Therefore, Marx was for ever stressing that in life as it is lived, the law, for various reasons, gets corrected, modified, altered or curbed. (He noticed, for example, 'the counterpoise of the Factory acts' and visualised things taking 'a form more brutal or more humane'). Therefore, when Marx spoke of 'laws' governing historical processes or, more specifically, the capitalist mode of production, it had none of the 'determinist' implications even of the sort which a probabilistic understanding of natural science attributes to its laws. Thus he indeed wrote in *Capital* of 'the absolute general law of capitalist accumulation' – the term 'absolute' is here used, it may be noted, in the Hegelian sense of 'abstract', it has no immediately concrete or any determinist implications – but he had immediately added: 'Like all other laws it is modified by a number of circumstances....' and these, for Marx, would include, among others and above all, human action, which could be working class struggles, capitalists' political practice or intervention by the state, etc. Structural logic of capitalism is modifiable by all kinds of historical factors and special conditions. Marx's formulation, with its combination of 'law' and 'modifiability' indeed raises the much larger question of, not the possibility, but the nature of general or specific law-like explanatory generalisations in social science. Not the possibility, because it is simply inconceivable that social reality as such be unamenable to any explanation at all. Real issue is the greater or lesser validity, 'the objective truth' content, of a particular 'law' or explanation. This is not the issue I would like to pursue here. (One indeed misses Marx's proposed work on *Dialectics*, even 'a few printers pages', which he later on so desperately wanted to write but could not). The immediately important point is that, notwithstanding Marx's occasional determinist or inevitablist language in *Capital* or elsewhere (at the theoretical level anyway), his 'laws' have a conditional, tendential character. In a substantive sense, these 'laws' are to be understood as 'laws of tendency' as Gramsci underscored them; and it is part of the very point of the concept of tendency that it is conditional upon other factors, situations, triggering or countervailing conditions. It is necessary, however, to distinguish between 'trends' and 'tendencies', the former are strictly conjunctural, relating to a specific situation or conjuncture of factors, the latter are of a deeper and general nature, indicating, as it were, near-necessities or *strong* probabilities over a period of time and therefore also suggestive of real possibilities, and more effective human action, in a given historical situation or a particular period of history.

No doubt, to speak of 'laws' which are at the same time identified as 'tendencies', which are yet seen to be 'working and asserting themselves with iron necessity', makes for a certain incoherence of thought. But that Marx is far from any 'determinist' or necessitatarian position is made absolutely clear by the qualifications he immediately adds about his 'laws' being 'modified by a number of circumstances'. (This, incidentally, is precisely the point Marx makes in the letter he wrote to the editors of *Otechestvenniye Zapisky* which we have noticed earlier.

In this connection, it is interesting, as well as instructive, to note that Karl Popper, in making out Marx to be 'determinist', quotes Marx's above passage on the 'law of capitalist accumulation' but chooses to omit the immediately succeeding qualifying sentence. Marxism is thus turned into the 'most dangerous historicism', a doctrine now 'worth attacking' as Popper himself says, that is, a strawman, easy to knock down. Equally selectively, Oakeshott interprets Marxism as the very opposite of 'historicism', a dangerous 'rationalism', that is, yet another strawman easy to knock down).

Meszaros has written:

> As is well known, Marx's bourgeois critics never ceased to accuse him of 'economic determinism'. Nothing could be, however, further removed from the truth. For the Marxian programme is formulated precisely as the *emancipation* of human action from the power of relentless economic determinations.
>
> When Marx demonstrated that the brute force of economic determinism, set into motion by the dehumanizing necessities of capital production, rules over all aspects of human life, demonstrating at the same time the inherently *historical* – i.e. necessarily *transient* – character of the prevailing mode of production, he touched a sore point of bourgeois ideology: the hollowness of its metaphysical belief in the 'natural law' of permanence of the given production relations. And by revealing the inherent contradictions of this mode of production, he demonstrated the necessary *breakdown* of its objective economic determinism....

III

Far from being a determinist or necessitarian, Marx never missed an opportunity to underscore that human beings are the real subjects of history. Quite early, in his famous third thesis on Feuerbach, Marx had stated: 'the materialist doctrine that men are products of circumstances and that, therefore, changed men are products of other circumstances and changed upbringing, forgets that it is men that change circumstances and that the educator himself needs educating'. Again, still more explicitly, Marx wrote: 'History does *nothing*. It "possesses *no* immense wealth", it "wages *no* battles". It is *man* – real living man – who does everything, who acts, possesses and fights; ... history is nothing but the activity of man pursuing his aims'. Marx stood by this position throughout his life, in theory and in practice, as he went on to light up the historical processes and the possibilities of conscious human intervention in them, with his doctrine of historical materialism.

Marx's emphasis on history being 'nothing but the activity of man pursuing his aims' is no contradiction or abandonment of his historical materialist theory which accords a paramount place to 'economic necessity' or 'objective determinations' in the critical processes of social and historical development. On the contrary, properly understood, and not interpreted in a vulgar economistic or determinist manner, Marx's theory makes for a more effective determination of their own history by human beings, for now they do so in full awareness of objective necessity and therefore of real possibilities. As in relation to nature, so in social life, recognition of necessity sets human beings free, free to act more purposefully and even transcend necessity. That is how Marx's theory sought, in Thompson's words, to free humanity 'from victimhood to blind economic causation and (extend) immeasurably the region of choice and conscious agency'.

IV

Marx's theory – in relation to questions of 'historical determinism' or 'base and superstructure' – is really an argument for a proper recognition of the complex interaction of objective economic structures and historical agency, of 'imposed necessity and cultivated desire'. It does not assimilate one to the other, neither structure and agency nor materiality and culture in general. For Marx, as we have argued earlier, objective material conditions or economic-structural processes constitute the basis for human activity and intervention; it is within the necessities and constraints imposed by them that possibilities and choices for human activity or intervention arise and exist. More precisely, the economic or material realm or structures posit boundaries for human praxis, set its context, outer limits or parameters, the 'economic' defining, so to speak, the terrain and horizon, 'the conditions of existence' for the non-economic, the so-called superstructure. But this does not even remotely imply any determinist reduction of the non-economic realm, the superstructure, to some epiphenomenal manifestation of the economic base, or a refusal to recognise the autonomous reality and more or less effective role of its various aspects or parts, including the political, in social and historical processes. Besides, as Marx had insisted: 'the concrete is the product of many determinations'. Responding to the charges of 'reductionism' or 'determinism' Engels had once, on the one hand drawn attention to Marx's *Eighteenth Brumaire* which deals almost exclusively with the *particular* part played by political struggles and events, of course within their general dependence upon economic conditions at a particular juncture in the history of France, and to the section on the history of the bourgeoisie in Chapter XXIV of *Capital*; on the other hand he had rhetorically asked: 'why do we fight for the political dictatorship of the proletariat if political power is economically impotent?' The metaphor of 'base and superstructure' does not undermine but enhances the position of human beings as subjects of history. It is not merely that it is human beings, and not any 'economic base', who 'act, experience, think, and act again', but opting for revolutionary politics, they can use political power to change and transform the economic base itself, that is, overcome the limits or 'imposed necessity' of economic structures, and thereby make possible a freer and better life for themselves. This is how politics, and not economics, has primacy in Marxism. The much quoted 'determination by the economic in the *last* instance' is an eminently useful proposition for social scientists and historians, concerned with interpreting or explaining things, but as a revolutionary doctrine, for those who as Marxists would also change the world, Marxism essentially posits a 'determination by the economic in the *first* instance' only, for according to it whatever then happens or ultimately, including a revolutionary transformation of the economic base or structure itself, is determined by the activity of human beings in pursuit of their aims.

Outside of revolution, or revolutionary politics changing the structural base of society, the logic of this base indeed asserts itself as a decisively conditioning factor in society. In other words, for the supposedly normal conditions of existence of society, the Marxist idea of *determination* of superstructure by economic structure remains very much valid as a generalisation. But even so it does not mean a direct reflection, a one-to-one or unique affair. The determination involved is essentially a *correspondence* and this allows any amount of diversity or variability of expression. For example, Marxism views the state as the organiser of society in the long-term interests of the class (exploitative) structure as a whole. But states can and do have more or less 'relative autonomy' from the exploiting class in their pursuit of these interests, just as the forms of state may vary from the most democratic to the most dictatorial. Speaking of 'the political form of sovereignty- dependency relationship', that is, 'the specific form of the state', Marx had written: '...due to innumerable different empirical circumstances, natural conditions, relationships among races (tribes, & c.), outside historical influences, etc., the same economic basis – same in terms of the main conditions – can show endless variations and gradations in the phenomenon, which can be made out only by analysis of these empirically given circumstances'.

There is thus nothing positivist or unconditionally determinist about how Marxism posits the relation between 'economic base' and 'superstructure'; the relation is far more open, it is a dialectical relationship, which leaves the superstructure very much a realm of *real* choices and possibilities. In a relevant passage, this is how Gramsci saw it: 'It may be ruled out that immediate economic crises of themselves produce fundamental historic events; they can simply create a terrain more favourable to the dissemination of certain modes of thought, and certain ways of posing and resolving questions involving the entire subsequent development of national life.' The economic structure even as it conditions also serves as an indication of real possibilities; as a limiting horizon for superstructural developments, it is also suggestive of the need for the extension or transcendence of this horizon. How far the horizon is extended, or even transcended, and *which* possibilities are eventually realised depends on human beings and them alone.

Marx, who argued that fundamental conflicts or contestations in society have their roots in the economic structures, also pointed out that human beings fight them out in the realm of superstructure, in philosophy, politics, law, art and culture, or morality, and not the least in religion, 'the sigh of the oppressed'. He says as much in a statement which also touches on another relevant aspect of the subject under discussion. We have earlier noticed that, as against the economic, the realm of the non-economic, the superstructural realm in general, remained largely *untheorised* by Marx. But in a famous passage, though only as a passing reference, Marx draws our attention to the *differing* amenability of the levels of *base* and *superstructure* in society to scientific treatment. Speaking of the historical transformations set off by the conflict between 'the material productive forces of society' and 'the existing relations of production', and involving 'the economic foundation' and 'the entire immense superstructure', Marx wrote: 'In considering such transformations, a distinction should always be made between the material transformation of the economic conditions of production, which can be determined with the precision of natural science, and the legal, political, religious, aesthetic or philosophic – in short, ideological forms in which men become conscious of this conflict and fight it out.' The implication is that this fight and its outcome, that is, the superstructural developments, are largely unamenable to 'determination', least of all 'with the precision of natural science' in the words of Marx. Not that within the framework of the reasonably adequate scientific generalisations that Marxism provides about the structure and dynamics of society, and given requisite data and delicacy of analysis, more or less viable, historically specific, explanatory statements about the superstructural realm cannot be made. Even so the fact remains that human beings and their choices, all the diverse factors, elements, variables constituting, as it were, the *subjective* dimension of society, always a most vital part of social reality, are yet not calculable as the *objective* dimension is. This leaves the superstructural realm proper largely devoid of certainties and predictabilities, that is, relatively open and undetermined. Causal connections are surely there, but it makes more sense than any notion of 'determinism' or 'necessity' to see this realm as open for determination by human beings, subject, of course, to 'determination by the economic in the *first* instance' as we have posited and explained above.

Men and women indeed 'fight it out', they choose and act, and struggle to determine their history. But, as suggested above, the outcome of concrete historical class struggles is not predetermined, cannot be predicted in advance, least of all 'with the precision of natural science', as Marx put it. There are thus no inevitabilities in Marx, only *real* possibilities and *strong* probabilities. Marx always disclaimed any determinist or neccessitarian belief in revolution or socialism coming of its own accord. If socialism was seen as 'inevitable', it was so, as Milligan once wrote, only 'in the sense of being that which, under conditions already existing or coming into existence, sufficient men with sufficient power seem certain to will sufficiently to win'. Socialism, for Marx, was a 'necessity' that men and women will come to recognise and acting on the basis of that recognition struggle for it. At heart a child of the optimistic 19th century, Marx may have been unduly hopeful about the future of socialism but he offered no guarantees of its victory. In fact Marx was much too knowledgeable and wise to believe that there are any guarantees in history. In the *Communist Manifesto*, even as he emphasised, at the very beginning, that 'the history of all hitherto existing society is the history of class struggle', Marx had immediately added that this struggle 'each time ended either in a revolutionary reconstitution of society at large or in the common ruin of the contending classes'. And his optimism about it notwithstanding, Marx is not without alternatives in future which, pursuing his argument about the long-term consequences of capitalism, Rosa Luxemburg summed up as 'socialism or barbarism'. Indeed, it is the ideologues of capitalism who are today blindly deterministic about our future with their political slogan, 'there is no alternative'!

Thus Marx was no determinist and whatever determinism there is in his Marxism, is a most conditional one, which accords primacy to human praxis, to revolutionary politics. If attention was drawn to the economic-structural necessities underlying the historical processes, it was for enhancing the freedom for *praxis*, for not foreclosing but liberating human practice, for freer choices by humans, free not in some abstract or metaphysical sense, but in the only possible *human* sense of men and women choosing and acting with the fullest possible knowledge and consideration of the necessities of the objective material situation or circumstances. Such is the dialectics of freedom and necessity in Marx.

V

It is of the nature of the structured and changing character of the social process that the relation between freedom and necessity, the ratio between them, varies from one period to another in the development of society. This touches on an issue that the age-old question of 'historical determinism' has invariably involved, namely, that of its opposite, 'voluntarism'. On this, in a brief but contemporaneously very relevant comment, Paul Sweezy has written:

> The determinist position holds essentially that the conditions which exist at any given time uniquely determine what will happen next. This does not necessarily mean that every individual's thoughts and actions are uniquely determined, but only that in the given circumstances only one combination of thoughts and action can be effectively put into practice. Individuals can choose but societies cannot. At the other extreme, what is often called the voluntarist position holds that anything can happen depending on the will and determination of key individuals or groups.
>
> Marxism is neither determinist nor voluntarist; or, if you prefer, it is both determinist and voluntarist...; at any given time the range of possibilities is determined by what has gone before (determinism), but within this range genuine choices are possible (voluntarism). This very general principle, however, by no means exhausts the Marxian position. Even more important from our present point of view is the idea, which is of the very essence of

> Marxism as a revolutionary doctrine, that in the life of societies there are long periods of relative stability during which a given social order unfolds and finally reaches the end of its potentialities, and that these are followed by periods of revolutionary transition to a new social order. This theme is of course familiar to all students of Marxism, especially from the famous Preface to the *Critique of Political Economy*. What does not seem to have been widely recognised is the clear implication that the ratio of determinism to voluntarism in historical explanation necessarily varies greatly from one period to another. Once a social order is firmly established and its 'law of motion' is in full operation, power naturally gravitates into the hands of those who understand the system's requirements and are willing and able to act as its agents and beneficiaries. In these circumstances, there is little that individuals or groups can do to change the course of history: for the time being a strictly deterministic doctrine seems to be fully vindicated. But when the inherent contradictions of the system have had time to mature and the objective conditions for a revolutionary transformation have come into existence, then the situation changes radically. The system's law of motion breaks down wholly or in part, class struggles grow in intensity, and crises multiply. Under these circumstances the range of possibilities widens, and groups (especially, in our time, disciplined political parties) and great leaders come into their own as actors on the stage of history. Determinism recedes into the background, and voluntarism seems to take over.

Be that as it may, 'determinism' in Marxism, though regularly raked up by critics, is really a tired theme today, which is not to deny, however, that the general problem of agency and structure – which also involves the problems of voluntarism and determinism, men and circumstances, freedom and necessity, revolution and science – retains its importance in social theory and political practice, including theory and practice of Marxism. For my present argument it would suffice to conclude with a restatement of Marx's clearly non-determinist, non-evolutionist, essentially revolutionary position, which found one of its clearest expression in his famous proposition in the second paragraph of the *Eighteenth Brumaire of Louis Bonaparte*: 'Men make their own history, but they do not make it just as they please; they do not make it under circumstances chosen by themselves, but under circumstances directly encountered, given and transmitted from the past.' I would like to add that this is the position which Lenin, thinking and acting in the authentic tradition of revolutionary Marxism, accepted and endorsed. Demarcating himself from the scientistic, evolutionist Marxism of the Second International as it expressed itself among the 'orthodox Russian Marxists', the Mensheviks, who believed that 'history is the product of material forces acting though the process of evolution', Lenin wrote: 'I think, with Marx, that man makes history, but within the conditions, and with the materials given by the corresponding period of civilisation. And man can be a tremendous social force'.

VI

Marx's theory and practice is full of valuable insights for such history-making, that is, pursuit of revolutionary politics, relating to issues that remain as significantly relevant as ever – such as the place or importance of theory in revolutionary politics, the revolutionary ethics, independent class politics and self-emancipation of the working people, the relation of reform to revolution and economic struggle to political struggle, the class character of the state and the relation between state and revolution, the contradictions-laden nature of the epochal transition from capitalism to communism, etc. etc. These insights were born of his lifelong interest in and active association with the radical or revolutionary movements of his time spread over several continents. But it is an aspect of his 'unfinished project' that just as he was unable to write his proposed work on politics, *The State*, he never came to theorise his rich political experience or practice. Hence there are far too many loose threads and 'empty spaces' in Marx's theory of politics. But on an issue of immediate concern to my argument in these notes, he is quite clear and historically specific. Insofar as socialism for Marx involves a revolutionary overthrow of capitalism – which is not necessarily the same as a violent overthrow, though even in a 'peaceful' revolution which Marx saw as a possibility under certain favourable circumstances, he never expected the ruling classes to submit without a last ditch 'pro-slavery rebellion' as he called it – at least two distinct theories of revolution emerge from his writings. His main, supposedly 'orthodox' theory of socialist revolution is quite well-known – its non-occurrence has been in fact the staple of commonplace anti-Marxism for decades now. This theory was based on Marx's view of the historical tendencies of advanced capitalist development in Europe, initially in countries like England and France. Here capitalist relations of production were already becoming fetters on the forces of production developed within them; 'the contradiction between socialised production and capitalist appropriation' was manifesting itself in the recurring 'crises of over-production'. The inhuman consequences of unrestrained industrialism had sharpened the 'antagonism of proletariat and bourgeoisie'. Capitalism, even as it was daily manifesting its essential irrationality and inhumanity, appeared to have also prepared the ground for a transition to the more rational and humane social order, namely, socialism. It had not only created the objective material basis for it in the developed forces of production but also produced 'above all its own grave-diggers', as Marx called them, in the proletariat. Marx expected the proletariat of the advanced capitalist countries to acquire the requisite socialist consciousness and, sooner rather than later, carry out its historical task, that is, overthrow capitalism and, through a socialist transition, move on to build a communist society.

As Marx visualised it, each nation is 'dependent on the revolutions of the others' and 'communism is only possible as the act of the dominant peoples "all at once" and simultaneously, which presupposes the universal development of productive forces and the world intercourse bound up with them'. The terrain on which Marx expected these simultaneous revolutions to be made was the industrially advanced Europe. A socialist transformation could be envisaged there because capitalism's productive potentialities had created the *objective* material basis for it and the antagonist contradictions of the system were fast generating the necessary *subjective* forces.

Even as Marx remained hopeful about 'the social revolution of the nineteenth century', he became aware of a problem with the way he had visualised it. Little was yet visible of the monopolistic development and imperialistic expansion of capitalism but Marx noticed the growing ascendancy of capitalism – 'one cannot deny that bourgeois society lives its second 16th century', he wrote to Engels in 1958 – and the problem it posed for the revolutionary process in Europe. As he put it in this letter to Engels: 'For us the difficult question is this: the revolution on the Continent is imminent and its character will be at once socialist; will it not be necessarily crushed in this little corner of the world, since on a much larger terrain the development of bourgeois society is still in the ascendant.' This is how the Paris Commune of 1871 was indeed encircled and crushed in the European 'little corner of the world' (as were any number of socialist revolutions around the world later by an ascendant bourgeois power). 'The difficult question' noticed by Marx was suggestive of the possibility of another, alternative socio-historical perspective as compared to the one advocated by him. Marx, however, for the most part, held on to the prospects of socialism coming to fruition through a major – non-isolated – social revolution in Europe accomplished by the working classes of the advanced industrial countries.

Apropos this view of Marx, it is important to notice his emphasis on the adequacy of the objective material basis for a socialist transformation. 'The development of productive forces', he wrote, 'is an absolutely necessary practical premise, because without it privation, want, is merely made general, and with want the struggle for necessities would begin again, and all the old filthy business would necessarily be restored...' The emancipation of the working people from the rule of capital is feasible, Marx said, only if the objective conditions of its emancipation are fulfilled whereby 'the direct material production process is stripped of the form of penury and antithesis', giving way to the 'free development of individualities'. The quantitative dimension of the material emancipatory requirements is central to Marx's main theory of social revolution. Socialism, with Marx, presupposes 'a great increase in productive power, a high degree of its development'; without it, as just noticed, 'privation, want, is merely made general, and with want the struggle for necessities would begin again, and all the old filthy business would necessarily be restored.' With 'penury and antithesis' characterising the material base of society, the 'free development of individualities' that socialism seeks is impossible.

Since overcoming the conditions of 'privation' and 'want', of 'penury and antithesis', necessarily implied the highest development of the forces of production, successful social revolution, one capable of building socialism successfully, had to be envisaged by Marx in capitalistically advanced countries.

VII

These considerations, central to Marx's main theory of social revolution are valid, by themselves and in their implications, for successful struggle for socialism anywhere. They do not, however, exhaust Marx's thinking on the subject. Alongside his main theory, the unrealised possibility and for that very reason much noticed by the critics, Marx had another theory of socialist revolution, which finds expression in several of his writings both of the early and the late periods, suggestive of alternative perspectives and possibilities.

If there is no economic or any other determinism in Marx, there is no theory of necessary stages of historical development either. He specifically disclaimed any such 'super-historical' view of social or historical processes. For him there is no unique path of historical transitions, no pre-determined or unilinear, stage-by-stage social development, either *to* capitalism or *from* capitalism. Marx's social theory recognised a multiplicity of roads of social transformation within the global framework of mutual and differential impact. In the *Grundrisse* he explicitly accepted it for the pre-capitalist past; he saw it in terms of plurality of modes of production developing under the influence of specific local, geographic, ethnographic and historical circumstances, each one an independent discrete entity needing to be analysed in terms of its own categories and own logic of development. For Marx *Capital* itself was 'his historical sketch of the genesis of capitalism in Western Europe' only; he had strongly protested when a Russian commentator sought to 'metamorphose' it, in Marx's words, 'into a historico-philosophical theory of the general path every people is fated to tread, whatever the historical circumstances in which it finds itself'. And late in his life in the 'Chronological Notes' – a massive conspectus of Marx written in 1880-82 – he equally explicitly assumed a plurality of paths for the post-capitalist future. It is not surprising therefore to find in Marx what may well be described as his subsidiary theory of revolution, indicating a dramatically different course of revolution or social progress for our times as against the one postulated by his much-noticed main theory of socialist revolution in advanced capitalist Europe. Not well-theorised but explicitly stated on more than one occasion, this other theory, typical of Marx, concerned itself with socialist revolution elsewhere, with the revolutionary possibilities in the relatively backward countries, the countries of 'belated' or 'retarded', non-classical capitalist development.

Intimations of this theory are there in the same work of 1845 (*The German Ideology*) in which Marx spoke of the simultaneous 'act' of the 'dominant peoples'. Here Marx also considered, as an exception to the rule, the possibility of a socialist revolution erupting in an *underdeveloped* country as a result of *uneven development* – an exception that literally became the rule in the 20th century. Marx not only hinted at this possibility of socialist revolutions in less advanced countries, he developed that idea in other contexts, especially in his correspondence with Vera Zasulich, with regard to the specific conditions – and potentialities – of Russia where the anticipated revolution later in fact unfolded.

VIII

At the very beginning, in the early 1840s, we find Marx taking note of the belated bourgeois development in Germany and therefore of the belated bourgeois revolution developing there. And hinting at the necessarily limited or partial character of its possible victories, he pointed out, already in 1844, that 'Germany will not be able to emancipate itself from the Middle Ages unless it emancipates itself at the same time from the partial victories over the Middle Ages'. 'Germany', he wrote, 'can only make a revolution which upsets the whole order of things'. Four years later, we have the celebrated passage in *Communist Manifesto:* 'The Communists turn their attention chiefly to Germany because that country is on the eve of a bourgeois revolution that is bound to be carried out under the more advanced conditions of European civilization, and with a much more developed proletariat, than that of England was in the seventeenth and of France in the eighteenth century, and because the bourgeois revolution in Germany will be but the prelude to an immediately following proletarian revolution'.

As expected the German revolution indeed occurred in 1848, but it failed rather rapidly even as a bourgeois revolution, and the possibility of moving from a bourgeois to a proletarian revolution, as visualised by Marx, never became real (as it in fact did later, with Lenin and Russian Revolutions of 1917). We may yet note Marx's perspective on this possibility for its activist orientation. Concerning the proletarian programme or tactics in such (and therefore similar) revolutions, Marx wrote:

> While the democratic petty bourgeois want to bring the revolution to an end as quickly as possible, achieving at most (their own) aims, it is our interest and our task to make the revolution permanent until all the more or less propertied classes have been driven from their ruling positions, until the proletariat has conquered state power and until the association of the proletarians has progressed sufficiently far – not only in one country but in all the leading countries of the world – (and) competition between the proletarians of these countries ceases and at least the decisive forces of production are concentrated in the hands of the workers. Our concern cannot simply be to modify private property but to abolish it, not to hush up class antagonisms but to abolish classes, not to improve the existing society but to found a new one...'

Failure of 1848 notwithstanding, Marx continued to hold on to the view that the unresolved tasks of the bourgeois revolution could be and will need to be solved by a proletarian revolution. And as regards this revolution, in 1956, he wrote to Engels: 'the whole thing in Germany will depend on the possibility of backing the proletarian revolution by some second edition of the Peasant's War.' It is equally worth noting in this connection that, apropos the outcome of the French revolutions of the period, Marx once spoke of *Paris* being defeated by *France*. He hoped for the French peasantry, disillusioned in due course, turning away from the bourgeoisie to find an ally in the proletariat and wrote: 'and thus the proletarian revolution obtains the chorus without which, in all peasant countries, its solo becomes a swan song.'

Obviously the perspective of this subsidiary theory is, if not a departure from, certainly a most significant modification of the general principles which underlay Marx's main theory, namely, that it is the expansion of the productive forces, generated by a certain necessary development of capitalism, which leads to an epoch of socialist revolutions. Decades later, after the death of Marx, looking back on 1848, Engels did write: 'the state of economic development on the continent was not, by a long way, ripe for the elimination of capitalist production.' However valid as a retrospective historical assessment, this observation is yet amenable to economistic interpretation, coming as it does from Engels who was, as we know, more than Marx a man of his own generation, more open to its evolutionist, 'naturalistic' or 'positivist' beliefs. It should not, however, be allowed to obscure the truly remarkable insight of Marx in suggesting that a country could, despite being backward or perhaps because of being backward, come to the forefront of revolutionary process, that the reserve forces of a bourgeois revolution could improve the prospects of a socialist revolution. What is more, this insight had a most important implication which became explicit in unmistakable terms in the work of late Marx – where Marx now posited the possibilities of different models of socio-economic development in our historical times, different that is, from the western pattern, followed in Europe and North America, and which has been almost invariably presented as necessary and desirable for the so-called developing countries of the third world. However, even as we recognise the world-historical importance of this insight of Marx and its implications, it is important to note that for Marx's own historically specific concerns, the context for the realisation of these different yet socialist possibilities, for the eventual success of such a revolutionary enterprise, was, even if a bit ambiguously, the above noted revolution involving 'all the leading countries of the world', that is the industrially advanced countries of Europe.

IX

As foreseen by Marx and Engels in *Communist Manifesto*, the revolution occurred in Germany, progressed rather shakily, was soon compromised by the bourgeoisie and ultimately defeated. Marx, along with Engels, participated in the revolution and even as the developments were taking place, analysed them. This analysis, expressive of Marx's method as well as his political commitment, exceptionally rich in the lessons flowing from it, was to be most relevant for the revolutions of the 20th century which followed. Even today, it retains its meaning and insightfulness for the political processes in the countries of belated or retarded capitalist development, including India. A brief digression therefore will not be out of place.

Marx wrote of the German bourgeois revolution in relation to its earlier counterparts, the bourgeois revolutions of England (1649) and France (1789). (The fetishisation of quantitative methodology and the explicit anti-Marxism of mainstream social science has recently expressed itself in much scholarly analysis questioning such class characterisation of these revolutions. Allergic to considerations of origins and political-outcomes, it has been focussing on the personnel, the actual participants, etc. – this however is not a subject to be pursued here). Marx saw the bourgeoisie as victorious in these earlier revolutions and noted that 'the victory of the bourgeoisie was at that time the victory of a new social order'. But in Germany, according to Marx, the bourgeoisie was not revolutionary, not any more, for now the proletariat, 'this class *behind* it', was knocking at the gates. The German bourgeoisie could not be relied upon to make even its own bourgeois-democratic revolution for fear of the eventual socialist revolution. The conclusion was obvious: the two tasks, the bourgeois and the socialist, would have to be telescoped, unlike the pattern of the earlier bourgeois revolutions in England and France. In other words, even the bourgeois-democratic revolution, for its completion, would require the leadership of the proletariat.

Marx's analysis was of seminal importance later to the Bolsheviks in Russia in working out their political line of what Lenin described as 'uninterrupted' or 'continuous' revolution; this is how they moved from the February to the October Revolution in 1917. And Mao's *new* democratic revolution, as the opening phase of China's revolution, was new precisely as distinguished from the old successful democratic revolutions, in which the bourgeoisie overthrew feudal domination in Europe; China's bourgeoisie, weak, vacillating and fearful of popular revolt simply could not do so. Insofar as the crux of a successful bourgeois revolution is the anti-feudal agrarian revolution which is a precondition of any proper or adequate capitalist development, Marx's analysis was more than vindicated by the historical experience of the revolutions of the 20th century, as much by the Marxist-led ones in Russia or China, or the bourgeois-led ones, say in India, where more than fifty years after winning independence the rulers are still occupied, rather pretending to be occupied, with the carrying out of land reforms!

In this connection Marx's assessment of the German bourgeoisie of the period is both interesting and instructive. He wrote:

> The German Bourgeoisie had developed so sluggishly, so pusillanimously and so slowly, that it saw itself threateningly confronted by the proletariat, and all those sections of the urban population related to the proletariat in interests and ideas, at the very moment of its own threatening confrontation with feudalism and absolutism. And as well as having this class *behind* it, it saw *in front of* it the enmity of all Europe. The Prussian bourgeoisie was not, like the French bourgeoisie of 1789, the class which represented the *whole* of modern society in face of the representatives of the old society, the monarchy and the nobility. It had sunk to the level of a type of *estate*, as clearly marked off from the people as from the Crown, happy to oppose either, irresolute against each of its opponents, taken individually, because it always saw the other one in front of it or to the rear; inclined from the outset to treachery against the people and

> compromise with the crowned representative of the old society, because it itself already belonged to the old society; representing not the interests of a new society against an old but the renewal of its own interests within an obsolete society; at the steering-wheel of the revolution, not because the people stood behind it but because the people pushed it forward; at the head of the movement, not because it represented the initiative of a new social epoch, but only because it represented the malice of an old; a stratum of the old state which had not been able to break through to the earth's surface but had been thrown up by an earthquake; without faith in itself, without faith in the people, grumbling at those above, trembling before those below, egoistic in both directions and conscious of its egoism, revolutionary in relation to the conservatives and conservative in relation to the revolutionaries, mistrustful of its own slogans, which were phrases instead of ideas, intimidated by the storm of world revolution yet exploiting it; with no energy in any respect, plagiaristic in all respects; common because it lacked originality, original in its commonness; making a bargaining-counter of its own wishes, without initiative, without faith in itself, without faith in the people, without a world-historical function; an accursed old man, who found himself condemned to lead and mislead the first youthful impulses of a robust people in his own senile interests – sans teeth, sans eyes, sans taste, sans everything – this was the nature of the *Prussian bourgeoisie* which found itself at the helm of the Prussian state after the March revolution.

It needs to be noticed that German bourgeoisie's fear of a revolution from below, its vacillations, its propensity to seek change through bargaining and through compromises with the forces of the old order, and much else that Marx said about its character and historical role, was far from being unique. With due concession to the historically specific differences – which remain most important – all this was to become typical of the bourgeoisie in the countries of belated colonial or post-colonial capitalist development. Reflected in its struggle for power, it is as much reflected in the capitalism it builds when in power, where, in the words of Karl Marx, we 'suffer not only from the development of capitalist production but also from the incompleteness of that development. Alongside of modern evils, a whole series of inherited evils oppress us, arising from the passive survival of antiquated modes of production with their inevitable train of social and political anachronisms. We suffer not only from the living but from the dead.' Given the essentially *secondary* character of such bourgeois development, we may as well also remember Marx's statement: 'as is well-known secondary diseases are more difficult to cure, and at the same time, ravage the body more than original ones'. As an example, we need to take only a cursory look at the Indian bourgeoisie, its historical role, and the capitalism it has built, to recognise the truth of the insights of Karl Marx.

X

Marx, throughout his life, continued to hope for an European revolution; he continued to regard the conditions in the advanced capitalist world as sufficiently ripe for the socialist revolution he expected to take place. Ten years after 1848, he wrote to Engels: 'on the Continent the revolution is imminent and will also immediately assume a socialist character'; though, as already noticed, he did not rule out the possibility of its being crushed 'in this little corner of the world', considering that in a far greater territory the movement of bourgeois society was still on the ascendant. About this time, Marx has been interpreted to be speaking of the possibility of a socialist revolution only after capitalism in its further development exhausts its potential and is beset by problems engendered by this development. Yet twelve years later he declared: 'The English have all the material requisites necessary for a socialist revolution: what they lack is the spirit of generalisation and revolutionary passion.' Still later, as the 1882 Preface to *Communist Manifesto* clearly indicates, 'a proletarian revolution in the West' remained a real possibility for Marx. But over the years Marx had also grown progressively less sanguine in this regard and his interest had increasingly shifted eastward, to the coming revolution in Russia. It is in this eastward shift of late Marx that the non-evolutionist, non-determinist, and truly revolutionary character of Marx's social theory best manifests itself.

Before I explore this shift, it bears repeating that even during the post-1848 period of hopefulness about an European revolution, Marx's thought was immune to any kind of determinism or evolutionism about a transition to socialism. In addition to what has been already stated, specifically relevant evidence here is a little noticed aspect of his analysis of the Paris Commune (1871). As we have seen, although Marx maintained that the socialist revolution could only be led by the proletariat, he was far from ruling out the possibility of socialist revolutions in countries where the majority of the population were still peasants; and he consistently stressed that the success of such revolutions depended on winning the support and participation of the peasantry. Such was now the case with the Paris Commune where the peasantry still constituted the greater part of the population in France. For its success or further progress, Marx argued for a worker–peasant alliance. He recognised that 'the Commune does not do away with the class struggle, through which the working classes strive for the abolition of all classes'. But he held that the Commune 'affords the rational medium in which the class struggle can run through its different phases in the most rational, humane way'. Marx had warned that the proletariat 'must not hit the peasant on the head' but win its support and take steps to ease the peasants' transition to socialism. Had the Commune survived, that is, had it been able to win the French peasantry to its side, Marx believed that the working class could have gone on to build socialism in France. It may be added that Marx's view of the peasantry was always complex – because historically nuanced. If he saw the French peasantry as a class playing a reactionary role in Napoleon III's Second Empire, he also saw it capable of revolutionary initiatives. Marx distinguished the revolutionary from the conservative peasantry. The former he described in heroic terms as 'the peasant that strikes out beyond the condition of his social existence, the smallholding'. The revolutionary peasant, for Marx, was characterised by 'enlightenment' and represented the future, the 'modern Cevennes'. (Cevennes, a mountainous region in France, was the site of a large uprising of Protestant peasants at the beginning of the 18th century).

Marx continually stressed the forging of a worker–peasant alliance in 'all peasant societies'. He never argued that the triumph of socialism in any particular country required the proletariat to be a majority (as opposed to a more or less sizeable portion) of the population. Instead, he searched painstakingly for those conditions in which workers could join with other oppressed classes to take political power and initiate the further protracted transformation to socialism/communism.

Marx's theoretical model of a worker–peasant alliance, postulated specifically in the aftermath of the Paris Commune, was and remains an important guiding principle in the struggle for socialism in the less developed or 'developing' countries of the capitalist world. It was later developed and put into practice by Lenin as strategy and tactics in the Russian revolution and was an integral part of his project for a socialist transition in Russia.

XI

Marx's eastward shift was not any kind of altogether new turn in his thinking. It is true that Marx, in the better worked yet unfinished part of his theory of capitalist development, focussed on the 'highly developed capitalist form'. Later on, not only was this taken as substantially the whole of his theory of capitalism, it was also taken for granted, despite Marx's explicit disclaimers, that as capitalism gets a foothold in other parts of the world, they would experience the same kind of development as the advanced capitalist countries. It was commonplace to quote selectively and refute out of context passages from Marx that lent support to this view: such as 'the country that is more developed industrially only shows to the less developed the image of its own future', or 'the bourgeoisie... compels all nations, on pain of extinction, to adopt the bourgeois mode of production... to become bourgeois themselves. In one word, it creates a world after its own image', etc. But this can be and has been quite misleading. From the very beginning Marx saw capitalism as a global system and noticed its structural compulsion to globalise in several truly prophetic passages in the *Communist Manifesto*: 'the need of a constantly expanding market for its products chases the bourgeoisie over the whole surface of the globe. It must nestle everywhere, settle everywhere, establish connections everywhere', or 'the bourgeoisie has through its exploitation of the world market given a cosmopolitan character to production and consumption in every country', etc. But Marx pointed out an aspect of this capitalist globalisation which the above noticed interpretations have invariably ignored. In the *Communist Manifesto* itself Marx had written: 'the bourgeoisie has subjected the country to the rule of the towns... Just as it has made the country dependent on the towns, so it has made.... nations of peasants (dependent) on nations of bourgeois, the East on the West'. A little later Marx was to write: 'The profound hypocrisy, and inherent barbarism of bourgeois (rule) lies unveiled before our eyes, turning from its home where it assumes respectable form to the colonies, where it goes naked.' He was scathingly critical of the devastation, the misery and suffering British rule caused in India. It is in an article on India that Marx wrote of 'human progress' under capitalism resembling 'that hideous pagan idol who would not drink the nectar but from the skulls of the slain'. Years later, in a letter to Danielson in 1881, with reference to India, he described colonialism as 'a bleeding process with a vengeance'. In a limited sense and in some situations Marx did see a certain 'progressive' side to colonialism, but he, along with Engels, always positively assessed, even celebrated, resistance to colonialism, to 'civilisation-mongers' as Engels called them.

In *Capital*, even as Marx analysed 'the highly developed capitalist form', Marx also wrote: 'A new and international division of labour, a division suited to the requirements of the chief centres of modern industry springs up and converts one part of the globe into a chiefly agricultural field of production for supplying the other part which remains a chiefly industrial field'. Obviously as capitalism spreads outward, the bourgeoisie of the more developed countries does not create a world after it own image in the less developed parts of the world. In other words, Marx was aware of this reality of capitalism as a global system, the causal relationship between development of capitalism in Europe and the particular character of the skewed economic development elsewhere, the development of the underdevelopment as the reverse side of the coin of development under capitalism on a world scale. Marx was coming to see capitalism as a global system where the progress of the advanced section was at all stages the cause of retrogression, absolute or relative, in the remainder, with its corollary that the colonies or post-colonial states with their crippled and dependent economies could produce nothing other than crippled and dependent bourgeoisies devoid of any radical hopes or potentialities.

Marx thus had the basic elements, in however fragmentary a form, of a theory of capitalism as a global system, though he never lived long enough to develop this theory – it was left to Lenin to really pioneer the theory of capitalism as a global system, consisting essentially of a core of advanced industrial countries surrounded by a vastly larger and more populous peripheral countries, colonies, semi-colonies, neo-colonies, in varying states of dependence on each other and ultimately on the centre. Nevertheless, in his eastward shift during the last decade or so of his life, Marx turned his attention to the related question of historical interdependence of peoples and countries in different periods of global history and confronted a set of fundamental problems which, entirely new to Marx's generation, would be nowadays easily recognised, as Shanin has argued, 'as those of "developing societies", be it "modernization", "dependency" or the "combined and uneven" spread of global capitalism and its specifically "peripheral" expression'; at the centre of it all lay 'the newly perceived notion of "uneven development", interpreted not quantitatively (i.e. that "some societies move faster than others") but as a global interdependence of societal transformations'. Involved in this effort was Marx's perception of structures unique to backward capitalism as well as his actual anticipation of the radical potential of the peasantry which, however, was nothing new for him. All this is of topical contemporary importance, especially for peripheral and semi-peripheral societies of global capitalism. But my concern at the moment is with the fact that it is in this connection, rather late in his life, but as alert intellectually and politically as ever, Marx again turned to the theme of what we have described as his subsidiary theory of socialist revolution, providing evidence, more clearly than ever before, that he did not believe all peoples were fated to tread an identical path to socialism.

Now, in 1981-82, of course following his earlier interest in Russia, Marx was, along with Engels, looking forward to the coming revolution in Russia. The issue arose in the context of Marx's interest in the peasant Commune (*Obschchina*), and as a consideration of the historical options available to what was then universally regarded as backward Russia. If ever evidence were needed that in Marx there is no evolutionist or unilinear thinking, no determinist or stageist view of historical processes, it is here, present in a most explicit form. The issue, as just mentioned, concerned the possible historical options for Russia. And for Marx and Engels, it arose as the question whether the communal ownership among the peasantry in Russia would be destroyed by the development of capitalism in Russia or whether it could, at a higher level, facilitate and hasten the transition to socialism, providing 'the finest chance ever offered by history to a people' to pass directly from a feudal to a communist phase of development. Marx believed that it could, provided there was an early revolution in Russia, early enough to save the peasant commune from being destroyed. Marx specifically distanced himself from his 'disciples' in Russia, Plekhanov and others, whose strictly evolutionist Marxism saw history as constituted by necessary stages and postulated the necessity of a capitalist stage in Russia's advance to socialism. Marx found their doctrines 'boring' and referred to them derisively as 'Russian capitalism admirers'. Marx's position also involved a new recognition of the great revolutionary potential of the peasantry.

The issue is broached in Marx's now well-known correspondence on the subject. In the first draft of his proposed letter to Vera Zasulich in 1981, Marx wrote: 'If the revolution occurs in time, if it concentrates all its forces... to ensure the free flowering of the rural commune, then the latter will develop itself before long as an element in the regeneration of Russian society, as a point of advantage when compared to the nations enslaved by the capitalist system'. There was no reference here to any essential preconditions in the technological achievements of capitalism or the material help from a victorious revolution in the West. Marx seems to be moving away from such views – how far if at all he had moved in this direction will for ever remain a matter of debate. In the fourth and final draft, the reply finally sent to Zasulich, Marx was still convinced that 'the commune is the fulcrum for social regeneration in Russia'. And the only qualification he added was: 'But in order that it might function as such, the harmful influences assailing it on all sides must first be eliminated, and it must then be assured the normal conditions for spontaneous development'. Engels however was quite explicit in regarding, apart from an early revolution in Russia, a revolution in the industrially more advanced Europe as a necessary condition for realising this option. 'The possibility undeniably exists of raising this form of society (Russian communal ownership) to a higher one,' Engels wrote, 'if before the complete break-up of communal ownership, a proletarian revolution is successfully carried out in Western Europe, creating for the Russian peasant the preconditions requisite for such a transition, particularly the material conditions which he needs if only to carry through the revolution (necessarily connected therewith) of his whole agricultural system.' In other words the Russian communal ownership could be saved to become the basis of a socialist development if together with a Russian Revolution, a proletarian revolution occurred in the more advanced Europe – a position which Marx too came to adopt finally in the Preface to the 1882 Russian edition of *Communist Manifesto*, whether persuaded by Engels or otherwise; the Preface said: 'If the Russian Revolution becomes the signal for a proletarian revolution in the West, so that the two can supplement each other, then the present Russian communal land ownership can serve as a point of departure for a communist development'. Be that as it may, Marx in any case was still hopeful of a European revolution and saw in it, if not an absolute precondition, as Engels did, certainly an absolute favourable factor for a Russian regeneration based on and facilitated by the commune.

The coming Russian Revolution was expected to trigger off precisely this European revolution. Marx and Engles regarded

Russia in the 1880s 'as the vanguard of revolutionary activity in Europe'. With truly remarkable historical insight Engels wrote in 1885 that 'the Russians are approaching their 1789' and 'when 1789 is once launched in such a country, 1793 will not be far away'. He clearly foresaw both 1905 and 1917. He noticed the accumulated contradictions – economic, social and political – that constituted the inner dynamics of backward Russian society, the utter weakness of its 'civil society' and the rottenness as well as isolation of its state structures, the gathering anger of the people and exceptional maturity of its revolutionary movement, making Russia, as he wrote 'one of the exceptional cases where it is possible for a handful of people to make a revolution, i.e. by giving a small impetus to cause a whole system, which (to use a metaphor of Plekhanov) is in more than labial equilibrium, to come crashing down and by an action in itself insignificant to release explosive forces that afterwards become uncontrollable.'

Engels continued to believe that a Russian Revolution, once started, would be sure to be followed by a German Revolution: 'We have in Germany a situation which is certain to move toward a revolution at an increasing speed and push our Party to the forefront within a short period of time.... One thing we want is an immediate impact from without. It is the situation in Russia that will provide this for us.' And this in turn was to open the way for the realisation of the socialist option for backward Russia. As Marx and Engels' famous Preface to the 1882 Russian edition of *Communist Manifesto* put it: 'If the Russian revolution becomes the signal for a proletarian revolution in the West, so that the two can supplement each other, then the present Russian communal land ownership can serve as a point of departure for a communist development.'

To sum up, it was the conviction of Marx, his main theory of anti-capitalist revolution, that it was the industrially advanced countries of Western Europe which would be the setting for the socialist revolution and the subsequent building of socialism. But he also had a subsidiary theory which postulated the occurrence of a socialist revolution in the backward counties of the capitalist world. But the construction of socialism there was conditional upon the help and support of the victorious proletariat of the industrially advanced countries. In the concrete historical situation of their times, Marx and Engels saw the imminent revolution in backward Russia as the first possible breakthrough against capitalism which would be a signal for a general European revolution in which both revolutions would supplement each other and the revolutionary proletariat of the industrially advanced countries would help the Russian proletariat and people, despite their backwardness, build socialism without having to pass though a prolonged period of capitalist development.

XII

In the event it is Marx's subsidiary theory of revolution which became the main theory in the world historical process – socialist revolution occurred but only in one backward underdeveloped country after another. This one possibility, well foreseen and worked for by Marx was indeed realised. But the other possibility, the necessary favourable factor, if not a precondition of its further socialist progress, a 'supplementing' revolution in the industrially advanced capitalist countries the way Marx visualised it never materialised – even when it occurred did not survive – making all the difference to the present and future of socialism in our time. This is the trick that history has played on the doctrine of Karl Marx. Indeed, as Engels once said, 'history is about the most cruel of all goddesses'.

It needs to be remembered that, as anticipated by Marx and Engels, a German, indeed a European revolution, triggered off by the Russian revolution did occur in the aftermath of the First World War. We had, alongside Russia, revolutions or near revolutions in Germany, Finland, Hungary and Bavaria, in Austria and North Italy, and a powerful revolutionary wave elsewhere in Europe. But this European revolution could not withstand the powerful offensive of capitalist counter-revolution; much of it was aborted or betrayed and surrendered by Social Democracy. Most significant for the future of socialism was the betrayal and surrender of the revolution in Germany, industrially the most advanced among these countries. The nature and role of social democracy in Europe, its degeneration, found a typical expression in the statement of its leader in Germany, Scheidemann, who, responding to the German reaction's charge of being responsible for the revolution filed a law suit for libel in a Berlin court in 1922 and declared: 'The imputation that Social Democracy wanted or prepared the November revolution is a ridiculous, stupid lie of our opponents'! Quite a contrast with the Bolsheviks in Russia, and indicative of how far social democracy had strayed from its original aims. The consequences for the future of socialism, as visualised by Marx, were disastrous. These developments and their analysis is not our concern here. The significant point to be immediately noticed is the context in which the question of actual construction of socialism first appears on the historical agenda. Of the Europe-wide revolutionary upheaval, only the revolution in backward Russia survived, thanks to an exceptionally favourable combination of factors – of history, geography, contemporary international situation, but above all the political leadership provided by Lenin and his Bolsheviks, who, as Rosa Luxemburg said, had done everything that could be done 'within the limits of historical possibilities' and thus saved 'the honour of international socialism'. But this also confronted the revolutionary Bolsheviks, their Marxist leadership and the common Russian people with an almost, though not entirely, impossible task of pioneering the path to socialism, history's 'most radical rupture' as Marx called it. They were called upon to pioneer it not just in a backward, war and civil war ravaged country, with a small, civil war-decimated working class, but also alone and in the midst of a most powerful, implacably hostile capitalist encirclement which did not allow their enterprise a single day of peace. For the Soviet Union it was war or threat of war throughout its seventy odd years of existence. In his optimism about the future, Marx had indeed argued that the overthrow of the old system must lead to a better one, because 'mankind always sets itself only such problems as it can solve'. But with the social democratic failure in the more advanced Europe, the problems which mankind, rather the Bolsheviks had to set for themselves in Russia were not quite soluble in the circumstances of their time and place. Not that the problems were entirely insoluble or that what ultimately happened was inevitable. The ways in which problems were sought to be solved, the inadequacies of theory and practice, were surely the ultimately decisive factors in what has happened; in effect, it was a human failure. Still behind this failure lies the inexorable historical fact: not prepared to build socialism, the Bolsheviks and the Soviet people were yet called upon to build it. Herein lay the origins of what I had described, in mid-1989, as their 'truly historical predicament'.

In the years to come, while revolution in the advanced capitalist world further receded, it is Marx's subsidiary pattern which, in one historical variation or other, repeated itself in the revolutions of the 20th century which followed in China, Korea, Cuba or Vietnam, in the generally backward Eastern Europe, or in Africa and similar places elsewhere, thereby reproducing the same predicament. Emulation or imposition of the 'Russian model of socialism' as it came to be, if it helped in some ways also made any genuine escape from it impossible. This only added to the problems and further confounded the predicament of 'actually existing socialism' everywhere.

3

History's Trick on the Doctrine of Karl Marx–II

The 'historical predicament' that confronted the Bolsheviks and the Soviet people is still very much with us. To understand it better, it is well worth our while to take another look at history's trick on the doctrine of Karl Marx that lay behind it, and seek its explanation in terms of that doctrine itself.

Marxism, we have seen, never saw socialism as 'a vision' to be pursued by well-meaning people. As against the idealist or utopian view, for which, as Engels put it, socialism is 'the expression of absolute truth, reason and justice and has only to be discovered to conquer all the world by virtue of its own power', it was distinctive of Marx to assert (or perhaps re-emphasise what is really an old idea born of the historical experience of people's struggles) that it is exactly those on the receiving end of a given form of oppression who are the primary agents of its liquidation, that genuine social liberations are not (as a rule at any rate) delivered to people by someone else. Marx saw socialism as the 'self emancipation' of the working people – 'socialism from below' as Hal Draper once called it – a process of revolutionary social transformation in which those who are exploited and oppressed by capitalism liberate themselves rather than rely on some other agency to liberate them, that is, to win socialism for them.

Marx certainly directed our attention to the most important

characteristic of capitalist society, namely, that it is fundamentally divided between the dominant classes – so defined by virtue of their ownership or control of the main means of domination, the means of production, administration and coercion and of communication and persuasion as well – and the dominated classes – so defined by their relative or absolute lack of such means and who thus come to be dominated, exploited and oppressed. But Marx also insisted that domination, exploitation or oppression are not unalterably inscribed in the human condition and that they can be overcome by the collective endeavours of the dominated classes themselves. Such indeed is the story of human progress.

More specifically, Marx argued that by its very nature an irrational and oppressive system generates social forces which, precisely because they bear the brunt of its irrationality and oppression, will sooner or later seek to change it. A revolutionary change in an exploitative social order is fought for and carried out, above all, by those who, as its worst victims, need such a change most, provided of course that they are able to win requisite understanding of their *real* situation, and then organise and struggle for the change they need. In case of capitalism, Marx identified this social force for revolutionary change, for socialism, in the working class, the class of the proletariat.

Socialism represents the *long term* interests of the entire people, that is how Marx visualised it, but he equally visualised it as a real historical possibility growing out of the existing social order, the productive achievements of capitalism and the opposing class interests and struggles generated by it. Socialism had come on the historical agenda because there existed for the first time in history, not only the forces of production that made socialism possible but also a class with interest and capacity to realise it, to create a classless society – a class whose own specific conditions of existence as well as strategic location at the very heart of capitalist production and exploitation gave it a collective interest as well as force and capacity for collective action which made socialism possible and practicable. And a class without property or exploitative interests of its own to protect, could not fully serve its own class interests without abolishing class exploitation and classes altogether. It is thus that the working class was seen to have a specific, objective, class interest in socialism, its conditions of existence, experience and strategic location were seen to give it a specific class capacity and therefore, as compared with other potentially radical forces, a special, privileged position in the struggle for socialism, and socialism was seen as making possible the emancipation of the *whole* people – an objective which in other times could never be more than an abstract, utopian dream. This is how Marx also saw the proletariat as the 'universal class'.

I shall be discussing the question of *agency* in the struggle for socialism today later in these notes. Immediately, it needs to be specifically noted that Marx's identification of the proletariat as a potential revolutionary force was no arbitrary choice of his Marxism. It involved no teleological privileging of the proletariat, nor any kind of idealisation of the proletariat and its class consciousness. Rather it is capitalism, as it were, that can be said to have 'chosen' the proletariat for a revolutionary role. This is how Marx and Engels put it in a crucially important passage rather early in their political life:

> If the socialist writers *ascribe* this world-historical role to the proletariat, this is not at all because they consider the proletarians to be *gods*. Rather the opposite. Because the destruction of all humanity, even the *appearance* of humanity, is empirically complete in the fully developed proletariat; because all the existential conditions of the present society are concentrated in their entire inhuman extremity in the living conditions of the proletariat; because the human being has lost itself in the proletarian at the same time having not only won the theoretic awareness of this loss but also been forced by inescapable, unvarnishable, imperative misery, that practical expression of *necessity* to revolt against this entire inhumanity – this is why the proletariat can and must emancipate itself. But it cannot abolish its own condition of existence without abolishing all the inhuman conditions of the present society which find their concentrated expression in the situation of the proletariat... It is not a question of what this or that proletarian or even the whole proletariat, at the moment *regards* as its aim. It is a question of *what the proletariat is,* and what, in accordance with its *being*, it will historically be compelled to do. The aim and the historical action of the proletariat are laid

> down in advance, irrevocably and obviously, in its own situation in life and in the whole organization of contemporary bourgeois society.

Again, speaking of 'dissolution' of capitalism Marx wrote:

> Only inasmuch as it produces the proletariat as proletariat, the misery which is conscious of its spiritual and physical misery, the dehumanisation which, because it is conscious of its dehumanisation, will abolish it.

It needs to be clearly noticed that central to Marx's argument assigning the proletariat its historical role are two considerations, both of which are undeniable. First, that it is necessarily and unavoidably the worst victim of exploitation and dehumanisation under capitalism and cannot escape this fate except by a revolution carried through to the end; and second, that potentially it has the power to overthrow the rule of capital, once it is able to win 'the theoretic awareness of its loss'. These two considerations, however, provide no guarantee that the proletariat will understand its situation and act accordingly.

II

Marx himself was certainly optimistic in this regard – rather too optimistic and mistaken critics have said, for no revolutions that he hoped for have occurred in the advanced capitalist Europe. That historical development has rendered the classical vision of the role of the proletariat not obsolete but problematic is not to be denied. It needs to be critically examined and made relevant for our times. Yet Marx was not *that* wrong in his assessment of the revolutionary potential of the early industrial proletariat as is sometimes made out by the critics. This potential was fully demonstrated in the post-first world war upheaval in Europe, especially in the German Revolution of November 1918, where it was not the proletariat which failed Marx but the social-democratic leadership which failed the revolutionary proletariat. So it was elsewhere in Europe. Even more significant here is the case of the revolution in Russia. No doubt, an important factor in the situation was the role of the bourgeoisie as presaged by Marx in his analysis of the revolutions of 1848 – 'the greedy and cowardly Russian bourgeoisie', as Trotsky described it, 'too late on the scene, prematurely a victim of senility, afraid to lift its hand against feudal property...' Also, it was the genius of Lenin to draw upon this analysis of Marx for his strategy and tactics in the bourgeois revolution, go on to combine 'a peasant war' with 'proletarian revolution', to obtain for the latter 'the chorus' Marx had spoken of. But decisive for the success of the Russian Revolution was the part played by the proletariat, a proletariat, politically conscious, fully revolutionary in its commitment and steeled and organised through decades of revolutionising practice. Under the leadership of Lenin and the Bolsheviks, it played a role and produced a result that fully accorded with the expectations of Karl Marx – and at the same time confounded the evolutionist orthodoxies of the Second International. (Incidentally, this proletariat virtually perished in the early post-revolution years of war, counter-revolution, civil war, and economic disintegration, with serious consequences for the future of socialism in Russia.)

Again, Marx may have been optimistic about the revolutionary potential of the proletariat, but he had no illusions about it either. The 'class-in-itself' had to transform into 'class-for-itself' before it could play its historical role. Believing as Marx did in the liberating quality of human praxis, the self-transforming nature of revolutionary activity, he knew that the potential will be realised only through unremitting struggle and organisation over a long period. In a passage, distinguishing between the propaganda of his group in the Communist League and that of an opposed minority group, and using the metaphor of 'civil war' for class struggle, he wrote:

> While we say to the workers: you have to undergo fifteen, twenty, fifty years of civil wars and popular struggles not only to change the relations but to change yourselves and prepare yourselves for political mastery, they tell them on the contrary, 'We must come to power immediately, or we can forget about it.' While we make a special point of emphasizing to the German worker the underdeveloped state of the German proletariat, they flatter his

> national feeling and the craft prejudice of the German artisan, which to be sure is more popular.

'The proletariat, which will not permit itself to be treated as rabble', said Marx in 1847, 'needs its courage, its self-confidence, its dignity and its sense of independence more than its bread.'

Marx thus expected the proletariat to change itself in the process of its struggle against capitalism in order to be able to change society. He never ceased to stress that workers make themselves fit to found society anew only through the process of struggle. Nor did he entirely underestimate the difficulties here, coming from the dominant bourgeois ideologies, indeed from the capitalist mode of production itself. 'The ruling ideas of each age', he had written, 'have ever been the ideas of its ruling class' and the proletariat is daily exposed to them. And he was aware how the nature of human beings is produced or moulded within an economic system, how the very process of capitalist production reproduces workers who view the necessity of capitalism as self-evident. Thus even as he noticed in *Capital* how under capitalism 'the detail worker of today (is) crippled by life-long repetition of one and the same trivial operation, and thus reduced to a mere fragment of a man', Marx had written: 'The advance of capitalist production develops a working class which by education, tradition and habit looks upon the requirements of that mode as self-evident natural laws. The organisation of the capitalist process of production, once it is fully developed, breaks down all resistance'. Hence Marx's emphasis on 'revolutionising practice'. Viewing 'revolution' as revolutionising practice, a 'practical movement' which is a process of revolutionary schooling as it were, Marx and Engels had written:

> Both for the production on a mass scale of this communist consciousness, and for the success of the cause itself, the alteration of men on a mass scale is necessary, an alteration which can only take place in the practical movement, a revolution; this revolution is necessary, therefore, not only because the ruling class cannot be overthrown in any other way, but also because the class overthrowing it can only in a revolution succeed in ridding itself of all muck of ages and become fitted to found society anew.

This view of the situation alone helps us understand and explain Marx's life long theoretical, political and educational activity, with and on behalf of the proletariat.

III

The highly significant experience of the success of Russian Revolution and the failure of the European, more specifically, the German Revolution notwithstanding, and despite the life-work of Marx and his successors, the proletariat in Europe has not developed the way anticipated by Marx in the advanced capitalist countries. And this is what gives substance to the argument that Marx overestimated the revolutionary potential of this proletariat. Whatever the validity of this argument, the more significant fact, however, is that Marx underestimated the potential of capitalism for further development and expansion and gave it only a short lease of life. His optimism with regard to the proletariat is almost a corollary of this other undeniable underestimation, which also meant an underestimation of the difficulties likely to come up in the way of the realisation of the proletariat's revolutionary potential. Marx underestimated not only the productive potential of the market-based system of private enterprise but also the capacity of capitalism to both adjust itself to the demands of a permanent technological revolution and accommodate the social and political demands made on it in a capitalist society, of course often with the help and intervention of the capitalist state. In other words, capitalism has proved to have a great deal more expansive and adaptive power than Marx suspected. The most important, ultimate consequence of capitalism's productive and prolonged existence has been the succumbing of the proletariat in industrially advanced countries to 'economism', which is even otherwise natural to it; it came to be mainly concerned with fighting to maintain or increase its share of the capitalist pie, without questioning in Macpherson's words, 'the methods of the bakery'. Its leaderships too, instead of 'helping' the proletariat transform into a 'class for itself' committed to the socialist cause, themselves got transformed into economistic reformers.

It is not that the advanced capitalist countries don't have

vast masses of people for whom in Marx's words, 'the destruction of all humanity, even the appearance of humanity, is empirically complete'. Nor either that these victims of capitalism are necessarily passively resigned to their fate. But for the proletariat as a whole it has certainly not been true for quite some time, as it was in Marx's days in mid nineteenth century; nor is it that, as the *Communist Manifesto* put it, 'workers have nothing to lose but their chains'. They have since successfully made gains for their standard of living, which gains, incidentally, were in tune with capitalism's own internal logic of 'self-expression' or expansion; they were in fact among the dynamic factors in capital's self-expansionary process. These gains, together with the extended domination of bourgeois ideologies and the collateral absence of requisite revolutionary consciousness and organisation, went a long way to ensure that the proletariat is not 'forced to revolt' any more. As Paul Baran has put it:

> Bad as its condition has been, (the proletariat) was able to rise above the 'inescapable, unvarnishable, imperative misery' which was observed by Marx, and which he expected would be accentuated with the passage of time. Although its social and cultural existence is in essence as inhuman as it was in Marx's time, it has largely failed to 'win the theoretical awareness of its loss' and has tended to succumb to bourgeois ideology and to adjust itself to its degradation.

IV

Factors underlying this historical turn in the development and destiny of the proletariat in the west, its failure to become what Marx called 'the universal class' – a class whose consciousness of its own exploitation and alienation would turn into a revolutionary consciousness and revolutionary action – are now well-known. Nevertheless it will not be out of place to specifically mention a few of these factors, for, beyond the question of social revolution in the West, these factors remain more or less relevant in the struggle for socialism everywhere.

In the economy, leaving out the specificities of its current phase of globalisation that we will take note of later, the overall trajectory of capitalist development in the days after Marx, overtook quite a bit of the visionary analysis of the *Communist Manifesto*. Marked by an extraordinary growth of capitalism as a global system with intensified imperialist exploitation of the periphery overlaid with the consequences of scientific-technological revolutions and an international economic restructuring, a worldwide integration of markets, finance and command centres of production and increasing transfer of real decision-making process to centres beyond even the conventional democratic control, the decline of the relative weight of industry and manufacturing as against finance and service industries, new methods of organisation of the labour process and fragmentation of the working class within and across countries, growth of middle classes, labour aristocracies and new individualistic intellectual professions on the one hand and immigrant labour and marginalised groups on the other, etc., etc., this development was and remains full of trends that not only increase the power of capital but simultaneously decimate the ranks of industrial workers, destroy working-class communities and culture, weaken unions and defeat parties of the Left; in short, these trends have been massively subversive of the traditional organisational and cultural bases of anti-capitalist politics in countries of advanced capitalism.

Outside of economy, 'democratic politics' so-called has been an important factor in sustaining the capitalist order. Fought for and won by the working people (and always needing to be defended and expanded by them), democracy as it came up yet turned out to be, in Bagehot's words, 'the way to give the people the greatest illusion of power while allowing them the smallest amount in reality'. It was (and remains) useful to the ruling classes in many ways, above all in helping them divert popular opposition into safe parliamentary channels and gain legitimacy for the established order. As parliamentarianism 'civilised' even its revolutionary leadership, the working class accommodated and constrained itself in accordance with whatever was possible within the framework of bourgeois democracy.

These developments in economy and politics underpinning it, the 'welfare state' has played its own important role in the continued survival of capitalism. Realised and maintained through the struggles of the working people, but made possible on the one hand by capitalist-imperialist expansion and the extraordinary productivity of social labour (that allowed for concessions or social benefits that democracy demanded) and on the other by a certain civilising influence exercised on capitalism's predatory nature by the very existence of Soviet Union and the forces of 'historical communism' as it has been called, the 'welfare state' acted, as John Saville put it, as a 'shock absorber' against threats to the system from below. It was not only that the working class in the West no longer had 'only chains to lose' as the *Communist Manifesto* said. Its concern with securing and safeguarding the gains it had won, with improving or even just maintaining the attained standard of living, etc., made this working class interested and involved in the survival and success of capitalism and complicit, as a beneficiary, in the continued exploitation of the third world. This is how 'welfare statism' also sustained and legitimised the class-collaborationist politics of the working class leadership in the West to the benefit of the capitalist system.

Beyond economy and politics, capitalism's most important defence against any revolutionary challenge has been the extended ruling class ideological domination through the massively grown ideological state apparatuses, 'culture industries', 'opinion businesses' and 'hidden persuaders' of all sorts that, thanks to the recurring 'communication revolution', daily and increasingly more effectively, shape, transform and manipulate politics and culture, and everyday mass consciousness in the societies of advanced capitalism, all the time 'hitting below the intellect' as Oscar Wilde once put it, and swamping whatever possible 'emancipatory interests' there be in society with the 'compensatory interests' of capitalist consumerism.

Apropos this extended ideological domination of the ruling classes, we must take note of the 'ugly face' which socialism came to acquire in the Soviet Union, making its own contribution to proletariat in the advanced West turning away from socialism and succumbing to capitalism – just as this proletariat's initial failure to make or sustain a socialist revolution (that is, turning away from the socialist option), in its own way, contributed to Soviet socialism's acquisition of an 'ugly face' and its ignominious surrender now to capitalism. The deformation that was the 'actually existing socialism', did provide a certain basis, but more an excuse, to ideologues of capitalism – not that they really needed it – for their 'anti communism', which in itself became a potent ideological weapon in the hands of the ruling classes in the west, used by them to prevent the working people taking a critical look at the 'actually existing capitalism', and get them to acquiesce in the manifold ugliness of the capitalist social order. Anti-communism simply demonised all those people and groups who in any way represented political opposition to the capitalist social order. It had 'this peculiar property', Joel Kovel has written, 'which causes all distinctions to be melted in the heat of its ideological furnace' – 'the *black hole effect*' he has called it: 'Viewed against this diabolical force (communism) all moral and rational comparisons disappear, like light sucked in by the virtually infinite gravity of a cosmological black hole'. Anti-communism was an important factor in the western proletariat succumbing to capitalism and missing out on the historical role visualised for it by Karl Marx.

These details do explain a few things, but what is important is that as a result of it all, in the final analysis, the two basic premises of Marx's hope for a socialist revolution in the west came to be almost entirely undermined. Whatever their initial situation or revolutionary potential, the working classes as they developed later in the countries of advanced capitalism were neither the worst victims of capitalism's irrationally and inhumanity, nor were they able to win 'the theoretic awareness of the loss' that they were nevertheless suffering as 'human beings' under capitalism. They were transformed into a reformist, at times even a conservative political force. The proletariat in the west, while retaining an objective *class interest* in socialism, simply failed to acquire the requisite *class capacity* to struggle for and win socialism.

V

Marx and Engels were certainly aware of some of the economic, political or ideological developments we have mentioned, though it must be recognised that many of them became fully significant and adversely effective only long after Marx, or even Engels (who passed away in 1895) had departed from the scene. Even as Marx wrote of how developed capitalism 'breaks down all resistance', and lamented English proletariat's lack of 'spirit of generalisation and revolutionary passion', Engels too noticed that 'the English proletariat is actually becoming more and more bourgeois, so that this bourgeois of all nations is apparently aiming ultimately at the possession of a bourgeois aristocracy and a bourgeois proletariat as well'.

Engels more than once deplored the fact that, objectively in a strong position, the English proletariat (since at least the downfall of the Chartist Party in the 1850s) lacked an independent political party of its own and was content to trail behind the upper classes. But he also found it understandable: 'This is understandable in a country in which the working class has shared in the advantages of the immense expansion of its large-scale industries. Nor could it have been otherwise in an England that ruled the world market, and certainly not in a country where the ruling classes have set themselves the task of carrying out parallel with other concessions, one point of the Chartists' programme after another...' Again: 'There is no workers' party here.... there are only Conservatives and Liberal-Radicals, and the workers gaily share the feast of England's monopoly of the world market and the colonies'. We also know that Marx and Engels throughout struggled for *independent* working class politics and 'political position', and waged a consistent battle against reformism in the working class movement. Just as from the other end, they fought against Blanquism, anarchism or anarcho-syndicalism of their times. But the fact remains that such awareness or struggle on their part never became sufficiently important for them theoretically; they never came round to assess or theorise the implications of these developments for their theory of socialist revolution in the countries of advanced capitalism.

Insofar as, rather to the extent, Marx erred in overestimating the revolutionary potential of the industrial proletariat, it needs to be appreciated that the mistake stemmed, not from inherent errors in Marx's approach or assessment, but from what has been described as 'the inherent difficulty of extrapolating from a moving platform'. Making a concrete study of capitalism, Marx saw a possibility for the future, or ventured a prediction if you like, based upon where he stood at the time. But according to Marx himself, with the further growth and evolution of capitalism, that is, with the changed circumstances, this possibility or prediction was open to be affected in different ways, to be altered, or modified, or even proved mistaken. Therefore what has happened poses no problems at all for Marxism. It only draws attention to an aspect of the evolution of capitalism and, therefore, of the working class.

As James O'Connor has written, what Marx initially saw and theorised was the coming to power of the capitalist *economy*. Installed in the factory system and utterly ruthless in its exploitation, it yet nested, so to speak, in a precapitalist society where workers of Marx's day still retained their communitarian values and solidarities and which provided them a matrix from which to resist and rebel. (It is in this context that Marx wrote in 1844, of 'communist artisans' with whom 'the brotherhood of man is no mere phrase.... but a fact of life.' Again, a year later: 'To.... communist criticism corresponded immediately in practice the movement of the *great mass* against which history had so far developed. One must be acquainted with the studiousness, the craving for knowledge, the moral energy and the increasing urge for development of the French and English workers to be able to form an idea of the *human* nobility of that movement.') But as it evolved, capitalism not only expanded and adapted, even more significantly, it matured into a capitalist *society*, with capitalist relations penetrating into all spheres of life. Workers are now not merely economically exploited, they are also embedded in capitalist society, surrounded by capitalism on all sides which comes to define, as it were, the very limits or horizon of their existence. These workers can see no alternative to capitalism and simply go quiescent. Rather strongly put, but essence of the matter all the same.

Marx himself was not unaware of this development. On the contrary, his awareness of what was happening is implicit in his entire analysis of capitalism, including his powerful ethical-aesthetic critique of the emergent bourgeois society and explicit in passages where Marx spoke of capitalism '(breaking) down all resistance', and working class 'by education, tradition and habit' coming to look upon 'the requirements' of capitalism 'as self-evident natural laws'. Marx was in fact brilliantly insightful about the all-encroaching and all-penetrating power of capitalism. But he never recognised it as the threat it later turned out to be for his socialist project. Always optimistic, and giving capitalism only a short lease of life, he hoped for working class to break through capitalism's socio-economic and ideological barriers and redeem itself.

It needs to be added however that optimism or hopefulness notwithstanding, Marx, as also Engels, never believed that the proletariat was capable of developing, exclusively by its own effort a revolutionary *and* socialist consciousness; they did not attribute any revolutionary socialist spontaneism to the proletariat. Their lifelong practice – theoretical, educational and organisational – and emphasis on revolutionising 'practical movement' and 'popular struggles' to produce men with altered, socialist consciousness, would be simply incomprehensible if they had held such a view of the character of the proletariat. It would certainly be difficult to understand why Marx believed that the political economy of the working class elaborated in *Capital* was so important that it was worth sacrificing his 'health, happiness and family'. From the Communist League in the 1840s through the First International to Engels' last years, when he acted as consultant to socialist parties all over the world, they were tirelessly active in their efforts as revolutionary intellectuals and leaders to develop a revolutionary socialist consciousness among the proletariat. Only, as mentioned earlier, they never came round to subject this activity of theirs to serious theoretical treatment. In the meantime as the economistic degeneration of Second International soon showed, the question of 'socialist consciousness' had already become one of decisive importance for the socialist movement.

VI

The crucially important task of theorising the problematic of socialist consciousness was not carried out even when it became obviously urgent in the period after Marx and Engels – the Second International as a whole simply opted for wholesale economism, reformism or social patriotism. Lenin was the only exception and he, following in the footsteps of Marx and Engels, essayed the problem with remarkable success in Russia, developing further the revolutionary tradition of classical Marxism. His achievement is well expressed in his classic *What Is To Be Done?*, written in 1902. Written in response to problems facing the revolutionary struggle in Russia, Lenin's work was more than a response to these problems; it countered a whole trend of distortion and vulgarisation of Marxism in the European socialist movement which (represented in Russia by the opportunist evolutionism of Plekhanov and others) had emasculated it into a fatalistic theory of self-propulsion of historical processes. Lenin literally restored life to Marxism as a revolutionary doctrine, insisting that socialist revolution is something to be actively pursued and that Marxism is above all about *making* history. It is this vital truth that Franz Marek underlined when he, very rightly, assessed this work of Lenin 'as the most important book published after the death of Marx and Engels on the fundamental problem of the Marxist philosophy of history'. It is as part of an active pursuit of socialist revolution or making of history that Lenin focused on the critically important question of working class *political* consciousness, of 'mass consciousness in theoretical as well as in political and organisational work'.

Lenin pointed out that 'economism' comes naturally to the proletariat: 'The history of all countries shows that the working class, exclusively by its own effort, is able to develop only trade union consciousness, i.e., the conviction that it is necessary to combine in unions, fight the employers and strive to compel the government to pass necessary labour legislation, etc.' For it to become a revolutionary force, Lenin argued, the proletariat needs to be educated into its real, objective interests, into socialist political consciousness, the necessity of overthrowing capitalism and replacing it with an entirely different social order. This was, for Lenin, not a question of only imparting political education or theoretical understanding to the working class. It was far more a matter of putting *socialist* meaning into its experience, imbuing its struggle with socialist consciousness, that is, not 'injecting' something, but helping the working class develop and acquire socialist consciousness as it struggles against capitalism. The development of ever sharper socialist consciousness among the working people is, according to Lenin, a prior necessity for any successful revolutionary politics, and therefore the prime responsibility of a revolutionary party, whereby alone it can function as a revolutionary party, helping working classes raise their economic struggles to the level of political struggle and leading them in revolution, 'the highest form of class struggle', as Marx described it. Needless to emphasise that their struggle remains central to the socialist transformation of the working classes. In other words, not capitalism as such, or economic struggle against it, but the revolutionary struggle for overthrowing capitalism will transform the proletarians into men endowed with the capacity to overthrow capitalism and begin construction of socialism. For Lenin, as for Marx and Engels, revolutionising practice was the practice of revolution. This was indeed the governing principle in his theory of organisation.

VII

Lenin's theory of organisation, dealing with the basic problems of the social superstructure (the state, the party, ideology, class consciousness, etc.) was a deepening of Marxism, a decisively important constitutive element of what Mandel has called 'the Marxist science of the subjective factor'. It was a remarkably successful answer to the problems of revolutionary struggle in Russia, and continues to remain basic to such struggle anywhere else. Even so, Lenin's is still a partial response to the problematic of engendering socialist consciousness. The issues involved are too many and complex in this age of massive bourgeois ideological dominance, and the need for more adequate theory in this area is obvious. Particularly important here are the issues relating to the pursuit of revolutionary politics and the struggle for socialist transformation in bourgeois-democratic political regimes with more or less strong civil societies. Here a pioneering but, again, a historically specific exercise, which acknowledges Lenin's contribution, has been that by Gramsci. Between 1929 and 1935, a prisoner of fascism and destined to die, struggling against constant ill-health and fascist surveillance, compelling him to use secret codes and phrases (where Marxism is 'philosophy of praxis' and Lenin some 'Ilici'), Gramsci wrote down thoughts which represent a most outstanding contribution to Marxism. If, partly to escape the censor, he referred to it as 'the philosophy of praxis', the name yet grasps and reveals the very essence of Marxism. Gramsci directly confronts the complex issues which together constitute the problem of non-occurrence of socialist revolution in the countries of advanced capitalism in Europe; of course he does so in the context of Italian history, which was for him the long-term historical context of 'a failed nationalism and a triumphant fascism' in Italy and the more recent one of the isolation and defeat of the Turin working class and the subsequent victory of Italian fascism. For Gramsci, this confrontation was a revolutionary project, a reconstitution of Leninism as it were, for building a successful socialist movement in the advanced capitalist countries of Europe. As part of his project Gramsci focused on the complexity of political power in the parliamentary or constitutional states of the West, with their strong civil societies, in contrast to the more openly coercive or autocratic regimes, and pointed out that in the former the bourgeoisie maintains its rule over the subaltern classes in two ways, that is, not only through domination that state as an apparatus of coercion secures, but also through hegemony that mobilises the consent of the subaltern classes in favour of bourgeois rule. The latter is a system of class domination in which class power has no clearly visible point of concentration in the state but is diffused throughout society and its social and cultural practices. Insofar as the essence of hegemony is to ensure willing acceptance of capitalism's domination in society, it consists in so constituting civil society and the state that alternatives to capitalism cannot be taken seriously. Gramsci reformulated the concept of civil society, as received from Hegel and Marx, by marking it out as a terrain of social and cultural practices, institutions and relations – generally neglected by old Marxist left – that sustain bourgeois hegemony and therefore, for Gramsci, also the terrain of a new kind of struggle which would take the battle against capitalism not only to its economic foundations or state structures but to its social, cultural and ideological roots in society. This is where multi-dimensional counter-hegemonic battles have to be fought and won for socialist 'commonsense' or 'world view' in society, if the socialist movement has to advance. This is how Gramsci's appropriation of the concept of civil society as an important organising principle of socialist theory was a part of his revolutionary project.

It is important to underscore this and affirm Gramsci's position within the tradition of revolutionary Marxism. While Gramsci accomplished much in the sphere of culture or superstructure that Lenin could not, due above all to the exigencies of his revolutionary tasks, Gramsci's thought rests upon the prior achievement of Lenin, as he himself acknowledged; it needs to be seen as a *development* of Lenin's views on such issues as 'economism', 'socialist consciousness' or struggle in the sphere of ideology and culture. Noticing that Gramsci called Marxism 'the philosophy of praxis (from the Greek, to do, practice)' and that 'Lenin is the greatest modern theorist of practice', Karl Marzani, a most perceptive scholar of Gramsci, has written: 'Gramsci is the analyst of the superstructure, par excellence. In area after area – sociology, politics, mass psychology, literature, etc. – he deepened Marxism, sometimes going further than Lenin, for in many areas Lenin *acted* as a Marxist but did not write and develop the lessons of his experiences.' Incidentally, Marzani has also suggested: 'The deeper one's Marxism the less one's dogmatism. But a prerequisite for deepening one's knowledge of Marxism is to take Marxism seriously. This is the foundation of Gramsci's thought, as it was Lenin's.'

Gramsci's problematic was never seriously pursued after

him, not even in Italy. Comintern orthodoxy was content with freezing the Stalin-interpreted Russian experience into a dogma, and Moscow sanctioned 'official Marxism', deliberately silent on Gramsci, took care of any other similarly creative exercise within the European communist movement. The consequence has been a tragic poverty of theory concerning the pursuit of revolutionary socialist politics in the advanced capitalist countries of Europe, which, along with other factors, contributed to the persistently weak presence of revolutionary socialism there and the stagnation and ultimate decline of the communist movement. 'Euro-communism', even as it addressed a real problem, was only a good example of this poverty of theory, and now with the Soviet collapse, we are witness to the virtual disappearance of 'communism' in the capitalist West. After years of retreat from revolutionary Marxism, the old, once heroic, communist parties have almost everywhere degenerated into plain social democracy of our times.

VIII

Gramsci's many contributions to socialist theory and practice are not our concern here, but one subsequent development deserves to be immediately noticed. If Comintern orthodoxy virtually disowned Gramsci, the revolutionary theorist, and sent him into oblivion, in more recent years, Gramsci has been a staple with academic Marxists of different hues, hyphenated ones particularly; they have owned and appropriated him for all sorts of 'democratic', non-revolutionary or anti-revolutionary purposes. Gramsci has become safe, tame, denatured – a wisp of his revolutionary self. Academics, seeking justification or alibis for their retreat from socialist commitment and politics, have in the name of Gramsci, gone in for highly abstruse theories, creating fanciful illusions about their 'counter-hegemonic' activity. Ignoring the facts that Gramsci was a revolutionary, the leader of possibly the largest proletarian uprising in Europe (Italy's 'two red years') in the aftermath of the first world war and Bolshevik Revolution, and a key founder of the Italian Communist Party who remained a communist militant to the very end, they have created a mythical Gramsci who holds views he never did, and even stands so apart from Lenin as to be opposed to revolutionary socialist organisation of the sort that he, following upon Lenin (code-named 'Ilici' in his prison writings) in fact held indispensable. They have thus appropriated Gramsci's thought by first reducing him to a *thinker*, a maker of *concepts* only, then detaching his concepts – such as 'hegemony' 'national popular', 'war of position', 'passive revolution', etc. – from his political project, that is, his revolutionary purposes, and finally using these concepts for their own academic theorising or reformist and anti-revolutionary purposes.

Two aspects of such appropriation of Gramsci may be briefly mentioned. Gramsci did make the important distinction between 'civil society' and the state. Since then, as Gramsci became a fashion with academics, not only on the left, 'civil society' has come to be theorised as a realm of freedom, of voluntary associative life and human emancipatory aspirations, as against the state which continues to be seen, with a new emphasis, as a coercive institution, the location of all really dangerous forms of power. One will readily concede that the distinction involved can be constructively used to oppose statism, check state's rampant abuse of power, defend human rights and freedoms, free popular or participatory initiatives, and so on. Such use has indeed come up as 'civil society activism' of recent years. A positive development, it still needs to be critically looked at for its limitations, even negative aspects, as we shall do later in another context. Immediately what needs to be noted is that the theorists concerned have gone far beyond such legitimate use of the concept of 'civil society'. While Gramsci had made the distinction primarily to mark out civil society as the terrain of bourgeois hegemonic power which supplements, supports and strengthens its other, more obviously coercive expression in the state, these theorists have used it to posit a simple dichotomy between state and civil society, where state is uniquely a site of coercion, a 'public' presence which is quintessentially oppressive and civil society, equally uniquely a free space, a 'private' realm of freedom and voluntary action. As Ellen Meiksins Wood has pointed out, this view of civil society as the anti-thesis of state obscures not only that civil society may be the site of any number of non-state oppressions of its own, but, more importantly, also the fact that coercion, though of a different kind, is one of the constitutive principles of civil society itself – the 'private' realm has a distinctive 'public' presence of oppression flowing from its economic structures. For, whatever else it is, civil society is also the realm of private property, class exploitation and market imperatives. Even when 'economy' is seen as one among a multiple of non-state institutions, relations and practices in civil society, it is not recognised as *capitalism* with its ruthless totalising logic, a system of appropriation, exploitation and domination detached from any public authority and social responsibility, a unique structure of power which gives private property and its possessors command over people and their lives that goes far beyond their economic activities, and would be the envy of any autocratic state; the freedoms of civil society are, directly and otherwise, regulated or circumscribed by the dictates of the market, the necessities of competition and profitability, even as they may also serve to 'manufacture consent' for the ruling classes. It only needs to be added that the coercive functions of the state, in large part, have been occupied with the enforcement of this capitalist domination in society, the 'public' coercion by the state sustaining 'private' coercion of capitalism in civil society.

The concept of civil society, as it has gained currency in recent years, has come to obscure all this. Despite the appeal to Gramsci's authority, which has been a staple of contemporary theorising on the subject, the concept in its current usage has nothing of what E.M. Wood has described as 'Gramsci's unequivocally anti-capitalist intent'. This usage in fact so dissolves capitalism into civil society that its totalising logic and coercive power become simply invisible, and, thus, whatever its other uses or usefulness, the concept of 'civil society' has been eminently serviceable in conceptualising away the problem of capitalism. Civil society becomes, as it were, an alibi for capitalism. You no longer even *think* capitalism, leave alone struggle against it, only theorise about civil society. An understandably comfortable perch for the neo-liberal theorist, it is also a good enough reason, rather excuse, for the disoriented or opportunist left intellectual's political retreat from socialism.

The other important aspect where, apart from his concept of civil society, Gramsci's thought has been stripped of its revolutionary charge is a post-structuralist appropriation of Gramsci which reduces Gramsci, the revolutionary theorist, to a cultural critic 'on the model of Methew Arnold, Julien Benda, Michel Foucault, Jacques Derrida' etc., as one comment has it. Ignoring that Gramsci's concern with culture or the superstructural realm was part of his response to the strategic dilemmas of the Italian communist movement and that his remarkable insight here lay in positing it as the terrain of a decisively important struggle against capitalism, a culturist reading is imposed on his thought and Gramsci is represented as the theoretician of cultural superstructures for whom the realm of culture is not just relatively autonomous but so primary as to have no basis in objective economic conditions or class structures and therefore no necessary relations with either class politics or any revolutionary transformation of society – concerns which were central to the life and work of Gramsci. One consequence of this interpretation of Gramsci as a culturist has been the rise and spread of a left-wingish culturalism, often Marxism lapsing into cultural studies, where the cultural has been increasingly treated as essentially autonomous of economic and social determinations and thus safely dissociated from any concern with radical politics. In fact, losing whatever critical edge it had initially, in the main, cultural studies have tended to itself become one of those many styles of consumer capitalism that it set out to study and criticise.

Gramsci's thought was unambiguously intended as a weapon against capitalism, not an accommodation to it. It speaks volumes for the hegemonic reach of capitalism that this thought has been so accommodated and Gramsci himself appropriated as to turn him into, in the words of historian T.J. Jackson-Lears, 'the Marxist who's safe to bring home to Mother'.

Of course the accommodation can never be complete and Gramsci survives. But what has happened underlines the relevance of Gramsci's Marxism and the importance it attached to the counter-hegemonic struggle against capitalism, which importance has increased manifold in view of recent developments, particularly the collapse of 'socialism' (that is, 'actually existing socialism') in the Soviet Union. Capitalism is today a truly global and universal system, not merely in the conventionally understood terms of growth of multinational corporations or the supposed undermining of the nation state, but in the sense that capitalism itself, with its structural logic of accumulation, profit-maximisation and commodification, its all-encompassing market imperatives, has come to penetrate every aspect of our lives as never before, not only in the advanced capitalist countries but, in however varied or lumpenised a form, in the rest of the world as well. Capitalism is now visibly present in our social relations, in our politics and policies of the state, in the prevailing morality and culture, in the diverse practices and ideologies of the ruling and producing classes, in literally everything, everywhere. In other words, capitalism has come to acquire an all-pervasive, coercive hegemony in society, well facilitated by the elite controlled and operated information technologies, enormously expanded and well oiled public relations industry and evergrowing tribe of hack journalists, each in its own way busy shaping our culture to suit the interests of business, manufacturing consent for the capitalist system, or 'market economy' as they prefer to call it, and marginalising positions critical of the existing order, even as they are all themselves governed by imperatives of the market. The official ideologies defending capitalism may no longer convince any one, but its hegemony ensures that alternative ideologies are either not allowed to be propagated or disseminated in such fragmentatory or distorted forms that they can be easily shown to be inadequate as genuine alternatives. Capitalism may not be able to resolve its objective contradictions and the rulers may not even want to face and solve its growing problems, but capitalism's ideological hegemony means that despite the all too obvious economic failures of capitalism, the struggle against capitalism stays weak and paralysed. 'There is no alternative' becomes the ignorant refrain in society, as it indeed has these days. It is in this situation that counter-hegemonic struggle against capitalism that Gramsci focussed on acquires a decisive importance if the socialist movement is to advance and put socialist revolution back on the agenda of history.

IX

Marx himself throughout his life, continued to regard the conditions in the capitalist world as sufficiently ripe for the socialist revolution he expected to take place. We have already noticed that even as late as 1882, 'a proletarian revolution in the West' remained a real possibility for him – and it indeed occurred, later, in the aftermath of the first world war, though it did not survive. Obviously therefore, so far as Marx himself is concerned it is not the conditions, 'the material requisites' which failed him, but the proletariat and its leadership in the West: it simply failed to attain the requisite class consciousness and organisation, that is, the class capacity to make and sustain a socialist revolution. Russia stood out as an exception, thanks to Lenin and his Bolsheviks. The failure and the exception together with our reference to Lenin and Gramsci draw our attention to possibly the most crucial factor in the situation we have been discussing: the hegemony that the dominant classes have come to acquire in societies of advanced capitalism, combining their coercion of the working people with a massive 'engineering of their consent' through means and in forms ranging from the most sophisticated and subtle to the most stridently demagogic. This ideological hegemony is not a matter of some sort of lying, deception or deliberate mystification, though these elements are never entirely absent. It is essentially what the working people are persuaded to accept and adopt and through which they 'interiorise' the values and norms which dominant classes have themselves adopted and believe to be right. What is more, they are persuaded that whatever they may think of the prevailing social order, however oppressive or alienating they feel it to be, no alternative is possible, it could even be catastrophically worse. The working people simply come to reject any notion that there could be a radical and viable alternative. It is thus that consolidation and popular ratification of the prevailing capitalist order is secured.

Marx and Engels had always recognised the power and influence of bourgeois ideology. 'The ideas of the ruling class are in every epoch the ruling ideas', they had stated. As historical materialists, they were also aware of the plasticity and mouldability of human nature, of the fact that human beings are powerfully influenced and shaped by the social order within which they are enclosed. But, giving capitalism only a short lease of life, they had tended to discount the possibility of any wholesale succumbing of the proletariat to the dominant bourgeois ideology – which it is well to remember, is seldom, if ever, all of one piece, but is generally constituted by all sorts of competing and even contradictory ideas and doctrines which yet supplement each other, above all, in their practical implications, and hold together to serve the same bourgeois or ruling class interests. They had expected the proletariat, despite all odds, to grow into a 'class-for-itself', to organise and struggle for socialism. It is clear now that having seriously underestimated the possibilities of further growth and expansion of capitalism, they had also underestimated the extent of the dominance that bourgeois ideology may come to acquire as its consequence. Pointing out the extraordinary scope and depth of *habit* formation resulting from centuries of capitalist development, Baran thus wrote of the expanded role of bourgeois ideology in societies of monopoly capitalism: 'Bourgeois ideology no longer serves merely as a break on people's striving for a better society, it no longer represents merely a barbed wire entanglement keeping people from satisfying their basic needs and potentialities – it has now reached what may be called it ultimate target: it has crippled that striving itself, it has driven a powerful wedge between human *needs* and human *wants*.' Not only has the mentality of the dominant class become undisputedly the dominant mentality – this was to be expected and was fully foreseen and analysed by Marx and Engels – but 'with bourgeois taboos and moral injunctions internalized, people steeped in the culture of monopoly capitalism do not want what they need and do not need what they want.'

It is here on the terrain of ideology, more than anywhere else, that the battle for socialism, that Marx had visualised, was lost in the advanced capitalist countries of the West. But Marx was more than vindicated in the East.

X

As capitalism grew into a global system of exploitation and oppression, the proletariat in the advanced capitalist countries was neither the worst victim of its irrationality and inhumanity, nor was it able to win 'the theoretic awareness of its loss' – the two necessary conditions Marx had postulated for it to become the historically destined revolutionary force for socialism. But this very global expansion of capitalism soon reproduced these existential as well as ideological conditions elsewhere. With due concession to historical specificities and differences, the conditions postulated by Marx came to be realised among the dispossessed masses of the much more numerous and populous dependencies in the periphery and semi-periphery of the global capitalist system. Here was that increasing mass of human beings who came to conform closely to Marx and Engels' description of the 'fully developed proletariat' in the *Holy Family*, whose 'living conditions' represented 'the focal point of all inhuman conditions in contemporary society'. The basic similarity in the existential situation of the proletariat in Marx's time to that of the dispossessed masses of the periphery in our times is obvious – the new proletarians were to be found in the rapidly increasing mass of dehumanised humanity in the third world. They were the ones to bear, and who continue to bear, the brunt of the irrationality and inhumanity of capitalism, the worst victims of capitalist-imperialist exploitation and oppression. At the same time, they were not exposed to the same extent as in the advanced capitalist countries to the corrupting impact of bourgeois ideology and culture. This made for a much wider acceptance of Marxism there and explains the remarkable fact that Marxism starting as a specifically European phenomenon became more truly universal in its acceptance than any other body of ideas, secular or religious, in the history of humankind. The people in the third world were thus, in a manner of speaking, in a better position to win what Marx had described as 'the theoretic awareness of their loss', and launch powerful revolutionary movements. Subject to the specificities of history, national situation, class structures within and political conjunctures within and without, many of them indeed proceeded to launch them. Drawing inspiration from the Marxist-led October Revolution in Russia, and given favourable historical conjunctures and effective Marxist leadership, some of them even made successful revolutions under the banner of Marxism. In this sense, these movements and revolutions in the periphery of capitalism were certainly proletarian, notwithstanding a mixed-class leadership and a mixed, predominantly rural class composition of the movements, the particular mixture in each case depending on the history and class structure of the country in question. It is here, as in the 'backward', 'less advanced' Russia earlier, that Marx's basic premises for a socialist revolution came to be realised.

This is how the Russian Revolution, even as it was in one sense the last of the European revolutions of the 19th century, also became the first of a new wave of revolutions which unfolded in the 20th century in the peripheral 'backward' countries of the world – altering the geography, the spatial pattern, of the progress of world socialist revolution, making it very different from the one anticipated by Marx.

This wave has receded today – much defeated, it is in fact in full retreat. This is not to be denied. But as an epochal transition, world revolutionary process was never visualised without its ups and downs, its reversals, failures and defeats. And it should not be difficult to recognise that Marx's argument which worked in the past still continues to work with compelling logic, in the 'backward', 'dependent' or 'developing' countries of the periphery, which may yet provide the most potent challenges to the currently triumphant global capitalist system.

The altered geography of socialist revolution, however, also produced the 'historical predicament' of the countries thus called upon to pioneer the road to socialism. Not prepared to build, they were yet confronted with the task of building socialism. As Marxists, the Bolsheviks in Russia did not believe they could build socialism on there own in their single backward country. But, the revolution having failed to survive or spread in Europe, they had the choice between surrender and a holding operation. Surrender their revolution they would not, and a holding operation is no recipe either for staying in power long enough or for persuading people to stay inspired waiting for a revolution in the West and hoping to build later. So the Bolsheviks went on to build and others followed – and now, what they built, as socialism, has collapsed.

If only a few made the point earlier, many more are now arguing that it was in any case impossible to build socialism in an industrially underdeveloped, backward country. It was doomed as an effort to 'skip the stages', indeed to usurp history. Some of them, with their academic and scholastic interpretation of Marx's doctrine, are even seeing the current collapse or failure as a vindication of 'the science of Marxism'. Scientism or evolutionism dies hard with the sophisticates of Marxology. But history is not only a cruel goddess, it also does not come neatly packaged or according to the book. The failure or collapse in the Soviet Union was not inevitable. The pioneers and their successors could certainly have done better. Those who come after them, as they are bound to, better placed or still subject to compulsion of the altered geography of socialist revolution, can only draw lessons from the successes and ultimate failure of this first experiment and strive to build better, that is, build socialism or societies in transition to socialism, as Marx would have done in their place.

4

Bolsheviks and the October Revolution

While Marx had visualised the possibility of a 'socialist revolution' in a backward, 'less advanced' country, his speculations concerning the Russian Commune notwithstanding, he never seriously explored the implications of such a possibility, that is, of this revolution ending up in the necessity of building socialism in such a country, lacking as it would be in the necessary material and social prerequisites which were seen to be created by advanced economic and social development of capitalism. This, however, was not Marx's problem, and to his way of thinking such problems of the future are best left to men and women of the future. In any case, for Marx, the context of such a possibility as well as necessity ultimately remained a successful socialist revolution in the advanced industrial countries of Western Europe. As we have already noticed, Marx's view that late 19th century Russia might develop directly from a primitive agrarian society to socialism, through a revolution based on the peasantry and its communal traditions, was premised upon not only the survival of the Russian Commune but also a 'supplementing' 'proletarian revolution in the West', whose victorious working class could provide the necessary support and help, and exert as it were a gravitational pull on backward Russia. Viewed in this way, the possibility of building socialism in an economically backward country remained a part of the main Marxist tradition, its theoretical design of a proletarian revolution which would, on the basis of advanced forces of production created by capitalism, initiate a fairly speedy transition to socialism, marked particularly by democratic power for the mass of common people, a power which would be, *á la* Paris Commune, far more democratic, economically, politically and socio-culturally than that of the most democratic of the bourgeois states. For Marx socialism or communism, in its transcendence of capitalism, would be the inheritor of all the positive tendencies and possibilities inherent in capitalism, of its economic wealth, political freedoms (albeit very partial) and socio-cultural gains. The material and cultural achievements of capitalism were to be the take-off points of a successful transition to socialism.

As Marx saw it, 'the emancipation of labour', and with it of the people in general, was feasible only when the objective material conditions of its emancipation are available whereby 'the direct material production process is stripped of the form of penury and anti-thesis', as he put it, giving way to the 'free development of individualities' which socialism seeks to ensure. That is why in the *Communist Manifesto, Anti-Duhring* and elsewhere, Marx and Engels insisted that socialism could only be built on the mature basis already laid by capitalism. In *The German Ideology*, discussing the essential material premises of a socialist transition, even as they also observed that socialism would require social revolutions in at least several of the most developed countries, they wrote: 'the development of productive forces is an absolutely necessary practical premise because without it *want* is merely made general, and with *destitution* the struggle for necessities would begin again, and all the old filthy business would necessarily be reproduced'. On the subject of the limits placed by objective economic conditions on a revolutionary socialist enterprise we have a truly remarkable observation from Engels in his *Peasant War in Germany*. Referring to the situation of Thomas Münzer, the leader of the Peasant War of the early 16th century, he wrote: 'Not only the movement of his time, but the whole century, was not ripe for the realization of the ideas for which he had himself only just begun to grope. The class which he represented not only was not developed enough and incapable of subduing and transforming the whole of society, but it was just beginning to come into existence. The social transformation that he pictured in his fantasy was so little grounded in the then existing economic conditions that the latter were a preparation for a social system diametrically opposed to that of which he dreamt'. Collaterally, Engels had even warned that 'the worst fate that can befall an extreme leader is to be compelled to take over a government in an epoch when the movement is not yet ripe for the domination of the class which he represents'.

It should however be remembered that, however profound, these are yet retrospective historical assessments. As a revolutionary, Engels also knew that history does not come neatly packaged as decreed in the book and had, therefore, firmly concluded that nevertheless Münzer was right in acting as he did, in pursuing his revolutionary purposes as best as he could.

II

All this is in fact elementary Marxism. Obviously you cannot build socialism whenever and wherever you want, regardless of conditions – this would be plain idealism or utopianism, something totally alien to Marxism. However, those who see Marxism only as a 'scientific' doctrine and fail to recognise that it is a revolutionary doctrine as well, particularly those given to its evolutionist or economistic interpretation, have used this argument about the necessary 'ripeness' so-called of objective economic conditions for socialism, to reject the entire Bolshevik revolutionary enterprise, including the October Revolution itself. Contemporary Mensheviks and stalwarts of the Second International like Kautsky and Plekhanov onwards, this argument has been the staple of critics of Bolshevism and there have been, of course with due variations, any number of Social Democrats, Austro-Marxists, Council Communists, Liberal Socialists, Left and Right Oppositionists, East European revisionists, Western Marxists, New Leftists, Euro-communists, etc., etc., down to more recently, Rudolf Bahro, Boris Kagarlitsky, etc., who have questioned the basic strategy and tactics of Lenin and his Bolsheviks, charged them with impermissible revision of Marxism and seen the Russian Revolution as a premature break, an abortive attempt to force the pace of historical change. Bolsheviks are seen, in a manner of speaking, as a case of usurping history. Quite understandably, now, with the collapse of 'Soviet Socialism', this critique is being recycled with a new vigour and vehemence by critics from within the left, by Marxists and socialists, ex-Marxists and ex-socialists, and even by yesterday's Stalinists, recycled everywhere including the erstwhile Soviet Union itself. Even Gramsci is being roped in for his most particular and partial description of the October Revolution as 'the Revolution against "Capital"' (i.e. Marx's *Das Kapital*), totally obscuring the fact that even as he recognised the intractable problems confronting the post-revolutionary Russia, Gramsci not only saw Lenin and the Bolsheviks as entirely within the Marxist tradition, he expressly sympathised with their activist revolutionary strategy and politics. Thus, the entire revolutionary tradition of Marxism is sought to be jettisoned by one-time Marxists and socialists, 'Waking from history's great dream', as he describes it, Eric Hobsbawm writes: 'For about half a century, from 1914 to the aftermath of the Second World War, the world passed through a period of cataclysm, producing all manner of freak results, of which the Russian Revolution is probably the most long lasting'. It was indeed 'premature'. Arguing that Lenin should not have made the October Revolution, Hobsbawm once again reminds us: 'There were indeed Marxists – the Mensheviks, Plekhanov, other people – even in Russia who took this view'. If Martin Jacques, editor of the now defunct *Marxism Today* informs us that 'it is the end of the road' for not only 'Stalinism' but also 'most of Leninism', Robin Blackburn, editor of *New Left Review*, goes further to argue: 'Marxism cannot escape implication in the fate of the Russian Revolution'. Lenin, we are told, cannot 'escape the charge' of having laid the ground for Stalin, partly because Lenin was not, after all, 'a systematic thinker'! Critics have indeed traced it all, all the evil, back from Lenin to 'utopianism' of Marx and Engels and forward from Lenin who is now guilty of sowing the seeds of destruction in the very first days of the Bolshevik Revolution, whose politics 'inevitably and necessarily led to an elitist form of government'. A Nina Temple, speaking for a collapse-shattered British Communist Party simply asserts: 'If you look at Russia since the revolution, things went wrong from the start', etc., etc. And in interpreting what has happened to the 'socialist world', 'Marxist scholarship' has not been wanting in seeing the collapse of Soviet socialism even as a victory and vindication of 'the science of Marxism'. Thus, for example, we have Michael Buroway, who even as he questions '"The Marxism is dead" school', celebrates 'the death of Marxism-Leninism', and pointing out that 'after all, the social democratic wing of Marxism, in the tradition of Eduard Bernstein, G. Plekhanov and K. Kautsky, was forever condemning the Bolsheviks for usurping history,' writes: 'As to Marxism's status as a science, far from being a refutation of Marxism, Soviet Communism's failure to realize the promises of socialism is a powerful vindication of Marxism'!

Incidentally, it is interesting to note that this argument around 'the ripeness of conditions', 'sufficiently developed productive forces', or 'necessary economic basis', etc., the repeated insistence that 'ripeness is all' and the theoretical contributions sustaining the positions noticed above, have overwhelmingly come from the Marxist intellectuals (ex-, post-, or any other) in the advanced capitalist West, where such 'ripeness', indeed 'over-ripeness' has been a major fact of socio-economic existence for a pretty long time now, but socialist revolution remains as far away as ever. Surely none of the loudly proclaimed arguments about the impermissibility of socialist transition in backward countries need apply there. If the Russian revolution was indeed mistaken, premature, a usurpation of history, because it took place in a backward country, then the same injunction cannot apply in countries of advanced capitalist development. Surely these Marxist or socialist intellectuals should argue for and support socialist revolution in their advanced capitalist countries. Yet they are today as forcibly opposed to a revolutionary strategy there as they are to the Bolshevik strategy in 1917. Obviously all their 'Marxist' theorising about 'premature' October Revolution, about its 'usurping history', is only an excuse born of expediency and not an expression of their commitment to any kind of socialism. In fact, most of them, in their retreat from socialism are ending up as supporters and apologists for what can at best be described as social-democratic capitalism.

III

Lenin and his Bolshevik comrades were Marxists. They knew their Marx and Engels well, as well as any one else, in fact a lot better than their contemporary or later Marxist critics. They fully shared the basic positions of classical Marxism concerning proletarian revolution and the building up of socialism. But they were revolutionary Marxists in the tradition of Marx himself and not the evolutionist Second International. They were fully appreciative of the perspective of Marx's historical materialism which was principally concerned with the broad development of civilisation in the world as a whole, and not with particular, necessarily subordinate developments within one or another country, large or small, except insofar as Marx and Engels were themselves immediately concerned with them as part of their ongoing revolutionary activity, their Marxist theoretical and political practice. And here, as we have noticed earlier, there was no dogmatically settled trajectory or path of transition to socialism. As Lenin himself put it: 'We do not at all regard the theory of Marx as something complete and inviolable.... We think that it is particularly necessary for socialists independently to analyse the theory of Marx, for this theory provides only general guiding propositions which must be applied differently in England from France, in France from Germany, in Germany from Russia according to the particular circumstances'.

In other words, the Bolsheviks also recognised well, as Marxists, the dialectics of a general principle and its concrete application to different, historically specific situations. What is indeed striking is the way in which Marx's thinking was mirrored so faithfully in the theory and practice of the makers of the Russian Revolution, both before and after October 1917. Thus, even as they saw the difference separating the socio-economic reality in Western Europe from that in pre-revolutionary Russia, they were fully alive, like Marx and Engels before them, to the revolutionary possibilities in their own country. Lenin had fully assimilated Marx's seminal analysis of the events of 1848. He insisted on 'learning from the experience of Germany as elucidated by Marx' and wrote: 'With the proper allowances for concrete national peculiarities and with serfdom substituted for feudalism, all these propositions are fully applicable to the Russia of 1905'. He made explicit the thesis, implicit in Marx's analysis, that in the conditions then prevailing in Russia, a bourgeois-democratic revolution could only be carried through to completion under the leadership of the proletariat. He spoke of 'uninterrupted' or 'continuous' revolution (Marx's phrase was 'permanent revolution') and wrote: 'At the head of the whole of the people, and particularly of the peasantry – for complete freedom, for the consistent democratic revolution, for a republic. At the head of all the toilers and the exploited – for socialism'. Again, with Marx, Lenin regarded the coming revolution in Russia as a catalyst for a socialist revolution at least in Germany and possibly in all of Central and Western Europe. As he visualised it, it was to 'carry the flame of revolution into Europe'. Later on, he was most emphatic: 'the bourgeois-democratic revolution in Russia is now not only a prologue to but an indivisible and integral part of the socialist revolution in the West', indeed 'a prelude to and a step towards the world socialist revolution'.

Lenin was neither 'an economic reductionist', nor a 'voluntarist organisation man', as he is sometimes made out to be. In the tradition of Marx' own work, especially *Capital*, and following upon its remarkable insights about the developing global capitalist system, Lenin pioneered Marxist study of imperialism and monopoly capitalism, with their multiple internal contradictions and economic and political consequences – colonial exploitation, impoverishment of vast masses of people at home and even more so abroad, wars, political authoritarianism, general instability in the capitalist world as a whole etc., etc. This study was a decisive element underlying Lenin's belief in what Lukacs called 'actuality of the revolution', that is not only the necessity but the possibility and immediacy of revolution in Russia as well as Europe. And as the contradictions of imperialism exploded in the First World War, Lenin argued in 1915 that since 'uneven economic and political development is an absolute law of capitalism', victory of socialist revolution 'is possible first in a few or even in one single capitalist country'. His concern with the possibility of revolution in Russia inevitably involved not only a study of the development of capitalism in Russia but also a detailed concrete analysis of the impact of capitalism on the specificities of the Russian class structure, including the problems of highly differentiated and uneven development of class consciousness. It was this concern again which led him to analyse the political conditions in Russia (nature of state, levels of repression, etc.), to work out the type of political party and organisation needed and to recognise the centrality of ideological and programmatic debate in the party and socialist consciousness and clarification within the workers' movement – all this as part of an active preparation for the forthcoming revolution in Russia which, as with Marx, Lenin well anticipated. That backward and alone, Russia could also be called upon to pioneer the path to socialism, as it turned out to be, was of course, again with Marx, never anticipated as a real possibility.

IV

Whatever Lenin's innovations or contributions to the theory and practice of Marxism, including his supposed 'revisionism', it can never be too much stressed that, both before and after the October Revolution, he stayed, in essentials, very much within the framework of classical Marxist understanding of historical processes, including issues concerning revolution and socialism. He was unequivocally committed to the classical Marxist view of the global character of socialist enterprise. Writing in 1915 ('On the Slogan for a United States of Europe') he categorically stated that

> A United States of the World (not of Europe alone) is the state form of the unification and freedom of nations which we associate with socialism – until the time when the complete victory of communism

> brings about the total disappearance of the state, including the democratic.... The *political form* of a society wherein the proletariat is victorious in overthrowing the bourgeoisie will be a *democratic republic,* which will more and more concentrate the forces of the proletariat of a given nation or nations, in the struggle against states that have not yet gone over to socialism. The abolition of classes is impossible without a dictatorship of the oppressed class, of the proletariat. A *free union of nations in socialism* is impossible without a more or less prolonged and stubborn struggle of the *socialist republics* against the backward states.

Even as he based his strategy for breaking the 'weakest link of the chain' – that is, for a revolution in Russia – on his interpretation of the law of uneven development, Lenin insisted that '*political* revolution can under no circumstances whatsoever either obscure or weaken the slogan of a *socialist* revolution', and the perspective for him remained 'a socialist revolution' which, he wrote, 'should not be regarded as a single act, but as a period of turbulent political and economic upheavals, the most intense class struggle, civil war, revolutions and counter-revolutions'. In this perspective a revolution in Russia was expected to open up precisely this period of world-wide – or at least Europe-wide – revolutions which alone could secure the conditions for a victory of socialism.

For Lenin, as he prepared, fought for, and finally won the victory of socialist revolution in his country, Russia was yet only the 'weakest link' in the chain that was the global capitalist system and he clearly recognised that socialism was unviable here without the help of the more advanced European proletariat. Over and over again, with unequalled force and clarity, and as much before as after October 1917, Lenin insisted that revolution in Russia could not succeed or sustain itself unless it led to revolution in the West. As he put it, 'the workers of the most backward country will not be able to hold that banner unless the workers of all advanced countries come to their aid'. He categorically stated that a revolution in Russia cannot be 'in itself' socialist, that 'the Russian proletariat single-handed cannot complete the socialist revolution', that 'the final victory of socialism in a single country is of course impossible'. After the revolution had taken place in Russia,

Lenin was convinced that without a revolution in the West, the Russian Revolution would not survive. He believed, with Marx, that the proletariat of the advanced capitalist countries will help and show the way forward once the revolution in Russia triggers off an European revolution. And the focus of prime interest here was Germany with its developed capitalist economy, material resources and technical knowledge, and a politically educated and advanced proletariat. Even as he wrote that 'it is the absolute truth that, ...if the German revolution does not come, we are doomed', he also, with the hopefulness of a revolutionary, believed that 'Germany plus Russia equals communist Europe'. Where Marx had once hoped for an internal triumph of the proletariat in advanced Paris accelerating the then retarded German development, Lenin and the Bolsheviks were counting on the triumph of revolution in industrial Germany to consolidate and carry forward the gains of revolution in backward Russia – and they remained hopeful about it till the mid-1920s. As Lenin wrote: 'The German proletariat is the most trustworthy and the most reliable ally of the Russian and the world proletarian revolution'. There was a strong, near universal feeling among the Bolshevik leaders that a victory in the highly industrialised Germany would be in the best interests of international socialism, and for this they were even willing to risk a temporary loss of the newly constituted Soviet Union. Such was the spirit of internationalism among the founders of the Bolshevik Party at the time. Lenin and his Bolsheviks saw the Soviet Union as a base of struggle for international socialism, and that is how they addressed the oppressed and exploited people the world over. Such was the driving impulse behind the founding of the Communist International. Lenin wrote: 'Our contingent of workers and peasants which is upholding Soviet power is one of the contingents of a great world army'. Even as, in opposition to the reformist perspective and politics of the leadership of the Second International and still hopeful about the revolutionary potentialities of the 'advanced countries of Western Europe', Lenin argued in defence of 'the Russian model' of revolutionary politics, he wrote: 'It would be erroneous to lose sight of the fact that, soon after the victory of the proletarian revolution in at least one of the advanced countries, a sharp change will probably come about: *Russia will cease to be the model* and will once again become a *backward country* (in the "Soviet" and socialist sense).'

Thus Lenin's Marxism was no more optimistic about the final victory of socialist revolution in Russia or the prospects of socialism in one country than any of his contemporary or later Marxist critics. He was most categorical about his classical Marxist perspective: 'It is not open to the slightest doubt that the final victory of our revolution, if it were to remain alone, if there were no revolutionary movement in other countries, would be hopeless... Our salvation from all these difficulties, I repeat, is an all European revolution'. And this was the perspective of the Bolshevik leadership as a whole. In the very midst of the revolution, Trotsky, speaking for the Bolshevik government, said: 'If the people of Europe do not arise and crush imperialism, we shall be crushed – that is beyond doubt. Either the Russian revolution will raise the whirlwind of struggle in the West, or the capitalists of all countries will stifle our struggle'. Stalin too thus summarised the essential difference between Lenin and his opponents on the issue of making the October Revolution: 'There are two lines; one sets the course for the victory of the revolution and relies on Europe, the second does not believe in the revolution and counts only on being an opposition'.

Such then was the avowed revolutionary perspective of Lenin and the Bolsheviks, before, during and after the October Revolution. This is how Lenin and the Bolsheviks with him, as Marxists, thought and acted even as the revolution in Russia fought for life against civil war and counter-revolution backed by fourteen invading armies from the capitalist world, waiting all the time for an European revolution to come to its rescue. As the eminent historian E.H. Carr, speaking of the perspective of Lenin and the Bolshevik Party, has pointed out, it was 'the European revolution, on which the confident calculations, not merely of a few optimists but of every Bolshevik of any account, had been based'.

V

The Bolsheviks were not alone in looking to a European revolution. Even Kautsky and other socialists of Western Europe self-acknowledgedly did the same, maybe in traditional deference to the views of Marx and Engels who had done so long before them. As Kautsky wrote: 'the Bolsheviks must not be too much blamed for expecting a European revolution. Other socialists did the same, and we are certainly approaching conditions which will sharply accentuate the class struggle, and which may have many surprises in store. And if the Bolsheviks have till now been in error in expecting a revolution, have not Babel, Marx and Engels cherished a like delusion? This is not to be denied'. Needless to add, with their evolutionist Marxism, Kautsky and these 'other socialists' were only prepared for surprises. They did nothing to prepare for this revolution. Only Lenin and his Bolsheviks, as revolutionary Marxists did. For them the perspective of an European revolution was never a delusion or baseless optimism, an exercise in 'Marxist utopianism' as accused by latter day critics. On the contrary, it was based on a solid analysis of contemporary capitalist system. Lenin and the Bolsheviks were alone in developing a theory of imperialism which could explain the nature of capitalism as a single global system, with its contradictions, crises and wars, its sharpened class struggles and 'weak' links, etc. It is this analysis which helped them grasp the international scope of the class struggle this global capitalism was generating, including the strong probability of an European revolution. It is significant that there was no comparable effort in the European socialist movement, despite its claims to be the main inheritor of the legacy of Marx, of the classical Marxist tradition of theoretical and political practice.

The Marxist analysis and prognosis was proved to be correct. As expected, revolution occurred in Russia in the aftermath of the first world war and was soon followed by an Europe-wide revolutionary upheaval. If Germany, Finland and Hungary, Austria and Italy were the major storm centres of this European revolution – as Victor Serge recorded, 'from the Scheldt to the Volga the councils of workers' and soldiers' deputies – the soviets – are the real masters of the hour' – hardly any important country in Europe escaped being convulsed by popular unrest and class struggles. This is how Victor Serge, a revolutionary, saw it:

> The newspapers of the period are astonishing... riots in Paris, riots in Lyon, revolution in Belgium, revolution in Constantinople, victory of the soviets in Bulgaria, rioting in Copenhagen. In fact the whole of Europe is in movement, clandestine or open soviets are appearing everywhere, even in the Allied armies; everything is possible, everything.

At the other end of the political spectrum, Lloyd George saw it no differently:

> The whole of Europe is filled with the spirit of revolution. There is a deep sense not only of discontent but of anger and revolt amongst the workmen against the pre-war conditions. The whole existing order in its political, social and economic aspects is questioned by the masses of the population from one end of Europe to the other.

The Marxist prognosis about the European revolution was more than vindicated, but the hopefulness about its outcome was belied. This is how John Rees sums it up, even as he takes note of the Bolsheviks' last-ditch effort, through the Third International, to intervene and salvage the revolution in Europe:

> What was lacking in these revolutionary upheavals was not the objective Europe-wide crisis. Neither was it the willingness of workers to struggle for power. What was lacking was a leadership of sufficient clarity and an organization with a core of sufficiently experienced members to successfully lead these movements to power. This was the decisive difference between the German and Russian revolutions. It was a weakness which the Bolsheviks laboured heroically to overcome in the Third International. It was certainly not a struggle that was doomed to failure in advance.
>
> The Bolsheviks correctly predicted a European revolution and they strained might and main to provide that revolution with a leadership which could bring it to a successful conclusion. They were right to try. As Marx once observed, 'world history would indeed be very easy to make, if the struggle were taken up only on condition of infallibly favourable chances'.

In retrospect it is possible to argue that Lenin overestimated the possibility of a rapid and successful extension of the revolution to the European continent, but as John Rees has pointed out it was certainly not doomed to failure in advance. The fact is that it was aborted, betrayed or surrendered by the European social democracy – in Germany the counter-revolution was in fact planned and led by the reformist SPD, paving the way for the eventual rise of fascism. And once this had happened the revolutionary tide simply ebbed away. In the event, out of the post-first world war revolutionary upheavals, thanks above all to the leadership of Lenin and the Bolsheviks, only the Russian Revolution survived.

VI

It is necessary to reiterate at this point that the October Revolution was a genuine people's revolution. It was not some 'Bolshevik coup', 'the product of the organisational skill of a ruthless conspiratorial minority' – a view which, despite evidence to the contrary adduced by several old authentic accounts and more recent specialist studies, has been regularly propagated by the hostile critics, and, with the wide currency given to it by the western media come to inform the conventional wisdom on the subject the world over. After the Soviet collapse, this view seems to have acquired a new lease of life thanks to the growing number of repentant Marxists and socialists everywhere, including the erstwhile Soviet Union – all of them feeding into the ruling classes' constant effort to take people's history away from them, especially the history of their successful struggles and victories.

To put it most briefly, the October Revolution was not a quick, smooth royal road to power for the 'conspiratorial Bolsheviks'. Behind their ultimate rise to power lay decades of hard political and theoretical work and the building up of the party, class and mass organisations. Nearer to the event itself, between the generally admitted spontaneous mass uprising of February 1917 and the Bolshevik organised mass uprising of October 1917, lies the long period of internal political polarisation and the threatened counter-revolution during which the Bolsheviks had to fight with and against *all* other socialist parties to gain political ascendency among the increasingly more militant popular masses and to make the revolution possible. Of course, the programme and tactical flexibility of the Bolsheviks were essential to this end. But that is only part of the story. The remainder and more important part is how the other parties responded to the deepening economic and political crisis in Russia and, in the process, steadily lost in the estimation of the mass of workers and peasants as they failed to give adequate answers to the most pressing issues posed by the revolution, particularly the issues of ending the war and bringing the Russian soldiers home, the distribution of land to the peasants and the control of the factories by the workers. Only the Bolsheviks provided the requisite answers. As the economic and political paralysis of successive regimes led or participated in by these parties drove a wedge between them and the mass of workers, peasants and soldiers, as they were all in turn discredited in the eyes of the latter, earning only people's contempt for their timidity and temporising, for trying to limit or freeze the revolution in its belated 'bourgeois' character, often with the help of their scholastic theorising, the Bolsheviks, closer to the people and more in tune with their militant mood, saw the soldiers, peasants and workers acting for themselves – 'voting with their feet' against the war, seizing the land, occupying the factories – and provided them with necessary programmes – 'Land, Bread and Peace' – as well as organisation and leadership, and through it all educated them politically on a mass scale. In fact such was the shifting of popular support to Bolsheviks that at one stage, in his famous *April Thesis*, Lenin even postulated the possibility of a peaceful road to power, which possibility was however soon aborted by counter-revolution's armed attack on revolution. Throughout this period, it was the Bolsheviks who prepared the people to defend the revolution against the emerging counter-revolution. As the developing situation soon posed the choice: either revolution or counter-revolution, the Soviets, as organs of people's power, disillusioned with the Provisional Government of Kerensky without and with the moderate socialists within, increasingly looked to the Bolsheviks for leadership. As the other parties, including moderate socialists of different hues lost their purchase on reality and with it confidence of the popular masses, the Bolsheviks' vital role in organising the defeat of Kornilov's counter-revolution gave them the support of the majority in the Soviets, and they moved on to practical military preparations for the successful armed insurrection of October 1917, which ended the dual power, emerging from the February revolution, finally in favour of the Soviets.

VII

It needs to be recognised that Lenin had all along insisted that the insurrection could only be the crowning act of the mass revolution and not a party coup – a difference on which he had to repeatedly argue with not only the Mensheviks but his own comrades including leading Bolsheviks like Zinoviev and Kamenev. Lenin was variously accused of Jacobinism, of being a follower of the anarchist Bakunin or the conspirator revolutionary Blanqui. Lenin's answer to such accusations is worth quoting. Far from planning the mounting of a coup, it indicates precisely the preconditions for revolution which had been achieved by October 1917, Lenin wrote:

> Military conspiracy is Blanquism, if it is organised not by a party of a definite class, if its organisers have not analysed the political moment in general and the international situation in particular, if the party had not on its side the sympathy of the majority of the people, as proved by objective facts, if the development of revolutionary events has not brought about a practical refutation of the conciliatory illusions of the petty bourgeoisie, if the majority of the soviet-type organs of revolutionary struggle that have been recognised as authoritative or have shown themselves to be such in practice have not been won over, if there has not matured a sentiment in the army (if in wartime) against the government that protracts the unjust war against the will of the whole people, if the slogans of the uprising (like 'All Power to the Soviets', 'land to the peasants', or 'Immediate offer of a democratic peace to all the belligerent nations'...) have not become widely known and popular, if the advanced workers are not sure of the desperate

situation of the masses and of the support of the countryside, a support proved by a serious peasant movement or by an uprising against the landowners and the government that defends the landowners, if the country's economic situation inspires earnest hopes for a favourable solution of the crisis by peaceable and parliamentary means...

John Rees has commented:

> When Lenin believed that these conditions were *not* present, during the July Days, he bent his every effort to *prevent* a premature rising. Many other revolutionaries in Europe, as the German Revolution would show, were to pay with their lives for not being able to make a similar assessment. But by October even Lenin's political enemies were forced to admit that he was no Jacobin. The Menshevik N.N. Sukhanov writes: 'To talk about military conspiracy instead of national insurrection, when the party was followed by the overwhelming majority of the people, when the party had already de facto conquered all real power and authority was clearly an absurdity. On the part of the enemies of Bolshevism it was a malicious absurdity, but on the part of the 'cronies' (Zinoviev, Kamenev) an aberration based on panic. Here Lenin was right...' Or as Robert Service (very much a liberal historian) simply expresses it: 'What really counted was that the Bolshevik political programme proved steadily more appealing to the mass of workers, soldiers and peasants as social turmoil and economic ruin reached a climax in late autumn. But for that there could have been no October Revolution.' Martov (the leading Menshevik) wrote: 'Understand, please, that before us after all is a victorious uprising of the proletariat – almost the entire proletariat supports Lenin and expects its social liberation from the uprising'.

Again, John Rees has rightly pointed out:

> Ultimately October was not a great contest between Menshevism and Bolshevism, not between bourgeois democracy and Soviet power, but between bourgeois reaction and military dictatorship on the one hand, and Soviet power on the other. The Mensheviks did not understand this ... The Bolsheviks' ability to prevail lay in the fact that they did understand this.

Those who today dream that there could have been a 'third way' which would have prevented the 'premature' revolution of October 1917 need to think on two issues. Firstly, such a course was offered to the workers of Russia in 1917 and they rejected it and, secondly, they rejected it in part because they saw behind the vacillations of Kerensky the bayonet of Kornilov. Trotsky was right when he insisted that 'fascism is the price paid by those who toy with revolution'.

VIII

As postulated by the revolutionary perspective of the Bolsheviks, a European revolution indeed occurred but it found the social democratic leadership of the European working class totally unprepared for it. In the final analysis the European working class certainly helped save the Russian Revolution and the young socialist state from strangulation at birth by imperialism, but its own revolution was let down, aborted, betrayed and surrendered by reformist social democracy. The October Revolution indeed survived but as a beleaguered fortress, surrounded by a hostile though temporarily exhausted enemy and under intolerable pressure of its internal backwardness and externally imposed isolation. The Bolsheviks were called upon to not only save the revolution but take, as best as they may, the road to socialism! In terms of classical Marxism it was an entirely unanticipated and unprecedented situation.

Lenin, in his own way, knew and well understood what had happened. Even as he expected an European revolution, he was, as always, fully aware of the difference in the objective socio-economic situation of backward Russia and the advanced capitalist West from the standpoint of beginning and continuing a socialist revolution. Like Engels before him, Lenin recognised the extreme weakness of 'civil society' in pre-revolutionary Russia which had facilitated the revolutionary capture of power by the proletariat led by the Bolsheviks. As he said: 'In such a country it was quite easy to start a revolution, as easy as lifting a feather... But to start without preparation a revolution in a country in which capitalism is developed and has given democratic culture and organisation to everybody, down to the last man – to do so would be wrong, absurd'. Referring to 'our enemies' in Russia, Romanovs, Kerensky and the Russian bourgeoisie, he wrote: 'Do these enemies amount to anything compared with the international bourgeoisie, who have turned all the achievements of the human mind into a weapon to suppress the will of the working people'. He had concluded: 'That is why it was so easy for us to start the revolution and more difficult to continue it and why over there in the West it will be more difficult to start and easier to continue'. This was an understanding which well ties up with Gramsci's theory of hegemony in society, with its focus on the nature of ruling class domination, its dimensions of coercion and consent, and civil society as the terrain of hegemonic struggles that any preparation for a socialist revolution in the West must take note of. About two decades after Lenin, Gramsci was to write: 'In Russia, the State was everything, civil society was primordial and gelatinous; in the West, there was a proper relation between State and civil society and when the State trembled a sturdy structure of civil society was at once revealed. The State was only an outer ditch, behind which there stood a powerful system of fortresses and earthworks ...' Hence the immediately relevant conclusion for the struggle for socialism in the countries of advanced capitalist development: here 'the resistance' of civil society has to be overcome 'before hand', that is, 'before the attempt to seize power'. That is how Gramsci argued more than fifty years ago. In view of the developments in the world since then, including the experience of the now collapsed 'communist regimes', Gramsci's argument and conclusions, properly interpreted and extended, have a near-universal validity now for the struggle for socialism in our times.

IX

I have spoken of the 'trick' that history played on the doctrine of Karl Marx. This is not to be interpreted too literally, for, as we have seen, there is nothing mysterious or inscrutable about what happened. Even so history did leave the October Revolution, its Bolshevik leadership and the Russian people alone and isolated within capitalist encirclement and faced with the near-impossible task of attempting a socialist transition in backward Russia – one could even say impossible, because in the classical Marxist perspective, such a transition could be successfully carried out only on the basis of the achievements, economic, political and cultural, of advanced capitalist development and these were simply absent in the newly constituted Soviet state. Lenin had hoped, as it were, to combine the political potential of the 'weakest link' with the economically mature conditions of the 'advanced' capitalist countries. The failure of revolution elsewhere in Europe, especially in Germany, simply crippled this hope and the possibility it involved.

As we have already noticed, Lenin or the Bolsheviks had no illusions about building socialism in a single backward country like Russia. The perspective with which Lenin had initially led the Bolsheviks into the October Revolution, which was also the perspective with which he valiantly struggled to ensure the survival of the Soviet state as long as possible, was the classical Marxist perspective. And this found expression, yet again, in the very last piece of his writing ('Better Fewer But Better') in March 1923, where he stated that his struggle could not really succeed till there was a new wave of revolutionary upsurge embracing the developed capitalist countries. For him there could be no real advance towards socialism in Russia, unless there was a more or less simultaneous movement in at least Germany, if not a number of developed capitalist states of the world. A Marxist, he knew that the objective material conditions for socialist emancipation whereby, in Marx's words, 'the direct material production process is stripped of the form of penury and anti-thesis', were simply not available in backward Russia. Socialism postulated 'an association where free development of each is a precondition for the free development of all' – this was simply impossible for Russia to attempt. The inadequacies of the *objective* material conditions were only too obvious – and very soon war, civil war and counter-revolution, even as they added to these inadequacies, took their toll of even the available *subjective* conditions, the class conscious proletariat of Russia and the Bolsheviks Party itself, those who had made the revolution. Yet the Bolsheviks could not be expected to surrender the revolution. They had no choice but to begin, to initiate a socialist transition in Russia. Lenin and the Bolsheviks were fully aware of their predicament as they were called upon to take the road to socialism in one country, to attempt history's most 'radical rupture' as Marx described it, for the first time, in 'backward Russia' further devastated within, economically and politically, by war, civil war and counter revolution and in the midst of a most hostile capitalist environment. Not prepared to build, the Bolsheviks and the Russian people yet sought 'to build socialism' in their country.

X

Before I proceed to explore the ensuing *problematique* of this attempt and its outcome, there is one historically significant point which needs to be more specifically underlined than I have done so far. For the future of humankind, equally significant with the success of revolutionary Marxism in Russia (regardless of its later, but not necessary or inevitable degeneration) was the failure of reformist social democracy in the West. History has already taken its sweet revenge on the proletariat of these advanced capitalist countries with the degeneration and ultimate collapse of the first effort to build socialism – to replace capitalism with a more rational and humane social order – even if they still do not know or understand it. History has also exacted a very heavy price for this failure from the common people everywhere. As Trotsky was to put it later, 'the peoples of the world will pay for the historic crime of reformism'. And they have indeed paid with imperialist exploitation and wars, with fascism and political dictatorships, with economic depressions and mass unemployment, with first world poverty and inequality and third world hunger and destitution, with racism, sexism and fundamentalism of all kinds, with the material and moral–cultural ravages wrought the world over, at the centre and even more in the peripheries, by the continued existence of capitalism over these eighty odd years. And if the threat of nuclear self-destruction has somewhat receded with the defeat of Soviet Union in the cold war and its ultimate disappearance, it still remains real, and additionally now there is the imminent threat of an ecological disaster, daily looming larger over the future of humankind. The scientific and technological revolutions of our time, given their planned *socialist* use, hold for humankind, for the first time in its long history, the possibility of moving from the hitherto existing civilisations of scarcity to a civilisation abundant enough to not only satisfy the genuine needs of all on this earth but provide for a 'truly rich' human life that Marx wrote of. But capitalism knows or recognises no such human purposes, its accumulative logic, the market-driven pursuit of profit and privilege for the few, will only continue to blight humankind's hope of a better life for all.

Capitalism, even as it survives beyond its historical time, is today more of a fact in the world than it ever was in its history – and people are paying the price for it. But failures of the past notwithstanding, this must not be allowed to obscure that other fact, indeed history's most important fact which has always been a promise too, that people continue to hope and struggle for a better life. The collapse in the Soviet Union, this historical turn in the destiny of socialism, is no end of any history. For the same reasons as before, men and women will continue to struggle against capitalism, and they can well ensure a different outcome for their struggle next time. The dialectics of historical processes may well see, sooner that most people think, in the advanced capitalist countries as much as elsewhere in the world, a recovery of revolutionary Marxism and a renewed struggle for socialism, socialism that Marx argued for. Capitalism surely continues, now more predatory than ever before; but however dimmed at the moment, the fire kindled and fanned by the October Revolution still burns in the breasts of the victims of capitalism, everywhere. The promise of October Revolution still holds, a promise that found eloquent expression in the unique economic emancipation, unprecedented political freedom and popular participation, the cultural and artistic explosion, the sexual and national liberations and so much more that was the distinctive feature of the early days of the October revolution. All this can yet be, again, and more permanently. The October remains our past, but not only that, it is our future too. We must not relinquish the legacy of Lenin's October Revolution.

5

Lenin's Project of Socialist Transition in Russia

Not prepared to build the Bolsheviks were yet called upon to build socialism in Russia. Therein lay their historical predicament.

Every revolution has the two-fold aspect of overthrowing the old power structures and building a new social order. The former opens the way to the latter as a possibility but does not necessarily guarantee that this shall be successfully realised. This obviously depends on the strength and understanding of the new forces which gain power through the revolutionary process, the adequacy of the objective material conditions as well as the obstacles they have to overcome, including the opposition offered by the defeated but still far from dead supporters of the old social order. The October Revolution under Leninist leadership, certainly carried out the first task, thereby proving the validity, under the specific conditions of Russia in 1917, of the Marxist theory of revolution in the relatively backward countries of the capitalist world. The Russian proletariat, as it developed in the decades before the first world war, fitted the classical Marxian conception very well. Though relatively small in relation to the population as a whole, because of belated capitalist development, it was concentrated in major cities and was able under the sustained and resolute leadership of the Bolsheviks to overthrow the bourgeois regime which had come to power in the February Revolution. As visualised by Marx and now realised by Lenin, it led in making the revolution 'permanent' to itself seize state power in the socialist revolution of October 1917. But the building up of a new social order now was a different proposition.

The classical Marxist tradition always visualised the building up of socialism on the basis of the conditions created by advanced capitalist development. Here two conditions were seen as absolutely necessary for any transition to socialism, namely a sufficiently numerous, politically conscious and well organised, revolutionary working class and a high level of development of the productive forces. Though not numerous, such working class was available in Russia in the *immediate* aftermath of the revolution, but most of it soon perished in the civil war that followed, or disintegrated in the economic chaos that accompanied it. As for the second condition, Soviet Union had neither the industrial development or technological resources, the management skills and the necessary trained intelligentsia, nor sufficiently skilled labour force to undertake a socialist reconstruction of Russian society. The Bolsheviks had throughout looked to the proletariat of the industrially advanced countries of Europe, particularly the more advanced German proletariat, not merely to come to their aid but lead in the anticipated international process of revolutionary socialist transformations. But no such aid or leadership from outside was forthcoming to help overcome the weaknesses within. The European revolution had failed and fast receded in the West. The Bolsheviks of course managed to save their own revolution, but this only left them alone and beleaguered in backward Russia, confronting a totally unanticipated situation and an equally unanticipated and truly formidable task, which yet they had no choice but to undertake, that is, attempt the construction of a new social order in Russia.

Bolsheviks' making of the October Revolution and their attempt to build socialism in a single backward country has been questioned by critics on the left, all the more frequently since the collapse of the Soviet Union. It needs to be clearly understood, however, that defeat of October revolution or surrender of power by the Bolsheviks would have meant power passing on not to other left wing groups (Socialist Revolutionaries, Mensheviks or any other Russian version of social democracy) but to the forces of reaction; it would have meant not some from of bourgeois democracy but a bloody counter-revolution. And being in power Bolsheviks could not have retained it for long in the name of some 'holding operation', awaiting 'a world revolution', or lesser revolutions elsewhere. Such indeed was Lenin's initial strategic concern in the aftermath of the October Revolution: to 'hold the fort' until the situation became favourable with the hoped–for revolution in the advanced European countries which would enable the Bolsheviks 'to lay hold of the advanced productive apparatus and set it in motion'. But this could not be done indefinitely. The very legitimacy of the Bolshevik possession of state power depended upon an affirmative answer to the question of possibility of socialist construction in the economically backward and internationally isolated Soviet Union. Besides the Bolsheviks were revolutionaries willing 'to dare'.

II

The task was indeed unanticipated by the Bolsheviks. They were called upon to do what they had previously, in the tradition of classical Marxism, deemed virtually impossible, namely, to make an attempt 'to complete the socialist revolution' literally 'single-handed', to do something which they still thought not justified or feasible theoretically – contrary to what latter-day Stalin-era theorisation would have it – but had become a practical, political necessity. No matter how difficult or remote the realisation of their ideal of socialism, as Marxist revolutionaries they had no choice but to set about realising it. Unanticipated, it was a formidable task too. The socialist transition they set out to carry was, in Marx's words, 'the most radical rupture' in human history and they were called upon to carry it out for the first time, in a most backward, war and civil war-devastated country of Europe, and in the midst of an actively hostile, overwhelmingly powerful capitalist encirclement. In other words, an underdeveloped and devastated country was called upon to make, in isolation and encirclement, the great leap forward on its own for the whole of mankind.

The hostile capitalist encirclement persisted throughout Soviet Union's seventy odd years of existence, and along with its economic and political coercions, war or threat of war over *all* these years was a fact of life for the Soviet people, which compelled grievous distortions in the socialism that was built and contributed to its ultimate failure. Socialism in the Soviet Union needs to be understood as the product of a capitalism dominated world system as much as of internal economic backwardness and political forces. No doubt the idea of socialism was the Bolshevik inspiration when they set out on their pioneering enterprise, but the real historical socialism as it came up in the Soviet Union was not a gradual putting into effect a socialist idea. This socialism grew through an historical dialectic with the forces of world capitalism within the framework of a global inter-state system. It could not but internalise the distorting logic of this dialectic.

The situation in post-October Russia was most unfavourable for the Russian proletariat, having led in the October Revolution, to now lead in the construction of socialism. Unfavourable, but not altogether impossible. It is certainly possible to visualise that, if the ensuing period had been even halfway peaceful, the Russian proletariat could have established itself as the ruling class and led by the Bolshevik Party (and possibly other radical parties in alliance with it) initiated the transition to socialism along the lines sketched in the classical Marxist theory. Admittedly, the Russian proletariat would not have found the task easy, it could yet have failed. But at least it could have had a chance. This chance or possible opportunity however was virtually destroyed during the years of civil war, foreign invasion and counter-revolution which followed the October Revolution, whose terrible and bloody struggles largely decimated and dispersed the Russian proletariat which was already so small to begin with, took their toll of the Bolshevik Party itself, and further devastated the poor, technologically underdeveloped Russian economy already much ruined by the first world war. And whatever survived – the proletariat, its party and the economy – was now subject to the unrelenting military, economic and political pressure of a hostile encirclement by the world capitalist system.

It is elementary Marxism to expect that, under the circumstances, socialism sought to be built in the Soviet Union was going to have more than its share of 'inevitable defects' that Marx spoke of. That it in fact came to be rather grossly deformed was known, except to the 'faithfuls', in the years that followed. How permanently or disastrously was the question till it finally collapsed. Three decades back, noticing this deformation, and the 'altogether new and exciting vistas' that await a society moving into socialism from a comparatively more advanced economic, political and cultural base and in a world at peace, I had written:

> In judging the *possibilities* inhering in socialism, one must remember that the development of socialism in the Soviet Union, carried out under exceptionally difficult and unfavourable circumstances, has been much distorted... The historical conditions surrounding the first great experiment in building socialism: Russia's past history and habits; its vast peasant environment of rural idiocy and lack of democratic consciousness and traditions; the need for rapid industrialisation beginning from scratch in an illiterate and technically backward society; constant military, economic and political pressure of hostile, counter-revolutionary western capitalist encirclement; therefore, the necessity of building socialism not on the achievements of capitalism, except when borrowed or copied, and not with the help of the more advanced societies but in the teeth of their opposition; serious theoretical or ideological errors and weaknesses together with the character of the men who led, etc. – all these have left their mark on what has been built in the Soviet Union.

The mark proved more deadly than I, with many others, had then thought, and what was built has now collapsed, primarily under the weight of its own contradictions. Even so, it is well to remember Anna Louise Strong's cryptic observation. Speaking of the 'evils' that went with the Russian experiment in socialism, she had written:

> Most of all they came because the democratic and technically developed working-class of the West left the first building of

> socialism to an illiterate, technically backward peasant people, who knew that they were not ready for the task and yet who built.

III

As Bettelheim has pointed out, the revolutionary forces in post-October Russia were too weak – weak within and without any political and economic assistance from more advanced countries – and unavoidably perhaps, too lacking in theoretical and practical understanding based on relevant historical experience, to solve the enormously complicated and difficult problems involved in replacing the old order by a new, genuinely socialist society in Russia. Lenin was aware of this weakness, indeed of the entire predicament created by the lone survival of the revolution in Russia, as he grappled with these problems during the few years that he himself survived the October Revolution.

A socialist revolution had been carried out in Russia, but its survival and further progress, a 'lasting' victory for it, was seen by Lenin and Bolsheviks as 'exclusively' dependent on 'world revolution', in effect a European revolution. On the morrow of revolution itself, in March 1918, Lenin stressed that there was 'no hope of the ultimate victory of our revolution if it were to remain alone, if there were no revolutionary movements in other countries'. Conscious of the difficulties ahead, he repeated: 'our salvation from all these difficulties is an all-European revolution'. As the Bolsheviks struggled to save their revolution from counter-revolution, they had expectations of help from the spread of revolution to Europe. The revolution in Europe however failed to sustain itself, leaving the Bolsheviks isolated even as they managed to save their own revolution in Russia and even set up the Soviet Republic. The Bolsheviks hoped their isolation would prove temporary. It did not; the European revolution, let down by social democracy, receded and finally disappeared in the West. Soviet Russia, equally finally, stood alone, encircled by global capitalism. Still hopeful, this is how Lenin saw the situation as late as July 1921:

> Actually, however, events did not proceed along as straight a line as we had expected. In the other big, capitalistically more

> developed countries the revolution has not broken out to this day. True, we can say with satisfaction that the revolution is developing all over the world and it is only thanks to this that the international bourgeoisie is unable to strangle us, in spite of the fact that, militarily and economically, it is a hundred times stronger than we are...
>
> As for our Russian Republic, we must take advantage of this brief respite in order to adapt our tactics to this zig zag line of history.

At the same time Lenin was realistic enough to argue:

> When we started the international revolution, we thought: either the international revolution comes to our assistance, and in that case, our victory will be fully assured, or we shall do our modest revolutionary work in the conviction that even in the event of defeat we shall have served the cause of the revolution and that our experience will benefit other revolutions.

The October Revolution survived without a revolution in Europe on which the Bolsheviks had staked their chances. But its victorious survival also meant that what had seemed inconceivable previously had now become possible. As Lenin put it: '...is the existence of a socialist republic in a capitalist environment at all conceivable? It seemed inconceivable from the political and military aspects. That it is possible both politically and militarily has now been proved.' Again, neither Lenin nor any one else among the Bolsheviks, including Stalin, had thought of the possibility of building socialism singly in Russia before or immediately after the October Revolution. But now, while they still held on to their classical internationalist perspective, they had no choice but to begin a socialist transition in Russia. However difficult or previously inconceivable the task, it had become a political necessity for Lenin and the Bolsheviks.

As in case of the October Revolution, this choice was questioned, among others by the 'orthodox' Marxists of the Second International. But as revolutionaries in the classical Marxist tradition, it was not an easy choice to make for the Bolsheviks themselves. The issue became the subject of intense political debate within the Bolshevik Party before the necessity of this choice was recognised and accepted and the decision to begin a socialist transition in Russia was made. E.H. Carr has pointed out that in the early stages of inner-party debates on the question of socialism in Russia, there was no unbridgeable gulf between the proponents of 'socialism in one country' and their opponents. He says: 'Theoretically the differences between the two views seemed almost to disappear under the weight of the argument. The supporters of socialism in one country did not at this stage dare to pretend that the building of socialism could be completely achieved in a backward country, but laid stress on the process of building. Its opponents did not deny that some progress could be made, but emphasised the inconclusive character of the work and the impossibility of bringing it to completion'. Lenin himself never really abandoned his view that socialism will have to be 'created by the revolutionary co-operation of the proletarians of all countries'. And whatever the later theorisation or its validity, it needs to be noticed that as late as April 1924, after Lenin's death, even Stalin did not equate 'socialism in one country' with fully developed or complete socialism. He said (on 30 April 1924):

> But to overthrow the power of the bourgeoisie, to establish the power of the proletariat in one country does not mean the complete victory of socialism. The principal task of socialism – the organisation of social production – has still to be fulfilled. Can the final victory of socialism be achieved in one country without the joint efforts of the proletarians in several advanced countries? No, it cannot.

IV

The decision to begin the transition to socialism was made but the future still remained uncertain. Lenin's very last piece of writing for publication, 'Better Fewer, But Better' which appeared in *Pravda* on 2 March 1923 is quite instructive in this regard. While justifying the Bolsheviks' historical initiative in overthrowing the bourgeois state power and setting up the Soviet state, Lenin held that 'it is not easy for us, however, to keep going until the socialist revolution is victorious in more developed countries'. And then he raised the crucial issue: 'Thus at the present time we are confronted with the question: shall we be able to hold on with our small and very small peasant production, and in our present state of ruin, until the West-European capitalist countries consummate their development towards socialism?' But he noted that 'they are consummating it not as we formerly expected', while 'we lack enough civilisation to enable us to pass straight on to socialism, although we do have the political requisite for it'. He saw the continuing threat from global capitalism and asked: "Can we save ourselves from the impending conflict with these imperialist countries? May we hope that the internal antagonisms and conflicts between the thriving imperialist countries.... will give us a second respite'. Still convinced about a world socialist revolution in future, he wrote: 'But what interests us is not the inevitability of this complete victory of socialism but the tactics which we, the Russian Communist Party, we, the Russian Soviet Government should pursue....'. It was still a question of 'respite', which the Soviet Union really never had, what with war, threat of war and constant economic and political pressure against it throughout its seventy odd years of existence. But it was even more a question of 'tactics', of the policies to be pursued during whatever kind of 'respite' became available, in the short and the long run, on which hinged, in the final analysis, the future of socialism in the Soviet Union.

It was thus that the Bolsheviks opted for their modest yet heroic enterprise and entered the uncharted territory that was a socialist transition in Russia. Lenin was aware that it was going to be a slow and tortuous process. He had, in *State and Revolution*, already recognised that the necessary economic structures and work ethics would not be available or could be immediately developed.

He had written: 'If we are not to fall into Utopianism, we cannot imagine that, having overthrown capitalism, people will at once learn to work for society without any standards of right, indeed, the abolition of capitalism does not immediately lay the economic foundations for such a change.' He knew, as we have already noticed, that the hardest task in Russia was not the overthrow of old, exploitative feudal-capitalist social order and its dominant classes, it lay ahead in the post-revolutionary task of constructing the new exploitation-free social order. At the very beginning he made it clear: 'I have had occasion more than once to say that compared with the advanced countries, it was easier for the Russians to start this Great October Proletarian Revolution but that it will be more difficult for them to continue it and carry it to complete socialist society.' He had also had the occasion to note what he described as 'the specific feature of the situation in Russia at the present time': 'an exceptional situation' where the Russian proletariat was 'in *advance* of' any other in Europe 'as regards strength of the workers' political power', but was '*behind* the most backward West European country as regards our level of culture and the degree of material and productive preparedness for the introduction of socialism'. And now such 'introduction' was the task history had imposed on the Russian proletariat and its Bolshevik leadership. But there were no illusions all the same. Even as Lenin spoke of their 'historic victory', he insisted: 'But for us, members of the Communist Party, this meant only opening the door. We are now confronted with the task of laying the foundations of socialist economy'. 'The foundations' only and not 'the completion' of socialism – a classical Marxist position which however did not rule out a historically conditioned socialist transition in Russia.

V

Marx, with Engels, was aware of the difficulties that any post-revolutionary regime would face after the old order has been overthrown, even if, given their historical materialist outlook, they were not in a position to provide any guidance beyond some general suggestions for the ensuing task of constructing a socialist society. And here, beyond the more obvious economic and political problems, perhaps their most significant suggestion concerned the human material involved in the process of socialist transition. Marx had once spoken of 'the tradition of all the dead generations (that) weighs like a nightmare on the brain of the living'. This was never more true than of Lenin's Russia. And even of the proletariat of the countries of advanced capitalist development they had written: 'Only through years of struggle can the class which overthrows cleanse itself of the mire of the old society and become fit to create a new society'. Aware of this and the additional 'weight' of war and civil war-ravaged Russian backwardness and the state of its further decimated and dispersed proletariat, Lenin wrote in early 1919:

> The workers were never separated by a Great Wall of China from the old society. And they have preserved a good deal of the traditional mentality of the capitalist society. The workers are building a new society without themselves having become new people, or cleansed of the filth of the old world; they are still standing up to their knees in that filth. We can only dream of cleaning the filth away. It would be utterly utopian to think this could be done all at once. It would be so utopian that in practice it would only postpone socialism to kingdom come.
>
> No, that is not the way we intend to build socialism. We are building while still standing on the soil of capitalist society, combating all those weaknesses and shortcomings which also affect the working people and which tend to drag the proletariat down. There are many old separatist habits and customs of the small holder in this struggle, and we still feel the effects of the old maxim: 'Every man for himself, and the devil take the hindmost.'

Elsewhere he noticed 'the forces and traditions of the old society' that gripped the Russian peasantry and wrote: 'The force of habit of millions and tens of millions is a most terrible force.' He warned that these 'millions and millions of small owners ... by their ordinary, everyday, imperceptible, elusive, demoralising activity, achieve the *very* results which the bourgeoisie need and which tend to *restore* the bourgeoisie.'

Obviously initiating a socialist transition in Russia was going to be a difficult task, carrying more than the normal load of Rosa Luxemburg's paradox, the contradictions that arise from building the new with the materials of the old, for the old in this case happened to be war and civil war-ravaged Mother Russia.

VI

The difficulties of the situation, both objective and subjective, were compounded by the fact that there was no guidance here in classical Marxism, nor any significant historical experience to go by except the time and territorywise all too limited experience of the Paris Commune, and that too only at the level of general principles. Marx had indeed pointed out that a transition to socialism even under the best of circumstances is not an easy task. The new society comes, Marx had written, 'in every respect, economically, morally and intellectually, still stamped with the birth marks of the old society from whose womb it emerges'. It carries and suffers from 'inevitable defects'. There were other relevant statements and propositions in Marx and Engels which Lenin knew and accepted as axiomatic and which provided him with an overall orientation in his enterprise. But important as general principles, they did not on their own add up to much by way of specific policies, alternative social models or worked out programmes. In fact the question of 'socialist transition' was possibly the most significant of the 'silences' or 'empty spaces' in Marxism that we mentioned earlier. Of course, given his historical materialist outlook, it was not Marx's problem. But even after him it remained 'a familiar Marxian absence': the destination of a new society, but uncharted by any detailed map. It was an area of 'theoretico-political darkness', common to all currents within the socialist movement, so that while abstract or ad hoc responses or proposals abounded to be followed later by all sorts of post-facto critiques, even crucial issues like those of proletarian or socialist democracy, of democratic, that is, genuinely socialist planning, or of enterprise democracy, that is, socialist transformation in relations of production at workplace, were not theorised, they remained politically nebulous, underdeveloped and institutionally underdetermined. Far more significant is the fact that these issues never came to be critically theorised, in truly Marxist terms, even in the Soviet Union – only apologetics abounded – with consequences that were to prove ultimately disastrous for its socialist enterprise.

Lenin, who knew that socialism anywhere 'requires a long, difficult, and stubborn class struggle', was aware of this 'empty space' in Marxism but, in tune with the classical tradition, seemed content in his earlier theoretical work to leave it to men and women of the future, who actually undertake construction of socialism, to fill it up. In *State and Revolution*, written on the eve of the October uprising, which contains possibly the most detailed description of the socialist future Lenin ever allowed himself before the socialist revolution got underway, he wrote: 'By what stages, by means of what practical measures humanity will proceed to this supreme aim we do not and cannot know'. Therefore, Lenin's awareness of the problem notwithstanding, the need for necessary Marxist theory in this area went unrecognised. There was also the fact that Lenin shared with Marxists and socialists in general a tendency to underestimate the problems that must arise in the organisation and administration of society as it transits from capitalism to socialism, and saw it, initially at least, as a relatively easy task. Thus, in the same *State and Revolution*, we find Lenin expressing a view that was to change soon and fast once the Bolsheviks came to power. He had written:

> We, the workers, shall organise large-scale production on the basis of what capitalism has already created, relying on our own experience as workers, establishing strict, iron discipline backed up by the state power of the armed workers. We shall reduce the role of state officials to that of simply carrying out our instructions as responsible, revocable, modestly paid 'foremen and accountants' (of course with the aid of technicians of all sorts, types and degrees)... Such a beginning, on the basis of large scale production, will of itself lead to the gradual 'withering away' of all bureaucracy, to the creation of an order... under which the function of control and accounting, becoming more and more simple, will be performed by each in turn, will then become a habit and will finally die out as the *special* functions of a special section of the population.

However valid as a long-term perspective or as an expression of democratic commitment, this is no answer at all to the immediate practical-political needs of a revolutionary party in power.

VII

Marx had posited the possibility of a socialist revolution in a backward country, but he had never visualised its being called upon to build socialism by itself. This in any case was not a problem for him to theorise. In a major theoretical advance Lenin had argued that 'uneven economic and political development is an absolute law of capitalism' and therefore socialist revolution 'is possible first in a few or even in one single capitalist country', while 'others will for sometime remain bourgeois or pre-bourgeois'. But this theme was never seriously pursued by him, certainly not the implication that this may result in the possibility, indeed the necessity of attempting a transition to socialism in one country. His consequent primary concern remained elaborating a strategy for 'breaking the weakest link of the chain', in the hope of initiating a chain-reaction of revolutions elsewhere in the advanced countries of Europe. Lenin did write that 'the victorious proletariat of that country having expropriated the capitalists and having organised socialist production would stand up against the rest of the capitalist world, attracting to its cause the oppressed classes of other countries, raising revolts in these countries against the capitalists and in the event of necessity coming out even with armed force against the exploiting classes and their states'. But this was only so much rhetoric about a revolution in the future, and even so 'that country' was never meant to be backward Russia. Insofar as Lenin expected a revolution in Russia, and he was not too optimistic about it in the immediate future till the February revolution occurred, it was as part of a European revolution. Of course he prepared for it and with an exemplary initiative and understanding seized the opportunity when it arrived to make a successful socialist revolution. But he was not at all theoretically prepared to rule and build socialism in Russia 'all by itself'. Lenin had well-theorised the making of a socialist revolution, the overthrow of capitalism, but had no complementary theory, as it were, of the construction of socialism, least of all its construction in a backward country like Russia. Involved in this theoretical 'absence' was a most fundamental question of our times: what does a poor, backward country, seeking a better life for its people – which, I believe, ultimately only a transition to socialism makes possible – do in a situation of global domination of capitalism? This question still remains largely untheorised in Marxism.

Here it will not be out of place to notice a related issue of extraordinary theoretical importance which Lenin raised in his truly remarkable last piece of writing ('Better Fewer, But Better'), but did not live to pursue. Looking forward to a world revolution in the future, Lenin pointed out that 'precisely as a result of the first world war, the East has been definitely drawn into the revolutionary movement... into the general maelstrom of the world revolutionary movement' and added, rather optimistically: 'In the last analysis, the outcome of the struggle will be determined by the fact that Russia, India, China etc. account for the overwhelming majority of the population of the globe...so that in this respect there cannot be the slightest doubt what the final outcome of the world struggle will be.'

At several points in this argument and its view of the future, Lenin's meaning is not altogether clear. But there is no doubt that, like Marx before him who in his later years had turned Eastward in his search for anti-capitalist revolution, Lenin too was turning away from the traditional Marxist concern with revolution and socialist future as an affair of the advanced capitalist countries, tying up the fate of the rest of the world with the success or failure of their proletarians. This obviously demanded a systematic, scientific study and analysis of a whole series of new problems for Marxist theory which had remained ignored or only incidentally treated earlier because of the traditional Marxist focus on the development of advanced capitalism, – above all the problems of the possible future course of development of countries which belonged to capitalist system as colonies or dependencies of advanced capitalist countries. If Lenin had lived, such theoretical work, in many ways a further development of his pioneering study of imperialism, might have been undertaken right then and the international communist movement better provided with the crucially important understanding of the functioning of capitalism as a global system of exploiting and exploited nations so necessary for the pursuit of revolutionary politics in countries situated in the periphery and semi-periphery of the global capitalist system. But Lenin died soon after and despite Mao's achievement in China and valuable, theoretical work elsewhere, this still remains a major task for socialists, a vital requirement for successful revolutionary practice in countries of the third world.

I would like to add that in the aforementioned article Lenin views the national liberation movements, arising from within the global imperialism, as a new revolutionary subject, an ally of the working class as it were, that helps in the progress of world socialist revolution, as indeed these movements proved to be when led by Marxism. Even as we need to take a critical look at these movements, especially their outcomes since then, Lenin's argument here has implications for other 'revolutionary subjects' – those rising up against other forms of oppression in contemporary capitalist societies, related to gender, race, caste, national, religious or ethnic minorities etc. – whose struggles need to be recognised as part of our struggle against capitalism, needing to be articulated with class struggle in any revolutionary socialist movement.

VIII

If the events that culminated in the October Revolution had moved with unexpected speed, the situation resulting from its survival was entirely unanticipated and without a theory to cope with it, creating a truly historical predicament for the Bolsheviks. Lenin could only respond pragmatically to the whole series of new issues and unforeseen problems that this predicament posed. He struggled, on the whole with remarkable success, grasping the essential feature of each particular moment in the rapidly changing situations and identifying the main link in a long chain of political tasks, so as to not only continue to survive but, using whatever resources were available, move forward in a highly unequal battle and against the heaviest of odds. It is significant that throughout this period, Lenin was fond of repeating Napoleon's famous dictum, 'we shall fight and then we shall see', a credo which well reflected the inadequacy of theory and difficulties of practice arising from it. So much of

Lenin's writing in the period immediately preceding the October Revolution is fragmentary, aphoristic and tentative responses to rapidly changing conditions and events. This is even more true for the period after 1917 when, with the isolation of the October Revolution, he came to confront a literally unanticipated situation in terms of classical Marxism. Therefore the theoretical status of these writings should be carefully considered before arguing or acting on their basis. Though one must hasten to add that whatever Lenin said or did during these periods yet bears the mark of a great Marxist and a revolutionary genius. And the most distinguishing feature of what Lenin said or did in the post-October period was the consistency of both the awareness of the predicament as well as the revolutionary boldness in confronting the problems posed by the predicament, which *in effect* meant struggling for, and theorising, a socialist transition in backward Russia. Along with his, ever relevant, other theoretical and political achievements, best expressed in the making of the successful October Revolution, it is a singular contribution of Lenin to Marxism to theorise, necessarily inadequately, during the few years of active political life still left to him, that a socialist transition might in fact be possible in a backward country, that is, one without an adequate basis in prior capitalist development. The Soviet collapse notwithstanding, this is a contribution whose particular importance for countries of the third world can never be overemphasised. That Lenin viewed this transition or the struggle for it as part of his perspective on 'the world revolutionary movement' only enhances the significance of his contribution.

IX

The inadequacy of theory was indeed a problem. But guidance was not entirely lacking in classical Marxism. There was the central principle, the life impulse as it were of a socialist transition anywhere: the self-emancipation of the working people. Marx had repeatedly emphasised that 'the emancipation of the working classes is the task of the working classes themselves'. After him, the principle found possibly its most eloquent expression in Rosa Luxemburg. Like Lenin, she recognised: 'Far from being a sum of ready-made prescriptions which have only to be applied, the practical realization of socialism as an economic, social and juridical system is something which lies completely hidden in the mists of the future. What we possess in our programme is nothing but a few main signposts which indicate the general direction.' Underlining the basic principle behind these 'signposts' for rebuilding the society, she wrote: 'This rebuilding and this transformation cannot be decreed by some authority, commission or parliament; they can only be undertaken and carried out by the mass itself.' And: 'Socialism will not be and cannot be inaugurated by decrees; it cannot be established by any government, however admirably socialistic. Socialism must be created by the masses, must be made by every proletarian.' A socialist society, Rosa Luxemburg argued, must rest on genuine 'moral foundations'– the 'highest idealism in the interests of the whole', 'a true public spirit' – as against the 'dullness, egoism and corruption' that underpin capitalism. 'All these socialist civic virtues, together with the knowledge and ability to manage socialist operations, can be acquired by the working class only through their own activity, their own experience.'

Lenin could not have agreed more. For him all this was axiomatic in any construction of socialism. 'Concrete analysis of concrete conditions' was, for Lenin, always the essence of Marxism. Beyond that, in the midst of all the hostile circumstances and handicaps, the guidance, he repeatedly insisted, could only come from the people, from their 'collective experience' as Lenin put it. At the very outset, immediately after the October Revolution, in his address to the All Russian Central Executive Committee on 17 November 1917, he said: 'Socialism cannot be decreed from above. Its spirit rejects the mechanical, bureaucratic approach; living creative socialism is the product of the masses themselves.' Again, interpreting 'the dictatorship of the proletariat' as a radical working people's democracy – 'democratic for the proletariat and the propertyless in general and dictatorial against the bourgeoisie' only – he pointed out:

'Creative activity at the grass roots is the basic factor of new public life.' Yet again, at the Second Congress of the Soviets: 'Experience is the best teacher and it will show who is right... We must be guided by experience; we must allow complete freedom to the creative faculties of the masses.'

Such was the governing orientation of Lenin and the Bolsheviks as they entered the uncharted territory that was a socialist transition in Russia.

X

Under the circumstances then obtaining within the country and without it, Lenin visualised the socialist transition in Russia as a rather modest enterprise, a realistic advance over a most difficult terrain. He opted for a slow, cautious advance to socialist transformation with the willing cooperation of the peasantry and a general rise in the cultural level of the working class and the Russian people as a whole. As *the* key tactics in this effort, 'to save ourselves' as he put it, he advised: 'We must strive to build up a state in which the workers retain the leadership of the peasants, in which they retain the confidence of the peasants, and by exercising the greatest economy remove every trace of extravagance from our social relations'. As Bukharin, a leading Bolshevik himself, was to put it later: 'We shall not be able to fulfil our task by single decrees, by single compulsory measures... A prolonged organic process...a process of real growing into socialism will be required....For many decades we will be slowly growing into socialism.'

Lenin of course did not guarantee success in this conjoint, worker-peasant undertaking to hold on and transform. He could only repeat as he often did, Napoleon's famous dictum, 'We shall fight and then we shall see'. He could even write:

> Either the international revolution comes to our assistance, and in that case our victory will be fully assured, or we shall do our modest revolutionary work in the conviction that even in the event of defeat we shall have served the cause of the revolution and that our experience will benefit other revolutions.

To his partymen he said:

> Those Communists are doomed who imagine that it is possible to finish such an epoch-making undertaking as completing the foundations of socialist economy (particularly in a small-peasant country) without making mistakes, without retreats, without numerous alterations to what is unfinished or wrongly done. Communists who have no illusions, who do not give way to despondency, and who preserve their strength and flexibility 'to begin from the beginning' over and over again in approaching an extremely difficult task, are not doomed (and in all probability will not perish).

And he seemed to sum it all up on the fourth anniversary of the October Revolution. He wrote:

> We have brought the bourgeois-democratic revolution to completion as nobody has done before. We are advancing towards the socialist revolution, consciously, deliberately and undeviatingly, knowing that no Chinese wall separates it from the bourgeois-democratic revolution, and knowing that *struggle alone will determine* (in the long run) how far we shall advance, what portion of this immeasurably great task we shall accomplish...

Lenin had thus no illusions about successful building up of socialism in Russia; he had only the option, and the hope and optimism of a revolutionary's willingness to struggle for it, to at least prepare the path towards socialism. Despite his confidence and a certain overestimation of possibilities, this was Lenin's dominant perspective once the European revolution had finally receded, 'Struggle and struggle alone decides... how far we shall advance' was his constant refrain in those early years.

In retrospect, we now know that even though initially they advanced a great deal against the heaviest of odds, and indeed accomplished 'a tremendous amount' as Lenin said, the struggle, especially after the departure of Lenin, was simply not adequate enough to overcome the logic of Russia's backwardness and the consequences of the historic failure of the proletariat in the West.

XI

The struggle for socialism as it came to be waged in the Soviet Union was not adequate enough but its relevance as our legacy in the continuing struggle for socialism makes it well worth our while to take another brief but more focussed look at the politics and economics of the socialist project in Russia as Lenin had visualised it, during the few years that he survived the October Revolution.

Lenin saw the struggle for socialism in Russia as a democratic process. The centrality of politics as a principle in the construction and working of socialism, as against 'market' which structures and governs the functioning of capitalism, found its expression in the centrality of revolutionary *socialist* democracy in effecting a socialist transition. For Lenin 'socialism is impossible without democracy'; it 'cannot consolidate its victory and bring humanity to the withering away of the state without implementing full democracy'.

The absence of theory or practical guidance for the construction of socialism was indeed an important 'empty space' in classical Marxism. But there are scattered statements and propositions in Marx and Engels which Lenin took as axiomatic principles for his socialist project. Most importance of these served to underline freedom and democracy as unalienable parts of a socialist transition. Marx had bitterly attacked press censorship, curtailment of people's rights and the arbitrary exercise of state power. His criticism of Jacobinism and Bonapartism was animated not only by hostility to politics that sought to usurp social forces but also deep commitment to a popular democratic basis for any revolutionary politics. Proletariat has to 'win the battle of democracy' as part of the socialist revolution and sustain it as part of the socialist enterprise. Marx and Engels had always argued for the accountability of political representatives and, further, specifically warned against 'everything promoting the superstitious worship for authority' within the Party, against people 'treating party officials–who are their servants–as impeccable bureaucrats, rather than criticising them'. Lenin knew his Marx and Engels well and these were his principles too.

Both Marx and Engels had, no doubt, recognised the need for a revolutionary state 'to break down the resistance of the bourgeoisie', 'to hold down one's adversaries by force' and so on. And of the post-revolutionary period Marx had written: 'Between capitalist and communist society lies the period of the revolutionary transformation of the one into the other. There corresponds to this also a political transition period in which the state can be nothing but the revolutionary dictatorship of the proletariat'. This, however, was a statement, as we have already explained, about the social content of public power, the essential class character of the state in a transitional socialist society. It had absolutely no implications of any dictatorial form of government or politics. The Paris Commune, with its unparalleled practice of democracy was a 'dictatorship of the proletariat' as Marx and Engels saw it. The had visualised this 'dictatorship' as a most advanced form of democracy for the people. Lenin fully endorsed this Marxist position. He wrote:

> The forms of bourgeois states are extremely varied, but their essence is the same: all these states, whatever their form, in the final analysis are inevitably the dictatorship of the bourgeoisie. The transition from capitalism to communism certainly cannot but yield a tremendous abundance and variety of political forms, but the essence will inevitably be the same: the dictatorship of the proletariat.... Simultaneously with an immense expansion of democracy, which for the first time becomes democracy for the poor, democracy for the people and not democracy for the money bags, the dictatorship of the proletariat imposes a series of restrictions on the freedom of the oppressors, the exploiters, the capitalists. We must suppress them in order to free humanity from wage slavery, their resistance must be crushed by force; ... Democracy for the vast majority of the people, and suppression by force, i.e., exclusion from democracy, of the exploiters and oppressors of the people – this is the change democracy undergoes during the transition from capitalism to communism.

If Lenin saw the new Soviet state as 'dictatorial against the bourgeoisie', as 'creating conditions in which it will be impossible for the bourgeoisie to exist, or for a new bourgeoisie to arise', it was to be 'democratic for the proletariat and the propertyless in general'. Again: 'socialism can be implemented only through the dictatorship of the proletariat, which combines violence against the bourgeoisie, i.e., the minority of the population, with full development of democracy, i.e., the genuinely equal and genuinely universal participation of the *entire* mass of the population in all state affairs and in all the complex problems of abolishing capitalism'. Hence also the metaphorical statement that 'any cook should be able to run the country'.

It was in fact the established Marxist tradition that the historical fate of socialism was inextricably linked to the advance of democracy, social, economic and political. Wrote Lenin: 'Whoever wants to reach socialism by any other path than that of political democracy will inevitably arrive at conclusions that are absurd and reactionary both in the economic and political sense'. Lenin certainly saw the transition to socialism as essentially a democratic process. The 'empty space' was yet not a shortcoming only, it was the space of democracy, a resource whence guidance in the construction of socialism could come, through whose diversity, debate and experiment, criticism and correction alone socialism could be created.

Of course, Lenin saw capitalist democracy as 'curtailed, wretched, false... for the rich, for the minority', etc. Even when 'bourgeois democracy is invaluable for educating the proletariat and training it for struggle', and the workers are urged by him to make full use of bourgeois democratic rights, but 'in the spirit of the most consistent and resolutely revolutionary democracy', he regards it as 'always narrow, hypocritical, spurious, and false; it always remains democracy for the rich and a swindle for the poor'. As against it when 'the proletariat takes power, becomes the ruling class', it 'gives real freedom and democracy to the working people ... gives them not just the "right to" but the real use of what has been taken from the bourgeoisie'. He visualised the 'dictatorship of the proletariat' as 'an immense expansion of democracy, which for the first time becomes democracy for the poor, democracy for the people.'

We may in this connection note a most important aspect of Lenin's *State and Revolution* written during the very heat of the revolutionary struggle, on the eve of the preparation of the October seizure of power, and published *after* the revolution in 1918. Like all Lenin's writings it was practically motivated, by the *political* needs and exigencies of the times as he saw them. Far from being a 'utopian' or 'anarchist' text it is often interpreted to be, it was really a needed blueprint, however rough in its guidelines, for constructing the proletarian state of the future. In fact the objective of a large part of Lenin's writings in 1917, as expressed in *State and Revolution* and most of his major articles of the period, was to expose the bourgeois mythology around the question of political power and wean his social democratic followers away from their superstitious regard for the state. To this end he had to offer alternatives for the transcendence of conventional politics and the initiation of the mass of the people into the practice of their own self-government. And these alternatives did not even remotely involve rule by one party, vanguard or any other. We know how well and how successfully Lenin had argued (in *What Is To Be Done?* and elsewhere) for the role of the party in the making of revolution. It is significant that his *State and Revolution*, published after the revolution, has hardly a couple of references to party; it is virtually silent about party in relation to making of the new state. This is, however, no aberration or deceitfulness on Lenin's part as certain critics would have it, who, defying all evidence to the contrary, persist in portraying Lenin as elitist in his conception of politics, where acting in the name of proletariat or people, the party supposedly pre-empts all politics for itself and necessarily makes for one party rule under socialism. Lenin's silence regarding the role of the party in the proletarian state is in fact a most obvious refutation of such misrepresentations. This silence is not difficult to understand if it is recognised that in Lenin there is no substitutionist politics ever, which would replace self-acting proletariat or people with party, or self-governing people with one party rule.

XII

In his search for alternatives Lenin on the one hand went back to classical Marxism and on the other to the contemporary experience of the revolutions of 1905 and 1917, above all their spontaneous creation, the Soviets. Classical Marxism had envisaged the transition from capitalism to communism taking place within the frame work of a state embodying the most radical kind of democracy and had pointed to the Paris Commune as the exemplar, the requisite 'political form' indeed. In *The Civil War in France* Marx praised the Paris Commune of 1871 for dismantling the bureaucratic apparatus of the capitalist state and replacing it with organs of popular self-government. It was no matter of chance that only a few weeks before the October Revolution which was to make the issue of a proletarian state the most crucial for the hoped for socialist transformation, Lenin made a special effort to restore this, by then long-ignored and almost forgotten part of Marxist teaching about state, socialism and bureaucracy contained in Marx's account of the Paris Commune. On the eve of revolution itself, in his *State and Revolution*, Lenin visualised a state in the image of the Paris Commune, 'a state without a standing army, without a police opposed to the people, without an officialdom placed above the people', and proposed to 'organise and arm all the poor, exploited sections of the population in order that they themselves should take the organs of state power directly into their own hands, in order that they themselves should constitute these organs of state power'. It was to be a state that would open up unheard of democratic vistas: 'Under socialism much of "primitive" democracy will inevitably he revived, since, for the first time in the history of civilised society, the mass of the population will rise to taking an independent part, not only in voting and elections, but also in the everyday administration of the state. Under socialism all will govern in turn and will soon become accustomed to no one governing'. Lenin spoke of running the country through 'public meeting democracy' and expressed his idea of the state in that famous aphorism: under socialism or in a proletarian dictatorship, the administration should become so simplified that every cook should be able to manage state affairs. Important here is not so much the detailed or aphoristic expression as the revolutionary commitment of Lenin, his immediately democratic vision which, as 'actually existing socialism' later came to be, was either discreetly ignored in practice or in severely bowdlerised form held out as the very long-term objective of full communism.

Apart from the example of Paris Commune, drawing on the more advanced experience of the Russian revolutions of 1905 and 1917, Lenin saw the alternative, socialist form of exercise of political power taking shape in the original Soviets, the councils of workplace delegates spontaneously thrown up by workers, as well as by peasants and soldiers, in the course of their struggle. A vital workers' and peasants' democracy which indeed triumphed, however temporarily, in October 1917, emerged and organised itself in the Soviets which was indeed a superior form of democracy which united political and economic power, unlike parliament that leaves the most important power of the bourgeoisie, its economic power, essentially untouched, which brought under democratic control the administrative and legislative functions of government, again unlike parliament which leaves the civil service, army and police in unelected hands, and which, most of all, served as organs of power, directly responsible to the will of workers and peasants, and capable of organising their struggles and defending their interests. Lenin's view of people's self-activity exercised through a multiplicity of independent communes or Soviets, learning through their own mistakes and experience how best to resume control over all their affairs – this view of the socialist project in Russia found in the Soviets already existing and available popular institutions. Through them the people in arms could appropriate to themselves initiatives and processes which the state had progressively taken away from them. In the long run, they could be the means to realise the aim of dissolving economic, administrative and political power in the mass of people themselves, which was the express object of the socialist revolution, its occasion, its imperative, its ultimate justification. Marx had hailed the Commune as the model of socialism, 'the political form at last discovered under which to work out the economic emancipation of Labour'. For Lenin, following in his footsteps, Soviets was the form for the purpose, the authentic organs of socialist construction.

XIII

It is necessary to remember and recognise that Lenin's belief in the Commune form of state did not disappear with the success of the October Revolution. On the contrary it fully informed his activities immediately after the Bolshevik seizure of power. The Soviet state began its existence as a proletarian democracy. The whole power in the initial period vested in the 'Councils of Workers', Soldiers' and Peasants' Deputies', or the Soviets. Members of the Soviets were freely elected by popular vote and controlled by the masses. In the Soviets, decisions were taken by majority vote. The minority had the right of discussion and criticism, on condition that in practice it carried out the resolutions of the majority. In this way the Soviets reflected the mood and the will of the working people, assuring them the freedom to influence and determine the most important affairs of the state – a witness to the democratic commitment of Lenin and the Bolsheviks.

A most significant expression of the Bolsheviks' commitment to democracy was the way they broke up 'the prison house of peoples' that was the Czarist state, and stood up as a whole for the right of self-determination of the formerly oppressed nationalities – a most advanced democratic position, beyond anything the liberal-democratic theory had to offer, ever. Further evidence is there in the way they, moved by the early socialist ideals, treated the more than 100 nationalities, minorities or ethnic groups of all kinds that came to constitute the Soviet peoples and who spoke more than 700 languages and dialects – making them into nations they were not before 1917, raising them all, even those with the primitive and pastoral backwardness, to the threshold of contemporary levels of advancement in terms of economic development and social security, literacy and education, health, art and culture, and so on. As E.H. Carr has pointed out, it was for the first time that they came to enjoy 'the full development of their language and of their national culture'. Despite distortions by 'the Great-Russian chauvinism' that Lenin always condemned and resisted most resolutely, and reversals and deformations of the later Stalin era due to excessive centralisation of power and policies of lopsided and unequal development – 'a single socialist nation', 'Russification', etc. – this was a signal achievement; (though, one must add, in one of those ironics of history, given the later deformations, this, in its own way, contributed to the final break-up of the Soviet Union). Lenin had insisted: 'Every nation must obtain the right of self-determination', and for him the real essence of the policy lay in 'consistent democracy', that is, 'political and civil liberties and complete equality'. And he fought for this policy against the reservations of Bukharin, Stalin and others. As elsewhere, democracy was central to his solution of the specific problems of national oppression too. He wrote: 'by transforming capitalism into socialism the proletariat creates the possibility of abolishing national oppression; the possibility becomes *reality* "only" – "only" ! – with the establishment of full democracy in all spheres including the delineation of state practices in accordance with the sympathies of the population'.

Democracy was in fact a pervasive feature of Soviet life and activity in the immediate aftermath of the October Revolution. Not only did the Bolsheviks share power with other political and social tendencies including Mensheviks and a section of the left socialist revolutionaries, as in the Soviets, internal democracy was a characteristic feature of the functioning of the trade unions and the Bolshevik Party itself. Even in 1920-21, the Menshevik opposition led by Martov, apart from being active in the Soviets, could present its own political platform at trade union congresses. And within the Bolshevik Party a plurality of views continued to be debated. Even during the most difficult moments of the civil war, important economic and political problems were the subject of wide discussion in which even Lenin was at times in a minority. Nobody even dreamt of the sanctity of the leadership. Of course, a leader of Lenin's status and proven ability had enormous authority but it was not the will of the 'infallible leader' that prevailed, but the democratically expressed wish of the majority. Such Leninist practice of proletarian democracy in so many spheres and institutions in no way hampered the Soviet state in surviving the most difficult period of the civil war and counter-revolution, armed or economic blockade, and widespread famine in the country. On the contrary, it constituted the newly-born Soviet state's main strength. Indeed, the revolution as a whole manifested itself as a democratic upsurge which saw an extraordinary afflorescence of the creative genius of the Russian people in every sphere, a many-splendoured revolutionary ferment in arts and literature, in education and gender relations, in social sciences and elsewhere which represented and further generated powerful social forces and trends to become part of Lenin's project of socialist transition with the active support and participation of the working people.

This is how Neil Harding has summed up the powerful democratic and emancipatory thrust of Lenin's socialist project:

> The objective of the socialist revolution was, as Lenin once pithily put it, 'an end of bossing' and this, in a nutshell, was the message of *State and Revolution*. Its challenge was the promethean one, born of the impeccable line of Marx's romantic view of man as actor, the forger of his own world. It ran directly counter to that other Saint Simonian development of social democratic Marxism which saw the individual as the beneficiary of an efficient state-directed philanthropy. To the war-weary, to the hungry, to the indentured workforce and the oppressed peasantry Lenin projected in 1917 a vision, a challenge... – power is yours, take it and use it; the land is yours, take and use it; the factories are yours, take them and use them – get off your knees and be men, rule yourselves. This was the message... encapsulated in his slogan 'All Power to the Soviets'. It was an extraordinary platform which called not for the capture of political power by a political party but for the dissolution of the state in an infinitely varied system of soviets and communes.

Such was Lenin's project. It was indeed launched in the period immediately following the October Revolution. But it lasted barely six months. What actually happened over the next few years was something quite different. The immediate exigencies of the infant Soviet state struggling for survival in its isolation took precedence over everything else. Battered by the white armies of foreign intervention, civil war and counter-revolution, ruined industrially and facing economic chaos, threatened with hunger and starvation by famine at home and imperialist blockade from abroad, and all the time confronting the inexorable logic of Russian backwardness, the new Soviet state desperately struggled to stay alive. The social and political pressure, internal and external, was enormous and almost intolerable. And the Bolsheviks' own resources to cope with it were fast getting depleted, seriously blunting the edge of any effective *socialist* political intervention in the situation. Lenin's project, with all its early promise, though never abandoned in theory, simply floundered.

Part of the tragedy of Lenin was that, as within Russia and without not his hopeful predictions but worst fears came to materialise, as civil war, famine and economic collapse consumed the country and the Bolshevik dream, no matter how valiantly he struggled, Lenin was himself increasingly compelled to retreat, and to compromise. And he did not live long enough to recover and regain the initiative. The assassin's bullets, first incapacitated and finally claimed him in January 1924. Nevertheless, his project and his struggle retain their importance, as Lenin hoped, for 'other revolutions' of the future.

XIV

I would like to touch upon a couple more issues concerning Lenin's politics before turning to his response to the economic problems of a socialist transition in Russia as he confronted them in the early post-October years. Obviously, most important for Lenin's project was the key instrument for carrying it out, the new state, and yet this was to soon become the site of his most serious problems. He saw the situation clearly enough: 'The new state organization is being born in travail, because it is far more difficult, a million times more difficult, to overcome our disruptive petty-bourgeois laxity than to suppress the tyrannical landowners and the tyrannical capitalists... When proletarian organization solves this problem, socialism will triumph completely'. This problem never came to be solved in the Soviet Union.

Lenin also recognised the toll taken by the continuing civil war; not only was the Bolshevik Party and the proletariat which made the revolution being decimated, but with the accompanying industrial collapse, the initially small working class, now still smaller and dispersed, was getting 'declassed' in every sense of the word. And within this overall situation was the problem Lenin specifically noted: 'The key feature is that we have not got the right men in the right places; that responsible Communists who acquitted themselves magnificently during the revolution, have been given commercial and industrial functions about which they know nothing; and they prevent us from seeing the truth, for rogues and rascals hide themselves magnificently behind their backs'.

The 'rogues and rascals' had made their entry into the new state almost inevitably. Given the initially poor and now further depleted Bolshevik resources, it was indeed inevitable that the major instrument available to them was 'the old machinery of the state' which the Bolsheviks had to perforce take over – 'our misfortune' is how Lenin described it. Bureaucracy, a stratum of 'privileged persons standing above and apart from the masses', as Lenin saw it, was rapidly emerging powerful in the state. When fellow Bolsheviks, including Trotsky, identified the new state with the working class and invoked the proletarian state, Lenin was quick to point out that it is still 'an abstraction'. Even in December 1922, as he neared the end of his active political life, he wrote of 'our administrative machinery, which is pretty bad... inherited ... in effect from the old regime, for it was absolutely impossible to reorganise it in such a short time, especially in conditions of war, famine etc.' Far from being workers' state proper, it was so bureaucratically deformed that even as the workers were bound to defend it as their state, Lenin said they needed to defend themselves against it. By and large it was, in Lenin's words, 'that same Russian apparatus which... we took over from tsarism and slightly anointed with Soviet oil... it is a bourgeois and tsarist hotchpotch'. Paul Sweezy, drawing upon the work of Bettelheim, has thus described the situation:

> The weakness of the Russian revolutionary forces stemmed from many sources. Their social base of course was the urban industrial working class, and their leadership was provided by the Bolshevik Party. The problem was not that these forces, so based and so led, were lacking in revolutionary spirit or experience. If that had been the case, the October Revolution would never have taken place at all. The trouble was that the proletariat was small relative to the

population as a whole, and the Bolsheviks had few links and almost no influence in the countryside where the vast majority of Russians lived. Added to this basic situation were the terrible losses and disruption of the civil war years (1917-1921)....

In these conditions it is obvious that the Bolshevik leadership, even where it was strongest and most experienced, lacked the resources to replace the old Tsarist administration and bureaucracy with a new revolutionary apparatus: while in the countryside where it was weakest, it could do almost nothing to influence the course of events. The result was that it had to struggle along as best it could with the sprawling, inefficient, corrupt state machine inherited from the past. It is crucial to understand, moreover, that not only did this inherited state machine have the qualities just listed; it also had an indelible class character. In its essence it was a *bourgeois* state machine, built up over many generations, possessed of a dyed-in-the-wool bourgeois mentality, wedded to bourgeois ways of doing things, and profoundly hostile to the ideology and purposes of the revolutionary power it was forced to serve. As evidence of the latter and reflecting the class nature of the state machine, Bettelheim cites an inquiry conducted in the summer of 1922 which showed that only 9 per cent of the old officials and 13 per cent of the new ones were favorable to the Soviet regime.

It was absolutely unavoidable that this government apparatus, which the Bolsheviks were obliged to add to and expand as the state assumed new functions previously reserved to the private sector, should be and remain a fertile field for the preservation and resurgence of bourgeois relations not only within its own confines but also throughout Soviet society. And ironically, not a few of the measures taken by the leadership to control and counter these developments tended to have the opposite effect. In particular, honest revolutionaries assigned to positions in the state apparatus with a view to implementing officially adopted policies were more often than not assimilated by their new environment and transformed into ordinary bourgeois bureaucrats. This does not mean that they deliberately betrayed the trust put in them. On the contrary, it is probably safe to assume that in most cases they tried their best to do what was expected of them but that, even in so doing, they acquired the ways of thinking and acting of those around them. Working-class men and women might resist these pressures longer than others, but it is of course a fallacy to assume that class origin is a lasting determinant of ideology and behavior. In this connection, Lenin, who was extremely sensitive to this range of problems – far more so than most of his colleagues in the Bolshevik leadership – had recourse to a telling analogy. In Bettelheim's words, he drew an analogy between the situation of the Bolshevik Party, which occupied the leading positions in the state but could not really govern, and that of a conquering people which had apparently subjugated another people but, in the long run, though sill occupying the latter's territory, became subject to it, because 'the vanquished nation', being 'more civilised', 'imposes its culture upon the conqueror.'

Confronted with this situation Lenin again and again warned the leaders against faulty methods of work, born, apart from lack of requisite knowledge, of conservatism, egoism, indiscipline and other habits of mind inherited from the old society and wanted them to reeducate themselves through close contact with the masses so as to respond to their needs and draw them too into the work of the government. This last was indeed of decisive importance. As Lenin again and again insisted: Bureaucracy 'can be forced to retreat only if the proletariat and the peasants are organised far more extensively than has been the case upto now, and only if real measures are taken to enlist the workers in government'.

XV

Lenin knew, as Marx had emphasised before him, that a socialist transition demands 'the alteration of men on a mass scale.' In *The German Ideology* Marx and Engels had argued:

> Both for the production on a mass scale of this communist consciousness, and for the success of the cause itself, the alteration of men on a mass scale is necessary, an alteration which can only take place in the practical movement, a revolution; this revolution is necessary, therefore, not only because the ruling class cannot be overthrown in any other way, but also because the class overthrowing it can only in a revolution succeed in ridding itself of all the muck of ages and become fit to found society anew.

Marx had thus viewed revolution as a process of class struggle and not merely its definitive outcome, a revolutionary schooling of the working people, as it were, to acquire the capacity to rule and build a new society. Marx had also written in one of his famous theses on Feuerbach: 'the materialist doctrine that men are products of circumstances and upbringing, and that, therefore, changed men are products of other circumstances and changed upbringing, forgets that it is men that change circumstances and that the educator himself needs educating. The coincidence of the changing of circumstance and of human activity can be conceived and rationally understood only as *revolutionising practice*'. 'Revolutionising practice' is where Lenin sought the answer to the problem of 'altered' or 'changed' men and women who are fit enough 'to found society anew', as he insisted on raising the cultural level of the working people not only for, but even more through, their active participation in the affairs of the state. This indeed is the theme to which Lenin returned at the last Congress of his party which he attended (in 1922) and which he continued to pursue till the end – the theme of a 'cultural revolution' involving the masses of the Russian workers and peasants; 'This cultural revolution', he wrote, 'would now suffice to make our country a completely socialist country'; though, as a Marxist in the classical tradition, he also pointed out: 'but it presents immense difficulties of a purely cultural (for we are illiterate) and material character (for to be cultured we must achieve a certain development of the material means of production, must have a certain material base).' Such was the initial perspective of Lenin, and the Bolshevik leadership shared in it, though it betrayed a strong tendency to interpret it in a simple, instrumental manner. Trotsky thus argued that if 'culture was the main instrument of class oppression... it also, and only it, can become the instrument of socialist emancipation'. And sharing the Leninist perspective of the time, Stalin wrote: 'The surest remedy for bureaucracy is raising the cultural level of the workers and peasants. One can curse and denounce bureaucracy in the state apparatus, one can stigmatize and pillory bureaucracy in our practical work, but unless the masses of the workers reach a certain level of culture, which will create the possibility, the desire, the ability to control the state apparatus from below, by the masses of the workers themselves, bureaucracy will continue to exist inspite of everything.... This is the sense and significance of Lenin's slogan about the cultural revolution.' A little later, reiterating the unequivocally democratic intent of Lenin's 'cultural revolution', Stalin said: 'Lastly our economic organizations... How are we to put an end to bureaucracy in all these organizations? There is only one sole way of doing this, and that is to organise control from below, to organize criticism of the bureaucracy in our institutions, of their shortcomings and their mistakes by the vast masses of the working class.'

The Leninist perspective on the politics of socialist transition in Russia was distinguished for its total commitment to democracy and popular participation, and to correction of the emerging bureaucracy from below. We have already noticed the factors in the objective situation which were seriously undermining its practice. In the years that followed, more particularly the later Stalin era, this perspective was entirely lost. Stalin continued to use Leninist language. As an old Bolshevik and in his own way loyal to Lenin, maybe he meant it all too. But his practice entirely diverged from it as he opted for 'a revolution from above'. Democracy and popular participation literally vanished from state and party structures and insofar as he checked bureaucracy, he did so not 'from below' but, essentially, and ineffectively, from above, often by use of terror, as he went about building what he believed to be socialism. Once he departed from the scene, such terror-driven control from above was also gone, leaving the bureaucracy, long entrenched in the party and state structures, free to consolidate itself as a new ruling class, and this in a system which the party and people continued to believe was socialism.

XVI

'The grandeur and powerful attraction' of Lenin's perspective, as Hannah Arendt once described it, is not to be denied. This however is not to overlook that Lenin's own thought had its 'blind spots' and the Bolshevik practice, even in Lenin's lifetime, showed grave departures from democratic principles. Lenin himself made mistakes or compromises which undermined the radical socialist democracy which was his goal – even disastrous mistakes and compromises, especially in the civil war period of 1918–1921, that he himself recognised even as he also sought to make amends and rectify as best as he could. We will later take a closer look at what happened with Lenin and after him. But immediately it needs to be clearly understood that these departures or mistakes or compromises are not the product of any theory or inadequacy of commitment to democracy. If anything they were departures from theory and its principles compelled by the objective circumstances of the prolonged civil war that followed the October Revolution, by the need to defend the revolution against the attack of a ferocious counter-revolution backed by foreign invasion. Refusing or failing to recognise such historical compulsions, Kautsky onwards, even socialists in the west (with so many others in tow elsewhere) have regularly criticised and condemned the Bolsheviks as inherently anti-democratic, intolerant of opposition, politically authoritarian and repressive and so on. Such criticism and condemnation has become quite the fashion after the recent Soviet collapse, with all sorts of out of context references to Lenin and even to Karl Marx. What these 'scholarly' socialists and sundry other socialist or ex-socialist critics forget is that they never had to prepare, organise, make and defend a revolution as the Bolsheviks had to, that their own failure as socialists was, and continued to be, the single most important *objective* circumstance behind the isolated Bolsheviks' historical compulsions, that the reasons for this failure of theirs are precisely those which for the most part Lenin took care of in his preparation, organisation and carrying out of the first successful socialist revolution in Russia....

Incidentally it is interesting to see these socialist critics roping in Rosa Luxemburg too in their attack on the Bolshevik theory and practice, in the process reducing this revolutionary Marxist to a liberal democrat. The above observations are relevant in her case too – the 'freedom' or 'democracy' she wanted were hardly appropriate as policy (if that is how her criticism is interpreted) in the special conditions of the phase immediately after the Bolshevik seizure of power in October 1917 or during the civil war and struggle against the counter-revolution. And so far as the differing organisational theories of Lenin and Luxemburg are concerned, they faced their acid test in the post-world war I revolutionary upsurge. The party that Lenin built was able to lead the masses to power in Russia. In Germany, the absence of a similar cohesive, trained, educated and disciplined party and leadership proved fatal to the German revolution and to many of the courageous revolutionaries themselves, including Rosa Luxemburg herself. This is not to deny the long-term legitimacy of Rosa Luxemburg's criticism. There is no doubt that a vigorous return to original principles was imperative once the counter-revolution had been defeated and this never happened, the lost Soviet democracy was never recovered. I will come back to this question later for a somewhat detailed comment. But immediately the important fact to note is that Rosa Luxemburg was in total sympathy and solidarity with the Russian Revolution. She recognised the Bolshevik seizure of power as a necessary part of the world revolutionary process, something they accomplished under the most difficult of circumstances. She spoke of 'the party of Lenin' as 'the only one in Russia which grasped the true interest of the revolution in that period'. Even in her most critical pamphlet, she hailed the Bolsheviks for doing everything that could be done 'within the limits of historical possibilities', thus salvaging 'the honour of international socialism'. It is indeed interesting and instructive to see Rosa Luxemburg being selectively roped in for anti-Bolshevik tirade; for, leave aside the right-wing critics, these socialists or ex-socialists, in the West or elsewhere, would never dream of endorsing any other word written by her!

XVII

We have noted that democracy from below, 'revolutionising practice', was integral to the politics of Lenin's project for a socialist transition in Russia. It is equally important and instructive to note how he viewed the economics of this transition during the few years that he survived the October Revolution.

For the Leninist project, the problems in the realm of economy – now constituted, as Lenin noticed, by no less than five different economic systems or structures: the patriarchal economy, small commodity production, capitalist production, state capitalism and socialism, all devastated by war and civil war – were no less intractable than those presented by the dominance of bureaucracy in the state. In theoretical terms, the prevalence of bureaucracy meant the continuance of bourgeois social relations and attitudes in the state apparatus. In the economy the bourgeois relations were even more dominant, not only in industry, transportation, and finance, etc., that is, the branches of the economy transferred to state ownership, but, and particularly, in agriculture too, where the revolution, by abolishing feudalism, had established and strengthened a regime of small peasant ownership which in turn provided the basis for a characteristic capitalist accumulation process and the rise of a class of rich peasants or kulaks. Having overthrown the former dominant classes, the Bolshevik government was now faced with the much harder task of not only destroying the former social relations in the economy, the basis of the old exploitative system, but to prevent these relations from being reconstituted on the basis of those elements of the old which continued to persist in themselves or within some of the new social relations.

This is how Lenin saw this problem, and its answer, soon after the October Revolution:

> The abolition of classes means not only driving out the landlords and capitalists – that we accomplished with comparative ease – it also means abolishing the small commodity producers, and they cannot be driven out, or crushed; we must live in harmony with them; they can (and must) be remoulded and re-educated only by very prolonged, slow, cautious organisational work.... The dictatorship of the proletariat is a persistent struggle – bloody and bloodless, violent and peaceful, military and economic, educational and administrative – against the forces and traditions of the old society. The force of habit of millions and tens of millions is a most terrible force. Without an iron party tempered in the struggle, without a party enjoying the confidence of all that is honest in the given class, without a party capable of watching and influencing the mood of the masses, it is impossible to conduct such a struggle successfully. It is a thousand times easier to vanquish the centralized big bourgeoisie than to 'vanquish' the

> millions and millions of small owners; yet they, by their ordinary, everyday imperceptible, elusive, demoralizing activity, achieve the very result which the bourgeoisie needs and which tends to restore the bourgeoisie.

XVIII

Given the severe constraints that Russian backwardness imposed upon the Bolsheviks, their immediate economic programme, in the aftermath of the October Revolution, was very modest. They did not, deliberately, go in for wholesale nationalisation. They sought instead a control over commanding heights, workers' participation, mixed joint stock companies, etc., that is, a proletarian state controlled economy which necessarily continued to have a significant degree of capitalist presence within it. Such was Lenin's strategy, a slow, cautious and measured path to get a ruined economy going again, as well as to win a breathing space for the revolution to gather its forces before moving forward more effectively to create the 'material foundation' and supersede 'penury' in order to advance along the path to socialism. A great deal of necessary as well as unavoidable nationalisation did take place on the initiative of the state, but a great deal more was the result of the workers' initiative from below, often fuelled by the resistance of the capitalists, their politics-governed lockouts, etc. Lenin in fact recognised the enormous strain that such nationalisation was putting on the workers' state. Already in April 1918 he complained, 'if we go on expropriating capital at this rate, we shall infallibly be beaten'.

In agriculture too, having given land to the peasant, the Bolsheviks were in no hurry for socialisation or cooperativisation. This was simply impossible economically, and more so in view of the need to maintain the worker-peasant alliance, so necessary for both revolution's survival and any socialist transition in Russia. The Bolshevik perspective was to use the industrial strength of the cities to improve the productivity of the peasants and thus win them as allies of the working class and its revolutionary state. There had to be a more or less equal exchange between town and country. As Lenin was to put it: 'The correct policy of the proletariat exercising its dictatorship in a small peasant country was to obtain grain in exchange for the manufactured goods the peasant needs.'

Such was the cautious Bolshevik perspective immediately after the October Revolution. But the ferocious counter-evolution mounted by the old ruling classes, backed by the armed allied intervention and economic blockade changed all that and led to, as an economic historian has put it, 'the inexorable expropriation of large scale capital and capital generally, the confiscation of the property of the ruling classes, the suppression of the market and the construction of an all-embracing proletarian organisation of political economy, which depended on overcoming the market, and its exploitation'. This was necessarily accompanied by stricter labour discipline, the drive for greater productivity and the replacement of the workers' committees which ran the factories by 'one man management'. In the sphere of agriculture the most significant consequence was the abandonment of the principle of equitable exchange between town and country. The overall outcome of the intensified pressure of civil war, of counter-revolution and imperialist intervention, was the emergence of a siege economy – a 'war communism' as it came to be called.

In the towns and cities workers, more conscious politically and better led, accepted, even if unhappily, the new rigours of this 'war communism' as necessary for the defence of their revolution. But in the countryside where the Bolsheviks never had an independent political base, with its emergent middle peasant economy, it was altogether different. The grain was needed for the Red Army at the front and fighting the civil war, and for industrial workers and others in cities and towns, and soon enough even to ward off large-scale starvation there, but the peasant who had it now, for the most part, would not give it willingly. And there was no time to persuade. It could only be taken from him by force. Given the peasants' reluctance and resistance, the only alternative available was to seize grain by sending out requisitioning and roadblock units from the towns. The Bolsheviks would far rather have avoided it, if for no other reason than it threatened to split the alliance between the workers and peasants, the very basis of the new Soviet state. Lenin had continually stressed the need for a 'class alliance of the working (middle) and exploited (poor) peasantry with the working class'. In the midst of the crisis itself (at the Eighth Congress of the Party in March, 1919) he declared: 'Nothing is more stupid than the very idea of applying coercion in economic relations with the peasant.' But for the Bolsheviks it was now a question of the very survival of the revolution. Indeed all that stood between the infant workers' state and its destruction by the counter-revolution was grain requisitioning.

Such was 'War Communism' as it came to be practiced, an act of desperation, a major policy retreat, a necessity forced on the Bolsheviks, as Lenin said, 'by extreme want, ruin and war'. It was part of the Bolsheviks' achievement that they recognised the necessity and met it face to face. But it was no dogmatic attempt to 'communise the economy', to 'suppress the market', etc. that critics continue to charge the Bolsheviks with, though, apart from wrong implementation of policies on the ground that Lenin himself admitted and regularly warned against, there was an understandable occasional inclination to make virtue of necessity and even claim its harsh measures to be 'socialism' itself. As Lenin most categorically stated: 'It was war and the ruin that forced us into War Communism. It was not, and could not be, a policy that corresponded to the economic tasks of the proletariat. It was a makeshift'.

By the end of the civil war, the policy of 'War Communism' was also totally exhausted. It was time to return to the proper 'economic tasks of the proletariat' in the new situation. Already in 1919, Lenin had pointed out that 'theoretically there can be no doubt that between capitalism and communism there lies a definite transition period which must combine the features and properties of both these forms of social economy'. Now, in 1921, Lenin in part even argued: 'the alternative [to War Communism] (and this is the only sensible and best possible policy) is not to... put the lock on the development of capitalism, but to channel it into state capitalism'. The answer now found was the New Economic Policy which involved major concessions to private enterprise in the economy, to petty commodity production, internal markets and so on. (The notion of 'state capitalism', it may be noted, was visualised by Lenin as a very limited phase strictly supervised by the proletarian state, wherein, within the framework of the New Economic Policy, the government could 'lease out concessions' to foreign and local capitalist enterprises, which 'concessions' however would remain under the control of the Soviet state. This, along with much of Lenin's argument against 'Left Communists' was not so much a matter of *theory* as part of a pragmatic or tactical response to 'the present state of affairs in our Soviet Republic', as Lenin put it. Lenin later acknowledged that 'concessions have not developed on any considerable scale', and abandoned the term and the accompanying tactical approach altogether. Within his overall revolutionary perspective, the strategies of 'cultural revolution' and 'cooperation' became the focus of his interest and hope, providing a more positive definition of Russia's road to socialism).

The New Economic Policy, retreat of yet another kind, did not however in any way abandon or bypass the issues of socialist transition. (It was no 'adjusting into capitalism' as some former Marxists and socialists or Gorbachevian ideologues, missing out on the heroism of Lenin's modest effort, have been making out). Economic considerations apart, its most important underlying principle was the need to re-secure a firm basis for the much-damaged worker-peasant alliance. The sustenance of this alliance and the need to survive and secure an adequate economic basis for constructing socialism, saw Lenin laying an overriding emphasis on rapid industrial development. He wrote:

> If we see to it that the working class retains its leadership over the peasantry, we shall be able, by exercising the greatest possible thrift in the economic life of our state, to use every saving we make to develop our large-scale machine industry, to develop electrification, the hydraulic extraction of peat, to complete the Volkhov Power Project, etc.
>
> In this, and in this alone, lies our hope. Only when we have done this shall we, speaking figuratively, be able to change horse, to change from the peasant, muzhik horse of poverty, from the horse of an economy designed for a ruined peasant country, to

> the horse which the proletariat is seeking and must seek – the horse of large-scale machine industry, of electrification, of the Volkhov Power Station, etc.

And we have Lenin's famous metaphoric response: 'Communism is Soviet power plus the electrification of the whole country'.

XIX

Certain economic practices connected with 'War Communism' along with its occasional rationalisation in socialist terms, the concessions made in the New Economic Policy to capitalism along with certain economistic ways of thinking which accompanied it, together with the some out of context references have been the basis for charging Lenin with what he himself characterised and rejected as 'economism' – a theoretical interpretation of Marxism which unilaterally subordinates the transformation of social relations to the development of the forces of production, which is then even traced back to Marx and Engels. There is no doubt that there are 'economistic' or 'productionist' elements in Marx and Engels, though they constitute, especially with Marx, only a most minor part of their work as a whole, notwithstanding the fact that they became dominant in European Marxism with the Second International because of the specific socio-economic features of its historical environment. And even if it is argued that Lenin's concessions to 'economistic' ways of thinking and acting were often forced upon him by overriding circumstances, it has to be conceded that his Marxism was not immune to economism. He was quite capable of counting 'modern large-scale capitalist engineering' among 'the conditions necessary for socialism', praising Taylorism in the workplace, or saying that his party's task was 'to study the state-capitalism of the Germans, to spare no effort in copying it and not shrink from adopting dictatorial methods to hasten the copying of it... even more than Peter hastened the copying of Western culture by barbarous Russia', and even add, 'we must not hesitate to use barbarous methods in fighting barbarism'. To concede this however is not to deny that his theory and practice *as a whole* was least influenced by economism. His lifelong practice of *revolutionary* Marxism is evidence enough. And it remains true of the way Lenin now *recognised* the economic problems of post-civil war Russia, even if given the constraints of the objective situation, he was unable to effectively pursue the *politics* which flowed from such recognition.

In this context we may briefly look at two issues, one concerning social relations of production involving workers in a factory and the other relating to socialist transition in a predominantly peasant country, as Lenin confronted them in the historically concrete Russian situation, which, in different ways, indicate how revolutionary politics governed Lenin's practice even in the post-October period.

In proper Marxist understanding of socialism, what is crucial is not the form of property ownership but the real relations among the groups and individuals involved in the processes of production and distribution. Public ownership opens the way, and is a necessary prerequisite, to the transformation of these relations. But taken by itself it neither constitutes nor guarantees such a transformation, which can come about only as the result of a long and difficult struggle. In the Soviet Union, during 1918–1922 under the difficult conditions of the period of War Communism and later the New Economic Policy, industrial organisation had necessarily come to be dominated by the principles of director's absolute authority, privileged role of experts and specialists, material bonuses and rewards, etc. – principles which derived from the kind of hierarchical division of labour which lies at the heart of the capitalist mode of production. The practice of such principles may have corresponded to the requirement of a specific stage of the Russian Revolution, but Lenin was always aware that this was in no sense a move towards socialism. In fact he interpreted the decision to strengthen the authority and raise the pay of specialists in precisely the opposite sense, and wrote:

> It is clear that this measure not only implies the cessation – in a certain field and to a certain degree – of the offensive against capital (for capital is not a sum of money, but a definite social relation); it is also a step backward on the part of our socialist Soviet state

> power, which from the very outset proclaimed and pursued the policy of reducing high salaries to the level of the wages of the average worker.

This assessment or criticism obviously implied the need to take a step forward which could only be political democratisation that would strengthen the real power of the workers relative to that of not only the bourgeois technocrats but every economic and political authority in the factory. Only such a step could create 'a new and higher social bond, a social discipline, the discipline of class-conscious, united working people' which Lenin, as against reliance on directors, experts and specialists, deemed imperative to raise the productivity of labour. Only such a step, a move towards *socialist* relations of production could provide the requisite environment for the emergence of a truly socialist labour, not 'single acts of heroic fervour' but 'mass heroism in plain, everyday work'. This is indeed what, at the time, the free and voluntary labour of the communist *subbotniks* had come to symbolise, of whom Lenin wrote:

> Evidently this is only the beginning, but it is a beginning of exceptionally great importance. It is the beginning of a revolution which is more difficult, more tangible, more radical and more decisive than the overthrow of the bourgeoisie, for it is a victory over our own conservatism, indiscipline, petty bourgeois egoism, a victory over the habits left as a heritage to the worker and peasant by accursed capitalism. Only when this victory is consolidated will the new social discipline, socialist discipline be created; then, only then, will a reversion to capitalism become impossible and communism become really possible.

As Bettelheim has pointed out, the necessary step backward of 1918–1922 was never followed by the even more necessary and possible Leninist step forward. On the contrary, the weight and authority of the factory director and of the factory party secretary –authority which was not subject to review by the workers – became more powerful over the years, a development which, one might add, received new impetus during the period of rapid industrialisation that followed in the Stalin era. Against Lenin's hopes, what got consolidated were 'the relations of authority and command between administration, cadres, specialists, and technicians on the one hand and the direct producers on the other'. It is these which together with the bourgeois relations rampant in the apparatuses of government ultimately scuttled Lenin's socialist project and provided the basis for the later emergence of a distinctive class-exploitative society in the Soviet Union.

The New Economic Policy provides example of a different kind of the pre-eminence of revolutionary politics in the theory and practice of Lenin.

Lenin was aware of the problems of creating a base of modern large-scale industry in backward, war-devastated Russia, so essential for the socialist transformation of the country. At the end of civil war and wars of imperialist intervention, the situation had become even more desperate and the Bolshevik Party was constantly occupied with the problems of economic recovery and reconstruction, and of carrying out by themselves their country's unaccomplished task, its industrial revolution. Isolated, surrounded by enemies, the Soviet Union had to achieve in as short a time as possible – because the threat of armed attack was both permanent and immediate – what in the West had taken over a century with the help of colonial plunder and at the expense of a ruthlessly uprooted peasantry. The highly contradictory and un-Marxist concept, 'primitive socialist accumulation' – un-Marxist because 'accumulation', primitive or any other, is alien to socialism – elaborated and given currency by Yevgenii Preobrazhensky, summed up not only the terribly difficult and completely unexpected task thrust on the revolutionary agenda, but also in a way the tragedy of the Bolshevik Marxism. The concept was in common use; Bukharin, Trotsky, Preobrazhensky, all spoke of 'primitive socialist accumulation', though the thrust of the policy advocated in each case was different. While ridiculing the transposition of the concept of primitive accumulation from the early phase of capitalist evolution to that of socialist transformation, Lenin was generally sympathetic to Bukharin's approach to the essential problem. In Bukharin 'the mobilisation of living production power' was 'the basic moment of primitive socialist accumulation' and he saw it as 'the dialectical negation of capitalist private accumulation'. Lenin, on his part, never contemplated that the problems of socialist industrialisation should or could be solved at the expense of the peasantry. On the contrary, from the beginning of 1919 till he wrote the last published piece of his life ('Better Fewer, But Better') on 2 March 1923, his most important concern was how to 'strive to build up a state in which the workers retain the leadership of the peasants, in which they retain the confidence of the peasants...', just as he also argued for 'exercising the greatest economy (to) remove every trace of extravagance from our social relations'. For Lenin, in constructing socialist economy in Russia, the burden must be shared by both the working class and the peasantry, and priority was to be given to the immediate improvement of the 'conditions of the working people', that is, industrial workers as well as peasants. As he put it: 'All the peasants and all the workers will have to exert themselves to the utmost; our machinery of the state which is still working very inefficiently, must be improved and made less costly so that we may improve the conditions of the working people and, to some extent at least, restore our economy.'

Again, central to any effort at socialist economic construction was the question of Soviet political power, the defence of which under certain conditions did require retreat on the strictly economic front. Such, as we have seen, was the essential nature of War Communism – a retreat from the policies adopted immediately after the October Revolution. And soon the Bolsheviks were called upon to undertake retreat of another kind in the New Economic Policy (NEP) inaugurated in 1921, a retreat from War Communism, involving as it did economic concessions to private enterprise, small traders and producers (who became known as Nepmen), to foreign investors, and above all to the peasantry. NEP was in Ryazanov's phrase 'a peasant Brest-Litovsk'; like that agreement which sanctioned the German occupation of Ukraine in order to buy the desperately needed peace for the revolution, it was a necessary surrender and concession to the country's most numerous class and one on which the revolution had to depend for sheer physical survival. In Lenin's words: 'Only an agreement with the peasantry can save the socialist revolution in Russia until the revolution has occurred in other countries'. Even as he sought 'an economic breathing space...to preserve the rule of the proletariat in Russia', looking to the future he wrote: 'Here industrial workers are in a minority and petty farmers are the vast majority. In such a country socialist revolution can triumph only on two conditions. First, if it is given timely support by socialist revolution in one or several advanced countries.... The second condition is agreement between the proletariat... and the majority of the peasant population'. We know that this revolution, hoped to be only delayed, never arrived, but Lenin stood firm in his commitment to 'the second condition'. And the immediately important issue is that this is how the overall nature of the NEP needs to be understood. There were many people in Russia at the time, both in and out of the Bolshevik Party, who saw NEP essentially as a temporary 'retreat', a package of concessions to the peasantry (and other non-proletarian segments of the population) to get the economy going, indeed a tactical manoeuvre to be abandoned at the earliest opportunity, as soon as it had accomplished its purpose. Lenin's view, however, and for that matter the official view of the Party of which he was then the acknowledged political and ideological leader, was entirely different. Economic considerations were of course important. But decisively important for Lenin was the politics of the situation. He noticed the entirely unanticipated nature of the situation in Russia as also the need for an innovative departure, if need be, from what was widely believed to be the received doctrine. In his report to the Third Congress of Communist International, Lenin dwelt at length on 'the problem of the relations the proletariat should establish with this last capitalist class in Russia' (namely, the class of small producers including the small farmer) and wrote: 'All Marxists have a correct and ready solution for this problem in theory. But theory and practice are two different things, and the practical solution of this problem is by no means the same as the theoretical solution.' In the given situation, 'the practical solution' in relation specifically to peasantry was 'alliance with the peasantry', which was not the conventional or the supposedly orthodox Marxist answer. This is how Lenin put it:

> For the first time in history there is a state with only two classes, the proletariat and the peasantry. The latter constitutes the overwhelming majority of the population. It is, of course, very backward. How do the relations between the peasantry and the proletariat, which holds political power, find practical expression in the development of the revolution? The first form is alliance, close alliance.

XX

Decisive in Lenin's perspective on the NEP was its political purpose, which was to restore the worker-peasant alliance while at the same time setting in motion the process of transforming the peasantry along the lines which Marxian theory held to be essential for a successful transition to socialism, that is, to transform the peasantry, through economic help and voluntary cooperativisation, from isolated petty producers into socially conscious members of the society as a whole, increasingly assimilated into the working class and in a mutually supporting alliance with it actively involved in the construction of a socialist society. A most significant and creative response to the Russian situation, Lenin's politics here developed and put into practice Marx's theoretical model of a worker-peasant alliance that Marx had postulated in the aftermath of the Paris Commune, which he saw as a proletarian revolution occurring in a country where peasantry constituted the greater part of the nation. Recognising that this alliance did not end the class contradiction involved – non-antagonist as Mao would call it later – Marx had written: 'The Commune does not do away with the class struggle, through which the working classes strive to the abolition of all classes...' But he held that the Commune 'affords the rational medium in which that class struggle can run through its different phases in the most rational and humane way'. Marx had warned that the proletariat 'must not hit the peasant over the head'. Instead, the perspective, though all too briefly suggested, was that of winning over the peasantry and easing its transition to socialism through helpful economic and political measures – a position shared by Engels when he later wrote of doing 'everything at all permissible to make his (the small peasant's) lot more bearable' and facilitate his voluntary 'transition to the cooperative....' This was now Lenin's perspective too. For Lenin, the only way to socialism in the Soviet Union was through helping the peasants and in doing so convincing them that their own best interests would be served by working together with the workers and the Soviet state and not separately. That is why when, at the Eleventh Party Congress (April 1922) Lenin proclaimed an end to the 'retreat' phase of the NEP, it was not to be an end to the NEP itself. Even as he, once again, insisted that 'the central feature of the situation now is that the vanguard must not shirk the work of educating itself, of remoulding itself, must not be afraid of frankly admitting that it is not sufficiently trained and lacks the necessary skill', he argued that from then on NEP was to be the vehicle for a new advance. 'The main thing now', said Lenin, 'is to advance as an immeasurably wider and larger mass, and only together with the peasantry, proving to them by deeds, in practice, by experience, that we are learning and that we shall learn to assist them, to lead them forward.' Thus, for Lenin, the NEP, properly understood, was in no sense a tactical manoeuvre but rather the crucial element of the Bolsheviks' long-term strategy for achieving socialism in their peasant-dominated country.

Crucially important in this strategy, it may be noticed, was the role of the cooperatives, the means whereby the Bolshevik Party was to 'lead them (the peasants) to socialism'. Lenin indeed argued that 'cooperation under our conditions nearly always coincides fully with socialism'. In one of his very last articles, 'On Cooperation' (January 1923), Lenin wrote:

> Indeed, since political power is in the hands of the working class, since this political power owns all the means of production, the only task that remains for us is to organise the population in cooperative societies.... Indeed, the power of the state over all large scale means of production, political power in the hands of the proletariat, the alliance of this proletariat with the many millions of small and very small peasants, the assured proletarian leadership of the peasantry etc. – is this not all that is necessary to build a complete socialist society out of cooperatives, out of cooperatives alone... It is still not the building of socialist society, but it is all that is necessary and sufficient for it.

Indeed, wrote Lenin: 'Now we are entitled to say that for us the mere growth of cooperation... is identical with the growth of socialism.' Lenin emphasised 'how vastly, how infinitely important it is now to organise the population of Russia in cooperative societies'. Seeking 'to build socialism in practice in such a way that every small peasant could take part in it', he saw in cooperativisation a 'transition to the new system by means that are the simplest, easiest and most acceptable to the peasant'. He urged every possible state help to 'produce the civilised cooperators', and wrote: 'And given social ownership of the means of production, given the class victory of the proletariat over the bourgeoisie, the system of civilised cooperators is the system of socialism'. Lenin urged the party to get the peasants 'into the work of cooperatives through NEP', and thus hoped that 'NEP Russia will become socialist Russia'.

XXI

Such now was Lenin's perspective of a socialist advance in the Soviet Union. But, once again, as with his project of socialist transition with the active support and participation of the workers, this other advance visualised by Lenin did not take place. The NEP was already in trouble. Lenin doubted that communists were guiding the bureaucracy and even asked rhetorically: 'who is leading whom?' As he put it:

> Well, we have lived through a year, the state is in our hands, but has it operated the New Economic Policy in the way we wanted in the past year? No. But we refuse to admit that it did not operate in the way we wanted. How did it operate? The machine refused to obey the hands that guided it. It was like a car that was going not in the direction the driver desired; but in the direction someone else desired; as if it were being driven by some mysterious, lawless hands....

In the event the original Bolshevik perspective of a workers-led alliance with the peasantry did not survive Lenin, nor did the economic policies it decreed, whose necessity as well as viability has been well established by Bettelheim and endorsed by Sweezy and others. The actual course of Soviet economic development in the post-Lenin period not only followed the path suggested by Preobrazhensky's 'primitive socialist accumulation', but went much beyond the parameters set by its original author, who had carefully set out a host of qualifications, limitations and conditions and sought to answer the question 'how much?' in terms of long range interests of the country. The crude and harsh interpretation of the Stalinist leadership simply dropped the prefix 'primitive', and 'socialist accumulation', as Mao was to argue three decades later, became part of the 'measures which squeeze the peasants very hard'; peasants' surplus was forcibly appropriated to secure funds for rapid industrial development. In other words, the class struggle involved was far from conducted in 'the most rational and humane way' that Marx had visualised and was part of Lenin's project of socialism in Russia. Later collectivisation of peasantry, which was a most forcible and bloody process, not only irretrievably damaged the worker-peasant alliance but put a premium on methods of coercion and command from above to break and discipline the working people which greatly aided the emergence of a non-democratic, ruthlessly authoritarian state in the Soviet Union – the very antithesis of a free and democratic society of 'associated producers' or 'civilised cooperators' postulated by Lenin's socialist project.

XXII

The Leninist project of a socialist transition in Russia – with its exceptional democratic thrust, emphasis on 'revolutionising practice', programmatic concepts of 'cultural revolution' and 'growth of cooperation' from below, and much else – was a creative Marxist response to the entirely unanticipated situation resulting from history's trick on the doctrine of Karl Marx: instead of socialism being built on a base provided by the economic, political and cultural achievements of capitalism, a backward country, Russia, was called upon to build it. There never are any guarantees in history. But given his genius as a Marxist and a revolutionary, one can visualise Lenin pursuing his project to a successful conclusion. But that was not to be. The assassin's bullets fired at him by the Socialist Revolutionary Fanny Kaplan at the height of the civil war (August 1918), finally incapacitated him in 1923 and caused his death in January 1924. Lenin's socialist project did not survive him.

There were compromises and departures from principles even in the early years when Lenin was still alive. But his mistakes and inadequacies of Bolshevik theory notwithstanding, these were primarily compelled by circumstances and were seen as temporary concessions to a difficult situation. After Lenin, more particularly in the Stalin era, such compromises and departures not only took on a more grievous turn, at times themselves became the principles. Stalin, a Bolshevik leader in his own right, interpreting Lenin selectively or as he understood him, proclaimed a full-fledged theory of 'socialism in one country' and implementing it almost as a national economistic enterprise, instead of building socialism from below, opted for a 'revolution from above'. Of course there were the continuing compulsions of the objective circumstances, the initial economic backwardness and the varied pressures of a hostile capitalist environment, the threat of war that soon became a reality and yet again continued as a cold war – all of which so distorted things as to make any kind of 'organic' development of socialism almost impossible. But decisive for the outcome and the ultimate failure of the socialist project in Russia were the inadequacies of theory and political leadership. The situation demanded a truly innovative Marxist response, in the Leninist tradition, to cope with these objective compulsions and carry forward the socialist project – but this was simply not forthcoming. What took over as theory instead was really a gross theoretical distortion – a nationalist shift away from Lenin's resilient and creative Marxism to a Marxist scientism with 'economism' as its hard core, which was the dominant Marxism of the Stalin era, and after him ceased to be any kind of Marxism at all. The Soviet Communist Party, degenerating with the passage of years never recovered its lost Marxism. The absence of democracy in the party and state structures ruled out any kind of corrections from below or outside. The outcome was a deeply deformed socialism. The Stalin-era inadequacies of theory and political leadership were only compounded in those Stalin left behind. And now the deformed socialism that was built has collapsed.

The 'actually existing socialism' has ceased to exist and, at the end of seventy odd years of chequered existence, a finally defeated Russia has been sucked back into global capitalism.

This was not inevitable. Lenin had seen the building of socialism in backward Russia as a struggle, where 'defeat' was a distinct possibility, but nothing inevitable. 'Struggle, and struggle alone decides .... how far we shall advance', he had said. Obviously, the struggle, especially after the departure of Lenin, was not adequate enough. And it has now ended in a defeat. Nevertheless, we have its 'experience (to) benefit other revolutions', the least that Lenin had hoped for in the event of `defeat. This experience is our legacy not only for the pursuit of revolutionary politics in behalf of socialism but also for the perspective and practical guidance or lessons it provides for the socialist transitions of the future, a legacy for revolutionary socialists everywhere, especially in the poor and backward countries of the third world where people continue to be the worst victims of capitalism and where they today confront the choice: socialism or further peripheralisation within a global capitalist system.

6

The Damaged Beginnings

It was indeed very difficult but certainly not impossible for the Soviet people to travel the road to socialism even in the absence of the much-hoped for European revolution. But the already limited resources of the Bolsheviks for the purpose were soon so destroyed and grievously depleted by more than three years of civil war, foreign invasion and the imperialist-backed counter-revolution as to make the task near-impossible.

The havoc played by these years with the Soviet economy and society, the new democratic institutions and state structures, above all with the support base, organisation, ideology and political practice of the Bolshevik Party, needs to be noticed in order to understand the later course of development of the October Revolution, the deformations that came to characterise the construction of socialism in the Soviet Union. The continuous external pressure of a hostile capitalist world is of course important, but given the grave inadequacies of theory and political practice of especially the post-Lenin period, it is the internal deformation which was to prove decisive in the later crisis and ultimate collapse of 'actually existing socialism' in the Soviet Union and the eventual disintegration of the Soviet Union itself.

The October uprising was a decisive turning point in the progress of the Russian Revolution: Bolsheviks, led by Lenin ensured what in 1850 Marx had called 'the revolution in permanence' – a democratic revolution immediately going over into a proletarian revolution. But in the very nature of things, it was far from being the end of the struggle for power among the contending forces. Soon the civil war broke out all over the country already much devastated by the first world war. The old exploiting classes, though defeated, counter-attacked, supported by armed invasion by 14 countries including all the imperialist powers and their economic blockade of Russia. It was a most bloody and brutal period, following upon the remarkably peaceful revolution carried out by the Bolsheviks.

The brutality of the White Terror unleashed by the counter-revolution was well expressed by one of its major leaders, General Kornilov: 'The greater the terror, the greater our victories'. 'We must save Russia', he declared, 'even if we have to set fire to half of it and shed the blood of three-fourth of all the Russians'. Starvation, disease and death followed in the wake of the economic devastation caused by the civil war. All kinds of counter-revolutionary plots were hatched with the help of foreign diplomatic and secret-service agents, including the selected assassination of Lenin and other Bolshevik leaders. Many of them were indeed assassinated; though the attempt on Lenin's life did not immediately succeed, it hastened his early death. On many occasions the life of the Soviet regime hung by a thread. The choice for the Bolsheviks in this period was reduced to a capitulation to the Whites or a defence of revolution by whatever means were at hand. The alternative to this defence was only a bloody counter-revolution and never, at any stage, any kind of democratic regime. The situation simply ruled out any kind of normal politics or democratic methods. Barbaric methods had to be used to counter local and world reaction's barbaric attack on the revolution. Red Terror arose as the answer to the White Terror of the counter-revolution. The Red Terror was certainly brutal and it had its excesses, but unlike the White Terror it was not directed against the mass of workers and peasants in the name of an old discredited social order. That is why the Bolsheviks enjoyed the fierce and virtually undivided loyalty of the workers in the cities, and even in the countryside; while the peasants, like the workers, bridled under the regime of War Communism, they fought to the death to defend the revolution against the Whites. That is also why, despite being subjected to the most draconian forms of coercion, we yet saw the most conspicuous acts of individual and mass heroism on the part of the workers, peasants and soldiers during this period.

The revolutionary counter terror was certainly not something welcome to Bolsheviks, it was a most unwelcome necessity, which was abandoned as soon as the situation improved. As Lenin later reported at the All-Russian Central Executive Committee on 2 February 1920:

> We were forced to use terror because of the terror practised by the Entente, when strong world powers threw their hordes against us, not avoiding any type of combat. We would not have lasted two days had we not answered these attempts of officers and White Guardists in a merciless fashion; this meant the use of terror, but this was forced upon us by the terrorist methods of the Entente.
>
> But as soon as we attained a decisive victory, even before the end of the war, immediately after taking Rostov, we gave up the use of the death penalty and thus proved that we intend to execute our own programme in the manner that we promised. We say that the application of violence flows out of the decision to smother the exploiters, the big landowners and the capitalists; as soon as this was accomplished we gave up the use of all extraordinary methods. We have proved this in practice.

Lenin tried to limit the ferocity of counter-terror while it lasted, and frequently intervened personally in cases where its excesses were brought to his notice. It is significant that his first words after recovering consciousness from the socialist revolutionary assassin's bullets were 'Stop the Terror'. Yet Lenin, as a revolutionary also recognised: 'How can one make a revolution without firing squads? Do you think you will be able to deal with your enemies by laying down your arms? No one attaches any importance to this during a civil war when each side hopes to win.'

Lenin was aware of the experience of earlier revolutions, including the French Revolution and later revolutions in France. He knew his Marx who, in 1848, in reaction to 'the cannibalism of the counter-revolution' had argued that there was 'only one means to curtail, simplify and localise the bloody agony of the old society and the birth pangs of the new, only one means – the revolutionary terror'.

Bolsheviks were also knowledgeable about Marx's warning in this regard to the revolutionarics of the Paris Commune. Even as he hailed them for 'storming heaven', he had questioned their moderation and 'conscientious scruples' in confronting the counter-revolution, and forewarned: 'If they are defeated, only their "good nature" will be to blame'. They were defeated, and ruthlessly crushed, literally mass massacred in a most violent and bloody counter-revolution. This was warning enough to Bolsheviks now facing a counter-revolution of their own.

II

It is a tribute to the Bolsheviks' revolutionary commitment, their political consciousness and will power, their politics and organisation, that they took the measures that were necessary, withstood the most savage siege for so long, won the civil war and thus ensured the survival of the revolution. But they could do so only at enormous cost. At the end of it all the country stood battered and bloodied, its economy, both industry and agriculture, in utter ruin, and, as Ilya Ehrenberg was to put it later, its 'everyday life' had become 'prehistoric', 'the everyday life of the cave age'. One ominously dangerous element in the situation was the burgeoning revolt of the peasantry against grain requisitioning, its exasperation with the War Communist regime finding explosive expression in the revolt of the now predominantly peasant sailors at Kronstadt which, as Lenin said, was 'like a flash of lightening which threw more glare upon reality than anything else'. The worker-peasant alliance stood almost irretrievably damaged. The Kronstadt revolt was crushed, a tragic necessity, but not without producing the banning of factions within the Bolshevik Party, and the disaster this spelled for its democratic traditions. Drawing the necessary lessons, Lenin moved fast from War Communism to New Economic Policy, above all in order to reconstruct the worker-peasant alliance, the very basis of Soviet power and the possibility, if any, of a socialist transition in Russia. The civil war, however, left another equally, if not more important, tragic legacy, which despite Lenin's desperate efforts and warnings never came to be repaired even tentatively. The revolutionary regime indeed survived, but the freedom and democracy which characterised life and politics in the first period of Soviet power and which the Bolsheviks, like everyone else, took for granted, had disappeared, never to return. The necessity of restoring democracy for a *socialist* reconstruction of society went simply unrecognised by the Bolshevik leadership as a whole, more especially after Lenin's departure.

The vice-like pressures of civil war had in fact transformed the Soviet regime in so many ways. The soviets, trade unions, political party system including the Bolshevik Party, literally all the democratic institutions of the post-October period, were badly hit by the White Terror and the civil war, they emerged out of it transmuted and grievously deformed. The weight of the bureaucracy, of the army, of the Cheka ('sword of revolution' against counter-revolution) from their modest beginnings, grew enormously during the civil war. Without these institutions the October regime would have been swept away in a bloody counter-revolution. With them the October Revolution had now become sclerotic and authoritarian. The measures taken by Bolsheviks to save the revolution had the dual effect of halting counter-revolutionary attacks but only at the cost of contributing to an early phase of centralisation of power and bureaucratisation of state structures. The political military apparatus that grew during the civil war, while giving stability and some direction to the revolution, had also the consequence of foreclosing democratic development – what with the curtailment of diversity and democracy in general and within the revolutionary camp, the banning of rival parties and formal suppression of factions within the Bolshevik Party, the establishment of Party control over every institution including the soviets and the trade unions, their bureaucratisation and constant distancing from the rank and file workers and peasants and the consequent steep decline in the self-activity of the working people which is the necessary basis for any genuine socialist enterprise. The persistent fear that counter-revolution could easily stage a come back only sustained and reinforced this undemocratic turn in the fate of the October Revolution. In noting all this, which involved a series of departures from Bolshevik principles, it needs to be remembered that the alternatives available at the time were worse than those resulting from the Bolshevik departures; the 'movements', which, on paper, appeared to have a more democratic programme (Workers' Opposition, Kronstadt, Makhno, etc.) were either frauds (Makhno) or utopian. Nevertheless it was the tragedy of the early 1920s that the Bolsheviks had defeated the counter-revolution, but in the process the basis on which they themselves stood had been destroyed. At the end of the civil war, the objective premises of *State and Revolution*, of the Leninist view of how to go about constructing the new proletarian state and begin building socialism simply lay shattered.

III

Of crucial importance in this turn was the havoc wrought by the civil war on the Russian proletariat and its vanguard, the Bolshevik Party. The pre-1917 revolutionary proletariat, organised, trained and led by the Bolsheviks, virtually perished in the struggle against counter-revolution and foreign intervention. Conscription may have been necessary to build a mass army in a peasant country, but it was the most active and class-conscious workers, above all the Bolsheviks, who volunteered again and again for the most dangerous tasks and lost their lives. Others had to be drafted, necessarily, into the new state structures and most simply dispersed with the disruption of the urban economy. The working class as a whole was thus reduced to an atomised, individualised, politically demoralised and exhausted mass, a fraction of its former size, and no longer in a position to exercise the collective power that it had exercised in 1917. In the turmoil and chaos of the period, working class and its traditional institutions all got disrupted and dislocated beyond any possibility of rapid or early recovery and recomposition. By 1921, writes Isaac Deutscher, 'the old, self-reliant, and class-conscious labour movement, with its many institutions and organizations, trade unions, cooperatives, and educational clubs, which used to resound with loud and passionate debate and seethed with political activity – that movement was now an empty shell'. This is how Lenin described the situation: 'The industrial proletariat... owing to the War and to the desperate poverty and ruin, has become declassed... dislodged from its class groove, and has ceased to exist as a proletariat'. Thus, at the end of the civil war, the working class base of the new workers' state, the rock on which the Bolshevik power stood, had disintegrated, and the social force that the Bolsheviks, above all Lenin, counted on to prevent the development of bureaucracy and keep the revolution on its socialist course was cut from under the feet of the Bolshevik Party.

The Bolshevik vanguard fared no better. At the end of the civil war it too stood decimated, as decimated as the revolutionary proletariat and for the same reasons, (the best of what survived was to later perish in Stalin's purges). It was no longer the old Bolshevik Party. Demands of the civil war had necessarily led to excessive and rigid centralisation of authority on the one hand and a series of restrictions on inner party democracy on the other. The new entrants to the now rechristened Communist Party were, in their massive numbers, post-revolution entrants; along with those inspired by revolution's ideals, as a party in power it had attracted all sorts of indifferent careerist or opportunist elements too. An overwhelming majority of these members, having served in government and party apparatuses or the army, often in positions of political and military authority, when they later assumed leading posts in the local Soviets, in the economy, in education, etc., tended to introduce everywhere, as Trotsky noticed, 'that regime which ensured success in the civil war'. One important consequence of the now changed character of the working class and the party was that the long-established relationship between class and party stood largely dissolved. And with the increasing erosion of the support of the peasantry, party also stood much isolated from the mass of the people. The Bolshevik Party, once a true revolutionary vanguard, now found itself lacking adequate class or mass base, but with responsibility for governing and leading a country with an overwhelming peasant and petty-bourgeois majority, which almost inevitably made for its undeniable vanguardism or substitutionism after 1921, where Party or State exclusively led by it take over the place of self-acting working class or people. This only accelerated the slide towards bureaucratic degeneration of the Party, as also of the State where unavoidable but dangerous concessions to former bourgeois and tsarist bureaucrats, technologists, officials, etc. had already gone into constituting a new bureaucratic stratum, which was finding its political leadership in the Party itself. All this further contributed to the transmutation of Party's nature and role as a revolutionary vanguard.

The Party, in exclusive control of state power, even as it led them, increasingly became a ruler over the people. This was perhaps the most tragic of the deforming developments of the period because, in the situation, Party alone could be expected to provide a corrective political intervention in the much deteriorated economy and politics of the country. Instead 'dictatorship of the proletariat' became synonymous with the dictatorship of the Party. No longer a revolutionary vanguard, but using all the resources of the Bolshevik tradition, this 'dictatorship' was to accomplish epic feats of industrialisation and prepare for the inevitable onslaught of imperialist powers; but as it did so, economic and political bureaucracies proliferated in the Soviet economic and political state structures. The project of transcending the state, of 'dictatorship of the proletariat' as the anti-thesis of the bourgeois state, simply came to be abandoned. A style of work emerged which, as Lenin lamented, owed more to tsarist bureaucratic traditions than, the ritualistic lip service apart, to the ideals of the revolution. A vast bureaucratic administration was established which was increasingly independent of Soviet or any other democratic control, and therefore, all the more arrogant in its claims and unchecked in its growth. The military methods of the civil war persisted and necessarily led to an accentuation of a centralising and authoritarian approach. The Commune vanished even from Lenin's vocabulary, even as he valiantly but unsuccessfully struggled against such deformations in the Soviet regime and kept looking for democratic correctives to the very end of his life.

It needs to be reiterated that these centralising and bureaucratising deformations were not something foisted by the leadership on the Party or by the Party on the Russian society. They were overwhelmingly caused by the force of objective circumstances. The Bolsheviks had arrived at a point far distant from the goals of 1917 – it had been a massive retreat for them. But they had travelled this road in opposition to their own theory, not because of it – no matter what theoretical justifications were given at the time, or later, to gain legitimacy for such departures from theory in practice.

IV

There were indeed departures from principles but these were not a product of any principles of Bolshevik theory or Marxism or of Lenin's Leninism, as critics including some on the left, continue to allege. A look at some specific issues would further establish the point I am wanting to make.

We have already noticed the Bolshevik commitment to democracy, which was massively demonstrated at the very beginning of the Soviet experiment in socialism, with Lenin's project of a Commune-type state. Regardless of the issues of long-term practicability, the necessity of transitional or institutionalised forms, or the still nebulous and under-determined nature of the concept of proletarian democracy, this unprecedented practice of democracy of the working people was initially remarkably successful; if it did not develop into a functioning, alternative system of socialist democracy (as against bourgeois democracy) this is obviously because it was soon wrecked by the civil war. Again, the Bolsheviks certainly did not have any well-worked out or systemised ideas about enterprise democracy, an inadequacy they shared with the wider Marxist, in fact entire socialist tradition, including Anarchists and Anarcho-syndicalists. But it was not the Bolsheviks' substitutionism or statism or Machiavellian politics, as alleged by hostile critics, but the decimation and dispersal of the proletariat which threw the movement for workplace democracy into complete disarray. Even otherwise the initial expropriation of the capitalists, often forced by the workers themselves, made for a new type of centralisation of control. It is noteworthy that the number of factories activity seized by the workers was much less than those where they *asked* Soviets to nationalise them – reflecting a certain economic and political weakness of the working class even in this early period. Thus, if the demands of the civil war in a situation of growing industrial crisis resulted in 'one-man management', 'militarisation' of the working class, top-down control of workplaces and of the production process, etc., the weakness of the proletariat, with its extreme particularism, 'parochial' or 'local' outlooks, internal divisions and conflicts, shifting political allegiances – all this having strong negative effects on productivity as E.H. Carr has pointed out – too played its part in the ultimate disappearance of 'enterprise democracy'. At the end of the civil war, the working class had simply lost the strength, the unity, collective vision and political consciousness and determination to rule over itself; it could neither defend or practise 'enterprise democracy', nor offer any adequately comprehensive, realistic vision or perspective on its place as part of the process of transition to socialism.

Again, it was no part of either Marxism or Bolshevik theory to have an authoritarian or one-party system as the political form of the transition to socialism. The extreme democratic character of the early Soviet power apart, it was a power shared with other socialist parties. Seats were allotted to socialist opposition in the Central Executive Committee of the Soviets and the Left Socialist Revolutionaries were partners of the Bolsheviks in government till they left it in March 1918 in protest against Brest-Litovsk treaty, and eventually joined the other side in the civil war. Even when in opposition, these parties continued to function as legal parties. Roy Medvedev, the long standing anti-Stalinist dissident Soviet scholar, has pointed out that an analysis of Lenin's speeches and articles during 1917–20 shows that he did not assume the existence of a one-party system in Soviet Russia, nor a complete ban on the other left or socialist parties; in fact he even offered places in the government to other left parties and was rebuffed. But the pressure of circumstances imposed its own choices or options. In times of civil war, democratic rights or practices always tend to be a casualty. And in a civil war as brutal as in Russia the choices or options turned out to be exceptionally harsh. The party of Cadets, violently hostile to revolution and resorting to armed action against the Bolshevik government, could not be allowed to function in the revolutionary interior. The Bolsheviks had initially no intention of banning the socialist opposition, but bans and even Red Terror followed as this opposition, the Socialist Revolutionaries being the foremost among them, moved over to the counter-revolution, attempted sabotage and insurrections, even assassinations of Bolshevik leaders. It was a Socialist Revolutionary, Fanny Kaplan, who shot Lenin twice at point-blank range, bringing him close to death and ultimately resulting in his premature demise. Even so, these bans and curbs, and Red Terror, were declared to be temporary measures, unwelcome but necessary, and they were indeed withdrawn or rescinded whenever and wherever possible even during the civil war, though often only to be reimposed. It is thus that ultimate damage was done to Soviet democracy during 1918–1921. It is worth noting that the Soviet Constitutions of 1918 and 1924 gave no recognition or privileged position as the sole ruling party to the Bolsheviks. One-party rule was a contingent product of the civil war and was formally institutionlised only in the 1936 Constitution.

The Bolshevik's monopoly of power was thus established by virtue primarily of the fact that, one by one, the parties which stood in opposition to them, with the sharpening of issues and polarisation during the civil war, passed over to the camp of armed counter-revolution. E.H. Carr has noted: 'If it was true that the Bolshevik regime was not prepared after the first few months to tolerate an organised opposition, it was equally true that no opposition was prepared to remain within legal limits. The premise of the dictatorship was common to both sides of the argument.'

V

Most significant for the future development of the Soviet Union was what happened to the Bolshevik Party, for here was possibly the best available resource for the necessary recovery from the damage done by the civil war. Yet the civil war had not only physically decimated the Party, its experience had badly sapped its inner life; it emerged from the civil war increasingly centralised, bureaucratised and lacking in internal democracy.

While we must recognise the existence of internal tensions in the Bolshevik tradition, we need to reject the notion now being recycled by anti-communists and others that Leninism is basically elitist and authoritarian in its principles of societal or party organisation. The notion is not only untrue, there is a basic continuity in Lenin's organisational conceptions of the Party or society and state throughout his active political life, and this continuity is based on their essential democratic character. The authoritarian features appear in the practice of Lenin and Bolsheviks only under the desperate objective conditions of war, civil war, foreign intervention and blockade, when they are compelled to adopt increasingly restrictive measures not only in the country as a whole but within their own party as they wait for a revolutionary triumph in the West that will end the desperate isolation of their beleaguered and impoverished country. Thus the anti-democratic bureaucratic transformation of the Party, of its 'disciplined quantity into authoritarian quality' in Le Blanc's words, did not result from Lenin's ideas in 1902 when he wrote *What Is To Be Done?*, or later on. If there was one principle which throughout governed Lenin's thinking on the subject, it was his commitment to internal debate and democracy in the Party. The process of anti-democratic bureaucratisation was set in motion by the historically contingent situation that followed upon the heels of the October Revolution, that is civil war and the threat of foreign-backed counter-revolution.

Lenin's early insistence on discipline and organisation in *What Is To Be Done?* was a product of the chaos and anarchy that reigned in the revolutionary movement in Russia at the time. Lenin responded to the weaknesses of the movement by demanding a party press in place of stray leafleting, professionalism (especially under illegal conditions) in place of amateurishness, coordination and centralisation in place of localism, and most important, socialist politics in place of syndicalism and economism, and so on. All this so obviously demanded a democratically active, participatory membership and not a passive, obedient one. In fact, well after the principle of democratic centralism had been constitutionally enshrined, Lenin suggested in 1906 the 'institutionalisation of a membership referendum on key political questions', which, for various reasons, was never put into practice. Democratic centralism itself was no original or inevitable source of bureaucratism (or of latter-day Stalinism) as the critics continue to allege. Encapsulating the twin principles of 'freedom of discussion' and 'unity of action', as Lenin put it, it insured decision making that was informed by experience and criticism from below and effective implementation of the decisions taken, and thus also provided the organisational basis for a self-correcting and self-redeeming politics. It is thus that Lenin laid the foundation for a highly disciplined and internally democratic party organisation suited for revolutionary assault against the Czarist state. This Leninist concept of organisation was put to its decisive test in the revolutionary upsurge of 1917. It was not merely its discipline but equally its internally democratic character (that is democratic centralism) which enabled the Bolshevik Party to respond, with truly remarkable flexibility to the rapidly changing objective situation and subjective moods of the people, attract the more militant sections of the working class to itself (and grow tenfold in six months), gain increasing popular support and approval and thus, establishing its political superiority over the rival parties, carry out, no cleverly manipulated 'coup' as enemies and critics including right-wing Soviet or post-Soviet historiography and some leftwing anti-Leninist analysts continue to misrepresent, but a genuinely popular social revolution.

VI

Conditions of illegality of course imposed their demands, but all through from 1905 to 1917, the Bolsheviks were a party in which heated discussion and debate was the norm. They divided over boycotting or participating in the Duma, over working in the police-inspired trade unions, over philosophical dispute between Lenin and Bogdanov, and a host of other more or less important issues. In 1917 itself, the Bolsheviks divided over the very nature of the revolution, over the April Thesis and peaceful road to power, over if and when to call for a second revolution, over the question of armed insurrection itself; and later, over such issues as coalition with other socialists, the Constituent Assembly, the Brest-Litovsk treaty with German imperialism, over military policy during the civil war, over the role of trade unions under socialism, over nationality policy, and repeatedly over economic issues like War Communism and the difficult transition to New Economic Policy, over even democratic centralism (at the 9th Party Congress). This listing of issue or debates is only illustrative. And throughout 1918–21, the traditional authoritative bodies like Party Congress and Central Committee continued to function with full power – they met and thrashed out the policy issues regularly. Tension and conflict was the rule not the exception in the Party, the Committees were more often called to account from below rather than above, activists could freely express themselves at general open meetings and through periodic elections, factions were regularly formed, and dissolved once the context changed. There was no 'official' leadership other than the elected bodies and no concept of 'dissent' or 'deviation'. Internally, democracy gave full recognition to tendency and faction rights within the Party.

Lenin all along insisted on the cultivation of the spirit of criticism and self-criticism inside the Party, accommodating in the process a plurality of opinions as long as they are concerned with issues of socialism and revolution. No one, not even Lenin, was sacrosanct in this ruthless practice of internal democracy. Lenin himself could be and was in fact outvoted on several occasions. There was no 'great leader' who knew everything, or came along or down to clear all doubts. The only means that the leadership had to persuade others was the power of argument and the record of its previous decisions. And the majority decisions prevailed. Recognising that correct answers can be found only through fierce and vigorous debate and that people are integral to their verification and successful implementation, Lenin wrote:

> there can be no mass party, no party of a class without full clarity of essential shadings, without an open struggle between various tendencies, without informing the masses as to which leaders and which organisations of the party are pursuing this or that line. Without this a party worthy of the name cannot be built.

Incidentally, Lenin's method of countering his opponents was not that of suppression but of theoretical reasoning as is clear from his handling of his contemporaries, of the Mensheviks once and later of Trotsky, Bukharin and others in the Bolshevik Party. An outstanding feature, for example, of the immediately pre- and post-October period was free, open and uninhibited exchanges, even angry polemics without any intimidation, within the Bolshevik leadership, which alone made it possible for it to effectively change tactics, even make dramatic turns, to shift from one economic or political strategy to another, during a period of unprecedented complexity and rapid change. (In its early period the newly-formed Communist International too was characterised by similar free and divergent expression of views as could be seen in the famous exchanges between Lenin and M.N. Roy in assessing national liberation movements.) The rich quality of debate and discussion within the party was made possible by and reflected the fact that the Bolsheviks had over the years developed a high level of agreement on general politics and a wide knowledge of the Marxist tradition among the leadership and the ranks. The eminent non-Marxist historian E.H. Carr, in his classic *A History of Soviet Russia,* has specifically commented on the unique quality and vibrancy of political debate within the Bolshevik Party in its hey day, even when it came to enjoy governmental power in the aftermath of the October Revolution, something unmatched by any party anywhere, bourgeois democratic, socialist or any other, before or since. To this day none of them has so recognised tendency and faction rights within the party or practised such freedom and publicity of discussion. (Needless to add, it is only such practice of internal democracy in the party which provides the best check on, among other evils of organisation and politics, the formation of a durable political elite able to manipulate other levels of party membership).

It is important to note that it is precisely its practice of thorough-going internal democracy which enabled the Bolshevik Party to build and strengthen its links with the working class, to register and respond to its pressure from below, to learn from its experience, the real source of all theory, in discussing and formulating its economic and political policies. Along with its undoubted discipline, it was its open and democratic character and rootedness in the working class which on the one hand enabled the Bolsheviks to overcome the organisational conservatism which even the most revolutionary party inevitably develops and on the other provided their Party with necessary stability as well as flexibility to respond effectively to changing situations and mass moods at all times, absorbing the 'courage, initiative, and freedom from bureaucratic routine' that characterise the living mass movement, and expressing the party's ideas in terms which fitted the experience of those engaged in the struggle. As Trotsky was to note later: 'Lenin's strength did not lie so much in his ability to build a machine – he knew how to do that too – as in his ability at all critical moments to utilise the living energy of the masses for overcoming the limitations and the conservatism characteristic of any political machine'. (The contrast with Rosa Luxemburg's Spartacus League and its failure in Germany is obvious. As in Russia, in the German revolution too the proletariat set up workers councils or soviets after November 1918. But whereas in the Russian Revolution the question of dual power was resolved in favour of the working class, in the German Revolution it was resolved in favour of the bourgeoisie, with disastrous consequences for the future of socialism in the Soviet Union and elsewhere in the world).

VII

Even as the civil war, in depleting and dispersing the workers on the one hand and decimating the Bolshevik Party on the other, shattered the dialectical relationship between the Bolsheviks and the working class, it also led to the silencing of opposition within the party itself and a gradual withering away of its long tradition of debate and discussion within – it became first a monologue of the party with itself and then merely a dispute among leaders of the party, till Stalin forcibly or otherwise dispensed with even such disputation. (It is this together with bans on the opposition parties – recognised as undemocratic departures and declared to be only temporary measures – which strengthened the tendencies towards monolithism and bureaucratism in the political system and led to the transformation of what had hitherto been a functional bureaucratisation into a relatively stable social layer, in a position to gain a strong position in the party itself). Decisively damaging for the inner-party democracy of the Bolsheviks was the decision to ban the existence of factions within the party, taken at the 10th Party Congress in March 1921. Once again it was not a product of theory, of any principles of party organisation. On the contrary it was a desperate departure from the long-defended and long-practised principles, compelled by the Kronstadt mutiny which, occurring in the midst of the appallingly difficult economic situation resulting from the crisis of war communism, was seen as posing a threat to the very survival of the revolution and which was believed to be instigated or fuelled by 'disagreements' and factionalism in the party. As Lenin, seeking to stop his 'sick, feverish' party from tearing itself apart under the pressure of circumstances, put it:

> there should not be the slightest trace of factionalism – whatever its manifestations in the past. *That* we must not have on any account... [when there is a] tremendous preponderance of peasants in the country, when their dissatisfaction with the proletarian dictatorship is mounting, and when the demobilisation of the peasant army is setting loose hundreds and thousands of broken men who have nothing to do, whose only accustomed occupation is war and who breed banditry... The atmosphere of the controversy is becoming extremely dangerous and constitutes a direct threat to the dictatorship of the proletariat.

It needs to be noticed that the resolution prohibiting factions in the party was adopted (*i*) only after the discussion was over, the delegates had been elected on the differing platforms and majority decisions taken; (*ii*) the leader of the Workers' Opposition, Shylyapnikov, against whom the resolution was primarily directed, was not removed from his post and representatives of his position were taken into the Central Committee; (*iii*) the platform of the Workers' Opposition had appeared in the central organ of the Bolshevik Party in no fewer than 2.5 lakh copies; (*iv*) a Discussion Sheet was established so that it could provide a forum for the expression of different opinions.

Even so the ban on factions was not total nor was it permanent. Lenin made it clear that it was a temporary measure till the situation improved; for him it was an unfortunately necessary, episodic act of self-defence. When one senior Bolshevik leader tried to get the Congress to agree to a ban on separate platforms in Central Committee elections – there were no fewer than eight different platforms put forward by different groups and individuals at the 10th party Congress – Lenin replied:

> We cannot deprive the party and the members of the Central Committee of the right to appeal to the party in the event of disagreement on fundamental issues... Supposing we are faced with a question like, say, the conclusion of the Brest Peace? Can you guarantee that no such question will arise? No, you cannot. In the circumstances, the elections may have to be based on platforms.

What happened to party democracy is indeed typical of developments in this post-revolutionary period. The ban on organised factions in the party was proposed and adopted in the context of the Kronstadt mutiny as an emergency exception, a deviation from the desirable degree of democracy, justified only by the life-and-death needs of the moment. But having been adopted for this reason, like the ban on the opposition parties, it stayed and became accepted as a norm which not only served to provide a basis for the dictatorial règime of the later Stalin era and beyond, but also became a principle of communist party organisation throughout the world. Obviously such Stalinist monolithism was neither written into the original Leninist theory of organisation, nor was it in any meaningful sense inevitable. Indeed the history of Soviet politics during this period is a history of 'exceptions', of distortions regularly turning into norms, departures themselves turning into principles. A process of internal degeneration took over which deformed every concept and institution of workers' democracy, including 'dictatorship of the proletariat'. Even for Lenin, as we know, it ceased to denote a workers' state, subject to the democratic rule of the working people. It was rather reduced to a specially organised dictatorial regime, still defended or justified in terms of its revolutionary purposes and increasingly counterposed to abstract democracy, so that instead of going beyond the formal freedoms of bourgeois parliamentarism into *real* freedom which allows 'associated producers' to become their own rulers, it retreated backwards to become a single-party dictatorial regime.

VIII

Certainly, in understanding the process of authoritarian degeneration of the Bolshevik Party and the Soviet state, it needs to be recognised that the compulsions of objective circumstances were indeed overwhelming in the early period of 1918–21: the civil war and its imperatives, the massive economic dislocation, famine, physical decimation of the proletariat and the party, the increasing erosion of worker-peasant alliance, the failure of the revolution in Europe and its struggle for survival in Russia, etc. This explains and justifies, even if not in every case, the authoritarian shift in the policies pursued by Lenin and the Bolshevik Party. But the continuance and even acceleration of authoritarian degeneration in the period after the civil war cannot be similarly explained or justified. It is true, as Moshe Lewin and others have pointed out, that carried over from the earlier period, even after the civil war was won, 'the prevailing psychology was one of the struggle for existence'. There was also the questionable assumption that the threat to the 'dictatorship of the proletariat' – now increasingly identified with the dictatorship of the party – and the possibility of the capitalist restoration was even greater. This may explain but does not justify the ruthless party dictatorship which Lenin, Trotsky and the Bolsheviks continued to practise even in the post-civil war period. In other words, it will not do to explain everything away in the name of 'the compulsions of the objective situation'. The Red Terror too was a product of the civil war but it virtually disappeared soon after. But the ban on opposition parties and on factions within the party was never lifted even when it had become counter-productive. We have earlier noticed the explanations and controversies, the questions of retreat and advance on the economic front, which characterised the debate on New Economic Policy, focussed on the need of restoring the worker–peasant alliance, which was deemed essential for the construction of socialism in Russia. But there was no similar debate on the retreat and advance on the political front, focussed on the need of restoring democracy which Bolshevik theory always recognised as integral to any socialist project.

There is no doubt that inadequacies and errors of Bolshevik theory and practice in their own way contributed to this process of authoritarian degeneration of the revolution. But what is most questionable about the authoritarian measures and actions of the Bolsheviks – self-admittedly 'exceptions' and deemed to be temporary – beyond their justification as unfortunate necessity, is the occasional embellishment or rationalisation of this necessity in theoretical terms. As an effort to gain legitimacy for such measures and actions by establishing a line of continuity with the pre-October Bolshevism, such rationalisation may have something to be said for it during the civil war. But not so afterwards, during 1921–23, when in order to justify the Bolsheviks holding on to power in the name of a decimated working class and a peasant population increasingly hostile to Bolshevik rule, there was a totally unjustified attempt by Lenin (and others including Trotsky and Stalin) to provide a longer term theoretical rationale for such authoritarian practices, which in effect meant justification of a substitutionist vanguardism – the party substituting for the working class and ultimately the mass of the working people, which was never a part of the original Bolshevik scheme of things. This had very negative consequences for the future of socialism in Russia. Such theorisation, defence of 'exceptions' that were really grave distortions, by Lenin and other Bolshevik leaders was invoked repeatedly – though, again, not entirely or always without justification – by Lenin's successors to defend jacobinist notions of vanguardism, political and bureaucratic concentration of authority in the party and state, and worse, in the later period. It is here that connecting links or threads with the later fully consolidated Stalinist authoritarianism can indeed be discerned, lending substance to the charge of Lenin having himself in some degree at least prepared the ground for it. And again, it is here, in the context of bureaucratic authoritarianism later becoming an accepted structural component of Soviet socialism, of degeneracy eating into the very vitals of the Soviet party and state, that the essential relevance of Rosa Luxemburg's criticism of Lenin and certain Bolshevik practices of the period lies; though interpreted as suggestive of alternative policies during the civil war, Rosa Luxemburg's criticism was completely mistaken.

IX

As noticed earlier it has been fashionable for critics of all sorts, including ill-informed anti-Leninists on the left, all the more so after the Soviet collapse, to rope in Rosa Luxemburg in their attack on Lenin and the Bolsheviks, to present her as an opponent of Russian Revolution and turn her, a revolutionary to the depth of her being, into an anti-communist or some special kind of 'democratic' socialist, if not just another liberal polemicist against Leninism. It is important to note that Rosa Luxemburg's criticism of some of the policies of Lenin and Bolshevik government was outlined in an unfinished draft – 'The Russian Revolution' – written while in prison in 1918, in a situation of isolation and highly restricted access to information. Out of prison, during the last few months of her life before she was murdered in January 1919, with better access to information, Rosa Luxemburg changed her mind on most though not all of the issues involved. She never published or tried to publish her pamphlet in her lifetime (It was published by a former colleague Paul Levi on his own in 1922, only after he was expelled from the German Communist Party and, as Lenin wryly put it, now wanting 'to get into the good graces of the bourgeoisie').

Rosa Luxemburg had watched the unfolding revolution in Russia with great enthusiasm and, condemning the Mensheviks as 'Russian Kautskys' stood up for the Bolsheviks, their 'seizure of state power' and the strategy to consolidate it among the vast masses of the Russian peasantry as well as non-Russian nationalities. She recognised the essential greatness of the October Revolution, the world historic task the Bolsheviks had accomplished 'within the limits of historical possibilities' – 'they have contributed whatever could possibly be contributed under such devilishly hard conditions'. She saw it as her prime responsibility to defend the Russian Revolution, mobilise support for it among the German proletariat and struggle to aid and supplement it with a revolution in Germany. When she concluded her pamphlet by saying 'the future everywhere belongs to "bolshevism" ', she meant exactly that. She was alive to the context of the Bolshevik policies even as she was critical: 'They are not supposed to perform miracles. For a model and faultless proletarian revolution in an isolated land, exhausted by world war, strangled by imperialism, betrayed by the international proletariat, would be a miracle'. Again: 'It would be demanding something superhuman from Lenin and his comrades if we should expect of them that under such circumstances they should conjure forth the finest democracy, the most exemplary dictatorship of the proletariat and a flourishing socialist economy'. Again, even as she recognised the necessities of the situation, she specifically pointed out that 'there is no doubt either.... that Lenin and Trotsky... have taken many a decisive step only with the greatest inner hesitation and with most violent inner opposition', and wrote: 'Bolshevik terror is above all the expression of the weakness of the European proletariat', adding that this 'sore too can only be healed through the European revolution. And this is coming'. Finally: 'Whatever a party could offer of courage, revolutionary farsightedness and consistency in a historic hour, Lenin, Trotsky and the other comrades have given in good measure. All the revolutionary honour and capacity which western social democracy lacked was represented by the Bolsheviks. Their October uprising was not only the actual salvation of the Russian Revolution, it was also the salvation of the honour of international socialism'.

From the other end, even as he argued with or against Rosa Luxemburg and pointed out her mistakes, Lenin wrote (in 1922):

'...inspite of her mistakes she was – and remains for us – an eagle. And not only will Communists all over the world cherish her memory but her biography and her *complete* works will serve as useful manuals for training many generations of Communists all over the world'. Lenin in fact upbraided the German Party for its slowness in publishing her collected works. (Needless to add, they were not thus published even later in 'socialist' Poland or East Germany, and far from her memory being cherished, like Gramsci, Rosa Luxemburg too remained consigned into oblivion in the Soviet Union under Stalin and his successors, with little or no recognition in official Marxism).

It is within this context and framework that Rosa Luxemburg voiced her criticism and in this context alone can her criticism be properly understood. This criticism is not so much a suggestion of alternative policies as a description of what hopefully would or could have been the optimum course of action if conditions were different, with the beleaguered Russian Revolution getting better support from the German proletariat and the situation easing with an European revolution which Luxemburg believed was coming. Beyond that, along with her life and work as a whole, it has a continuing relevance as an expression of revolutionary socialism's principled commitment to democracy, and more specifically, an assertion of socialist democracy as the essential content of a 'dictatorship of the proletariat' – and thus a legacy for revolutionary socialist movement everywhere.

X

Rosa Luxemburg asserted that for the movement she belonged to 'personal opinions.... (are) sacred'; it 'demands complete freedom of conscience for every individual and the widest possible toleration for every faith and every opinion'. 'Freedom of the press... the right of assembly and of public life' are "sacred rights" of the people, the most important democratic guarantees of a healthy public life and of the political activity of the labouring masses'. As she told the Bolsheviks, 'the exclusion of democracy' cuts off 'the living sources of all spiritual riches and progress', and 'the only way to rebirth is the school of public life itself, the most unlimited, the broadest democracy and public opinion'... She pointed out that 'without general elections, without unrestricted freedom of press and assembly, without a free struggle of opinion, life dies out in every public institution, becomes a mere semblance of life, in which only the bureaucracy remains as the active element'. More specifically, she insisted: 'Freedom only for the supporters of the government, only for the members of one party – however numerous they may be – is no freedom at all. Freedom is always and exclusively freedom for the one who thinks differently. Not because of any fanatical concept of "justice" but because all that is instructive, wholesome and purifying in political freedom depends on this essential characteristic, and its effectiveness vanishes when "freedom" becomes a special privilege'. Reaffirming a most valid principle, she wrote: '...socialist democracy is not something which begins only in the promised land after the foundations of socialist economy are created; it does not come as some sort of Christmas present for the worthy people who, in the interim, have loyally supported a handful of socialist dictators.... It begins at the very moment of seizure of power by the socialist party. It [socialist democracy] is the same thing as the "dictatorship of the proletariat"', and so on.

XI

Rosa Luxemburg's critique had a directly prophetic relevance for what later went wrong in the Soviet Union when under Stalin and his successors, absence of democracy, in party, state and society, became a most grievous structural deformation of socialism as it came to be built in the Soviet Union, and, in a gross misrepresentation of Marxism, also came to be defined and defended as 'dictatorship of the proletariat'. But there was nothing in it for Lenin to disagree with as he went on to himself recognise the departures from principles he was compelled to make in practice (which he always saw as temporary in nature) or point out the mistakes Rosa Luxemburg had made in what she wrote in prison (most of which she herself corrected after she was released). Notwithstanding his departures and their unjustifiable rationalisation, the fact remains that the political culture of the Bolsheviks during Lenin's time was, as we have already seen, totally different from that of the later Stalin period. Refusing to see that Leninism under Lenin was an entirely different affair, critics have continued to trace the origins of the later-day Stalinist authoritarianism in Lenin and early Bolshevism. Part of the answer was provided, decades back, by the anti-Stalinist revolutionary Victor Serge. He has written: 'It is often said that the germ of all Stalinism was in Bolshevism at its beginning. Well, I have no objection. Only, Bolshevism also contained many other germs – a mass of other germs – and those who lived through the enthusiasm of the first years of the first victorious revolution ought not to forget it. To judge the living man by the death germs which the autopsy reveals in the corpse – and which he may have carried with him since birth – is this very sensible?'

But this is obviously not a very satisfactory answer for, as Mandel has pointed out, the judgment of what was authoritarian in 'essence' or 'tendency' in Lenin or Leninism is almost invariably based on the abusive use of the privilege of historical hindsight. Therefore what needs to be recognised is the basic fact that its overall commitment to democracy and democratic values apart, the pre-Stalinist Bolshevism presented a picture of thoroughgoing inner-party democracy, political debates of the highest quality, open disagreements between party leaders even during the height of the civil war. Thus, for example, Stalinist purges of the later period, the brutal elimination of real or perceived dissidence within the party, would be simply inconceivable for the earlier Bolshevik culture. In other words, in its highhandedness and repressiveness – the Terror, the Gulag, the purges, etc. – the Stalinist system was qualitatively different from various emergency measures, conceived as temporary and not called socialist, that the Bolsheviks (not always wisely or justly) took during the period of revolution, civil war and their aftermath. Lenin and his comrades certainly made mistakes but these were precisely that, only mistakes, a minor blemish on their long and heroic record, which were turned into a calamity under the later leadership of Stalin as he forged his system and imposed it on an obedient international movement as the undisputed model of Socialism.

To conclude, the most significant aspect of the process of overall political degeneration early in the life of Soviet socialism is the manner in which so many original ideas and institutions, concepts and principles, were crushed out of shape, discarded or distorted as a consequence of the internal and external pressure on the new state, for pressure always tends to deformation and distortion. What is more, 'temporary' measures, admittedly neither democratic nor socialist, designed to meet recurrent crises, gradually hardened into articles of faith. As Hal Draper has argued, quite often the principles were first distorted by the strain of emergency exceptions, and then the distortions were turned into principles. Departures from principles thus themselves became the principles to serve as the basis for building a most deformed form of socialism, which could be described at best only as 'actually existing socialism'.

XII

Lenin clearly saw what was happening, the political degeneration that was engulfing the Bolshevik Party and the Soviet society. He was sick and dying and did not live long enough to cope with it, but we do not need to speculate what Lenin would have done had he lived longer. The few years that Lenin survived the revolution, for whose survival he had struggled so hard, were devoted almost entirely to the struggle against the bureaucratic degeneration that was taking place all around him.

Lenin died before the actual construction of what came to be built as 'socialism' in the Soviet Union had really begun. But he was fully aware of the consequences of the isolation of revolution in backward Russia and the damage done by the civil war, the most important of which was the authoritarian and bureaucratic degeneration that had set in the Bolshevik Party and the Soviet state system, to which some of his own decisions and actions, the ad hoc and emergency exceptions, together with his forced theorisation in defence of them, had contributed. Though sick and dying and often incapacitated physically, the remaining two years of Lenin's life are a saga of struggle, however belated or unsuccessful, against this political degeneration of the October Revolution.

The legacy of Lenin during the brief post-revolutionary period that he survived the revolution, is both multifaceted and ambiguous as the Bolsheviks moved through a difficult, entirely uncharted territory. Its difficulties or ambiguities however have little to do with Lenin's peculiar character or that of his Bolshevism, or some specific, determining 'Russianness' of the situation. The decisive conditioning factors are still the compulsions of overall objective circumstances of the situation in Europe as a whole, including Russia, and the understandable but momentous 'silences' or 'empty spaces' within Marxian thought or tradition, the limited theoretical arsenal of Bolshevism itself, on issues of socialist transition. Insofar as there is a certain disintegration of the coherence of Lenin's thought in the period after the revolution, including a divergence between theory and practice, it has to be seen primarily as a consequence of the failure of his theoretical predictions – made entirely within the tradition of classical Marxism – to materialise, which isolated the Russian revolution, and in a situation entirely unprecedented for classical Marxism, forced it to rely upon its own ruined resources to survive and build. Thus it is that even as Lenin tried to fight the danger of growing bureaucratisation, he was to an extent also instrumental in undermining or preventing the emergence of social institutions or organisations, within the Party and outside it, which could have helped him in stemming the rot, though, it has to be recognised that left to themselves, to their own devices, as plans or programmes, these possible levers of regeneration within the party, in their utopianism, limited visions or narrow sectarianism, were leading, and could have only led to a further disintegration of the regime. That is how Democratic Centralists, the Left-Communists, or Workers' Opposition came to be put down, the Soviets or the trade unions were emasculated, and Lenin was left with virtually no allies when he began his somewhat belated struggle against bureaucratic degeneration of the party and the state, Nevertheless, he struggled to the last.

It needs to be clearly understood that Lenin, throughout this period, never lost sight of the original project of socialism in Russia, with its essential emancipatory thrust. For him socialism always remained not merely an economic but 'an emancipatory' project. And thus, he continuously wrestled with the problem of bureaucracy. There was his entire project of dealing with the problem through separation of party and state, through decentralisation, through a policy of granting necessary privileges to state, economic or scientific functionaries and regularly stripping them down in the interest of egalitarianism, through placing trusted revolutionaries in important state positions (in Red Army this took the form of the political commissar system), and so on. Measures were contemplated, even if not always instituted or carried out, to deal with the hostile, bourgeois character of the state and the political degeneration of the party. Throughout 1922, Lenin became increasingly scathing in his attack on the ineptitude of the party and the state apparatuses, and voiced demands for radical changes in both places, even as Stalin was emerging as the leader of bureaucracy and consolidating his control of the party as a machine rather than the effective *political* organisation Lenin had built in an earlier period. Lenin and doubtless many others in the Bolshevik leadership in these early post-revolutionary years understood what was happening to the party and in the state, but while they struggled, they lacked the power and resources to take effective counter-measures. Lenin's illness was an important factor in isolating him from the politics around him and undermining his ability to effectively intervene.

Much as he had feared, 'dictatorship of the proletariat' notwithstanding, Lenin saw revolutionary power pass from the proletariat to the Party and from the Party to its central leadership even as the Party was losing both its class character and democratic functioning. It was Lenin's consistently held view during 1921–23 that the Party had degenerated – it was contaminated by the legacy of its immediate past and by the all-pervasive petty-bourgeois environment of peasant Russia; its level of culture was too low and its expertise too ill-developed. He repeatedly noted that its supposed base, the proletariat, was virtually 'declassed' in every sense of the word, and the 'bulk of the present membership... insufficiently proletarian'. It was falling prey to careerism, to the corruption of power and privilege, patronage and personal aggrandisement, to worst forms of the old style, tsarist ways of work, red tape, high handedness and arrogance.

Lenin, as we have noted earlier, was equally clear about the problem with the newly constituted Soviet state:

> We took over the old machinery of the state, and that was our misfortune. Very often this machinery operates against us. In 1917, after we seized power, the government officials sabotaged us. This frightened us very much and we pleaded: 'Please come back.' They all came back but that was our misfortune. We now have a vast army of government employees, but lack sufficiently educated forces to exercise real control over them. In practice it often happens that here at the top, where we exercise political power, the machine functions somehow; but down below government employees have arbitrary control and they often exercise it in such a way as to counteract our measures. At the top, we have, I don't know how many, but at all events, I think, no more than a few thousand, at the outside several tens of thousands of our own people. Down below, however, there are hundreds of thousands of old officials whom we got from the Tsar and from bourgeois society and who, partly deliberately and partly unwittingly, work against us.

Central to the problem was the growing bureaucratisation of the state apparatus. Lenin recognised bureaucracy as a stratum of 'privileged persons standing above and apart from the masses' even as he found the 'throwing out' of bureaucracy far more difficult than throwing out the Tsar, the landowners or the capitalists. Indeed, shortly before his death, Lenin admitted that 'we effectively took over the old state apparatus from the Tsar and the bourgeoisie', only it had been 'smeared in red', as he had put it earlier in 1921. In a bitter comment, he wrote: 'the apparatus we call ours is in fact still quite alien to us; it is a bourgeois and Tsarist hotchpotch and there has been no possibility of getting rid of it in the course of the past five years...' Russia in the 1920s, said Lenin, was very different from the society the Bolsheviks had hoped to create in 1917. The Soviet Republic, far from being a 'continuation' of the Paris Commune it was proposed to be, was already 'a workers' state with bureaucratic distortion', a 'bureaucratised workers' state'. In such circumstances of degeneration of party and state, other grave distortions were bound to follow. Possibly the most serious of these, noticed by Lenin, was in the sphere of the Soviets' nationalities policy. Tsarist Russia was, as already noted, a 'prison-house of nations' that Lenin led the Bolsheviks into breaking open. What followed, the impulses for freedom and development that were released, constitute – despite, what happened later – a remarkable achievement of the early, heroic period of the Russian revolution. Yet Lenin was already witnessing the dangers of 'great-Russian chauvinism' emerging from within the Communist Party and state bureaucracy which compelled him to say that 'in such circumstances the "freedom to secede from the union", by which we justify ourselves, will be a mere scrap of paper, unable to defend the non-Russians from the onslaught of that really Russian man, the Great-Russian chauvinist'. Lenin denounced 'the Great-Russian chauvinist, in substance, a rascal and a tyrant, such as the typical Russian bureaucrat is'. This was the terrain of yet another battle of Lenin in his last days. So grave was the shift away from the original Leninist or Bolshevik principles here – the basis for later centralisation, repression, inequalities, etc. – that in one of his very last writings Lenin apologised to the workers of Russia for failing to act decisively on the nationalities question.

Incidentally, the major culprit here was the Georgian Stalin whom Lenin publicly denounced for his 'great-Russian chauvinism', even calling him a 'great-Russian gendarme'. Not only that. Lenin saw the bureaucratic degeneration manifested in the personality and practices of Stalin who was already emerging as the central leader of party and state bureaucracy. Lenin was also concerned over the growing conflict between Stalin and Trotsky and warned the party about it. It was, he said, a trifle but 'a trifle as may acquire a decisive significance'. Lenin's grasp of men and politics was superior to others and as a historical materialist he did not underestimate the significance of individual in large historical processes. So great was Lenin's alarm over all this that, as he lay ill and dying, in what has come to be known as his Last Testament – a carefully phrased statement that looked beyond personal conflicts or immediate concerns – Lenin recommended Stalin's removal from power, from the post of Secretary-General of the Party. He wrote: 'Stalin is too rude, and this defect ... becomes intolerable in a general secretary.... I suggest that the comrades think about a way of removing Stalin from that post and appointing another man (who is)...more tolerant, more loyal, more polite, and more considerate to the comrades, less capricious, etc...' Lenin wanted to have someone else as his deputy or as secretary of the Party. Trotsky was a possible choice, but he allowed himself to be outmanoeuvred; he preferred to avoid confrontation with Stalin. (After Lenin's death, he even agreed that Lenin's Last Testament need not be published.) As Roy Madvedev has put it, in the conflict with Stalin 'Trotsky simply opted out'. In any case, with Lenin ill and isolated, it was perhaps already too late. The full immensity of the consequences is only too visible today.

Painfully aware of the dangers that bureaucratic degeneration and authoritarian involution of Soviet state and society posed for the future of socialism in Russia, Lenin yet never lost sight of his original, emancipatory and libertarian vision of socialism in Russia. In his last writings there is a desperate return to the anti-statist theme of *State and Revolution*, and 'a society of free cooperators' is a phrase that comes up with increasing frequency in his works of this period. Even as he attacks the autonomy and arrogance of the new Soviet bureaucracy, he cries out that it is cultural revolution, education, civilisation, socialist training and popular participation and control, indeed 'all the riches which mankind has created' which are needed, more than anything else, for a socialist transition in Russia. Lenin's concern with the question of the machinery of state, which he described as 'deplorable, not to say disgusting', grew almost to the point of becoming an obsession with him during his last days. It is to this that he devoted all the energies of his remaining years. But he could see or find no adequate or effective answer to this question.

XIII

Lenin clearly recognised, international isolation apart, the shrinking internal social base of revolution and the hoped-for socialist project. The sphere of self-activity which, with the October Revolution, had begun by embracing the people as a whole had shrunk and virtually disappeared. Proletariat itself, decimated and demoralised, was dislodged from its class groove and historical mission, and had lost the support of the peasantry. Party, badly mauled by civil war, acting as a proxy for the exhausted and scattered proletariat, was itself a mere drop in the ocean of the people as Lenin repeatedly reminded his comrades. Moreover it had degenerated and fallen prey to the traditions of the old bureaucracy. All initiative and self-activity had thus moved from mass to class, to a degenerating party which was no longer equal to its tasks. On the other hand 'rotten bureaucracy', as Lenin called it, had grown, enormous in numbers and very powerful. In another of his bitter comments of the period, deploring that 'we don't know how to conduct a public trial for rotten bureaucracy', Lenin wrote of the 'stinking bureaucratic and Soviet bourgeois atmosphere' and warned: 'for this, all of us... should be hung on stinking ropes... and I have not yet lost all hope that one day we shall be hung for this, *and* deservedly so'.

In such a situation, in the absence of free press, free Soviets or trade unions, other political parties or independent non-party organisations, or even rival factions within the Party, when all other avenues were closed to him (some of them closed by himself in defending the revolution), Lenin made one last effort to salvage something at least of his initial vision of socialism. He looked for a carefully chosen small band of men, the most dedicated and resolute, far-seeing and determined men, unsullied by corruption or thoughts of personal gain and endowed with superordinate powers to assume the mantle of the guardians of the socialist cause, that is, to oversee, supervise, control and hold to account power-holders in the state and the party, at all levels, in all localities. He sought to rally all the sound or exemplary forces in the Party and the administration to create an embryo out of which the self-administration of the peasants and workers might yet develop.

A People's Commissariat for State Control established in 1919, transformed a year later into the Workers' and Peasants'

Inspectorate (Rabkrin), was to be revitalised as the state-body created to combat bureaucracy and corruption in the state apparatus. In 1921, as part of Lenin's last desperate effort to save the soul of socialism in Russia, a Central Control Commission was set up within the Communist Party which fused with Rabkrin was to perform a similar function with respect to the party apparatus. The methods visualised or adopted to check bureaucratic abuse of power were specially characteristic of Lenin's approach. Thus, for example, local control commissions held public meetings open to Communists and non-Communists alike, at which the conduct of all members of the Party, from the highest to lowest, was submitted to searching examination. Those found guilty of misdeeds could be rebuked or, in extreme cases, expelled from the Party. The idea was that the people should have the power not to accept or reject the dictatorship of the Party as such, but to control the behaviour of the particular people who ruled in the name of the Party or the Soviet state. Even Lenin's jacobinism had at its heart the principle of direct democratic check on the rulers by the people.

As earlier during the civil war, so later, under Stalin's leadership, Rabkrin was not at all effective. It did not escape the fate of other government agencies, becoming merely one branch of the bureaucracy pitted against others. In that truly remarkable last essay he ever wrote ('Better Fewer, But Better'), noting that Rabkrin 'does not at present enjoy the slightest authority' Lenin felt obliged to denounce it in the strongest terms. Nor was the Control Commission any more effective. In fact in later years it was turned into the opposite of an organ of popular control and became instead an instrument of the Stalinist purges. Aware of what was happening, Lenin would still not give up. As E.H. Carr has reported, towards the end of 1922, repeatedly expressing 'his horror and fear of the growth of bureaucracy in the Soviet apparatus', Lenin proposed 'a block against bureaucracy in general and against the Orgbureau' (i.e. the party organisation). And then illness finally struck him down. With Lenin's departure from the political scene, and death soon afterwards, the road was more or less clear for Stalin to use the Soviet state power to build socialism as he understood it. And the Party involved in the task was no longer the Party of Lenin. Within a few years it was moulded into a party of another kind, Stalinist party, which became the model for communist parties elsewhere so that whatever be their undoubted contribution to the socialist cause, when in power the consequences have been generally disastrous.

It is interesting to speculate on what further Lenin might have done to remedy the situation if he had lived and been able to resume active leadership of the party and the state in the Soviet Union. But there is sufficient indication in E.H. Carr's summing up of Lenin's final position. He has written: 'If Lenin was driven by practical necessities to recognise a constantly growing concentration of authority, there is no evidence that he wavered in his belief in the antidote of "direct democracy"'.

XIV

I would like to digress here to take note of one related aspect of the experience in China where three decades after 1917, history's 'trick' on the doctrine of Karl Marx produced, now under Mao Tse-tung's leadership, yet another Marxist-led revolution in a backward country – a country even more backward economically and socio-culturally than Tsarist Russia – confronting it with similar problems of socialist transition off its own resources. (The Russian model, if not a hindrance was not of much help either, and early Soviet assistance, however ambiguously helpful initially, when later withdrawn as an act of great power chauvinism, had only grave distorting and disruptive consequences). Many were the accomplishments of Mao Tse-tung as one of history's greatest revolutionary figures – in the realms of thought, military strategy and tactics, and political leadership. But in a long-term historical perspective, possibly the most significant contribution lay in his understanding of and the emphasis on the need of constant struggle against the recurring danger of degeneration in a revolutionary party, not only in the pre-revolutionary phase but far more importantly, after the revolution, when it comes to power.

Like Lenin after the October Revolution, Mao was fully aware of the difficult, near-impossible tasks facing the Chinese Revolution. This is how he put it most explicitly as the People's Liberation Army was about to win its final victories in March of 1949:

> To win country-wide victory is only the first step in a long march of ten thousand *li*. Even if this step is worthy of pride, it is comparatively tiny; what will be more worthy of pride is yet to come. After several decades, the victory of the Chinese people's democratic revolution, viewed in retrospect, will seem like only a brief prologue in a long drama. A drama begins with a prologue, but the prologue is not the climax. The Chinese revolution is great, but the road after the revolution will be longer, the work greater and more arduous.

Mao was already warning not merely of the economic difficulties ahead but also that revolutionaries who had not been conquered by enemies with guns might succumb to sugar-coated bullets, the temptations that come with status and privilege that being in power confers.

'Learning from the Soviet Union', which was a cardinal principle in China in the first years after the takeover of power in 1949, naturally meant copying the Soviet model's central strategy of economic development, though the Chinese soon discovered that it put demands on the agricultural sector which could not be met and which threatened the alliance between workers and peasants, as essential for the construction of socialism in China as it was in the Soviet Union (where it came to be later destroyed with disastrous consequences for that country's socialist enterprise). And in a significant shift of policy, China under Mao, putting emphasis on the peasantry and industry associated with the peasantry, opted for the principle of 'walking on two legs'. However, of immediate interest to our argument is the fact that the revolutionary regime in underdeveloped China faced the same developmental problems as the Bolsheviks in the 1920s, and in trying to solve these problems was beginning to spawn similar political and economic bureaucracies, which tended to evolve in the same way as their Soviet counterparts did before them. Bureaucratic and elitist practices were permeating all sections of Chinese society, including its economy and politics and political system as a whole. These were very much in the tradition of age-old Confucian habits of thought and action and hence were easily assimilated by those newly in authority.

Mao's truly significant achievement was the effort, regardless of its ultimate outcome, not only to break away from what may be called the tyranny of the Soviet model and seek to pioneer a somewhat different road to construction of socialism, but, as a part of this pioneering exercise, confront this problem of bureaucratic degeneration of socialist revolution.

It is not necessary to review the history of what later came to be known as the 'two-line struggle' in the Chinese Communist Party in the period between 1949 and the Cultural Revolution, which can even be traced back to inner-party struggles of the long pre-revolutionary period of the Communist Party. It would suffice to focus on the fact that the issue now was the shape of the new order being built in China, with Liu Shao-chi and others opting for the Soviet model and all that went with it and the Maoists struggling for a different path that sought to deepen the revolution in the direction of greater equality and fuller participation by the masses in controlling and managing their own lives. Most significant here was Mao's understanding and analysis of the problem of contradictions, and therefore of classes and class struggle, in post-revolutionary society. As Lange has pointed out, 'it has been the merit of Mao Tse-tung to have recalled with emphasis (that) socialist society too develops through contradictions'. Mao's awareness of this problem in China was certainly sharpened by his critical assessment of the experience of October Revolution and its outcome in Russia. He survived the revolution longer than Lenin, though not long enough, and saw more clearly than any other revolutionary Marxist leader before him the process of post-revolutionary class formations and therefore the paramount importance of a *comprehensive* class struggle during the period of transition to socialism. Mao's innovative Marxist thinking has important implications for not only understanding what ultimately happened in Russia or China but all revolutionary processes of the future.

After the revolutionary overthrow of an old bourgeois or bourgeois-feudal regime, the old exploiting classes continue to exist, resist and counter-attack in various ways; they have to be fought to the end, the class struggle continues. Even more important is the fact that the ideas, values and habits of thought and behaviour of the old ruling classes continue to persist, embedded in all strata of society, including intelligentsia and even revolutionary leadership. As Marx expressed it, 'the tradition of all the dead generations weighs like a nightmare on the brain of the living'. Changing all this through revolutionising practice on the part of the revolutionary leadership and the working people was recognised by Mao as the central problem of the transition to socialism. The struggle, really a cultural revolution to change human beings, was also for Mao in a very real sense class struggle, more important and difficult than overthrowing the old classes, nationalising property, building heavy industry or raising material living standards of the people, important or difficult though all these things are. But even more specifically innovative was Mao's understanding that administrators, managers, technicians, experts of various kinds, together with political leaders required for running a post-revolutionary society, especially a backward one, having, necessarily as it were, higher incomes and the ability to dispose over substantial perquisites and power, soon develop a vested interest in maintaining them and helped by conservative, even counter-revolutionary, ideological inheritance tend to become a ruling (and exploiting) class. It was not merely a question of bureaucracy, to be reformed from within as Lenin tried, who despite his deep abhorrence for it saw it as a necessary, even if transient evil to be checked and controlled and made more socially responsible – 'you cannot "throw out" the bureaucracy in a peasant country... You can only reduce it by slow and stubborn effort... for many years to come'. It was the question of a class that needed to be eliminated altogether to achieve a genuinely non-exploitative classless society. In other words, the class enemy to be struggled against in the post-revolutionary society is not only the old ruling classes with their old ideas, habits, etc., or seemingly transitory new managerial or bureaucratic strata or elites still subject to old ideas and habits, but it could well be new ruling and exploiting classes produced (and incessantly reproduced) by the social formation which had emerged from the revolution itself. This struggle obviously has to be a class struggle in the fullest possible sense of the term.

Paul Sweezy has well summed up this particular contribution of Mao and its implications. Revolution, he has argued, does not constitute, as is generally believed, a decisive turning point, after which progress, however slow and painful, involves overcoming the terrible heritage of the past and could only be in the direction of the higher stage of communism of which Marx wrote in his *Critique of the Gotha Programme*. On the contrary,

> post-revolutionary society contains not only contradictions inherited from millennia of class-driven society, but it produces and reproduces its own contradictions. The revolution provides no final solutions. It only opens the possibility of moving forward *in the direction* of eliminating classes. But the existence of this as a possibility implies its opposite, the possibility of moving backward towards the re-entrenchment of an exploiting class based not on private property in the means of production but on control of an all-encompassing repressive state apparatus.

According to Maoist understanding this is precisely what happened in the Soviet Union.

As mentioned above, no one understood this process of post-revolutionary class formation better than Mao Tse-tung. In 1968 Mao told the French writer Andre Malraux: 'Humanity left to its own devices does not necessarily restore capitalism... but it does re-establish inequality. The forces tending towards the creation of new classes are powerful'. For this very reason he saw the effective overthrow of capitalism as occurring over a long period of time, even centuries, with all sorts of ups and downs, reversals and even capitalist restorations. He wrote:

> Socialist society covers a considerably long historical period. It constitutes the revolutionary period of transformation from capitalist society to communist society... In the historical period of socialism, there are still classes, class contradictions and class struggle; there is the struggle between the socialist road and the capitalist road; and there is the danger of capitalist restoration.

> We must recognise the protracted and complex nature of this struggle...

In China itself Mao had the insight and the courage to expose the ongoing antagonistic class struggle at the very core of the Communist Party. He saw the possibility of capitalist restoration taking place essentially through the agency of capitalist roaders within the party and he fought them to the best of his ability. To pre-empt such a possibility was at the heart of his many intra-party struggles, rectification campaigns, etc. within the Chinese Communist Party after 1949. Mao insisted that the party itself is only an instrument involved in, but not dominating, the dialectical process of continuous revolution, that the party does not stand outside the revolutionary process with foreknowledge of its laws, that 'for people to know the laws they must go through a process. The vanguard is no exception'. Revolution, he argued, could only be saved by mobilising the mass of the people, the real creators of history, to take on and to rectify the party. Even earlier Mao had regularly stressed that there can be no successful guerrilla army seeking political power which does not fully mobilise the masses through simultaneous economic, political and cultural strategies. And now, emphasising the uninterrupted character of the revolutionary process, he attacked commandism and bureaucracy and called for 'the mass line', for respect for the initiative of the masses, for their critical and creative input on a regular, and often a daily basis – a call which well tied up with the best in the revolutionary Marxist tradition, with Marx's political–educational work among the working classes and emphasis on revolutionising practice, Lenin's direct appeal to people and their 'collective experience', and Rosa Luxemburg's concern for a mass line approach in order to sustain the revolutionary character of any socialist enterprise, be it a movement, organisation or social reconstruction. With an eye to the Soviet Union, Mao warned, in 1961–62, against a situation where 'the state is to be managed by only a section of the people, (or) that the people can enjoy labour rights, education rights, social insurance, etc. only under the management of certain people'. A couple of years later, in the Sino-Soviet ideological controversy, the existence of 'vested interest groups', 'a privileged stratum' in the Soviet Union was clearly recognised as essentially a 'new bourgeois element' whose interests could finally lead to a 'capitalist restoration' there. It could happen in China too. As Mao commented, if 'the cadres were to be corrupted and demoralised, then it would not take long, perhaps only several years or a decade or several decades, at most, before a counter-revolutionary restoration on a national scale inevitably occurred and the whole of China would change its colour'.

Mao's answer to this threatening possibility was 'the mass line'. The Maoist phrase 'from the masses to the masses' was, as Gurley has put it, 'a method of involving the masses in policy formation'. Like Lenin, Mao never lost sight of socialism as an emancipatory project and insisted that it is necessary at each stage of development to keep the final objective in mind. And in order not to lose sight of the final objective, he all the time argued for greater equality in society, particularly between workers and peasants, and for greater mass participation.

At the centre of the ideological struggle as it developed in China was the issue of base and superstructure, of the contradiction, as Mao's opponents, proponents of the Soviet model put it, 'between advanced social relations and backward productive forces'; hence the major task is to 'develop the productive forces'. 'The revolution is over', they said, 'let's get on with production'. But Mao saw the relation in both cases as not one-sided or mechanical but dialectical and intricate and urged the revolutionisation of the superstructure in order to change the material basis of society, and egalitarianism in social productive relations to ensure against the emergence of new bourgeois elements which may lead to capitalist restoration. That is how he argued for 'grasping revolution and promoting production'. Against Liu Shao-chi and others who wanted economics or technique in command, Mao insisted on putting 'politics (or class struggle) in command', which has nothing to do with any facile 'voluntarism' but is the essential principle of any socialist transition where, by definition, not economics, not market, capitalist or any other, but revolutionary politics commands economy and its production processes and the central objective is changing of human beings and relations among them. A socialist economy above all demands *socialist* relations of production. That is why Mao warned: 'If our country does not establish a *socialist* economy, the dictatorship of the proletariat will be transformed into a bourgeois dictatorship, into a reactionary fascist type of dictatorship'.

As the Chinese revolution progressed, Mao noticed its bureaucratic and capitalistic degeneration, the formation of a new Mandarinate in the party and the state, the Communist Party itself becoming the crucible of a new bourgeoisie. He was deeply disturbed by the regression he saw taking place all around him – weakening of the rural collectives, enlargement of private plots, reopening of market fairs, piece-work rates and bonuses in the factories, etc., etc. Agitated by the emergence of an ever more aloof and self-indulgent bureaucracy, he chastised cadres who feared the masses and curbed their activism, and denounced the authoritarian first secretaries as tyrants. Castigating the bureaucracy, he wrote: 'The bureaucratic class is a class in sharp opposition to the working class and the poor and lower middle peasants. How can these people who have become or are in the process of becoming bourgeois elements sucking the blood of the workers be recognized for what they are? These people are the objects of the struggle....' Mao struggled against all this but his efforts fell short of their purpose, they could not prevent the growing bureaucratisation or the rise of 'capitalist roaders' in the Party. His first initiatives in this regard, such as the Socialist Education and Four Cleans campaigns, were softened and reshaped by Liu Shao-chi and the bureaucracy, and achieved little. Failing again and again, like Lenin before him, but now on a massive scale, he sought direct people's intervention to purge and control the governing apparatuses in China. Mao sought a 'cultural revolution' in the country. The term itself came from Lenin; but while Russians in the post-Lenin period, interpreted it instrumentally as education of the masses in cultural values, etc., Mao, more correctly assumed that what Lenin had meant was the wholesale involvement of the working people in the ongoing political processes and socio-economic development, a truly creative appropriation by the masses of cultural leadership. (The intellectual premises of the assumption that Lenin and Mao shared can be traced back to *Grundrisse* of Karl Marx). It is thus that, in the significant historical context of the worldwide revolutionary ferment of the 1960s, Mao made his last desperate bid, the 'Great Proletarian Cultural Revolution' with its call 'to struggle against and overthrow those persons in authority who are taking the capitalist road'. He told the party members and the people 'It is justified to Rebel' and asked them to 'Bombard the Headquarters'. It is characteristic of Mao that he saw this struggle as a very prolonged one. At the very height of the Cultural Revolution, in 1967, he said:

> The present Great Proletarian Cultural Revolution is only the first of its kind. In the future more such revolutions must take place... The issue of who will win in the revolution can only be settled over a long historical period. If things are not properly handled, it is possible for a capitalist restoration to take place at any time... Let no one in the Party or among the people in our country think that everything will be all right after one or two cultural revolutions, or three or four. We must pay close attention, and we must not relax our vigilance.

The Cultural Revolution was launched in 1966 specifically aimed at 'those in the Party who are in authority and are taking the capitalist road'. Mao's perspicacity lay in recognising that the antagonistic contradiction blocking socialist construction lay inside the Party. And the method he chose to resolve it was truly astonishing and unprecedented. He chose to wage his struggle not through political intrigue and manoeuvring but through a massive mobilisation of people, within the party and outside, inviting them to 'bombard the headquarters' and rectify the party from below, to confront power holders, particularly capitalist roaders, to overthrow the traditional hierarchy, and to build a new government structure starting with revolutionary committees composed of citizens, cadres and soldiers. As with Lenin earlier, the guidance once again came from the Paris Commune. As the basic decision on the Cultural Revolution said: "It is necessary to institute a system of general elections, like that of the Paris Commune, for electing members to the cultural revolutionary groups and committees and delegates to the cultural and revolutionary congresses...' It gave people the right of recall, a Paris Commune principle. And the vanguard party was to lose its monopoly of authority. The emerging cultural revolutionary groups, committees and congresses were to be 'permanent standing mass organisations', 'organs of power of the cultural revolution'. In Mao's words 'a wholly new form of state structure' was to be devised. The Cultural Revolution simultaneously sought a change in the cultural values of people towards a radically egalitarian ethics and introduction of a new political system empowering the masses.

The Cultural Revolution swept through China like a storm, evoking idealism of the youth, popular participation in politics and support for Marxist ideas and ideals of democracy, manifested in such phenomenon as the embryonic emergence of the Shanghai Commune. But soon Mao lost control over of this massive upheaval and things went awfully awry. There was sabotage from within by his opponents – the counter effort of the establishment under attack was able to delay, divert, misdirect, or carry to absurd extremes every initiative from Mao's side. Lacking an effective organised basis, the cultural revolution itself went off the rails. It degenerated into excesses of intellectual nihilism, rampages of destruction of all so-called 'olds', mindless xenophobia and brutal persecutions; in contradiction to the declared goal of extending democracy, there was increasing Maoist commandism in the movement; the political intervention from below, intended to counteract party and government bureaucratisation, gave way to subjection of the people to mindless recitation of officially sanctioned slogans and 'quotations' that could only dull their political senses; the PLA published the *Little Red Book* and other Mao glorifications in millions of copies and pushed the quasi-religious cult of Mao, who became the Great Helmsman and the Reddest Sun in Our Hearts as well as the greatest Marxist-Leninist of our times; far from creating a new democratic form of government the movement bogged down in unprincipled power struggle and factional strife that exhausted everyone and led nowhere. Mao's own authoritarian and other errors contributing, all this had long-term devastating consequences for China's material as well as spiritual and intellectual life.

Mao saw the anarchic 'turmoil', 'the havoc' around him but had no means to rectify the situation. He yet talked of 'the road we still have to travel', of more cultural revolutions in future but was helpless in salvaging the one he had initiated. As Mao lost control, temporised and even retreated, the weakened and humiliated establishment asserted its necessity and justification; the bureaucracy went on to redefine 'party consolidation' as the goal of Cultural Revolution and the PLA, busy restoring order, redefined the goal of Cultural Revolution as simply to 'study Mao Tse-tung Thought', in effect discouraging any action on it. The revolutionary effort and élan that characterised its early period were never recovered, though Cultural Revolution is officially supposed to have lasted ten years, a 'decade of turmoil', as they later called it. At the end of it all, Mao's last desperate effort to stem the capitalistic and bureaucratic degeneration of the Chinese revolution too failed, succumbing as much to its inherent limitations and the momentous, even tragic, inadequacies of a Marxist theory of socialist transition as to the logic of Chinese backwardness and the attraction of the Soviet model. The failure of the Cultural Revolution laid the groundwork for 'a great reversal' of policy in all fields. It left the road clear to 'market-Stalinism' of Deng Xiaoping and the rest.

The Cultural Revolution failed. Mao himself when he launched it knew well that it might fail; he had on more than one occasion said that it might take more than one, perhaps even many, cultural revolutions before China would become a socialist society. Even as he accepted the failure of the first one, Mao continued to struggle for a number of specific left initiatives. Late in life, he again seized on the idea that the bureaucracy was the new ruling class, but, crippled by amyotrophic lateral sclerosis and hemmed in politically, he could do nothing about it. In 1975 he wrote a poem to the dying Zhou Enlai which concluded:

The struggle tires us,

and our hair is grey,
You and I, old friend,
can we just watch our efforts being washed away?

It has been fashionable with critics to focus, one-sidedly, on the failure of the Cultural Revolution, on its chaos and turmoil, its devastation, destruction and stupidities, and 'Mao's personal dictatorship'. Literally every aspect of the Cultural Revolution is condemned. Sympathetic ones have questioned its absence of preparation and well-thought out programmes, the lack of institutions to carry it through. One does not have to deny the validity of such criticism or defend everything that happened during the Cultural Revolution to point out its positive aspects and valuable principles underlying it: a different view of development of socialism (from that of the Soviet Union) and reaffirmation of fundamental socialist ideals like egalitarianism; that building an alternative to capitalism is a matter of long, very long struggle and socialism is about not production forces but production relations; the idea of 'politics in command', that is people, *their* politics has to be in command for building socialism; an unprecedented assertion of democracy – even though authoritarianism was in control, the idea that people can *thus* speak up against their leaders, challenge and question them, was indeed a new thing altogether, and so on – these are issues of vital importance as people continue or renew their struggle for socialism. And central to it all was the key issue that lay at the very heart of the Cultural Revolution, the degeneration of revolutionary leaders when they come to power and the need for democratic checks and correction. Maurice Meisner has well observed:

> The Cultural Revolution raised profoundly important questions about the means and ends of socialism in the twentieth-century.... At no time in world history have the consequences of the transformation of revolutionaries into rulers been exposed so clearly.... Rarely has there been so searching an inquiry into the sources of inequality, elitism, hierarchy, and bureaucracy.

XV

Lenin's or Mao's struggle against the emergent bureaucratic

oligarchies or capitalist roaders in the party and the state, that can well arise even behind a Marxist-Leninist facade, their struggle to save the vision of socialism they had for their countries indeed failed. But even in its failure, their struggle remains a part of our collective legacy, bound up with the fate of socialism in future. Their struggle opened up problems and perspectives that retain their relevance for us. Mao, it may be repeated, saw farther and delved more deeply than any one before him into this particularly important problem of a socialist transition – which has also been a necessary but questionable aspect of the dialectics of human and societal development so far. Mao's analysis went to the very heart of the problem that revolutionaries in a post-revolutionary society face. Along with this analysis it is important to recognise the essential principle that lay behind Lenin's struggle or Mao's Cultural Revolution: a resort to 'direct democracy' to combat such degeneration of the revolution. It remains a vital guide for revolutionaries of the future. Capitalism may be universal today. But it is also now a totally destructive force, wholly incapable of meeting the long-term survival needs of either the human species or its natural habitat. Therefore, in the years to come, new waves of revolution are inevitable, and where there is revolution, the need for a Leninist struggle against bureaucracy and Mao's cultural revolution will follow, vindicating the historic significance of the struggle that Lenin and Mao waged.

However, in thus assessing the historic significance of this struggle, the continuing validity of the accompanying analysis and the principle espoused, it also needs to be recognised that the problems involved are much too complex to be solved by resort to either revolutionary Jacobinism or anarchist popular intervention. Obviously it is impossible to institutionalise such 'solutions'. Of course direct people's intervention to counter the emergent deformations remains the basic principle. But what is required is an early institutionalisation of the modes of popular action or intervention – this is central to any adequate solution to the problem of emergence of bureaucratic oligarchies or capitalist roaders. It could be argued that, stray suggestions apart, the problem was not even theorised adequately by Lenin or Mao in Marxist terms, in terms of a theory of democratic institutionalisation of political arrangements in the period of socialist transition. In his initial bid for a commune-type democracy, Lenin was, like the Paris Communards, directly storming the gates of heaven rather than building a pathway to the portals; he did not visualise that, as in other spheres, well institutionalised transitional political arrangements would be necessary. Indeed he was later to admit this as part of his error in October 1917 and in the months thereafter. Similarly periodic mass campaigns of criticism, mass mobilisation by a charismatic leader, that a cultural revolution visualised, is too dependent on the leadership itself to provide a good solution to the problem of oligarchy formation – and even a leadership of the status of Mao failed. Such revolutions, or revolutionary Jacobinism, may sometimes be necessary but an institutionalisation of popular participation and intervention is the real need – an institutionalised democratic political system, a democratically controlled socialist government, so controlled by workers and peasants, is imperative for any socialist transition, for keeping the revolution going steady on its socialist course. Nevertheless, by the very nature of their last desperate efforts, the solutions they attempted and the argument around them, Lenin and Mao had in their own way focussed on the key issue: the need for a genuine empowering of the people, which alone could be an effective check on the men in authority in order to ensure a responsible exercise of power. Always necessary, it was even more so during the period of a socialist transition, an uncharted territory where no 'laws of economics' but politics commands, where, even with a more adequate theory, the only real guide is the people, their own experience. In other words a socialist transition demands the fullest possible freedom and democracy for the working people.

XVI

This is the vital truth that Rosa Luxemburg underlined in her criticism of the Bolsheviks that we have noticed above. Not that Lenin was not aware of it. The issue, however, is important enough for a return to Rosa Luxemburg before I conclude the argument with a return to Lenin.

Rosa Luxemburg, as noticed earlier, stood in solidarity with the Bolsheviks in their seizure of power in October 1917, saw them 'as an example' and hailed them for having 'dared' and saved 'the honour of international socialism', even as she warned them against making a virtue of necessity in offering the circumstances-dictated limitations or peculiarities of the Russian Revolution as an example for the movement at large, and further argued – as the Bolsheviks well knew – that so far as realisation of socialism is concerned, 'in Russia the problem could only be posed but not solved, because it can only be solved internationally'. She criticised certain practices of the Bolsheviks even as she recognised them as 'distortions' or 'false steps' 'forced upon them by necessity', products 'in the last analysis... of the bankruptcy of international socialism in the present World War', including 'the failure of the German proletariat', and accepted that 'elementary conceptions of socialist politics and an insight into their historically necessary prerequisites force us to understand that under such fatal conditions (as the Bolsheviks faced) even the most gigantic idealism and the most storm-tested revolutionary army are incapable of realising democracy and socialism but only distorted attempts at either....' It is also the case that unlike the Bolsheviks she never had to make or save a revolution and her Spartacus League failed miserably when called upon to defend one in Germany at the end of 1918; and the freedom and democracy she advocated was simply impossible as an appropriate policy in the specially chaotic conditions, the 'devilishly hard conditions' as she herself called them, that followed immediately after the Bolsheviks seized power. Nevertheless Rosa Luxemburg was right in asserting the need to stick to socialist principles for the sake of revolution and in order to show an example and prepare the ground for coming generations and revolutionaries of the future. And it is certainly incontrovertible that once the soviet society had regained relative calm and stability a few years later, these socialist principles could surely be put in practice – when unfortunately, undemocratic practices justified by the exigencies of the earlier phase, became a permanent feature of the new society.

Pleading for the 'active, untrammelled, energetic political life of the broadest masses of the people', for reliance on their 'idealism and social activity', Rosa Luxemburg had specifically warned:

> With the repression of political life in the land as a whole, life in the soviets must also become more and more crippled. Without general elections, without unrestricted freedom of the press and assembly, without a free struggle of opinion, life dies out in every public institution, becomes a mere semblance of life, in which only the bureaucracy remains as the active element. Public life gradually falls asleep, a few dozen party leaders of inexhaustible energy and boundless experience direct and rule. Among them, in reality only a dozen outstanding heads do the leading and an elite of the working class is invited from time to time to meetings, where they are to applaud the speeches of the leaders, and to approve proposed resolutions unanimously – at bottom, then, a clique affair – a dictatorship, to be sure, not the dictatorship of the proletariat, however, but a dictatorship of a handful of politicians....

Reinforcing this warning was another equally if not more basic consideration. 'The communist revolution', Marx had said, 'is the most radical rupture with traditional property relations'. It seeks to abolish all private property-based exploitation and all classes, whereas earlier revolutions were against and for different forms of private property, with new classes replacing the old and subjecting the society at large to their own conditions of property-based exploitative appropriation. And as Trotsky put it, October Revolution had 'penetrated deeper than any of its predecessors into the holy of holies of society – into its property relations'. However the more important fact to be noted here is that earlier, new class systems, class modes of production and appropriation grew *within* the old order, the new classes had 'their already acquired status' within it before they went on to acquire dominance. But it is different with socialism. Capitalism indeed prepares the conditions for socialism, but there is no development of socialist mode of production and appropriation *within* capitalism. It follows only *after* the socialist revolution. And this is the task that the Bolsheviks were called upon to carry out, for the first time, alone, in their most backward country and in a most hostile environment. This situation had its own unprecedented problems, which Lenin recognised as did Rosa Luxemburg too.

Knowing that so far as 'a thousand questions' pertaining to capitalism are concerned, Marx had provided the answers, this is how Rosa Luxemburg, still speaking to the Russian Revolution, summed up the situation, the real question and its answer for those travelling the uncharted road to socialism:

> We know more or less what we must eliminate at the outset in order to free the road for a socialist economy. But when it comes to the nature of the thousand concrete practical measures, large and small, necessary to introduce socialist principles into economy, law and all social relationships, there is no key in any textbook. That is not a shortcoming but rather the thing that makes scientific socialism superior to the utopian variants. The socialist system of society should only be, and can only be, an historical product, born out of the school of its own experience, born in the course of its realization, as a result of the developments of living history... The negative, the tearing down can be decreed; the building up, the positive cannot. New territory. A thousand problems. Experience alone is capable of correcting and opening new ways. Only unobstructed, effervescent life falls into a thousand new forms and improvisations, brings to light creative force, itself corrects all mistaken attempts. The public life of all countries with limited freedom is so poverty-stricken, so miserable, so rigid, so sterile, precisely because through the exclusion of democracy, it cuts off the living sources of all spiritual wealth and progress...

Building socialism, said Rosa Luxemburg, is something which 'the whole mass of the people must take part in'.

XVII

This is also how Lenin thought. Rosa Luxemburg herself, even as she was critical of some of his emergency measures, recognised: 'No one knows this better than Lenin'. For the simple reason that Lenin never lost sight of socialism as an emancipatory project. We have noticed his earlier commitment to democracy and its fantastic, unparalleled affirmation in the immediate aftermath of the October Revolution. And as he struggled to save his project to the very last, he told the

Communists: 'In the sea of the people we are after all but a drop in the ocean, we can administer only when we express correctly what the people are conscious of. Unless we do this, the communist party will not lead the proletariat, the proletariat will not lead the masses, and the whole machine will collapse'. Again: 'our administration and our politics rest on the ability of the entire vanguard to maintain contact with the entire mass of the proletariat and the entire mass of the peasantry...' Disclaiming all 'handbooks' or any other guide, he pointed out that 'socialism cannot come into being through orders given from above' and, more specifically, wrote: 'the forms of transformation and the rapidity of the development of the concrete reorganisation we could not know. Only collective experience, only the experience of millions can give decisive indications in this respect.' He repeatedly insisted: 'living creative socialism is the work of the creative masses themselves.'

This obviously demanded, as already suggested, freedom and democracy for these masses – thus alone they could help find 'a thousand solutions' to 'a thousand problems' of the world's first attempt at transition to socialism, thus alone could socialism in Russia have been a 'living creative socialism', 'the work of creative masses themselves'. The grounds for Lenin's or Rosa Luxemburg's optimism here were not very different from those of Marx or Engels before them, or Mao, Ho Chi Minh, Gramsci or Che Guevara after them, or of the countless martyrs of the world communist or revolutionary socialist movement. They lay in the reliance on the creativity of the vast masses of human beings. But then freedom and democracy in the Soviet Union decayed and perished all too soon and was never regained. One does not have to deny either the continuing momentum of the October Revolution or the tremendous achievements of the Soviet Union under Stalin's leadership to recognise that under the same leadership bureaucratic degeneration of the revolution continued, the departures from principles themselves grew into principles, and as the party and the state regressed along this path, in time, the Soviets ceased to be effective organs of popular power, single-party state came to be institutionalised, trade unions were fully subordinated to party control, major oppositional trends within the party were tamed, defeated and finally destroyed, even physically at times, and the party itself bureaucratised and de-democratised to the point of a 'polit-bureaucratic' dictatorship, even 'personality cult' of one man, Stalin, and so on. In short, freedom and democracy simply disappeared in the Soviet Union.

Ill and dying, never losing sight of his original socialist project, Lenin devoted all the remaining energies of his last years to fight the growing degeneration of the revolution. He failed. For him it was already too late. But his warning remained. Writing of the Soviet state as 'Tsarist machinery painted red', of 'rotten bureaucracy', the 'stinking bureaucratic and Soviet bourgeois atmosphere', Lenin had warned, as if prophetically: 'for this, all of us.... should be hung on stinking ropes.... and I have not yet lost all hope that one day we shall be hung for this, *and* deservedly so'. The Soviet people may be said to have taken seventy long years to wake up to this task, but, in one of those ironics of history, they have ended up hanging themselves, and damaging the cause of socialism everywhere.

7

Stalin and After

I

We have noticed how the beleaguered workers' state established by the Bolsheviks went down the path of regressive bureaucratic degeneration. Lenin's struggle against it, his struggle to recover the original emancipatory project of Bolshevism was not continued, nor ever resumed later on, when the conditions were more favourable for such a struggle; the party leadership had simply lost the understanding and the will to undertake it as other compulsions of the situation took over. The October Revolution had inspired millions of Russia's common people, given them self-esteem and a belief in their own strength. The struggle to defend the revolution, and its early achievements had given these people a sense of being in control, a consciousness of themselves as participants in historic events rather than onlookers. Therefore, degeneration notwithstanding, the Soviets, Factory Committees, Trade Unions, inner-party debates and discussions, retained some of their eroding vitality till at least the end of 1920s. The overall 'revolutionary impulse' lasted – in one form or another, even as 'Soviet patriotism' – much longer and was a major factor in the later successes of the Soviet Union. But the exigencies of the objective situation, inadequacies of theory, Lenin's own ambiguities of thought and action, and compromises, the personal flaws and failings of individual leaders – all such or similar factors contributing, by the end of the 1920s, what later came to be called *Stalinism* consolidated itself, marking a break-off with the earlier, revolutionary phase of post-October development of the Soviet Union. Stalinism was a *turning point* and not a further development of the revolution despite the continuity with certain ambivalent policies of the earlier period. The years 1928-29 saw the beginning of Stalin's 'revolution from above', which was a definitive departure from the way Lenin had visualised the building of socialism in the Soviet Union.

Already by the time of Lenin's death, in January 1924, the scenario was very different from what it was in October 1917. Soviet democracy no longer existed. The authentic organs of people's power that arose and grew in the wake of the revolutions of 1917, mainly the Soviets and factory committees, were in decay, giving way to the absolute rule of the Bolshevik Party, (increasingly its central leadership) at all levels of the new regime – the Soviets or factory committees or trade unions, all were subordinated to party control. As E.H. Carr has described it:

> Before the end of Lenin's life the authority of the party over every aspect of policy and every branch of administration had been openly recognised and proclaimed. The party exercised in such organisations as the trade unions and co-operatives, and even in the major industrial establishments, the same function of leadership as it performed in relation to the state... It was the Russian Communist Party (Bolsheviks) which gave life and direction and motive power to every form of public activity in the USSR and whose decisions were binding on every organisation of a public or semi-public character.

Particularly significant here was the fact that the industrial proletariat, the heroes of the October Revolution, now decimated by the civil war in both numerical and political strength, had lost the capacity for political initiative and action which distinguished it in 1917. As Isaac Deutshcher has written:

> As the working class was bodily not there, the Bolsheviks decided to act as its *locum tenentes* and trustees until such time as life would become more normal and a new working class would come into being. Meanwhile they considered it their duty to exercise the 'proletarian dictatorship' on behalf of a non-existent or almost non-existent, proletariat.

As a self-proclaimed 'vanguard' of the proletariat, the party was effectively accountable to no one except itself. What is more it itself became increasingly as monolithic and totalitarian in its principles of organisation and functioning as it was in its practice of leadership over society. Of course this happened over a period of time. This transformation was a major break from the authentic Bolshevik tradition, which indeed died hard and just as it evoked resistance from Lenin himself during the last months of his active political life in late 1922 and early 1923, there was resistance and dissidence and intra-party strife later on too. Even in the 1930s party was far from monolithic, it divided over such issues as the pace of industrialisation, treatment of opposition, the relations between the party centre and local units, and so on. And if there was division in the upper ranks, the lower units were, understandably, disorganised and chaotic. But as Stalinism consolidated itself, the break and the transformation finally occurred. The Bolshevik Party which even in the 1920s was what Moshe Lewin calls an 'alliance of factions', rather than the monolith of liberal or Stalinist myth, was transformed into an apparatus of power, terrorised and terrorising, with purges thrown in, by the end of the 1930s.

The absolute party rule over society found its institutional expression in the newly established state power, one-party state, with its special organs of repression, and autonomous in relation to the people. It was a situation where, if capitalist class was destroyed, working class was still fragmented and weak, making for enormous growth in the power and longevity of post-revolutionary bureaucracy, particularly so against the background of economic backwardness and relentless hostility of the surrounding imperialism. (This is reminiscent of the 'mutual exhaustion' of the bourgeoisie and proletariat after 1848, which gave rise to the Second Empire of Louis Bonaparte in France, and the 'many-sided deadlock' between junkers, industrialists and workers in Germany which yielded the dictatorship of Bismarck's officialdom. It is this logic which explains part of what happened in the Soviet Union).

With the departure of Lenin, this dictatorial bureaucratic degeneration was no longer seen as such, and as something to be struggled against, but only as a necessity and was sought to be defended and justified (not always or entirely without justification) in the name of Lenin and more recent Bolshevik practice, often enough with the help of selective, out of context use, indeed absolutisation, of Lenin's historically-conditioned propositions or rationalising theoretical defence of ad hoc responses (including emergency repressive measures) that, for Lenin, yet remained unwelcome departures from principles. In fact a Lenin cult was launched with Stalin's liturgic 'Oath to Lenin' setting the tone for the new era – it included not only the renaming of Petrograd as Leningrad, the erection of his statues everywhere, a 'Lenin levy' recruitment into the party, etc. but the cultural obscenity of mummification of Lenin and creation of a mausoleum over his dead body!

Much of this was later imposed on or voluntarily accepted by an obedient international movement, against the explicit disavowal of Lenin, as the model of principled socialist practice, just as, still later, what came to be built on this basis was passed on to it as the undisputed model of socialism, with disastrous consequences. One is reminded of Rosa Luxemburg's fear and warning in 1918: 'The danger begins... when they (Bolsheviks) make a virtue of necessity and want to freeze into a complete theoretical system all the tactics forced upon them by these fatal circumstances, and want to recommend them to the international proletariat as a model of socialist tactics'.

Such was the grossly distorted political framework within which the post-Lenin Bolshevik leadership under Stalin set about reconstructing their devastated country and building socialism. That no *democratic* correction was sought, that even the threat of growing bureaucracy, which Lenin died fighting against, was no longer seen as a problem – though Leninist language continued to be used, here as elsewhere – was indicative of a most serious flaw in this leadership's understanding of a socialist transition – a flaw not fatal immediately or necessarily, though it proved to be so in the end. This does not mean that in abandoning or turning away from the Leninist project of socialism, Stalin or Bolshevik leadership had no theory at all to guide them. Deeply committed socialists and in their own ways well-versed in Marxism, they had a theory which, however, was not a conscious strategy of socialist transition well worked out in classical Marxist terms; it was far more an economistic response from within Marxism in relation to the unanticipated situation they were facing.

Before we take a look at this theory, it needs to be explicitly noted that the creation of the new order in the Soviet Union did not flow entirely from any such theory. The Soviet regime had gained a precarious existence because the world military-political balance was not propitious for its suppression. Western leadership of world capitalist system, apart from exhaustion at the end of war, was facing an advance of revolutionary movement throughout Europe, and therefore settled for a defensive strategy, unlike the earlier armed intervention. But the threat and hostile encirclement remained and survival was still the categorical imperative for the new regime, and its tragic isolation after the defeat of the German Revolution forced on it an autarky which imposed its own disciplines, economic and political. Therefore, the outcome in the Soviet Union was the result of many pragmatic decisions, impelled by an acceptance of the proposition that the survival of the Soviet Union required, as the top priority, that it be capable of armed resistance to attack and that this capacity required rapid industrialisation. It may be added that the rise of fascism in Europe, especially Nazism in Germany, and the need of the Soviet Union to catch up ('We have ten years' said Stalin prophetically in 1931) can be said to have spurred the breakneck collectivisation and industrialisation in the post-revolutionary Soviet state. The nature of the coming attack and thus the criterion of defensive reaction were not much open to Soviet choice.

Thus the external political factor, compounded of military threat and hostile capitalist encirclement was dominant in the initial stages of the socialist experiment and remained dominant throughout its history. The political, economic and at times military forces of the developed capitalist world were mobilised to harass, destabilise and defeat this experiment. The real historical socialism thus was not the gradual putting into effect of a socialist idea, however much this idea, and the theory accompanying it, may have been flawed in the post-Lenin period. Real socialism, 'actually existing socialism' as it came to be called, grew through a historical dialectic with the forces of world capitalism within the framework of a global inter-state system. Theory apart, it was the product of the world system – a capitalism dominated system – as much as of internal political forces. As such it had internalised the marks of this historical dialectic. The post-Lenin Bolshevik theory simply failed to cope with this awesome historical dialectic.

II

It is only in this context that the issue of 'socialism in one country' which Stalin vigorously championed, can be understood. Of course, literally interpreted as it came to be, it contradicted the classical Marxist conviction shared by Lenin and other Bolsheviks, that properly speaking socialism could be successfully built only internationally. But obviously, it was impossible for the Bolshevik leadership to just hang on to power, hoping for better days to come internationally. Given the historical situation, they *had* to build, even if initially at least from above, and not through working people's self-activity from below. And here, in certain important respects, Stalin could legitimately appeal to Lenin, and what he sought to do was in accord with the feelings and desires of the great majority of the party's membership. The really decisive issue was not to build or not to build but the precise nature of *what* had to be built, *how* the historically specific socialist transition in Russia was conceived. Lenin had more than once stressed that 'we, the Russian proletariat... are behind the most backward West-European country as regards our level of culture and the degree of material and productive preparedness for the introduction of socialism' and therefore insisted that 'the work of learning practically how to build up large-scale production is the guarantee that we are on the right road, the guarantee that the class-conscious workers in Russia are carrying on the struggle against small proprietary disintegration and disorganization, against petty-bourgeois indiscipline'. He saw this as guaranteeing 'the victory of communism'. The dangers of 'small proprietary disintegration and disorganisation' were indeed real and Lenin was right in insisting on large-scale production as a necessary material prerequisite for a successful socialist development, though, obviously, this by itself is no guarantee of 'the victory of communism'. With Stalin we have the additional emphasis on the 'primacy of the production of means of production', this has to be the essential thrust of the national economy: 'the national economy cannot be continuously expanded without giving primacy to the production of means of production'. Furthermore state or public ownership was established and proclaimed as the only and highest form of 'socialist property,' bypassing or obscuring both the distinction between real and juridical social ownership and the crucially important issue of transformation of relations of production in the economy. Thus theoretically armed, Stalin set out on the road to 'socialist development' by giving priority to large-scale production (heavy industry, etc.) and production of means of production so that one can even speak of his production policy in terms of production for production's sake.

In effect, the theory that now came to guide the 'socialist development' in the Soviet Union was the economistic version of Marxism that was widely prevalent in the Second International and the workers' movement in the West. This economism and the related productivist bias is there, though as a very minor element, in Marx and Engels too; and Lenin himself did not entirely break away from it. Thus Stalin neither originated nor forced this economistic Marxism upon the Bolshevik Party, though his great prestige as leader and chief spokesman of the Russian Revolution after Lenin's death not only gave added weight and authority to such Marxism but as 'Economism' – with its implicit beliefs that the public ownership of the means of production can be equated with, or is bound to be followed by the socialist transformation of the relations of production, or that a massive development of the productive forces is an essential precondition for the achievement of socialist relations of production – made it the dominant theory underlying the socialist construction in the Soviet Union.

This economistic Marxism or Economism which came to flower after the introduction of the First Five-Year Plan, well meshed in with the needs of the objective situation. Opposed to any capitalist restoration, but losing hope or interest in any world revolution, Soviet leadership opted for a strong centralised state to rebuild the economy and survive the capitalist encirclement – the option very much reminiscent of Engels' view of the state as 'the executor of the economic necessities of the national situation'. At the heart of Stalin's plan of economic reconstruction was a programme of rapid industrialisation, the so-called 'forced marches' on the road to progress. As he was to put it: 'We are fifty or a hundred years behind the advanced countries. We must make good this distance in ten years. Either we do it, or we shall go under'. Ten years later Germany invaded the Soviet Union.

Set this task the Soviet people and communists responded magnificently – with great acts of heroism and sacrifice, performing miracles of socio-economic reconstruction, transforming the very face of backward Russia within literally a decade, making it the industrial and military power capable of taking on and defeating the anticipated counter-revolutionary attack, the armed might of world fascism. The revolution was young, its liberationist thrust still alive among the people as was the hard-won prestige of the Bolshevik Party. The much-noticed evils and crimes of the period notwithstanding, it was a saga of people in action. No action is possible without conviction, and action of this magnitude and historical significance required inspired faith. Such faith was supplied by Marxism-Leninism, its vision of a new society, egalitarian and without classes, fulfilling the betrayed promises of the French and all other revolutions of the past.

A historical account of the period or its achievement is not my concern here. It would suffice to mention, especially in the contrasting context of the deepest-ever recession in the contemporary capitalist west, that, as noted by R.W. Davies, the foremost economic historian of Soviet Russia, the country underwent a transformation which 'in terms of speed and scale has neither precedent nor successor anywhere in the world';

and the overall achievement was summed up by the Webbs as *'A New Civilisation'*. It needs to be added that in all this Stalin led and inspired. In its own way his theory had worked even if the outcome was not the construction of socialism as visualised by classical Marxism. If the achievement really belonged to the Soviet people and communists, Stalin shared in it and also inevitably got much of the credit plus the enormous prestige that went with it, which was, in the same way, later reinforced by the Soviet victory over fascism and the post-Second World War reconstruction, lending added sanctity to principles and practices of what came to be summed up as Stalinism. If these principles and practices meant that the cost of Soviet achievement was equally enormously high in human terms, one can only repeat, the Soviet people built with Stalin and despite Stalin.

III

As just mentioned the details and complexity of the historical processes of the Stalin period do not concern us. For my argument it is necessary only to take note of a minimum of relevant facts to indicate the implications of the dominant economistic Marxism especially as it finally manifested itself in what came to be built, and later collapsed in the Soviet Union.

The Bolsheviks, as we have already noticed, had to either give up power or begin, best as they may, the construction of socialism in a single, backward country. Given the increasingly economistic perspective on this construction in the post-Lenin period, this in effect meant presiding over the industrial revolution of Russia. And time was of the essence of the situation. The situation around the mid-1920s was in every other way too a difficult one. Even as the country recovered somewhat from the devastation caused by the war and the civil war, the New Economic Policy which had in its own way helped in this economic recovery had also generated significant capitalistic elements and classes in the rural and urban sections of the economy. Not only was the old revolutionary proletariat decimated or dispersed, the emerging new working class was small, politically immature and in a state of flux. The Bolshevik

Party – now called Communist Party (Bolsheviks) – bled white by the civil war, with its social base depleted and class composition much changed, had become somewhat ambiguous in its fulfilment of the self-proclaimed vanguard role. Furthermore while the party continued to occupy all the leading positions in the Soviet government, it did not really control state power, for the state apparatus was staffed by elements predominantly hostile to socialism and the Bolshevik revolution. Compounding these difficulties was the serious inadequacy of theory which now came to govern the Bolshevik policy and practice. Of course the Bolsheviks being an urban working-class party not only lacked knowledge and experience with respect to agriculture, they did not, all the more so after Lenin, really understand the needs or the potentialities of the peasantry for a socialist transition. As a result, despite paying lip-service to Lenin's conception of the NEP and its relation to the peasants, especially the worker-peasant alliance, they lacked either the understanding or the will (or both) to implement it, and in effect treated it not as part of a strategy for achieving socialism, as Lenin had visualised, but as a tactical economic retreat to be abandoned as soon as conditions would permit. (Their brand of Marxism indeed carried within it a certain distrust of peasantry.) Supplementing as it were such lack of understanding of either peasantry or agriculture, was the Bolsheviks' strong predilection for the most rapid possible expansion of modern large-scale industry, perceived as the best way to promote the development of the forces of production and increase the size and weight of the proletariat. The ideological preference for large-scale production, in fact, was to become a permanent feature of Soviet economic practice at all stages of development. A blanket priority was accorded to growth of Department I (as the economists call it), and Stalin later wrote as if this was to be a permanent feature under socialism – the so-called 'law of balanced (proportionate) development' seemed to consist essentially in *assuming* this priority, 'because the national economy cannot be continuously expanded without giving primacy to the production of means of production'. It has even been suggested that the economistic Marxism of the post-Lenin era had a strong tendency to identify socialism with large-scale machine-industry and its associated working class.

It is thus that, subordinating almost everything to economic development, a crash programme of industrialisation was seen as the necessary basis of survival as well as 'socialist construction'; the priority in the allocation of productive resources was to be given to build the infrastructure of an industrial economy – energy, steel and heavy industry, transportation and communication, and the required education, etc. – and a military-industrial complex that was needed for defence of the country. The Soviet economy in the coming years indeed came to be operated as a war economy in which certain priorities are accepted as given, and costs are not counted, or rather all other objectives are subordinated to the main one. Obviously such an economy, propelled by its relatively simplified demands, was eminently amenable to what has come to be described as administrative-command system. Centralised command planning, however rough and ready or crude, however wasteful of human and material resources, and without any kind of democratic control from below, was yet a reasonably adequate instrument for its basic purposes. This policy succeeded remarkably well in its own terms, its achievements were indeed impressive and they looked all the more impressive when capitalism was flat on its back after the Great Depression of 1929. The Soviet Union grew as a great industrial power, it could take on the full might of world fascism and defeat it, and after the post-Second World War reconstruction, emerge yet again as the second largest industrial economy and a super power in the world, able in some sectors – notably the military and space sections – to match if not surpass the efforts of its more advanced American rival. Even so, the heroic, revolution-inspired labour of the Soviet people and communists notwithstanding, it was primarily an economistic achievement. Its economistic nature, the bias away from socialism, was more than evident in its governing slogan – to 'catch up' with advanced capitalism; its evaluation of progress in terms of the visible material progress of capitalist countries – per capita production of steel or electrical energy or the quantity of pig-iron produced in comparison to the United States; its use of capitalist technological devices or methods to secure maximal exploitation of labour – piece-work-system, competitive Stakhanovism, etc., indeed, as Harry Braverman was to later note: 'the organisation of labour in the Soviet Union... differs little from the organisation of labour in capitalist countries'; its one-sided training of work abilities of the mass population of producers as against the socialist goal of all-sided development of the creative capacities of each individual; its overall concern with *quantitative* targets or criteria in production whereas a socialist economy is essentially concerned with the *quality* of chosen ends, a recognition of genuine human *needs* and their fulfilment; its coercive disciplines (economic, political as well as ideological) in the workplace so that Marx's term 'free association of producers' either disappeared or lost all meaning in the 'socialist' discourse in the Soviet Union... As a path of 'socialist construction', what happened was a reversal of the original Leninist path. It turned its back on the worker-peasant alliance which Lenin had considered absolutely imperative for Russia's transition to socialism and it obscured and virtually throttled the more basic liberationist or emancipatory thrust of a socialist transition.

IV

Let me clarify this with a brief reference to a few issues of history and theory. At the very beginning of the Soviet economic development, the immensity of the task confronting the Bolsheviks was well summed up in the contradictory nature of its definition – 'primitive socialist accumulation'. Initially argued for by Preobrazhinsky, and visualising development at the cost of 'small-scale production' of the peasant, the concept was seen as a necessary 'socialist' parallel to the 'primitive accumulation' in the course of capitalist industrialisation in the west which included apart from the colonial plunder, the ruthless mass uprooting of peasantry, a process spread over several centuries. This concept in a way summed up the tragedy of the situation the Bolsheviks faced, for this was an entirely un-Marxist concept; 'accumulation', primitive or otherwise, is alien to socialism. (The mistake probably arose from equating or identifying accumulation with expanded reproduction under socialism and Marx had quite categorically warned against it). Now this concept became the very foundation of Soviet model of development and its practice went much beyond the relatively mild, much qualified programme of its original author. Stalin, his early reservations about it notwithstanding, soon dropped the prefix 'primitive', labelled it simply as 'socialist accumulation' and in a reversal of Lenin's policy, tied it to his own programme of rapid break-neck industrialisation. It was to be industrialisation at the expense of the peasantry – who were to yield the 'surplus' for purposes of accumulation needed for industrial growth – and its dominant thrust was the building up of heavy industry, while concomitantly downgrading the development of light industry and the production of consumer goods. Stalin indeed spoke of the interests of workers and peasants lying 'along a common line', but this 'identity of interest' was by no means characteristic of Soviet socialist construction. 'Tribute' from the peasantry ('something in the nature of "tribute"' as Stalin put it in 1928) was frankly acknowledged to be a source of capital and this 'tribute' only intensified after 1928 with the drive for collectivisation. (Though, one must add, increasingly, accumulation also came from the working class through restricting real wages – via a much slower growth of Department II – through controlling supply and fixing prices and diverting surplus so obtained into Department I as capital.) This model of economic development had serious consequences for the future of socialism in Russia. If it ended all hope of an effective worker-peasant alliance and thereafter, given the overwhelming peasant majority in the population, the necessity of a severely repressive state, it thereby also jeopardised the possibilities of a socialist advance. And as this model soon ran into the economic impasse of 1927–28, the answer was found in the drastic 'revolution from above' launched in 1928–29 which pushed the Soviet economic and political development still further away from its professed aim of 'building socialism'.

Until 1926, the NEP worked quite well as an economic recovery programme, though, despite Party's reiterated declarations of adherence to the Leninist concept of the NEP, very little was attempted and even less accomplished towards transforming productive (and hence also social) relations in the countryside, as Lenin had visualised, that is, achieving a 'socialist society out of cooperatives'. NEP was seen and implemented as an economic and not also a political measure. With the NEP various capitalist elements – traders, rich peasants, speculators, etc. – too had surfaced and a nexus was growing between NEP-era traders, state bureaucrats and party bosses leading to a massive growth of bureaucratic privileges. But more significant in the immediate context are the problems NEP was producing in the countryside, which manifested themselves above all in the stagnation of agricultural production as well as a decrease in the marketed surplus of grain, threatening the food supply of the cities and undermining the country's export capability, and hence also its ability to import much-needed industrial products. As a result of the break-up of the great estates following the October Revolution and consequent economic developments, there was a very significant rise in the number of middle peasants and, especially as a result of the NEP, also a moderate increase in the number and clout of rich peasants or kulaks. Peasantry as a whole, after centuries of deprivation, was not only eating more and feeding more to the livestock, but with the stagnation of agriculture also more unable or unwilling to bring surplus to the market. The real cause of the difficulties here, however, lay not in the NEP, or agriculture itself, or even the kulaks, but in the industrialisation policies of the Soviet government, aimed not only at an accelerated *rate* of industrialisation but also a particular kind of industrialisation. The rapid pace of industrialisation was accompanied by the problem of financing it which, the way it was done – extracting 'tribute' from the peasantry – could only exacerbate the situation in the countryside. And the kind of industrialisation meant concentration on modern large-scale urban industry and neglecting or even cutting-back on all other kinds of industrial production including not only production of consumer goods but also of relatively simple types of means of production which are so crucially important to the functioning of peasant agriculture – hoes, shovels, carts, axes, hammers, saws, wire, nails, etc., etc. – it literally starved the village and rural handicrafts. It needs to be noticed that the potentialities of the peasant agriculture as it existed in Soviet Russia in the mid-1920s had by no means been exhausted. What was required was rather a policy of providing the peasantry with the wherewithal to expand production on the existing basis. Further progress of agricultural production needed a more ample supply of the tools, implements, and materials that would make possible a continued increase in the productivity of the peasant's labour so that, with increased production, they are able to buy consumer goods and have the incentive to sell what they manage to produce. But the Soviet leadership and the government did not see it this way. Underestimating the potentialities of Soviet peasant agriculture and overestimating the economic power of the kulaks, even seeing it as a counter-revolutionary threat, the party adopted (again intended to be temporary) 'exceptional measures' (in effect forced requisitioning) to increase the collection of grain to meet the needs of the cities and to export. The peasants reacted negatively, with the result that production faltered, the marketed surplus suffered further reverses, and even more stringent 'exceptional measures' became necessary. A vicious cycle had been set in motion, and the leadership could see no way to break out of it except through a crash programme of collectivisation combined with accelerated industrialisation. A supplementing reason of counter-revolutionary threat, threat of restoration of capitalism in Russia, was pressed into service. Massive collectivisation was thus viewed as simultaneously solving the biggest and most urgent problems confronting the Soviet government: guaranteeing an adequate supply of grain to the state and breaking the back of the counter revolution represented above all by the kulaks. It could also be legitimised as putting an end to the danger of 'small proprietary disintegration and disorganisation and petty bourgeois indiscipline' against which Lenin had warned. Such was the 'great change' (Stalin's term) of 1928-29. (Incidentally, Trotsky endorsed it all and wrote: '(The) Union of these small parcels into big tracts had become a question of life and death for the peasants, for agriculture and for society as a whole.') The aim of 'overtaking and surpassing' the advanced capitalist countries in the shortest possible time was reiterated once again. The forced collectivisation of agriculture separated the peasants from the means of production and provided the rapidly growing industry with its much-needed workforce. And harsh exploitation of vastly expanded working class made possible a very high rate of capital accumulation. The Soviet Union soon became a great industrial power in the world. It was, as noticed earlier, truly a case of 'driving barbarism out of Russia by barbaric means'.

The 'barbarism' involved in the forced collectivisation of agriculture raises an issue of crucial importance. Stalin acclaimed this collectivisation as the 'extension of socialism' to the countryside and the ruthless elimination of the presumed threat from the kulaks was regarded as a necessary part of this process. Apart from the fact that not just the kulaks but large masses of peasantry too suffered this ruthlessness, the real issue here is quite different and it relates to the question of socialist construction in Russia itself.

There is no denying the power of the kulaks in the countryside though, arguably, it was based not so much on their control of a grain surplus as on their role as moneylenders and local power-wielders. And to the extent that the power of kulaks was increasing in the late 1920s, the reason was not their inherent economic strength but rather the growing hostility of the middle and even some of the poor peasants to the policies of the Soviet government. The breaking of this power was of course essential to a socialist solution of the agrarian problem, but the way adopted in 1928–29 was not the only possible one. Again, small-scale individual cultivation certainly did not provide a foundation for the socialist development of agriculture. But that was true from the beginning and was fully understood by all Marxists: there was never any dispute about the eventual necessity of transcending small-scale individual cultivation. The real issue or the 'only' question, again, was how to do it. And here as already noticed, the Leninist perspective on the NEP was intended to provide the answer, which also contained part of the answer to the problem of kulaks, namely, creating a 'socialist society out of cooperatives'. In fact there was widespread receptivity to cooperative forms of organisation during the NEP, though most of what was accomplished was done by the peasants themselves with little or no help from the government. However limited in the context of the massive predominance of individual peasant farming, such popular initiatives by the poor and middle peasants, despite the absence of support from above and the hostility of the rich peasants, were indicative of the possibilities of transition to a socialist organisation of agriculture. This essentially voluntary cooperativisation, of course with necessary help and support from the party and the state, was precisely the course championed by Lenin, who believed that the worker-peasant alliance – which to him was the essence and the *sine qua non* of the dictatorship of the proletariat in Russia – required faithful adherence to the principle of non-coercion vis-à-vis the peasants. As Lenin might have predicted, therefore, the forced requisitioning of 1927–28 followed by the forced collectivisation campaign of 1928–29 effectively destroyed the alliance and barred the road to a genuinely socialist development of Soviet society.

Stalin's new policies of 1929–33, the 'great change' as they became known, certainly had overwhelming, even enthusiastic support within the party, its leadership as well as the cadre below. Nevertheless they were a radical departure from Leninist programmatic thinking. In fact no Bolshevik leader or faction earlier had ever advocated anything akin to imposed collectivisation, breakneck industrialisation, the destruction of the entire market sector, etc., all of which was necessarily accompanied by the widespread use of force, even terror, against the people. Far from being 'the shortest path' to socialism, Stalin's new policies did not merely slow down the movement towards socialism in the Soviet Union, they grievously, and we can now add, permanently damaged and distorted it .

The new policies – the 'great change' or the 'revolution from above' as they were approvingly termed by the Party itself – had rather fateful consequences for the Soviet peasantry and working class and therefore the socialist experiment itself. Of the peasant Paul Sweezy has written: 'Collectivisation combined with mechanisation (made possible by accelerated industrialisation) was supposed to initiate a rapid increase in agricultural output, and this in turn (was to) enable the peasantry to raise its standard of living and at the same time deliver the required amounts of grain to the state. But it didn't work that way, and history attaches little credit to good intentions. In fact Soviet agricultural output not only declined in the short run but entered into a long-run period of stagnation and crises....The new production relations in the countryside (the collective farms crucially buttressed by the state-owned and state-run machine-tractor stations) placed the peasantry back in the straitjacket very different in some respects from, and yet similar in others to, that in which they had been confined before the revolution. Only now it was not a rent-collecting landlord class which was the immediate appropriator of their surplus product, but a tribute-gathering central state.' (Sweezy has also noted: 'It is interesting that Stalin himself, in 1928 and 1929, spoke of the necessity of imposing "something in the nature of a tribute" on the peasantry to support the country's industrialisation. In this he was advancing essentially the same idea as the one he had rejected when it was put forward earlier by the Trotskyist opposition, and especially championed by Preobrazhensky, under the label of "primitive socialist accumulation."') Commenting on the negative aspects of the new situation of the immediate producers in the countryside, a foremost authority on the subject, Moshe Lewin, has said that it 'reminded them (the peasants) of conditions from which the revolution seemed to have redeemed them forever'.

Obviously the surplus which could be squeezed out of the peasant was too little to sustain the projected rate and kind of industrialisation. It soon became necessary to add the rapidly growing working class itself, the immediate producers in the industrial sector proper, to the sources of tribute. With the management of industries, indeed the economy as a whole, almost wholly free of rank and file workers' control and the latter subject to diverse non-economic constraints (certainly not self-imposed by workers themselves) it was soon a situation where, in fact, in Marx's famous paraphrase of Ricardo, 'the means of production employed the labourers, the labourers did not employ the means of production'. The undeniable social and material gains of the revolution notwithstanding, the developments here were to prove particularly disastrous for the future of socialism in the Soviet Union.

With the fast pace of industrialisation, whose nature, necessity or wisdom have remained debatable, a new working class indeed came into being, created rather fast, in a hothouse fashion out of the uprooted and transplanted muzhiks during the 1930s. Of this working class Isaac Deutscher has written: 'Twenty odd million peasants were shifted to the towns during the 1930s. Their adaptation was painful and jerky. For a long time they remained uprooted villagers, town dwellers against their will, desperate, anarchic and helpless. They were broken to the habits of factory work and kept under control by ruthless drill and discipline.' Obviously this working class was lacking in real proletarian character. And it is here precisely that the Soviet Communist Party simply failed its professed ideology. Relying on state coercion or material incentives, it remained distanced from the working class (or from the people in general). There was no significant effort at the revolutionary ideological schooling of this proletariat. In its economistic orientation, the Party simply failed to see the decisive role of ideological and political struggle, of revolutionising practice, indeed of a cultural class struggle or revolution, in moulding this proletariat into a politically conscious socialist working class. The workers' democracy which arose prior to and during the October Revolution in the trade unions, the party organisations and the local soviets had grievously declined. Insofar as these organisations survived, they were rigidly controlled from the top, being mere executors of decisions made at the level of the Central Committee and the Politbureau; the workers themselves, now a majority of the active population, had no rights of self-organisation or self-expression, and that most basic of workers' rights, the right to strike, was totally suppressed. As a result, the reconstituted and expanded proletariat which came with the forced-march industrialisation was a repressed and atomised proletariat, deprived of all means of self-expression and terrorised by an omnipresent secret police. Needless to add, fifty years later, the grandchildren or the great grandchildren of these new and raw muzhiks, semi-serf workers, were certainly an urbanised lot but altogether lacking in critical proletarian consciousness. They were not a 'class-for-itself' but only a 'class-in-itself', and therefore unable to either resist the lure of capitalist consumerism or to effectively intervene in defence of their own interests when Khrushchevs and Brezhnevs arrived, or Gorbachevs and Yeltsins were produced and promoted to power by the Communist Party itself to push the world's first experiment in socialism to final ruin.

The undoubted economic achievements of the 1930s must not obscure the fact that even as claims of having built socialism successfully were being made, the Soviet Union was already on the road to becoming a *sui-generis* class exploitative society. Here, in tracing back to the causes of the failure of the Soviet working people to intervene effectively to secure a change of course or to prevent the ultimate denouement, a particular political consequence of the 'great change' or 'revolution from above' needs to be underlined. Notwithstanding the initial, and occasionally even later, absence of compulsion in the campaign, and despite Stalin's much-quoted intervention, 'Dizzy with Success' (2 March 1930) – wherein he berated the party cadre for compelling middle peasants by force to join the *kolkhoz* – as a result of Party's overall policy of hastening the pace and the growing repressiveness of Stalin's politics in the 1930s, collectivisation of agriculture was a bloody process which not only ruptured the worker-peasant alliance but also necessitated the creation and development of a huge bureaucratic and despotic apparatus to suppress the peasantry. It naturally left its mark on the Soviet State, enhancing its repressive, anti-democratic character. And as the Soviet society itself began to acquire an exploitative class character, almost necessarily, coercion and command from above became the increasingly dominant way to discipline and control the working people and the everyday social life, which in its own way contributed to people's alienation from the system and further depoliticisation of the Soviet society as a whole.

VI

The course of historical development in the Soviet Union during the Stalin period had, as suggested above, a theoretical underpinning, mostly explicit but implicit at times, of what has come to be described as economistic Marxism which, in its own cramped and narrow manner, identified and defined socialism in term of ownership and control of production, replacing, as it were, the idea of socialism as a relationship amongst people by the idea of it as a relationship between things. In this view the distinguishing characteristics of socialism are state ownership of the decisive means of production and a comprehensive planning of the economy. Given this perspective, the situation in the Soviet Union, on the eve of the 'great change' of 1928-29 appeared as one in which the state sector, having taken over the commanding heights of economy (large industry, banking, railways, etc.) in the aftermath of the revolution and now subject to a certain amount of central planning, was in competition with the large, private commodity producing sectors (peasants, small producers, traders, etc.) which had acquired a new lease of life with the New Economic Policy (which incidentally was deemed absolutely essential to the physical survival of the people). As Stalin at the time put it: 'NEP is a policy of the proletarian state aimed at permitting capitalism while commanding positions are held by the proletarian state, aimed at increasing the role of socialist elements to the detriment of the capitalist elements, aimed at the victory of the socialist elements over the capitalist elements, aimed at the abolition of classes....' It was this struggle between the planned state sector and commodity producing private sector which was seen as the crux of struggle to achieve socialism. And the 'revolution from above' launched in 1928-29 was seen, in its outcome, as winning this struggle decisively for socialism. With the collectivisation of agriculture and the success of the first Five-Year Plan, the state sector finally triumphed over the private sector, and the Soviet Union became – not only in the eyes of its own leaders but also in those of its supporters and many others everywhere – the world's first socialist society. The road forward to a communist society was conceived in the same economic-productivist terms. As Sweezy has pointed out, having completed this part of the journey to socialism as 'the lower phase of communism', the Soviet leadership under Stalin saw as its primary task the promotion of maximum growth of the socialist economy: 'This was considered necessary to enable the country to defeat its foreign capitalist enemies, and to provide the material base in both production and consumption for the further advance to communism. This meant putting economics in command. All policies had to be judged by reference to their effect on economic growth: all were good that contributed to rapid growth, all bad that hindered it. *The advance to communism would be an automatic by-product of economic growth and need not be a direct concern of policy-makers.* The assumption, more often implied than spelled out, was that once socialism in this sense has been firmly established, *its own inner dynamic will automatically propel it forward on the next leg of the journey to communism.*'

Guided by this perspective, everything else, all ideology and politics, was subordinated to the most rapid possible economic development. Concentration of authority at the top everywhere, in government, party and economic enterprises, subjection of workers to wholesale regimentation and harsh discipline supplemented by an unbridled use of material incentives to secure maximum effort and productivity, the imposition of an extremely repressive political regime and rejection, except for purposes of propaganda and political mobilisation, of the human emancipatory thrust of socialism – these were some of the important aspects of this 'second revolution', 'the revolution from above'. The humanist, egalitarian vision of socialism of Karl Marx or Lenin was discarded and denigrated as petty bourgeois sentimentalism. For Stalin the very idea of equality was anathema. All manifestations of egalitarianism – such as the provision enacted in Lenin's time, which prohibited party members, no matter what position they held, from receiving more than skilled labour – were wiped out. He denounced such equalisation of wages and salaries at the 17th Congress of 1934 and carried out a bitter ideological campaign on the issue, questioning the very ideal of equality as a 'reactionary, petty bourgeois absurdity, worthy of a primitive sect of ascetics but not a socialist society organised on Marxian lines'. And at no time later did Stalin or his successors change their tune. For them putting economics in command was the very essence of Marxism. (To the extent Lenin's NEP put economics in command, it was visualised by him as an unfortunate necessity, to be reversed as soon as possible and even so, for him, as we have seen, it was always subject to its more basic political purpose, the resecuring of the badly strained worker-peasant alliance).

It should not be difficult to understand that the economic policy now pursued, while it did produce a rapid rate of growth, also produced, almost inevitably, increasing stratification of society and a progressive depoliticisation of the masses. Not only were these trends in and of themselves contrary to development towards communism, even more important, they made it relatively easy for the privileged groups in the bureaucracy, in the management of economic enterprises, in the professions, and in the party itself to consolidate their position in society and pass their advantages on to their children. In other words, these economic policies made it possible for those in positions of economic and political power to constitute themselves as a new ruling class over the mass of working people. A repressive, even terroristic bureaucratic state provided a most congenial political environment for this process of class formation. No doubt throughout this period from the 1920s to the 1950s, as later too, there were professions of Marxist orthodoxy, regular reference to Marx, Engels and Lenin, to socialist values and even so-called 'new Soviet man', etc., etc., but only ritualistically, on high and holy days, or for purposes of ideological manipulation and political mobilisation. Insofar as a serious view of classical socialist values was taken, their practice was put off until some future time when the forces of production would presumably have developed to the point of making general abundance a reality. The idea, assiduously propagated by Soviet ideologists, was that raising material living standards of the masses will by itself foster socialist consciousness. There was no recognition that the seemingly socialist forms, such as nationalised means of production and comprehensive economic planning, themselves need to be infused with genuine socialist content. This obviously cannot be done unless the economic process of constructing socialism goes hand-in-hand with the formation of socialist human relations, the socialist human beings themselves. Here the state or the party even if genuinely committed to socialism, cannot act in place of the people. As the classical Marxist view held, only revolutionising practice will produce transformed, socialist human beings. Masses must transform themselves while transforming the objective world, and they transform themselves only through their own experience of victories as well as defeats in the struggle to build socialism. Only thus they acquire a collective consciousness, a collective will and a collectivity capacity, that is, their freedom as a class or a people. Economism of the Soviet practice in the post-Lenin period simply led it away from the classical Marxist perspective on society's transition to socialism.

VII

This economistic or productivist version of socialism, a reductionism that tied it down to a state-directed rapid industrialisation, was supported or sanctified with a simplistic, rather scientistic Marxism with its mechanistic interpretation of the metaphor of base and superstructure, 'stages of historical development', 'laws of socialism' and so on. It was a 'rigidified Marxism', as Bettelheim has called it, which pervaded throughout most of the Soviet history and which denuded Marxism, its historical materialism, of its essential revolutionary character. Particularly relevant to our immediate argument are erroneous notions in three areas to which Bettelheim has drawn our attention. They concern (1) the foundation of class relations,

(2) the role of productive forces and (3) the withering away of the state. We will take a quick look at each of them.

With respect to class relations, the primary distortion of Marxism is to treat them as juridically defined and determined, a distortion which is not peculiar to Stalin and the Communist Party of the Soviet Union under his domination but was shared by many others including Trotsky and his followers who were on other grounds strongly opposed to Stalin. This distortion is clearly visible in what we have already noticed above, namely, the view that the abolition of private property in the means of production and its replacement by state ownership does away with the exploiting classes and makes for socialism. The 'public' (that is, mainly state) ownership is equated to 'socialist ownership' of the means of production and this ownership is seen as settling the question of production relations in the economy or society. Thus Stalin's 1936 statement to the Seventh Congress of the Soviets: 'The capitalist class in the sphere of industry has ceased to exist. The kulak class in the sphere of agriculture has ceased to exist, and the merchants and profiteers in the sphere of trade have ceased to exist. Thus all the exploiting classes have now been eliminated.' Therefore, it was concluded, there was no exploitation or exploited classes either.

It is on this basis that Stalin declared in November 1936: 'Socialism is something already achieved and won.' A party resolution echoing Stalin, qualified this 'socialism' as the 'first phase of communism'. (Much later, in his *Economic Problems of Socialism in the USSR*, Stalin was to argue that the contradiction between manual and mental labour, a characteristic feature of capitalism, 'has disappeared in our present socialist system', a statement based on no deeper analysis than the finding, ex cathedra, that since there was no longer any capitalist exploitation, 'today, the physical workers and the managerial personnel are not enemies, but comrades and friends, members of a single collective body of producers'; what indeed remained of the contradiction was only a 'distinction' to be eliminated mainly by raising 'the cultural and technical level of the workers.')

Furthermore, this view of classes and class relations as being essentially an emanation of the property system means that, short of the restoration of private property in the means of production no new exploiting class can arise. And it had the additional comfortable, but utterly un-Marxist, implication that since the abolition of private property in the means of production ushers in an essentially classless society, given a sufficient development of the forces of production, it will evolve in a harmonious way towards communism.

The true Marxist position, in contrast, is that classes have their existence in the *real* relations of production, and that it is only through a transformation of these relations that the class structure can be changed or, in the limited case, that classes can be abolished. And the fact of the matter was that these relations of production, while undergoing certain modifications, had not undergone any *socialist* transformation during this period in the Soviet Union. Consequently there was no socialism there in any proper Marxist sense and the question of any evolution towards communism simply did not arise. (What precisely came to be built in the Soviet Union, I will discuss later in these notes.)

The second erroneous notion concerned the role of productive forces. As already noticed, there were Marxists earlier, principal among them Kautsky and Plekhanov, who had argued for or defended the primacy of the productive forces over the production relations. Misinterpretation of historical materialism as 'technological determinism' has been common with friends and foes of Marxism. This mechanistic understanding, an over-simplification if not distortion of Marxism, was widespread in different sections of the Third International too and, once again, shared by Stalin with his opponents, including Trotsky. It expressed itself in the view that in the construction of socialism primacy belongs to the development of the productive forces. Within this view even 'law of the primacy of the production of the means of production over that of means of consumption' was formulated as one of the more important basic 'economic laws of socialism'. The development of the productive forces was indeed seen as the 'driving force of history'. Therefore, in the Marxist orthodoxy of the Stalin period, underlying its rapid industrialisation, was the doctrine that productive forces and not production relations will spearhead revolutionary change in Russia. The relation between the two, as between base and superstructure in general, was understood in a one-sided, most mechanistic manner. In this way, development of the forces of production was turned into a sort of universal panacea for all the ills and contradictions of society, and from this it followed that for a socialist society the highest and overriding objective for the foreseeable future must be the most rapid attainable development of the forces of production. Given this view of the road to socialism, Soviet economy was increasingly a case of production for production's sake, (not socialism's production for use), with the consequence that although the logic of 'accumulation' in the Soviet Union differed markedly from that of capitalism, the direction and outcome of its productive activity, including the spoliation of the environment, largely came to resemble the patterns of capitalist development.

This view was in its own way supplemented and sustained by the received Marxist notion about capitalism becoming a fetter on the development of the forces of production – a notion which seemed self-evident in the 1930s – whereas socialism ensures their unfettered development. A simplistic interpretation of this notion not only meant a continuing underestimation of the productive potential of capitalism but also had the effect of ignoring capitalism's other contradictions, and obscuring particularly the distinction implicit in Marx's argument – made explicit in recent years by G.F. Cohen and others – between development-fettering and use-fettering of productive forces by capitalism as a market-governed system, so that its profit-driven accumulative drive develops the productive forces increasingly as an 'economy of war and waste' and carries within it the possibility that, in its ruthless structural logic, capitalism might, so to speak, *overdevelop* the forces of production in self-destructive ways which could well mean a nuclear holocaust or a slow but almost inevitable ruin of its own natural base, and with it the ruin of human habitat on the planet earth. Marx had indeed warned, as later made explicit by Rosa Luxemburg: 'Socialism or barbarism'.

Incidentally, its implicit disregard or depreciation of the essential humanist dimension of any socialist enterprise apart, rank economism of the 'theory of productive forces', as the Maoist Chinese were to call it later, is evident in the way the 'forces of production' themselves were typically thought of, that is, in an extraordinarily narrow and obviously un-Marxian manner, almost exclusively in terms of science, technology, machines, etc., and hardly at all in terms of the workers themselves. The result was a heavy emphasis on developing the instruments of production with a corresponding neglect of the human agents without which these instruments are so much dead matter. Marx himself had written: 'Of all the instruments of production, the greatest productive power is the revolutionary class itself'. This obviously gives priority to human beings in the production process itself. And if 'forces of production' are interpreted in this manner, the conclusion can hardly be avoided that the very idea of separating forces of production from social relations, subordination of the transformation of social relations to the development of the forces of production was a fundamental departure from classical Marxism.

This departure, in the shape of an ideology of the productive forces, was most useful for the Soviet leadership. It took care of all current or emergent problems of conflict and class struggle in Soviet society. This ideology assumed a basic solution to such problems and saw the path to communism as a royal road built with the bigger and better productive forces and, in due course, strewn with a plenitude of consumer goods. As Paul Sweezy has put it:

> The great merit of this view from the point of view of the Soviet leaders was that it seemed to provide an explanation of all the troubles and contradictions which the country was experiencing: the forces of production were still too backward and underdeveloped to permit an advance to a harmonious, smoothly functioning socialist society. Though the foundation of such a society had been laid through the substitution of state and cooperative ownership for private ownership of the means of production (no more exploiting classes, hence no exploited either), the edifice itself could not be built without a decisive increase and improvement in the productive forces. Hence the slogans of the period: 'Technique decides everything' and 'Catch up with and surpass the most advanced capitalist countries'....

In other words the Soviet leadership put 'economics in command', when the imperative was to 'put politics in command', that is, subordinating economy to socialist purposes, giving active priority to transforming human beings and their relations to each other.

Economism of Soviet practice in effect meant an evasion of what is indeed the key task of any socialist construction which demands, even as it also makes possible, a transformation of human beings, of human nature itself, through 'revolutionising practice' on the part of the working people. As already noticed, this is what classical Marxism had always emphasised. Using the metaphor of 'civil war' for class struggle, Marx had made the general statement: 'We say to the workers: you have 15, 20, 50 years of civil war to go through in order to alter the situation and to train yourselves for the exercise of power.' In a pointed reference, apropos the Paris Commune, he had written 'The working class did not expect miracles from the Commune. They have no readymade utopias to introduce *par decret du peuple*. They know that in order to work out their own emancipation, and along with it that higher form to which present society is irresistibly tending through its own economic development, they will have to pass through long struggles, through a series of historical processes, in the course of which men, no less than circumstances, will be completely transformed.' Official Soviet ideology indeed recognised this and even invoked the making of a new 'socialist man' in the Soviet Union, but it was a promise honoured only in the breach. The failure here was particularly important because of the reason that socialism, unlike capitalism, does not grow and mature within the old order it seeks to replace, and therefore the requisite transformation of human nature is a task to be primarily carried out in the post-revolutionary society. In other words, the 'bourgeois man' was born and matured within the old feudal order; it is the centuries-long process of building capitalism within the framework of feudal society, the practical human activities involved in the establishment and expansion of capitalist economic and social relations, which gradually moulded human beings with appropriate attitudes, motivations, and 'instincts'

– cupidity, means-and-ends rationality, possessive individualism, and so on – and thus transformed men and women into human beings that capitalism simultaneously needed and made possible. A successful construction of socialism in the Soviet Union demanded a parallel 'revolutionising practice' for a socialist transformation of human beings. 'Economics in command' simply disabled the Soviet practice in facing upto this key task of socialist construction.

It only needs to be added that 'putting politics in command' does *not* mean downgrading or neglecting the development of the productive forces. On the contrary, it is the best and, in the final analysis, the only way to develop the productive forces as they need to be developed under socialism and on the road to communism. Mao, more alive to this most vital issue of a socialist transition than any revolutionary or Marxist before him, never saw any contradiction or problem here, not even when he launched his Cultural Revolution. As Joan Robinson was quick to point out: 'The aim of the Great Proletarian Cultural Revolution is to revolutionise people's ideology and as a consequence to achieve greater, faster, better and more economical results in all fields of work... Any idea of counterposing the Great Cultural Revolution to the development of production is incorrect.' 'Politics in command' is indeed the very essence of a socialist transition anywhere.

The third erroneous notion pointed out by Bettelheim concerns the concept of 'the withering away of the state' – a concept without which the Marxist concept of the 'dictatorship of the proletariat' loses the most substantial part of its meaning. According to classical Marxism (Marx, Engels, Lenin), in a socialist transition, the state as an apparatus of repression would lose its *raison d'etre* and begin to wither away along with and roughly in proportion to, the abolition of classes in the post-revolutionary society. But the Soviet state, far from weakening, much less disappearing, had grown into a massive apparatus. While Stalin pronounced the concept of withering away of the state as 'incompletely worked out and inadequate', the existence and growth of the state in the Soviet Union was defended as necessary in order to protect the country and its socialist system against its external enemies, the hostile capitalist world. This argument certainly had its validity. But the overwhelming reality of the ever-burgeoning Soviet state, its Byzantine cultism and system of government, its gigantic and growing coercive apparatus, the omnipresent secret police, the magnitude and forms of repression, etc. – all this points to the utter inadequacy of such defence or justification, especially when it was claimed that class exploitation and antagonisms had been eliminated which would leave no class with interest in supporting counter-revolution, and the people themselves with every interest not only in defending their socialist country but also the ability to do so. The situation is better comprehended in relation to the policies pursued internally and any number of contradictions generated by them; Bettelheim even speaks of *'a class struggle which was both furious and blind'*. The Soviet state had indeed grown into a bloated, alienated and coercive, even terroristic power standing over and above the people, including the Russian proletariat, who had been deprived of democratic rights, of all avenues of self-organisation and self-expression. Instead of the state 'withering away' as the Marxist classics had expected, in the words of Klyuchersky, a Russian historian of pre-revolutionary era '... the state swelled and the people withered away' – with consequences which were tragically visible all over when its 'socialist system' collapsed in the Soviet Union.

VIII

Decisive for future developments was the way the struggle for socialism in the isolated and beleaguered Soviet Union was visualised in the post-Lenin period. Formulated as what is generally referred to as Stalin's theory of 'socialism in one country', it was a major departure from Lenin, exceeding in the magnitude of its consequences perhaps all other theoretical deviations of that early period. The real issue here is not the attempt to build socialism in the Soviet Union which, as we have argued, was fully justified, but the way Stalin implemented his theory which involved a definitive retreat from internationalism to nationalism in the emerging politics of the new Soviet state. Lenin had, following Marx and Engels, over and over again, with unequalled force and clarity, both before and after 1917, insisted that Revolution in Russia could not succeed and sustain itself to build socialism unless it found an ally in revolution in the West. This was the theoretical perspective which underlay Lenin's view of the struggle to survive and build socialism in the Soviet Union – it was to be a part of an ongoing international class struggle. Explicit in his last writings and the way he worked with the Communist International to advance the revolutionary struggle in the advanced capitalist as well as colonial parts of the world, Lenin held on to this perspective even as he confronted the unanticipated task of attempting a socialist transition in Russia. In fact, as part of the Bolshevik leadership, Stalin himself had shared this internationalist position. In *The Foundations of Leninism* (April 1924), outlining and endorsing Lenin's views on the building of socialism, he had written:

> The overthrow of the power of the bourgeoisie and the establishment of a proletarian government in one country does not yet guarantee the complete victory of socialism. The main task of socialism – the organization of socialist production – still remains ahead. Can this task be accomplished, can the final victory of socialism in one country be attained, without the joint efforts of the proletariat of several advanced countries? No, this is impossible. To overthrow the bourgeoisie, the efforts of one country are sufficient – the history of our revolution bears this out. For the final victory of socialism, for the organization of socialist production, the efforts of one country, particularly of such a peasant country as Russia are insufficient. For this the efforts of the proletarians of several advanced countries are necessary. Such, on the whole, are the characteristic features of the Leninist theory of the proletarian revolution.

But by the autumn of 1924, Stalin chose to depart from this position. The first edition of his book was withdrawn from circulation and the relevant passage was re-written as: 'After consolidating its power and leading the peasantry in its wake, the proletariat of the victorious country can and must build a socialist society'. Later (in November 1926), after he had won Party's approval for his theory, Stalin put it even more explicitly as the 'starting point' of Bolshevik thinking on the subject (which it was not): 'The party always took as its starting point the idea that the victory of socialism in one country means the possibility to build socialism in that country, and this task can be accomplished with the forces of a single country'. (In retrospect, the essential meaning of this shift lay not in its affirmation of the decision to build socialism in the Soviet Union but in the implied abandonment of the original internationalist for a nationalist perspective on it and the way Stalin conceived the building of this socialism.) This theory or project was then retrospectively grafted on to Lenin, and even in his case some of his more unequivocal warnings on the subject were later expunged from the published writings. Thus ideologically armed, Stalin went on to build his socialism within a decade!

The policy of 'socialism in one country', the way it came to be implemented, changed the entire orientation or emphasis of Bolshevik political practice. It replaced the interest in and reliance on the international class struggle and viewing the Soviet politics and its socialism-building as part of this struggle, with interest in and reliance on the power of the Soviet Union as a nation state. And given the scientistic or economistic understanding of Marxism in general and socialist construction in particular, the new Soviet state increasingly came to be 'the executor of the economic necessities of the national situation' – a phrase Engels had used to describe the role of the pre-revolutionary Tsarist state in promoting economic development in Russia. And Stalin's own role, in important ways, fitted in more with the ruthless tradition of Peter, the Great, a character out of Russian history, than with that of a leader of a world-wide revolutionary movement. It is not entirely without justification that a scholar like Tucker could later write: 'Stalinism as revolution from above was a state-building process, the construction of a powerful, highly concentrated, bureaucratic, military-industrial Soviet Russian state'.

IX

Stalin obtained approval of his theory of 'socialism in one country' at the fourteenth Congress of the party in 1925 and it soon gained wide acceptance. Explaining this turn in Party's position, particularly in relation to Trotsky's theory of 'permanent revolution', Isaac Deutscher has written:

> The truly tragic feature of Russian society in the twenties was its longing for stability, a longing which was only natural after its recent experiences. The future had little stability in store for any country, but least of all for Russia. Yet the desire at least for a long, very long, respite from risky endeavours came to be the dominant motive of Russian politics. Socialism is one country, as it was practically interpreted until the late twenties, held out the promise of stability. On the other hand, the very name of Trotsky's theory, 'permanent revolution', sounded like an ominous warning to a tired generation that it should expect no Peace and Quiet in its lifetime.

As Stalin's theory matured with the passage of time, the initial steps of a socialist transition were seen to represent the achievement of socialism, socialism itself came to be visualised as a distinct social formation with its own laws of development, and its transition to the 'second' or 'higher stage of communism' was to be an almost unproblematic, science-and-technology driven process, something, as Stalin suggested in his *Economic Problems of Socialism in the USSR*, that was indeed imminent in the Soviet Union – each of these propositions, needless to say, was not just a departure from but a caricature of Marxist understanding of transition from capitalism to communist society of the future.

Marx was in fact specifically jettisoned in this his last lengthy writing intended as the theoretical elaboration of the problems of 'socialist' political economy in the Soviet Union. Writes Stalin:

> I think that we must also discard certain other concepts taken from Marx's *Capital* – where Marx was concerned with an analysis of capitalism – and artificially pasted on to our socialist relations. I am referring to such concepts, among others, as 'necessary' and 'surplus' labour, 'necessary' and 'surplus' product, 'necessary' and 'surplus' time. Marx analysed capitalism in order to elucidate the source of exploitation of the working class – surplus value – and to arm the working class, which was bereft of means of production, with an intellectual weapon for the overthrow of capitalism. It is natural that Marx used concepts (categories) which fully

> corresponded to capitalist relations. But it is strange, to say the least, to use these concepts now, when the working class is not only not bereft of power and means of production, but, on the contrary, is in possession of the power and controls the means of production.

The flawed, indeed apologetic nature of Stalin's theorising is best evident in the last sentence of the above quotation: the *juridical* overthrow of capitalism, the elimination of capitalist ownership of the means of production is relied upon to brush aside the crucial question, in Meszaros' words, 'of who *controlled* the allocation of labour power as regards both the adopted production targets and the distribution of the total social product – i.e. whether it was allocated by the associated producers themselves, exercising their control within the framework of a fully co-operative mode of production and distribution, or under the new personifications of capital who ruthlessly enforced their system's imperatives through an authoritarian state machinery....'

Not only is 'the antagonism arising from the structural subordination of labour to the established hierarchical system', which was already a fact of life in the Soviet system, thus disposed of, the same underlying assumption is used to postulate the abolition of the opposition between mental and physical labour in the Soviet Union, suggestive of the imminence of the arrival of 'communism', the radically new socio-economic system that Marx had visualised as succeeding capitalism. Stalin argues:

> The economic basis of the antithesis between mental and physical labour is the exploitation of the physical workers by the mental workers. Everyone is familiar with the gulf which under capitalism divided the physical workers of enterprises from the managerial personnel. We know that this gulf gave rise to a hostile attitude on the part of the workers towards managers, foremen, engineers and other members of the technical staff, whom the workers regarded as their enemies. Naturally, with the abolition of capitalism and the exploiting system, the antagonism of interests between physical and mental labour was also bound to disappear. And it really has disappeared in our present socialist system. Today the physical workers and the managerial personnel are not

> enemies, but comrades and friends, members of a single body of producers who are vitally interested in the progress and improvement of production.

That is how Stalin theorised as his slogan of 'socialism in one country' became the compulsory wisdom for communists at home and abroad to which, henceforth, all theory and political practice was to be subordinated.

X

A most important subordination, *the* departure from the earlier Leninist position and perspective was, as mentioned above, a definitive retreat to nationalism in the emerging politics of the new Soviet state with grievously damaging consequences for its socialist construction, its nationalities policy within and pursuit of socialist politics abroad.

The nationalist, rather nationalist-statist shift not only strengthened the distorting economistic thrust of Soviet socialist construction but carrying the mark of Great-Russian chauvinism as it inevitably did, even otherwise marred the socialist experiment *within* the Soviet Union. More particularly, it involved a departure from the original Bolshevik perspective which had a genuinely socialist position on national and ethnic issues. Marxist theory had from the very beginning held that a nation which oppresses and dominates other nations simultaneously deprives itself of its own freedom. The ending of national oppression was advocated for the benefit, not only of the oppressed, but of the oppressor as well. Demanding freedom of Poland in the interests of Germany itself, Engels had said (in 1847): 'A nation cannot be free and at the same time continue to oppress other nations.' For Marx (apropos British oppression of Ireland) 'the people which oppresses another is forging its own chains'. Lenin fully adhered to this Marxist position. Like Marx and Engels he saw the structurally entrenched inequality between the oppressor and oppressed nation as a practical challenge and had insisted that

> internationalism on the part of oppressor or 'great' nations, as they are called (though they are great only in their violence, only great as bullies), must consist not only in the observance of the

> formal equality of nations but even in an inequality of the oppressor nation, the great nation, that must make up for the inequality which obtains in actual practice. Anybody who does not understand this has not grasped the real proletarian attitude to the national question.

The Bolsheviks, accordingly, proclaimed principles of national sovereignty and autonomy, including the right to secession. The initiative flowing from this position, especially during the early years, made for unprecedented material and cultural advancement of different nationalities, regional or ethnic identities in the Soviet Union, leading ultimately even to the growth of new modern nations. There was significant centrally planned economic development (though not without a certain built-in lopsidedness) and local languages and cultures flourished as never before. Local schools used their own languages, and quotas ensured admission to universities for the different ethnic groups. 'Rooted nationalities', as they were called, assumed high positions in government and usually controlled the republics where they were dominant. The Soviet state in fact practised its own form of 'affirmative action', so that if you were a member of a rooted nationality in a given region, joined the Communist Party, and came from a working class or peasant background, you were likely to be promoted ahead of the Russians who lived and worked in the same region or republic.

But while much was achieved, problems flowing from the contradictions of the multi-national state inherited from tsarism and the compulsion to build a strong state in order to survive and construct a new social order had a logic of their own, pushing the Bolshevik policies in the other direction including Great-Russian chauvinism. Already in 1920, Stalin, the old Bolshevik, author of *Marxism and the National Question*, and now the Commissar of Nationalities, was speaking of 'the centre and the border regions' and defining 'Soviet autonomy' as the 'ensuring of a revolutionary union between the centre and the border regions' insisting: 'We are against the secession of the border regions from Russia, because secession in that case would mean a weakening of the revolutionary might of Russia.' Lenin, aware of the emerging problem, wrote of the bureaucratic state apparatus which 'we took over from tsarism and slightly anointed with Soviet oil. The apparatus we call our own is, in fact, still quite alien to us', adding: 'it is quite natural that in such circumstances the "freedom to secede from the union" by which we justify ourselves will be a mere scrap of paper, unable to defend the non-Russians from the onslaught of that really Russian man, the Great-Russian chauvinist, in substance a rascal and a tyrant, such as the typical Russian bureaucrat is.' He specifically warned against the failure to live up to the socialist principle of real national equality, putting into relief the consequences of Stalinist policy on the national issue for socialist development in no uncertain fashion:

> The Georgian (Stalin) who is neglectful of this aspect of the question, or who carelessly flings about accusations of 'nationalist socialism' (whereas he himself is a real and true 'nationalist-socialist', and even a Great-Russian bully), violates, in substance, the interests of proletarian class solidarity, for nothing holds up the development and strengthening of proletarian class solidarity so much as national injustice.

This was a matter of major concern for Lenin in his last days, an important reason behind his request to the Central Committee for the replacement of Stalin as General Secretary of the Party. Lenin however died before he could work out effective measures to deal with the worsening situation, its departures from the principle of national equality, the continuing degradation of the promised autonomy or right to secession.

With the bureaucratic degeneration of the socialist experiment as a whole and the Great-Russian chauvinism – much curbed initially by Lenin's interventions but never completely eliminated – acquiring a new lease of life in the 'Soviet nation' as Stalin now also called it, not only the original Bolshevik initiatives faltered but nothing necessary was done to deal with deep-seated cultural and social issues, the biases and prejudices of ordinary Russians, or of other national or ethnic groups. No programmes or policies were forthcoming for dealing with historic hostilities, conflicts and tensions that permeated the different societies and cultures of the Russian

Federation and the Soviet Union. Here little actually changed at the grass roots or community level of Soviet society. Instead of actively working for alleviating many of the historic socio-cultural antagonisms, the approach to the national question became a formal, legalistic affair and a sort of 'Russification' took over in the form of domination of the ethnic Russians in the life of the party and state institutions of the non-Russian republics or regions of the Soviet Union, imposition of the Russian language on and the settlement of large Russian population in the Baltic and Central Asian states. There was an element of economic discrimination too in the form of introducing monoculture in agriculture and promoting only light industries in the Central Asian regions. The elites of rooted nationalities that were promoted in the government and party tended to separate from their national bases to become part of the Soviet system. The ruling stratum in the Soviet Union had its share of men from these nationalities, they had been, as it were, co-opted and 'Russified'. What the Soviet leadership in effect succeeded in doing was creating just enough of a Soviet consciousness to sustain construction of what it believed to be socialism, where, again, survival in the midst of capitalist encirclement apart, consolidation of the system and defence of the interests of the ruling stratum were increasingly the major concerns determining the approaches to the problems of economy and culture. It may be added that the undoubted Stalinist-era repression, even terrorisation, of ethnic groups was governed primarily by a concern to consolidate and defend the system; it was not part of any calculated campaign against non-Russians or any particular race. The upshot of it all was that Soviet nationalities policy, over the years, turned from an instrument of freedom into one of domination by a strongly centralised bureaucratic ruling stratum under the hegemony of Russian nationality. Far from the nationalities question being completely solved and the Soviet Union become a country of 'fraternal Socialist Nations', as Stalin declared it to be, the new policy generated deep contradictions within, which, with the release of ideological and political repression, later exploded into disintegration of the Soviet Union itself. Even so, the conflicts that have ensued since then must not be seen, as is conventionally done, simply as the product of repression under the old Soviet system. What has happened in fact, in its own peculiar way bears witness to not only the failure but also a certain success that was Soviet Union – for when the Party collapsed and virtually the entire system crashed, the only institutions or identities that were able to pick up the pieces were its republics; though, containing one or several minorities, these republics are also now the sites of new and often bitter ethnic conflicts within, and are even otherwise vulnerable to all sorts of other regressive developments.

XI

If national-statist departures were damaging enough within Soviet Union for its nationalities policy and socialist construction as a whole, their consequences without were disastrous for the world revolutionary movement. These departures were soon evident in Soviet foreign policy. Having lost faith as well as interest in world revolution, it was no longer designed to promote it. On the contrary it involved not merely an abandonment of international class struggle but its subordination to the *national*, not necessarily socialist, interests of the Soviet Union. In fact the interests of international revolutionary movement, insofar as, as a historical legacy, they were still a theoretical or political consideration, were identified with the interests of the new Soviet state, the 'socialist Fatherland' now governed by narrow nationalist considerations. In its Stalinist form it was a policy that managed or sought to contain the revolutionary potential of October wherever, subsequently, class revolutions occurred or appeared possible. The most visible and forceful expression of the shift away from internationalism and socialism to nationalism came during and after the Second World War. The heroism of the Red Army and the Soviet people was invoked in the name of Mother Russia and it was called the 'Great Patriotic War', not the 'proletarian war for socialism', or the war in defence of the only socialist state, as the allied communist parties the world over believed. This was accompanied by the revival of old ranks and insignia in civil and military areas, sanctifying the privileged officer caste. In 1944 the *Internationale* was replaced by a new national anthem; in 1946 Stalin rebaptised the Council of People's Commissars as the Council of Ministers, a title Lenin always abhorred; in 1947, he changed 'Red Army of the Workers and Peasants' into 'Armed Forces of the USSR', etc. In this renovating process, at the 19th Congress of the Party, even the qualification 'Bolshevik', which had hitherto linked it to its internationalist revolutionary past, was suppressed.

The nationalist shift almost inevitably meant recourse to *raisons d'etat* in Soviet foreign policy. Only thus, for example, can we understand the obviously dubious aspects of the Stalin–Hitler pact before the war and still more the *realpolitik* of post-war politics, with its compromises or deals with imperialism and surrenders in France, Italy, Greece, etc. Soviet policy was cautious and essentially defensive of national interests, even after the stunning victories of the Red Army. The chief concern of the Soviet leadership was not world revolution which its senior diplomat Maiskii (in his 1944 Memorandum) blithely wrote off as the 'music of the future', but the far more practical aim of obtaining a *Peredyshka* or recuperative breathing space in order to recover from the wartime destruction of their country. Stalin wanted post-war stability in Europe and a durable place in the world to concentrate national energies on domestic reconstruction and development. He and the Soviet leadership did not want any confrontation with the victorious capitalist powers, now led by the United States. Instead, hopeful about continuation of wartime accords (Teheran Conference, etc.), and viewing Soviet Union as a now arrived conventional Great Power, they primarily, if not only, sought recognition of its security concerns within its own sphere of influence in Eastern Europe – 'our sphere of influence has been recognised' by the wartime allies, Molotov even boasted in traditional great power terms in August 1945. In pursuit of its essentially national or great power interests, the Soviet leadership headed by Stalin was prepared to make concessions to imperialist powers, for example, reciprocally respecting Britain's security concerns in the Mediterranean; Stalin's strategy towards Poland in fact differed little from British policy towards Greece, both seeking to ensure that a regime friendly to the regional hegemon came to power. To the same end, this leadership was willing to curb, if not throttle, any revolutionary impulses in Eastern Europe or in the non-Soviet Communist Parties elsewhere.

As against the eventual incorporation of the recently liberated strategic periphery into a Soviet bloc or 'the socialist world', allaying Western fears, Eastern Europe was visualised as regimes of an intermediate stage of development, 'people's democracy', as distinct from socialism or any 'proletarian dictatorship'. Thus, for example, 1944 onwards, Moscow repeatedly frowned upon, warned against, and imposed restraint upon the radical agrarian strategies of the Polish Workers' (i.e. Communist) Party, condemning them as 'sectarianism'; any attempt at 'sovietisation' (collectivisation of agriculture, etc.) could only lead to Poland becoming 'a bone of contention between the Teheran powers', something Moscow was keen to avoid at the time. Again, in Bulgaria throughout 1945 and 1946 Stalin sought to dampen the ardour of a Bulgarian party that he clearly considered excessively revolutionary, wanting to move too fast, and thus a disruptive influence on Soviet relations with its wartime allies. He urged them to opt instead for 'a democratic republic', a 'path through a parliament', a 'transition to socialism in a special manner without a proletarian dictatorship'....

It was no different in Germany, if Wilhelm Pieck, the veteran German Communist and former Comintern functionary is to be believed. This is how Patrick Flaherty, an independent scholar with access to evidence now becoming available, has reported it all:

> Among many historical gems, Pieck provides a running account of a June 1945 dialogue of Stalin with the leadership of the German Communist Party that mapped out the character of post-war reconstruction. Stalin laid down the law to the German delegation: their primary objective was to be the 'completion of a bourgeois democratic revolution' and the establishment of a 'bourgeois democratic government.' This self-limiting revolution translated no more and no less into 'breaking the power of the landlords'

> and 'eliminating the vestiges of feudalism' that had provided the backbone of German militarism in the past. Pieck's notes on Stalin's marching orders confirm a more detailed summary of the stern instructions issued to the top leadership of the German Communist Party immediately before its departure from Moscow: The political task in Germany is not to implement socialism or initiate socialist development. This tendency should be viewed as detrimental and resisted. Germany confronts a bourgeois-democratic restructuring that in its content and essence will be comparable to the completion of the bourgeois democratic revolution of 1848.

Stalin's objective was not any sovietisation or socialism in Germany, or a Sovietised regime in the Eastern occupation zone, but rather a permanent post-war demilitarisation of Germany which, if anything, could even be a capitalist parliamentary democracy. As with significantly radical or revolutionary impulses elsewhere in Eastern Europe, the chief worry of the Soviet leadership in Germany was that the revolutionary tradition to which the old KPD (Communist Party of Germany) was heir would interfere with the Teheran settlement with the United States and Great Britain.

It may be added that, along with what has been noted above, as late as mid-1947, Stalin, still hopeful about his accords with wartime allies, was persuaded to take a positive view of Marshall Plan aid for war devastated Europe, including his allied regimes in Eastern Europe, and only sought elimination of some objectionable aspects of this foreign aid plan. But his wartime allies had other ideas. The United States, now the pre-eminent capitalist power in the world, was all set to bulldoze its way towards world empire. The US Assistant Secretary of War, John J. McCloy made explicit the hard core of the moralising rhetoric of US foreign policy, the perceived strategic interests of the rulers of the United States, when he declared in May 1947 that the United States 'ought to have our cake and eat it too'; that is, it should feel free to claim all the conventional prerogatives of a regional power within its own hemispheric sphere of influence while simultaneously exercising the right to intervene at will everywhere in the world. The reality dawned on the Soviet leadership that Cold War against the Soviet Union was on, in fact it had already been declared with the atom bombing of Hiroshima and Nagasaki which, as Professor Blackett, the eminent scientist, pointed out long ago, was not so much the conventionally claimed last act which ended the Second World War as the opening act of the new Cold War. It is this global imperialist drive of the United States (and not Stalin's expansionist aims) which made Stalin and Soviet leadership to change tack and opt for the hard line. The imposed 'sovietisation' of Eastern Europe, their full-fledged incorporation in the Soviet bloc or 'socialist world', which ensued after the summer of 1947 was a product of the Cold War (and not its cause). Especially after the Tito crisis broke out, a coercive regimentation was seen as the most reliable means of lashing together a ramshackle geopolitical bloc to take care of Soviet security interests and otherwise meet the challenge of a vastly superior United States. Whatever the name given to the new order, the states in Eastern Europe were now called upon to 'carry out the functions of a proletarian dictatorship', as Stalin himself now told a delegation of Bulgarian Communists in December 1948! (Of course this was to be a 'proletarian dictatorship' as Stalin understood it and not what Marx and Engels had argued for.)

XII

A concern for Soviet national or state interests was equally evident in the surrender of revolutionary possibilities elsewhere in Europe, say in France or Italy, and of a virtual revolution in Greece in the Balkans.

The Communist Party's leading role in the anti-fascist resistance, the prestige and popular support it had thus acquired, its organisational resources and capabilities together with the changed balance of forces in society in favour of the Left had created a 'revolutionary possibility' in both France and Italy at the end of the war. The Spanish communist leader Fernando Claudin has written: 'in the conditions of 1945, with the Red Army on the Elbe, the confirmation of the "revolutionary possibility" created in Italy and France would have meant the victory of the revolution in continental Europe and a radical change in the world balance of power to the detriment of

American imperialism, the only large capitalist state which had come out of the war strengthened...' But this was not to be. After years of subservience to the Soviet Union and practice of reformist politics under its aegis, the leaderships lacked the requisite revolutionary political line and the will for a revolutionary transformation of society – the 'party of martyrs' (*parti des fussillés*), as the French Communist Party had deservedly come to be called, could not become the 'party of revolution'. The 'revolutionary possibility' was frustrated. Claudin has observed: 'it is impossible to exaggerate the negative effect of the frustration of this possibility on the further development of the world revolutionary movement. Without any exaggeration, it can be compared to the consequences of the defeat of the German revolution in 1918-19.' Patrick Flaherty has thus reported on Stalin's role in 'the frustration of this opportunity' in France:

> In a November 1944 meeting with the leaders of the French Communist Party, Stalin again intervened personally to rein in the resistance movement and adjust its political program to the strategic objectives of the Soviet Union. Stalin's main concern was to persuade reluctant French Communists to dissolve their armed partisan militias and submit themselves to the authority of a 'government recognised by the allied powers.' Stalin urged French Communists to abandon what he deemed a confrontational sectarian strategy and soft-pedal their program to appeal to the 'average Frenchman.' Above all, the PCF was told to avoid isolating itself from the political mainstream and concentrate on pulling together a 'left-wing bloc' that should be ecumenical enough to encompass socialists, liberals, trade unions, and all sympathetic groups. Stalin went one step further than the Maiskii Memorandum when he advised French Communists to drop the term 'Popular Front' out of deference to the sensibilities of a bourgeoisie still smarting from the working-class insurgencies of the 1930s. To enable the PCF to dissolve into this broad coalition, Stalin tacked on the suggestion that French Communists stop flying red flags in their parades and refrain from the use of the term 'communist' in their programmatic literature. In the post-war world, Stalin had his heart set on doing business with the 'democratic fraction of capitalists' on the basis of the wartime anti-fascist alliance.

> Warning French Communists not to overestimate their own strength, Stalin wanted the leadership to forswear even the theoretical option of revolution and commit itself exclusively to the parliamentary path. To the PCF, Stalin assigned the primary task of preventing a discredited collaborationist right from rehabilitating itself and returning to power in a 'reactionary government' hostile to the Soviet Union. The best guarantee against a resurgent anti-Sovietism was for the PCF to become an indispensable part of a broad coalition government. The cooperative strategy outlined by Stalin for the PCF was geared towards cultivating the respectable political credentials required to play this role. Stalin's insistence on the PCF abandoning even lip service to revolutionary goals was but an aspect of the broader geopolitical strategy intended to forestall a global bipolarization that would plunge the Soviet state back into a hostile capitalist encirclement.

As in France and Italy, thanks primarily to their heroic struggle against Nazi occupation, the Communists and the Left in Greece were, towards the end of the war, the dominant political force in society, indeed in a position to carry out a successful revolution. But they were soon sacrificed to the exigencies of Russia's foreign policy. Stalin was interested in doing a deal with the British over the disposal of the Balkans and did not want the Greek Communists to hinder or compromise the negotiations. Put simply, Soviet representatives pressured the Communist leadership into accepting British terms even though they were extremely damaging. Soon afterwards, Stalin got his deal. On 9 October 1944, he and Churchill reached a secret agreement, 'the Churchill-Stalin Pact', whereby the fate of the Balkan peoples was settled, their future sacrificed at the altar of great power politics. Stalin conceded Britain a 90 per cent interest in Greece, in return for a 90 per cent interest in Romania and a 75 per cent interest in Bulgaria for Russia. Influence in Yugoslavia and Hungary was to be split fifty-fifty. Stalin had abandoned the Greek Communists and effectively handed them over to the tender mercies of Winston Churchill. What is particularly remarkable is that the Greek Communists were completely unaware of the deal that had been struck, and the bloody assault by the Right-wing (including Nazis and their collaborators) on the Communist-led National Liberation Front (EAM) that soon followed took place with the knowledge and agreement of Stalin. The decisive blow came on December 30 when Stalin appointed an ambassador to the Greek Government even as ELAS (the Greek National Liberation Army) was fighting for its life on the streets of Athens. While there were protests against British conduct in both Britain and America, the Russians remained silent. Of course, West's Cold War offensive against the Soviet Union soon changed the situation in the region and compelled a change in Stalin's perspective on politics in the post-war world. But, for the moment, Stalin had honoured his deal with Churchill, sacrificing the Greek Communists and the Greek Left in a breath-taking display of realpolitik. They never recovered from this sell-out.

XIII

Focussed as it was on its own economic and political (including security) concerns, Soviet foreign policy reflected a rather negative view of global revolutionary change. Bids for power by communist parties were discouraged and those pursuing an independent revolutionary politics were distrusted. A good example is China where, towards the end of the war, a socialist revolution under communist leadership was fast maturing but all that Soviet Union hoped and looked for was the establishment of a friendly, nationalist or non-communist government in China, allowing for spread of Soviet influence there. No wonder, for the success of Chinese Revolution, while professing conventional loyalty, Mao kept his distance from the Comintern, where Soviet interests indeed became a matter of decisive, when not sole importance for the world communist movement. In fact bureaucratic pressure and material aid so confined and intensified Russian domination of the Communist International that no dissent or difference over policies or politics was possible. It was diverted from its original purpose of promoting world revolution and turned into an extended arm of Soviet foreign policy. And when this policy so dictated, it was unceremoniously dissolved (1943), or for that matter, later resurrected as Cominform (1947). Internationalism, that hallowed, defining principle of the communist movement was freely manipulated as a tool for the great-power interests of the Soviet Union. Indeed, with the patronage of a Comintern subjugated to the objectives of Soviet policy, the very understanding of internationalism was subverted. The demand for safeguarding 'revolutionary achievements of the first socialist country' was imposed, rather than the need for reinforcement of the revolution. By submitting everything to this idea, the Comintern pursued an international policy which stifled the world revolutionary movement. Again and again, the communist parties abroad – which most faithfully saw the Soviet Union as a 'Socialist society', as not one, however important, but *the* centre of the world-wide revolutionary movement, whose communist party was still the 'Party of Lenin' and its leadership infallible practitioners of 'science of Marxism' – were reduced to playing the role of 'frontier patrols' for the Soviet state, often acting only as reformist pressure groups on their respective bourgeoisies or ruling classes, down-playing revolutionary politics for fear of alienating potential friends and allies of the Soviet Union. With the power, prestige and funds available, the Comintern and most of its parties were entirely in the hands of thoroughly reliable Soviet or local party *apparatchiks*. Even as the rank and file and the common people with them struggled, suffered and sacrificed, the communist parties, increasingly bureaucratised, themselves staffed and led by a hierarchy of officials, as a matter of faith or other considerations, willingly subordinated their revolutionary interests to the interests of the powers that be in the Soviet Union. The degeneration of revolution in the Soviet Union apart, the subordination of the world revolutionary movement to the Soviet *raison d'etat* or national interests was a most important reason for disorienting this movement and, despite unparalleled heroism and sacrifice of the communists the world over, led to its stagnation and ultimate disintegration.

XIV

The nationalist-cum-statist shift in the Soviet socialist project only facilitated its growing deformation, above all its ongoing bureaucratic degeneration which was soon most grievously manifest in what came to be built as socialism under Stalin. But however away from, if not in defiance of what Marx or Lenin had said on the nature of socialism (or its development internationally and over an entire historical period), and even as power struggles intensified in the party and his opponents stigmatised it as surrendering the advanced revolutionary base of the world working class and liquidating the revolution, Stalin's own position gradually matured into one of steady advance into socialism. And finally, in November 1936, he proclaimed:

> Our Soviet society has already in the main succeeded in achieving Socialism: it has created a Socialist system, i.e., it has brought about what Marxists in other words call the first, or lower, phase of Communism, Socialism. Hence, in the main, we have already achieved the first phase of Communism .... for the USSR Socialism is something already achieved and won.

But while feats of heroic labour had been performed and there was tremendous economic and material advance, what was won was not socialism as classical Marxism had visualised it.

What had been built as socialism in the Soviet Union was not even remotely a translation of classical Marxist ideal into reality – that is, a society of 'freely associated producers' (as Marx had called it) or of 'civilised cooperators' (Lenin's more specific description for Russia), with mastery over their labour and their fate. Far from being an expression of worker's self-rule, the self-directing life-activity of freely associated individuals, it was more a forced association of human beings ruled over by an increasingly alien political force. Its politics was an authoritarian state distinguished by a single party dictatorship which dominated all public life. And its economics was a 'command-administrative system', not Marx's conscious *social* plan which regulates the totality of the life-process of society through the full involvement of the freely associated individuals but far more a one-sided technocratically processed administrative or bureaucratic imposition, without any effective control from below, that is, a mere economic plan – and often unfulfilled at that. Not socialism, it was not even a society in transition to socialism, as Marx or Lenin had visualised that process. In its beneficial aspects, it resembled far more what Neil Harding has called 'that other Saint Simonian development of social democratic Marxism which saw the individual as the beneficiary of an efficient state-directed philanthropy'. Central to the existence and functioning of this socialism was a massive bureaucracy, grown over the years in the Soviet state system, a stratum whose interests had come to be directly opposed to the interests of the mass of workers and peasants, even as it imposed or led in the non-capitalist crash modernisation programme of the Soviet Union. This bureaucracy had every interest in promoting the development of the state sector, and within the state sector that of large-scale modern forms of technology and organisation. It therefore reinforced and made full use of all the mistaken biases and tendencies which the Bolshevik leadership had inherited from the past or the limitations of their current theory concerning socialist transition. These biases and tendencies, and limitations of theory, were thus not only the causative factors operating through the old Bolsheviks in leading positions, but also the expression of the very real and active interests of a social stratum which was in any case rapidly expanding its power and influence; they fitted in well with the needs and aspirations of the bureaucrats now dominating the economy and politics of the country.

It is most significant that this bureaucratic degeneration of revolution, of post-revolutionary state and society, including its economy, was not viewed as Lenin had done who, notwithstanding certain ad hoc or ambiguous concessions here, always saw it as spelling disaster for any socialist project and who had therefore died fighting against it. During the post-Lenin period, if at all the problem of bureaucracy was recognised, whatever its undesirable qualities or tendencies or growing powers and privileges, it was seen as a temporary and transitional phenomenon, a necessary product of Russian backwardness. The abolition of private property in the means of production having taken care of the question of exploiting classes, in the new 'socialist' setting, with the inevitable development of the productive forces, the conditions necessitating a bureaucracy too would gradually disappear and so would this stratum in due course. In the meantime – and this is a crucially important point – the struggle against bureaucracy would take the form of measures to control excesses and inculcate in bureaucrats a greater sense of social responsibility. In other words, unlike Lenin, bureaucracy was not seen and struggled against as the threat it was to the socialist project. We may here note an observation Academician Vladimir Kudryavtsev made much later in 1990 which is tellingly indicative of not only the overall character of Soviet politics and political system but also the apologetic nature of Marxism in the erstwhile Soviet Union, all the more tellingly indicative if one remembers the classical Marxist injunction about 'ruthless criticism of everything that exists (which) will not shrink either from its own conclusions or from conflict with the powers that be'. Writing of 'ways of combating bureaucracy' and deploring the lack of development of what he calls 'Marxist political science' in the Soviet Union, Kudryavtsev has written: 'It is necessary to point out that the only national monograph devoted to this subject was published in Moscow in 1906. Not a single serious study dealing specifically with this issue was carried out during all the years of Soviet power'! Bureaucracy was simply accepted as a necessary fact of life. The argument in a nutshell was that such elites are inevitable for a long time to come (until they more or less automatically disappear), but they ought to be well-behaved elites. Such at least was the explicit or assumed theory, and it was the Party, the repository of socialist values, which was to serve as a check to ensure bureaucracy's good behaviour and its ultimate disappearance. But this never happened.

XV

On bureaucracy, Party and related issues, till the very end, Stalin continued to use the Leninist language and appeal in the name of Leninist principles. Thus he rejected any kind of 'substitutionism', which substitutes Party rule for working class or masses. Upholding the leading role of the Party, he yet recognised 'the dictatorship of the proletariat' as 'wider and richer in its scope than the leading role of the Party'. He regularly spoke of strengthening 'criticism and self criticism' in the Party: 'A party which hides the truth from the people, which fears the light and fears criticism, is not a party, but a clique of impostors, whose doom is sealed.' Arguing for 'ruthless criticism of its own shortcomings', he recognised the need to purge the Party (and associated Soviet institutions and organisations) 'of the foulness of bureaucracy': 'There can be no doubt that bureaucratic elements exist not only in the economic, cooperative, trade union and Soviet organizations, but in the organizations of the Party itself. Since the Party is the guiding force of all these organizations, it is obvious that purging the Party is an essential condition for really putting new life into and improving all the other organizations of the working class. Hence the slogan of purging the Party'. And so on, till the very end, when at the 19th Congress of the CPSU in 1952, the last in Stalin's lifetime, the Report on the work of the Central Committee prepared under Stalin's guidance stated: 'the Party cannot close its eyes to the fact that whenever criticism and self-criticism are suppressed and control by the masses over the activities of organisations and institutions is weakened, then such ugly features as bureaucracy and degeneration, and even the corruption of individual sections of the party apparatus invariably appear'.

Such good old Leninist principles were indeed reiterated on every possible occasion but with the consolidation of Stalinism in the Party and the state, Soviet political practice was increasingly diverging from them. Even the purges Stalin carried out were of *another* kind which only further decimated what was still left of the 'Party of Lenin'. Far from being able to act as an effective check on bureaucracy, the Party itself was fast degenerating – the disappearance of internal democracy, poverty of theory, corruption of power, Stalinist purges, all contributing to its rapid decay as a revolutionary 'vanguard'. A party is not a 'vanguard' (or for that matter, even proletarian, revolutionary or socialist) by law or self-proclamation. It is so, above all, by virtue of its actual work, political role and social endorsement. And here disastrous erosion had occurred by the end of the

Stalin period. In *appearance* the same, but in *reality* little trace of the old Bolshevik Party of Lenin remained. As Moshe Lewin has noted: 'the party became an organization of an unprecedented type: a bureaucratic political administration, highly centralized and geared to mobilization, regimentation, and control, entirely different from what it had been under Lenin'.

Stalin's other theoretical-political limitations or mistakes apart, his entire conception of proletarian revolution or socialist construction was vitiated by an outlook of social engineering managed from the top. Thus while Lenin always recognised the role of 'the Russian proletariat', 'peasantry' or 'part of the peasantry', of the people or classes in the October Revolution, Stalin would speak of the role of 'a handful of Bolshevik members of the Petrograd Soviet' or 'we, this small group' in the revolutionary process. Stalin's conception of politics primarily as an organisational affair is well expressed in his early boast about the Bolshevik Party as 'A party which without fear of confusion in its ranks is able at a wave of the hand of the Central Committee to reform its ranks and march against the enemy'. A fetishism of organisation was indeed a marked future of Stalin's 'revolution from above', where not creativity of people and politics but organisation had primacy in the construction of socialism. All that was needed to transform society was an iron will and ruthless leadership at the top of the party using the ramified organisational structures below (trade unions, soviets, etc.) as its 'transmission belts'. Voluntarism implicit in this view of social engineering – 'there is no citadel which Bolsheviks cannot storm' – not only involved search for shortcuts without awareness of economic reality, but, almost invariably, took little or no account of the real human and material costs of such shortcuts, however much all this otherwise contradicted the dominant belief in the mechanical progress of productive forces which, on their own, were to give birth to a socialist society.

This essentially non-Marxist, instrumental orientation was fully reflected in the Party as it came to be, just as it was in the construction of socialism as 'a revolution from above'. With barrack-like obedience, unquestioning compliance with orders from above, and publicly proclaimed sycophancy, the Party had become a docile instrument, indeed a machine at the disposal of a small clique at the top, and finally Stalin himself – 'the Leader', 'the Teacher', 'the Father of the Peoples', 'the Radiant Sun', etc., etc. With the absence or disappearance of democracy within, the Party ceased to be any kind of legitimate 'demiurge' of revolutionary transformation. Instead, it was itself transformed from an organised *means* of revolutionary struggle into an *end in itself*, almost a metaphysical entity with the attribute of infallibility, justifying itself through a characteristic establishment of an apriori, nominal, definitional link between what the Communist Party does and what it is supposed to do or that which is worthwhile and desirable to work for (the liberation of the proletariat, democracy, socialism-communism, etc.) Its Marxism *ideologised*, the Party saw itself not as it was or had become, but rather as a moment of an optimistic, deterministic, teleological and historical scheme. History on its side, it was inexorably marching towards victory. For it only the past changed but the future remained fully certain and the present did not need any kind of critical assessment. Its democratic moorings lost, the Party stood transformed from its original conception and role of the Leninist times.

This transformation of the Party was preceded and accompanied by the absence of democracy in the Soviet society as such – the working masses were deprived of the right to criticise and discuss or to take decisions affecting the political life of the country, they were gagged in their factories and farms, trade unions and soviets, threatened with charges of 'wrecking' and 'counter-revolution', and terrorised by a ubiquitous police system. The 'essence of Stalinism', as Deutscher wrote, 'lay precisely in the fact that it did not allow any independent opinion to form itself or any opposition to crystalise'. This only undermined and ultimately destroyed any living links the party had with the people. The Party, thus degenerated ideologically, as well as organisationally, and itself bureaucratised, could hardly serve as a check on the powerful and ever-proliferating bureaucracy. On the contrary, without a social base in the proletariat or support of the peasantry, a machine increasingly penetrable by opportunists and careerists, the Party came to find a social base in the growing bureaucracy itself. And this gave the latter the opportunity, in turn, to infiltrate the Party, gradually taking it over as its own instrument of rule and adapting its ideology, by now an ossified and strongly economistic form of Marxism, to the needs of the new situation. Bureaucracy had always needed and sought protection of the Party, whose membership, especially posts in the hierarchy, had long become a gateway to career advancement. With the crystallisation of a bureaucratic faction at its top under Stalin, the Party eventually became the site of political leadership of the bureaucracy. There arose a bloc of higher echelons of the party and state bureaucracy including the technocratic or managerial elite – really a class-in-the process-of-becoming, an incipient ruling and exploiting class, well aware of its privileged status and with a strong interest in perpetuation of its power. Its membership came from diverse social backgrounds, but internal conflicts notwithstanding, it had common interests, though it was not yet fully conscious of them or clear about how to pursue them. By the very nature of its origins it lacked traditions or an ideology of its own. Nevertheless, to be described later as 'party bourgeoisie' (Bettelheim) or perhaps more accurately as 'state bourgeoisie' (Sweezy), it already had important class-like characteristics and played an essentially class role in the history of the period. Among the reasons why it was not recognised as such was the fact that in the prevalent or accepted theory, classes were entirely defined and circumscribed by the property system, that is, ownership of the means of production. And the emerging privileged stratum or class did not legally own them. The juridical insistence on the leading role of the Communist Party also provided a cover for the replacement of the working class as the mainspring of power by a privileged group, a proto-neo-bourgeoisie. Vulgarised Marxism too was rushed in to provide whatever faltering legitimisation it could – the already noticed Stalinist notion that egalitarianism is foreign to 'a socialist society organised on Marxian lines' well served as an ideological rationalisation for the established privilege and the emerging class rule.

Some of the negative features or potentialities of this bureaucratic degeneration were, paradoxically, held in check for a time by, if not the Party, the terror practised by Stalin: a bureaucrat abusing his position too blatantly was likely to find himself in a labour camp, if not worse. But after Stalin's death these restraints were largely removed, and the true nature of the situation was soon revealed. The Party with Stalin at its head, for all its faults or terrors, had retained a certain ideological commitment and successfully mobilised people for 'socialist construction', and then for the anti-fascist war, and after the war for post-war reconstruction. But by the late 1950s and 1960s, all pretensions to vanguard role, to lead or mobilise the people were over. Even the Party of Stalin had become the party of Khrushchev and Brezhnev, all set in its progressive degeneration to become the party of Gorbachev and Yeltsin, that is no Communist Party at all, only a parasitic part of Soviet privilegentsia. During the Brezhnev period, when the insecurity of the ruling cadres was finally relaxed, the reality finally emerged: the *nomenklatura* – of course together with state-bureaucratic and managerial technical elites – had become a stable ruling and exploiting class.

Trotsky has written of the Stalinist 'Thermidor', which however is not a fully adequate understanding. The actual Thermidor happened only after Stalin's death – or, rather, even after Khrushchev's fall – with the Brezhnev years of 'stagnation' when the *nomenklatura* finally stabilised itself into a 'new class'. Stalinism proper is better viewed as the enigmatic 'vanishing mediator' between the authentic Leninist revolutionary outburst and its Thermidor. Trotsky, however, is right in his prediction from the 1930s that the Soviet regime could end only in two ways: either a workers' revolt against it, or the *nomenklatura* would no longer be satisfied with only political power but would convert itself into a capitalist class which directly owned the means of production. This second scenario is what effectively happened: post-collapse, the new private owners of the means of production in the ex-socialist countries, especially in the former Soviet Union, were, in their large majority, the members of the ex-*nomenklatura*.

Accepting Trotsky's view of the Soviet Thermidor, Kagarlitsky has written:

> By the 1930s, the Soviet Union was no longer ruled by a 'revolutionary regime'. Trotsky correctly called the new political order the Soviet Thermidor, in which the new elite no longer srved the 'proletarian revolution' but looked after itself. In the 1940s, with the rise of the Soviet super-power, the regime increasingly took on Bonapartist features. Though gravely weakened, the revolutionary impulse still made itself felt, and this was the secret both of the socio-economic success of the USSR in the post-war period, and of the attractiveness of our country to the developing world. Nevertheless, this impulse was finally extinguished. By the late 1980s we had a huge country with an inefficient super-centralized – and not particularly planned – economy, and a bloated, hypertrophied bureaucracy that was dreaming of acquiring property as well as power. The epoch of the 'Soviet Thermidor' had come to an end. The time had come for restoration. This historical task was taken on by the Yeltsin regime, with support from the West.

XVI

The degeneration of revolution was inevitably accompanied by a degeneration of Marxism in the Soviet Union, the two naturally facilitating each other. We have already in different contexts referred to the initial inadequacies of Bolshevik theory in coping with the entirely unanticipated post-October situation in Russia and the rigidly scientistic and economistic form Marxism acquired in the post-Lenin Soviet Union. But in view of the centrality of the theoretical failure in the deformation and ultimate disintegration of the socialist experiment in the Soviet Union, a brief additional comment will not be out of place.

During the post-Lenin period of planned economic development, war against fascism, and post-war reconstruction, there was remarkable ideological mobilisation under Stalin's leadership which saw the Soviet people and communists perform great acts of heroism and sacrifice. This mobilisation had the leadership claiming Bolshevik legacy and speaking in the name of Marxism and its ideals, making for a faith that continued to inspire in the 1920s and 1930s and retained some of its substance in the 1940s and early 1950s. But this Marxism was fast becoming an ideology in the service of the state. An important factor here, that Marx himself had explicitly warned against, has been thus noticed by Victor Serge: 'Whatever may be the scientific value of a doctrine, from the moment it becomes governmental, interests of State will cease to allow it the possibility of impartial inquiry [and] lead it.... to exempt itself from criticism.' Marxism is a critical theory of society; therein lies its inherent strength. 'Our task', as Marx put it, 'is ruthless criticism of everything that exists, ruthless in the sense that the criticism will not shrink either from its own conclusions or from conflict with the powers that be'. But now, far from providing the much-needed 'ruthless criticism' of Soviet society, Marxism was called upon to deny or rationalise the violations of its own core principles and commitments, even hide or justify the emerging class contradictions. Petrifaction inevitably followed. As 'Marxism-Leninism', it was transformed from a critical science, a living and developing practice-oriented doctrine, into a fixed dogma, virtually a secular religion, dividing the world into the good and the evil, the believer and the unbeliever, and providing all clarity and every certitude. As a 'way of breaking' the revisionist orthodoxy of the Second International, scientistic orthodoxy of Stalin had full rein; dialectics itself, its radical categories now frozen as 'laws' in official Marxism, came in handy for 'use by the Party leadership to justify its decisions', as Althusser later acknowledged. In its Stalinised version Marxism-Leninism become a rigid. schematic, catechistic codification of basic principles totally incapable of providing what was most needed: an adequate theory of transition to socialism in a backward and beleaguered Soviet Union, and correctives to its errors, deviations and distortions. On the contrary, incapable of confronting Soviet reality with reason, it became a legitimising ideology whose primary function was to evade or mask this reality, or to serve as a means of ideological manipulation and control of the people (even as the Party, increasingly bereft of any clear or consistent class base or popular support, was coming to rely more and more on its control over the powerful security apparatus and the armed forces to retain its domination in society).

The bureaucratised party and state leadership were remarkably successful in appropriating an appallingly distorted version of the vocabulary of Marxism, via official Marxism-Leninism. The success of this appropriation may be partly attributed to a stultifying system of indoctrination at every level of education in which people were forced to regurgitate obviously dishonest material from textbooks of catatonic dullness and to confine their intellectual work to the limits set by official ideology. Creative original texts of Marxist theory were not used in this education; not only Trotsky but Rosa Luxemburg and Gramsci too were out, and the best Marxist work from the West or elsewhere was ignored or banned because of its critical attitude towards the Soviet Union, even when it was basically friendly or concerned writing. Nor was creative Marxism permitted within the country. A vast mass of self-styled Marxist texts and formal Soviet academic commentaries continued to pour from the Party's publishing houses but it is significant that Soviet Marxism made no major contribution to Marxist theory in the 20th century. It did not produce a single Marxist thinker of any stature, nor a single *Marxist* study of Soviet social formation. The contrast with classical tradition of Marxism, its intellectual and moral quality, is only too glaring. The writings of Marx and Engels were indeed available, but the citizen was, as it were, inoculated against their effect. Thus when Gorbachev's spokesman, Gedenny Gerasimov, told editors of the conservative *National Review* in 1990 that resistance to *perestroika* was due to the fact that 'Some people read too much Marx', he was completely wrong. Marx was little read in the Soviet Union, either by the people or their leaders. The Soviet leaders, for understandable reasons, were indeed printing, publishing, distributing or selling Marx worldwide, including the Soviet Union, but they, including Gorbachev, had themselves stopped reading him a long time ago. What better evidence of this 'Marxlessness' of the latter-day Soviet leadership than the fact that Gorbachev and his colleague and crony Kavlev, political bureau member in charge of ideology in the CPSU at that, charged Marx, of all things, with lack of concern for 'human values'! And this when Marx's *Economic and Philosophic*

Manuscripts of 1844 was already among the most discussed books of the post-war decades and scholars in Gorbachev's much-admired marketised West, discovering in Marx 'the flowering of western humanity' were busy claiming him, the 'humanist' and 'freedom loving' Marx of the *Manuscripts*, as West's very own – of course as against the revolutionary Marx of the *Communist Manifesto* and *Capital*.

XVII

For the purpose of these notes, it is not necessary to attempt any overall assessment of the historical role of Stalin. It would suffice to make a few concluding observations on 'the Stalin phenomenon' as it has been called, whose complexity relates to both his achievement in what was built as socialism in the Soviet Union as well as his contribution to its crisis and ultimate disintegration.

Stalin was an old Bolshevik, a leader of the October Revolution in his own right, a great organiser and essentially a political being with a revolutionary commitment to build socialism, as *he* understood it, in the Soviet Union. With all his personal failings, limitations of theory and subject to grave compulsions of objective circumstances, socialism in the Soviet Union is indeed what he aimed at. In Bialer's words, his was 'the principal role' as a 'revolutionary transformer and restorer' in changing backward Russia, its economic and technological topography, beyond recognition and this at a rate surpassing anything achieved anywhere else in the world. The achievement was indeed unparalleled. As Churchill put it, 'he inherited a Russia with a wooden plough, and left it with atomic weapons.' If critics have not been wanting, scholars like E.H. Carr, Maurice Dobb, Alec Nove, R.W. Davies and others, have upheld Stalin's perspective on industrialisation, which was, it needs to be recognised, widely shared within the Party as a whole. Appreciative of Stalin's 'accomplishments in the domain of industrialisation' Issac Deutscher has written of the 'positive historical function of Stalinism' which made possible rapid economic development in an underdeveloped nation. At the same time, while the door to education, culture and better life was opened by the October Revolution, the new system ensured that basic goods and amenities, work or livelihood and social security were available for the entire population, men and women alike. It had a built-in-bias in favour of expanding the domain of literacy and education, of music and culture, of sports and athletics, of civilised life in general for the people. The occupational structure of the entire population underwent a rapid change; with new educational and social mobility, a new intelligentsia arose from among the workers and peasants. The Soviet people, loved and admired everywhere, came to be the cynosure of the world's eyes. And however grievously flawed its 'international proletarianism', the new Soviet state, under Stalin's leadership, yet stood up in its name for peace, popular causes and third world liberation and against western imperialist powers in general, which is such a contrast with the capitulation and surrender to imperialism typical of the latter-day Soviet rulers, especially during the Gorbachev era. As Alain Badiou has pointed out, 'actually existing socialism' was the only political force that – for some decades, at least – seemed to pose an effective threat to the global rule of capitalism, really terrifying its representatives, driving them into paranoid reaction. It may be added that today when capitalism defines and structures the totality of human civilisation, every 'communist' territory was and is a kind of 'liberated territory' as Fredric Jameson recently put it apropos Cuba; even in their failure the 'communist' regimes opened up a certain space, the space of utopian expectation which, among other things, enabled us to measure the failure of actually existing socialism itself and, for that matter, now enables us to measure the failure of 'actually existing capitalism' as well.

The 'socialism' that Stalin built is thus not without its achievement. But this achievement exacted a very heavy price from the Soviet people. If the forced collectivisation of agriculture visited untold ruin and suffering upon the Russian peasantry, the break-neck industrialisation involved colossal waste of both human and material resources. A failure as a model of socialism, it was a tightly regimented society whose administrative-command economy had its political counterpart in a centralised one-party state, dictatorial and even terroristic towards the people, the terror not sparing even the Communist Party itself which came to be ruthlessly purged and decimated within – 'Self-Destruction of the Bolsheviks' or 'The Party Commits Suicide' is how scholars Getty and Naumov have recently described this Stalinist terror against the Soviet Communist Party. Lucio Colletti has wryly remarked, Stalin 'had more communists on his conscience than had hitherto been exterminated by the entire world bourgeoisie'.

There could be no greater contrast than that between the 'socialism from below' sketched out in the Marxist classics and embodied in the October Revolution and Lenin's own socialist project for Russia and the Stalinist system as it took its final shape in the 1930s, a society ruled from the top, all political, economic and cultural power concentrated in the hands of the *nomenklatura*, the privileged layer of officials at the apex of the party and state hierarchies –a regime whose repressions resolved no contradictions of Soviet society, only confirmed them. Stalinism as ideology and practice reflected the degeneration of the October Revolution, it was a repudiation of not only the classical legacy of Marxism but of the Leninist Bolshevik heritage as well. It is significant that while it lasted, 'actually existing socialism' of Soviet Union was never seen, in the West or elsewhere, as a superior alternative, *at all levels*, to even the most advanced capitalist societies, as classical Marxism had always visualised it; it was best seen as an alternative model of a social-welfarist rapid economic development for the post-colonial societies of the third world – which, one may add, in its own paradoxical manner, summed up both the failure and achievement of Soviet socialism.

It is rightly emphasised that decisive for its failure as socialism was the failure of Soviet socialism on the plane of democracy which, as we have seen, was integral to the classical view of socialism. Even so it needs to be recognised that in the period 1928–38, during the war against fascism, and for the post-war reconstruction, Stalin had immense popular support – Soviet economy functioned and secured its successes because it could secure the cooperation of workers. As even a critic like

Nove has concluded: 'Clearly, this was not just a matter of combination of terror and propaganda.' The *glasnost*-produced Soviet critics of Stalin too have recognised the depth of popular support for him. Thus Latsis has observed that among millions, especially the youth till at least 1937, there was real enthusiasm: 'Among the people there was both hatred and reverence towards the Leader and the Teacher'. If Stalin's forced collectivisation and industrialisation programmes were driven forward in a quasi-military manner there was also a massive mobilisation of cadres from below who were yet inspired by the proclaimed ideals of the revolution and who, in a hostile world, saw Stalin's 'general line' as essential to the survival of their Party and the state it controlled. They indeed responded with courage and dedication. No doubt the simplification of economic tasks during the early phase of industrialisation, war-time and post-war reconstruction helped, but the CPSU under Stalin's leadership was still able to demand sacrifices from its cadres, members and supporters among the people. The need to meet threats of foreign intervention and to realise the promise of a happy future were enough to persuade even such a man as Andrei Sakharov to give of his best and to weep when Stalin died.

Thus, as I have mentioned before, the Soviet people indeed built with and despite Stalin. And I would like to add that in the overall historical situation of the times, despite all that had gone wrong, yes, even horrendously wrong, it was morally right and more legitimate to take sides with Stalin and defend what had been built than act otherwise. Of course one could have been more critical even when hopeful of a change for the better. And certainly, now that its ignominious collapse has grievously damaged the cause of socialism everywhere, one needs to be ruthlessly critical to be able to draw the necessary right lessons from what has happened. Even so the currently fashionable Stalin-bashing (or, for that matter, bashing of his successors as the ultra-left generally does) will not do – it is no Marxism, or any other kind of legitimate historical analysis. What was built had its unparalleled achievements and Stalin was undoubtedly a great man. Critics as far apart as Winston Churchill, M.N. Roy and Issac Deutscher have recognised it. He was a Bolshevik leader in his own right, a close comrade of Lenin, and a great organiser and inspirer of people. It is necessary to take a balanced view of his place in the history of our times. We may here recall the assessment of E.H. Carr, who questioned those interested simply in 'throwing stones at Stalin' and concluded:

> Stalin's role in history thus remains paradoxical and in some sense contradictory. He carried out, in face of every obstacle and opposition, the industrialization of his country through intensive planning and thus not only paid tribute to the validity of Marxist theory, but ranged the Soviet Union as an equal partner among the Great Powers of the western world. In virtue of this achievement he takes his undisputed place both as one of the great executors of the Marxist testament and one of the great westernizers in Russian history. Yet this *tour de force* had, when studied and analysed, a supremely paradoxical character. Stalin laid the foundations of the proletarian revolution on the grave of Russian capitalism, but through a deviation from Marxist premises so sharp as to amount almost to a rejection of them. He westernized Russia, but through a revolt, partly conscious, partly unconscious, against western influence and authority and a reversion to familiar national attitudes and traditions. The goal to be attained and the methods adopted or proposed to attain it often seemed in flagrant contradiction – a contradiction which in turn reflected the uphill struggle to bring a socialist revolution to fruition in a backward environment. Stalin's ambiguous record was an expression of this dilemma. He was an emancipator and a tyrant; a man devoted to a cause, yet a personal dictator; and he consistently displayed a ruthless vigour which issued, on the one hand, in the extreme boldness and determination and, on the other, in extreme brutality and indifference to human suffering. The key to these ambiguities cannot be found in the man himself. The initial verdict of those who failed to find in Stalin any notable distinguishing marks had some justification. Few great men have been so conspicuously as Stalin the product of the time and place in which they lived.

XVIII

It is possible, and in its own way quite legitimate to see Stalinism as a consequence of 'Russian backwardness' and the accompanying 'heritage of oppression, misery and ignorance', the 'low cultural level of the country', the 'social composition of the population', 'the pressure of a barbaric world imperialism', etc., as Trotsky and many others have done. Scholars like Carr and Deutscher, in recognising and even appreciating Stalin's historical role, have also emphasised a certain 'impersonal' aspect of his personality and noted the more basic and powerful socio-historical pressures that manifested themselves through the instrumentality of Stalin's personality. Thus, Carr plays down the elements of personal conviction or originality of conception in Stalin's 'revolution from above' and characterises him as 'the most impersonal of great historical figures'. Deutscher calls Stalin a man of 'almost impersonal personality' and sees him as a great improviser who responded to the pressure of extremely adverse national circumstances in 'an unpremeditated, pragmatic manner'. Certainly Stalin had no blueprint of the kind of society he wanted to create which then governed his policies. While considerations of theory or conviction did play some role, Stalin actually improvised as he went along, rather than following a preconceived strategy. During the crucial formative period of the society he built, between 1928 and the end of the Second World War, Stalin was probably mainly motivated by fear of external attack and a supposed need, in the face of this danger, to industrialise through forced marches and to crush all actual or potential internal opposition. Thus it can even be argued that the kind of socialism created in the Soviet Union during these years was in a real sense a by-product of policies designed to accomplish other ends.

But to thus emphasise the objective situation and its compulsions, external or internal, or the 'impersonality' of Stalin as a historical figure, almost absolves him of any responsibility for the ugliness and cruelties of what happened in the Soviet Union during this period, the enormous deformities of what come to be built as socialism. And this is wrong. For what happened or was built was nevertheless the outcome of conscious decisions and acts of the party leadership for the most part after Stalin took over; these were policies in whose formulation and pursuit Stalin's was the decisive role. And this is a crucially important point, for these policies could have been different. Other, better options *were* possible.

The policies to be adopted were a matter of discussion and debate in the party before Stalinist policies or options came to prevail. Such was the Leninist tradition in the party. While the October Revolution had opened up all kinds of possibilities to begin building a new social order, in the situation that developed in its aftermath the Bolsheviks vigorously discussed and debated among themselves and made difficult choices between different policies. Oppositional groups or trends – the 'Left Opposition', the 'Workers' Opposition', 'Left-wing communism' in general – continued to exist and argue for the policies they wanted to be pursued. Lenin was not the only individual responsible for decision-making, opposition did not cease to function despite a ban against factions decided at the Tenth Party Congress in 1921, and there was always the possibility of critically reviewing party policy. Lenin himself engaged in it constantly, especially towards the end of his life. Even after Lenin, until at least the mid-1920s, various factions of the 'Left Opposition' remained active, the 'Workers' Opposition' continued to advocate the idea of a power takeover by the working class, and the Factory Committees, Soviets and trade unions discussed alternative policies and enjoyed a certain autonomy of action. In fact, compared with the 1930s, when Stalinism finally established its domination in the party, the situation in the 1920s was markedly different in its opportunities for a specific kind of political pluralism, of course within an overall commitment to build socialism. If Stalin's collectivisation programme had the support of Trotsky, it was vigorously opposed by Bukharin. Trotsky's opposition group had its alternatives to offer to several of Stalin's policies. The concept of 'permanent revolution' properly interpreted, carried with it a different policy perspective for the building of socialism in the Soviet Union. It is a fact that Stalin continued to be confronted by a strong opposition till the very end of the 1920s. And this included warnings by old Bolshevik leaders against the growing bureaucratisation and loss of ideological commitment and revolutionary élan in the party. Sounding the alarm – 'in good time', as he said – 'on the terrible decline of the spirit of activity of the working class and on their increasing indifference towards the destiny of the dictatorship of the proletariat and of the Soviet state', Christian Rakovsky – an old Bolshevik who later fell victim to the Stalinist terror – asked (in 1928):

> ....what has happened to the spirit of revolutionary activity of the party and of our proletariat? Where has their revolutionary initiative gone? Where their ideological interests, their revolutionary values, their proletarian pride have gone? You are surprised that there is so much apathy, weakness, pusillanimity, opportunism and so many other things that I could add myself? How is it that those who have a worthy revolutionary past, whose present honesty cannot be held in doubt, who have given proof of their attachment t the revolution on more than one occasion, can have been transformed into pitiable bureaucrats?

All this is only to suggest that policies other than those adopted by Stalin were possible. Of course as Stalin consolidated his hold on the party in the 1930s, the possibility ceased to exist. But this is not to argue that the Stalinist policies were the only possible policies, so decreed by the objective situation.

Paul Sweezy has written:

> What is crucial is that these policies were deliberately decided upon and in no sense a mere reflex of an objective situation. They could have been different. The goal they were intended to achieve could have been different, and the combination of means designed to achieve the goal actually chosen or another goal or set of goals could also have been different. And the result ..... could have been a different society operating with a different internal logic and following a different course of development.
>
> These are not mere armchair speculations. We *know* that different courses were possible in the decisive years after Lenin's death because we know that great struggles and debates racked the Bolshevik Party in that period. Nothing requires us to believe that Stalin's victory was inevitable, or that if the Left or Right Opposition had won out it would necessarily have followed the same course he followed.

Pointing out that the options were real and the Soviet Union came to be what it was because some were embraced and others rejected, Sweezy adds:

> Stalin was certainly right to make preparations to repel external aggression the number one priority, but ... a different choice of means could have produced better results in the short run and much better results in the long run. More equality and fewer privileges to the bureaucracy, more trust and confidence in the masses, greater inner party democracy – these, we believe, could have been the guiding principles of a course which would have ensured the survival of the Soviet Union and pointed it toward, rather than away from the luminous vision of a communist future.

So long as 'actually existing socialism' continued to exist, there was always the hope for rectification, for a correction of course, that is, a turn in the direction of genuine socialism. But realisation of such a possibility was, at the very least predicated upon a recognition that what was built was not socialism but, at best, a deeply deformed or distorted version of it, and a return to classical Marxism not only to recover the original socialist project but to acquire the theoretical resources necessary for such rectification of course. This was indeed a very daunting task and, in the circumstances, it demanded a very high quality of leadership in the party and the state in the Soviet Union. In retrospect, it is only too obvious, such leadership was never forthcoming.

XIX

Lenin's political practice, in its essentials, throughout remained within the authentic tradition of classical Marxism, above all its revolutionary commitment, its internationalism and its vision of socialism as an emancipatory project. During the few years that he survived the October Revolution, compelled by the most adverse circumstances to make ad hoc, even dangerous departures from principles, he yet recognised them as departures to be rectified at the earliest. Facing an entirely unprecedented task from the standpoint of classical Marxism, namely, to struggle for a socialist transition in the backward, isolated and beleaguered Russia, he sought to provide, however inadequately, a guiding theory for the purpose, spelling out some at least of the basic principles of this transition such as the maintenance of the worker-peasant alliance, struggle against bureaucratic degeneration, commitment to democracy within the party and outside, need to stay and struggle with the people and learn from their experience, and so on.

With Stalin a self-conscious search for an adequate theory of socialist transition in Russia took a back seat. Lenin's insights or principles were soon abandoned or violated in practice, and even as earlier departures from principles themselves became principles helped by the compulsion of objective conditions, Leninist project was virtually swamped by a nationalist-productivist view of socialist construction. Even so, Stalin had grown up in the tradition of Lenin's party. His 'revisionism', if we may so describe this shift, still had some vestigial remains of the old Bolshevik tradition. As once on 'the national question', or later in his reports to the Party Congress, and then towards the end about the 'problems of socialism' in the Soviet Union, Stalin could still write theoretically interesting things. His direct heirs, men like Khrushchev and Brezhnev however were reared in the political milieu of Stalinist revisionism, untrammelled by any Bolshevik reflexes. As survivors from Stalin's purges, they expressed the very essence of this revisionism, distilled in its most purified form. And in its most important aspect, they were bereft of any Marxist theory worth the name. And finally, symptomatic of the degeneration of the party and Stalin's tragedy of his own making, (as indeed of the nature of the system built in the Soviet Union) is not only the fact that the change in the leadership of the Soviet Communist Party after Stalin was pulled off by a virtual coup – first by Malenkov and then by Khrushchev ousting Malenkov and killing Beria in the Central Committee itself, but that beyond Khrushchev or Brezhnev, it ultimately spawned within its ranks specimens such as Gorbachev and Yeltsin who were able to reach the highest rungs of the party hierarchy despite being all along totally bereft of any communist commitment or Marxist theory.

Stalin had proclaimed in 1936 that in the Soviet Union 'socialism is something already achieved and won'. And this was the socialism that he imposed in Eastern Europe after its liberation in 1945. This became a dogma with Khrushchev and later Brezhnev and those who followed them in the Soviet leadership. It was to be kept in place in the Soviet Union and maintained, if necessary by force, in Eastern Europe – as for example in Germany (1953), Hungary (1956) and Czechoslovakia (1968). Unable to take a critical look at it, far from seeing it as a most deformed, if not failed model for building socialism, they simply mouthed theoretical inanities about 'developed socialism', even 'full-scale communist construction'! Its growing difficulties or malfunctioning in the Soviet Union or the allied countries was seen entirely as an economic problem, a problem of economic production or management which provoked Mao's legitimate protest: 'They (the Russians) only talk about production and not about revolution'. Critical as Mao was about such matters as Stalin era's 'distrust of peasants', or 'measures which squeeze the peasants very hard', or 'lopsided stress on heavy industry to the neglect of agriculture and light industry', his basic objection was: 'Stalin emphasised only technology, technical cadre. He wanted nothing but technology, nothing but cadre; no politics, no masses.' Again, apropos Stalin's *Economic Problems of Socialism in the U.S.S.R.*: 'This book by Stalin has not a word on the superstructure from the beginning to the end. It never touches on man. We read of things but not man. His basic error is his distrust of the people. I think the Soviets have not seen clearly the relationship between long-term and immediate interests... They believe technology and cadres decide everything. They emphasize specialization but not redness, cadres but not the masses...(They) ignore superstructure, politics, and the role of the people. Without a communist movement it is impossible to attain communism'. And significantly enough, when the economic problems of the Soviet economy mounted, instead of turning left, towards people and classical socialism – that is finding a solution in such measures as weakening bureaucracy, politicising the masses and entrusting increasing initiative and responsibility to the workers themselves – they turned rightward and the remedy was sought in reforms based on assigning a growing role to capitalist forms and criteria in the management of the economy, no matter how irrelevant all this was to the real problems ailing the Soviet economy. Instead of resolving the contradictions that had got built into the system, particularly the key contradiction – the structural subordination of labour to the material and political imperatives of the system that had been built as socialism – they went in for 'scientific management of society' where 'scientific' was only a synonym for 'capitalist'. Literature on the subject by planners, reform-minded economists or plain party ideologues proliferated like anything in the Soviet Union. A fetishism of technology took over; system's social antagonisms were sought to be eliminated through technical devices, 'new instruments' and 'improved mechanisms'. No wonder such reforms or remedies did not work and the crisis of the system only deepened. The resulting popular discontent was met in classical ruling-class fashion, by making superficial concessions on the one hand and accentuating repression on the other. (Later, when under Gorbachev similar reforms or remedies only got the system into a deeper mess, they opted, characteristically, for the restoration of capitalism).

Along with these internal developments went a transformation of Soviet foreign policy, characterised by an increasing abandonment of whatever socialist features it once had. Not long after denouncing Stalin in his secret speech as a monstrous tyrant, Khrushchev ordered the bloody suppression of the Hungarian uprising in October 1956. And after twelve more years of openly declared 'destalinisation' and 'democratisation', his successor Brezhnev – the new party boss who had deposed him – emulated him in putting a brutal end to Dubcek's 'socialism with a human face' in Czechoslovakia in August 1968. Such use of direct force in Eastern Europe apart, brutal if unsuccessful pressures were brought to bear on China and Albania to force them to submit to Soviet hegemony. On the world stage the Soviet Union increasingly played the part of a 'great power', entering into both competition and collaboration with the United States as the other great power, with its own sphere of influence and not hesitating to send its armed forces into other countries in order to uphold its great power interests. The huge armaments race growing out of this situation, even as it contributed to the great post-war boom in the United States, Western Europe and Japan, burdened the

Soviet Union with massive, wasteful military expenditure, forcing it to devote a far larger share of its productive resources to arms than ever before in peace time, something that the Soviet economy could immediately ill-afford and proved disastrous ultimately.

This accelerating political degeneration, within and without, was inevitably accompanied by a further degeneration of Marxist theory in the Soviet Union. Under Stalin Marxism in the Soviet Union had for the most part become a rigidified set of doctrines, which was more ideological than scientific. Far from being a tool of serious analysis, it had, as 'Marxism-Leninism', become more and more an instrument of ideological manipulation and domination of the people. Under Khrushchev it degenerated even by Stalin's standards, and by the time of Brezhnev it had become only so much demagogy, totally divorced from any of its roots in classical Marxism. Indeed we had the absurdity of a ruling oligarchy hiding, justifying and legitimising its rule in the name of Marxism – a quintessentially revolutionary doctrine.

Already with Stalin, while principles of socialism were being trampled upon, its vocabulary was retained. The dream, as it were, was lumped together with reality when the reality was increasingly a violation of the dream. Thus, the Soviet Union was a 'proletarian dictatorship' even if the workers exercised no power whatsoever, or the year of the great purges and of terror at its highest, 1936, was also the year when 'the most democratic' constitution was promulgated. This yawning gap between theory and practice, expressed in Orwellian newspeak, was only perpetuated by Stalin's successors, and as the reality moved still further away from the dream, losing whatever legitimacy it still had in the Stalin era, it was a major factor in demoralisation of the people, their resentment and cynicism and ultimate rejection of socialism itself. After all this was the only socialism the Soviet people knew. A parallel process was at work in relation to Marxism, in whose name this 'socialism' was built and sought to be legitimised. As the demagogic or clichéd expression of ideals of Marxism contrasted with the ugly class character of Soviet social reality, as the awful gap between proclaimed principles or values and practice on the ground was revealed, it only bred cynicism and hostility among the people. Yet this was the only Marxism they knew. It is not surprising therefore that the final discrediting of the system meant a massive discrediting, along with socialism, of Marxism itself. And the ideological vacuum thus created was ultimately filled in by capitalist consumerism, religious revivalism, national or ethnic chauvinism, even anti-Semitism, indeed by all kinds of reactionary ideologies. (Of course, the ruling elite had already transited to neo-liberalism, and it is worth noticing that almost all the ideologues of capitalism in pre- or post-collapse Russia and East European countries had studied in Communist Party schools with Marxism as a compulsory subject!)

XX

The multiple contradictions of socialism built under Stalin's leadership, dormant or suppressed earlier, first clearly surfaced, as a crisis of the system in the post-Stalin period, significantly enough just when it had gained extraordinary legitimacy and credibility for its performance in the struggle against fascism and seemed to have not only stabilised itself after the post-war reconstruction, but, with revolutions in Eastern Europe and China, expanded into an alternative 'socialist world'. The emergent crisis posed the crucial question: whether the forces of social transformation in the Soviet Union could draw adequate and appropriate lessons from their own experience and the reality around them to correct their mistakes (and to atone for their crimes in certain cases) with a view to moving forward in the right direction. This was a possibility that socialists the world over hoped for. But the bureaucratic degeneration of the system had already gone too far and with the quality of leadership that Stalin had left behind, it remained only a theoretical possibility – even the warnings in Hungary (1956), Czechoslovakia (1968) or still later Poland (1980) went unheeded and whatever promise they held was ruthlessly extinguished, presaging the explosive denouement of our times when as a writer in the then Moscow periodical, *New Times*, put it: 'To the surprise of the world the 'socialist camp' has collapsed in one autumn'. This was in November 1990 and the reference was to Eastern Europe. A couple of years later Soviet Union itself collapsed out of existence.

Khrushchev in a way symbolised both the crisis of the system as well as the utter lack of resources within to cope with it, that is, to recover and regenerate the system along genuinely socialist lines. This found an eloquent expression in Khrushchev's famous report to the 20th Congress of the CPSU (1956) which in laying all the blame on Stalin – the 'cult of personality' – also provided irrefutable evidence of the utter poverty of theory on the part of the new leadership. It literally proclaimed the fact that CPSU had abandoned Marxism. As Althusser pointed out, the 'pseudo-concept' of the 'cult of personality' did expose 'certain practices', 'abuses', 'errors' and 'crimes' but it explained 'nothing of their conditions, of their causes, in short their internal determination and therefore their forms'. While Stalin's role or that of other leaders was indeed important, the policies and practices of the Stalin era needed to be explained in terms of the system that had been built, by the social relations that had come to prevail which facilitated the accession to power of such leaders and gave them the ability to operate their policies. This pseudo-explanation made it abundantly clear that the post-Stalin leadership was incapable of analysing and understanding their society in Marxist terms or of tackling the task of transforming the real social relations which had given rise to the evils now being verbally condemned. Such an 'explanation', together with concepts like 'state of the whole people', 'developed socialism' or the 'stageist-view' of transition to communism, only served to hide and help consolidate the class relations that had emerged which concentrated economic and political power in the hands of a minority, and which far from alleviating them, only further deepened the contradictions within the system that had been built. In the meantime while the old clichéd theoretical positions were regularly reiterated and demagogic declarations of 'burying capitalism' were made, other fashionable concepts of this period, 'peaceful coexistence', 'peaceful competition', 'peaceful transition', etc. had no Marxism nor any socialist vision about them; they were really an explicit renunciation of international class-struggle and its subordination to the 'national interests' of the Soviet Union – a definitive departure from the Leninist foreign policy of proletarian internationalism, which visualised an alliance with the revolutions or revolutionary struggles of the advanced countries and with all oppressed peoples against the imperialists. This departure had its beginnings in the Stalin era and later, almost inevitably, ended up in Gorbachev's ultimate surrender to imperialism.

No one took such concept-mongering seriously except the 'fraternal' communist parties. Insofar as there was indeed anything like theory underlying the essentially pragmatic practices of the post-Stalin period, it was a productivist, scientistic-technological view of the struggle with capitalism and the transition to socialism/communism itself.

In the long Brezhnev period, even the Khrushchevian pretensions to theory disappeared. The half-hearted attempts at reform too were abandoned, leading to a situation of all-pervasive bureaucratic stagnation. As the ruling elite lived off the fat of the economic achievement of the past, only the regular reiteration of old clichéd 'theoretical' positions remained. This theoretical degeneration, which was to soon reach its denouement in the Gorbachev era, was only a complementary aspect of the political change that had now occurred in the Soviet system. Brezhnev's coup against Khrushchev had not only put an end to the limited de-Stalinisation of the Khrushchev period but also removed the threat that Khrushchev's proposal to revamp the leadership every few years had posed to the smooth life of the ruling elite. This elite was now finally free from the tensions and personal uncertainties of the Stalin era. Leadership groups and stratum of officials and managers, the privileged bureaucracy in the party, state and economy felt more secure than ever before. Their access to positions of prestige and power was guaranteed. The chances of their children to accede to the status of their parents were enhanced. In other words, the so-called *Nomenklatura*, whose hierarchy was reminiscent of the Tsarist 'Table of Ranks', had finally emerged as a relatively stable ruling class. The people's passivity or acquiesance was won through a subtle and not so subtle combination of political repression, ideological control and, of course , material concessions which allowed a certain rise in their living standards, even as the economy was tending to be stagnant. As a ruling class it was interested in perpetuating its rule at home and, in a grossly vulgar expression of internationalism, playing super-power politics abroad, supporting all kinds of regimes with Marxist labels or otherwise that its presumed national interests demanded. The disastrous decision was taken, in the name of countering USA, to compete with it in strategic nuclear and space research, falling into the American trap to strain and ruin the Soviet economy. The strain of being a super-power, the massive waste of resources which could be put to better economic, political and military use certainly contributed to the Soviet economy virtually reaching a dead end by the time the Brezhnev era ended.

Even as this was happening, the gap between the rulers and the ruled further widened. As the bulk of the people stood in the never-ending queues, or, disillusioned and alienated, turned to religion or vodka or both, communist rulers were busy 'serving the people' from their marble palaces. Corruption that inevitably goes with unchecked political power reached new heights. All the while the likes of Leonid Brezhnev and his cronies pinned endless medals on one another and surrounded themselves with a peasant's or *nouvo riches* notion of luxury. There is no evidence that in the last decades of Soviet Union the Soviet ruling elite, the bureaucracy as a whole, was motivated for a better performance of the system, interested in improving production or optimising output. All evidence since *glasnost* shows the opposite, a growing indifference towards overall economic performance, at the plant level as well as at macro economic level. It had became a non-functional, indeed a dysfunctional ruling class, notable only for its somewhat new ways of extracting surplus from the direct producers, the Soviet workers and peasants, and living off it. In its parasitic existence, this ruling class had no *integral* relation to the system it presided over, it was ready to desert it at the first opportunity for the greener pastures of capitalism.

The system was indeed in decay, ripe for disintegration. All that was needed was a touch of genuine mediocrity. And this final touch was provided by Gorbachev, as true-blooded an *apparatchik* as any produced by the bureaucratically degenerated Soviet Communist Party, come up the way they now did in that party giving all the hostages to fortune on the way. Gorbachev's arrival to power also provided conclusive evidence, if any was still needed, of the long-time decay and degeneration of Marxism in the Soviet Union and its Communist Party. If anything characterised the debates around his *glasnost* and *perestroika*, it was, except at the most negligible fringes, its total Marxism-lessness. And one has only to look at the altogether easy manner in which, in 'a renewal of socialism', Gorbachev transited from his own 'bull-shit' Marxism to the bull-shit liberalism of a Reagan or a Bush.

The 'actually existing socialism' of the Soviet Union finally disintegrated. It was wracked by internal structural contradictions it could not cope with. It was also subject throughout its history to relentless imperialist pressure – there is truth in Chomsky's suggestive observation about the United States taking seven days to take care of Grenada and seventy years to take care of the Soviet Union. Even so its disintegration was not inevitable. Even the capitalist dictatorial regimes do not collapse so ignominiously as the Soviet regime did. Of course, at least in retrospect, it is clear that however viable theoretically, a socialist rectification of the system had become practically impossible. The political and ideological resources for it had been regularly destroyed or squandered over the years and while a new ruling class had consolidated itself, the system itself had reached a dead end. Decisive in the final disintegration was the role of small, generally mediocre, vision-less men who sought to rectify the system, essentially as it had come to be, in their own class interest, but did not know how to go about it, and as it got into a deeper mass, had no compunction in deserting it for capitalism. They were true and ultimate heirs of the very bureaucracy that set the Soviet Union on the road to degeneration and against which Lenin, though ill and dying, had fought to the last. As we have noted earlier, writing of the 'stinking bureaucratic and Soviet bourgeois atmosphere', of 'rotten bureaucracy', Lenin had warned, as if prophetically: 'for this, all of us ... should be hung on stinking ropes.... and I have not yet lost all hope that one day we shall be hung for this, and deservedly so'. The Soviet people may be said to have taken seventy long years to carry out this belated hanging. But in an irony of history they have only hanged themselves.

XXI

Lenin had recognised the trick that history had played on the doctrine of Karl Marx: instead of socialism being built on a base provided by the economic, political and cultural achievements of capitalism, a single backward country was called upon to build it. In responding to this call, together with fellow Bolsheviks he had seen this as a struggle where defeat was a distinct possibility, in which case, he had written, they will have left behind 'experience (that) will benefit other revolutions'. This experience is indeed rich with lessons for the world revolutionary movement. We will later take a close look at what was built as socialism in the Soviet Union, its difficulties and contradictions as they surfaced in the post-Stalin era and its ultimate crisis and disintegration under Gorbachev. The particular lessons to be learnt are implicit in our account, so far and later, of how and why of what has happened, and I will also be explicit about some of them, particularly in the area of democracy, though I reject the widely prevalent but all too simplistic notion that 'all that Soviet system needed was the addition of democracy'. Here, even though it involves a certain amount of repetition, I would like to conclude with a few basic generalisations in this regard.

In any valid assessment of the Soviet experiment in socialism, it is imperative to take account of the extremely adverse circumstances in which it was carried out – a situation entirely unanticipated in classical Marxism. Not prepared to build, the Soviet people under Bolshevik leadership were yet called upon to build socialism – history's most 'radical rupture' as Marx called it – for the first time and that too in a single backward country besieged by global capitalism. The complexity of such an assessment must include not only the severe historical limits of Russia's backward feudal-capitalist economy, the economic, social and cultural determinants involved, but also the fierce resistance and opposition of the rulers of the capitalist world from which it had broken away. Indeed in many vitally important ways, the situation emerging from the October Revolution came nowhere near fitting the classical Marxian schema. The Bolshevik leadership, which had all along regarded a socialist revolution in Russia viable, recognised the immensity of the new, unanticipated task, but were left with no other choice and decided to struggle for socialism in Russia. For them the economic and cultural backwardness of Russia and its isolation within a global capitalist encirclement did not imply any postponement of this struggle. They were undoubtedly right in their decision. In the event this struggle did not prove to be adequate enough and we are now witness to its ultimate failure.

In understanding or explaining this failure, it is indeed legitimate to recognise the harsh logic of the objective historical situation, its myriad internal and external pressures. This not only closed certain desirable paths or options in the struggle but also contributed to the emergence of grave distortions and deformations in what came to be built, and to the ultimate failure of the socialist experiment. But validity of such argumentation notwithstanding, exaggerated emphasis on such historical compulsions, the offering of exclusively objectivist explanations of earlier distortions, or later crisis and collapse, carries within it a certain fatalism or 'inevitablism' which is entirely alien to Marxism. Marx's recognition of 'historic necessity' so-called or emphasis on 'compulsions of the economic', even as it was a warning against false 'voluntarism' or dangerous search for shortcuts, was always combined with the still more important recognition of 'political will' and emphasis on 'men making their own history'. For Marxism, the necessities and constraints of a given objective situation only constitute a 'determination in the *first* instance' as it were; what finally happens, the historical outcome, is ultimately determined by human action, at its best by *revolutionary* action. Therefore, importance of the objective circumstances notwithstanding, revolutionary socialists need to focus on the *subjective* dimension of the historical experience and its outcome in the Soviet Union. That is where the really vital lessons lie. And the most important of these, determining as it were the *quality* of struggle for socialism, concern the *theory* guiding this struggle. In other words, more than anything else, we need to focus on issues in the area of theory of socialist transition – socialist transition anywhere in the world including particularly backward countries in a situation of global domination of capitalism.

XXII

We have had the occasion to notice the areas of 'silence' or 'empty spaces' in classical Marxism. And, for quite understandable reasons, 'socialist transition' is one such area. Therefore, especially when confronted with the task of attempting a socialist transition in backward Russia, the Bolshevik theoretical arsenal was extremely limited and poor. Lenin, in the few years left to him after the revolution, facing what he repeatedly recognised as an entirely unanticipated situation, valiantly tried to cope with this condition of ideological limitation or theoretical poverty. His tentative response to this new, rapidly changing, and often deteriorating economic and political situation, yet contained elements of the much-needed theory of socialist transition. For example, his insistence on democracy, on staying with the people and seeking guidance in their experience, his absolute emphasis on maintaining the worker-peasant alliance, or the necessity of a continuous and successful struggle against the emerging bureaucracies in post-revolutionary society for the very survival of the socialist project, etc., etc. Valuable as an initial effort, these elements yet did not constitute an adequate theory and soon Lenin was no more. In fact, under the pressure of circumstances, Lenin's own political practice had degenerated, there were emergency departures from principles which, with help from the till then most minor authoritarian and substitutionist components and a certain 'organisational fetishism' of pre-1917 Bolshevik tradition, came to provide the basis for a persistent authoritarian and bureaucratic degeneration of the party and the state in the Soviet Union; and when the awareness was recovered that full democracy, both in the party and in the Soviet institutions was the only way to prevent such degeneration, it was already too late. In the post-Lenin period, instead of being further developed, the positive elements of early Leninist theory and practice, lip service apart, were simply abandoned and in place of a search for a genuinely Marxist theory of socialist transition, a vulgar scientistic and economistic Marxism came to prevail. Not changing the social relations of production, but developing the forces of production became the principle of socialist transition. Not politics, that is revolutionary *socialist* politics, but economics came to command the construction of the new socialist society. Such was the overall character of Marxism in the Stalin era. After him, with 'socialism' declared to be already achieved, and that too in less than a decade, the issue of a theory of socialist transition simply disappeared. The Khrushchevs and Brezhnevs who followed, even as Stalin's slogan 'to catch up and overtake' remained their goal, started talking in the still more theoretically vulgar economistic and scientistic-technological terms of a 'transition to communism'! Soon even such pretence to inherited theory disappeared with Gorbachev's own transition to 'bullshit liberalism', the long-discredited capitalist orthodoxies of yesteryears. If the crucial concerns or preoccupations of Marxism had been already for long reduced to a liturgy used on rare festive occasions, the vision of a socialist society was itself now nothing more than consumerist capitalism with a certain degree of social security and welfare.

XXIII

A socialist transition, the creation of a new social order even in the best of circumstances, which are most unlikely to obtain, is bound to be a very difficult enterprise, full of hard choices and great tensions. A prolonged process of social development, it has to reckon with the specificities of the old society, an exceedingly entangled whole with its own history, socio-economic complexity and, invariably, its own 'muck of ages' too. Once embarked on the transition, challenges from within and without to its socialist objectives will arise over and over again during the many years and decades of transition. Problems of building the new on the basis of the old, the future with materials of the past, as Rosa Luxemburg saw it, will come compounded with the constant conflict between the practical and the ideal, making it necessary all the time to make compromise in order to advance, to find alternative ways of dealing with old and new contradictions, ways which would avoid or limit corruption of the ultimate goals. Most important new contradictions will be around the emergence of new social strata and interest groups mainly responsible for shaping and executing economic and political policies and tending, by virtue of their control over the use of society's surplus, to get consolidated into a class. Inequalities or class differences among the people (and discrimination along regional, racial or ethnic, etc. lines) are all the more likely to grow and become ingrained in society if maximising the rate of economic growth becomes the overriding goal. A socialist transition has to consciously work against such deformation; it has to not only do with the old class system but also frustrate the formation of new exploiting classes or social strata. Adequate vigilance and institutional safeguards will be needed to ensure that opportunism, careerism and corruption do not creep in to vitiate the socialist ideals. Insofar as egalitarianism is among the most vital of these ideals, the task here cannot be interpreted in a purely material sense, a matter of changes in the legal ownership of the means of production or income policies. Needing to overcome the crippling heritage of ages, including centuries of capitalism, it demands changes in many other aspects of society, including the entire educational system and the forms of organisation of production and government. A necessarily long process, it will involve not only bitter struggles – which can only be characterised as class struggles – at every step but also paying a more or less high price in terms of immediate productivity or efficiency in order to advance towards greater equality.

Two areas of struggle are crucially important in any socialist transition: changing popular consciousness and practice of democracy. The fact has to be recognised that habit and tradition, deeply encrusted beliefs and ancient prejudices, inherited patterns of thought and behaviour form a stubborn part of reality. They have a remarkable capacity to endure and generally tend to be conservative, at times even reactionary, in their effect on human practices. While all the resources for radical change in society's popular traditions need to be explored and utilised for socialist purposes, an overall change in popular consciousness is imperative for any real progress along the socialist path. Of course, under even the best of circumstances, a change in consciousness is bound to be a long, very long process. But if thoughtless voluntarism here can be counter-productive, exaggerated caution or evasion will be disastrous; witness the dangerous resurgence of long suppressed or ignored national, ethnic, religious and such other sentiments in post-communist regimes (and not only there). A properly nuanced but unending multi-faceted struggle for socialist consciousness is integral to a socialist transition. Equally integral to it, indeed to the generation of this consciousness and to the ongoing uninterrupted revolutionary practice that must permeate a transitional society as a whole, is democracy, a democracy that is really democratic, involving richly-arrayed affirmative action to bring the common people into the corridors of power, releasing their long denied or suppressed creativity, enabling them to call leaders to account and prevent corruption of socialist ideals.

In a most perceptive discussion of the problems of a socialist transition, emphasising that a socialist project to be socialist, even as a transition, has to be a democratic project, ensuring full participation by the people, and that such participation demands an increasingly transformed social consciousness on the part of the people, Harry Magdoff has written:

> If a new social order can only work and be meaningful if it is shaped and directed by the will and consent of the people, the role of the leadership, especially its upper echelons, their life style and behaviour has its own importance, especially during the transitional period. We know from the experience of 'actually existing socialism' how, especially in a situation of economic

> scarcity and backwardness, privileged bureaucracies arise even after capitalism is overthrown, how new classes and social strata emerge from among the state and party officials, enterprise managers, professionals and intellectuals etc. and become consolidated almost as a self-reproducing ruling class that dominates and benefits from the use of the surplus produced in the economy. A socialist transition, therefore, needs to consciously work not only to do away with the old class system but also to frustrate the formation of such new classes or social strata. This can be ensured only by an uninterrupted revolutionary practice and mass struggle, by empowering the people and their active involvement in checking and holding the leadership accountable. This means not only eternal vigilance in defence of the revolutionary cause but institutionalised democratic arrangements at every level that can serve as effective safeguards against pragmatism, opportunism and careerism of the leadership. More convenient or seemingly 'efficient' authoritarian ways or formal democracy that leadership would generally prefer will not do. The absence of such institutionalised democracy and the repressive practices of the regimes of 'actually existing socialism' were surely obstacles to initiatives by the masses to struggle against corruption of socialist ideals. A socially conscious, awakened and actively involved people are the best defence of a socialist system against both internal subversion and external aggression.

All this is only suggestive of what, in the light of our experience, has to be basic in responding to the problems of a society in transition to socialism – problems which will come compounded in case of a society which is economically backward, where the socialist project will involve undertaking, as it were, two major transformations *simultaneously*, overcoming the economic-material backwardness and effecting a socialist transition, that is, developing the forces of production and changing the social production relations simultaneously. Apropos the problems of a socialist transition in general, it may be added that such a transition anywhere will develop and proceed through serious contradictions of its own. Socialists have always dwelt on the contradictions of capitalism, and have been right to do so, but experience shows that attention has also to be paid to the contradictions which are an inescapable part of the socialist enterprise. Hence the need for a theory that can help understand

and cope with these contradictions, provide guidance for the class struggle which remains necessary in all spheres of life – economy, politics, culture, etc. – of a society in transition to socialism.

XXIV

Central to a theory of socialist transition, to its class struggle or struggles, is the principle of 'putting politics in command' – a principle which found explicit expression in Mao when, rather belatedly and therefore without success, he struggled to chart out a different path of development for China as against the capitalist and Soviet practice of putting 'economics in command'. Understood in proper Marxist terms, this principle demands not only the introduction of socialist relations of production along with, rather than subsequent to, the development of forces of production, but also a constant keeping in sight of the long-run goals of a socialist and communist transformation of society. 'Economics in command' in a post-revolutionary society invariably means the eventual exclusion of these goals, the loss of a socialist vision in the planning process which reduces the ability of the leaders or decision-makers to recognise discrepancies between what they are doing and the ideal that socialism represents. The real choice here is not between two techniques, capitalist or socialist, that would enable the economy to 'progress' but between two different political courses. The core of 'putting politics in command' is that the transitional practices be governed, no matter how slow the progress, by the long-term communist goal of eliminating 'three great differences', between mental and manual labour, between industry and agriculture and between city and country. It aims at egalitarianism in the widest and deepest sense of the term, that is, the reduction and ultimate elimination not only of differences in income but also differences in knowledge, power, privilege and everything else that divides people and sets them against each other, either as groups or as individuals, and thus makes it impossible for them to live together in solidarity and happiness. It must always be borne in mind, even in an economy of shortages, that socialism as a practicable ideal seeks a reduction in socially necessary labour time, a shift in the balance of human activity from the realm of necessity to the realm of freedom, whereby human beings produce sufficient to satisfy basic human needs, the necessities of material existence, without absorbing all their time and effort. Its basic thrust is away from productivism and towards securing an increasing margin of time and effort, over and above the satisfaction of basic needs, for the pursuit of 'truly human', 'emancipatory interests' as against the 'compensatory interests' of consumerism under capitalism. Such is the essence of Marx's thinking about socialism as an 'emancipatory project'. He never conceived of the new, higher form of society as merely more productive of economic goods and services; in his view, it would be above all more human, more just, more productive of good life for all people.

Viewed thus a socialist transition demands and aims at transformation of human beings. As Che Guevara put it: 'a new man must be created simultaneously with the material base'. In his polemic with Proudhon Marx had pointed out that 'all history is but the continuous transformation of human nature'. Regarding the transformation now postulated this is how Marx, in the third of his *Theses on Feuerbach*, posed the problem and its resolution:

> The materialist doctrine that men are products of circumstances and upbringing, and that therefore changed men are the product of other circumstances and changed upbringing, forgets that it is men who change circumstances and that the educator must himself be educated.... The coincidence of the changing of circumstances and human activity can be conceived and rationally understood only as *revolutionizing practice*.

It is thus, through revolutionising practice, through participatory activity involving masses of people at the level of the state and of civil society that people transform themselves even as they transform the society around them into one of expanded autonomy and self-organisation at every level, a society whose routine workings are structured by the working people themselves rather than by a governing body placed over them. To be revolutionary, this practice, activity or organisation, needs to be suffused with socialist ideology, politics and culture; without it, even autonomy and self-organisation may only create organisations for the collective ripping off of society. Hence the centrality of ideological, political and cultural struggle in the class struggles of a socialist transition. What is required, in other words, is a rebuilding of consciousness requisite for a socialist development, which is possible only when it is reinforced by daily experience at work, at home, at school and at play. This is how people imbibe the socialist values and rise, culturally, politically and even technologically to a new higher level. If it is through revolutionising practice that people are moulded into a revolutionary force for the overthrow of an old social order, this is also how they are moulded for the building of the new socialist society. Even those economistically inclined need to recognise that reorganisation of consciousness and work relations is a prerequisite even for realising the economic or productive potential of socialism. Marx had with good reason insisted that of all the productive forces, the most revolutionary are such transformed people. In its comprehensive Marxist sense, such are the implications of 'putting politics in command'.

Let me here add an argument of more general nature. In any struggle for socialism, as much after as before the rise to power, it is the *quality* and *comprehensiveness* of class struggle which determines the outcome. And at the heart of this class struggle lies politics – the cutting edge of social revolution or transformation – which, as I have argued earlier, has primacy in Marxism as a revolutionary doctrine. In the light of our historical experience, one can well insist that the quality of politics or political practice assumes even greater importance in the post-revolutionary period when essaying to move through the entirely uncharted territory that is the transition to a socialist society, its problems compounded by the shift from oppositional revolutionary politics to politics of governing with a view to build socialism. The fact that in the transitional societies, or at least in a particular phase of development of the transitional societies, the 'determinist' elements in historical causation are weakest and the 'voluntarist' elements become most significant only adds to this importance. Apropos relatively backward countries attempting a socialist transition, I would even hazard the proposition that given the immaturity or inadequacy of the *objective* (material) conditions necessary for a transition to socialism, there is the compensating need as it were, for that much more mature or adequate *subjective* contribution by human agency, which means, above all, that much more innovative and dynamic – revolutionary democratic as against bourgeois or bureaucratic – political intervention in order to soften and overcome, as much and as far as possible, the economic, cultural and other handicaps in the situation, to resolve the historically produced new or old contradictions, or, to phrase it differently, to work out the dialectics of circumstances and men in favour of a socialist transformation of society. Politics during this transitional period, far from being something merely superstructural – which revolutionary politics never is – could even be the means, the necessary condition or sustaining framework *within* which the requisite material, i.e. economic-structural base for socialism may have to be built up. This may sound a 'voluntarist' argument. But then it was Marx who wrote: 'World history would indeed be very easy to make, if the struggle were taken up only on condition of infallibly favourable chances'. Or, one might add, on condition that history arrive neatly packaged according to the book!

XXV

It is indeed in the lack of an adequate Marxist theory of socialist transition and therefore in the grievously flawed political practice of the leadership that *the prime cause* of the crisis and subsequent collapse of the regimes of 'actually existing socialism' has to be located and not in the initial decision of Lenin and the Bolsheviks to struggle for 'socialism in one country', or in the compulsions of the objective circumstances, and still less in the personal limitations of post-revolutionary leaders, or later in some immaculate 'cult of personality', or still later in poor, corrupt, even treacherous leadership or secret machinations of capitalist powers, etc., etc. What has happened was certainly not foreordained. With a more adequate theory and political practice, other, better possibilities were always there. It is not necessary for me to discuss this complex subject any further to again insist that there was no inevitability about what has come to be described as 'Stalinist deformation' with its political purges, concentration camps and Byzantine cult of the leader or its legacy in a Khrushchev or a Brezhnev or later in a Gorbachev or a Yeltsin. It was only one among other possible choices or alternatives. The central command system did not have to degenerate into a colossal and frightful bureaucracy over time; bureaucratic planning was not the only option. Leadership did not necessarily involve monopoly of political power, party and state system did not have to be necessarily non-democratic and authoritarian; democracy and pluralism are possible of maintenance even under most adverse circumstances. National chauvinism was certainly not a socialist invention; with active promotion of internationalism and institutionalisation of democracy and equality, the outcome would surely have been different. Again, Marxism need not have been reduced to a legitimising ideology, a ritualistic state religion, or a stupid and boring compulsory teaching in schools. All this degeneration or deformation was neither necessary nor inevitable and it was not even remotely a part of Marxist ideology.

In an economistic interpretation of what has happened, it has been sometimes argued that the post-revolutionary regimes rushed too fast and far away from capitalism, disregarding things like 'market', etc. There is also the associated view which has charged them with 'utopianism' in pursuit of socialist ideals. While there is room for a nuanced use of market (but not *capitalist* market as such) during the transitional period and there certainly was the need for more appropriate theory and practice in this or related areas, one really wonders about the charge of moving away from capitalism too fast and far, or of socialist utopianism. Did Stalin dream of equality, or a society of 'associated producers' of Marx or 'civilised cooperators' of Lenin, or, in 'catching up' with America, of qualitatively different patterns of production and consumption? Did he try to tackle the social division of labour, to abolish the hierarchical order, to dismantle the mighty state? Was Khrushchev's de-Stalinisation a 'thaw' to restore democracy in the party or establish socialist democracy in the country? Were Brezhnev or Chernenko or Gorbachev driven by the goal of socialist revolution? To ask such questions is to raise a laugh. The real criticism here would be that these regimes did not depart enough, away from capitalism, to realise the real potential of socialism. They remained all through far too much within the basic paradigm of capitalism. And whenever the contradictions of *their* socialism caught up with them, they sought answers in capitalism and not a turn to socialist ideals. This was precisely because, with them, it was always 'economics in command'.

XXVI

The emphasis on economic development, on the development of the forces of production to 'catch up', overtake and surpass world capitalism economically and the promise of more abundant goods and services to the people, in effect relegated the socialist issues on the agenda to the background. Attractive enough, especially in a poor, backward country, it was yet competition with capitalism, conducted on the latter's own terms, according to capitalist rules: work to be rewarded with more consumption. To the extent that such capitalist criteria remained unchallenged, the failure to overtake centuries-old, still dynamic global capitalism in production, other failings of the post-revolutionary regimes apart, could only mean defeat and ultimate loss of legitimacy of the system in the eyes of the people at home and abroad. For a coherent socialist system, superior to capitalism in classical Marxist terms, what was needed was an effective challenging of the terms of competition, the breaking of the hegemony of capitalist aspirations, with alternative patterns of consumption and standards for validating people's lives as satisfactory and fulfilling. With the gains of the revolution, its early achievements and continuing thrust born of original motivation for it – all of which meant relative equality, priority of social consumption in education, health and culture, the absence of unemployment and cyclic crises, a commitment to a rational planned development serving basic human needs – an adequate basis indeed existed for a viable set of alternative socialist aspirations and ways of thinking, feeling and acting, for an alternative socialist mode of life as a whole. This could and needed to be supported by conscious effort, an effective ideological struggle to confront capitalist consumerism and cultural domination on a world scale, to reorganise an alternative socialist consciousness. Efforts made in this regard were most partial and sporadic, often a matter of propaganda and exhortation, when what was required was a reinforcement of such consciousness by reorganised work relations and changed patterns of daily experience at work and out of work. Such socialist agenda was indeed much spoken and written of, but, in effect, its realisation was deferred to a distant communist future. In a mechanistic interpretation of base-superstructure metaphor, this realisation was deemed possible only when objective economic development, material abundance, permitted it. Thus the valid idea that the full development of socialist democracy and 'socialist man' requires a material base became the justification for a single-minded pursuit of economic growth in the here and now and a callous disregard for the self-determination of the people in the present – indeed a denial of the socialist content or direction of the transition away from capitalism. To insist once again, if the 'primacy of economic' lies at the heart of capitalist power, this power has to be confronted with the assertion of the 'primacy of politics', of socialist politics, in any transition to socialism. Only thus can capitalism be effectively opposed, a transition genuinely away from it in a socialist direction ensured and its restoration in any form prevented.

All this is not to suggest even remotely that you can build socialism, attempt a socialist transition anywhere, anytime, regardless of conditions or circumstances, or that there can even be an easy, unproblematic transition to socialism, free of conflicts and contradictions, mistakes and distortions – least of all in a single backward country. That would be an impossible, utterly un-Marxist position. It would be plain idealist utopianism. In fact the expression 'transition to socialism' is far from being adequate to the complex reality it pretends to describe, for it evokes a 'forward movement', of which the destination, more or less assured, would be socialism, when what is really involved is a historical period which can be more accurately characterised as being that of 'the transition *between* capitalism and socialism' (in proper Marxist terms 'between capitalism and communism'). Such a period need not lead to socialism in a linear fashion. It may lead there but it can also lead elsewhere to another form of capitalism, or more likely to a new form of class-exploitative society. In other words, the transition period is a two-way street. Mao indeed spoke of the possibility of 'restoration of capitalism', a possibility that Marxist scholars like Sweezy and Bettelheim too had come to recognise by the mid-1960s. Beyond these considerations it may even be that given the circumstances, travelling the road to socialism was never possible in a particular country. But for revolutionaries nothing is thus settled in advance. Theirs is the obligation to think and act as revolutionaries, as Marx would have done in their place. And failure is not a foregone conclusion, notwithstanding the crisis or collapse that has overtaken the first experiments in socialism so far. Revolutionaries of the future can and must do better in their struggle for socialism.

The point of my argument concerning the adequacy of theory guiding practice during a socialist transition is not that with it anything or everything is possible, it has no implications of idealist voluntarism or utopianism. It is only that a self-conscious and reasonably adequate theory would help ensure that there would be less of mistakes and distortions (which are bound to be there) and that they would be amenable to discovery and rectification so that no matter how slow or halting, or contradictions-laden, the overall *direction* remains clear, that it is indeed a transition to socialism, and not to an economically stagnant, bureaucratically ossified class-exploitative regime, with its rulers totally alienated from the people, and the people full of yearning for capitalism after more than seventy years of 'socialism'!

8

What was Built and What Failed in the Soviet Union

Not prepared, the Soviet Communists and people yet sought to build socialism, to attempt history's most radical rupture as Marx saw it, involving a transition from the traditional, long class-disfigured to a transformed, classless society; they sought to make this transition, to build socialism, for the first time in history, in a country which in its backwardness lacked all the objective conditions postulated for the purpose and whose only political tradition was autocracy and which, additionally, stood totally isolated and under constant threat from a globally dominant capitalism. Into this building went a mix of Bolshevik inheritance and socialist principles, an essentially economistic understanding of Marxism (whose idiom or language nevertheless constantly invoked Lenin, if not Marx), 'the economic necessities of the national situation' in Russia, and plain pragmatism of survival. Decisive for the success of this pioneering enterprise was the quality of socialist theory and political leadership. And these, as we have already noticed, came to be not merely inadequate but seriously flawed. Therefore while there were spectacular social, economic and technological achievements (often enough through 'forced marches') the socialist project itself steadily degenerated.

As we look back on the collapse in the Soviet Union and Eastern Europe, central to this degeneration was, after the early heroic efforts, the erosion and then the virtual disappearance of democracy, always visualised as absolutely integral to the socialist project. Marx had indeed spoken of 'dictatorship of the proletariat' as the political form of the period of transition from capitalism to communism. But it was a statement about the social content of political power during this period, and not its form of government. In its essential contradictory character, if it recognised the need for political repression of the old exploiting classes, their inevitable efforts at counter-revolution, it was to be the broadest and the deepest possible democracy ever for the formerly oppressed and exploited common people. As a concrete example of such 'dictatorship', Marx (and Engels) had pointed to the Paris Commune, whose principles and practice were a democracy for the people, more profound and active than anything witnessed so far. And Marx had specifically written:

> The Commune does not do away with the class struggles through which the working classes strive for abolition of all classes and, therefore, all class rule, but it affords the rational medium in which that class struggle can run through its different phases in the most rational and humane way.

In the Soviet Union 'dictatorship of the proletariat', under compulsions of objective circumstances, and with the help of apologetic theorising, instead became a form of government, a dictatorship over the people in the worst bourgeois sense. Whatever its revolutionary role in an earlier period of successful confrontation with the counter-revolution, in its further development, it had become itself a counter-revolutionary factor in Soviet society.

Orthodox Marxism or political theory of the Stalin era simply glossed over this historical evolution of the Soviet State, it covered up the reality of *what is* with a simplistic reiteration of *what ought to be*: the proletarian revolution overthrows the old exploitative social order and gives rise to a government which abolishes private ownership of the means of production and sets about building socialism; this government, as a 'dictatorship of the proletariat', has to necessarily repress the old exploiting classes and thwart the inevitable efforts at counter-revolution, however, for the people, the workers and peasants, it is, has to be, a democracy much more genuine than the freest bourgeois democracy anywhere; as socialism gets built, classes and class struggle, gradually disappear, the state will be all set to 'wither away' in the classical Marxian sense; it will continue to exist, as an apparatus of repression, only for defence against capitalist intervention or counter-revolution from abroad; within, with socialist democracy assured, the society will move on to transit to communism, subject only to the adequacy of the development of forces of production... Soviet theory's such reiteration of classical Marxist position was however an exercise in apologetics. For the reality was entirely different. Whatever the aberrations of the early post-revolutionary years when repression was not directed only against the deposed exploiting classes or to defeat the counter-revolution, with the passage of time, internal repression against large sections of the Soviet population came to be a characteristic feature of Soviet society. The 'dictatorship of the proletariat' had become a dictatorship over the proletariat and the people of the Soviet Union.

By the time the other revolutions of the 20th century followed and other 'socialist' regimes came into existence, the Soviet economic and political development, along with the achievements as well as degenerations of 'the Stalin era', had become a model to be emulated by these new regimes. And the characteristic feature noticed above, namely, the gross distortion of Marx's concept of 'dictatorship of the proletariat', came to be, to a greater or lesser degree, a definitive feature of the political systems of the new post-revolutionary states.

Of course the process was complex and there were important differences of history, national traditions, political conjunctures, and above all of political leadership. In many countries, notably China, North Korea, Yugoslavia, Cuba, Vietnam, the revolution was essentially, as in Russia, internally generated which made for a certain independence or divergence of action and behaviour. In China particularly, drawing lessons from the negative aspects of the Soviet experience, Mao even sought to pioneer a different road to construction of socialism.

He failed but his effort, with its interrelated principles of 'politics in command', 'class struggle in the realm of superstructure', 'cultural revolution', etc., remains a valuable legacy for the revolutionary socialist movement every where. Elsewhere, the revolution was not always or entirely an internal or people's affair. In most of Eastern Europe, it had an important aspect of imposition from above by Soviet Command, carried out with the help of the Red Army. Stalin's armies, like Napoleon's once, altered the social order in the countries they crossed, this time eliminating factory owners and uprooting landlords. This was their revolutionary heritage and their progressive function. But this made the revolution an imported product and the fact of external imposition of both the revolution and the Russian model, not only accentuated certain national contradictions but also created other problems, most significantly those of the legitimacy of the new regimes in the eyes of a majority of their citizens. Again, while Czechoslovakia and to a certain degree East Germany had achieved a certain level of economic development, and the former had a significant democratic tradition and a strong Communist Party of its own even before the second world war, the rest of Eastern Europe was not only economically backward, often abysmally so, but was also politically and culturally backward and almost without exception subject to authoritarian rule of one sort or another. And as elsewhere, here too the hostility of the surrounding capitalist world was a fact of daily life.

Indeed, almost all the socialist revolutions of the 20th century has had to struggle with a heavy weight of socio-economic backwardness as well as economic and military encirclement by global capitalism. This economic-military political factor always remained dominant in the economic and political development of all post-revolutionary societies. 'Capitalist encirclement' and 'counter-revolution' may have been used to rationalise post-revolutionary dictatorships and the accompanying incompetence, but the forceful reality of such pressures must always be recognised. The political, economic and at times military forces of the developed capitalist world always remained mobilised to promote counter-revolution and to harass, destabilise and defeat efforts to consolidate socialist revolutions and build a more just and egalitarian social order that is socialism. As Franz Schurmann once put it: 'In each of these countries, these leaders told their people that the new society was mortally endangered from aggressive forces abroad and subversive forces at home. In every instance, these threats were real. From the time of the October Revolution, powerful foreign countries, fearing the spread of revolution or the march of red armies, did what they could do to weaken or destroy the socialist countries'. One consequence everywhere was the distortion of priorities – the revolution lost its initial emancipatory thrust and instead of carrying out the promised *socialist* transformation, increasingly turned into a means of rapid economic development which in a situation of economic backwardness and threat from abroad almost inevitably made for authoritarian rule. This is how the East European regimes too, especially with the Soviet hegemonic connection, reproduced in local conditions some of the worst features of Soviet experience, which in political terms meant one party-dictatorship, police repression and even Moscow-like trials, etc., etc.

This is not to deny that revolutions in East Europe were indeed genuine social revolutions, for they did result in a massive revolutionary transformation of economic, social, political and cultural life in their countries. The new rulers in control of state power, even when they did not come to power with the active support or participation of the people, yet sought to change the pattern of class dominance over the state and the economy in favour of the dominated classes, above all the workers and peasants, enabling the hitherto excluded and suppressed layers of the population to assert their elementary interests. Fundamental changes in property relations were carried out, eliminating both the social basis of the traditional ruling classes and all property based inequalities and privileges. State structures were transformed, giving, at least in the initial stages, access to power to the long marginalised, oppressed and excluded people. More or less rapid growth of economy took place, covering all social sections and resulting in massive changes in the occupational structures. Vast changes were sought to be carried out in the whole national culture. And most important of all, lavish state subsidies in the form of free education, health care, cheap housing and access to culture, combined with universal employment, gave the working people a sense of social security unheard of under their previous regimes or even in the advanced countries of the capitalist world. Women joined the workforce in large numbers and benefited considerably from increased access to education and health care. But notwithstanding these and other gains of revolution, which paralleled those of the October Revolution in Russia, as in the Soviet Union, in fact modelled on it, their political system was anything but democratic even when it claimed itself to be a 'socialist democracy'. Together with the Soviet Union, they were for all practical purposes one-party regimes, with the ruling party enjoying a monopoly of political power and exercising comprehensive control over society including its administrative-command economy. It was a power heavily concentrated at the top, extremely repressive and intolerant of dissent, at times both expressing and caricaturing itself with practicing a 'cult of personality' which often reached incredible heights, or depths.

It needs to be noted that at the beginning of the revolutionary process, the new rulers in these post-revolutionary societies, given their socialist origins, intentions or commitment, did recognise that the essence of socialism after the revolution is the replacement of the bourgeoisie as the ruling class by the proletariat. As revolutionary parties, under Marxist, communist or any other names, they not only enjoyed considerable popular support or prestige and provided genuine leadership, they were also committed, in the language of classical Marxism, to the 'political supremacy' of the proletariat in the post-revolutionary period, to 'the state' being 'the proletariat organised as the ruling class', to 'the dictatorship of the proletariat' 'as the transition to the abolition of all classes and to a class-less society'. But it never worked out this way in practice in the Soviet Union or any other of these 'socialist' countries. It was not merely a question of the proletariat not being numerically large enough, or politically and culturally developed enough, to function as a hegemonic class. The 'altered geography' of world revolution and devastation of war and civil war had in any case taken care of that. It is that the 'political supremacy' in these countries came to be achieved by tightly organised revolutionary parties. They exercised it in the name of the proletariat, representing, at least initially, its objective historical interests which included those of other exploited and oppressed classes, and carrying out, besides defending the revolution, its immediate historical tasks, above all making 'despotic inroads into the property rights and bourgeois relations of production' as the *Communist Manifesto* had put it. But this *necessary* situation never came to be 'transcended in course of the movement' as expected or hoped for. Instead, no matter by what complex historical processes or for which reasons it happened, every such party not only increasingly moved away from any such class representation but also, almost unavoidably, identified itself with the state, giving rise to a single-party state in possession of absolute monopoly of power. The economic development, where 'social ownership' came to be reduced to a relation of juridically ordained state-ownership only, brought in another essential element into the power-structure, the managerial technocracy, producing a highly privileged power bloc at the top of society, made up of *party apparatchiks* or *nomenklatura*, state bureaucracy and managerial technocracy which in due course became a rigid, oppressive, and constraining force in society, an increasingly dysfunctional and parasitical ruling elite, cut off from those below, and because of the general lack of democratic traditions and very weak institutionalisation of the popular democratic participation of the early revolutionary period, not accountable either to the working classes or the people at large in any meaningful sense of the word. The post-revolutionary state thus was in no sense 'the proletariat organised as the ruling class', nor the resulting situation even remotely 'the transition to the abolition of all classes and to a class-less society'.

It is thus that not socialism as such or any imperatives of socialist theory, but inadequacies of political leadership and compulsions of objective circumstances became structural in the politics of these 'socialist' societies, and the process of political degeneration first in the Soviet Union and then in Eastern Europe, and variously elsewhere too, settled into what Ralph Miliband has called its 'primal mould':

> Even though Communist regimes have differed from each other in various ways, they have all had two overriding characteristics in common: an economy in which the means of economic activity were overwhelmingly under state ownership and control, and a political system in which the Communist Party (under different names in different countries), or rather its leaders, enjoyed a virtual monopoly of power, which was vigilantly defended against any form of dissent by systematic – often savage – repression. The system entailed an extreme inflation of state power and, correspondingly, a stifling of all social forces not controlled by, and subservient to, the leadership of the party-state. The 'pluralism' which formed part of the system, and which involved the existence of a large variety of institutions in every sphere of life, from culture to sport, was not at all intended to dilute the power of the party-state, but on the contrary to reinforce it, by turning these institutions into organs of party-state control.

It is within this mould that 'socialism' was built in the Soviet Union and then, treated as a model, imposed from outside in Eastern Europe and freely adopted, to a greater or lesser degree, in other post-revolutionary societies. While the basic *social gains* of the revolution remained and were enhanced, there was, despite bureaucratic degeneration, spectacular economic progress too, and the model came to have great attraction for power holders in poor countries of Asia and Africa, facing their own vast and intractable problems of socio-economic development. Bolshevism, if not socialism itself, seemed to have turned into an ideology for rapid welfareist economic progress for countries in which the conditions of capitalist development were weak or non-existent. In its interim success, the Soviet Union indeed provided an economic model for the decolonised third world, including countries like India which had no sympathy for its dictatorial politics. But the model had nothing to do with socialism in the original Marxist meaning of the term. Its exceedingly undemocratic and arbitrary form of rule, concentration of power at the top, denial of elementary human rights and decency, its gross brutality and callousness, even its paternalism which brooked no dissent nor any promotion of self-government and independence of the masses but only furthered, in Kautsky's words, 'the Messiah-consciousness of leaders and their dictatorial habits' – all this made it abundantly clear that while these post-revolutionary regimes were born of genuine social revolutions, what those presiding over them had, ultimately, made of these revolutions was a harsh, bureaucratic system of power and privileges, which simply made it impossible for them to build anything which could legitimately be called socialist.

II

'Socialism' in the Soviet Union – what was being or ultimately built there – has been the subject of debate over these seventy odd years among enemies and friends, and friendly critics as well. The mainstream Sovietology in the West produced a plethora of 'theories of the Soviet system' which, apart from being cognitively flawed, almost invariably had, despite academic or scientific pretensions, more than their share of ideological blinkers. Far too many scholars used that theoretically most suspect concept, 'totalitarianism', to describe Soviet Union as 'a totalitarian system', a 'directed society' fully controlled from above by a self-appointed bureaucracy. If some were inclined to categorise it among 'developing societies' of the third world by emphasising shared concerns for rapid economic growth, 'modernisation' or 'nation-building', others located it in the spectrum section of 'industrial societies', exemplified by the developed countries of the first world. Quite a few even postulated a growing convergence between these seemingly antithetical systems. A sympathetic perspective on the post-Stalin period saw the emergence of better textured theories viewing Soviet Union along pluralist lines as an increasingly complex, rule-governed and stable system. Eclecticism was a characteristic feature of these academic exercises. But historically the most important thing about western Sovietology as a whole was its growth as a 'demonology' feeding into the overarching official ideology of the capitalist West, legitimising capitalism via the 'black hole' effect of anti-communism we have already noticed – wherein any and all questioning of capitalism was interpreted and blocked as involving a loss of political freedom and 'open society' as they called it, the only alternative being a Soviet-type totalitarian society!

The debate among Marxists and socialists, the friends and friendly critics, has been no less widespread or partisan, and particularly intense after 1956. And quite understandably, the focus of discussion has been the precise nature and dynamic of the post-revolutionary society as it definitively came to be during the Stalin era, and then continued with its few ups and many downs till the final collapse in 1991. It is significant however, and quite indicative of the quality of Marxism or the overall character of social science scholarship in the Soviet Union (and other 'socialist' countries) that over all these years, except for some persecuted or marginalised and rather fragmentary dissident writings, either had little or nothing of any theoretical value to offer on this subject. (Mao was the odd exception here in virtually pioneering, as we have already had the occasion to note, a Marxist theory of post-revolutionary society in his critique of the Soviet and Chinese developments.) Instead, we had an infinite number of cliché-ridden apologetics rationalising and defending, even extolling the existing state of affairs, the new established order, as socialist – a plethora of books which, it is clear now, made little sense to the people at home, but were avidly lapped up by the official Communist Parties, their leaderships and cadres, abroad. The general flight from Marxism also meant a characteristic evasion of Marx's basic principle in such matters: 'Our task is ruthless criticism of everything that exists, ruthless in the sense that it will not shrink either from its own conclusions or from conflict with the powers that be'. Abandoned long ago in everything but words, Marxism, for all practical purposes, had come to be reduced to 'a state religion' imposed on the people, or a bunch of clichés to be invoked on high and holy days, and thus rendered utterly impotent for any confrontation with reality, for a critical analysis of what had been built as socialism. Thus, while bureaucratic degeneration of the state and the party was to prove disastrous, as Lenin, who indeed died fighting against it, had warned, it was never even recognised or engaged with as a serious problem, and symptomatic of the situation, of the state of Soviet Marxism or scholarship as a whole is the fact that, as the Soviet Academician Vladimir Kudryatsev has recently (1990) informed us, 'not a single serious study dealing specifically with this issue (of bureaucracy) was carried out during all the years of Soviet power'!

Marxists outside 'the socialist world', however, witness to the continuing and deepening crisis of the prevalent models of socialism – all too visible in the cumulative evidence of their persistent economic problems, their social stagnation and decadence, their repressive and even reactionary political character, etc. – were and have been making genuine efforts to understand what had happened or was happening, to describe and assess the outcome of these first experiments in socialism. And more than 30 years of debate on the left concerning the nature of what was built in the Soviet Union, has produced a variety of answers. In general terms we have propositions like: 'a dictatorial tendency whereby revolutionary elites seized control of societies', 'a flawed movement for the self-emancipation of the working class', 'an expression of messianism', 'a product of oriental despotism', 'a failed developmentalist project', etc. One judicious author, Perry Anderson, (quoting Carlo Ginzburg) has recently suggested that 'communism may end up being comparable to the Jesuit experiment in Paraguay, a rational attempt at insulating a section of the world from international pressures and sustaining an alternative development path, and one that was much idealised by intellectuals at the time but one which was in the end to collapse almost without a trace'. Somewhat specific answers have been: 'actually existing socialism', 'state socialism' 'proto socialism' 'bureaucratically deformed socialism', 'authoritarian socialism', 'degenerated workers state', 'bureaucratised workers state', 'dictatorship of the proletariat', 'dictatorship of bureaucracy', 'command-administrative system', 'centrally planned economies', 'capitalism', 'state capitalism', 'capitalism without capitalists', 'post-capitalist state', 'social imperialism',

'Stalinist system', etc., etc. We have Stefan Heym's 'pioneering socialism' and Issac Deutscher's epigram: 'socialism in a backward country is backward socialism'. Quite a few have, analogically, reminded us of the 'crude communism' that Marx had himself attacked in the *Economic and Philosophical Manuscripts of 1844* and elsewhere. And so on. Perhaps no society anywhere has ever been burdened with so many different loaded descriptions or names, forcing many to opt for a neutral or purely descriptive expression, a 'Soviet type society', that is, a *sui generis* 'post-revolutionary society'. It is obvious that such a plethora of descriptive or explanatory names, of terms with quotation marks to describe the 'Soviet type' societies, partly at least reflects our theoretically poor or inadequate understanding of these societies, of the nature and dynamics of what was built as socialism in the Soviet Union.

'Socialism' or 'socialist' has been conventionally used to designate states generally run by the Communist Parties and this fits the terminology many of them used (or still use as, for example, in China) to identify themselves. But, obviously, beyond a certain point of origin or intent, it can be most misleading. The widely used 'actually existing socialism', apart from being cumbersome and now somewhat redundant or outdated, suffers under the double disadvantage that the noun never applied and the adjectives have ceased to apply. The suggested alternative, 'real or really existing socialism' is not much of an improvement either. 'State capitalism' or 'social imperialism' rely on somewhat dubious theories that capitalism had been restored in the Soviet Union. The terms which properly place 'bureaucracy' in the centre, fail to differentiate from bureaucratised modern capitalism. Those focusing on the 'state' seem to ignore the role of the Party as a shadow-state. Even the much used adjective 'Stalinist' risks the misunderstanding that the terror of high Stalinism characterised the system throughout, which it did not; the system, democratic initially, in most of its career was merely repressive. The other terms used too are inadequate in their own ways. This only underlines, once again, what Lenin used to emphasise, namely, life, social reality and historical processes are much too rich, complex, and diversely colourful for any theory to grasp with the help of mere labels, definitions or even concepts. More or less helpful in providing points of entry into understanding the 'Soviet-type' societies, quick labelling, defining or conceptualisation of this sort has also often bypassed complex theoretical issues involved and instead of resolving them only created the illusion of a solution.

It is not necessary for my purpose to attempt a review of the debate concerning the nature of what was built as socialism in the Soviet Union. Among others, we now have Charles Bettelheim's outstanding multivolume study of the subject, *Class Struggles in the USSR*. Though it is necessary to add that the historical and factual material, the evidence adduced by him and others, is amenable to more than one interpretation, and the controversy among Marxists is likely to continue for quite some time, even if much of it has been overtaken by the cataclysmic collapse of this 'socialism' in the Soviet Union and Eastern Europe. A very brief and necessarily partial survey of some of the major themes or theoretical issues will suffice for understanding what was built and has now collapsed in the Soviet Union.

III

There was the Soviet self-definition as socialist, widely accepted by the common people and the ruling classes abroad, by most friends and almost all enemies, and assiduously propagated by the associated communist parties. It was accepted at home too; the rulers at the top believed they had got socialism and were quite content, even happy, at least till recently, in their enjoyment of it. (The pre-Gorbachev Soviet state in fact viewed itself as an embodiment of 'developed socialism' – a stage in socialist construction between the revolution and full-fledged communism. Soviet Union was claimed to have entered this stage in the 1960s, and the Constitution of 1977 proclaimed that a developed socialist society had been built in the USSR). But the people below, as we now know only too well, though persuaded of the self-definition, certainly had other ideas. Underlying this self-definition, at an abstract theoretical level, was the generally accepted Marxian-view that in historical development socialism follows capitalism, that capitalism will be overthrown by proletarian revolutions and these revolutions will establish socialist societies. Born of a proletarian-led revolution, the Soviet society was almost automatically assumed to be or identified as a socialist society. More particularly, this society, identifying what Marx called 'capitalist private property' uniquely with individual private property in capital, had abolished such private ownership and established public (mainly state) ownership of the means of production as well as centralised control and planning of the economy, its production and distribution mechanisms, in the process abolishing or severally 'regulating' the market mechanisms characteristic of capitalism. The public or state ownership was identified with 'social ownership' and, given the job security and extensive social gains of revolution and the assumption that the workers had collective possession of the means of production, use of labour power as commodity, the existence of commodity form of labour, was denied, though differential wage form of labour remuneration was deemed necessary in the transitional 'first phase of communism' in the sense of Marx. That is how the Soviet Union was considered, by itself and by many others, a socialist economy or society.

The public or state ownership of the means of production has been the most basic premise of the argument for the socialist character of Soviet economy or society. And it is precisely here that its most basic flaw lies. For a legislative or *juridical* change of one form of ownership into another does not necessarily mean a *real* change in either ownership or the concerned relations of production. More specifically, the flaw lies in equating the *juridical* abolition of (individual) private property in the means of production with the establishment of *real* public or social ownership of these means and on this basis asserting the end of capitalist relations of production, their replacement by socialist relations and thus claiming the establishment of socialism. Which is simply not the case. Marx and Engels had already shown that capitalism and capitalist relations of production were quite compatible with state ownership, that state ownership does not deprive 'the productive forces of their character as capital', that the real issue was the 'social appropriation' of the means of production, i.e. real possession and decisive control over the means of production and the production processes by 'associated producers', that is, the active working class. Nor does planning by itself distinguish socialism. In fact capitalism can and does have a great deal of state sector, and planning too, without ceasing to be capitalism; all public ownership or planning is not necessarily socialist. The argument really confused *form* with *content*. In the eyes of those arguing in the above manner, 'socialism', or even 'dictatorship of the proletariat', is *assured* by the existence of certain forms (a certain juridical form of ownership or proletarian rule, a certain organisational form of the Party or the State, a certain form of ideological expression, etc.) and not by concrete social and political relationships, which are really the essence of the situation according to classical Marxism.

But the form acquired or seemed to acquire a certain socialist substance from the early social gains of revolution, successes of planned economy in the midst of the capitalist crisis of the 1930s, various achievements of the Soviet Union as a non-capitalist power, (including its ability to manoeuvre and survive, to counter, more or less successfully, the global ascendancy of capitalism in different parts of the world and decisive role in the defeat of fascism) and, in its own way, even from the fierce and sustained hostility of the capitalist world throughout as well as from people's hope and search for an alternative to capitalism. Thus, attributing its failings or ugly features, earlier to low level of productive forces and later only to 'mistakes,' distortions' or 'deviations' of policy, or more generally to 'inevitable defects' in the new society as it emerges from the old capitalist society that Marx had spoken of, the view could still be held that the Soviet Union was a developing socialist society or democracy modified only to the extent necessary to defend itself against external counter-revolutionary intervention.

There were others who took a more serious view of the failings or 'aberrations' of the Soviet system and saw them as affecting its socialist but not the essential anti-capitalist character.

Thus, taking note of its grave 'bureaucratic degeneration' under Stalin, Trotsky chose to describe Soviet Union as a 'degenerate workers' state' where such basic gains of the Revolution as socialisation of the means of production had survived but along with *nomenklatura* a parasitic bureaucracy had emerged and taken hold of the state apparatus. In other words, democratic control over bureaucracy which was considered unavoidable in a situation of backwardness that characterised traditional Russian society but dispensable with the overcoming of this backwardness, had failed and *nomenklatura* had usurped the political power of the working class, without, however, affecting the basis of the post-capitalist society in the shape of a state-owned economy. Trotsky viewed the Soviet order under Stalin as an unstable, transitional formation between capitalism and socialism whose further progress to socialism would require revolutions in the advanced capitalist countries as also a political (not social) revolution in Soviet Union through which 'the workers would overthrow the bureaucracy' and restore a genuinely proletarian regime. In 1936, against those who argued that the Soviet transitional regime could only move in the direction of socialism, Trotsky did rather firmly suggest that 'in reality a backslide to capitalism is wholly possible'. But he did not theoretically elaborate this insight and continued to expect a solution from a political revolution in the Soviet Union. As Mandel, representing the orthodox Trotskyist position, later argued, the Soviet economy with the state ownership of the means of production and the suppression of the right to private appropriation, centralised economic planning and state monopoly of foreign trade, the absence of generalised commodity production or the sale of labour power as a commodity, still retained its potential for socialism. It was postulated that the bureaucratic usurpation would end, either, as Trotsky himself believed, with a second, purely political revolution, or as Isaac Deutscher hoped, especially after the death of Stalin, through gradual democratisation of Soviet society as the educational and cultural levels of the Soviet peoples rose as a result of the growth of the Soviet economy. Political power thus restored to the working people, they would find, rather resume their way to a genuine socialist development. In this view, though not socialist, the Soviet Union under Stalin, or later, despite its 'bureaucratic degeneration' was still seen as a workers' state, as a 'transitional society between capitalism and socialism'. However plausible this view may have been in the 1930s or even later after the death of Stalin, it is now obvious that it grievously underestimated the rot that had set in the Soviet society, where it was no longer a case of bureaucracy temporarily deflecting the proletarian state from its natural, socialist course of development, but of a process wherein the entire socialist inheritance of October Revolution had been or was being negated.

Over the years, while sympathetic works on the new Soviet social order proliferated (including some exceptionally influential non-Marxist writings like those of the Webbs and Dean of Canterbury) we also had critics like Rizzi, an Italian Marxist, who, going beyond Trotsky's characterisation of Soviet bureaucracy as a mere parasitical excrescence, described it as a new ruling class based on a mode of production which involved a form of exploitation similar to that in slave societies. The Soviet system was also seen by more than one scholar as an attempt by a bureaucratic ruling class to industrialise and modernise 'mother Russia' of the Czars, using collective and authoritarian methods bolstered by a pseudo-socialist ideological rhetoric. In the immediate post-Stalin period we had Yugoslav dissident Djilas' much noticed account of the nature of this class which traced the source of its power to the monopolistic control it exercised over the means of production.

IV

Given the economistic distortions that set in early and soon took over the socialist enterprise in Russia, it is not surprising that right from the 1920s we have theories characterising Soviet economy as 'capitalist'. Any number of thinkers on the left have written upholding this view, including K. Korsch and later A. Bordiga, R. Dunayevskaya, C.L.R. James, T. Cliff, and most recently C. Bettelheim whose *Class Struggles in the USSR* contains so far the most comprehensive analysis of the origin, development and nature of 'capitalism' in the Soviet Union. Of course there are more or less important differences among them as also more or less important shifts within their own thinking over time. They have written of the confusion of 'statisation' with 'socialisation', the loss of proletariat's control over the state, the 'Stalinist counter-revolution' inaugurating a 'state capitalist economy', and so on, and generally tended to describe Soviet economy as one or other form of state capitalism and the Soviet ruling class as a 'state bourgeoisie'. Bettelheim's argument is even accommodative of the notion of a 'party capitalism' under a 'party bourgeoisie' to distinguish it from 'state capitalism' in other countries where the party does not play as central a role as in the USSR. 'Capitalism without capitalists', the expression used by Engels to describe the whole project of German Social Democracy and later by Lenin for a similar purpose, has also been used by scholars to describe the Soviet system.

Whatever their differences or internal shifts of thought, these critics from the left have seen the means of production in the Soviet Union as 'collective capital' directed by the state or the party, or more precisely by the state or party bourgeoisie, with the workers having no control over these means, nor their products; they were simply workers, sellers of labour power against wages and thereby producing surplus value for the masters of the means of production. Bettelheim has even sought, more elaborately than others, to demonstrate the existence of capitalist competition and the working of the laws of capitalist accumulation and profit generation in the Soviet economy. The central argument for the 'capitalist' thesis, however, remains the 'radical separation' of the immediate producers from the means and conditions of production so that, in the words of early Bettelheim, 'under cover of state ownership, relations of exploitation exist today in the USSR which are similar to those existing in the other capitalist countries, so that it is only the *form* of these relations that is distinctive there.'

It is important to note that these critics differ as to when to situate the beginning or 'restoration' of capitalism in the Soviet Union. For a small minority, USSR was neither socialist nor non-capitalist but had always been capitalist, right from the seizure of power by the Bolsheviks, and therefore there is no question of 'restoration' of capitalism. For most others, as with those adhering to the non-capitalist thesis, Soviet Union before the consolidation of the Stalinist power (roughly the final years of the 1920s) was basically a proletarian, if not a socialist regime, and the 'restoration' proper was a product of the following period of high Stalinism. For the rest, it came about in the post-Stalin period of Khrushchev and Brezhnev. Chinese polemics on the subject, Mao's significant departures apart, indeed tended to suggest that it was the sole responsibility of a 'revisionist renegade clique', rather than the product of five decades of Soviet history. Be that as it may, these critics are agreed that, originally or otherwise, 'Soviet Union was a capitalist society with all essential characteristics of capitalism'.

For all its attractions or the scholarship backing it, the 'capitalist' thesis is theoretically flawed and incapable of explaining the system or its collapse in the Soviet Union. Except for the traditional communists or the old faithfuls on the one hand and the opponents of socialism on the other, it is now generally agreed that what we had in the Soviet Union was neither socialism, nor in any meaningful sense a transitional society between capitalism and communism as these concepts are understood by Marx and Engels or other Marxists in the classical tradition, including Lenin and Mao. But nor was it, as argued by the critics on the left whom we have just noticed, some form of capitalism, originally so or restored later, as this social formation, that is capitalism, has been traditionally understood in Marxism. It is simply not true, as claimed by these critics, that the Soviet system had all essential characteristics of capitalism. Besides, if the Soviet Union was capitalist or had capitalism, ever since the 1920s or afterwards, why the need, indeed the desperate effort of Gorbachev and his successors to restore capitalism? A restoration, it may be added would have required a reasonably well-defined victory of the counter-revolution, for which there is little evidence. And if it was originally, or even otherwise a capitalist system, the trauma and turmoil of its final years and ultimate collapse, the way it has occurred, is not easy to explain; a move in the direction of increasing the sphere of market or even private ownership of the means of production, that is, of more capitalism, need not have had such a disruptive effect on the functioning of a capitalist system. In view of the absence of any revolutionary threat from within or the nature of its outcome so far, it does not make much sense to speak of the collapse of a long established, even 70-year-old, capitalism in the USSR. And a collapse of capitalism into capitalism at that! Bolshevik seizure of power was no beginning of a 'capitalist revolution', and what has happened in the Soviet Union is so obviously better understood as the result of developments internal to the October-born revolutionary regime itself. In fact the evidence adduced in behalf of the 'capitalist' thesis, including Bettelheim's own version, is amenable to a different, more viable interpretation which would regard the Soviet Union, as it came to be, as a new social formation, standing on its own foundations of a *sui generis* class-exploitative economy which, not socialist, was not capitalist either.

It has been suggested that passing through a stormy transition period from 1917 to 1953 which included not only revolution, civil war, capitalist encirclement, force-marched collectivisation and industrialisation, war against fascism and post-war reconstruction, but also the bitter inner-party struggles of the 1920s and 1930s and Stalin's purges that wiped out what was left of the old Bolshevik leadership, the Soviet Union came to be a society which was neither capitalism nor socialism as these social formations have been traditionally understood by Marxists, nor was it as most Trotskyists maintained, a transitional society between the two which had been temporarily stalled by a bureaucratic deformation. Instead it had become a social formation which was neither foreseen nor easily accounted for by any of the existing versions of Marxist theory. In fact the received orthodoxies of conventional Marxist doctrine, with its strong 'economistic' or 'formalist' orientation, simply could not provide adequate theoretical framework for analysing and understanding the historically novel forms of society resulting from the proletarism revolutions of the 20th century in one backward country after another. The novel form of society that had so emerged in the Soviet Union was really a *sui generis* class-exploitative society with enough basic differences from both capitalism and socialism to be considered and studied as a new social formation in its own right. Such is the position taken by Paul Sweezy, who has, basing himself above all on the path-breaking work of Bettelheim, and like him writing much before the final collapse in Eastern Europe and Soviet Union, offered what in my opinion is so far the most adequate Marxist analysis of the nature of this new social formation which has, in his view, now failed as much because of its own internal weaknesses and contradictions as a non-capitalist but class-exploitative society, as because it was confronted by a more powerful rival which put enormous pressure on it, militarily and economically.

V

It is an unfortunate fact that while Marxists have learnt to dig deep below the surface to uncover underlying relationships and processes of capitalism to understand its functioning, a similar effort to understand the dynamics of the now collapsed 'socialist' societies has been all too rare throughout. If Soviet Marxism or scholarship as a whole had been literally without exception apologetic in character, the critics have been all too often content with 'Stalin-bashing' – the failure of socialism in the Soviet Union itself is now seen as the fault of evil men; Stalin in the first place, or, as with the old faithfuls, the evil men of the *nomenklatura* – Khrushchevs, Brezhnevs, Gorbachevs, etc. who followed him, even as they continued to claim possession of the 'truth' of socialism. To move from such concern with the appearance of things to the reality that was the Soviet system, we need to share whatever authentic Marxist understanding is available and to deepen and extend it to decipher the denouement that overtook 'socialism' in the Soviet Union. The external context has been generally noticed and rightly stressed – a hostile global capitalism had besieged Soviet socialism throughout and made it vulnerable to its enemies. What is on the whole lacking and vitally needed is a critical analysis of this socialism internally, in terms of Marxist method of historical materialism and class analysis which helps us to understand this failed experiment in socialism and grasp the implications of its failure for the future of socialism in our time.

Using the material available, particularly the outstanding work of Bettelheim, and presented mainly in a series of articles in the *Monthly Review*, mostly through the 1970s – that is, long before the Soviet collapse and therefore almost prophetic in its implications – Paul Sweezy's argument, typically lucid in its statement, remains the best point of entry for such a Marxist critical analysis, helping us better understand the nature and dynamics of the Soviet system while it lasted as well as its growing crisis and denouement in 1991. Sweezy distinguishes the Soviet system from capitalism, rejects the 'capitalist' thesis and points to its specificities as a new social formation standing on its own foundations, which, not capitalist, was yet a new kind of class-exploitative society. Much of the immediately following argument is based, at times literally, on the analysis and assessment of Paul Sweezy.

By way of introduction to our discussion of what was or came to be built in the Soviet Union, I would like to share these two relatively recent statements from him:

> I have no doubt whatever that the Russian Revolution and the ones that followed – with a few obvious exceptions like the Iranian revolution – were genuine socialist revolutions with deep roots in an international movement that traces its origin back to the first half of the nineteenth century. The parties and their leaders who headed the revolutionary struggles were for the most part seasoned Marxists whose mission in life was to overthrow an unjust and exploitative system and to replace it with one based on the principles of socialism as expounded by Marx and Engels and their followers in the late nineteenth and early twentieth centuries. Under these circumstances the revolutionary regimes that came to power were clearly socialist in character, and any attempt to deny or obscure this well established fact is a falsification of history.
>
> After the revolutionary seizure of power comes the struggle to shape the post-revolutionary society.... My central thesis, reduced to its barest essentials, is as follows: All the socialist revolutions of the twentieth century took place under extremely

> unfavorable conditions and against the fierce resistance of the leaders of the capitalist world from which they had broken away. The new revolutionary regimes were able to overthrow and expropriate the old rulers, and to this extent they succeeded in laying the foundation for a socialist society. But the life-and-death struggle to develop and protect the embryonic new society gave rise – whether inevitable or not remains a matter for debate – to a military-style cleavage between the leaders and the people which in time, and against the will and intentions of the original revolutionaries, hardened into a new self-reproducing system of antagonistic classes. This was obviously not a restoration of capitalism: that would have been the result of a victory of the counter-revolution, not of a development clearly internal to the revolutionary regime itself.
>
> In the Soviet Union this process lasted roughly for a decade and a half, coming to a climax with Stalin's purges of the mid-30s that wiped out what was left of the old Bolshevik Party. The character of the post-revolutionary society was now established – neither capitalist nor socialist, an authoritarian class society with state ownership of the main means of production and central planning....

Again:

> ....to my way of thinking, the problem of the revolutions of the twentieth century is that they did not bring to power the proletariat organized as a class. What they did bring to power is tightly organized revolutionary parties drawn from elements of various sections of society. Those parties expropriated the traditional bourgeoisie but did not do away with the capital-labour relation as such. They substituted the state for the private capitalists as the employer of labour, unifying the many capitals which had grown up independent of each other in the course of capitalist history. That is not to say that all units of capital were put under one management, of course – only that all the separate managements became subject to the same ultimate authority, which now assumed the life-and-death powers that had previously been exercised by the impersonal forces of the market.
>
> The question then arose of what we should call these states. They weren't socialist, but were they capitalist? Charles Bettelheim and I had an exchange on this point, among others, that lasted a period of some years. Bettelheim thought that we should call the Soviet Union a capitalist society, but I thought that would

> introduce into our analysis preconceptions, expectations, and biases which would inevitably influence our findings and cause much confusion. To my way of thinking, the power, prestige, and privileges of the Soviet rulers did not derive from the ownership of private wealth but from unmediated control over the state apparatus and hence over total social capital. The Soviet Union, though a class society and not the socialist society it claimed to be, had none of the economic laws of motion comparable to those of capitalism. For example, there was nothing like the chronic unemployment typical of the West.

To proceed with our discussion, Soviet Union was not a capitalist society for the simple reason that, appearances apart, it did not share in all the essential features that characterise capitalism. A capitalist economy, analytically speaking, is characterised by three interlinked and interacting features which determine its essential nature and functioning:

(1) Ownership of the means of production by private capitalists; (2) separation of the total social capital into many competing or potentially competing units; and (3) production of the great bulk of commodities (both goods and services) by workers who, owning no means of production of their own, are obliged to sell their labour power to capitalists in order to acquire the means of subsistence. Of these, Soviet system shared only the third feature with capitalism which however did not make it a capitalist system.

This feature, the capital-labour relationship, operating through the market, whereby workers work to produce surplus value to be appropriated by the capitalist class as profit, is of course a basic feature of capitalism. But as Sweezy has emphasised:

> capital-labour relation, while a basic and necessary feature of capitalism, is not by itself sufficient to define the capitalist system in its full historically developed form... for such a definition it is necessary to add that capital exists not as a single entity... but as many capitals organised separately and acting independently of one another....

In the marketplace, capitalism faces the property-less working class in the form of many private capitals which compete with each other. This is where and how profits are produced, maximised and used for the further expansion of capital. Marx had identified competition as 'the essential locomotive force of the bourgeois economy' and pointed out that 'competition executes the inner laws of capital; makes them into compulsory laws towards the individual capital'. The functioning of capitalism thus is governed by economic 'laws' which are generated by the mutual interaction of competing capitals on the one hand, and of capitalists and wage labourers on the other. No overall direction exists or is needed: the system runs itself as long as capitalists act to maximise their profits and use their profits to expand their capitals. This is indeed the basic motivating principle of capitalism where 'production is merely production for capital'. Its driving force is this compulsion to accumulate. 'Accumulate, Accumulate! That is Moses and the Prophets!' wrote Marx. The mechanism of competing capitals, together with capital-wage labour relationship is crucial for realising the 'laws of motion' of capitalist economy, which come together in its most basic law, the all powerful dynamic of capitalist accumulation, the drive towards maximum extraction and accumulation of surplus, which simultaneously generates the characteristic contradictions of capitalism, expressed in business cycles, the reserve army of labour, degradation and dehumanisation of work, and, above all, a polarisation in each country of capitalism and in the increasingly globalised capitalist system between wealth and opulence at one end and poverty and squalor at the other.

It needs to be specifically noticed that in capitalism, as distinct from pre-capitalist social formations, the economy comes to be radically separated as an autonomous domain from the other domains of social life (politics, religion, etc.) and even as it achieves an overall dominance in society, it acquires a momentum and logic of its own and is subject to its own laws and 'blind' forces of the market. It is via the market, that is *economically* (and not politically or by force as in other class-based social formations) that surplus labour of direct producers is extracted and appropriated. And it is the market, again, which provides, when necessary, the 'correctives' for its normal functioning.

The state is of course involved in the process as the guarantor of the underlying property system and enforcer of the rules of the competitive struggle. It also typically plays a role in strengthening the hand of some interests against others and in acting to contain or resolve the contradictions to which the system periodically or irregularly gives rise, or to ameliorate the suffering that is endemic to capitalism in order to retain or secure legitimacy for it. At times the state even intervenes, as it were, to save capitalism from the capitalists – left to themselves they would have, perhaps, destroyed capitalism a long time ago. In brief, state manages 'the common affairs of the whole bourgeoisie' as Marx put it, organising society in the long-term interests of the capitalist system as whole, which incidentally also means that more than being an 'organ' or 'instrument' of the capitalist class, the state also needs to have relative autonomy from this economically dominant class to be able to pursue or promote its common affairs or long-term interests. But the state is never autonomous from the socio-economic structures of a capitalist society, and in the economic sphere the state is dragged along by the laws of value and capital accumulation and the special interests they create; it remains subservient to the market and its logic of profit-making, a servant and never a master of capitalist economy. To use a mathematical analogy, in a capitalist system the economy is the independent variable, the state the dependent variable – a situation radically different from, indeed the opposite of, what obtained in the Soviet Union.

Thus as Sweezy has argued, of the three defining characteristics of capitalism, Soviet system shared only the third one with capitalism, namely that relating to the position of workers in the economy – subject however to *a significant difference* to which we shall return later – which more than anything else turned it into a class-exploitative society, yet not a capitalist society.

A notable argument along the same lines has come from Istvan Meszaros. Working with his own theoretical framework, with its focus on *capital* rather than capitalism, he has argued that 'the Soviet Union was not capitalist, not even state capitalist' because of the differences 'between capitalism and the post-capitalist form of managing the socio-economic metabolism' in the Soviet Union. Meszaros points out that 'the capitalist formation extends only over that particular phase of capital production in which: (1) *production for exchange* (and thus the mediation and domination of use-value by exchange-value) is *all-pervasive*; (2) *labour-power* itself, just as much as anything else, is treated as a *commodity*; (3) the drive for *profit* is the fundamental regulatory force of production; (4) the vital mechanism of the *extraction of surplus-value*, the radical separation of the means of production from the producers, assumes an *inherently economic form*; (5) the economically extracted surplus-value is *privately appropriated* by the members of the capitalist class; and (6) following its own *economic imperative* of growth and expansion, capital production tends towards a *global integration*, through the intermediary of the world market, as a totally interdependent system of economic domination and subordination.' He adds: 'out of these essential defining characteristics only one – number four – remains, and even that in a *radically altered* form in that *the extraction of surplus-labour is regulated politically and not economically*.' This, again, turned Soviet Union into a class-exploitative society but not a capitalist society. As Meszaros says, 'the Soviet system was very much dominated by the power of capital: the division of labour remained intact, the hierarchical command structure of capital remained.' But it was still not capitalism or state capitalism.

VI

The private capitalist ownership of the means of production was abolished early in the Soviet Union and declared to be replaced by social ownership of the means of production. This was a departure from capitalism which however needs to be looked at critically, in the light of classical Marxism, for herein lay a most significant specificity of the Soviet economic formation accounting for its exploitative character. The abolition was a fact but replacement, social ownership, was in law only, and as we have already noticed, the *juridical* must not be confused with the *real*. Ownership does not necessarily coincide with legal title, the real issue is one of *effective* power over persons and productive forces. Classical Marxism always recognised the distinction involved, and Marx and Engels were always concerned with the *real* relations of production, whatever the legal form might be; they never confused juridical categories with real social relations, though these may in due course get 'finally sanctioned as an explicit law'. That property forms can conceal as well as articulate real social relations is a commonplace of Marxism. Marx, for example, had written: 'In England, serfdom had practically disappeared in the last part of the fourteenth century. The immense majority of the population consisted then, and to a still larger extent in the fifteenth century, of free peasant proprietors, whatever was the feudal title under which their right of property was hidden.' For Lenin too the existence of a 'legal relation' to the means of production, 'fixed and formulated by law' does not come into the actual definition of classes – it is a possibility which may conceal as well as articulate real social relations. Nor, again, is individual private property the only form of capitalist ownership. This is what Marx wrote more than a hundred years ago with regard to the growth of corporations within capitalism: 'Capital, which rests on a socialized mode of production and presupposes a social concentration of means of production and labour powers, is here directly endowed with the form of social capital (capital of directly associated individuals) as distinguished from private capital, and its enterprises assume the form of social enterprises as distinguished from individual enterprises. It is the abolition of capital as private property within the boundaries of capitalist production itself.' Needless to add, we have today massive state ownership of the means of production in capitalist societies – certainly not *private* ownership, yet just as certainly a form of capitalist ownership.

It is thus that juridical social ownership of the means of production in the Soviet Union had come to be their *real* ownership by the state. In a rather crude but revealing formulation made about the parallel situation in the erstwhile German Democratic Republic (G.D.R.), this is how Gregor Gysi, chairman of the Party of Democratic Socialism (the successor to Socialist Unity Party) put it after the collapse in Eastern Europe: 'G.D.R. society was non-capitalist, but at no time achieved the quality of a socialist society... The means of production were, finally, not more highly socialised, because the state property designated as people's property was governed by a centrally organised state, that is, in the last analysis the man at the head of the party and state was perhaps the only one who could feel like an owner.'

As a result of this specific feature of Soviet social formation, the juridical illusions created by 'state ownership' notwithstanding, the immediate producers were *in reality* separated from the means and conditions of production. Production was carried out by property-less wage earners; the social surplus, at least a considerable part of it, continued to be produced by them, but they had little, if any, influence on its composition or distribution. Vast majority of working people had indeed no control whatever, either individually or collectively, over the use of the means of production, the way social surplus was produced or utilised; they remained effectively excluded from all decision-making processes – 'alienated from ownership, from power and from the results of (their) labour' as the Soviet Academy of Sciences itself recognised (in the journal *Voprosy Teorii*) two years before the collapse.

In other words, while as a result of the revolution, the expropriation of the established bourgeoisie or ruling classes did take place, the capital-labour relationship as a whole was not significantly altered, let alone abolished in the Soviet system as it came to be. The change that in effect occurred was that the state came to be substituted for the private capitalists as the employer of labour and appropriator of the surplus, along with, of course, the surplus produced by the peasantry. As Sweezy has put it:

> The expropriation of the established bourgeoisie did not do away with the capital-labour relation as such; it simply substituted the state for private capitalist as the employer of labour.

It is the specificity of the social relations of production (and not ownership relation or form) which most crucially defines the character of a social formation. Capitalism is so by virtue of its social relations of production being based on the separation (alienation) of the immediate producers from the conditions of production. In the same way the social relations of production in socialism – which classical Marxism saw as the antipode of capitalism – are based on the free union of the immediate producers with their conditions of production to which corresponds the 'associated mode of production' as opposed to the 'capitalist mode of production'. Obviously, with one significant difference to be noticed later, the Soviet social formation came to share its social relations of production with capitalism, and hence was not socialist in its essential character.

To put the argument differently: although not always explicit in the classical analysis, it is surely obvious that the abolition of exploitation cannot mean just that the surplus product is no longer privately appropriated. It must also mean that the direct producers have some control over the production process and the use of the social surplus – through some form of worker self-management together with democratic control over the state and other institutions through which decisions over the use of productive capacity and social surplus are made. It is evident that the way the state system of economic administration and the political system were organised or functioned, the workers in the Soviet Union had no control in either of these senses. It was the state that owned the means of production, employed the workers, appropriated the social surplus and decided upon its use. The Soviet Union was thus an exploitative society in the strict Marxian sense.

The ruthless suppression of workers when they came out to protest against their exploitation during Gorbachev's *glasnost* revealed the essential exploitative character of Soviet society as no amount of scholarship could. As a worker, Petr Suida, commenting on the brutal repression of the protesting workers at the time (1988), said:

> The mask was torn from the regime that claimed it was a popular government and that the enterprises belonged to the people. The events showed that our society is, in fact, *antagonistic*, that the state stands above the people. It's not the people's state. It exists

to protect a class of exploiters – the party-state bureaucrats, whose platform is Stalinism. The class of the exploited stands facing them, left with nothing but the ideals of the revolution as a sort of pacifier.

VII

Marx himself had, in different contexts, pointed out such or similar possibilities, involving the appropriation of the social surplus by the state power. Pre-capitalist modes of production were characterised by a kind of unity of economic and political power, specifically in the sense that exploitation was carried out by 'extra-economic' means – that is, by means of political, juridical, ideological (religious) and/or military power. This unity existed in a very wide variety of forms including variously buttressed state power. Many ancient empires employed state power to collect tribute from subject peoples, including their own peasants, and imperial office was the principal means of acquiring great private wealth. Marx had noticed that it was not necessarily private property owner (landowner) but 'as in Asia, the state which confronts them (the direct producers) directly as their landowner...' Elsewhere he had written of 'the tribute-collecting state' in the Orient, and, apropos the 'earlier modes of production', spoken of 'the principal owners of the surplus product...namely the slave holder, the feudal lord, and the state (for instance the oriental despot)...' The tributary relationship, a relationship between the producers on the one hand and the ruling political powers on the other, is directly a relationship of exploitation, not between two classes of civil society, the producers and private-property owners as is *essentially* the case with slave, serf or wage-labour relationships, but between the producers and *the state itself directly*, in a way fusing the economic exploitation and political rule in the same hands. As Engels once put it, state simply comes to 'unite in the same hands, economic exploitation and political oppression'.

The proper question to ask in such matters is not 'who holds formal title to the means of production?' but rather 'to whom the actual advantages of ownership accrue as contrasted with the non-owner?' And in the 'Soviet-type society', where exploitation was mediated primarily through political-administrative processes, the advantages accrued to those at the top of this society's authoritarian economic and political (state and party) structures. Their control over state or public property not only gave them economic and political power but also provided a 'splendid cover for private appropriation', even as they could pass the risks and liabilities along to the people below. It was a case of extracting the surplus from direct producers, not by economic means, as in capitalism, but by non-economic means, by means of political power, by force, not merely physical force which was of course important but also by force of ideology, tradition and culture, including, ironically enough, the ideology of socialism. The situation had an obvious parallel in pre-capitalist societies where the extraction of surplus took the form of a tribute imposed by non-economic, that is political-ideological means. As a matter of fact, in a sophisticated analysis along these lines, the American Marxist historian, Robert Brenner, has treated the USSR as comparable to pre-capitalist social systems, such as feudalism, since, as he says, 'the bureaucracy constitutes itself and reproduces itself as a class by virtue of its ability to take a surplus *directly by force* from the collectivity of the direct producers, the working class'. Hence the aptness of Kalecki's observation, noticed in the *Prologue*, about another Soviet-type society: 'Here in Poland we have successfully abolished capitalism; all we have to do now is to abolish feudalism'!

It has been suggested over the years, more recently by Bahro among others, that 'socialism' in the Soviet Union and Eastern Europe resembled 'the Asiatic mode of production' in that its form of domination of economy and extraction of surplus was based on an autocratic state. The suggestion is not to be denied. The concept postulates the land and the system of irrigation in the ownership of a despotic state, which means – if we don't reify the state – in the group ownership of a class of state administrators who extracted the surplus and participated in its distribution in a manner proportionate to their place in a totally centralised hierarchy, usually with a monarch at the head, while the peasants below lived and laboured in their isolated communities, paying taxes to the state in the form of their agricultural product and labour power for public works (primarily for the construction of irrigation projects). This is not the place to argue for or against, to accept or reject, the idea of 'Asiatic mode of production'. The important and altogether legitimate point to be noted is the extraction and appropriation of surplus by the state, with the clear implication that the ruling or exploiting class does not necessarily have to be the private owners of the means of production.

It is interesting as well as significant that such an interpretation by critics was found embarrassing as striking rather close to home, and Stalinist orthodoxy had officially banned 'Asiatic made of production' from public discussion for more than a generation! (A conference at Leningrad in 1931 rejected the relevance of the concept of 'Asiatic Mode of Production' to the analysis of Asian societies. The decision was confirmed by Stalin's adherence to a mechanistically uniform or unilinear perspective on history. The critics have argued that the communist leadership suppressed the concept because the idea of a ruling class controlling the means of production without ownership of private property indicated a continuity of political power from Tsarist despotism to Stalinist Russia, with a party-state bureaucracy replacing the traditional officialdom. Blame for the suppression of the concept and implantation of a unilinear evolutionary scheme of historical development is frequently assigned to Stalin – and major proponents of 'Asiatic Mode of Production' including Riazanov and L. Madiar indeed disappeared during the purges of the mid-1930s. It must however be added that unilinearism in history, an evolutionary scheme in which historical stages – primitive communism, slavery, feudalism, capitalism, socialism – followed each other in a 'succession' according to necessary laws, really a mechanical or vulgar interpretation of Marx's conception of historical materialism, predates Stalin, and has continued long after him).

VIII

The evolution of the Soviet Union from a proletarian democracy it started with to a class exploitative society it came to be had deep social causes and was a prolonged process. We have noticed different aspects of this process earlier and only need to recapitulate it briefly in the present context. Out of the early post-revolutionary problems of economic and political management, there came into being a new privileged bureaucratic-technocratic stratum which already existed in Lenin's time but was as yet far from consolidating its hold on political power. Over the years it gradually strengthened its control over governmental and economic apparatuses, usurping all possible privileges and powers for itself to the detriment of the proletariat – it emerged as what later came to be described by Bettelheim and others as 'state bourgeoisie' (at times even 'party bourgeoisie'). Parallel and linked to this degeneration of the proletarian state was the degeneration of the Bolshevik Party that had become the single governing party in the Soviet Union. It had started as a genuine, revolutionary party of the urban working class and as such led the way to the seizure of power in the Russian Revolution. With the decimation and dispersal of this class in the years of civil war, however, the established relation between class and party (now christened 'communist') was largely dissolved, and for a number of years (roughly the 1920s and 1930s) the party ruled through its control of the armed forces and the security apparatus together with a certain degree of ideological support from the people, but without any clear or consistent class base. This situation, the turmoil and conflicts of the period, only helped *further* the permeation of the party, both ideologically and numerically, by the growing 'state bourgeoisie', thus putting an end to its ambiguous position as an unwilling and unreliable instrument of the dictatorship of the proletariat that it claimed to be. The logical end of this process of hardening degeneration of the Soviet state and the party, which included the liquidation of the old Bolshevik leadership of the party, was the eventual emergence of a new ruling class, which ruled not through private ownership of the means of production, as in capitalist society, but through occupying the decision-making positions in the party, the state, and the economy. It ruled in the name of the Communist Party, and lacked independent roots in the socio-economic structure but it was a ruling class nevertheless which exploited the workers, disposed over their surplus product in its own interest rather than in theirs, maintained the hierarchical division of labour in the economy as well as the methods of organisation and management developed through centuries of capitalist existence, and, depoliticising the masses, used its absolute political power to obtain and keep its material privileges, free itself from any control from below, brutally repress its opponents and cultivate the legend of its own infallibility. It was as much an exploiting class as is the private property-owning bourgeoisie in any capitalist country. As against the rise of this ruling class, the position of the proletariat steadily deteriorated from that of a class holding a revolution-bestowed monopoly of state power – on the use of which, however, there were always severe limitations – to a position very similar, subject to a qualification to be noted later, to that of the proletariat in any capitalist country, an exploited class forced to sell its labour power to acquire the means of livelihood and lacking any possibility to control the processes or the products of its labour. Marx had once written: 'Whenever a part of society has a monopoly of the means of production, the labourer, free or not free, must add to the working time necessary for his own maintenance an extra working time in order to produce the means of subsistence for the owners of the means of production, whether this owner be the Athenian aristocrat, Etruscan theocrat, Roman citizen, Norman baron, American slave-owner, Wallachian Boyard, modern landlord, or capitalist'; or for that matter, we may add, 'the Soviet state bourgeoisie'. It is thus that we had a class exploitative society and a corresponding ruling class in the Soviet Union.

It is important to note that the new ruling set-up, squeezing surplus value from the workers by virtue of its political power, was not merely 'a dictatorship after the bourgeois image' that Rosa Luxemburg had warned against in her fraternal critique of the Bolsheviks in 1918, which could yet be in its own way revolutionary, or at least well-intentioned. It had instead solidified into an authoritarian and repressive regime, increasingly devoid of any positive social role, almost entirely parasitical and dysfunctional. It was 'a formalised hierarchy of material rewards corresponding to a formally stratified and quite rigid ladder of importance and power' whose members, having long forgotten something called 'revolution' and unrestrained by any democratic checks from below, embarked on an orgy of personal accumulation, self-aggrandisement, and criminal abuse of power. The extravagant and corrupt lifestyle of the new rulers is now well-documented: the special privileges and perks, pensions, warrants and 'sealed envelope' payments, privileged housing, personal palaces, country houses and hunting lodges, luxury holiday resorts, personal vehicles, special shops and exclusive eating places, expense accounts, to say nothing of embezzlement of public funds, bribery, black-marketing, hoarding, illegal villas and luxuries, Swiss bank accounts, and nepotism of the worst kind – all witness, in Moshe Lewin's words, to the degenerative process by which not leaders but rulers were formed in the Soviet Union.

Incidentally, as noticed earlier, some of the negative potentialities of this system were paradoxically held in check for a time by Stalinist terror and purges; a member of the hierarchy abusing his position too blatantly was likely to find himself in a labour camp, if not worse. After Stalin's departure these restraints were gone and the ruling elite was released from any kind of submission to Party such as Stalin had enforced. But with his departure, the true nature of the situation also stood clearly revealed. If the extreme methods of repression in use under him were abandoned, Stalin's departure also signalled the arrival of the new ruling class in the Soviet Union. The failure of Khrushchev's half-hearted effort to discipline it only confirmed this arrival. The following Brezhnev period more than confirmed it: the Soviet Union finally had a ruling class in full sense of the term.

Long before the collapse in 1991, Charles Bettelheim had thus written of the class character of the Soviet system as it had come to be:

> The privileges that .... were regarded as having been imposed by the conditions of the moment, by the needs of accumulation, are today officially recognized elements in the system of social

> relations within which it is claimed the Soviet Union is 'building the material foundations of communism.' For the Soviet Communist Party there is no question of dismantling this system; on the contrary, it seeks to reinforce it. There is no question of allowing the Soviet workers to exercise collective control over the utilization of the means of production, over the way current production is used, or over the activity of the party and its members. The factories are run by managers whose relations with 'their' workers are relations of command, and who are responsible only to their superiors. Agricultural enterprises are run in practically similar ways. In general, the direct producers have no right to express themselves – or rather, they can do so only when ritually called upon to approve decisions or 'proposals' worked out independently of them in the 'higher circles' of the state and the party.
>
> The rules governing the management of Soviet enterprises are to an increasing degree copied from those of the 'advanced' capitalist countries, and many Soviet managers go for training to the business schools of the United States and Japan. What was supposed to give rise to increasingly socialist relations has instead produced relations that are essentially capitalist....
>
> The producers are still wage earners working to valorize the means of production, with the latter functioning as collective capital managed by a state bourgeoisie. This bourgeoisie forms, like any other capitalist class, the corps of 'functionaries of capital', to use Marx's definition of the capitalist class. The party in power offers to the working people only an indefinite renewal of these social relations. It is, in practice, the party of the 'functionaries of capital', acting as such on both the national and international planes.

And here is an equally insightful passage on the making of the ruling class in the Soviet Union by one of the leading western historians of Soviet society. Discussing the incredible difficulty of governing an economy and society as huge, backward, and divided as the Soviet Union was, Moshe Lewin has written:

> The problem was not just one of getting enough specialists and managers. There was the parallel problem of promoting a powerful class of bosses, the different *nachal'stvo*, composed of top managers in the enterprises, and top administrators in state agencies. The *nachal'stvo*, ...the state's ruling stratum was the key group which

the system continued to foster. The rewards for being admitted, especially in a country in a state of penury, were very considerable and the power over subordinates very great. Some of the privileges were openly acknowledged: *personal'naia mashina, personal'naia pensiia* (personal car and special pension) and separate eating places were public knowledge. But much was hidden: for example, closed supply networks offering goods on *spets-paiki* (special rations); special warrants; a graduated scale of expense accounts and perks; privileged housing; well-sheltered resorts; and, finally, the 'sealed envelope' with money over and above the formal salary. All these were slowly developed into a formalized hierarchy of material rewards corresponding to a formally stratified and quite rigid ladder of importance and power.

The *nachal'stvo* class was born from the *edinonachalie* principle (one-man rule), especially as it developed in the workplace after 1929. The creation of a hierarchical scaffolding of dedicated bosses, held together by discipline, privilege and power, was a deliberate strategy of social engineering to help stabilize the flux. It was born, therefore, in conditions of stress, mass disorganization and a struggle for order and compliance in a state of social warfare. *Nachal'stvo* members were actually asked to see themselves as commanders in battle. The party wanted the bosses to be efficient, powerful and harsh, and endowed them with prerogatives and appropriate encouragement. It was the top party bosses of the Stalinist school who got results whatever the cost..., impetuous and capable of pressurizing ruthlessly, who were the models offered to the growing squad of *nachal'niki*.... The promotion of the despotic manager, increasingly the regime's style of leadership, was a process by which not leaders but rulers were formed. The fact that many of them were themselves quite insecure as to their jobs made the despotic traits of their rule probably more rather than less capricious and offensive. Occasional purges of 'enemies' within the *nachal'stvo* were probably intended to shake up, destabilize and prevent the hardening of a crust of powerful officials forcing the leadership to recognize their power, and increasing their influence in the state machinery generally. Destablizing purges, however, did not prevent the *nachal'stvo* from developing a distinct organization, style and 'mentality'. Shifts of central policy and police raids affected its personnel in the offices, but the impersonal features of a bureaucratic pattern kept coming to the fore. These could be neither purged nor sentenced for 'wrecking'.

To complete the picture we need to take note of two observations of Paul Sweezy: (1) 'after Stalin's departure from the scene the practice of purging the leadership cadres was discontinued. The result was to release this group from the kind of subservience to the party which Stalin had been able to enforce. With this change, the party was in effect transformed from being the master of its top functionaries to being the key instrument through which they exercised their rule over the country'; (2) 'I would include in the ruling class only the upper echelons of the party, state, and military apparatuses. And I would argue that they are drawn from a reasonably homogeneous group with all the essential attributes of a class, including the ability to reproduce itself (through the way they socialize their offspring, through differential access to education, through networks of 'connections', even through the formal device of the *nomenklatura*).... (and) evidence unmistakably points to the existence of a deeply class-divided society in which consciousness of the 'we-they' division on both sides of the great divide is at least as strong as it is in Western capitalist societies'. Sweezy further adds that 'the division of society into classes does not preclude, either theoretically or historically, mobility across class lines in both upward and downward directions. In fact, as Marx was at pains to emphasise, the strongest and most dangerous ruling classes are precisely those which best know how to co-opt and integrate into their own ranks the ablest and most vigorous members of the dominated classes.'

X

If 'state ownership' of the means of production, far from being socialist, is or can be yet a relationship of exploitation so far as the direct producers are concerned, and this was a feature that Soviet-type society had in common with capitalism, the other two defining features of capitalism we noticed earlier were simply not present in this society. There was no ownership of the means of production by private capitalists; most of the means of production were owned by the state or, in the case of the collective farms which were formally cooperatives, closely controlled by the State. And there was no separation of total social capital into many competing capitals; the units into which the means of production were divided for managerial and administrative purposes were not autonomous and did not relate to each other in the manner of competing capitals. Instead they formed parts of a hierarchical structure of decision-making and control which reached its peak in the top political organs of the state. The guiding force in this system was therefore an overall plan which, however well or badly articulated, was a set of directives having the force of law and not merely, as under capitalism, indicators designed to help the autonomous units of capital to act more rationally in their own interest.

This had important, non-capitalist implications for the Soviet economy. Under capitalism, Marx had pointed out, 'capital and its self-expansion appear as the starting and closing point, [and] production is merely production for capital'. And, as already noticed, this self-expansion or accumulation of capital, via appropriation of surplus value produced by labour, is assured by the economic mechanism of competing capitals and the working of the law of value in the market, where economy directly commands the capitalist dynamic, which is then expressed through the play of economic laws which seem to impose themselves on society as laws of nature. Hence also the overall opaqueness of economy under capitalism. In this overall economy-determined functioning of capitalism, the state acts only as a public complement to the dominance of private capital; the state is the servant, and never the master, of 'autonomously' working private capitalist economy. In the Soviet society it was entirely the other way around, the state was the master of economy. This was indeed the most important difference between capitalism and the Soviet social formation. With the establishment of state control over it, the economy lost the 'autonomous' character it has in capitalism, and the overwhelming dominance of capital through the market was replaced by the direct rule of a new ruling class which derived its power and privileges not from ownership and/or control of capital but from the unmediated control of the state and its multiform apparatuses of coercion. Supporting the new rulers at the top were subordinate interest groups, specially created political and economic institutions, and an accommodating ideology – all of which influenced the patterns of accumulation. But no blind forces of a capitalist economy were at work, which had been in large measure eliminated. In other words, the ultisation of society's surplus – though produced, as under capitalism, by a propertyless working class – was no longer governed by laws that govern it under capitalism – the laws of value and capital accumulation. It was subject to no economic-structural logic, no 'laws' of any kind, including the so-called 'laws of socialism'. It was governed instead by overall planning which, even as it makes for greater transparency in economy is also primarily a matter of politics, of more or less open or hidden class struggles. In other words, the historically unique set of socio-economic relations which determine the specific form of the economic-political nexus under capitalism no longer existed in Soviet society. It had been replaced by a different one which, since it lacked an autonomous economic base and its ruling class did not have a structural location, role or responsibility *within* the economy but controlled it from above or outside, was not capitalist. It was rather, or formally at least, akin to that which existed in feudal and other exploitative pre-capitalist societies.

That is why it is not possible to analyse the Soviet-type society in terms of 'capitalism' or its 'laws of motion'. It was not subject, like capitalism, to economic-structural compulsion to accumulate for the sake of accumulation, either at home or abroad. There was no *economic necessity* for it to polarise the society *within* into antagonistic classes or to go imperialist *without*, to exploit and despoil other national economies or plunder and ravage global economic resources as is the case with capitalism. War though terrible is also, as Lenin said, 'terribly profitable' for capitalists, but it was not so for the Soviet-type economy. Soviet Union indeed detested the Cold War imposed on it because, as Professor Pessen said, 'it condemns them to continuing deprivation'. Political or ideological needs or compulsions, however understood or interpreted, are different from the economic-structural needs or compulsions of capitalism, though their pursuit may have a similar trajectory and consequences. The Soviet Union indeed chose to go in for massive capital accumulation, seeking literally 'to drive barbarism out of Russia by barbaric means' (though it also involved extraordinary heroism and dedication on the part of Soviet people and communists). But this was the result of a deliberate political choice by the rulers, a choice compelled by the need to industrialise as rapidly as possible in order to survive and pursue their foreign policy interests in a hostile capitalist environment as also to build 'socialism' as they understood it, and where ideological considerations, born of a certain economistic or productivist bias in Marxism, decisively contributed to the making of the choice. It is in fact this 'autonomy' of politics as against 'autonomy' of economics of capitalism, 'the politicisation of the surplus-utilisation process' as it has been described, that permitted the Soviet society to introduce some rationality into economic management of society and to deal effectively (relative to capitalism) with some very basic problems affecting the lives of the masses – such as employment, education, health, social welfare and so on. Indeed whatever economic and social achievements the erstwhile Soviet Union had to its credit, they were the product of *political* decision-making and not the working out of any 'laws of socialism' or the structural logic of Soviet economy, certainly not of any Soviet form of 'capitalism'.

XI

It is not that all capitalism outside of capital-labour relationship was eliminated from Soviet-type society. The exploitative nature of capital-labour relationship itself had its all-pervasive capitalistic consequences in the entire society. Soviet Union was not capitalist, not even state-capitalist, but Soviet society was very much dominated, in however devious a manner, by the power of capital: the division of labour remained intact, so did the hierarchical command structure of capital. We have already noticed what Bettelheim has to say on the subject. Also the political line of 'catching up' with the more advanced capitalist west had all along taken its due toll. Besides, the laws of value and capital accumulation kept operating to the extent that private enterprise and free markets were allowed to continue in existence, mostly in the production and sale of agricultural products from the peasants' private plots. The individual production units in the state sector and concerned ministries too often strove to act as profit-maximisers and capital-accumulators. Nor do we need to deny the existence of what was well-recognised as a 'second' or 'underground' economy, including regular moonlighting by workers and professionals that had come into being, often with a certain official tolerance or support, to complement the official economy, a testimony as much to the spirit of private enterprise as to the initial economic backwardness of Russia and the backwardness of 'socialism' that was built. This economy certainly carried within it real tendencies towards development of private capitalism and provided a fertile breeding ground for corruption at all levels of society – both of which are fully manifest today in the post-collapse restoration of a *mafiosi* capitalism in Russia. But all such 'capitalism' that existed in Soviet society was much too minor, the capitalist role of such activities or tendencies much too restricted by the planning system and political control from above to seriously affect, much less to determine, the character of its economy as whole. The essential point being made therefore is not that all manifestations of capitalist behaviour patterns had been eliminated from the Soviet society – far from it – but that these had ceased to dominate the functioning of the economy and hence, directly or indirectly, to shape the objectives and tasks of political power.

It is thus that, as Paul Sweezy has argued, there was a great deal less of determinateness in Soviet economy and more potential flexibility possible for the Soviet rulers than is the case with capitalist societies which are narrowly constrained by the accumulation imperative, the structural logic of capitalism, which operates under all circumstances and regardless of the external environment.

XII

During the early years of the Soviet Union, attempt was indeed made to get on the road to socialism. Before long, however, the train got off on another track leading, as we have argued, to a social formation that was neither socialist nor capitalist but a *sui generis* post-revolutionary society. This unique new society succeeded in achieving a major forward leap in industrialisation without the aid of a capitalist economy, and at the same time fulfilling a number of significant social goals, including elimination of unemployment. But it also produced its own contradictions. In a celebrated passage Marx had pointed out: 'It is always the direct relationship of the owners of the conditions of production to the direct producers ... which holds the innermost secret, the hidden foundation of the entire social structure...' This relationship was also the foundation of the Soviet-type society which made it into a new form of class-exploitative social formation. Here indeed also lay the most basic of the contradictions of the new society: the exploitative relationship of the new owners of the conditions of production to the direct producers in the Soviet economy. Initially it meant a bureaucratic structure which operated at a far remove from the working masses and was so rigid and entrenched that it could sabotage reforms and radical initiatives by political leadership at the top which, among its other consequences, led to wide differences in living conditions among classes, republics and regions within each republic, with the new privileged social strata militantly striving for higher status and a way of life similar to that of the upper classes in the West. Eventually it meant the emergence of a new ruling class in monopolistic possession of privilege and political power presiding over an exploitative society where the working people, rendering surplus labour under conditions of near absolute political and economic powerlessness, came to be hopelessly alienated from the system as a whole. Ultimately it is this basic structural contradiction which, become endemic, underlay the manifold crises of the Soviet system in its later years and together with other more or less important contingent factors including gross political ineptitude of the rulers and a certain newly discovered class interest in capitalism among them, led to its collapse in the Soviet Union.

This collapse however had no systemic or any other inevitability about it. The Soviet economy had over the years, especially after the post-war reconstruction, run into deep difficulties, which indeed turned into a crisis of major proportions by the late 1970s which further intensified in the 1980s. But the political flexibility which the specific nature of their economic system permitted the Soviet rulers, provided them with a wide field of choices to cope with these difficulties or the crisis. As Sweezy put it, at least three macro-level options were always available to them, now or over the years past. They could opt for a policy of accumulation for the sake of accumulation *ála* Bettelheim, though it is hard to see why they would want to. Likewise, they could opt for a genuine socialist policy in the original Marxist sense, that is, a policy designed to facilitate a transition to a future communist society; but, again, it is hard to see why they would want to, since it would mean working for the eventual liquidation of their privileged class position. Finally they could opt for the goal of preserving, strengthening and improving the existing system, which they believed to be socialism, without in any way affecting their privileged class position. Obviously it is this last goal which had all along been the 'primary motivation' of the Soviet ruling class, through Khrushchev's 'destalinisation', Brezhnev's years of stagnation ('developed socialism') or Gorbachev's *glasnost* and *perestroika*. It was typical of their long entrenched economistic orientation and class concerns that in their attempt to solve the increasingly difficult economic problems, the Soviet rulers sought answers not within the classical tradition of socialism but in capitalism. Unable or unwilling to turn to the working people, who were already much too depoliticised over the years, they increasingly turned to capitalist techniques, vesting more power within the economic enterprises in managements, and relying for their guidance and control less and less on centralised planning and more and more on the impersonal pressures of the market. Almost inevitably the managerial elite among the rulers grew in power within the system, and as the more active part of the ruling coalition of state and party bourgeoisie, they naturally favoured the further and fast extension of market relations in the economy. This process implied an erosion of the power and privileges of the 'old' bureaucratic ruling stratum, conflicts between 'liberalisers' (new bourgeoisie) and the 'conservatives' (old bureaucrats), with the former pressing for rapid marketisation of the economy, and the latter, having no programme to cope with the society's mounting problems, left to defend their interests with the old 'socialist' ideology. This was the context for the arrival of Gorbachev at the head of the system with his own programme of reforms, well-laced with the ritualistic rhetoric of socialism. 'Gorbachev phenomenon' was fully illustrative of both the freedom of choice the Soviet rulers had as well as the option they had been choosing all these years since 'Stalinist socialism' was built, especially after its reconstruction following victory over fascism in the second world war. Gorbachev's was, his early references to Lenin and 'renewal of socialism', etc. notwithstanding, only a variant of the third option. That it ended as it did, in a collapse in the Soviet Union (as in East Europe a little earlier) was due as much to the depth of the economic and political crisis in the Soviet society as the understandable ineptitude of both the 'reformist' and 'conservative' sections of the Soviet ruling class. Indeed, as the crisis became unmanageable the Soviet rulers lost interest in preserving their 'socialist' system and beckoned by the greener pastures on the other side, simply deserted it for capitalism.

XIII

In arguing that the position of the workers in the Soviet society was essentially comparable to that of workers under capitalism, it was suggested that an important qualification has still to be made. In other words, while this society early acquired and retained one of the determining features of capitalism – production by property-less wage labourers – it was retained with a difference which had rather vital economic and political consequences for the functioning and future of Soviet society. It is time now to notice this difference and see how it entered into the basic structural contradiction of Soviet society, one between the producers and appropriators of its surplus. This involves taking another look at the working and ruling classes as they evolved or came to be in the Soviet Union and the relationship between them.

The Russian Revolution which brought the Soviet society into being was made in the name of the workers and peasants and under a leadership which genuinely represented their interests, was imbued with revolutionary Marxist ways of thinking and came to power on a programme of radical socio-economic, indeed socialist transformation. Naturally, the overthrow of the old order, in which the oppressed and exploited had themselves more or less actively participated, brought these common people important gains in terms of an improvement in their living conditions. In the early years of the new social order, their status, both economically and politically, was significantly improved so far as existing resources permitted. Among their most important gains was full employment and constitutional guarantees of the right to a job. In other words, Soviet workers, unlike workers under capitalism, could not be fired by managements except in extreme circumstances. This job security, won through revolutionary struggles and sacrifices of the workers, was something that no post-revolutionary regime could dare to abolish, regardless of what advantages, from the point of view of overall economic flexibility, might be gained by doing so. In fact the legitimacy of post-revolutionary regime to a large extent depended on the job-security system. What is more, the power that the state came to exercise over the economy made possible 'the politicisation of the surplus-utilisation process' mentioned earlier, which permitted the new regime, insofar as it was still governed by the socialist ideals, to add to these economic gains, through constitutionally guaranteed reforms, a wide ranging social security in matters of education, health, housing, culture and leisure, indeed achieve a kind of rationality in matters of human welfare which has been impossible for even the most advanced, 'progressive' or 'human faced' capitalist society. In this, no matter what happened later, the Soviet Union and other post-revolutionary societies do mark an important historic advance over capitalism. Herein lay, and still lies, their appeal outside, especially for the poor masses in the third world. As time passed these reforms were institutionalised: powerful bureaucracies were built around them, and the people came to expect not only their continuation but also their extension and improvement. Eventually even a new ruling class leadership, which had little in common with its revolutionary predecessor, had to accept them as integral parts of the society over which it presided. Any attempt to cut them back or undermine them would have called in question the legitimacy not only of the leadership *but* of the system itself.

While the politicisation of the surplus-utilisation process enabled the Soviet regime to cope with basic problems like poverty or unemployment which are endemic even to the most advanced capitalist countries and have reached intolerable proportions in the underdeveloped periphery of the global capitalist system, it cannot be said that the basic contradictions of its class society were eliminated. Indeed, the most fundamental of all these contradictions, the divorce of the real producers of wealth from any meaningful control over what is produced, how it is produced, and to what uses it is put, remained, giving rise to problems and conflicts which in the long run proved to be as intractable as any that beset a capitalist society. The important point here is that in the absence of even bourgeois forms of democracy, which could have somewhat softened, curbed or mediated these contradictions, the aforementioned social gains of the revolution, even as they provided legitimacy to the system, also came to undermine it.

XIV

The early gains of the revolution, further consolidated as part product of the politicisation of the surplus-utilisation process, certainly served to legitimise the new system even when it become a class exploitative one. The objective alliance between the *nomenklatura* and the industrial working class was cemented by the 'common pot' of what can be described as a welfare state, which enabled the ruling class to integrate workers into its political base. The full employment principle was part of a cooptive corporatist social contract – a system which granted job-security to the workers in exchange for their political passivity. But such legitimisation had its limits, and the political passivity of the working class had still to be ensured. Therefore to maintain the new class exploitative system there was the need for a policy towards the workers which would keep it powerless and docile. The monopolisation of power at the top, with the party and state bourgeoisie emerging as a ruling class, standing above and apart from the people, was thus accompanied by a process of depoliticising the working class (and the people at large too), depriving it of all means of self-organisation and self-expression, turning it into a mere instrument in the hands of an increasingly powerful state, to be manipulated with the help of both ideological and physical coercion. Its trade unions and other organisations were even more firmly co-opted into the system and the development of any independent, genuinely democratic or self-liberating movements among the people was precluded. Communist Party itself had degenerated as a revolutionary organisation and its leadership become a part of the new ruling class. The ultimate result was an unbridgeable gulf between the tiny minority of powerful rulers and the vast majority of the ruled who were fully depoliticised. As the contradictions within sharpened, the increasing alienation of the people made their tighter control even more necessary in a vicious circle, and the gulf between the rulers and the common people only further widened and deepened. Across this gulf, suffering the economic squeeze and political repression of a parasitic and dysfunctional ruling class, the working class was helpless in defending itself or fighting for its interests. It had not lost the gains made in its period of political ascendancy, for example in such matters as job sincerity and social welfare, but without access to political power and barred from any kind of independent self-organisation, it had even less influence on its conditions and methods of work than the working class in the bourgeois-democratic regimes of the capitalist world. Witness over the years to the increasing venality and corruption of the rulers, the yawning gap between their theory and practice, promise and performance as they continued to mouth the language of Marxism-Leninism and even claim, ad nauseam, to be on the socialist road to communism, the working class had grown cynical and resentful of all such rhetoric, rituals and appeals in the name of Lenin or Marx. As the country moved beyond post-war reconstruction and the Stalin era, it was now, increasingly, a demoralised, ideologically disarmed and depoliticised working class, without faith in itself or any ideals, utterly incapable of any heroic initiatives or positive intervention like its predecessor in 1917. It could only act as a negative check on the power of capital in the Soviet economy. This is precisely how its gains from the revolution, even as they had served to legitimise the system, also came to undermine it in a manner which the Soviet rulers, having long forgotten what Russian Revolution was about, simply failed to understand.

Capitalism as a mode of production works with its own system of incentives. And these incentives impose themselves in different ways, and to a greater or lesser degree, upon all classes of a capitalist society. At the heart of capitalist work ethics lies an essential selfishness and a complex of fears: fear of unemployment or bankruptcy, being fired or demoted, loss of income or status, and at the extreme even destitution and starvation, etc., etc. As a market system it ensures effectiveness at the level of the individual worker essentially through the disciplining role that a combination of unemployment and the 'threat of the sack' involves. The 'efficiency' of the market rests on ensuring incomplete workers' participation and the maintenance of a 'reserve army of labour'. One outcome of the revolution in Russia was the social gains won by the people, which did not merely mitigate these all-pervasive fears which are so functional to any capitalism. Not only was there no labour market in the strict sense of the term, where labour could be sold or bought as a commodity, guaranteed employment, assurance of job and income, together with comprehensive social security negated the very basic principles of capitalist incentives or work ethics, or discipline in the workplace. The fear of being fired or losing one's livelihood gone, the possibility opens that you work as little or with as little interest as you can get away with. There was not much incentive indeed, beyond one's own conscience, to work or innovate or take chances....

Socialism, based, as it must be, on a genuine 'social ownership' of the means of production, means replacing the *capitalist* with more humane *socialist* incentives, work ethics and discipline in the workplace. What was therefore needed in the Soviet Union was a radically different, alternative work ethics of socialism, a self-conscious and self-imposed discipline of workers freed from the impositions of capitalism, now working in conformity with, as Marx put it, 'associated labour plying its toil with a willing hand, a ready mind, and a joyous heart'. Such at least has to be the perspective of a genuinely socialist ethics of labour.

Obviously it did not happen this way in the Soviet Union except for the *Subbotniks* for a short period in the early years, a phenomenon to which I shall return later. The bureaucratic degeneration of revolution and an economistic Marxism made sure that socialist ethics never became a part of labour process in the Soviet economy. The 'social ownership' itself was only juridically so and therefore essentially spurious. It was not socialist even by the most minimum standards, democratic control over conditions of work, production and reproduction, and over decisions concerning the disposition of surplus, simply did not exit. And labour power, if not a commodity, yet continued to be exploited. Of course this exploitation was limited or contained because of the social gains of the revolution, particularly the guaranteed right to work, which was and had to be retained even when the Soviet Union had grown into a class exploitative society. Due to this right and the accompanying absence of a reserve army of labour, the Soviet workers did manage to assert a negative control over the labour process. But it was no substitute for a socialist ethics of labour.

The exploitative character of the labour process makes work boring, debilitating and degrading so that, while material incentives do help to an extent, workers have little interest of their own in what they are doing, and would perform as little work as they can get away with. This is essentially the case under capitalism. This came to be the case under Soviet Union's 'socialism' too. The Soviet workers, overwhelmingly ex-muzhik entrants into economy, for whom socialism was soon no more than a slogan, a passport to career advancement, or an externally imposed ideology, responded to the work situation as alienated producers. An economy will work only to the extent that its producers are motivated; these alienated workers of 'socialism', lacking motivation, had even less reason to work than the wage-slaves of capitalism. Besides being bribed by the enticement of a constantly renewed array of false needs, workers under capitalism are all the more effectively disciplined by the constant fear of unemployment, illness, and old age, a fear which forces them to ever greater exertions to avoid being fired and thus losing their means of livelihood. The alienated workers of what passed for socialism in the Soviet Union, enjoying economic and social security, had no such sword of Damocles hanging over them. They had neither the fears, nor even the material incentives of workers under capitalism to motivate their labours. And nothing else, no socialist incentives had been put in place of such or similar capitalist incentives. The workers simply had no interest nor any compulsion to work hard or better, only to produce more surplus value for their bosses.

XV

One response to this situation, especially during the early years of industrialisation, was the use of extreme measures of coercion, including deprivation of housing and food ration and even deportation to labour camps. While this succeeded after a fashion in moulding a mass of raw peasants into an industrial proletariat, it was obviously no answer to the real problem. On the contrary, such methods tended to reduce the productive capacity, intelligence, and independent initiative of the existing industrial workers to a minimum. The other response was a more genuine ideological mobilisation of the working people, in which still alive memories of revolution, Bolshevik inheritance, appeal of socialist ideals and their promise for the future, and the continuing, though weakening, relationship between the Communist Party and the working class, all played their part. But over the years as the revolution degenerated and the Soviet Union grew into a class society, all such resources gradually dried up.

While the growing complexity of the plan, and of the productive tasks it entailed, required more care, more commitment and more cooperation on the part of workers, the latter delivered less and less. With the exception of the war years and the period of recovery immediately afterwards, when survival needs and patriotic sentiments supplemented the Party's traditional appeals, most workers were never able to identify themselves with the planners or accept the plan as their own. And none of the Party's reforms to entice or force cooperation, or additions to the means of production, 'trebling the number of available machines' as Kautsky once caustically put it, seemed to make a difference (as was the case with the peasantry too, where for decades the state tried to make up for the lack of work spirit with tractors, fertilisers, and pesticides). Instead, the workers' response was a distrust of the announced goals and intentions of the Party leaders or management bosses. They viewed the reforms advocated in the name of greater efficiency of labour with suspicion and fear that they would cause unemployment. Indeed there came to exist a profound split between the 'economic managers' (i.e. the ruling bureaucracies) on the one hand and the workers on the other. The managers – of supposedly socialist enterprises – sought efficiency through techniques and methods of *capitalist* production and management and increasingly operated according to what are essentially capitalist standards. Their economic thinking and decision-making were directed to the goals of production, productivity, competitiveness in international markets; these were seen as ends, not as means. And the means to these ends were precisely the workers who were sought to be manipulated by propaganda and coercion and whatever capitalist tricks were possible to make them work harder for the benefit of their bosses, now seeking to 'catch up' with the advanced capitalist west in more ways than the originally intended. The workers reacted in what in a sense may still be regarded as classical proletarian manner. Without capitalist values or motivations, with job-security and an 'egalitarian bias' born of whatever kind of socialism they had, politically powerless and depoliticised, yet resentful about their rulers, they refused to oblige, especially when talk of international competition, balance of payment problems, foreign currency reserves, more GNP or less deficits, or any other abstraction which happened to dominate the calculations of economic planners or party bosses, simply made no sense to them. They were not good material for any capitalist purposes. Given a choice between a 'comfortable status quo' and working their heads and bodies off for something they were suspicious of or found incomprehensible, they preferred to choose the former.

In effect the Soviet society now operated under a kind of informal social contract understood and honoured by all concerned in which workers had job-security, stable consumer prices, and control over pace of work, in return for their passive acquiescence in the rule of whatever kind of political leadership there was. Workers had considerable structural power in the sense that their interests had to be anticipated and taken into account by the political leadership, though they had little instrumental power through direct participation in decision-making. Thus every one had a guaranteed job (even at the cost of hidden unemployment) and at least a minimum subsistence level so long as he showed up for work and seemed to exert himself. It was in this sense a lazy man's delight, a bargain in which many workers gladly exchanged minimal effort for minimal but secure wages. Others wanting to do better economically could moonlight or work hard on independent jobs in their off time and even look at their time in the factory as a rest period in which they could recuperate from the work that was really profitable. For most, however, there was no motivation to work hard at all.

Under capitalism demotivation of direct producers is partially at least compensated by the pressure and fear unemployment. Given the non-capitalist nature of the Soviet economy this whip did not work, even Stalin's terror could not really replace it. Thus depoliticised and demotivated direct producers became a permanent, near-structural feature of bureaucratically planned and centralised Soviet economy. As the economy stagnated, shortages of food and other consumer goods while the rulers wallowed in corruption and conspicuous extravagance only further undermined workers' morale and motivation, made them all the more resentful. In time the arrangement of passive acquiescence degenerated into an almost absolute cynicism, a situation where workers could well say: 'You pretend to pay us. We pretend to work.' (Later we had an equally cynical slogan in Eastern Europe when its communist regimes collapsed: 'Communism is Better than Working'!).

This was a situation tailor-made for low productivity of labour and technological stagnation. Obviously, bureaucratic control over economy or labour, the politically coercive extraction of surplus labour, is not what one might consider an ideal or optimal way of managing the labour process in order to increase productivity of labour and assure technological innovation and progress. Under capitalism it is the autonomous market economy which ensures both with a reasonable degree of effectiveness. In the Soviet economy, its system of production relations – where labour, subject to exploitation as in capitalism yet retained a lot of negative power in the form of laziness or indifference, defiance or sabotage, or moonlighting, etc. – it was simply impossible to achieve a comparable, competitive degree of productivity. And this undermined the very *raison d'etre* of the system as it came to be built under Stalin and was continued by his successors.

A *sui generis* social formation, neither socialist, nor capitalist, hostile to proletarian freedoms but incapable of making necessary concessions to capitalism, 'transitional' only in terms of its 'hybrid' and 'chaotic' dynamic, lacking 'stable' conditions for reproduction over the long term, Soviet Union had an economy, a system of production relations, in which almost everybody was a loser: the established ruling class, with decreasing returns in terms of the relative surplus it could extract, and with it the inability to provide the consumption levels it promised to the people, and therefore, faced with increasing loss of its legitimacy or hegemonic power; the technocratic-managerial elite (the more active part of the ruling coalition), with their unfulfilled plans and failure in management of economy and extraction of necessary surplus which would have given them pecuniary and consumption rewards comparable to their counterparts in the capitalist world; and the workers with their inability to positively control the labour process and promote own interests including their consumption aspirations. Herein lay the most basic causes of the consequent economic crisis in the Soviet Union.

XVI

As long ago as the 1920s, Preobrazhensky had written: 'the USSR has not the advantages of socialism but had lost the advantages of a capitalist economy'. This situation in a way continued to persist all along in the Soviet Union. But instead of recovering the advantages of socialism, Soviet leadership sought, differently in different periods, those of capitalism which became a determining factor in the grievously distorted 'socialism' they built and its ignominious collapse. However there was no inevitability about it. The Soviet leadership could have put 'politics in command' – which indeed lay behind the early social gains of the revolution – and opted for a truly proletarian socialist path instead of putting 'economics in command' and continuing with their essentially bureaucratic-capitalist relationship to direct producers (workers and peasants), or later on trying to slavishly follow in the footsteps of capitalists. They could have gone in for democratic rights and controls in the economy, offered the workers a different alternative of actively participating in building the new socialist society.

There is no reason, none at all, to assume *a priori* that socialist alternative or incentives would not have worked, or that freedom and workplace democracy are subversive of increases in productivity. One must recognise that a great deal of socialist idealism indeed inspired the Soviet working people – it was an important factor behind the achievements of the Soviet Union in the early heroic period of the revolution and even later during the economic construction of the Stalin era, war against fascism and post-war reconstruction. That socialist idealism and incentives or workplace democracy do work is evident from the concrete experience of the Russian Revolution in its early years, when politically more conscious of factory committees, led by the Bolsheviks or even otherwise, were at the vanguard of productivity campaigns, fighting capitalist sabotage and organising support for the war effort against counter-revolution.

More specifically, we have the example of the 'Communist Subbotniks', putting in voluntary, free labour on Saturdays out of their commitment to revolution, to *their own* socialist cause. This is how Lenin assessed this phenomenon in *A Great Beginning* (1919):

> Communist subbotniks are of such enormous historical significance precisely because they demonstrate the conscious and voluntary initiative of the workers in developing the productivity of labour, in adopting a new labour discipline, in creating socialist conditions of economy and life .... Communist subbotniks are extraordinarily valuable as the actual beginning of communism...

It perhaps says more about the actual démarche, rather degeneration of 'Soviet Communism' than anything else that these 'communist subbotniks', institutionalised as they were by managements and unions over the ensuing decades throughout industry, came to be called 'Black Saturdays' by the workers themselves. Far from unleashing the missing agent of 'the conscious and voluntary initiative of the workers' which even inspired Lenin's definition of communism in this context – 'Communism is the higher productivity of labour, compared with that existing under capitalism' – they came to be hated by the workers as compulsory, slave-like labour. It is not at all surprising, therefore, that the relaxation of controls during the Gorbachev era, found the workers going on strike over such management proposed work schedules. They had seized the first opportunity to finally rid themselves of these 'Black Saturdays'.

Apropos the issue being discussed, this is what Paul Sweezy wrote, ever so perceptively, way back in February 1980:

> What was needed, as socialists have long contended, was a radically different attitude towards work and workers, involving the workers in decision-making at all levels of the economy and society, and encouraging them to take upon themselves the task of humanizing the work process as the collective responsibility of free men and women. It may be of course that travelling this road was never possible in the circumstances prevailing in the Soviet Union. It could be argued that it would have required the leadership and guidance of a party deeply rooted in the working

> class and dedicated to its emancipation, and that what might have become such a party was consumed in the flames of civil war. But whether or not this is true – and we shall never know for sure – there can be no doubt that there was never the slightest chance that the new ruling class which emerged later on would opt for a course which, if successful, would lead to full-scale democratization and the loss of its monopoly of power and privileges.
>
> The ruling class, in keeping with what we know about its origins and nature, opted for a very different course, that of depoliticizing the working class, depriving it of all means of self-organization and self-expression, and turning it into a mere instrument in the hands of an increasingly powerful state. It seems to have worked so far (though it cannot be denied that this may be only an appearance based on ignorance), but this 'success' has had a very high price. A depoliticized working class not spurred on by a capitalist incentive system (a compile of fears, not only of being fired but also of being demoted, losing income and status, and much more) seems to be a working class which is not much interested in working its head off for goals – catching up with the capitalists, maximizing military power, or whatever – that are established by a ruling class with which it shares little but a long relationship of abuse and oppression.
>
> The result is that the performance of the Soviet economy, even in purely quantitative terms, has for some time now been lagging behind its leaders' ambitions and the potential of its human productive resources. Attempts are being made to turn the situation around by massive imports of capital and sophisticated technology from the advanced capitalist countries, but the real problems are human and social, not technological; and increasing dependence on capitalism, if allowed to go too far, could easily be a source of weakness rather than strength. It would perhaps be too much to say that post-revolutionary society, as represented by its oldest and most advanced exemplar, has reached a dead end. But at least one can say that it seems to have entered a period of stagnation, different from the stagflation of the advanced capitalist world but showing no more visible signs of a way out.

Perhaps, we can now add, it had indeed reached a dead end, though the capitalist option was still in the future.

It is significant that the Soviet rulers and their representative scholarship never came to recognise the basic contradiction of their society – the exploitative relationship of 'the owners of the conditions of production to the direct producers' in Marx's words – which was fatally corroding their system from within. Expressive of their ignorance of the real situation, of their theoretical poverty as well as class character or interests is the fact that, as the economic crisis indeed reached a dead end, they not only sought ever more capitalist answers to their problems but also blamed it all on the working class of the Soviet Union. Thus, a major theme with any number of official and other economists of the Gorbachev years, including members of his Presidential Council, Makarovs, Shmelyovs, Shatalins *et al* (all of them products of Soviet 'socialist', or shall we say 'Marxist' education) was the denunciation of the Soviet working class, full of an amazing degree of contempt and abuse for it. It was accused of 'apathy', 'indifference', 'irresponsibility', 'indolence', 'sloth', 'drunkenness', 'theft and lack of respect for honest work', and so on. And there was the inevitable argument about 'the economic harm that results from our parasitical certainty of guarantee of full employment'. Described as 'overemployment', it was blamed for a host of social ills ranging from poor labour discipline and low productivity to poor production quality and shoddy workmanship, 'the scourge of alcoholism' and even 'today's disorder', etc., etc. Equally inevitably the attention was drawn to 'the objective laws of economic life' and 'established age-old work incentives', and the manifold therapeutic advantages of a 'natural level of unemployment' and (thankfully) a 'comparatively small reserve army of labour.' The 'whip of unemployment' was advocated and yearned for in order to secure due leverage on the workforce... And all this in a state still supposed to be ruled by the working class, or by a party in the name of the working class! 'A dictatorship of the proletariat' indeed, for the faithfuls abroad!

XVII

Equally significant and expressive of their ignorance of the real situation, the theoretical poverty of their response as well as class interests, was the Soviet rulers turn away from planning to market as the salvation for all the economic ills of their society.

Immediately, I am concerned to make only one basic point in this regard.

Socialism, from a Marxist standpoint, is first and foremost a negation or anti-thesis of capitalism. Since capitalism is based on private ownership of the means of production and allocation of productive resources and distribution of products (as well as incomes) through a system of competitive markets, it follows that necessary conditions for existence of socialism are public ownership of at least the decisive means of production and the substitution of planning for the capitalist markets. These are necessary but not sufficient conditions for the existence of socialism. Socialism, it must be recognised, is more than a matter of economic ownership and planning. A prodigiously demanding negation of capitalism, it means: instead of the class exploitation of capitalism, economic equality and social justice; instead of the formal democracy of class-based bourgeois politics, a real and complete democracy; instead of an economy or society of alienated human beings driven by greed and fear, an economy characterised by willing mutual service and a society in which, as *Communist Manifesto* put it, 'free development of each is a precondition for the free development of all', that is, again in Marx's words, a 'truly rich human life'. Even so social ownership and comprehensive planning remain the necessary conditions for socialism. Without them, it is obviously impossible to leave capitalism and its market economy behind and take even the first steps on the long march that any transition to socialism is.

Given the state ownership of the means of production, even if it was only juridically and not really social ownership, planning in the Soviet Union was initially, in its own way, phenomenally successful, as has been attested by all discerning critics, including those who cannot be accused of being socialists of any kind. Besides its other gains, it transformed backward Russia into the world's second industrial power in virtually a single decade and then, overcoming the massive war-time devastation, into the world's only other super-power. And if this planning later faltered, and finally failed in its socialist purpose, the fault lay not with planning as such. It was a failure of the historically specific, Soviet model of planning.

In economic or material terms, Marx saw socialism as 'socialised humanity, the associated producers, regulating their interchange with nature rationally, bringing it under their common control, instead of being ruled by it as by some blind power' – as indeed happens in the market-based economy of capitalism, governed by its laws of capital accumulation. The advance or transition to socialism means precisely the increasing 'common control' by the working people over their conditions of existence, in the first instance, over their means of production and their products. This control can only be common, that is collective, and what is called an 'economic plan' is one of the means of ensuring this collective 'common control'. But this is possible only in certain politically determined conditions. And central to these conditions is a system of workers' democracy – as part of an overall democratic system – which precludes a separate class of bosses and managers controlling the economy. In the absence of workers' democracy the 'plan' can well become only a particular method used by a dominant class – distinct from the immediate producers and living off the product of their labour – to assure its own domination over the means of production and over the surplus produced by the working people.

There are no easy or ready-made answers to this question of workers' democracy. A crucial issue for any transition to socialism, it yet remains largely unexplored. It certainly does not mean the traditional syndicalist conception of workers' control. If the economy as a whole remains governed by the capitalist market, by the value relations of capitalism, control by workers over each enterprise could even transform them, or rather a privileged section among them, into a sort of collective capitalist pitted against other workers in a most dangerous way. Nevertheless the principle holds that in any transition to socialism, participation of the working people in the control and management of economy, of their work, workplace, production process and products, is absolutely necessary. However difficult or even limited to begin with, workers' participation should be constantly increasing within the context of a system which, in Paul Sweezy's words, 'as a whole is moving away from every kind of stratification and toward a situation in which the entire population constitutes a single homogeneous working class' – which really means the disappearance of all classes and hence of the working class itself. This can in fact provide us with the best possible criterion for judging and even measuring progress in a socialist (and communist) direction.

Bolshevik leadership of the October Revolution recognised the need for workers' democracy, 'the living regulation by the masses of the structure of the economy', as Trotsky put it, to ensure effective social direction of the economy. They originally intended and even attempted to realise it in their plan of transition to socialism. But for reasons we have already noted, as with Soviet democracy in general, they did not succeed. As the Soviet Communist Party and the government increasingly ceased to represent the interests of the workers in whose name they governed, a new ruling elite or class of bosses and managers emerged, a distinct group separated from the working people which acquired undisputed control over the economy and made all the decisions, including those concerning the economic plans and their administration. As part of an administrative command economy, planning became a centralised bureaucratic affair, the concern only of leaders, managers, experts. Without revolutionary or popular enthusiasm and mass participation, centralised planning became increasingly authoritarian and rigid with resulting multiplication of economic difficulties and failures. It is thus that, ultimately, the Soviet planning failed to produce results radically different from a capitalist system. If you don't have democracy, workers' control as part of people's control over the plan, a plan can be used just as well as capitalism and markets to exploit workers. In fact, given its centrality in the Soviet economy, the centralised bureaucratic planning, like the State and the Party itself became a form of alienation; instead of being a system of rational, collective human control over economic processes, it became a system that no one controlled but which came to control planners and producers alike, very much like capital under capitalism where people through their labour create something that becomes a power over themselves and their work.

The real issue or contradiction in the Soviet economy was, thus, not 'plan vs. market' as made out by the Soviet rulers, especially during the Gorbachev years, or by their supporters at home and abroad, including sundry bourgeois ideologues or plain apologists for capitalism, who blamed the ills of Soviet economy – its lagging labour productivity and technological stagnation, its irrationality in allocation of resources, its inefficiency, waywardness and wastefulness, etc. – on its planned character, who indeed perceived these ills as inherent in any system of planned economy, and thus argued for the virtues of a market economy. The real issue or contradiction was, so to speak, 'plan vs. people', it concerned the domination or 'common control' by the producers over the conditions and results of their work-activity or the absence of such domination or control.

Here we are really face to face with, possibly, the most basic question with regard to the Soviet economy. If planning, to be socialist, has to be democratic, socialism itself too, to be at all socialist, has to be democratic. We have already noted that democracy is integral to socialism and that the Soviet socialism was, in this respect, most grievously deformed – the absence of democracy and political freedoms had stifling consequences for creativity and innovation in all walks of life, not the least in the field of economy and material production. That lack of democracy denied the Soviet system a mechanism which could mediate, smoothen or contain its contradictions the way it does in bourgeois-democratic regimes, this also we have noted. But in the context of the above argument about the need for democratic control and accountability in a socialist economy, I would like to conclude with a specific argument on socialist planning and democracy.

Capitalism is a system of market-based economy. If capitalism or the capitalists go wrong state does nowadays intervene to contain the damage, at times even to save capitalism from the capitalists. But the basic correctives come from the 'laws of market'. It is indeed the market which corrects the malfunctioning of capitalism. Socialism is a negation of capitalism. By definition it is a system in which it is not market but politics which governs economic decision-making; here there is nothing equivalent to 'laws of market'. If its planning goes astray, the correctives can come only from democracy; only democratic intervention can contain the damage done and find answers to its problems. In other words, if a planned socialist economy goes wrong, it is the people alone who can correct. And this is indeed how it was visualised in the revolutionary tradition of classical Marxism. Marx onwards socialism's defining feature has been a reliance on the creativity of human beings, the knowledge and experience of the working people as they struggle, make revolutions and seek to build a new society. Of this last task Rosa Luxemburg, for example, had written: 'The negative, the tearing down can be decreed; the building up, the positive cannot. New territory. A thousand problems. Only experience is capable of correcting and opening new ways.... The whole mass of people must take part in it'. She had insisted that democracy and political freedoms are necessary for finding 'the thousand solutions' and correcting 'all mistaken attempts'. Confronting the task of building socialism in Russia, Lenin argued for allowing 'complete freedom to the creative faculties of the masses'. He had stressed that there was 'no key in any text book' to guide and insisted that guidance and correction will come from the 'collective experience' of the people. Indeed, as the Soviet central planning floundered, the corrections could only come from below, from people empowered enough to intervene and correct. What the Soviet economy needed was not market and its freedoms but freedoms of a socialist democracy.

XVIII

That Soviet system, in its crisis, lacked not freedoms of the market but democracy of socialism was however something impossible for the Soviet rulers to recognise. Such recognition and the consequent democratisation would have inevitably led to the loss of their monopoly of power and privileges. Instead, in a remarkable self-serving ideological exercise, which became a self-deception too, they rationalised away the very need for any democracy or popular intervention in the economy. They postulated that their society, or 'socialism' they had built, was a distinct social formation existing in its own right and governed by its own laws, the 'laws of socialism'. And 'laws' *are* laws. By definition they rule out any questioning or correction of them, and therefore, of their custodians, by the people!

The Soviet rulers believed that what they had built was socialism; and their economic achievement without being a capitalist economy, together with its social gains (especially the elimination of unemployment) and the Soviet domination of the world communist movement, persuaded millions all over the world that it was indeed socialism that had been built in the Soviet Union. At no time did they come anywhere near recognising that what they had built was, achievements notwithstanding, an awful perversion of socialism as visualised in classical Marxism, that it was a class society ruled by them as 'a large state and party bourgeoisie nurtured in the *nomenklatura*' as one description had it, and that the daily accumulating problems of this society were the product, above all, of the deep-seated economic and political contradictions of this bureaucratically structured non-capitalist but exploitative society which had created an unbridgeable gulf between them and the Soviet working people, that the rulers' ritualistic reference or appeals to the ideals of classical socialism had bred only cynicism for *all* ideals among the people, and indifference, hostility or contempt for the new rulers. The growing contrast between the ideals or claims and the reality, only too obvious to people within and even many friends without, went completely unrecognised by the Soviet rulers.

Class interests are always basic to any such refusal to recognise the reality as it really exists. At the same time, in the absence of an effective ideological defence or rationalisation which would cover up this reality, the underlying social and class conflicts of the society the rulers are presiding over, the situation can be not only uncomfortable for the rulers at the top but politically dangerous for them so far as the people below are concerned. It is not surprising, therefore, that, basically content with what they had built, as the new society stabilised itself the Soviet rulers and ideologues went in for a truly ideological, that is self-deceiving, exercise to produce and propagate such a defence and rationalisation of their new social order.

XIX

With Stalin and for nearly forty years after him, a massive 'Marxist' theorisation occurred in the Soviet Union to justify and defend the established state of affairs. Central to this exercise by Soviet ideologues was a theory which violated virtually every single principle of Marxism on the subject. According to this officially endorsed theory, uncritically accepted by defenders of this system at home and abroad, Soviet socialism, often described as 'advanced' or 'developed' socialism, was a distinct form of society, existing in its own right, consisting of two non-antagonistic classes of workers and peasants and one stratum, the intelligentsia, and with its own 'state of the whole people' – a society, non-antagonistic, peaceful and harmonious within itself, now almost unproblematically progressing on its way to communism, propelled forward by a benevolent 'scientific and technological revolution', with its promise of bigger and better productive forces and a plenitude of consumer goods! This is how Academician Fedoseyev, like so many others, taking liberties with Marxism, expressed this theory: 'With their keen theoretical insight into the future, Marx, Engels and Lenin foresaid that the victory of the socialist revolution would be followed by a period of transition from capitalism to socialism, after which society would go through two consecutive stages of the communist system – socialism and full communism... the principles of Marxism-Leninism in respect of the inevitability of, and the basic stages in, the transition to the communist social system remain in force...' etc., etc. All the relevant concepts of Marxism are there in this theory but virtually all of them without their original analytical or practical significance.

Insofar as classical Marxism referred to it – as, for example, Marx in his *Critique of the Gotha Programme* – it never saw socialism, 'advanced', 'developed', or any other, as a social formation existing in its own right; that would be plainly violative of its essential character as Marx defined it, that is *a transition between* capitalism and communism. As was common in his times, there is a certain loose usage of the term 'socialism' in Karl Marx. Quite often he used 'socialism' and 'communism' as synonymous terms, both referring to the same kind of society, that is, a 'cooperative society' or 'association' based on 'free associated labour'. More specifically, it is what Marx called 'the first phase of communist society' which later Marxists, including Lenin, came to describe as 'socialism' (as opposed to 'communism' proper). Marx, therefore, nowhere speaks of 'socialism' as a distinct stage or social formation or of 'transition between socialism and communism'. For Marx, as the new society emerges from the capitalist society itself, the former is obviously an integral part of the *same* new society, being its 'first phase' only chronologically, with the specific kind of developments corresponding to it. For him between capitalism and communism lies no stage or stages, only a transition, more or less prolonged according to circumstances, possibly a whole epoch or perhaps even more than one historical epoch. Lenin, though sharing the loose usage he often equated socialism with communism, was equally explicit in speaking of 'transition period between capitalism and communism'. Thus, he wrote: 'The transition from capitalism to communism (*perekhod ot Kapitalizina Kommunizmu*) of course cannot but yield a tremendous abundance of variety of political forms but their essence will inevitably be the same: the dictatorship of the proletariat.'

What is more, this transitional period was always viewed as full of contradictions and conflicts, with class-struggle remaining its decisive motive force – albeit running 'through its different phases in the most rational and humane way' in words of Marx – right up to the attainment of a classless and stateless communist society. Hence Marx's argument regarding the class character or social content of political power during this period: the state during this 'political transition period... can be nothing but *the revolutionary dictatorship of the proletariat*'.

Against this classical Marxist position we have the Soviet 'Marxist' theory: socialism as a distinct society in its own right, a 'state of the whole people', a transition from capitalism to communism via two, even three, basic stages, and the transition itself being an unproblematic, peaceful process, *sans* any class struggle, governed, above all, by the further development of productive forces!

XX

Perhaps the most interesting part of Soviet 'Marxist' theorisation about Soviet society, fully illustrative of its generally apologetic or ideological as against scientific character, was its utterly un-Marxist concept of 'laws of socialism'. Once the Soviet Union was visualised as a distinct social formation, different from and beyond capitalism, it was presumed to have its own distinct, comparable laws of operation. And following Stalin, the Soviet ideologues duly came up with the notion of 'laws' operative in 'socialist' society – laws which were supposed to be objective and discoverable in the same sense as 'laws of capitalism'.

Marx does speak of capitalism as a law-governed mode of production. He wrote of 'the economic law of motion of modern society', 'the absolute and general law of capitalist accumulation' ('the greater the social wealth... the larger are the masses of the workers whose misery is relieved only by an increase in the agony of toil', etc.) Though it is well to remember that he himself called attention to the peculiar 'approximate' character of such social laws and wrote: 'the general law asserts itself through the whole of capitalist production as the predominant tendency...' And he had specifically insisted that such laws are 'modified by a number of circumstances', which for him included the elements of human action, of class consciousness and political practice – a qualification which is ignored by critics (as, for example, by Karl Popper) in order to be able to foist a fatalist determinism or historicism on the doctrine of Karl Marx.

But 'approximate', 'modifiable' or 'laws or tendency' as laws of capitalism may be, they are yet objective laws, independent of aims, desires or wills of those active in the economy, asserting themselves as a natural necessity, even as a blind elementary force. The laws of capitalist development operate behind the backs of the people living under capitalism, both capitalists and workers, and, with profit-making and capital accumulation as the driving forces, there is not only ever greater concentration and centralisation of capital, the capitalist societies also repeatedly pass through economic crises and inevitably generate increasing inequality of wealth and income not only between classes and regions within each capitalist country but also between world's core and periphery nations. And this is so, above all, by virtue of the fact that in capitalism, as noticed earlier in another context, the economy becomes radically autonomous of other aspects of social life with a momentum and logic of its own – basically a self-regulating and self-reproducing market economy that steers and controls the state rather than being controlled by it, and whose working serves to 'execute' or 'realize' 'the inner laws of capital', laws that govern the processes of economic growth or development under capitalism.

In no pre-capitalist social system are the major aspects of economic life subject to objective economic laws – certainly not in the same sense as in capitalism. And they are not in a socialist system either, which is by its very nature a planned socialist economic system. The central purpose of socialism is precisely to overcome the blind laws of capitalism as a market-based economy and to subject the economy to conscious social control by the working people. Socialism involves replacing determination by the market with the conscious social direction of the economy. In other words, the economy comes to be governed by political norms, its primary goals are a matter of decisions which are subjective and political. If economic growth or accumulation remains a key goal, it is a political decision and not a systemic imperative; aiming at production for use and not profit, it can be a means and not an end in and of itself. In the same way alternative paths of economic development are open to political choice or decision. There are policy alternatives at every step; and the choice can always be coloured by group, sectional, and (ultimately) the choice-maker's own interest as distinct from, and therefore possibly opposed to or away from, the interest of the people at large. Thus, to take a specific example, is it to be the quantity and a certain quality of industrialisation as such, the putting of 'economics in command' which was the Stalinist choice or decision; or is it to be laying the groundwork for an eventual transition to communism through a long process that does entail industrialisation but of a type and rate greatly different from that involved in 'catching up with' or 'overtaking' the industrial achievement of one or the other advanced capitalist country in a specified number of years. Thus who controls the socialist state, and how, is the crucial question in determining the destiny of socialism, and not any blind economic 'laws' operating in a socialist society, and certainly none which would take it in one particular direction, that of advance. Capitalism alone has the historical specificity of being governed by 'laws', laws of the market. That is why it has been legitimately argued that political economy loses its role or character as a science with capitalism. Herein also lies the substantial meaning of Rosa Luxemburg's famous phrase that the proletarian revolution is the last act of political economy as a science. Needless to add that whatever happened in the Soviet economy was the result of conscious political choices or decisions and not of compulsions or guidance of any objective 'laws of socialism'. If indeed there were any 'laws', or more certainly genuine compulsions, that pushed this economy to the brink, and then ultimate disaster, they were primarily in the realm of politics and not economics.

Certainly Marx and Engels were concerned to emphasise the 'scientific' character of their socialism, especially against 'utopian socialism', but the primary purpose of this emphasis was to argue for its real possibility as well as necessity, now that objective material conditions for it had been created by the development of capitalism. And when Engels wrote that 'Socialism, since it has become a science must be pursued as a science', he had immediately explained it to mean: 'that is, it should be studied'. Certain loose or rhetorical sentences notwithstanding, and they occur in Lenin and Mao too, there never was any suggestion in Marx or Engels of 'laws of socialism', 'objective economic laws of socialist development' or 'scientific management of society', etc., which had been a favourite theme with Soviet scholars in the post-second world war period.

Again, it is true that elimination of commodity production or relations is among the historical tasks that have to be accomplished in the course of building socialism – for commodity relations, characteristic of capitalism, mean precisely the control of the bourgeoisie over immediate producers via market. And it is also true that this elimination cannot be an 'abolition'; it can only be the result of a struggle carried out over a period on several fronts, economic as well as political and ideological. This is so not only because there are economic limits linked to the existing state of the development of forces and relations of production but also because of corresponding ideological and political limits to the elimination of market categories and juridical bourgeois relations. That is precisely why the task of eliminating market relations in economy or society is understood as a historical task. And to the extent that they continue, that private enterprise, free market, or commodity production are allowed to continue in existence, and products in socialist society still possess varying degrees of commodity characteristics during the historically necessary transitional period, the laws of value and capital accumulation keep operating in the economy; they can even be utilised to eliminate wastage, practise frugality, adhere to a strict system of accounting, etc. to build socialist economy with greater, faster, better results at lower costs. But whatever be the extent of such continuing 'capitalism' in a transitional socialist society – obviously it will be a subordinate and diminishing affair, much too restricted by planning system and political control to determine the character of economy as a whole – and however this society adapts and uses these laws for its own purposes, they are the laws of capitalism and not of any socialism.

This is not to deny, as Magdoff has clarified, that there are objective limits to what can be accomplished in a socialist economy. Like any other economy, it is subject to all sorts of objective limitations, natural, human and technological: the amount and quality of arable land and other natural resources, the potential supply of raw materials, the size and skill of the available labour force, the available tools and other equipment, the transportation and communication facilities, etc., etc. All this has to be taken into account; the objective limits, constraints and compulsions in the economic situation certainly condition and circumscribe planning options at a given point of time. And here there is ample room for information, advice and expertise provided by specialists and others – which even permits them a loose usage of the notion of 'economic laws', to speak of the laws of production and reproduction in a social-economic system, or to denote the objective conditions that cannot be ignored, or technical balances between different aspects or material factors in the economy or branches of economic activity, etc., etc. But the crucial point is that these limits and constraints are not objective economic laws, well identified and defined forces that are objective in the sense of compelling a specific course of economic development, independently of the wills, the aims and desires of human beings participating in the running of the concerned socialist economy.

XXI

Such in fact has always been the orthodox Marxist understanding, which Lenin and the Bolsheviks fully shared. Even as they accepted Marx's general theory about the structure and dynamics of social and historical processes, or his more specific social scientific analysis of the capitalist mode of production, they knew in the aftermath of the revolution, that they had no 'science', or for that matter not even a reasonably well-grounded theory, but only general principles to guide them in the construction of socialism. There simply were no discovered or discoverable 'laws' governing socialist economic development or reorganisation. Instead, subject to objective conditions, the imperatives here, choices or decisions, emanate not from any economic laws but the freedoms of socialist politics, and people's experience, well-informed and democratically expressed, is the only true guide. As Lenin said: 'the forms of transformation and the rapidity of the development of the concrete reorganisation we could not know. Only collective experience, only the experience of millions can give decisive indications in this respect.' More specific but equally unambiguous, this is how Bukharin – who incidentally also held that political economy as a science of capitalism ends as and when capitalist system ends – put it: 'the social economy is regulated not by the blind forces of the market and competition, but by a consciously followed plan'. This remained the accepted position for more than three decades after the Bolshevik revolution. But following Stalin's *Economic Problems of Socialism in the USSR*, published in 1952, a complete shift occurs. Concerned with analysing and providing a supposedly scientific defence of what he had built as socialism, Stalin insisted upon the continued existence of objective economic laws in socialism – and an economic 'law', by definition, operates 'independently of our will'. Thus, for example, 'the basic economic law of socialism' is defined as 'the securing of the maximum satisfaction of the constantly rising material and cultural requirements of the whole of society through the continuous expansion and perfection of socialist production on the basis of higher techniques'. As a 'law' this does not just describe a goal to be achieved but states the objective inevitability of a continuously expanding production resulting from socialist ownership of the means of production. Now, as expressed by Engels, classical Marxism indeed had the perspective of an increase, 'under socialism', of 'the social productive forces and their yield by planned operation of the whole production in an ever increasing measure'. But this was viewed, as a possibility, not by virtue of any 'basic economic law of socialism', but as a result of 'conscious organisation (of production) on a planned basis' in a socialist economy freed of the crisis and waste of capitalism. Stalin's was clearly a departure from the classical Marxist position.

To take another example, Stalin proclaimed 'the law of balanced (proportionate) development of the economy, which has superseded the law of competition and anarchy of production', arguing that: 'In this same direction, too, operate our yearly and five-yearly plans and our economic policy generally, which are based on the requirements of the law of balanced development of the national economy'. Now, 'competition and anarchy' are, or can be legitimately treated as, *objective laws*, not of production, but of production under capitalism. But the proclaimed 'law' of proportionate or 'balanced development' has no comparable, law-like objectiveness or compulsion about it in a socialist economy – it is something that is desirable, at best a *requirement*.

Stalin's theoretical advance was however most welcome to the Soviet ruling elites as they consolidated themselves into a ruling class in the post-Stalin period. No longer the received loose formulations or historical flourishes emphasising the 'scientific' character of socialism, but 'laws of socialism' take over and become enshrined as an item of faith and a central component of orthodox thought, a staple of ideological consumption, repeatedly stressed in their speeches by party leaders and in textbooks or dictionaries on economic and national planning. In a definitive statement, the Director of the Institute for World Socialist Economy of the USSR Academy of Sciences declared:

> In the transition period from capitalism to socialism and in a fully socialist society, planning is a form of economic management by the state, based on the knowledge and utilization of objective socialist economic laws, independent of personal wills or desires. Given the necessary material prerequisites for planned economic development, the effectiveness of any planning depends on how correctly state bodies apply the basic economic laws.

XXII

This shift and the official canon it gave rise to speaks volumes for the state of Soviet Marxism under Stalin and after him, for even a passing look at these 'laws' is enough to expose their utter vacuity. Thus, with old versions furbished up or added to all the time, we have 'the basic economic law' which says 'the motto of social production is to produce everything for the sake of men (*sic*)', 'law of planned proportional development of the economy', 'law of distribution according to work done', 'law of socialist accumulation', 'law of population under socialism', etc., etc., Included under the rubric of 'socialist economic laws', worded or listed differently in different places, are such assorted propositions as: constant expansion of production, priority growth of the production of means of production, higher consumption standards, steady growth of labour productivity, economy of working time, etc.

It is obvious that these are no laws at all, only a set of generalisations amenable to a variety of interpretations. Many of them are no better than mere platitudes or justification of current practices. More often they are moral imperatives or exhortations. At best they are policy guidelines, prescriptions responding to the most obvious requirements of realism in planning and therefore specific to the concrete historical situation of the Soviet Union; for that very reason they are not only inappropriate elsewhere but most questionable, even harmful, if given universal currency as laws. At times the 'law', that is the prescription, is in flat contradiction with what a truly socialist transitional society should be seeking to ensure. Thus, 'distribution according to work' was for Marx a bourgeois principle or right, considered necessary only temporarily, in the early phase of communist society 'as it emerges from capitalist society (and is thus) in every respect, economically, morally, intellectually, still stamped with the birth marks of the old society'; the eventual goal for him is distribution according to needs which goes beyond not only 'distribution according to work' but, strictly speaking, any kind of principle of equality of distribution, according to work or otherwise. (Apropos Soviet leadership's practice of the principle that in the first phase of communism, a non-market society, remuneration should track labour contribution, 'to each according to his work', Jerry Cohen has suggested: 'Because of the difficulty of finding criteria for assigning product to individuals, Soviet bureaucrats often got away with defending their bloated salaries on the principle of reward to contribution. They sometimes implied that they would be failing in their obligation to help realize the lower stage of communism if they gave up their large dachas!')

XXIII

The theory of 'laws of socialism' had nothing to do with scientific analysis of planned 'socialist' economy of the Soviet Union. It was only a rationalisation and defence of what it had come to be. Its vapid generalisations, donning the mantle of 'laws' did not merely serve to conceal the conflicts of interest within this society – conflicts relating to planning decisions and priorities, distribution of scarcities, who gets what between classes and strata, city and country or regions, and so on – they also reinforced and sanctified the established order of things with its privileged ruling elites, economic and social inequalities and authoritarian politics. Insofar as plans were claimed to be designed in accordance with 'objective economic laws', which are independent of the will of individuals, only thing left was to carry them out. Whatever happened in the economy was basically what had to happen, and the economic development as it occurred came to acquire the character of something natural, inevitable. There was no choice but to accept it and whatever goes with it. What was in accord with objective laws could not be violated. Nor can they who are running the economy, that is operating these laws, be legitimately questioned. It is thus that, political repression apart, the negative or ugly economic, moral and intellectual aspects of Soviet society, the gross distortions of its 'backward socialism', came to be endorsed and continually reproduced. The massive Soviet literature on 'scientific management of society' bears witness to this caricature of Marxism.

The supposedly scientific theory of 'laws of socialism', by concealing reality and obfuscating the real issues only served as an ideology in the original Marxist sense of being a form of false consciousness that well served the interests of the Soviet ruling class.

Let me conclude with underlining the basic point emerging from the above argument. By definition, a planned socialist society is free of blind, objective forces of the marketplace that characterise the working of a capitalist system. Instead of a society subservient to the domination of the economy, here it is politics that takes charge; in a socialist society, politics is primarily the realm where public issues are identified and choices made, alternative paths of economic development debated and decided, actual or potential conflicts of interests recognised, and above all mistakes in economic policy, planning and practice corrected. And to be truly socialist, this politics has to be people's politics, the people would need to have the final say on what should be done with the available resources and technology. In other words, power should be in the hands of the people. The building of socialism thus demands a democratic, participatory effort of the working people. But, as it actually happened in the Soviet Union, it was not merely that control over the economy was concentrated in a state ruled by a small minority holding a monopoly of political power, but by treating this economy as governed by 'laws of socialism', interpreted as objective and therefore not subject to change or questioning, this minority made this economy and its own practices, in principle, immune to any kind of popular economic or political intervention. The denial of democracy to the Soviet people was legitimised, partly at least, by an appeal to objective 'economic laws of socialism' – the emerging economic problems were simply not allowed to be seen or recognised for what they essentially were, that is problems of and for a democratic Soviet politics. The denial of democracy not only distorted the entire process of socialist construction in the Soviet Union but, together with the rulers' repressive politics, also widened the ever growing gulf between these rulers and the Soviet people, and, supplementing the unique economic contradictions of Soviet society with potentially explosive political contradictions, finally pushed the Soviet system to and then over the brink into a most ignominious collapse.

Despite its undoubted achievements, the system ultimately failed. But it is 'the Soviet system', and not socialism, that failed in the Soviet Union.

9

Some Issues of Theory and History

What ultimately came to be built in the Soviet Union had little to do with either Marx's vision of freely associated producers gaining mastery over their labour and leisure, that is to say, their lives, or with the ideals and values of the October Revolution which this vision had inspired. It was a gross modification in theory and abandonment in practice of the elementary principles of socialism: genuine social ownership, democracy, equality and fraternity for all. Even so, for reasons mentioned earlier, it was widely believed to be socialism by friends and foes alike, and this 'socialism' had its achievements above all in a certain kind of rapid economic development, and even more in the exceptional reach of its basic social welfare functions, something impossible for any capitalist society. But achievements notwithstanding, even as 'Soviet socialism' stabilised itself after the post-second world war reconstruction, its accumulating problems became only too visible – Khrushchev's ineffective attempt at 'de-Stalinisation' only underlined their gravity. The problems persisted, leading to a continuing economic crisis mid-1970s onward, and finally the collapse in the early 1990s. Explanation of 'what went wrong?' with this socialism have varied. 'Everything', say the opponents, who believing that it was socialism, therefore, go on to argue that everything is wrong with socialism. A great deal of obloquy has been poured on Stalin who (with his 'Stalinism', 'cult of personality' and all that) has been all too often singled out as the one individual almost solely responsible for the ills and the final failure of the Soviet effort at building socialism. Others have argued that the trouble really began only after him with 'the renegade revisionists' of the post-Stalin period. Yet others have offered an 'economistic' theory of the decline of Soviet-style socialism, emphasising its inability to deal with the capitalist world, either in insulating itself from it, including its crises of the 1970s and 1980s, or in competing with it – 'Brezhnevite megalomania trying to compete', etc. Alternatively, the problem is located in 'the politics of socialism', seen as the pursuit of political power for its own sake – 'their failure was ultimately political'. Or it has been claimed that 'the central feature of the collapse' was 'the ideological dimension', it was 'the collapse of underlying self-confidence ... first among the leadership and then within the population as a whole'. It has also been viewed as, in many ways, 'A Singular Collapse', indeed a case of 'self-destruction'. And while the United States' role in it (via the imposition of a costly cold war, etc.) is generally conceded, many, especially among the faithful whose 'Marxism-Leninism' leaves them unable or unwilling to look for deeper causes, have blamed it all on Gorbachev and his *glasnost*, as part of a deep-laid conspiracy of American imperialism.

Obviously no explanation in terms of single or separate factors is possible. What has happened is the outcome of an overdetermined historical process in the Marxian sense, that is, of an overdetermination (of a variety of historically-produced economic, political, cultural and other contingent factors including those mentioned above) that proceeded powerfully conditioned by the basic economic contradictions, the underlying structural logic of Soviet society. As I have argued in another context, 'it is only within the necessities and constraints of the given objective, economic-structural situation, within "this determination by the economic in the *first* instance", that whatever happens is determined by men in pursuit of their ends'. It is in terms of such a 'dialectics of men and circumstances' that, like its emergence and development, the collapse of the Soviet Union has to be understood.

Marx had spoken of the basis or 'foundation' of a society and located it in the relation between the direct producers and those who, dominating the means and conditions of production, extract and appropriate the surplus produced by them. This is where the basic economic or class contradictions of a society lie. We have already taken note of the foundation of Soviet society – its mode of surplus extraction and appropriation and its dominant and subordinate classes – and therefore the entropic economic-structural or class contradictions that had come to lie at the very basis of this society and which conditioned its historical development. Over this foundation had come to be built a massively powerful, contradictions-ridden structures of command *from above*, especially in the economic and political spheres, within which the multiple contradictions of Soviet society matured into a crisis, and with different classes, groups, individuals playing their roles, culminated in the ultimate disintegration of this society. I do not have the competence to adequately analayse this complex historical process. I shall be content, in addition to my argument so far and with a certain unavoidable repetition, to draw attention to some of its more important aspects.

II

As already noticed, the Soviet socialist system, despite its many problems and negative features, was relatively successful as an economic system from its formation in the late 1920s and early 1930s through the mid-1970s. Turning vast masses of peasants into workers, spreading education and skills among them, it produced rapid industrialisation and urbanisation. Notwithstanding the initial narrow or low resource base, it achieved a fantastically high rate of economic growth, far outstripping the rate in the capitalist economies, not to speak of countries with a similar level of backwardness at the end of the first world war. The Soviet Union became the second industrial power in the world, with a military capacity which enabled the Red Army to resist and defeat the German fascist invasion and then liberate Europe from the Nazis. Certainly the Soviet Union and its allies had emerged as the political and military equal of the United States and its allies and could show phenomenal achievements in many fields, including science and technology, defence and space research (atomic and nuclear bombs, *sputnik* and Gagarin), sports, etc. A case can be made that, until about the mid-1970s, the Soviet system was succeeding in progressively narrowing the economic gap between itself and advanced capitalism.

This economic growth was accompanied by a significant rise in living standards and other gains in social and cultural fields. Unemployment was banished from the country, jobs were guaranteed with subsidised housing and blanket social security for all, basic needs of the people were met and the children and old people looked after as never before. In the countryside the insecurity and heavy work burdens traditionally attached to individual farming were mitigated through collective farming, and cooperative farmers, freed of market worries, material or social insecurity or anxieties over their own economic existence, had more free time for social and cultural pursuits. The Soviet Union indeed set up the most comprehensive educational, cultural, health and social security arrangements the world has ever witnessed, provided basic consumption goods to the multitudes in town and country at prices that remained unvaried for decades on end. The workers were provided with a range of social and economic rights and benefits; scientists and poets and dancers and musicians were provided with funds and the stimulus they needed to develop their creativity; millions and millions of copies of the works of Shakespeare, Pushkin and other world classics were distributed at nominal prices; and so were discs and tapes of Beethoven, Bach, Mozart, Tchaikovsky, and others – and so on. These achievements in economic, social and cultural spheres were real enough for the Webbs to write in the mid-1930s, against the backdrop of world capitalism in crisis, of 'a new civilisation' in the Soviet Union. It has to be conceded that behind these achievements lay not only the extraordinary idealism and sacrifice of the Soviet people and communists but also the use of capitalist methods borrowed from F.W. Taylor and the rest, and a highly repressive political regime. Even so, the history of the communist rule in the Soviet Union is not morally reducible to one of economic coercion or political repression as enemies have continued to make out.

Terrorism existed but so did immense enthusiasm. And besides the Webbs there were others, by no means sympathetic to or exclusively of the left, who were impressed and, indeed, urgent warnings used to be issued by many such people that the Soviet Union was launched on a course of development which would before long bring it level with and take beyond the West. Not only the Soviet but also western scholars believed that barring some unforeseen events, this was indeed a real possibility. For Stalin and later even Khrushchev, this was a hope they entertained. Someone who claimed that the future belonged to the Soviet system could, even as late as 1975, cite significant supporting evidence.

III

The successes of the Soviet system so far were evidently the result of planning guiding the economy; they bore witness to the fact that central economic planning had indeed worked in the Soviet Union. But it is an equally undeniable fact that these successes could not be sustained and what followed was a period of economic failures, of stagnation, shortages and long queues and a crisis that persisted to the point of final collapse of the system. This has given rise to a wide-ranging debate on the subject of 'planning' and there is a leading tendency among critics, including many radicals, to focus on the later period, ignore the deeper-lying causes and zero in on the presumably inevitable failure of central planning as the essential cause of the Soviet Union's economic troubles and the final collapse. This however is a mistaken view. It is important to recognise not only that the cause of Soviet system's economic failures and ultimate collapse lay deeper in the economic and political contradictions within and the hostile capitalist environment without, but also that insofar economic planning is involved the causes lay not in economic planning as such but in the historically specific character of economic planning in the Soviet Union.

The 'plan' is not, as a reifying approach would have it, an anthropomorphic entity which operates with an implacable logic of its own. Nor are phenomena like 'planning', 'economics laws', or 'the state' to be viewed as timeless, eternally equal to themselves. In their concreteness, they are always specific to a given historical situation, which also accounts for whatever meaning or relevance they have. Planning in the Soviet Union therefore must not be confused with planning in general. On the contrary it is important to recognise that Soviet economic planning evolved under very special historical circumstances which followed the success of the October Revolution. The Bolshevik leadership of the new Soviet state had pitifully little experience to go by and no time or opportunity at all for the trial-and-error experiments essential to the rational construction, for the first time in history, of a new economic system, which involved not just an attempt to build socialism but even more urgently to industrialise and survive in the midst of continuing actuality or threat of invasion by one or more hostile capitalist powers. If there were no blueprints of, or previous experience in, socialist construction, no personnel of socialist persuasion was available either. Revolutionaries, the few that survived the civil war, generally made for poor economic managers and the much needed personnel necessarily came from the old state apparatus with strong bureaucratic and semi-feudal traditions. As in case of the state apparatus in general, the economy too became a fertile ground for the emergence of a huge bureaucracy with special privileges and interest in protecting and extending them, and an ability to shape and control its members' ways of operation. This bureaucracy had in fact already emerged prior to the first Five-Year Plan, that is, prior to the turn towards forced collectivisation of agriculture and over-accelerated industrialisation, as part of an authoritarian apparatus of state and party functionaries controlling, under the all powerful Stalin-led Party Secretariat, all key aspects of social life in the Soviet Union – Lenin had seen the danger this posed to the socialist project, he warned against it and indeed died fighting against it. Within a bureaucratically deformed authoritarian political system, this bureaucracy, arrogating to itself all decision-making in the economy, in due course also made its power immune to any democratic participation or correction by supplementing the repressive authority of the state with an ideology rationalising its existence and powers as well as that of the system it served. It is thus that planning in the Soviet Union was introduced and practised by a ruling bureaucracy which, even as it built the economy, also sought to preserve and extend its powers and privileges – deemed necessary all along, in the last couple of decades of Soviet existence it is the latter purpose that was accorded primacy. 'Planning' was now visualised as a means of 'scientific management' of Soviet society. It was literally elevated to the status of a science, invented in the Soviet Union, guided by alleged 'laws of socialism' – 'laws' which only rationalised and justified the current policies and practices of the Soviet administrative command economy. (Incidentally, Engels had once described the Saint Simonian scheme of 'scientific management' of society as disguised capitalism).

It is crucial, therefore, to keep this historical specificity in mind and to reject any notion that Soviet economic policies and practices during its stormy career and central economic planning are one and the same, with its logical corollary that the crisis or collapse of the Soviet economy and society is also a crisis and collapse of economic planning itself. The truth is rather that what led to the crisis and collapse of the Soviet economy was precisely those aspects of economic planning that were peculiar to Soviet experience and not inherent characteristics of planning as such. It is necessary to distinguish between central planning and bureaucratic control of the economy.

IV

When the Soviet Union began its drive to industrialise in the late 1920s, it adopted technologies that had been developed by capitalism and it had the necessary human and material resources available within the country, that is, huge reserves of unutilised and under-utilised labour and an ample supply of fuel, minerals, other raw materials and 'virgin land' which could be mobilised and introduced into the system with relative ease, and 'regardless of cost'. Despite the crudeness of the economic command from above, planning functioned well because it was mainly concerned with setting up or coordination of a limited number of huge projects: dams, mills, power stations, railway lines; entire new cities that astonished the world in the 1930s came up, as did a powerful defence industry. This last is in fact a good example of where the Soviet-type central planning worked best: it was most able to meet 'consumer' need in those sectors where there was a single large customer able to place specific orders and reject the product if it is not of acceptable quality. Thus Soviet arms production often achieved global competitiveness, because the Soviet arms procurement ministries monitored the production process and had the power to reject sub-standard equipment. (The ordinary Soviet consumer was not in that position, he had no effective institutional representation, and this created problems when the economy grew more complex, and there was need to move from extensive to intensive phase of economic development). Incidentally, the readiness for war was in fact the primary goal of the Soviet Union from 1928 onwards – the threat of war was real and it did eventually materialise with the German attack in 1941.

For a small number of strategic objectives given over-riding priority, a centralised planning system in which the centre communicated its requirements directly to production units, was quite effective. Oskar Lange, taking note of this aspect, aptly described the Soviet system, including its very early period, as a *sui generis* 'war economy', its methods being necessary in a revolutionary period of transition, as also for rapid industrialisation and military build-up, though not intrinsically socialist. And this system of centralised planning that enabled the Soviet Union to industrialise so rapidly in the late 1920s and 1930s proved equally effective for the post-war tasks of reconstruction and building up a nuclear-weapons and ballistic-missile capability sufficient to maintain a rough balance of power with that of the United States and its capitalist allies.

A favourable factor behind the pre-war industrialisation was the possibility of borrowing with relative ease, on own terms, advanced technology from the capitalist world. The economic crisis of the 1930s made it profitable for capitalist countries, Germany, USA, UK and the rest, often in competition with each other, to export modern machinery on a large scale to the Soviet Union. In the 1930s and even 1940s to an extent, Soviet Union under Stalin was able, however crudely, to exploit contradictions within the world-capitalist system because these were sharp enough to even take the form of clashes between the most powerful capitalist states. The import of western technology during this period was an important factor in the Soviet growth up to the end of the 1950s. The relatively slow pace of internal technological change (except in the military field), in face of successive waves of technological innovation in the west, did not create any serious problems for Soviet economy in that period.

It also needs to be noted that while Stalin's coercive political practices, however costly otherwise, were a factor in the situation, Soviet successes, such as they were, in economy as elsewhere, owed a great deal to the motivation of the cadres in the enterprises and outside than is currently fashionable to recognise. What was built could not be built with only coercion or 'slave labour'. The administrative command economy of the Soviet Union, till the end of the 1950s and even for more than a decade later did quite well also because the early socialist ideological inspiration was still there, a certain patriotic urge for building and reconstruction still motivated the people, political discipline was strong and isolation from the growing consumerism of the market-based capitalist world could be maintained.

Soviet central planning was thus eminently successful in achieving the goals set by the political leadership. It helped ensure that the rate of growth of the Soviet economy during this period was on average high, much higher than that of the capitalist countries, providing Stalin, and even Khrushchev a little later, good reason to believe that they would 'catch up and surpass' the USA, Ernest Mandel has written:

It is wrong to represent (Soviet planned economy) as 'totally' or even 'basically' inefficient. It isn't. Nothing in the history of the Soviet Union allows such a judgement. It is based upon a misrepresentation of what really happened.

In all those fields where the bureaucracy chose priority goals, these were by and large implemented. The Soviet Union did build nearly from scratch a heavy industry which transformed a semi-agrarian backward country into the second industrial power of the world. It built a weapons industry which enabled it to defeat Hitler in the second world war (compare it to the performance of Tsarist Russia in the first world war and Japan in the second world war). It equalled the USA in spacecraft during a whole period. It developed the diffusion of classical world culture on a mass scale unprecedented in any major country of the world, including the USA, Germany and Japan. It educated more scientists than the whole of Western Europe plus Japan.

One can discuss whether these priorities were correctly chosen, what were the reasons for their choice, whether other choices would have been more meaningful, what were the costs endured (sometimes tremendous and absolutely out of proportion to the relative importance of a given prioritised goal). But by and large, the superiority of planning showed itself in the capacity of the system to realise those prioritised goals it had deliberately chosen.

V

This undeniable success of Soviet central planning was, however, soon followed by the equally undeniable fact of its failure for being a bureaucratic enterprise. As the Soviet Union moved into the period beyond the post-war reconstruction, Soviet economy ran into difficulties which bureaucratic Soviet planning found impossible to manage, not the least because it was now the instrument of an altogether degenerated political leadership. It is not only that some favourable factors of the earlier period had disappeared, the economy needed to make the transition from 'extensive' to 'intensive' phase of its development. The tasks of economic coordination became more complex as industrialisation advanced, the 'socialist camp' grew and, with the capitalist world uniting itself under American hegemony, the access to western technology ceased. By the 1960s growth began to slow down and by the 1980s stagnation had set in – new problems appeared, and many old ones surfaced with renewed vehemence as the Soviet society finally took shape as a *sui generis* class-exploitative society. Immediately the economic crisis itself stemmed from the exhaustion of the model of extensive growth adopted in the late 1920s which depended on the availability of ever new supplies of labour power and raw materials to maintain a satisfactory rate of growth, adequate enough to provide for the increasing civilian and military needs. Structural problems in their supplies apart, none of these were inexhaustible. Natural resources became depleted and the availability of labour power declined because of a variety of reasons – slowing down of the rate of growth of the population, war losses, exhaustion of the reserves of surplus rural workers. As the supply of new human and material resources dried up – which of course was bound to happen sooner or later – the 'magic' of administrative command economy, with its bureaucratised planning mechanisms, evaporated and the growth rate lagged, slowing down through late 1960s and 1970s to near zero in the early 1980s, the closing years of Brezhnev's rule, a few years before Gorbachev's election as General Secretary. The economy went into stagnation, hitting hard at the living standards of the people and the provision of social services. The Soviet economy became one of acute shortages and long queues for the common people.

With the need to turn from extensive to intensive growth, along with stepping up of their skill and training, motivation of workers had become more important than just bringing young people from the countryside into factories as semi-skilled labourers. And it is precisely this motivation which, steadily weakened over the years, now finally decayed. It was not merely that with its bureaucratic degeneration, the Soviet Union had finally stabilised into a class-exploitative, authoritarian society and therefore there was a general loss of whatever idealism or ideological inspiration there was in an earlier period, and, understandably enough, providing socialist incentives to work never become a real issue for Soviet planning or planners. It was also that, given its bureaucratically planned character, the Soviet 'extensive' economic growth with its internal disproportions, never developed anything akin to what has come to be called 'Fordism' in the market economies of the west, that is, a moving circuit of mass production and mass consumption. As consumer shortages emerged, the gross inequalities between the rulers and the common people were not rectified but only confirmed and enhanced by the rigidities of the bureaucratically administered system of distribution, made worse by the effects of under-investment in the necessary infrastructure. This situation certainly took its toll of workers' interest and involvement in production. Idealism had vanished and the other older methods – mostly a mixture of illusion, terror and propaganda, combined with fear of invasion from abroad – which for a time in the past did effectively mobilise the workers as well as the cadres and 'little cogs' in the economy could do so no more. As Kalecki has pointed out mobilisation of this type cannot be sustained for more than a decade or two. The more directly coercive methods, work through forced labour, was even more difficult to sustain, as Khrushchev found out soon after Stalin's departure, besides being extremely wasteful of valuable materials and machines as well as human lives. Indeed, the repressive apparatus itself had become a costly parasitic growth on the economy. And no better or more effective ways of mobilising the workforce were forthcoming. In the agricultural sector, with the forced collectivisation of the 1930s, more surplus may have been, for a time, seized from the peasantry but whatever the later contingent social gains (in collective health care, education, etc.) agricultural output was permanently damaged and agricultural productivity remained low due to super exploitation in the form of poor wages and conditions of work. In the industrial sector, with their employment guaranteed, there was near total erosion of motivation among workers at the point of production resulting in high absenteeism and moonlighting, low productivity and low product quality. As discontent with the deteriorating socio-economic situation mounted, increase in wages, in order to buy working class passivity, which neither domestic production nor imports were capable of soaking up and recycling, only fuelled inflation and thus worsened the economic situation, the continuing crisis of the Soviet economy. Soviet planning because of its bureaucratic character simply failed, as we shall see in some detail later, to cope with it.

VI

The highly bureaucratised central planning had obviously adverse consequences for technological advancement of the Soviet economy. The hypercentralisation of decision-making in production simply choked off modernisation and technological innovation except in the military field, where the remarkable achievements in space exploration and the high level of war material were obtained by giving them absolute priority and close supervision, unlike the lack of attention accorded to other, supposedly 'unimportant' areas, including the consumer goods industries. The situation was only worsened by the negation of Soviet democracy, in general and at the workplace, which inhibited innovation and the creative development of human productive powers, especially in the era of information technology; the free interchange between skilled workers and scientific investigators which so often characterises the frontiers of technical development never took off and at its worst, there was the almost terroristic imposition of the technical fantasies of pseudo-scientists like Lysenko.

Thus, on the whole, whereas technological change in the west became more and more accelerated, the Soviet economy, in this respect, fell further and further behind capitalism from one Five-Year Plan to the next. What is more, in sharp contrast with the advantages the Soviet Union drew from the fragmented world market of the 1920s, the 1930s and the early 1940s, in the period after 1945 the capitalist world became increasingly unified politically and economically and thus afforded few openings to Soviet diplomacy. Rather a lasting imperialist alliance against Soviet Union, under US hegemony, substituted itself for the deep inter-imperialist rivalries of the earlier period; these rivalries indeed persisted, but now they operated within this alliance. The old-style technological borrowing was no longer feasible. Keeping up with the west's technological change or challenge, in antagonism and not cooperation with it, became more and more difficult, if not impossible.

Technology apart, the unification of capitalism-dominated world market and the consolidation of anti-Soviet political alliance of capitalist powers under US leadership, came to exercise strong destabilising pressure upon the Soviet economy and society. The Soviet Union was on the winning side in the very hot Second World War. It was determined to hold on to the substance of what it had gained, with the cooperation of its war-time allies or without it. These allies under the US leadership were however equally determined that this should not happen. But that was not all. The 'spectre of communism' still haunting them, they continued to see in the Soviet Union a society organised on non-capitalist principles, the very existence of which was a standing threat to capitalism everywhere, especially in the emergent third world whose peoples struggling for a better life were increasingly seeing in the Soviet Union the promise and possibility of a better, alternative social order. Their objective was to contain and push the Soviets back and in the process to overthrow this form of society, as they had indeed sought since the time of the October Revolution. This was the objective behind the dropping of atom bombs on Japan, which indeed signalled a new (cold) war against the Soviet Union. Stalin's pre-emptive threat of occupying Europe in case of nuclear attack, soon followed by Soviet Union acquiring nuclear weapons of its own, ruled out any nuclear blackmail by the western capitalist powers. With the atomic option foreclosed, these powers, above all the hegemonic United State, had to work out a new strategy. The strategy chosen was to impose an open-ended arms race on the Soviet Union which the Western ruling classes shrewdly calculated could be sustained more successfully, at times even profitably, by their own economies than by the less developed Soviet economy.

As part of this strategy, the Cold War policies of the west – from Cocom to other forms of economic and military blockade – were designed not only to cut off the Soviet Union from western technology – which made its own contribution to the incipient stagnation of Soviet economy – but also, more specifically, to force Soviet planners to waste huge resources on military expenditures and thus ruin their economy. Such indeed was the explicitly proclaimed purpose of the later Reagan administration in the United States in stepping up the external pressures on the Soviets through a greatly increased arms programme. And it succeeded beyond its wildest hopes.

(Incidentally, the ruling classes in both East and West benefited from the Cold War notion of a powerful external enemy that could be used to consolidate power at home and as a rationale for controlling or silencing dissent. In the Soviet Union the forced march of arms race certainly strengthened the Soviet rulers' command structures and repressive apparatuses, gave authority to hardliners and generally served the rulers' need for social cohesion and discipline in society and legitimisation of an oppressive regime. Though, it must be added that, insofar as Soviet politics, in one of its important aspects, had come to involve a kind of class compromise between the Soviet 'state-party bourgeoisie' and the working class in which catching up with Western per capita GDP and consumption eclipsed the goal of a revolutionary- democratic transformation of socio-economic and political relations, the material basis of this compromise was squeezed by the arms race forced upon the Soviet Union by the United States, just as it was being squeezed in another way by the Soviet system's failure to go from the successful extensive growth of the first half of its existence to intensive growth now on the agenda).

Faced with economic and military pressure of US-led capitalist world, Soviet rulers were unable or unwilling to insulate their society from global capitalism, subject its economy *primarily* to imperatives of internal development and thus opt for more viable, socialism-oriented, economic policies. Instead, attempts were made to stimulate the Soviet and East European economies by opening up to the West which attempts were largely failures and resulted only in Third-World style indebtedness and a massive subversion by capitalist consumerism. The most direct and disruptive pressure came through the imposition of the confrontational politics of the Cold War which a wiser leadership would not have joined in the way the Soviet leadership did. It opted to play the role of a super power, and super-power rivalry led to further militarisation of the Soviet economy with disastrous consequences in the end. Military expenditure over race with the US, while it stimulated the US economy, or at least certain parts of it, strained the much smaller Soviet economy at the seams, draining its resources, diverting them away from badly needed consumer goods and light industries to build weapons it could ill afford and often, with the weaponry or defence capability it already had, did not need.

It bears repeating here that actual war or the threat of war, and, therefore, the preparedness for it, was a constant of Soviet history throughout, and a major factor not only in distorting Soviet socio-economic and political development away from socialism but also in the final disintegration of the Soviet system. Paul Sweezy has written:

> The centrally planned system was enormously effective early on, after the revolution, in solving the problem of making the Soviet Union a formidable military power. It never had succeeded in solving any of the problems of the peacetime economy, nor did it really try to, because the Cold War forced the Soviet Union to continue as a military-dominated dictatorship even after the Second World War. If, at the end of the Second World War, when the regime was popular and success had been achieved, it had been feasible to transform their economy into a peacetime economy and to loosen up the dictatorial regime, I think there would have been a chance for the Soviet Union to develop into something quite different.
>
> Instead, the Cold War ensued. The United States almost deliberately, as a matter of policy, imposed the Cold War with an intention of forcing the Soviet Union into an inescapable bind from which it could never really transform itself into an attractive socialist economy. Having missed that potentiality, the system from then on deteriorated. It did have the recuperative power to make good the damages inflicted by war. But after that it began to wind down. Out of necessity it used its resources, its best resources, its best man-and woman-power for military purposes. This began to take its toll, and I think that is at the origin of the stagnation of the 1970s and 1980s.

That the way the Soviet leadership joined the Cold War-dictated ever escalating arms race, proved disastrous for the Soviet Union is now almost universally recognised. But there was nothing inevitable about it. For the real failure here lay not in the realm of Soviet economy (or 'central planning') but Soviet politics, in the authoritarianism of its political decision making which made it immune to any corrections from below or anywhere else. Insofar as Soviet planning was involved, its bureaucratically centralised, commandist character too made any kind of necessary correctives impossible.

VII

The Soviet planning system was put into a definitive shape during the First Five-Year Plan period, and, certain modifications of techniques apart, it remained virtually unchanged in its essential character almost till the day when it finally collapsed, and this despite the fact that the Soviet economy had changed radically during this period, both in scale and complexity. As we have already seen, excessive costs notwithstanding, Soviet central planning served reasonably well during the early, extensive growth period of Soviet economy, when the priorities were clear, there were only a few basic inputs and little possibility of substitution, and therefore the problems of planning and calculation were, relatively speaking, easy and manageable. For the same reason it served well in the post-war reconstruction. But post-reconstruction, as the economy became more complex, with the changing social composition of the population and rising incomes, the texture of social needs too changed. The Soviet centralised planning, with its rigid command system, found itself incapable of dealing with the changed situation. What was needed was a shift from an extensive to an intensive growth model. But this was far beyond the capability of an inflexible, bureaucratic planning system which had never known anything but the extensive model of growth and was totally incapable of understanding or overcoming this model's deepening crisis. The political leadership itself had now grown sclerotic with privileges and perks of a dysfunctional ruling class and was therefore bereft of initiative or dynamism. As a result the economy began to falter, and eventually, in the 1980s, failed altogether.

More than ever before the need now was to set priorities democratically, after due public debate, and plan their fulfilment in a democratic manner. This was simply impossible for the old planning system. Instead all its flaws now surfaced with a vengeance, culminating in an ultimate failure. The command economy and its central planning could mobilise and guarantee the full distribution and use of resources, but it could not guarantee their efficient utilisation. The crudity of the links between macro-decisions and micro-decisions affected accountability adversely, making for a great deal of waste of resources, inefficiecy in their use and underutilised productive capacity. The principle implicit in socialist planning, the replacement of production for profit by production for use, presupposes some way of determining what production is socially needed or useful, some way for that information to be communicated to planners and production units and reasonable confidence that they will respond to it. The undemocratic character of Soviet planning only made for lack of such information or response. There was no feedback from below from consumers to planners so that priorities went wrong, mistaken decisions assumed vast dimensions before they were noticed, the political leadership could even congratulate itself with a flood of false success stories. Plans were often based on poor information and unrealistic assumptions and the mistakes when discovered could simply not be set to rights by the decisions of 'platoon sergeants and regimental commanders' – as one description has it – within the planning system, not even when they saw that the whole campaign was going wrong. It is inconceivable that the central command system, if it were transmitted the proper signals from below, would have failed to rearrange the priorities and improve the quantity and quality of consumer goods by cutting down the allocations elsewhere. But such signals were not forthcoming; the people lacked democracy and the party organisation was too far gone to become a decrepit and insensitive bureaucratic structure, reeking of evil machinations, and, one needs hardly add, drained of all socialist ideology or commitment. Again, a central problem in any economy is that of its proportional development. This was equally true of the centrally planned economy of the Soviet Union. Central planning can function efficiently only insofar as a certain minimum of proportional development between all main branches of the economy and sectors of social activity is realised and maintained. The Soviet planning system failed to realise or maintain these necessary proportions. They were negated through arbitrary decisions, mistaken policies, immediate economic or political compulsions, which resulted in 'overemphasis' on certain prioritised sectors so that the excessive weight of these priorities in overall planning goals led to an excessive number of underdeveloped branches and sectors, that is, to built-in disproportions in the economy. If the costs of military confrontation which the imperialist west was able to impose led to acute scarcity of resources and sectoral imbalances, there was the accompanying bungled allocation of priorities favouring the bureaucracy both at the micro-level of managerial decision making and at the macro level of central planning. Having lost the human purpose of gigantic expenditure of energy and resources that Soviet economy disposed of, or lacking the capacity to use the massive material resources available to it in a socially useful way, Soviet 'planning' simply imposed a thoughtless incrementalism, with each plant or enterprise seeking to increase its output of goods or services relative to the previous period. The disproportions thus perpetuated by Soviet planning were only another expression of Soviet economy's failure to make a transition from extensive to intensive industrialisation which, even as it inevitably resulted in rising social and ecological costs of whatever further industrialisation did take place, was an important factor in the overall crisis of the Soviet economic system. The absence of democracy in the system only ensured that no correctives were available or forthcoming. Herein indeed lay the basic cause of the failures of Soviet planning, which were as much a part of Soviet reality as were the undeniable achievements in the prioritised sectors.

An aspect of the fundamental disproportions in the Soviet economy which characterised Soviet central planning from the First Five-Year Plan onwards needs to be specifically underlined for, important in itself, this aspect, in its own way, is also illustrative of the economistic Marxism ('theory of productive forces') which guided, or rather misguided, the construction of Soviet socialism under Stalin's leadership and was dogmatically adhered to even afterwards. The planned reconstruction of economy assumed an initial and continued emphasis on the priority growth of producer as against consumer goods industries; even the induction of advanced technology in the latter was purposely held back, they were left to make do with obsolete equipment and low productivity, when the need was for a plan that would accord due priority to investment in consumption goods industries. There was no recognition of the fact that consumer goods and services for producers (workers and toiling peasants) are indirect producer goods; when they are continuously below expectations, the producers become unmotivated, leading to loss of productivity and still greater expenditure on 'controllers', that is, the bureaucracy in the economy and the coercive state apparatus. Instead, there was rigid adherence to the dogma of expanding production of means of production – shades of 'laws of socialism', with one 'law', 'the law of balanced (proportionate) development of the economy' proclaimed by Stalin giving way to another 'law', 'the law of the priority growth of the production of means of production'! – accompanied by a preference for the massive and the spectacular. Soviet economy very much looked a case of 'production for production's sake', such that while industrialisation suffered from gigantomania, there was shortage of consumer goods and the countryside was neglected and impoverished.

Disproportions in the economy were only one aspect of the crisis that Soviet economy entered when, the momentum of the extensive industrialsation of the period of post-war reconstruction having exhausted itself, thanks to bureaucratic nature of planning, it failed to make the needed changes, including a transition to an intensive technological revolution in the means of production. The crisis was only compounded by the failure of efforts to 'reform' it. These efforts of course had nothing socialist about them. By their very nature they were doomed to fail and compound the crisis in Soviet economy and society.

The efforts and the failure here, it may be noted, presaged the Gorbachev era and indicated the exhaustion of socialist commitment and the abandonment of even elementary ways of socialist thinking in the communist party leadership. The reforms suggested ranged all the way from the improvement of the technical devices of central planning to the idea of full 'marketisation'. The key thrust was on 'scientific planning', the resolution of the accumulating socio-economic problems through the device of a technologically and mathematically improved neutral mechanism which in the opinion of some at least of the party ideologues could go well with the 'rational mechanism' of the market. The Twenty Second Party Congress itself talked of building 'the material-technical basis of communism' with the help of 'new instruments of economic regulation'. The discussion of deep-lying contradictions of the system, its social antagonisms, remained under taboo, the questions of class and democracy never appeared in the reformist discourse, nor did the working class except as producers of surplus who were refusing to deliver, but with whom the most basic of underlying social antagonisms was finding expression as apathy and indifference, bordering on hostility to the system. Advocates of 'scientific planning' never got the message from examples like this one (reported by O.I. Antonov, a famous airplane designer, in 1965):

> two workers who were employed to unload bricks quickly from trucks did so by throwing them on the ground, usually breaking some 30 percent of them. They knew that their actions were both against the interests of the country and against simple common sense, but their work was assessed and paid on the basis of a time indicator. Therefore, they would be penalized – indeed would not be able to make their living – if they were to arrange the bricks carefully on the ground. Their way of doing the job was bad for the country, but, on the face of it, good for the plan! So they acted against their consciences and intelligence, but with a deep feeling of bitterness against the planners: 'You don't want it done in a way good husbandry would have it, you keep pressing only for quicker and quicker! Well then, get your bricks! Bang! Bang!' Thus, all over the country, decent and responsible citizens, perfectly rational beings, acted in wasteful, almost criminal ways.

Unable to recognise, much less address the basic problems, the fundamental social antagonisms generated by the system, the reforms inevitably failed, pushing the economy into a permanent crisis which only deepened as it moved into the 1970s and 1980s. It is interesting to note that all this while official Marxism in the Soviet Union continued, parrot-like, to talk of 'the general crisis of capitalism', its various stages, etc., ignoring or obscuring altogether the far more serious 'crisis of socialism' within, which had also become a major factor in holding up the anti-capitalist revolutionary movements in the world outside.

Incidentally, the perverse consequences of an excessively centralised and bureaucratised planning with huge built-in disproportions were so all-permeating and so vast that Soviet society as a whole, state's terror and propaganda notwithstanding, started to develop spontaneous reactions in order to escape the situation. One consequence, especially in recent years, was that alongside the planned economy, a whole private system of 'informal' economy, an unplanned and uncontrolled sector, developed in the Soviet Union, whose growing hidden or open market operations naturally brought along with them widespread corruption and criminalisation so that the *mafia* became a permanent feature of Soviet economy and society. Ironically enough, contrary to the common belief, the Soviet Union had come to suffer not from too much but too little planning in its economy!

VIII

However one defines the social formation that took shape in the Soviet Union after the mid-1920s, as a degenerated workers' state, or a particularly wasteful and inefficient form of state capitalism, or a *sui generis* post-revolutionary society, neither socialist nor capitalist, but ruled over by what could be legitimately described as a 'party-state bourgeoisie', the important point in the immediate context is that seventy odd years after the October Revolution it had virtually reached a dead end. Already in the 1960s, the Soviet academic Nemchinov had characterised the Soviet economy as 'an ossified mechanical system', and with remarkable insight into the future, written: 'An economic system so fettered from top to bottom, will put a brake on social and technological progress, and will break down, sooner or later, under the pressure of real processes of economic life'. Now, in the mid 1980s, with cumulative mistakes, failures and distortions from the past, the point of breakdown had been reached, the point at which Gorbachev took over. The rate of growth had come to hover effectively around zero (as in most countries of Eastern Europe), placing great strain on a political and social system already become anachronistic in its utter lack of democracy in economic and political life. There was popular disaffection and unrest and, perhaps just as important, a loss of morale on the part of the ruling elites themselves. The outcome was a general crisis of legitimacy. To put the situation in classical Marxian terms, in terms of one of the main axioms of historical materialism, it was a situation where the developing productive forces were in contradiction with the Soviet command economy: the intolerably repressive character of Soviet social formation apart, its production relations, expressive of its class-exploitative economic-structural basis, sustained and operated through its bureaucratically deformed central planning, had become obstacles to the dynamic of the forces of production and thus deserving of being swept away. The Soviet social formation had simply forfeited its right to survive. Old texts come to mind. Here is the famous passage from Karl Marx: 'At a certain stage of development, the material productive forces of society come into conflict with the existing relations of production.... From forms of development of the productive forces these relations turn into their fetters. Then begins an era of social revolution.' Only what began in the Soviet Union was not social revolution but an era of what may well be described as a social counter-revolution. Once again, ultimately, it was politics which decided. The old, fettering relations of production had to go. An adequate objective material base, in the shape of well developed forces of production, indeed existed for a turn to the Left, to socialist relations of production. But the degeneration of Soviet politics over a long period had left the situation bereft of the possibility of any such intervention from below, the necessary subjective intervention in behalf of socialism. The balance of forces in Soviet politics permitted only an intervention from above and to the Right, it made for a turn to capitalism and the magic of market relations, to a social counter-revolution.

I may add, the passage from Marx cited above, often treated as a quasi metaphysical formula by the learned Marxologists, once again acquired the freshness and substance of a literal, lived truth. The Soviet happenings readily fit the basic explanatory scheme of historical materialism and certainly suffice to ensure that reports of the death of Marxist theory, whether jubilant or despairing, are at least premature.

IX

In the 1960s, it was clearly being realised that the economic system of central planning was running into serious difficulties. It had shown itself to be much more capable of mobilising unutilised resources than managing an economy of increasing complexity. By early 1970s, it was building into a real crisis. And by the late 1970s and early 1980s, it was clear to important segments of the ruling elite that the well-trodden path was leading to a precipice. Throughout this period, therefore, there were debates in the Soviet Union (as also in East Europe and Cuba) on ways of improving the functioning of their economic system. While important issues were certainly at stake in these debates, the prevailing single-party state model was a restricting context, and the argument itself was settled by party diktat, or even by tanks, as for example, in Czechoslovakia where a somewhat different or better model, not necessarily socialist, was sought to be attempted. Even so, especially in the latter period, perhaps because of the urgency imparted by the deepening economic crisis, a certain more perceptive understanding of the situation emerged among Soviet scholars. A good example is the economist Abalkin who, in the mid-1980s, in the light of Soviet experience, insisted that production relations must not be 'analyzed in isolation from the real state of the productive forces and the practical activity of people, which results in a speculative, frozen image of production relations as an un-changing essence that is removed from reality'. He argued that 'the specific result of the progress of the productive forces is that the specific forms of production relations that have developed under certain historical conditions begin to age and thereby hinder economic growth, which makes it necessary to improve or replace them'. The task in the Soviet Union, therefore, was to develop new relations of production capable of promoting the further development of the productive forces. But this conclusion about exhausted the limits of Abalkin's 'Marxism'. As with other, similar or less pretentious theorising, the flaw was soon located in the state ownership of the means of production (equated with *social* ownership) and in Soviet planning (equated with central planning as such) which were seen as fettering the forces of production. Naturally enough their release, or that of the economy as a whole, was ultimately sought, away from social ownership and central planning, in privatisation and the market, that is capitalism, (We are currently witness to a similar process of theory and practice in People's Republic of China).

In fact a concern with *appearances* ('state ownership', 'planning', etc.) remained the major weakness of the Soviet debates on the emerging crisis of Soviet economy and society. There was little recognition that its real causes lay deeper in the foundations, the economic structural basis of Soviet society, not as it *appeared* or was apparently described, but as it had *in reality* come to be. They lay, above all, in the historically specific, class-exploitative nature of its relations of production and equally specific historically, the bureaucratic nature of its central planning. The October Revolution and the Bolshevik project under Lenin had aimed at socialism, that is, a transformation of the old feudal or capitalist exploitative relations of production into socialist relations of production. The evolution of Soviet society under Stalin, with its manifold distortions – an authoritarian and highly centralised state system, highly bureaucratised economic institutions, ideologically sanctioned inegalitarianism, absence of genuine democratic freedoms or processes in society and the party, etc. – had resulted in the transformation of relations of production in the Soviet economy but they were not socialist relations of production. Some of them were capitalist, some other even feudal, but all of them exploitative. Workers had certainly come to lack motivation. This was not, however, a natural by-product of guaranteed full employment, the once vaunted but later much-maligned feature of labour conditions under Soviet central planning. The problem, as noted earlier, lay in the fact that this planning created no affirmative work incentives to replace hunger and insecurity, the traditional prods to labour effort associated with capitalism. Material incentives provided were too weak because of consumer goods shortages, and moral exhortation failed because it was long emptied of any genuine class content; the workers had no control over workplace conditions, production decisions or even their labour organisations. Repression as a motivating factor was not adequate enough; it was not so even during the Stalin period. As long ago as 1942, Kalecki had pointed out: 'No socialist government can hope to succeed unless its efforts are seconded by a feeling of heightened tempo of development permeating the whole of society and, above all, of self-confidence amongst the workers and lower strata of society. Such a mood cannot be artificially created – it can be stimulated by propaganda but only if a real basis for it exists.' Whatever its reality or possibility once, such a basis was simply not there in the Soviet Union of the mid-1980s. What was needed was recovery of socialism as a great collective project in which an active majority of the population participates, as something belonging to the people and constructed by their own energies, where the setting of social priorities, that is planning, would be a part of such a collective project of all. The Soviet rulers could no longer opt for such a recovery of the socialist project. Their class interests indicated otherwise. Faced with an intractable economic crisis they chose to opt for the market. By definition, market is a project for the few, it cannot be a project of all.

X

Our account makes it clear that there is no monocausal explanation of what went wrong with Soviet economy, and why its dysfunctions grew over time into a fatal crisis. But within the context set by the deeper, ultimate economic-structural causes, one factor was of immediately decisive importance: the nature and interests of the Soviet bureaucracy as a relatively autonomous part of the Soviet ruling class – a group of (often incompetent) technocrats at the top and higher rungs of the

Soviet planning and managerial system, deciding what to do with the economy and despotically imposing their decisions on the society.

During an initial phase this bureaucracy had an obvious self-interest in building a broad industrial base in the country. It also meant a growth in its numbers and an increase of its power and privileges. But it was also subject to a certain degree of political control from above. But once, interpenetrating with the Party and state leadership, this bureaucracy had concentrated economic and political power in its hands, and at the same time reached a certain saturation of its privileged consumer demands, its attitude towards economic growth began to flag. And as it found managing this growth or the economy difficult, if not impossible, it simply went conservative, 'anything for a quiet life', of course with the privileges it had accumulated. Increasingly it became demotivated for speeding up, not to say optimising economic efficiency. Even otherwise bureaucratic planning had degenerated into an inert institutional structure, lacking in initiative or dynamism. The bureaucracy, indeed the ruling classes as a whole, turned parasitical. The system became one of generalised irresponsibility.

Caught between the unbreakable inertia of a huge bureaucratic machine on the one hand, and a largely atomised and demotivated mass of workers and peasants on the other, yet unable to replace bureaucratic management by generalised producers' self management, the system as a whole gradually ground towards stagnation. The rest is recent history. Strains within the stagnant economy and the pull of late-capitalist consumerism from abroad made it impossible to go on with the old order and the muddled attempt by the ruling elite to salvage and improve their privileged position by turning to the market only intensified the contradictions within and led to the collapse of the order itself into a mafiosi-capitalism.

Years before the final collapse in the Soviet Union, in the 1970s, this is how Paul Sweezy had posed the issue in Marxist terms:

> When the bureaucratically administered economy runs into difficulties (as it certainly must), there are two politically opposite ways in which a solution can be sought. One is to weaken the bureaucracy, politicize the masses, and entrust increasing initiative and responsibility to the workers themselves. This is the road forward to socialist relations of production. The other way is to put increasing reliance on the market, not as a temporary retreat (as was the case with the New Economic Policy under Lenin) but as an ostensible step toward a more efficient 'socialist' economy. This is in fact to elevate profit-making to the guiding role in the economic process and to tell the workers to mind their own business, which is to work hard so that they can consume more. It is to recreate the conditions in which commodity fetishism flourishes along with its associated false and alienated consciousness. It is, I submit, the road back to class domination and ultimately the restoration of capitalism.

That the Soviet rulers, led by their muddled theories and even more their class interests, finally chose to rely on the market does not in any way negate the fact that the other road was the only viable road in the interests of the Soviet people. And these people making their painful detour through capitalism may yet come to discover and travel this road in the not too distant future.

XI

The 'failure' of Soviet central planning has triggered off a vigorous debate, almost a political struggle, over the legitimacy or otherwise of concepts of 'planning', 'market', 'market socialism', etc. Soviet planning has been identified with central planning as such and both of them with socialism and the failure of Soviet planning has been interpreted as a failure of socialism itself. One consequence has been a massive surrender the world over, even on the Left, to the ideology of the market. Therefore, a few additional observations on the subject will not be out of place.

At the very outset, it needs to be recognised that planning as such has no necessary implications of socialism. In fact, as Galbraith and others have pointed out, planning has today reached advanced stages of development with capitalist firms.

And the capitalist states too have found planning useful and necessary from time to time, in their public or state sectors, in situations of economic crisis, or during their wars when the 'national' priorities are clear (e.g. military airplanes or civilian autos, tanks or home refrigerators, barracks or civilian homes, etc.). The question then is not 'whether planning?' but planning for whom? for what purpose? Bourgeois planning may have a partly mythical character but it can nevertheless be an instrument of bourgeois politics. To identify 'plan' with socialism and market with capitalism (which is true tendentially) may even aid the bourgeoisie in promoting capitalism and exercising its domination under cover of a 'plan' (or for that matter a 'state sector') in the name of which it gains legitimacy with the pro-socialism exploited classes and by which the exploitation of the masses can be still further increased. Soviet bourgeoisie was a good example (as in its own way the bourgeoisie in India and some other post-colonial states).

Both bourgeois and socialist 'plans' or 'planning' are possible. The real issue is not 'plan or market' but the nature of plan or planning. More specifically, it is the domination or non-domination by the producers or people over the conditions and results of their activity. A 'plan' or planning relations can prevent the producers or people from acquiring such domination, just as they may help its realisation. It needs to be recognised explicitly that it is only under certain social, political and ideological conditions – above all *genuine* social ownership of the means of production – that a plan can be an instrument of the domination by the producers and the people over the conditions and results of their activity. Furthermore, for it to play this role, the plan, taking into account the technical and general economic requirements as well as overall possibilities of the objective situation, must be elaborated and set in operation on the basis of the initiative of the masses, concentrating and coordinating their own experience and projects, which is one of the basic roles of centralism in planning. Otherwise, it will be a bourgeois 'plan', not the opposite of the market but its complement or provisional 'substitute', which permits the old relations of production and the attendant class domination and exploitation to continue and reproduce themselves.

Again, planning in general is a system of economic organisation, of resource allocation, based upon deliberate, conscious *a priori* choices *determining the key trends* of economic development. Crucial for central planning is society's decisive control over the social surplus product which alone can enable the 'planners', through the coordinating mechanism of a plan, to overcome the uncertainty associated with atomised decision-making of a private market economy, ensure effective inter-relatedness of decisions before they are implemented, and thus determine, in the medium and long run, the trends of society's socio-economic development. This control of the social surplus product in its political form can just as well be despotic as it can and needs to be democratic or socialist.

To continue, given the relative scarcity of resources, a centrally planned conscious allocation of resources always implies a deliberate choice of priorities, which can be realised only at the cost of not satisfying other, non-priority needs. If a plan's 'central' character tends to centralisation, even more importantly its *a priori* resource allocation has a tendency to neglect the non-priority areas and therefore almost unavoidably carries with it the possibility of 'disproportions' developing within the economy. In other words, there can occur 'overemphasis' or 'overinvestment' in the chosen priority sectors, and for that very reason, inadequate emphasis or 'underinvestment' in the other non-prioritised sectors of the economy. And since, in a complex modern economy, there is a high degree of interdependence between all main branches of the economy and all main sectors of social activity, the necessary logic of the process of reproduction, as first laid bare by Marx, inevitably asserts itself: as disproportions arise and persist, the planned economy runs into difficulties, even the priority sectors begin to stagnate, if not actually decline. This, as we have seen, was part of the manifold crises of Soviet economy, and as has been well put, 'No terror of Stalin, no boasting by Khrushchev, no benign neglect by Brezhnev, no cajoling by Gorbachev, could prevent these crises from developing'. Obviously, for the efficient and effective functioning of a central planning system, there is always the need not only to ensure a certain minimum of proportional development between all main branches of the economy and sectors of social activity and an appropriate balance between centralisation and decentralisation, but also to provide for correctives when disproportions or imbalances begin to develop in the economy.

This is where the advantages of a democratically planned socialist economy come in. It is really democracy acting as the economic regulator, the *driving mechanism* of the economy, ensuring not only its democratic organisation but also emancipation of producers as well as consumers from the economic 'coercions' of the market. Based on a genuine social ownership of the (major) means of production and properly institutionalised, it will be an economy where the people decide, after a pluralist and open debate, the main economic choices, the priorities of investment, the broad structure of resource utilisation between different branches of the economy and sectors of social activity, ensuring proportional development of the economy, and thus themselves determine the general direction of economic development of their society. Of course, at the central level only very broad priorities concerning development of economy including social welfare can be decided, setting the framework for the more detailed decision-making by decentralised self-governing bodies that would be characteristic of a self-governing socialist society. The open democratic political processes of this society will ensure that correctives will be available and forthcoming when disproportions, imbalances or other distortions occur in the economy.

Democratic socialist planning is an absolute necessity if the economy is to be subservient to society and not to the profit calculations of individual or corporate capitalists, if it is to serve the welfare of *all* the people and not a few, if poverty, underdevelopment and misery so rampant in the world today are to be eliminated. Beyond this, conscious human control of economic processes is necessary so that people are able to not only shape their own lives, but, with capitalism-threatened ecological disaster looming large, survive on this earth. For only thus can a sustainable relationship with the natural environment be maintained. Today this has indeed become a matter of life and death for the human species. It cannot be stressed too strongly that central planning, coordinated at a global level, is essential before it is too late for this planet to remain a liveable habitat for human beings.

XII

Our argument concerning planning in general and democratic socialist planning in particular should make it abundantly clear that it is a total misconception to equate socialism with central planning and central planning as such with the rigid, excessively centralised bureaucratic planning that ultimately failed the Soviet Union, and to argue on the basis of this failure that socialism or central planning are always bound to fail. There is no good reason to assume that the Soviet model is the only possible form of planning, central or any other, when it was but only one of its possible variants, a product of given historical circumstances, of very specific social forces and interests which governed its introduction and evolution. In fact the politics governing the 'socialist' central planning in Soviet Union, the politics-dictated requirement of accelerated industrial development, can be said to be as much driven by the imperatives of accumulation as market is by demands of competition and profit-maximisation internal to a capitalist economy. Therefore, if anything, the issue or need now is a critical examination of the failure of Soviet central planning in order to draw the necessary lessons for the future – an examination which would require much more attention to the politics and social policies involved than to central planning as such or to the techniques of planning, faulty as some of the latter may have been. Arguing that 'the Soviet experience be seen *within the framework* of relative backwardness, isolation and bureaucratic mismanagement of the USSR', Ernest Mandel had written:

> The problem is to determine to what extent the shortcomings of the Soviet economy result from the 'principles of central planning' in and of themselves, and to what extent they are rather the products of backwardness and bureaucratic despotism, which can

> be avoided under more mature circumstances. To give just one example: to what extent are the famous queues in the USSR the result of scarcities flowing *unavoidably* from 'central planning', and to what extent are they the products of the wrong decision systematically to neglect investment in transportation, distribution and agriculture as compared with investment in industry, especially heavy industry? Such a disproportion in investment is neither economically rational nor an automatic product of central planning. On the contrary, it is the proof of immature, wrong, lopsided, 'unplanned', incoherent, wasteful bureaucratic mismanagement. It could be avoided....

A critical examination of the Soviet experience will reveal that, as suggested above, the real issue here demanding attention is the dominant Soviet politics and the social policies flowing from it rather than the Soviet central planning. Surely, however centralised, bureaucratic, or otherwise faulty it may have been, the forced collectivisation of agriculture, the massive deportations of workers for absenteeism, the monstrous Gulag system with its forced labour, etc. were not because of Soviet planning, but far more the result of a ruthless, arbitrary and dictatorial, and often mistaken politics which made the search for alternatives or any questioning and correction of erroneous decisions in the economic or other fields, impossible.

The point is to draw the right lessons from the limitations and failure of Soviet planning. It was not the failure of planning as such and, therefore, we must reject the increasingly hegemonic ideology that all planning has to be necessarily bureaucratic and that the only antidote to bureaucratic inefficiency and oligarchical tendencies of a planning system is marketisation and privatisation. Really what is needed as part of a democratic society, is self-determination and self-government in the economic field too, and central planning is the only means we have to realise it. Only it has to be a genuinely democratic planning, which is certainly conceivable and feasible. It requires social control over the broad disposition of the means of production and the social surplus product, both at the level of the society as a whole and at the local or subsystem levels. Political democracy is necessary to determine overall social priorities, and system-wide planning is necessary to give effect to them within the overall framework set by this process; however, the detailed use of the means of production and the available social surplus then needs to be decided at each level by those most directly affected by that use. The required organisational structures or bureaucracies themselves need not be necessarily hierarchical or uncontrollable. This is not to underestimate the problems involved. But there is now extensive social science literature on participatory and democratic organisational forms. Central planning agencies can certainly be controlled by institutionalised democratic structures. And the socialist argument for self-administration in the economy and elsewhere presupposes increasing availability of ancillary social conditions such as guaranteed employment and social security, a shortening of working time, freely available elementary and higher education, a diffusion of information technology among groups of producers and consumers, wide access to the media of communication, and so on. Socialist democracy could be structured on a pluralist basis, both at local levels and in the form of a popularly elected government that decides the priorities in development and oversees the process of economic planning aimed at achieving these priorities as well as proportional development of the economy. Conflicts of opinions and interests would no doubt still arise, but pluralist democracy is precisely the means to resolve them. In such a state the trade-off between efficiency and equality or social justice could be decided democratically. This might not be optimal for 'success' in the socialist economy but it could easily provide a good living for all citizens and a political situation free from inequities and repression.

XIII

Plan or market? This is how the issue is often posed. In the final analysis the issue is quite simple. There is the obvious, inescapable fact that resources are limited. A choice must be made as to how they will be allocated. Basically there are two ways. Resources can be allocated via a market, where price and profits do the rationing. The alternative is to allocate basic resources in a way most suitable to meet social needs. And this is best done through central planning based upon articulated self-management of the working people, institutionalised within a pluralist political democracy. This is indeed how Marx visualised it when he wrote of society moving beyond capitalism to found a different civilisation where economic rationality is assigned a subordinate role in the service of non-economic, truly human ends. Even as he argued that 'the realm of freedom... lies beyond the sphere of actual material production', he recognised the necessities of this sphere and wrote: 'Just as the savage must wrestle with nature to satisfy his wants, to maintain and reproduce life, so must civilized man, and he must do so in all social formations and under all modes of production... freedom in this field can only consist in socialized man, the associated producers, rationally regulating their interchange with nature, bringing it under their common control, instead of being ruled by it as by a blind power; and achieving this with the least expenditure of energy and under conditions most favourable to, and worthy of, their human nature.'

This is precisely what socialist planning is all about. It is only another name for 'the associated producers', or as we could say today freely associated producers, consumers and citizens, 'rationally regulating their interchange with nature' in a manner 'worthy of their human nature'.

The other way, of being ruled 'as by a blind power' which is in so many ways most unfavourable to and unworthy of human nature, is the way of the market, the way that capitalism represents.

Capitalism is market economy par excellence where privately owned property predominantly exists in the form of 'many capitals' competing with each other in the market. Therefore, control over the social surplus product here is always fragmented. A lot of planning within capitalism notwithstanding, the capitalists do not have the power to decide in a conscious way how the economy or society will develop as a whole. This development is finally determined 'behind their backs', as those of the mass of workers and all other sections of society, by 'the blind forces', the objective laws of the capitalist market, above all by the law of capital accumulation. If in the absence of democratic planning where the concerned people themselves democratically decide priorities of development, the Soviet system could be justifiably described as 'state despotism', the setting of priorities by the automatism of the capitalist accumulation process can equally justifiably be described as 'market despotism'. Since a market economy like any other economy, also functions under conditions of relative scarcity of resources, it too poses the problem of priorities, of what demands will or will not be satisfied. Its law of capital accumulation, even as its produces and reproduces inequalities of wealth and income in society and therefore inequalities in the overall distribution of demand, also entails that the satisfaction of the demands of rich people (and of large firms) will be achieved at the expense of the demands of the mass of the working people, not to speak of the demands of the poor and impoverished. 'A good example', as Ernest Mandel puts it, 'is that of housing under contemporary capitalism. In the richer countries, millions are still homeless and waiting for cheap apartments, while in the meantime millions of "second residences", often unoccupied during most of the year, have been built. In the poorer countries, hundreds of millions are homeless or dwell in miserable shanty towns and slums, while the rich have villas built for them which equal those of the richest countries, and the super-rich live in estates and luxury compounds which more than 99% of even the richer countries' inhabitants cannot afford.' The capitalist market reflects the unequal and irrational structure of economic power in society and delivers accordingly. It inevitably tends to reward the strong, and to further disadvantage the weak. As the Bible has it, 'To him that has shall be given, and from him that has not shall be taken away even that which he has.' Such is the in-built tendency of the market. Governed by an insatiable profit-motive, only the so-called effective demand is satisfied, even if it is profit-stimulated 'artificial' consumerist demand or means wasteful use of resources, as is indeed happening on a massive scale today when all over the capitalist world the economic resources are being exploited in a short-sighted, wasteful and unrenewable way, regardless of the interests and needs of the future generations. The inexorable profit-maximising and accumulative drives of the capitalist market, accompanied inevitably by a needless and greedy consumerism, have today come to menace the integrity of the very life-world upon which the economy itself rests and thus become a threat to the future of humankind on this earth.

The market system, by its very nature, does not and cannot work either for providing the basic infrastructure for general human well being, that is, well being of common humanity, or for the better part of the totality of human needs. That would require major changes in the allocation of resources, the kind of changes a market system cannot allow or hope to achieve. No wonder that it is the state in capitalist societies which is called upon, in the interest of capitalism itself, to rectify some at least of the inherent inegalitarian logic of the market. And, given the nature of market-based allocation of resources, it is not surprising that the market economies, even when very rich, generally have had lower achievements in terms of standard indicators of quality of life – employment, health care, education, social security, etc. – than the poor but planned economies, such as those of the former Soviet Union and socialist countries of Eastern Europe, notwithstanding the bureaucratic nature of their planning.

XIV

In speaking of 'market' or 'market economy' in opposition to 'socialist planning' or socialism, we are really speaking of 'capitalist market' or 'capitalism'. For societies with markets, and trade, have existed throughout history, and as an institution to distribute consumer goods in a complex society, market will not doubt exist for a long time to come. It is in a capitalist society that market acquires a specificity, all its own. This market however is no arena of 'freedom', of 'free competition', as claimed by its ideologues. For one, there are the obvious limits to it imposed by the monopoly of private property claim, (belonging to some while others are excluded). That is why the economist Walrus, consistent in his defence of 'advantages' of market conceded that the true rule of the market implies the abolition of private property and even imagined an ideal of 'capitalism without capitalists' – a concept Engels saw reflected in the project of the Second International and which was taken up by the post-Stalinist Soviet 'reformers' of the Novossibirsk school. Be that as it may and the freedom-limiting power of private property apart, this market is no realm of much consumer choice or preferences either – what with the monopolies in control of production and products and their massive advertising campaigns, sales organisations, public relations programmes, etc., as part of capitalism's society-wide 'hitting below the intellect', as Oscar Wilde called it, in pursuit of profit.

Over and above everything there is the distinctive and dominant characteristic of the capitalist market that we have regularly referred to, the coercive logic of the capitalist market, the imperatives which subordinate every human need and practice to the requirements of profit-maximisation and accumulation, the so-called 'market disciplines' that global capitalism is today, through its new instruments – IMF, World Bank, WTO, etc. – trying to impose on other economies the world over. The capitalist market is not merely an economic space, it is a space, not of freedom or choice, but of domination and coercion.

The capitalist market's denial of freedom indeed goes much deeper than the word 'market' suggests. As Ellen Meiksins Wood has put it:

> Even when the market is not, as it commonly is in advanced capitalist societies, merely an instrument of power for giant conglomerates and multi-national corporations, it is still a coercive force, capable of subjecting all human values, activities and relationships to its imperatives. No ancient despot could have hoped to penetrate the personal lives of his subjects – their life chances, choices, preferences, opinions and relationships – in the same comprehensive and minute detail, not only in the workplace but in every corner of their lives.

At a more mundane level, 'freedom' of the market is much made of by its ideologues for its ability to provide automatic, impersonal solutions to the internal problems of the economy.

The example often cited is that of 'disproportions' that so came to plague the Soviet economy. The critics of planned economy have argued that as against it, a 'free-enterprise' or market economy possesses in the market a built-in mechanism to correct such disproportions. This, however, is not so simple as that. A market economy by its very nature is anarchic and produces on its own disproportions and waste on a huge scale, certainly comparable to those of bureaucratic planning. As for correction, this anarchy is still subject to the laws or the coercive logic of the capitalist market. These disproportions are 'corrected' through the market, but they are corrected by means of even bigger waste and outright destruction of productive resources. This is what periodic economic crises, with their downturns and stoppages, large-scale bankruptcies, massive unemployment of human and mechanical resources, are all about. Such is the disruptive nature and scale of these wasteful ways of registering and correcting error in a capitalist society that often state has to step in to prevent potentially dangerous breakdowns. In other words, the state finds it necessary to intervene and make corrections, at times to save capitalism from the logic of the capitalist market itself. (As for example, in the Great Depression whose recurrence remains a regular matter for anxiety in the capitalist world). These corrections are usually, though not always, approved by the capitalist class, which in any case is always strong enough to have its way in a capitalist economy. And so the cycle of wasteful registration and equally wasteful correction of error in a capitalist market economy goes on.

XV

It is significant that as soon as market economy matured into a dominant capitalist system, with it arrived a demand to check the depredations of its 'free market'. 'Regulation' of the market to modify its wastefulness, inegalitarianism, and essentially predatory, crisis-prone logic, has been a favourite theme with the economists and others concerned, since then. But more than 150 years experience of attempts at 'regulating' markets provides only one conclusion: all of them have failed to prevent periodic economic crises, periodic mass unemployment and regular production and reproduction of inequality in society. The market-based advanced capitalist countries have witnessed at least twenty-one business cycles since 1825 and are now witnessing it for the twenty-second time. Even a quick look at 180 odd years of 'actually existing' market economies makes it clear that there is no 'market without thorns' as the expression has it. The fact is that apart from its regularly generated inequalities and other ills, no market economy has been able to avoid the ills of periodic economic catastrophes like mass bankruptcies, mass destruction of capital or productive equipment, mass unemployment, periodically declining living standards and periodically increasing material and moral misery for millions, and periodic wars too. This, of course, is not accidental. It is related to the very nature of the market economy of our times, capitalism.

In more recent years, a recognition of the obviously anti-people character of the capitalist 'free market' has led to the advocacy, from high UN quarters downwards, of 'people friendly' markets. But wherever, and in whatever version, say in the erstwhile centrally planned economies of Eastern Europe or in post-Mao China, such markets have proved a failure from the point of view of ensuring a people-friendly growth of economy. However friendly to the people at the top, they have not been accessible to all, not equitable in distribution of their benefits, and not environment-friendly either. And they have invariably reproduced all the usual ills of a market economy, once again proving that indeed there is no 'market without thorns'. It is impossible to take their feasibility as the implied alternative route to pro-people economic development seriously.

Such having been the experience with the market, the 'regulated' or 'people-friendly' included, it is no wonder that a great part of the history of our time has been of a deep distrust of the market, it has been a history of successive social struggles, even revolutions against it – against slavery and the slave trade, for the eight-hour day, for trade union rights, against imperialism and the yawning gap between North and South, against ecological degradation, for socialism and socialist revolution, and so on. Indeed the market is no answer to the economic problems besetting humankind today.

XVI

Economics of the market apart, the morality or culture that flows from or inevitably accompanies the dominance of market in society is equally questionable. All material life and social reproduction in capitalism are universally mediated by the market. As a coercive force market subjects all human values, activity and relationships to its imperatives, which regulate not only economic transactions but social relations in general; they enter into the formation of socio-political institutions, personal attitudes and public and private morality itself. Reducing social relations to 'the cash nexus' (as the *Communist Manifesto* pointed out), respecting profit and personal gain above everything else, the market is the mortal enemy of community – indeed of any kind of fraternity among human beings. Market – with its imperatives and criteria of success – encourages some of the worst traits of humanity, for example, selfishness and greed, and discourages some of our best traits including selflessness and compassion. Its are 'the pseudo-moral principles' as Keynes once put it, 'which have hag-ridden us for 200 years (and) by which we have exalted some of the most distasteful of human qualities into the position of the highest virtues' – including 'greed and the war between the greedy – competition' as Marx once described it. These 'virtues', that is morality of the market, indeed play havoc with social and moral life. It dissolves 'the world of men into the world of atomised individuals, hostile towards each other', individuals alienated from fellow human beings, from nature and from themselves, their 'own active functioning' as Marx put it. It so commodifies life that, again in Marx's words, the very things which were once 'communicated, but never exchanged; given, but never sold; acquired, but never bought – virtue, love, conviction, knowledge, conscience, etc.' now become marketable and pass 'into commerce'; 'the *divine* power of money' overturns and confounds 'all human and natural qualities' in the marketplace. And so on.

I have already touched upon this subject earlier. I will only repeat that Marxism still provides the keenest insight into the moral and cultural damage that the capitalist market inflicts on human beings, and the argument has been never better stated than in the writings of Marx and Engels themselves. Marx's critique, made more than 150 years ago, stands more than vindicated in the social, moral, cultural and even psychological crisis of the contemporary late capitalist-market societies.

XVII

Most debate on the market has concentrated on the economy, particularly on the economic advantages and disadvantages (depending on who is talking) of organising production and exchange in this manner. Commodification of different areas of life and associated phenomenon of alienation that accompanies the market has also been well taken note of, especially in recent times. Its mystification of human nature, social relations, money, and freedom are also widely recognised, if not well understood. Less well known is the pervasive mystification of the whole sphere of production in a market-based economy, which, in terms of its extended effects is perhaps the most harmful mystification of all, and, therefore, deserves to be specifically noted.

Market economies have the effect, if not the main function of befuddling the understanding of those who live in them and thus misdirecting their frustrations and anger about social and economic inequalities, unemployment, idle machines and factories, ecological destruction, widespread corruption, exaggerated forms of greed, etc. that are the inevitable production of 'actually existing' market economies. Those living and suffering under them, failing to understand it all, are paralysed in their protest actions, or, at least, capable of only limited or partial struggles over issues of their immediate experience.

The key to the situation here lies in the fact of opaqueness or lack of transparency of a market economy, unlike the pre-capitalist class economies which were, in a manner of speaking, transparent so that mechanisms of production were visible and so was the fact of exploitation, which had to be maintained, visibly, by political, ideological and military, essentially extra-economic means, and not invisibly or economically via the market as in a capitalist-market economy. A market economy, in its opaqueness, makes it difficult for people to move beyond the *appearance*, their immediate experience, of things to the *nature* of things, the reality of exploiting and alienating processes of capitalist production. This of course underlines the importance of 'carrying' socialist understanding and consciousness to the people. But in the immediate context it is the ideological implication that needs to be noticed. Bertell Ollman has written:

> .... as compared to all other civilizations, capitalism suffers from a remarkable lack of transparency. While slaves, serfs, and even workers in Soviet-style command economies have no difficulty seeing who is doing what to them and why, the same cannot be said of those who produce the wealth of capitalism. Mainly responsible here is the capitalist market's role in developing a set of beliefs and way of thinking which – while highly functional in acts of exchange – also succeeds in mystifying most of the rest of capitalist society, emphasizing, in particular, a sense of freedom that hides far more than it reveals. The most serious impact is felt in the sphere of production, since it is there that the class character of society stands out most sharply, and in the exploitation and alienation that underlies the current operations of the market as well as its real history and potential for future change.... by distorting and occluding this whole range of phenomena, market mystification serves as the main ideological defense mechanism of capitalist society.

XVIII

To reject capitalist market economy for a democratically planned socialist economy, to argue against market as *the* answer to our economic problems, does not mean rejection of market or market mechanism as such at any stage of the development of a socialist society. (Though, as Lenin once said, any amount of market economy is a danger, like an infection that will spread; one has to be very watchful about it). In a Marxist perspective, a post-revolutionary society so described, must be seen as a transition from capitalism to communism. Marx had emphasised that as the new society grew on the basis of the old, market's principle of equivalent exchange must survive in a socialist society for a considerable period as a guide to the efficient allocation and utilisation of human and material resources. Though by the same token, the evolution of this society into communism requires an unremitting struggle against the principle, with a view to its ultimate replacement by the ideal 'from each according to his ability, to each according to his need'. Again, socialism is certainly viewed by Marx as a society without commodity production, for the precise reason that commodity relations meant domination of the bourgeoisie over the direct producers and the society as a whole. But he visualised the elimination of commodity production and therefore commodity relations as a historical task, and as such to be accomplished over a long transitional period, in the course of building socialism. Though, one must again hasten to added, just because it is a 'historical' task does not mean that it can even for a moment be safely neglected. The point of our argument is that the principle of equivalent exchange or commodity production cannot be immediately abolished in a socialist society because of its transitional character, though it is precisely this character which demands a constant struggle against both to contain and ultimately eliminate them. The notion of a 'direct' and 'immediate' abolition of commodity or market relations is as utopian and dangerous as the notion of the 'immediate abolition' of the state, and is similar in nature: it disregards the specific characteristics (i.e. the specific contradictions) of the period of transition which constitutes the period of the building of socialism. In this perspective the post-capitalist socialist society will not be one in which everything in sight would be nationalised or socially-owned and all private ownership and control will disappear. That would be an absurd and destructive proposition. On the contrary, its transitional nature, with the formerly exploited class or classes in control of state power, yet involves a 'mixed economy' but one in which the relative shares of the public and private sectors under capitalism would be reversed, the extent and pace of reversal being determined by the objective economic situation as well as the balance of forces in the ongoing class struggle. The public sector, under genuine social ownership, would thus be predominant. It should be absolutely clear that without such predominance, any talk of a new social order radically different from capitalism is just talk. Thus the main means of economic activity would be under one or another form of public, social or cooperative ownership, with the greatest possible degree of democratic participation and control. This is not a fashionable notion today, but such predominance and radical extension of the public sphere remains essential to the socialist purpose, a sine qua non for what is after all a cardinal aim of socialism – namely the dissolution of the existing and profoundly unequal system of power and the dangerous and uncontrolled dynamic of capitalism. Implied in this dissolution is the withering away of the market as the principal coordinator and allocator of resources in the economy.

The key task for socialist politics in a post-capitalist society would be precisely to explore the new complex of institutions that would be capable of replacing the major institutions of capitalism. In the economic field it would mean curbing and replacing the exploitative dynamic of the capitalist market. Here, obviously, democratic planning would be of decisive importance. But precisely because of the transitional character of society, its 'mixed economy', planning will not aim at anything like control of every aspect of economic life or activity. Subject to the overall requirements of central planning, the market can have a more or less important place in the economy as a whole. The rejection of the dominance of the capitalist market does not mean the rejection of all or any type of market. Market can have its usefulness in a transitional socialist society.

While addressing the problem of market in such a society, it is necessary to bear in mind the crucial distinction between market exchange and market forces. A market will be needed in a transitional socialist economy, but not 'market forces'. Thus, for example, about one kind, or use, of the market at least there should be little if any dispute. Under capitalism, however modified by history, state intervention, etc., market has three particularly important functions: it serves as a mechanism for allocating productive resources among various uses, as a way of deciding how much individuals and groups get paid for their labour or other assets they own, and as a means of distributing goods and services to consumers. In a post-capitalist planned economy, while the first two functions for the most part, and again with due modifications, would be performed through democratic planning which would determine the priorities of economic development and human welfare, the third can be for the most part entrusted to the market. A market would be needed and useful for distributing most goods and services to consumers. Wholesale markets for consumer goods and industrial supplies might also contribute to a smoother operation of the economy.

The real issue, therefore, is not market or no market but what kind of market, not even how exclusively the market is used but the degree to which the market guides the flow of investment or is used as an *independent* regulator of economy. As we have noticed earlier, a free market *in general* or central planning *in general* do not constitute either capitalism or socialism. The crucial questions are extent, control and who benefits in each case?, who controls the surplus and how it is allocated?, in pursuit of profit or to serve human needs? scarcities distributed by prices in the market or though rational planning?... Plan and market can coexist in a socialist economy as long as the former is able to control the parameters of the latter. The real issue, in other words, is not market as such but the precise role or use of market in a socialist economy. The one governing principle is that market cannot be allowed to dominate or dictate the overall pattern of economic and social life as happens under capitalism. Socialism means, among other things, that cash, the ability to pay, is not the means of access to health, education, and much else on which civilised life depends. It means, in other words, a progressive decommodification of life, the removal of the cash nexus as the core of social relations.

Subject to the basic purposes of socialism, sought to be realised through democratic planning, market can be used, but as a tool for operationalising the plan. Here it can be useful in diverse ways: in facilitating the overall responsiveness of the economy; in serving notice of people's needs or preferences, and of their relative strength by the direct pressure of supply and demand and thus ensuring, quantity and quality-wise, better distribution of goods and services; in providing an accurate idea of the costs of what is produced, though this will not govern the pricing policies of a socialist economy; in economic accounting of the individual and collective participants in the economy; in helping check the overall adequacy and rationality of planning and providing indicators to monitor optimisation, and so on. Arguing – in the Soviet context – that 'the living regulation by the masses of the structure of the economy' does not preclude the use of the market, Trotsky wrote: 'Only through the interaction of these three elements, state planning, the market and Soviet democracy can the correct direction of the economy of the transitional epoch be attained'.

The necessary use of market in a transitional socialist society does raise a host of difficult problems but none of these are in any sense impossible of solution. We have the experience of centrally planned economies, social-democratic exercises in planning and a large body of literature, especially since Lange's work on the subject, to guide us in the use of markets under the control of an overall plan whose fiscal, distribution-of-income and other policies can be so designed as to ensure that markets do not become instruments for giving advantages to those who happen to have more ability, more money, more property, more resources than others. Democracy, and therefore democratic planning are, of course, of decisive importance in this controlled use of the markets so long as they are deemed to be necessary.

To conclude, certain instruments and institutions now associated with the market can indeed be necessary and useful in a transitional socialist economy, but the moving force of the economy has to emanate not from the market but from democratic planning which, replacing the rationality of the market as the driving mechanism, ensures that the benefits of this replacement accrue not to workers alone but to people as a whole, benefits ranging from the terms and conditions of work and leisure to their larger implications for the quality of social life, culture, the environment, and in general those 'non-economic' or 'extra-economic' goods which, according to Marx, make for a truly rich human existence.

Incidentally, the currently fashionable neo-liberal argument about the inseparability of 'democracy' and 'market' as two fundamental requirements in society is self-contradictory. If there is democracy, then it is up to the people to determine whether or not (and to what extent) to use markets. It would be contradictory to leave the choice of institutions to the people, and at the same time, to pre-close that choice by insisting that the market form of organisation be, in fact, chosen. As Amartya Sen has put it: 'If democracy is to be an irresistible force then the market system cannot be an immovable object'. And it may be added that in the history of capitalism, market systems have cohabited most comfortably with dictatorial regimes.

XIX

The debate over 'planning' and 'market' has not been the only fall out of the crisis and collapse of the Soviet economy. There has been another equally notable debate, namely over 'market-socialism'. The unwarranted assumption, abstracted from Soviet experience, that central planning is necessarily bureaucratic planning, the turn to 'market' in the erstwhile or still existing 'socialist' societies (notably Gorbachev's Soviet Union and Deng's China), combined with the recognition of the necessary use of markets in a transitional socialist society as a general principle, has given rise to the notion of 'market socialism', which for its more enthusiastic advocates has become something of a talisman and indeed the only viable form of socialist society, a realistic alternative to traditional socialism. Others (like Roemer, for example) make no such claims or even view such socialism as something ultimately desirable, but argue for it as an immediately practical alternative to or advance over capitalism whose institutional arrangements may even help in a later transition to socialism proper. The notion, as Pat Devine has pointed out, remains at best, an inadequately theorised construct. It tends to avoid and certainly fails to give due attention to traditional socialist concerns. Its essential meaning is perhaps better conveyed by the notion of 'socialising of the market', which is often alternatively used to describe it (though, without clarifying how it is a different approach). The aim here is obviously to repair the damage wrought by the existing capitalist social order – 'a socialised market' could seek, by trial or error, to promote generally egalitarian and responsible, as well as reasonably efficient, outcomes. This, at best, means hoping or opting for a nice, humane, regulated capitalism.

At worst, the notion of 'market socialism' is a contradiction in terms because it seeks, in a wishful concept, to wed two distinctly different, indeed opposite, modalities in a stable relationship, the capitalist with the socialist. It is not suggested that certain institutions and practices associated with the market could not be adapted to a socialist economy – the market, for example, can certainly act as a signal, a source of information, a form of communication between consumers and producers, ensuring some 'rationality', some correspondence between what people want and what is produced, and guaranteeing that useless or inefficient enterprises will shape up or fall. Nor is it suggested that social democratic conception of the 'social market' in which the market's ravages can be curbed by state regulation and an enhancement of social rights, lacks all viability. But the market we are here concerned with is the one intrinsicably linked to the capitalist mode of production and thus means not an arena of freedom, not only super markets with lots of choice, but mass unemployment, poverty and degradation of environment, and much else we have noted above. In other words, the need is to recognise the historical specificity of the capitalist market and make the distinction between market *opportunities* and market *imperatives*. It is the failure to make this destination which underlies the mistaken belief in the endless possibilities of a socialised market. The market imperatives would undermine and eventually negate a socialist project, just as their negation is the very essence of socialism.

This basic issue apart, 'it is rather significant', as Mandel has pointed out, 'that neither Nove nor any other of the proponents of "market socialism" has much comment to make on the *inevitable* tendency of market competition to cut out the weakest competitors, i.e., to lead to monopoly, which in turn leads to competition between the monopolies on a higher level, which in turn leads to even larger (today essentially multi-national) monopolies. These processes of concentration and centralization of capital have regularly accompanied the development of market economy since the days prior to industrial capitalism, i.e., for at least four hundred years.' 'Can that practical experience of "actual existing market economy" be dismissed out of hand', he asks. Again, 'the market' cannot act as an economic discipline in society except on one condition, the commodification of labour power – a condition which places the strictest limits on the 'socialisation' of the market and its capacity to assume a human face. The market sought to be socialised acts not only as an 'impersonal' imperative but also as a direct instrument of class power, a medium through which capital controls and exploits labour at home, and the advanced capitalist economies, as a new imperialism, impose their exploitative 'disciplines' on the third world and on the 'new democracies' of the erstwhile socialist countries. To avoid or eliminate the ravages of market society will require greater transformations than 'market socialism' can accommodate. Yet again, socialism is not merely a set of humane economic arrangements, it is the promise of a non-alienated, truly rich human existence. For all its talk of harmonising social and self interest through a 'social market', the underlying structure of 'market socialism', 'the market' in 'market socialism', rules out the realisation of any such promise. Given the imperatives that go with the market, it is simply not possible to incorporate the socialist demands for an egalitarian distribution of income, social consumption and ecological protections into a model of 'market socialism' – much less realise through it the human emancipation socialism promises, 'the realm of freedom... beyond the sphere of actual material production,' in the famous formulation of Karl Marx.

While the debate continues, it is becoming clear that 'market socialism' (along with its variants like 'social market', etc.) does not provide an alternative to capitalism since, with or without a human face, market imperatives remain the driving mechanism. 'Market socialism' remains a utopian concept in the bad sense of the word, a non-starter really, in Laibman's words a 'call in a vacuum for a new third way' which would 'relegate socialism to a utopian cul-de-sac'. Gorbachev was a miserable failure and China's 'socialism with Chinese characteristics' has been all too rapidly acquiring the characteristics of a capitalist system.

The current vogue for 'market socialism' on the left in the West (an even elsewhere), especially among those claiming to be non dogmatic or realistic, only reflects the ideological hegemony of the new right, the fact that this section of the left has not gone beyond a legitimate rejection of statism or bureaucratic planning and, in the absence of any alternative, has fallen for the market. Yet today, when the predatory logic of a crisis-ridden late capitalism is becoming daily more manifest and 'market socialism' or 'social market' begins to look more utopian, less feasible, more of a contradiction in terms than ever before, it may be more rather than less realistic to think about genuinely radical alternatives. Socialism may turn out to be less unrealistically utopian than is a 'social' or 'socialised' capitalism.

It can never be too emphasised that beyond the issues concerning planning or market, important though these issues are, a socialist vision is about a rational and humane society, a society of justice and equality, and the issue of the market must be resolved in relation to such a vision. Way back in 1965 Che Guevara had written:

> there is a danger of not seeing the forest for the trees. Taking the wild idea of trying to achieve socialism with the help of the worn-out weapons left us by capitalism (the market place, profit making, individual material incentives, etc.) you come to a dead end. And you get there after travelling a long road along which there are many forks; it is hard to see where you took the wrong turn. Meanwhile the tampered-with economic base has left its mark on the development of the individual conscience. In order to build communism we must, simultaneously with the material base, make the new man.

XX

Advocated as a practicable systemic alternative to capitalism, 'market socialism' is indeed utopian. But viewed in more theoretical, classical Marxist framework, the term 'market socialism' is not entirely inappropriate. It is indeed self contradictory, the market being the central institution of capitalist society and socialism being a society which substitutes conscious control for blind automatism of the market. But, given Marxism's recognition of the necessary use of market in a transitional socialist society, the term can be seen as reflecting a phenomenon which is also self contradictory, that is socialism viewed as a *transitional* or passing form. The 'socialism-market' or 'plan-market' contradiction expresses the essential nature of this form and is itself the *surface effect*, as Bettelheim has called it, of a deeper contradiction which is situated at the level of the structure of production relationships and production forces of this transitional form and can be ultimately resolved only at that level. In other words, 'socialism-market' or 'plan-market' contradiction is not an absolute contradiction in the sense that the two forces cannot exist side by side; it is a contradiction in the sense that the two forces are in opposition to each other and are necessarily locked in an uninterrupted struggle for dominance. Therefore even as this contradiction will continue throughout the transition from capitalism to communism, the central issue of this transition is a resolution of this contradiction in favour of socialism. A key task but not an easy one. Experience, past as well as present, has shown that this contradiction constantly impels a 'socialist' society towards capitalism. Market has its own systemic logic, it generates inequality and sanctifies it; no wonder that, as once in the Soviet Union, now in China, the advocates of 'socialism with market' openly proclaim, indeed celebrate, the necessity of inequality in society. And market has a strong tendency to get out of control. Unless strictly hedged in and controlled by democratic planning, it invariably leads to retrogression and ultimate degeneration of a socialist system. The more a society relies on a market economy the more must that society become subservient to the market economy. This is no idle theory, but a proposition that has been proven over and over again during hundreds of years of first commercial and then industrial capitalist market economies and by the experience of failed socialism-building in our time.

Just as there are no blueprints of socialism in classical Marxism, there are no specific guidelines here for the use of markets and their ultimate elimination to resolve the issue of transition in favour of socialism. And this is not a matter of any economic 'laws', 'decrees' or 'proclamations', or of certain economic forms or abstract schemes put out in advance. It is primarily a matter of putting socialist politics in command and experience alone will be the guide in securing progressive extension of socialist relations and withering away of market and money relations in the economy – by means of *concrete* measures adapted to *concrete situations and conjunctures*. And progress along this path will provide the measure of *socialist* advance in the given society. Only thing certain is that it will involve class struggle in the fullest sense of the term, economic, political, ideological, over a very long period, even epochs. In this struggle, as on other fronts, there are bound to be strategic or tactical retreats, albeit temporary, on the economic front too. As Lenin saw it, NEP was precisely a retreat of this kind. It is important to recognise them as such and not understand or present them as 'reforms' or 'moves forward', approve them ideologically and legitimise as 'socialist advance' what is really or could ultimately be a defeat of socialism. Such was the case with 'turn to market' in the Soviet Union and Eastern Europe once, and is so now in People's Republic of China. Socialist aim remains the progressive elimination of market relationships in society. Needless to add, at the centre of the class struggle to eliminate them, is the question of state power, of political strategy and tactics that govern economic policies. The location, nature and use of political power remain decisive in a transitional socialist society. More than anything else it is politics which shall decide whether such a society moves forward to socialism or backward to capitalism. For an advance to socialism, politics of this transitional period has to be a genuine socialist-democratic politics, which Marx spoke of as 'dictatorship of the proletariat'. And Marx's 'dictatorship of the proletariat' is precisely what never happened in the Soviet Union. It was the most grievous casualty of the process of degeneration of the October Revolution in the Soviet Union.

The consequences were disastrous as we shall see, as we take another look at Soviet socialism's progress to perdition in the post-Stalin period.

XXI

The way 'dictatorship of the proletariat' was practised in the Soviet Union – as a form of government, a single-party authoritarian regime – transformed it into a decisive deformation in Soviet socialism. The socialist project, including its transitional 'proletarian dictatorship', as visualised by Marx, and by Lenin before and after the October Revolution, required free and active, self-directed participation and support of the people. But, in the Soviet Union, as this 'proletarian dictatorship' consolidated itself and in its degeneration ended up building a class-divided society, a 'socialism' with a ruling class and the ruled, one outcome was political passivity of the Soviet people, which, over the years, in sharp contrast with popular political resurgence of the post-October era, became a settled fact of Soviet life and, in its own way, a decisive factor in the degeneration of the socialist experiment and the final collapse of whatever had come to be built over seventy odd years.

In the earlier period, this passivity, though not yet total, could be, at least partly, traced to such factors as the decimation of the old revolutionary proletariat in the civil war, the final defeat of international revolution, lack of culture born of relative backwardness of Russia, the absence of any historical precedents or alternatives, etc. The most potent factor however was the rapid erosion of Soviet democracy followed by repression and terror of the Stalin era. The new generation of workers, peasants, intelligentsia, simply suffocated in the stale atmosphere of absolute barrack-like obedience and the idolatrous cult of Stalin. They had not gone through any school of genuine Marxist consciousness: they knew neither the theory nor the practice of the methods of mass or class struggle. All open political struggle, under clear ideological banners had ceased in the Soviet Union since the destruction of 'the communist opposition'. But in more recent years, this passivity was more effectively secured by combining reduced state repression with tactical economic concessions to the Soviet working class. The upshot was a society effectively depoliticised at all levels, hence *a fortiori* a non-revolutionary society, with concerns and motivations of individuals and families coming to be focussed on private affairs, individual interests and family consumption levels. The pressure of consumer goods shortages and other economic difficulties often, in its own way, plays a useful role *politically* for those interested in maintaining popular quiescence. People preoccupied with the material struggle for survival have little time or energy for sustained political activity. This is how the Soviet people stood depoliticised and powerless to seriously question the powers that be, to organise any resistance against the established social order.

Yet the Soviet society was changing all this while and had been transformed beyond recognition since the October Revolution, especially after the colossal changes of the 1930s and 1940s – the social composition of population had altered radically. It was a modernised and urbanised society; rural population had declined, working class had grown and a large, by Soviet standards sophisticated, middle class had emerged; there was an urban majority which was already second generation. Unlike the earlier generation of the muzhik-turned workers, the majority of the new working class were recruited from the working class families. The people were more educated, with a higher standard of living and culture for most of the population than ever before, with more free or leisure time which escaped the state regulation or organisation. A quarter of world's scientists were Soviet and 40 per cent of its working class have had some higher education. Gone were the days when important functions were filled by the so-called *praktiki*, workers whom the party trusted and who learnt their trade on the jobs; now the *apparatchik* himself had a higher education. A new intelligentsia, of working class and peasant origin, had come into being – a vast heterogeneous group, ranging from poorly paid elementary school teachers and shop assistants to grossly over-rewarded academicians, professionals (especially in science and technology) and party and state dignitaries. Soviet Union was a whole new society of better educated and more cultured people, its different sections better aware of the milieu around them and their collective interests, their dissatisfaction with their own work (including producing what no one wanted to buy) and their disabilities in the existing order of things. They were now desirous of voice and participation in the system, hopeful, however vaguely, of a change for the better. No doubt the hope once expressed by Bukharin that 'the abolition of the educational monopoly' would 'nullify the stability of the ruling groups' was not vindicated in the Soviet experience, but one thing was clear beyond doubt: a system designed, as it were, for illiterate muzhiks – silent and subservient, used to toil and survival – had become obsolete. Its peculiarly rigid political environment, the 'barrack-discipline' in the workplace and absence of elementary freedoms in society had become entirely counterproductive. 'Barrack socialism', as it had also come to be called, was an obstacle to further development of society.

Even in the absence of freedom or democratic institutions, the rulers had once enjoyed a degree of popularity with the people who had lived through the revolutionary period or had some memory or awareness of the conditions in pre-revolutionary Russia. As with Stalin, they had a certain historical prestige too, as leaders of the revolution. But the new rulers were different and the new generations had no reason to be reverential towards them. They considered the revolution's achievements, for which their parents were so grateful, to be part of the natural order of things. The revolutionary or even pre-war past was now too distant to be idealised for the new generations. There was only discontent now over the powers and privileges of the rulers, and a deep sense of alienation from them. The facade or rhetoric of socialism, or the pretentious claims of having obtained 'a harmonious state of the whole people that was free of primary contradictions', made the people only more cynical and resentful, still more alienated from these rulers.

The ritualistic incantations in the name of socialism apart, the Soviet leaders had in fact thoroughly 'deideologised' – a favourite expression of Gorbachev – the people so far as socialism was concerned. Over a long period of time, what they had been promising the Soviet people in the name of socialism, was nothing else but capitalist consumerism, which essentially means measuring the quality of life merely in terms of material wealth and security, by the quantity of goods one has. Material well-being is important, but socialism emphasises the democratic value of collective self-determination as well. More than this, socialism for Marx was a 'free association of producers' where material benefits flow from their self-organisation in economic as well as political matters, and, as communism, aims at a 'truly rich' human life that lies beyond 'the sphere of actual material production'. The Soviet rulers and ideologues indeed spoke of their system as 'socialism' – even of its transition to communism – and argued for its superiority over capitalism in terms of uninterrupted high growth rates, the resulting 'abundance' and the creation of a new type of 'socialist man', etc., etc. But even at their best what they were really offering the Soviet people was increased material wealth in exchange for autonomy, a similar trade-off to that presented to the majority in advanced capitalist societies, although with far less autonomy and a lower, though, so far as the overwhelming majority was concerned, more secure level of material well-being. This was the substantive meaning of the Stalinist slogan of 'catching up and surpassing' the West, or Khrushchev's promise or threat to 'bury' capitalism – really bury it under a superior avalanche of consumer goods.

The offer nonetheless worked to some extent as long as the standard of living rose through the early 1970s. But with the onset of economic stagnation in the 1970s, when growth rates fell from 8.9 per cent (inflated official figures) in 1966–70 to 4 per cent in 1981–83, to around zero in the following years, the offer could not be sustained any longer. The Soviet ideological perspective turned out to be what it really was, a fiction, and the Soviet society came to be afflicted by what has been called 'the contradiction of unfulfilled expectations'. Boris Kagarlitsky has even argued that 'the cultural level of the masses became on average somewhat higher during the 1970s than the cultural level of the ruling elite', giving rise to expectations that the system could not fulfil. Instead, while the changed character of the Soviet people demanded something better, even the old social welfare functions suffered a deterioration in late 1970s and through the 1980s – housing, health care, organised leisure and children's pre-school education, all became the insufficiently satisfied needs. As Kagarlitsky has put it: 'Under Stalin, when people's standard of living was extremely low and little attention was devoted to individual consumption, collective consumption, directly controlled by the State, developed comparatively swiftly... [But in the 1970s] a desire gradually arose for higher-quality work from the social services, the prestige of which (very high in the 1930s) suffered a precipitous decline.'

The failure here was traced, in a sense correctly, to bureaucratic centralisation, the 'administrative-command system', but there was no going to the roots of the problem in the light of Marxism or a Marxist understanding of socialism. Instead the people, especially the intelligentsia, had long identified the command economy as the differentia of a system which was neither democratic nor capitalist, hence, by elimination, socialist, something that the rulers were in any case proclaiming all the time. It was socialism therefore, which was seen to have finally failed. The Soviets had begun to lose the ideological war with capitalism.

Soviet Union's 'actually existing socialism' had decisively and violently disjoined the socialist project from issues of a superior morality and a fuller democracy to become a mere authoritarian developmentalism, promising not much more than economic security and rising living standards, very, though not entirely, similar to what capitalism does. Again, there is no law of nature or economics which says that the Soviet Union had to get into a rat race with the capitalist world, and thus subject its development to external imperatives flowing from it. It had the necessary resources, and technology and scientists too, to choose its own course and to proceed at its own pace subject to its own internal imperatives and together with the allied revolutionary regimes aim at constituting an alternative, essentially self-contained bloc to secure autonomous socialist development, that is, autonomous of the capitalist world. Yet the whole image of socialism as 'catching up with and surpassing' capitalism pushed Soviet Union into economic and military competition with capitalism on the latter's terrain. And in joining this competition Soviet leadership grossly underestimated the resilience and durability of its rival or enemy. It underestimated capitalism both in terms of its potential for continued expansion and in terms of its not having within it any catastrophist teleology. Surviving the Great Depression through 'new deal' on the one hand and war preparation on the other, capitalism witnessed unparalleled economic growth in the post-war period. This economic success was matched by its political success; the defeat of fascism, development of welfare state, shedding of formal colonial control in Asia, Africa and the Caribbean lent new legitimacy to liberal-democratic capitalism. Capitalism, again, acquired renewed ideological domination through the expansion of the mechanisms by which the rule of capital is maintained and protected and its values and institutions made hegemonic in society, noticeably communications (television, etc.) and consumerist culture (pop music, fashion, etc.). All this, the strength, durability and seductive potential of capitalism was underestimated by Soviet leadership and its ideologues; though, it must be added, this underestimation was shared by most communists and even critical socialists abroad who believed that the inherent weaknesses of late capitalism and the iniquities of new forms of imperialism would render even liberal-democratic, advanced capitalism a less attractive model for the people everywhere, including those in the Soviet Union, living under their deeply deformed 'socialism'.

It is not surprising therefore that the entire project of socialism as 'catching up with and surpassing' capitalism, really a grossly economistic caricature of the classical view of socialism, turned out to be deeply flawed. In the first place, the Soviet Union was not able to catch up with and surpass capitalism even in the narrowest most, traditional, quantitative terms such as overall industrial output or food production. As for engaging capitalism in a global military contest, the consequences were disastrous.

It has been throughout a part of global capitalism's tactics to use the enormous power it commands to condemn every country which ever attempted to introduce socialism to a perpetual war economy in order to strain or ruin the country and deflect it from its chosen path. So it was with the Soviet Union. Most significant here was the direct pressure generated by war or threat of war, which, causing or reinforcing its internal contradictions, so distorted the construction of socialism in the Soviet Union. As E.P. Thompson has underlined:

> ....war (1917–1921 and 1941–45 and the expectation of invasion in the 1930s) and cold war thereafter were necessary conditions for the historic formation of Stalinism and of its Brezhnevite aftermath: in the exaltation of military priorities, the imposition of command economies and suppression of consumer demand, the enhancement of ideological paranoia, the strengthening of internal security forces, the 'two camps' diplomacies, the outlawing of dissent, and all the rest.

The Soviet leadership however never saw it that way. It did not recognise the dangerous game of global capitalism, the distorting burdens it imposed on their economy. Defence against imperialist aggression was of course a most legitimate concern. But it did not demand or justify assuming the role of a super-power, which reduced or blowed up its legitimate need for self defence into a military contest with the capitalist powers, more particularly the United States. Towards the end, the Soviet desire to match every increase of arms or change in US defence policy, virtually enslaved the Soviet military-industrial complex to the external imperative and precipitated defeat in the cold war and eventually collapse of the Soviet Union. The US establishment has rightly acclaimed the role of Reagan's 'Star Wars' initiative in breaking up the Soviet state.

Possibly the most damaging aspect of the policy of 'catching up' with the West was that the ensuing competition with capitalism was conducted on the latter's terms, that is, the criteria or standards according to which the competition was being judged, not least by the population of Soviet Union itself, were those laid down by capitalism. And here capitalist society represented a success to which Soviet society was especially vulnerable. The Soviet Union could not compete economically in terms of output and technological change and even less in the newly promoted domain of consumerism and popular culture. It could not compete politically either, since its initially revolutionary successes, instead of developing into a functioning alternative and superior system of socialist democracy, had degenerated into, to use Bahro's phrase, a 'polit-bureaucratic' dictatorship. Soviet socialism in a sense, dug its own grave. As a sympathetic scholar has suggested: 'It has been defeated by its failure to meet its own standards. Unwilling to match the political freedoms of the west, let alone go beyond it, "socialist" regimes pegged their legitimacy to their ability to economically outperform advanced capitalism, where "performance" was to be judged in terms no different from the latter's extravagant consumerism'. It is this comparative or 'competitive' failure which provided an all-important basis for the collapse of 1991.

A contributory factor was the popular disillusionment resulting from the repeated failures of attempts to 'reform' the economic system, from Khrushchev to Kosygin to Gorbachev himself. This raised doubts about the viability of a system that people, along with rulers, identified as socialist and thus of the socialist ideal itself. Soviet intelligentsia fully shared in this disillusionment and the consequent abandonment of not only socialism but all ideas and ideals of the 'common good'. Socialism simply lost its special place in society as the collective repository of moral and political values. It has been legitimately argued that 'the full imperialist triumphs of 1989 were dialectically correlated with the Hungary of 1956, the Czechoslovakia of 1968, and the lapsing of the Khrushchev reforms within the Soviet Union; all available evidence seems to suggest that it was not in the age of Stalin himself but after the suppression of the reform movements that increasingly larger sections of the Soviet and East European populations and intelligentsias actually gave up on regimes of "existing socialism"'. As Tsypko, an ex-communist ideologue later said, communism died ideologically under Brezhnev – not under Stalin. Scholars have pointed out the shift in the position of Soviet intelligentsia 1960s onward, from a hopeful, occasionally even Marxist or leftist, criticism of 'actually existing socialism' to resistance in the 1980s and subsequently to liberal ideology, the choice for them finally getting reduced to dictatorship or liberal capitalism. The upshot of it all was that while Soviet 'socialism' was no inspiration for people in the west to move towards socialism, west's liberal capitalism, above all for its consumerist promise, had become attractive enough for the Soviet people to abandon this socialism altogether.

The Soviet adoption of consumerist values, which in a way betoken western capitalism's strength, was an explicit surrender to capitalism. If, objectively, the developed capitalist countries had been trying to force the Soviet Union to imitate their technology or join in a competitive arms race, subjectively, they had been trying to persuade the Soviet citizens, through various means, to imitate their consumption models. As the country moved into the 1980s, the expansion and globalisation of different kinds of networks and forms of communication, their new reach and power, gave a qualitatively new dimension to this persuasion. The cultural logic of late capitalism was able to ally itself with the electronic media in ways that proved to be beyond the post-Stalinist command economy of the Soviet Union. It was the 'culture of consumerism' all the way, the West was indeed the ultimate in cornucopia. Theorists of 'the postmodern' have written of the 'society of the spectacle'. The 'spectacle' was simply too dazzling for the Soviet citizens to resist. Its citizens – depoliticised, 'deideologised' and gone consumerist – exposed to a new capitalist offensive through the communications revolution, the Soviet surrender to capitalism was all set to turn into a rout. It was only a matter of time.

The Stalinist leadership was perhaps always aware of this danger; hence the extensive censorship which prevailed under the old system about conditions in the west, or the false, deliberately crude propaganda about them. But now it was no longer possible to keep the west out this way, that is, keep the people from knowing how much worse off they were in terms of comparison set by capitalism and accepted by them. The Soviet system was simply incapable of facing the challenge of the social convulsion resulting from the arrival, for example, of satellite television channels, the challenge posed by comparison with the consumption levels of the advanced capitalist west and the hegemonic assertions of its cultural products and aspirations daily beamed across through the now vastly expanded electronics media and new information technologies. Its own crude propaganda, reflecting no sophisticated understanding of contemporary capitalism, only a primitive or vulgar Marxist view at variance with its in many ways 'attractive' reality, boomeranged with a vengeance. The impact of it all was all the more devastating for a system suffering from a debilitating deficiency for a long time. Scientistic Marxism and economistic socialism had between them made sure of a major ideological-cultural neglect. The creation of 'a new man' – central to the revolutionary vision from Marx to Che Guevara – notwithstanding the hype over the 'Soviet man', never became a part of political agenda in the Soviet Union and remained excluded from its academic programmes; even the best of its educational effort aimed at assembly-line production of unalloyed technocrats who were supposed to fill slots within an unthinking, unquestioning bureaucracy. The overall cultural inertness of the Soviet system made it only too vulnerable to the cultural vitality of the capitalist world, however questionable some of its decadent or vulgar aspects may be. The Soviet authorities could no longer insulate their population from the cultural products of the west; on occasion they even actively promoted them to sustain their own lifestyle. Soviet society could less and less free itself from the desire of at least tens of millions of consumers to imitate the consumption pattern of the richer capitalist countries, with all the negative aspects of that pattern.

In this connection, it may be noted that it was about the time the consumption levels ceased to grow in the Soviet Union, in the 1970s, that social concepts of well being began to change under the demonstrative effect of western mass-consumption capitalist societies. Just when even 'old-style' consumers were beginning to get dissatisfied, 'new style' demands began to come up, at first in particular social groups such as scientific-technical elite and the new generation of better educated workers, especially the young, to become the general norm in 1980s. With the transfer of most families into their own apartments and colour television bringing images of the west – more cars, easy travel, and all those consumer goodies on the shelves – right into the home, the 'demonstration effect' acquired new significance and people began to compare their situation unfavourably with the west. In other words, in the ideological 'battle for the minds of men and women', the positive attraction of life-styles in the advanced western capitalism had become a major, if more subterranean, factor in undermining the viability of whatever still remained of the 'socialist' project as it had actually taken shape in the Soviet Union, (or for that matter, in the rest of 'the socialist world'). This attraction, now fuelled through every device provided by the communications revolution, virtually disoriented the entire Soviet society, the discontent grew as never before. With the coming in of Gorbachev's *glasnost* the dykes of this discontent simply burst open. The consumerist surrender to capitalism turned into a rout in behalf of capitalism.

XXII

It will be instructive to take a brief but somewhat specific look at the post-Stalin Soviet leadership's response to the emerging problems of their society, which accumulated into a dead end crisis in the 1980s and led to its ultimate disintegration soon afterwards.

From the very beginning till the end, the problems and the distorted trajectory of the Soviet experiment in socialism were the subject of sharp analysis and criticism within the revolutionary Marxist tradition abroad. (I am not here concerned with the bourgeois critiques, the best of which certainly had their share of insights, nor with the criticism within the Soviet Union which came to be ruthlessly suppressed as Stalin consolidated his leadership of the party and the state, setting the pattern for the future). Among others, the names of Rosa Luxemburg, Gramsci, or Trotsky in exile, come to mind. Trotsky was among the first to point out the emergence of a privileged and authoritarian bureaucracy separated from the masses, though he did not identify this stratum as a ruling class (When later, Djilas in his *New Class* did so, it was little more than a rhetorical expression). Mao's exceptionally insightful understanding of what had gone wrong in the Soviet Union even led him to struggle for a different road to socialism in China. More recently, as already noticed, we have had Bettelheim's classic 4-volume study, *Class Struggles in the USSR*, brief but remarkably perceptive analyses of Paul Sweezy and Harry Magdoff, and several similar critiques by Marxists outside the Soviet Union. It is significant that Soviet leadership, its 'theoreticians' and associated scholarship in the academy, simply refused to take note of this Marxist criticism. It was seen, if at all, as so many inimical exercises and dismissed as such. Social democratic criticism, like that of Kautsky and others fared no better. Even so, while socialist criticism from abroad was without any effect, the problems within the country accumulated and the need was felt to reform the system, believed to be socialism, from within – Khrushchev's and Gorbachev's were two major efforts to this end. But the inherent limitations of all such efforts, the resistance of the entrenched bureaucracy, together with the 'threat' from the capitalist west and therefore the need to 'defend' the system, continually delayed and aborted every attempt at self-reform. Once again, it is significant that in their efforts to understand or reform 'the socialist system', the Soviet leadership never turned to the theoretical resources of classical Marxism. The plain pragmatism of such efforts only meant moving still further away from socialism as visualised in the classical tradition of Marxism.

The problems of Soviet society, long ignored or suppressed, finally surfaced, demanding radical solutions, just as this society stabilised itself after the post-war reconstruction and after Stalin passed away in 1953. As Isaac Deutscher, hoping for a historical departure to the left in the post-Stalin Soviet Union, pointed out, such a departure was necessary due to the 'profound contradiction .... maturing between, to use the Marxian terms, the social and economic structure and the political superstructure of post-Stalin society'. The political system, dictatorship of the party leadership, propped up mainly by the all-powerful party machinery and the secret police, had become obsolete. Designed as it were for uprooted, half-illiterate muzhiks, it was no longer viable for a population grown more urban and better educated and cultured. The economy, more complex and more sophisticated, had rendered the crude dictates from the top, the party-bureaucratic centre, counter productive. And there was the disgruntled working class with guaranteed jobs and no incentives to work, and no political channels at its disposal (such as the right to strike) to bargain collectively, indeed no means to organise and express its class interests. Glaring social and regional inequalities and gross privileges of the leaders at the top made the situation still worse. The system could not be held together the way it was under Stalin. A departure had obviously become necessary.

The first attempt to reform the system was made by Nikita Khrushchev, survivor of Stalin's purges and as good a specimen as any of the kind of Communist Party Stalin had left behind, in every way indicative of the profound degeneration the Party had undergone from its pristine state of theoretical integrity and revolutionary commitment in Lenin's time, a degeneration which was to continue with Brezhnev and Gorbachev. And, typical of the system, he had come to power amidst rumours of murderous intrigues, through what can only be described as a palace *coup*, with no intervention at all from the base, which simply accepted the outcome. Half-peasant, half-townsman, and as such a symbol of the Soviet Union in transition, Khrushchev was also right in his understanding that its further progress demanded, above all, 'de-Stalinisation' of Soviet society, that is, ridding it of the political and economic ills inherited from the earlier Stalin era. But the utter inadequacy, indeed the theoretical poverty of this understanding lay in Khrushchev locating all these ills in a so-called 'cult of personality' – as un-Marxist a concept as there ever was, a gross departure from every canon of historical materialism. As Bettelheim has written:

> The contradictory reality of Soviet history and Soviet Society was not subjected to the least analysis. The aspects of reality which needed to be condemned and transformed were not explained in relation to the inner contradictions of the Soviet Union. They were

> presented as being 'Perversions' due to the actions of a certain 'Personality', namely, Stalin. The acceptance by the Soviet Communist Party of such a pseudo explanation testified to its abandonment of Marxism as a tool of analysis. This made the party incapable of helping to transform the social relations that had given rise to that which was being condemned in words.

This pseudo-explanation simply evaded the real issue of class relations in the Soviet society which had concentrated economic and political power in the hands of a minority at the top, engendering the contradictions that were plaguing the Soviet economy and society. (Khrushchev's 'theorising' about 'all people's state', 'peaceful transition', 'peaceful coexistence', etc. were equally suspect from a Marxist standpoint).

Khrushchev launched his reform project with the now well-known one-dimensional attack on Stalin's personality in 1956, pronouncing upon the tyrannies, mass persecutions and executions of the Stalin era. (Incidentally, in the autumn of the same year, he ordered the invasion of Hungary to crush the effort at self-reform there and a few years later cut off financial and technical assistance to China to penalise it for its refusal to fall in with his politics!) Underlying his attack on Stalin was the somewhat half-baked but official recognition that problems of Soviet society could not be overcome by periodic terror and violence against the people, that fear of concentration camp, coupled with moral exhortation was not enough to get the working classes to work honestly, that *overall* authoritarianism and corruption undermine efficiency and creativity throughout the entire fabric of society, as much in its culture, science, administration and politics as in the economy proper. When in the process of 'de-Stalinisation' millions were released from the Gulag in the 1950s, the reason was partly social pressure – but perhaps also partly that the forced labour system was proving cumbersome, expensive and inefficient.

It needs to be noted that Khrushchev's departure from the Stalin era was, contrary to the hope of Deutscher and many others, a departure to the right. His critique of Stalin, its other limitations apart, was a critique from the right (just as Mao's was a critique from the left). There was no returning to the basics of Marxist theory or a genuine practice of socialism. Instead of resolving the economic and social contradictions arising from the exploitative relations of production in the Soviet economy, its problems were seen primarily as 'economic problems' and solutions were to be sought in better 'economic management', in 'economic reforms' to make the system work better – the criteria in both cases being, almost inevitably, those seen to be successful under capitalism. Khrushchev argued that the Soviet Union had not made enough concessions to take into account constraints on the economy (the technological and scientific revolution, demands of global market, etc.) and their political implications (giving more power and stable control to the directors of the enterprises, factory managers and individual bureaucrats, etc.). The objective of reasserting control over the labour process, of getting people to work and do so efficiently, was to be secured through pecuniary incentives, consumer goods, etc. Physical coercion of the labour camps was no longer viable, and capitalist coercion based on the fear of unemployment being unavailable, the people were to be cajoled towards work and efficiency. As we have already noticed, the underlying social cause of the crisis of the old system was the absence of control over the economy's administrators, who had long usurped the power of the economy's official owner, the people, though without becoming full owners themselves. Under Stalin some control from above did exist. Purge or worse awaited a defaulting manager or bureaucrat. Khrushchev eliminated the terror but did not replace it with democratic control from below. As with Marxism or socialism, he only mouthed clichés about democracy.

Khrushchev's was a half-hearted, rather timid effort to reform the inherited system, to change it in order to preserve it, through a certain relaxation of the overall repressive control over the people, reduction of the arbitrary power of the authorities, a more rapid turnover among elected leaders at all levels, decentralisation of economic administration, induction of non-party intellectuals and scientists into the decision-making process, and so on. But even this 'de-Stalinisation', 'partial, self-contradictory, inadequate and hypocritical' as it was in the words of Isaac Deutscher, made the entrenched bureaucracy in the party and state system feel insecure and provoked its opposition. What is more, 'stuck in the mud of the past' as he was, this was precisely the constituency Khrushchev chose to implement his reforms – the heavily bureaucratised party apparatus, which was thus doubly unsuited to the task. The *apparatchiks* saw nothing wrong with the inherited system except Stalin's propensity to purge, even the faithful, periodically (which was, perhaps Stalin's bloody way to prevent crystallisation of a regular ruling class). What they, indeed all the privileged, wanted was Stalinism plus security of tenure. Even Khrushchev's haphazard half-measures were too much for them and when his reforms seemed to threaten their position, they toppled him, typically again, through yet another conspiracy at the top. The man they picked to replace him (who according to the then head of the KGB had even wanted to have Khrushchev killed) was Leonid Brezhnev, who made the unwritten pledge never to endanger the interests of the privileged. Herein lay the secret of his unexpectedly long reign. He kept his word and his job for 18 years. After a time, he also reached a social compromise with the state-dependent working class, making them concessions in exchange for their political passivity.

The price paid for Brezhnev's long reign was indeed heavy. With Khrushchev gone, all important reforms were shelved, there were no further attempts at any meaningful change in the economic, political or cultural life. The Soviet society was back at the pre-1956 impasse. The process of 'de-Stalinisation' was halted, though the earlier blind terror was replaced by a more 'rational form' of repression. Devoid of any vision, the new leadership came to be primarily concerned with assuring its own survival and privileges, with pursuit of narrow self-interest. With increasing corruption in public life, the chasm between the leadership and large segments of the intelligentsia and the people widened still further. The economy slackened and mid-1970s onward entered into a period of rapid decline. A massive conservative reaction set in which was deadly for politics, the human sciences as well as the cultural life.

Stagnation and a cynical and corrupt despotism was the price paid for the so-called stability of the Brezhnev era. It was becoming clear that the neo-Stalinist system was in historical terms doomed.

It is not that stagnation took over immediately with Brezhnev's accession to power. The momentum from the Khrushchev era persisted, the economic system had its potentialities, major advance could still be made on the chosen objectives. The sputniks were sent into the sky, yielding tremendous ideological gains to the new regime. As leader of the 'socialist bloc', it could proclaim the Brezhnev doctrine and invade Czechoslovakia, send its armies into Afghanistan, indulge in unbridled arms race and other military adventures. In other words, it could play super-power politics, though with disastrous consequences for the economy. As we have already noticed, drawing the Soviet Union into the Cold War and its ever escalating armaments race was a deliberate policy of the United States to push the rival economy to the brink. This was the hidden but now openly admitted rationale of Reagan's otherwise ridiculous 'Star Wars' project, to outspend the Soviet Union to its knees. And thanks to Brezhnevite megalomania it worked as planned. The Soviet economy collapsed; the leadership withdrew from the Cold War, defeated; the system disintegrated, the stampede to restore capitalism began. The United States could not have won a more decisive victory in the Cold War.

Incidentally, invasion of Czechoslovakia involved no 'defence of socialism', as claimed by the Soviet leadership. No doubt, in facing the difficulties born of the centralised bureaucratic planning – which had its origin in the Soviet Union during the Stalin period and was exported to the other Soviet bloc countries after the Second World War – the Czechoslovak reformers were turning to capitalistic methods – control of enterprises in the enterprises themselves with more power to the managements, coordination through the market, reliance on material incentives – and in that sense turning further away from socialism. This however is not to say that they were consciously moving towards capitalism, or that they were being hypocritical or insincere when they said that they were working to achieve democratic socialism. Strictly speaking, they could not even be said to be moving away from the Soviet-style socialism. For the fact is that the whole of East European bloc, including the Soviet Union, was moving in the same capitalistic direction, and for the same reasons. That was the essential meaning of the 'economic reform movement' which, in varying degrees and at varying speeds, had involved every member of the bloc – they were all, without abandoning state ownership, moving along market lines. In Czechoslovakia, as earlier in Hungary, what the Soviet leaders really feared was a threat to their 'national interests', that is, the interests of the national ruling class they represented and which interests included their own personal interests too. As Marxism has always held, foreign policy is ultimately the extension of domestic policy, for it is conducted by the same ruling class. Brezhnev doctrine was no exception.

Stagnation did not begin with Brezhnev's ascent to power, but it progressed rather rapidly under his rule. By the mid-1970s, its potentialities exhausted, the Soviet economy entered a serious crisis. Returns on investment diminished and the rate of growth declined. The technological gap with western capitalism, instead of getting narrowed widened and, significantly enough, even though a certain threshold had been reached, the Soviet Union was failing to generate its own technology except in the military field. With the slackening pace of economy there was a squeeze on housing and social welfare benefits. And this when, with new openings to the west, there was growing awareness of the still large difference in living standards between Soviet Union and the West. The new generation of workers, now less frightened and better educated and cultured, had been promised 'goulash socialism' but were getting neither goulash nor socialism. The Brezhnevian 'contract from above' in which steady rises in living standards were promised to compensate the people for leaving the ruling bureaucracy with its monopoly of political power, was breaking down. There were increasing signs of social breakdown (crime, juvenile delinquency, drunkenness, corruption), and growing internal political protest increasingly fuelled by the seduction of western consumerism. All these features of the crisis intensified over the next decade. The potentially explosive mixture of economic stagnation and social discontent could not last.

Brezhnev, as we have seen, came to power as the candidate of the bureaucracy which had resented and rejected Khrushchev's interference with its power and privileges, and had found allies in the political leadership to overthrow him. One consequence of this alliance or unwritten compact was that bureaucracy was increasingly freed of whatever outside political control existed during the earlier periods of Stalin and Khrushchev. Henceforth the administrators (especially at the top and middle levels) did not need particularly to fear punishment for any default or dereliction of duties. Real sanctions were reserved for those who violated the informal rules, the *esprit de corps* of the ruling bureaucratic caste mired in corruption. Growing over the years, a final coalescence of interests of ruling elites, of the party and state bureaucracies, had taken place. A class society with incipient class rule for long, it is in the Brezhnev period that the Soviet Union may be said to have acquired, despite factions within it, a ruling class in the proper sense of the term.

Representing the class power of the bourgeoisie now esconced in the party and the state, Brezhnev continued to speak of 'developed socialism' in the Soviet Union, and in yet another parody of Marxism, typical of the Soviet leadership over the years, 'theorised' the very issue of class out of power in a socialist society by redefining the dictatorship of the proletariat.

As we have argued earlier, what is decisive from the point of view of socialism is not the mode of 'regulation' of the economy, but rather the nature of class in power. It is not whether 'market' or 'plan' (and therefore also the state) controls the economy but the nature of the class which holds power. If the role of the state in directing the economy is seen as of decisive, definitional importance for socialism, then the truly essential question of whose state?, which class is in power?, comes to be obscured and relegated to the background. And this is precisely what Brezhnev's theoretical manoeuvre did. He proclaimed at the Twenty Second Party Congress that the dictatorship of the proletariat signifies 'state direction of economic construction' and thus dodged the question of the nature of state or class power in the Soviet Union. In other words, Marxian concept of 'dictatorship of the proletariat' was simply abandoned. A ruling class was the reality in the Soviet Union. One is reminded of a Chinese folk saying of the 1970s: 'The Sputniks went up and the Red Flag came down.'

Neither socialist nor properly capitalist, without any vision or larger purpose, this ruling class consolidated itself by draining all creative energy from Soviet society. Dysfunctional and parasitic on the system, it played super-power politics abroad and set about plundering the economy at home, in addition to the 'normal' exploitation – the 'extra-economic' appropriation of surplus from direct producers – which the Soviet economic structure had long involved. A most significant feature of the Brezhnev period was its rampant corruption, now equally entrenched in the structures of the state and party and all other social and political institutions. Not that corruption was unknown in the earlier periods; but now it underwent a qualitative difference. Brezhnev himself and many others in the *nomenklatura,* with his personal support, virtually looted the national exchequer, selling even imaginary crops to the state. Such corruption had no parallels in the earlier periods. For, under Stalin, the Terror acted as a strong deterrent. In the Khrushchev period, constant shuffling of top bureaucrats and rapid turnover in the Central Committee membership helped to curb it somewhat. But with Brezhnev it was an unbridled pursuit of private gains and unashamed whetting of ruling elites' consumerist appetites. It involved an unprecedented craving for conspicuous as well as expensive western goods, import of inessentials along with bribery by foreign suppliers to place excessive orders and heavy borrowing from western commercial banks to finance these imports. Dependence upon western technology and machinery in consumer goods sector only undermined confidence in domestic capability, as did the invitations to translational corporations for investments in the Soviet Union. There was a violent 180 degree turn from the traditional policy of self-reliance. The contrast with Stalin's proud refusal of Truman's Marshall Plan 'aid' at the end of the war was only too obvious.

The Brezhnev period saw a significant ideological shift among the Soviet intelligentsia on the subject of reform in the Soviet system. While dissidence in the Soviet Union had a 'motley-crowd' political complexion, 'stretching from "party democrats",...through liberals,...representatives of persecuted religions and oppressed nationalities to Great Russian chauvinists', as one description has it, the role of intelligentsia was crucial for any project of reform. In the 1960s, when Khrushchev opened up the issues with 'de-Stalinisation' and launched his reforms, the so-called 'thaw', the intelligentsia, recovering some of its traditional function in society, was hopefully responsive to it and expected further progress in this process of self-reform. Of course Khrushchev was no Marxist turning to authentic socialism, nor did the intelligentsia have any revolutionary fraction within it to struggle for such a turn. But it had a large fraction of liberals who were yet hopeful of combining liberal and communist ideologies in what they believed would be a democratic socialism. These 1960s-style liberals believed in the possibility of 'socialism with a human face', the historical ambiguities of such a project notwithstanding and however flawed their understanding of socialism may have been. Political repression in the Soviet Union made them all the more sympathetic to efforts at such self-reform within Soviet bloc countries, where their counterparts were more open and explicit in entertaining such or similar hopes. It needs to be noticed that till the 1960s the movements that challenged the existing social order in Eastern Europe (in Germany, Hungary, Czechoslovakia) did so in the name of socialism. (Even later, in the Polish uprising of 1970, the Gdansk workers held aloft the Red banner and sang the 'Internationale' as they demanded Gomulka's dismissal. And in 1980, the Polish Solidarity's programme still had a pro-socialist motivation). All these movements invoked a humane and democratic socialism which they felt had been distorted by Stalinism. They sought a renewal of socialism, even though one may question the way they went about it. The Soviet liberals viewed these movements with great sympathy and hopefulness. They had faith in a 'socialist' future for their country.

The failure of the Khrushchev experiment in the Soviet Union and the armed suppression of 'the Prague Spring' in Czechoslovakia in 1968, which radically reversed the above trajectory of reform in Eastern Europe and prepared the ground for future explosions, shattered this faith altogether. These two events were a crushing defeat for the hopeful liberals among the Soviet intelligentsia. There was widespread disillusionment and in the Brezhnev years they steadily lost whatever ideological hegemony they had. Unable to propose any strategic alternative to their society, they went on the defensive. One consequence was the utter indifference to Marxism and socialism of several generations of intellectuals. It has been suggested that the Khrushchev generation was possibly the last one to believe in the possibility of a renewal of Marxism or the socialist project in the Soviet Union. Now Marxism and the idea of socialism stood discredited with large sections of the intelligentsia. Thus, in the stagnant and conservative ethos of the late Brezhnev era, the situation was ripe for the spread of illusions about capitalism. Socialism being identified with the established order, the intelligentsia, or at least a large part of it, was now literally backward looking, hankering after an idealised capitalism, or nostalgically, after an even more distant past. Already in the 1970s, ginger groups of neo-liberal intellectuals were allowed to go on working at various academic institutions under the protection of influential apparatus 'uncles' like Andropov *et al.* From these safe harbours, they came forth to enter the reform struggle of the mid-1980s with the most coherent and well informed critiques of the old regime. These were the 1980s-style liberals who attained hegemony among the intelligentsia almost as the rightful heirs of the liberals of the 1960s, now intellectuals hungry for capitalist democracy or, perhaps, for the market and western capitalism in the name of democracy.

Towards the end of Brezhnev's 'age of stagnation' which was destructive of even the minimum creativity necessary to sustain any system, all the long-festering contradictions of Soviet economy and society came to a head. A change had become inevitable. His successor for a brief period, Andropov, moving away from the bureaucratic hard core in the party and state-apparatus – who preferred a bureaucratic solution to the problems – sought wider support among the intelligentsia, now largely gone pro-market, for his changes to bring the system alive. The *apparatchiks* showed their resistance to change by selecting the decrepit and discarded Chernenko – 'the man who sharpened pencils for Leonid Brezhnev' – as a stop gap leader to succeed Andropov. But the situation had become intolerable and by 1985 they had to resign themselves to the selection of a supposedly radical reformer, Mikhail Gorbachev, their own and yet more representative of the west-oriented technocratic elite among the Soviet rulers.

The Soviet economy, its bureaucratic centralism, had indeed reached a dead end. Mass apathy, faltering productivity, economic stagnation, widespread social discontent, restive counter-elites seeking to break into the closed structures of power – these and other symptoms of impending crisis were only too visible. Two responses were possible to this impossible situation. One was to recover the authentic socialist tradition of classical Marxism and the Bolshevik Party and launch an all-out campaign to rouse the working masses, raise the general level of political consciousness, revitalise the socialist ideals, democratise the planning system and empower the producers at all levels of decision-making. What was needed was not a new leadership which *claimed* to represent socialism and people's interest but a new regime which *in fact* represented socialism and people's interest, because it was under people's democratic control. It is certainly arguable that *objective* basis for a turn to socialism existed in the Soviet Union. The requisite material productive base was there and it could still count on a great deal of mass support, regardless of what the intelligentsia was after. That 'socialism' as such was not questioned in popular perception up to the early 1980s is substantiated by an opinion poll conducted by American scholars around 1985, among Soviet refugees who arrived in the US between 1979 and 1982, all of them now well established. One of the scholars, J. Millar, had concluded:

> The overall responses point to a desire for more political and economic diversity and for broader civil rights; but it is also clear that even after several years (on average) of life in the United States, only a few ....respondents were prepared to repudiate entirely the Soviet political, economic, and social system.

A genuinely socialist response to the crisis, however, demanded a decisive turning to the people, above all to the working class of the Soviet Union. But, his theoretical inadequacies apart, this was impossible for Gorbachev and the bureaucratic regime presided over by him, which was not only separated from the working class but was profoundly opposed to it in the same sense that a bourgeoisie is opposed to the working class in capitalist societies, and which was equally profoundly interested in preserving its power and privileges. In the event, therefore, while an *objective* basis was there, for reasons which are obvious, *subjective* forces, necessary for a turn to socialism, no longer existed in the Soviet Union. It was quite a contrast with the situation in 1917 when the Bolsheviks under Lenin led in the making of a socialist revolution in backward Russia. There was no one now, no party or group, capable of making a socialist response to the crisis of Soviet society, least of all a Gorbachev. His long apprenticeship as an *apparatchik* in the party, and the theoretical equipment thus acquired, had ensured that he would not even know what a socialist response could be. However muddled the reasoning or the unexpected outcome, he opted for the only other possible response to the crisis. Unable or unwilling to turn to the people and find answers in socialism, he turned to his ruling counterparts in the west and to the market and, whatever the conscious motivation, set his country on the road back to capitalism.

XXIII

In a long-term perspective, there was nothing inevitable about what happened in the Soviet Union though, as we have seen, there were deeper-lying contradictions in Soviet society which were almost inevitably impelling it towards its decay and ultimate disintegration. It were primarily the policies and practices of the post-October Soviet leadership, especially after

Lenin, which had led to the emergence, accumulation and exacerbation of these contradictions to the point of final collapse. If the economic command system originally failed in its socialist purpose and finally capsized, it was because of the wrong orders or directions transmitted from the top echelons of the political hierarchy. It functioned at the behest of the political leadership. As a critic has well put it: 'It is the dog of political decision-making which wagged the tail of the economic programme, and not the other way round.... The command economy did not fail the socialist polity; it is the latter which was the dominant element in the system that guided the impulses, and shaped the activities, of the economic command.' The failure of the Soviet Union, as socialism and otherwise, was a failure of its politics. And there are no inevitabilities here. The leadership could have made different, better choices.

Viewed in Marxist terms the Soviet society had indeed reached a situation in which the productive forces were clashing with the existing institutions and the rulers as well as the people were finding the situation impossible. But if the system collapsed it was not something inherent in the objective situation or due to personal failings of early Bolshevik leaders, or later some 'cult of personality', or still later in the poor or corrupt, even treacherous leaderships of Khrushchev, Brezhnev or Gorbachev. The cause of the collapse lay in more substantive subjective factors, above all in the overall quality of politics pursued, more specifically, the economistic Marxism that had governed this politics. At the end of its long economistic journey the Soviets seemed to have realised, or could be said to be aiming at realising, the Saint Simonian dream of scientifically managed society, 'capitalism without capitalists' Engels had once called it. Capitalist-style scientific management was the theory guiding the reformist programme of Gorbachev, it not entirely the earlier one of Khrushchev too. It was an untenable, utopian programme where a turn to the right could only end up in a transformation of the Soviet-style 'Party-State bourgeoisie' into a real bourgeoisie, a class of private proprietors. And it was only such a political intervention, Gorbachev's turn to the right, that was forthcoming in the Soviet Union. The consequence was the final collapse of the Soviet system as whatever kind of socialism it was. We may here as well notice the parallel global conjuncture in which even social democracy, let alone communism, had entered a period of secular decline throughout northern and western zones of Europe, giving way to openly right-wing regimes and pushing the remaining social democratic regimes further to the right. This directly increased the capitalist economic, political and military pressure on the communist regimes and indirectly, via the triumph of right-wing ideologies, helped to make them hegemonic in Soviet and East European politics too, leaving the Left there even less capable of offering any fundamental resistance to 'reform' programmes of marketisation, etc. A vigorous socialist Left in the West, in power or as movement, would have surely made a difference to the outcome in the Soviet Union. In other words, political failure of the Left in the West was a major contributory factor in sealing the fate of the Soviet Union and with it, as in 1917 and over the next seventy odd years, of socialism there and elsewhere in the world.

Those seeking an explanation of Soviet collapse in terms of economic failure of socialism, need to recognise that the central command structure of the economy, like so much else in the Soviet Union, had gone sour because socialism as classically understood had already gone sour with the Party and the State there. As part of the process of Soviet Union's slide into a class society and facilitating it, 'dictatorship of the proletariat' had early degenerated into dictatorship of the Party, and then into plain dictatorship – an authoritarian regime equipped with a massive apparatus of coercion, including extensive secret services (KGB, etc.), denying people democratic rights and freedoms and standing more over and above them than perhaps any bourgeois state ever did. The roots of this process of political degeneration lay in the degeneration of the Party into 'cult of personality' and all that. Increasingly bereft of idealism or revolutionary commitment, its principle of 'democratic centralism' become totally debased, shorn of all democracy and buttressed with every kind of centralism, a chasm had opened between the cadre and leadership, and following that, between the people and the Party. Party leadership, interpenetrating and overlapping with state bureaucracy and managerial technical elite, had become a ruling class, and the Party itself, home to all sorts of careerism, an instrument of ruling class control over the popular masses, complementing the work of the KGB, and forestalling the emergence of any organised resistance to its rule with a network of patronage, distribution of social advantages, even the most petty, and all sorts of corrupt practices – '"blat" (i.e. "connections") are stronger than Stalin' was a significant saying among people in Stalin's own time. The octopus-like *nomenklatura* thrived on exclusivity and the party card had become the coveted badge of privilege which entitled its owner to benefits not available to ordinary Soviet citizens.

There is an aspect to this degeneration of the Soviet Communist Party which needs to be specifically reiterated for it involves a basic issue or, if you like, a lesson for communists or socialists anywhere. The point I am wanting to make is that people suffer and forgive a great deal, including horrid political mistakes, if the leadership stays with them, shares and suffers with them in their difficulties, their trials and tribulations. Therefore, even as we refuse to see the denouement in the Soviet Union merely as a result of mistaken policies, bad implementation of good principles, 'wrong notions', 'distortions' or 'deviations', or sundry other reasons preferred by official Marxists or 'Party theoreticians', the role of Soviet leaders in this denouement has a centrality which cannot be underestimated. These leaders, become rulers, had moved so far, up and away from the people as to be completely isolated from them in their corrupt KGB cocooned existence. They had of course ceased to play any positive role in the economy or society. At once corrupt and incompetent, oppressive and irresponsible, impossible of being called to account in any manner, they were a wasteful excrescence on the economy and essentially dysfunctional and parasitical for the society as a whole, the source only of a succession of specific economic and political, social or moral crises in Soviet society. But more to the point in the immediate context is that they had accumulated vulgarly large material privileges for themselves, through their monopoly on the exercise of political power. They lived in a world entirely separate from that of the common people, enjoying rare privileges and a luxurious lifestyle, which we have noted earlier – special salaries, special canteens, special shops, export quality vodka, large apartments in special districts, dachas in the countryside, treatment in exclusive medical clinics, the central lane in the Moscow streets to drive to work in stylish, latest-model limousines....

Here are two random quotes on the lifestyle of Soviet rulers which was now regularly passed on to their progeny so that on the one hand there were the *zolotyie dietki* ('the gilded youth'), and on the other there were the *sieryie kryssy* ('the grey mice') and each group lived in a world that would not change for generations to come. Speaking of their privileges and perks, two Soviet scholars have written of 'agency-run distribution centres, polyclinics, sanatoria and recreation facilities, houses, cafeterias and even laundries that provide high-quality services.... at favourable prices or free of charge, but do not serve the man in the street for any kind of money'....Another Soviet commentator put it more cynically, but no less truthfully: the Soviet rulers' was 'a world of privileges, starting from their birth (special maternity homes) going on all through their lives (special shops, hospitals, hair-dressers' salons, canteens, toilets and what not) and not ending even with the end of their physical existence (special cemeteries). Yes, yes, special cemeteries for the rulers of "the first working class state in the world", where workers are not supposed to be buried.'

And this is what a one-time Party boss of Moscow and candidate member of the politbureau with Gorbachev, Mr. Boris Yeltsin – who, it is significant, won popularity with the people, in the early post-Gorbachev period, by thus attacking the Party – has to say:

> Take a man who climbs his way up the party career ladder. The system gives him first one class of special privileges; then, as he rises higher, another class; and the higher he goes the more special delights are handed out to him. Soon he begins to think he is an important person. He eats what ordinary mortals only dream of, he takes his holidays in places where the hoi polloi are not even allowed to come near the surrounding fence....

The higher you climb up the professional ladder of the Communist Party of Soviet Union, the more there are comforts that surround you and the harder and more painful it is to lose them. One becomes, therefore, all the more obedient and dependable....

Obsequiousness and obedience are rewarded in turn by privilege: special hospitals; special sanatoriums; the excellent central committee canteen; the equally excellent service for home delivery of groceries and other goods; the Kremlin-line closed telephone system; the free transportation....

(The system) satisfies their every whim, including a dacha (country house) behind a high green fence encircling spacious grounds alongside the Moscow river, with a garden, tennis courts and games pitches, a bodyguard under every window and an alarm network.

Even at my level as a candidate member of the politburo, my domestic staff consisted of three cooks, three waitresses, a housemaid, and a gardener with his own team of under-gardeners....the dacha had its own cinema and every Friday, Saturday and Sunday a projectionist would arrive complete with a selection of films.

As for medical treatment, the medicines and equipment are all imported, all of them the last word in scientific research and technology. The wards in the 'Kremlin hospital' are huge suites, again surrounded by luxury: porcelain, crystal, carpets and chandeliers...

There is also a wide choice of places at which to spend one's holidays: Pitsunda and Gagra, on the Georgian coast of the Black Sea; the Crimea; the midway between Moscow and Leningrad. The senior officer of one's bodyguard was given about 4,000 roubles just for out-of-pocket expenses. In other words, there was no need to spend any money on the holiday. These summer dachas are as luxurious as the year-round residences. One is driven to the beach by car, even though the distance is no more than a couple of hundred yards....

'The Kremlin ration', a special allocation of normally unobtainable products, is paid for by the uppermost echelon in the party at half its cost price, and consists of the highest quality foods. In Moscow, a total of some 40,000 senior party members enjoy the privilege of receiving these special rations to varying degrees of quantity and quality. There are whole sections of Gum (the huge state department store which faces the Kremlin across

> Red Square) closed to the public and specially reserved for the topmost elite, while for the officials a rung or two lower down on the ladder there are other special shops and so on down the scale, all of them graded by rank. All are called 'special': special workshops, special drycleaners, special clinics, special hospitals, special houses, special service. In the Soviet Union the word 'special' has a specific meaning, of which we are all too well aware. It is applied to the excellent food products that are prepared in special kitchens and are subjected to special medical tests; to the medicines packed in several layers of wrapping-paper and guaranteed safe by the signatures of several doctors....
>
> The joke is that none of this belongs to those who enjoy these privileges. All these marvellous things – dachas, rations, a stretch of seaside fenced off from everyone else – belong to the Soviet system...

Yeltsin asks:

> Why was it thought necessary to give material expression in such an absurd degree to the fantasies of property, pleasure and megalomania harboured by the party elite?...And who pays for all this?....

The question at the end is of course only rhetorical. For Yeltsin well knew the people did. It was the politically regulated surplus extracted from the Soviet working people that paid for all this, for the vulgar high living of a dysfunctional ruling class. It needs to be added however that these 'super-rich' of the Soviet Union whose lifestyle blatantly contradicted the official doctrine, were much less wealthy than their European or trans-Atlantic counterparts. Their concerns or appetites were no less egotistical than those of their western equivalents, just as their tastes were increasingly borrowed from the capitalist world, but given that there was no private ownership of the means of production, they were unable to increase their wealth, and indulge their western tastes, beyond a certain point. It was no surprise, therefore, that when it came down to it, they found west's capitalism far more attractive than their own socialism and were quite willing, indeed happy to ditch the latter for the former.

Such were the Soviet rulers and they had come to preside over a system which had now become an anachronism. It was anachronistic in its economy where, as a result of constant shelving of problems, social relations of production had become fetters on the forces of production, an absolute obstacle to further progress and development of society. And it was anachronistic politically in its utter lack of democracy and political freedoms, its one-party dictatorship and Byzantine ways of functioning. It was a system virtually ready for history's broom.

Most conspicuous and impossible about this anachronistic system was its autocracy, at once oppressive as well as parasitic and dysfunctional. Even the critical Marxists who refused to endorse Soviet socialism can be said to have underestimated the disastrous long-term consequences of this autocracy. Involving as it did a total lack of democracy in the Soviet system, it lay behind the failure of the system to correct itself to construct an egalitarian social space where problems could be openly faced and alternative ways of building socialism could be found. Later, when the system, away from socialism, evolved into a class-exploitative society, this lack of democracy meant non-availability of any means to indicate and smoothen its contradictions, to safe channel the growing discontent and put some check at least on the rulers. But if there was no democracy to check the rulers, the absence of democracy also deprived them of such legitimacy and avenues of ideological control as even formal democracy provides to the ruling classes in advanced and several even less advanced capitalist countries. They were never a strong ruling class in the sense that capitalists in developed capitalist countries constitute a strong ruling class with cultural and ideological hegemony over the dominated classes.

The lapse or failure of Soviet socialism with regard to democracy was indeed disastrous. It was disastrously significant too that the issue in its collapse became not the real and historically important choice between socialism and capitalism but a false and deceptive choice between socialism and democracy. That is how, once the fear of Soviet intervention was gone with Gorbachev, the people in Eastern Europe, in their urge for democracy and political freedom simply swept the autocratic system away, regardless of the consequences. As a commentator put it at the time: 'In the fire and fury against autocracy, the people even forgot the early years of socialist construction, which began on the ashes and debris left by the Nazi depredators, and abolished feudalism and capitalism. The modernisation of society, the spread of literacy, the building up of a public health system, the advance of culture at the expense of superstition and ignorance, etc., accomplished in phenomenally short duration, became for them, under the jack boots of oppressors, just a fading memory of a bygone generation.'

In the Soviet Union the denouement was a case of slow entropy culminating in a surprisingly rapid disintegration of the system. The system had continually proclaimed itself to be socialist, with a 'working class based' Communist Party in power. But the popular classes had long ceased to recognise themselves in Party's power and the Party itself was now a 'corpse that had been rotting for a long time'. Its long, often arbitrary exercise of power, use of repression and clientelism to secure people's political passivity, have had devastating enervating and depoliticising consequences so far as the popular masses were concerned. This together with the widely known personal corruption and the all-too-visible vulgarly luxurious and extravagant lifestyle of the leadership had left the people totally alienated from the system and the powers that be. Decades of indoctrination that the regime they were living under was socialist had only led to a loss of faith in socialism or any such ideals, leaving behind a tremendous ideological-cum-moral vacuum. But society, like nature, abhors a vacuum and, as soon revealed by Gorbachev's *glasnost,* it was now getting filled up with all sorts of ideological currents hostile to socialism – from bourgeois liberalism to religious fundamentalism, racist chauvinism, monarchism and outright fascism. It is not surprising, therefore, that when the system plunged into its deepest crisis ever, despite the advantage of over seventy years of monopoly on education, the media, etc. the party in power could not find a significant section of the class they claimed to represent (or for that matter, even a majority of its own membership) to defend it or its version of socialism. When the party finally lost power and was banned, the only thing remarkable about more than 18 million-strong Soviet Communist Party was their utterly impotent passivity; and when the entire system itself crumbled, none from among the apathetic masses was disposed to risk life or limb to save it. What is more, so pervasive was people's depoliticisation in the Soviet Union, or 'deideologisation' which Gorbachev professed, that like the intelligentsia, the popular masses too believed that what had been justifiably overthrown was socialism, and by this fact also accepted that capitalism was better. And as Gorbachev made way for his natural heir, they confirmed this acceptance by endorsing Yeltsin's usurpation of power and themselves bringing him to power a year later. It is another matter that the Soviet people, then, did not understand what they were really opting for.

Let me conclude this dismal story with one of the oldest and most beloved of Russian political jokes, passed down and updated from generation to generation, which soon made its reappearance in Moscow:

It asks how each leader since Lenin would solve the following problem: The train of state has come to the end of the tracks, far short of its destination. What order must be given to get it on its way again?

LENIN: Go out and organise the peasants, infuse them with revolutionary spirit and they will build tracks enough to carry us forward.

STALIN: Round up the peasants, shoot a few of them as an example, and they'll provide what is necessary.

KHRUSHCHEV: Pull up the tracks from behind the train, lay them out in front, and we'll continue our journey.

BREZHNEV: Close the curtains in the carriages, everybody rock back and forth, and no one will realise we're not moving.

GORBACHEV: We need glasnost! Run and tell the people that there are no tracks ahead of us.

YELTSIN: No more communist train rides! Fetch my horse and carriage....

10

The Gorbachev Years

It was typical of the repressive and depoliticised character of the Soviet system that the initiative for reform invariably came from the top, from the ruling elite and never from below, from the people who were the prime victims of the gross deformations of the system; therefore, it was also always a turn to the right and never to the left. And so it was with Gorbachev as he came to power in 1985 and faced what was the ultimate crisis in the brief history of the Soviet Union, where growth having fallen to 'a level close to economic stagnation' (as Gorbachev himself noted and his adviser Abel Aganbegyan concurred), the economy was unable to bear the burdens of Cold War abroad and Brezhnevian compromise with the working class at home; and this stagnation was accompanied by stratification and consolidation of privileges in society, crystallisation (though unacknowledged) of a ruling class increasingly aware of its interests, cleavages within the ruling party between the *apparatchiks* and the technical-managerial elite, 'the faithful and the doers', and a discontented population including an ambitious intelligentsia with no scope for further social advancement. The stage was set for a crisis which threatened the very existence of the system.

A privileged product of the system, indeed one of its important beneficiaries, with an *apparatchik* career of 30 years behind him, Gorbachev was moulded in the essentially conservative tradition of the *nomenklatura* and was not quite known for intellectual originality, or belief in and commitment to the vision of a new social order. And as an *apparatchik,* he had little experience in dealing with practical problems either in industry or agriculture. With the bureaucratic degeneration of the Soviet Communist Party under Stalin when anyone who might constitute the slightest threat to Stalin was removed and abject conformism and sycophancy had become the decisive considerations, selection of party leaders had gone so awry that, as Roy Medvedev has put it, 'instead of the best from the good, we got the worst from the bad'. Obviously no one could hope to climb to his position of bureaucratic pre-eminence without giving the necessary hostages to fortune, that is, 'dirtying' his hands in manoeuvres which were far from being principled or humanely sensitive. Only the poorer, mediocre stuff survived and surfaced for leadership purposes. It is thus that Khrushchev and Brezhnev, and now Gorbachev, along with Yeltsin, rose to top positions in the party hierarchy.

A product of the old *nomenklatura,* who had done his stint as a boss in the KGB, Gorbachev was at the same time a 'mutant' bred by the crisis of neo-Stalinist Soviet system. Narrowly elected as General Secretary of the Soviet Communist Party in 1985, he came to power as leader of a growing reform faction of the Soviet ruling class. His selection over more conservative rivals was a response to the deepening crisis of the system, showing an awareness within the top leadership that a radical reform of the system had become necessary. Counter-elites outside the *nomenklatura* too were pressing for reforms even as they were trying to break into the system's power structure which, with political inbreeding, increasing reproduction of power-holders across generations, its cooptative mechanisms and inherited rigidities of the Brezhnev era, had become ever more closed. The reforming elite within the *nomenklatura,* the new generation of 'energetic technocrats' brought to the centre of power by Gorbachev, had initially hoped and sought to turn a deteriorating economic situation with conventional remedies and rather timid reforms. But the effort proved futile, forcing Gorbachev to look for more radical reforms. This was his programme of *perestroika* and *glasnost,* wherein he saw himself burdened with a mission to reform the world as well. His book on the subject was titled *Perestroika: New Thinking for Our Country and the World* (1987).

Gorbachev had approved of the sacking of Khrushchev at the time (though he claimed that 'his view underwent considerable transformations' later on), and admired Stalin for 'safeguarding Leninism in an ideological struggle', even as he spoke of 'serious deformations' in Soviet society which 'made possible the omnipotence of Stalin and his entourage and the wave of repressive measures and lawlessness'. A reforming, even a 'visionary' bureaucrat – 'visionary' is the word his admirers were most fond of in describing him – he was a bureaucrat nonetheless and not, despite his self-image, a socialist in any meaningful sense of the word. That he believed the Soviet Union and therefore himself to be socialist is at the moment beside the point. His reformist initiative was not the free act or choice of an inspired leader but was compelled on the one hand by the crisis of the system he was presiding over – though he never realised its full gravity – and on the other by the needs of the ruling stratum he represented and wanted to save and strengthen. He never attempted any kind of critical systematic analysis of the past and present of this system, least of all a Marxist one; though, as first Secretary of the Party and Soviet President he claimed adherence to 'science of Marxism-Leninism' till he pronounced its 'strategic defeat' after he was thrown out of power. He had no understanding at all of the deeper structural causes of the problems plaguing the Soviet society. It has been said that 'he had just enough intelligence to change everything but not enough to see that everything would be destroyed'. More specifically, he spoke of 'renewal of socialism' in the Soviet Union, but simply lacked the theoretical equipment for the task. On the contrary, he was as good an example as any of the degeneration of Marxism among the leadership of the erstwhile Communist Party of the Soviet Union. In fact the entire spectrum of Soviet leaders in the late 1980s, all of whom came into prominence in the Brezhnev era, did not have the mental baggage to tide over the crisis and bring about socialist renewal in the Soviet Union.

There is no doubt that Gorbachev sincerely saw himself as a socialist. But we cannot take such professions at face value. He was socialist only in the sense that he believed that what had been built in the Soviet Union was socialism and saw himself as its defender. That is how Khrushchev, Brezhnev and the rest too were socialists. In traditional deference to this belief, like them, he too indulged in the conventional rhetoric. Gorbachev invoked 'October 1917', and spoke of 'socialism as a young social system', its 'great triumphs and accomplishments' and 'vast possibilities' for the future. In seeking reforms, he insisted: 'We are looking within socialism, rather than outside it, for the answers to all the questions that arise'. It was to be 'no restoration of capitalism', but a 'renewal of socialism', 'the real transformation of working people into the masters of all social production', indeed 'a return to Lenin' and 'Leninist style of work', etc., etc. All this could be seen as an expression of Gorbachev's honest commitment, but it could as well be recognised as meaningless rhetoric, a practice common with the Soviet leaders over the years. Gorbachev sought elimination of 'deformations' in the system but refused to recognise any 'crisis for socialism' in the 'difficulties and problems of the 70s and 80s', and was content with vague advocacy of 'more democracy and more socialism', that never went beyond *glasnost* and more specific economic-technocratic reforms in 'the methods and forms of social management' that characterised early *perestroika*. He spoke of assessing 'our successes and errors alike by socialist standards' but never spelt out what these standards were beyond loose references to 'a humane democratic socialism'. Gorbachev asked the CC of CPSU to give up 'the old dogmas', 'ideological blinkers' or 'obsolete views on the world revolutionary process', but carefully avoided mentioning which specific dogmas, blinkers, or views he was rejecting, and never acknowledged, while in power, that he had abandoned Marxism as he went on to offer his partymen the vacuous moralism of his 'new thinking'. Invoking Lenin in defence of whatever he was doing, was soon reduced to falling back on Lenin's thinking and experiments after the War Communism phase, inevitably concentrating on

NEP but making no mention of Lenin's repeated reference to NEP, in 1921 and 1922, as a planned 'retreat' to be followed by a 'bigger leap forward'.

But as the crisis deepened references to 'socialism' or 'Lenin' simply disappeared from Gorbachev's vocabulary. And if he must perforce yet speak of 'socialist choice' – he used this term for about eight months before finally dropping it too – such words were emptied of all meaning. Towards the end he was not averse to even dropping the word 'socialist' from the name of the country he was still presiding over. And when it was all over, he readily accepted the failure of socialism and announced the 'strategic defeat' of 'Marxism-Leninism'. Henceforth he was content to be only 'a confirmed supporter of the *idea* of socialism', an idea 'making a way for itself for many centuries', 'associated with Christianity and other philosophical tendencies' and 'many social and political movements', 'precisely an idea, which embraces values developed in the course of a search for a juster society and a better world'.

II

In the name of abandoning 'old dogmas' and 'obsolete views', Gorbachev had moved away from Marxism and any notion of scientific, that is, historically grounded socialism, indeed from any coherent understanding of either socialism or capitalism he may have had, and done so long before his final pronouncements. This was the essential meaning of the 'new thinking' he propounded in his book *Perestroika,* without abandoning, however, the conventional 'socialist' rhetoric of a Soviet party leader. Gorbachev's 'new thinking' was social theory degenerating into plain moralism. In a departure from whatever Marxism he ever knew of – though as First Secretary and Soviet President his adherence to 'the science of Marxism-Leninism' still remained intact – Gorbachev proclaimed the 'supremacy of universal human values over class values', and therefore the 'supremacy of a general human approach' as against 'the class approach' as he described it. While 'from the standpoint of basic Marxism', as Lenin put it, 'the interests of social development are higher than the interests of the proletariat', translated into historical terms, it saw the two as consonant for our times. But postulating a false contradiction between the two Gorbachev saw 'working class interests' as apart from 'those of humanity as a whole' and hence 'the conclusion that common human values have a priority in our age, this being the core of the new political thinking'. Even the residue of the language of class or class struggle disappeared from Gorbachev's moral discourse and there was no awareness that 'universal human values' could not be simply assumed in societies of destructive class and social antagonisms; they had to be first created through overcoming such antagonisms as visualised by the classical socialist project. There was no awareness either that moral rhetorics of 'universalism' easily conceal particular interests of exploiting classes, of bureaucratic, national, imperial or corporate elites. There was only the grotesque belief that values can be plucked out of thin air without any reference to their social basis, or to history. Gorbachev proclaimed that 'it is essential to rise above ideological differences' but refused to inquire into the conditions which alone could make this possible. Despite the author's disclaimer – 'in real politics there can be no wishful thinking' – Perestroika was a long wish-list of moral and political values – of course wrapped up in the customary party rhetoric of the First Secretary – without any attempt at showing how the desired moral and political objectives could be translated into reality. Perestroika was really an exercise in superimposing materially unfounded but wishfully declared values on the socio-historical reality of a Soviet Union in crisis, whose painfully evident contradictions, the projected values were supposed to resolve through the persuasive power of their self-evident rightness, as decreed by 'the new thinking'.

A most important aspect of Marxism is its rejection of utopianism in politics. Criticism of utopian thinking by Marx and Engels, regarding socialism or elsewhere, is common knowledge. In a general way Marxism enjoys a theoretical advantage in that its analysis or understanding of society and therefore its politics is a structural and a non-moralising one. In Marxism of Karl Marx, moral passion as part of revolutionary ethics is of course central to revolutionary politics, but by itself it generates only a most ephemeral kind of politics which is quickly reabsorbed and recontained by the system it seeks to question and transform. In fact, as historical experience reveals, a moralising politics tends to develop where a structural cognition and mapping of society is blocked. Or, as a scholar has well put it: 'voluntaristic wishful thinking – often wedded to a direct appeal to the authority of claimed moral imperatives – tends to predominate in politics precisely at times when the advocated political objectives are poorly grounded, due to the inherent weakness of those who promote them. Direct appeal to morality in such political discourse is used as an imaginary substitute for identifiable material and political forces which would secure the realisation of the desired objectives.' This obviously makes such political discourse, and politics based on it, extremely problematic. But it was not so problematic after all with Gorbachev. His dispensation, while discarding Marxism, had simply failed to project a different, new world view of its own. On the contrary, Gorbachev's 'new thinking' with its ethical rigmarole, 'a smorgasbord of pious hopes, high-minded platitudes and hollow slogans' as it has been described, was a capitulation to some very old thinking in the capitalist west. It was an ideological retreat presaging the economic and political retreat which immediately followed, culminating in complete surrender to the military might, technological prowess, economic clout, moral self-righteousness and cultural arrogance of western capitalism. Of course in an altogether different context, recognising that 'there is a morality of politics', Sartre had once said: 'and when politics must betray morality, to choose morality is to betray politics. Particularly where politics has taken as its goal bringing about the reign of the human.' Though no betrayal of morality was demanded in this case, Gorbachev's was a betrayal of emancipatory politics in the name of morality – insofar as he was at all sincere about either. For whatever their original intentions which helped to pave the way to Dante's hell, Gorbachev and his advisers ended up opting for the realm of capitalist oppression instead of 'bringing about the reign of the human'.

III

The three post-Stalin decades were not devoid of attempts to reform the Soviet system through 'marketisation' and 'scientific management'. There was thus nothing new in Gorbachevian reforms. They were indeed presaged by the attempts of the Khrushchev period. Gorbachev of course spoke of 'structural' change but, like the previous attempts, it was 'restructuring' without changing the structure itself, which was now the contradiction-ridden structure of a class-divided exploitative society. There was however a fundamental difference between the path followed by Gorbachev and his team and the earlier reform attempts. Gorbachev specifically rejected 'the half-hearted measures' of the past and decided to take 'the boldest steps' as he called them. In other words, he was prepared to go 'all the way' in pursuit of reforms whose general line, contradictory formulations and fluctuations on the way notwithstanding, was the shift to a market economy copied from the West. His talk of 'the human factor' and 'universal values' had nothing, even secretly, socialist about it and contrasted with his open declaration, 'there are no alternatives to the market', even as his advisers and 'Ideology Chiefs' went eloquent over virtues of the market, 'one of the greatest achievements of civilisation', and of the 'disciplined pursuit of profit', and even recognised in the United States a society which had achieved the 'first stage of communism', etc., etc. If, at home, it was still a market-oriented reform of the ossified 'socialist' system, abroad, the right even more than the left sensed the unmistakably *capitalist* thrust of Gorbachev's reform programme. His 'there are no alternatives to the market', along with the assurance: 'We are unanimous in our belief that perestroika is indispensable and indeed inevitable and that we have no other option', was very much in sync with Margaret Thatcher's 'there is no alternative' declarations about capitalism. The West went overboard promoting 'Gorbi mania'. Speaking for the capitalist West Thatcher said: 'we can do business with Mr. Gorbachev'. Gorbachev, on his part, was not only happy to do business with Margaret Thatcher or the capitalist West, but, unlike his predecessors in the past, was willing to do so on *their* terms and go 'all the way'.

IV

That this was indeed so soon became clear, first of all in the field of foreign affairs where Gorbachev was immediately most active (and remained enjoyfully most active throughout). Though, characteristically enough, Gorbachev had, in *Perestroika,* promised to 'ensure the Soviet Union's position as a superpower', he was pragmatic enough to realise that Soviet Union had lost the cold war, and rightly decided to call it off, end the arms race and cut down on costly commitments abroad, which included the dropping of the Brezhnev doctrine prohibiting the East European regimes from altering the prevailing social order under threat of Soviet armed intervention. But what should have been a planned retreat, thanks to Gorbachev's 'new thinking', turned into an abject surrender to western imperialism all along the line, beginning dramatically with the collapse in Eastern Europe and the consequent shift to capitalism there. Gorbachev had no policy on East Europe, unless absolute ideological and political non-intervention and the pious hopes of a moralist for self-reform there similar to what he took to be 'socialist renewal' at home, can be regarded as any kind of policy. It is noteworthy that as, with the withdrawal of Soviet support, one satellite regime after another fell in East Europe and one country after another took the road from 'socialism' to capitalism, Gorbachev maintained a deafening silence over these developments. He had no views, no analysis, no theoretical perspective of any sort to offer, not a hint about their possible implications for his own programme of reforms in the Soviet Union, which in a couple of years was to arrive at the same destination by a somewhat different Gorbachevian route. Smug in his failure to see anything beyond the passing of 'a variation of Stalin's authoritarian bureaucratic system, which we have ourselves discarded', Gorbachev was simply blind to the reality of class struggle in East Europe as, using its superior strength and in the name of 'democracy', western capitalism went on to force open the societies at least partially closed to it for forty odd years and bring them back into a capitalist Europe. This, incidentally, was one of the main purposes of the post-war Marshall Plan as originally proposed. The Soviet leadership then had understood the implications and rejected it.

Preceding, accompanying and following the collapse in East Europe, where he continued to yield further to the west, Gorbachev's international politics was an unabashed acceptance of *Pax Americana*, the western capitalist world domination, through all manner of compromises, unilateral concessions or straight compliance with American demands – on Afghanistan, Southern Africa, Central America, human rights, arms control, the INF treaty, Star Wars, right to the end on the Gulf War – always on unequal terms and without deriving even the benefits of normal realpolitik-based transactions. Instead, as peace emanated from Moscow, bellicose sounds echoed from Washington and in line with its past history, the United States went on to invade nations helpless to defend themselves (Grenada, Libya, Panama), engage in low intensity wars with those that offered some resistance (Nicaragua, Afghanistan, Angola), parade client regimes in Latin America and parts of Asia as democracies (which were really military terrorism underneath civilian government), or impose conditions for whatever aid or support for his reforms Gorbachev sought from the west, such as a clear move 'to embrace a real market economy', stop repressing the 'independence-minded' Baltic States, cut military spending and end aid to 'regimes that pursue internal repression' (the reference is to Cuba), etc., etc. As the US gave short shrift to any peacefulness or equity in its conduct of international affairs, Gorbachev virtually collaborated with it in the name of his newly discovered 'deideologised' internationalism. (President Bush [the senior Bush], giving much of the credit for the Sandinistas' defeat in Nicaragua to Mikhail Gorbachev, even went on record to tell the world that it was Gorbachev who twisted Daniel Ortega's arm to get him to fall in line with the American policy). All this was hailed by Gorbachev's admirers as the triumph of 'pragmatic approach' over the 'ideological approach', where 'not egotistic, but increasingly altruistic interests' had prevailed. As his eventually ill-fated foreign minister, Alexander A. Bessmertnykh said at the time: 'the essence of the new thinking (in international diplomacy) is to bring to the foreground not egotistic, but increasingly altruistic interests. Altruism ceases to be an attribute of the romantic school of diplomacy. It has suddenly become an element of modern thinking.'

As the victors of the Cold War behaved like victors – and why not?, pressurised Gorbachev economically and politically to give more concessions and sought to subjugate and humiliate him in various ways, in the process turning him from a 'statesman' he had been built up as and come to believe himself to be, into a suppliant to the west, Gorbachev was happy indulging in his 'modern thinking', in 'superpower diplomacy' and 'trumperies of summits abroad', where 'he had nothing to show and received nothing', except the honour of the invitations, and the spurious epithet of 'statesman'. He literally gave away everything, thereby losing both contact and credibility with the people at home. Yet, all this while, Gorbachev continued to declare his faith in the west and kept talking of 'our European homeland', the 'highway of world civilisation' which leads to the 'common European home', 'the joint solution of global problems,' 'making international relations more humane' by 'rising above ideological differences', etc., etc. There was no realisation at all that all such 'de-ideologisation' which he recommended was one-sided, only an unilateral ideological disarmament of the forces of socialism, of all those struggling against imperialism and capitalist domination of the world.

Gorbachev talked of the 'common European home', lamented Soviet Union's isolation from 'the mainstream of world civilisation' and wished for a 'return to the mainstream of world culture'. The utter parochialism here is obvious. Gorbachev had no awareness that such a view of 'mainstream' only idealised the European civilisation and culture, which is *today* more than anything else a *capitalist* civilisation and culture, and that a refusal to see Europe as a part of a more just and humane world meant a plea for turning one's back on the majority of humankind. Gorbachev identified with its 'concepts of freedom and the individual' and wrote of 'a deep, profoundly intelligent and inherently humane culture'. In its onesidedness, this view was sheer ignorance and humbug. It completely overlooked an inherent dimension of European culture and civilisation manifested in its multiple oppressions, wars, inquisitions, imperialist plunder, fascism, holocausts, etc., all a necessary product of its original and continuing class basis. There is a vital truth in Walter Benjamin's statement which is as applicable to European civilisation as any other so far: 'There is no document of civilisation which is not at the same time a document of barbarism'.

Gorbachev wished for 'a new type of world order' and appealed to the west for 'co-development, co-creativity and co-operation that are imperative in our times'. The naiveté underlying this appeal is truly unbelievable. Gorbachev simply refused to see that it is 'in our times', precisely in the early 1980s, that the west, in its continuing counter-revolutionary war against the Soviet Union since 1917, launched a major new offensive – 'Reagan doctrine', nuclear programme and 'Star Wars' project, third world interventions, economic and military pressure on pro-Soviet regimes, etc. – to weaken, paralyse and destroy the Soviet Union. And thanks to Gorbachev's 'new thinking', this offensive finally succeeded in destroying the Soviet Union.

Gorbachev wrote: 'The new political thinking has enabled us to appreciate more fully how vitally important to contemporary international relations are the moral values that have over the centuries been evolved by nations, and generalised and spelt out by humanity's great minds'. Having thus persuaded himself – another of 'humanity's great minds' – Gorbachev hoped for 'demilitarisation and humanisation of international relations with reason, knowledge and moral principles, rather than selfish ambition and prejudices' and claimed that Clauswitz and power politics 'now belong to the libraries', because 'for the first time in history, basing international politics on moral and ethical norms that are common to all humankind, as well as humanising interstate relations, has become a vital requirement'. But while Gorbachev kept repeating his moral sermons about priority of 'moral and ethical norms that are common to all humankind', about 'humanising interstate relations', his adversaries, or shall we say partners in 'the joint solution of global problems', asserted – in the Gulf and elsewhere – with the most brutal and open aggressiveness, their continued adherence to power politics and Clauswitz's well-tried principles.

Full of admiration for the high-tech economy and culture of the advanced countries of the west, Gorbachev argued for integration of the Soviet economy into the global capitalist network of trade and finance. As he reported at the 28th Congress of the Communist Party of the Soviet Union (1990): 'The incorporation of our national economy in the world economy is necessary not only for the modernisation of our own economy, but also for the joint construction with other peoples of the material foundation of an irreversibly peaceful period of history and for the resolution of the global problems of humanity.' Gorbachev had forgotten, if he ever knew, the time-honoured tenet of Marxist thought that a weak economy integrating into the advanced capitalist world economy does so on the latter's terms and cannot but acquire, often in a debased form, the values and institutions of the latter, and that a country with a weak economy which wants to maintain its independence and the possibility of charting its own course needs, not to integrate with but to protect itself against being overwhelmed and economically subjugated by the stronger capitalist countries. Gorbachev was blissfully unaware that in his willingness to incorporate the relatively weak Soviet Union into the capitalist world economy, he was opting for an adjustment of Soviet institutions and policies to the needs and preferences of its stronger partners, opening the road not to 'highways of world civilisation' but, more likely, to 'third-worldisation' of the Soviet Union, leading not to the 'common European home' but, more likely, to being left stranded like a poor relative on the steps outside.

It is hard to credit that Gorbachev and the powers that be in the Soviet Union could really believe in the pious nonsense dished out by 'new thinking' on international politics. But judging by their actions, they had certainly learnt to deceive themselves more effectively than they were able to pull the wool over the eyes of the public at home or abroad. It was a truly pathetic achievement.

V

It is significant, but not surprising, that while Gorbachev spoke of building what he somewhat picturesquely called a 'common home' based on 'principles common to humanity in the modern world', and equally picturesquely insisted that 'we are all passengers aboard one ship, the Earth, and we must not allow it to be wrecked', for 'there will be no second Noah's Ark', in his entire book, *Perestroika*, the word 'imperialism' did not find a single mention. On the contrary there is easy acceptance, even justification, of colonial and neo-colonial exploitation by the capitalist west, perhaps with the hope of soon sharing in it. Gorbachev wrote: 'I have explained on many occasions that we do not pursue goals inimical to Western interests. We know how important the Middle East, Asia, Latin America, other Third World regions and also South Africa are for American and West European economies, in particular as raw material sources. To cut these links is the last thing we want to do, and we have no desire to provoke ruptures in historically formed economic ties.' And this when the reality of imperialism, of the use of economic, political and military coercion to sustain a system of unequal interdependence among countries is so palpable the world over, and a severance of the 'historically formed economic ties', is an imperative precondition for any kind of pro-people economic development in the countries of the third world!

To Gorbachev, yearning for the 'common European home', the 'gains' from supporting liberation movements or struggles in the third world did not justify the 'costs' to the Soviet Union in terms of military and economic advantages; more was to be gained from a 'global historic compromise' with imperialism, for which purpose he was willing to make serious concessions in withdrawing such Soviet support from ongoing struggles and even overlooking American interventions against such struggles. The United States of course wanted its pound of flesh and demanded that the Soviet Union abandon revolutionary causes and struggles in the Third World (in Cuba, Nicaragua, El Salvador and elsewhere in Africa and Asia). Gorbachev, for reasons of both his 'new thinking' and western economic support was most willing to acquiesce in this demand, that is, explicitly repudiate any notion of class struggle in international relations. His crony and colleague in the Politbureau, Yakovlev, in fact said as much. The third world was told to come to terms with imperialism, and the Soviet Union shifted away even from the pseudo-Marxism of the 'non-capitalist path' etc. in the third world. And armed struggle was now, of course, only a historical relic.

Whatever be the ambiguities of his motivation, Gorbachev's theory and practice left the revolutionary socialist movements and regimes in the third world bereft of all Soviet support in the face of repression and counter-revolution – however ambiguous or self-serving this support itself may have been in the past. By sowing illusions about the potentially 'peaceful' nature of imperialism, by suggesting the possibility of resolving the major contradictions of our epoch not by class struggle but by class collaboration, by uncritically singing the praises of the market, Gorbachev's 'new thinking' and his collaborators brought grist to the mill of the international social democracy and even more to the free enterprise offensive of the international bourgeoisie. It was a surrender to the rules of the game of international capitalism.

A surrender to imperialism, no doubt, this turn in Soviet foreign policy dictated by 'new thinking' could also be viewed as a continuation by the new rulers of the old Stalinist policy of pursuit of perceived Soviet national interests (and not socialist internationalist interests) – of course in a different key; the old confrontation or rivalry was to be now replaced by the reciprocity of a non-ideological 'supra-system coalition' among states where, as Gorbachev put it, 'ideological differences should not be transferred to the sphere of interstate relations, nor should foreign policy be subordinated to them'! As a result the Soviet Union abandoned Cuba and backed away from its support, often erratic and cynical, for national liberation in the Third

World, notably in Nicaragua and South Africa, acquiesced to US pressure for withdrawal of Vietnam from Cambodia, was understanding and considerate towards the US military action against Iraq, and showed willingness for Soviet-Western cooperation – *a'la* James Bond! – in a 'struggle against international terrorism' which, for the west, always included 'intellectual communism'.

VI

A cover for surrender to imperialism abroad, Gorbachev's 'new thinking' became a cover for undermining and dismantling of the Soviet institutions at home, paving the way to capitalism, of whatever sort, in the Soviet Union. Gorbachev's reform programme, expressed above all in *perestroika and glasnost*, was indeed aimed at saving the system, even 'renewal of socialism' as he understood it. But it was based on no serious analysis of what had gone wrong under the long reign of Stalinism and neo-Stalinism in Soviet society. 'New thinking' was deemed an adequate substitute for such analysis, and the utter vacuity of its 'universal human approach' and the accompanying moralist discourse soon brought with it the absurd conclusion that the capitalistic market is the 'guarantee of the renewal of socialism', as Vadim Medvedev, Gorbachev's last 'Ideology Chief' (as he was officially called) put it.

The 'ideology of perestroika' involved abandonment of class analysis for what Gorbachev described as 'universal human approach'. As a Moscow city Party official, Yuri Prokofiev put it: 'It is not correct to give preference to any class or stratum of society. Human values come first'. Assumption obviously was that the Soviet state policy, with its official lawlessness and violation of human rights, was an expression of 'class values' or interests of the working class – when in reality it only expressed the values and interests of the Soviet rulers, the *nomenklatura* whom Gorbachev represented. But this 'theoretical' shift provided the Archimedean point for the ideological abandonment of working class values and 'class approach', of scientific socialist understanding and class struggle, and the consequent adoption, in the name of 'human values' and 'the universal human approach', of self-describedly bourgeois approach and values. Most significant implication of this shift, one decisive for the future, was soon visible in the voluble expression of faith in the 'magic of the market place'. Indeed, some of Gorbachev's economic advisers, who now 'discovered America', were so dazzled by the market as to perceive only its virtues and not its vices, missing the structural link between the two, just as they were otherwise missing the problems that will face the relatively weak Soviet economy when it integrates into the world capitalist economy. There was endless idealisation of the latter-day capitalism and virtues of the market which had more to do with bourgeois ideology, ancient or more recent, than with any reality anywhere at any time.

Gorbachev, ignorant of socialism, for this very reason, now betrayed an equal ignorance of capitalism; for him image was indeed the only reality. Gorbachev wrote of capitalism having absorbed 'many of the elements of socialist experience', and hopefully sympathetic to cooperation and convergence of the two systems, waxed loud about 'the advantages of the market economy (which) have been proven on a world scale' – 'the whole world experience proved the vitality and efficiency of the market economy'. And his co-thinkers, Vadim Medvedev and others, disregarding all historical evidence to the contrary, were soon eloquent about the capitalist commodity-money relations and the market being the instrumental embodiment of universal human values. Of course Gorbachev disclaimed making common cause 'with those who want to push the country back to capitalism'. But when the opponents of the Shatalin plan for rapid marketisation – 'Programme of Five Hundred Days' – termed it 'a deal with the devil' leading to 'the transition to capitalism', Gorbachev saw it as ushering in a 'planned market economy' and 'democratic humane socialism'. Gorbachev was simply unaware of the elementary Marxist proposition that whoever acts to strengthen the market, instead of struggling against the market, is, regardless of intentions, promoting capitalism and not socialism.

Gorbachev in fact came to evince a child-like faith in the cure-all properties of an ad hoc mixture of moral values and free market medicine. He did not know that there is no 'market without thorns', that there is a structural logic to market economy, a logic of unbridled individualism, selfishness and greed that generates wealth and affluence at one end and poverty and misery at the other, both at home and abroad, that it is an instrument whereby the rich and the powerful impose on whole societies a set of values and 'rules of the game' which reinforce inequality and injustice and dismantle all capacity for social solidarity. Laying bare the world market's interconnection between plenty at the centre and oppression, exploitation and misery in the periphery has been one of the more fundamental contributions of Marxist thought and economic writing in the recent decades. Gorbachev had no idea either of how the average standard of living in the affluent west, to which the East European or Soviet citizen aspired, is based on the market-propelled rape of a very large part of the world's resources, or that opting for a market economy Soviet Union could end up in a third world situation, instead of the western consumers' paradise that its modern citizens seemed to be dreaming about. He had no awareness at all that mass unemployment, poverty, and a withering social security system could well come to characterise a Soviet Union going for 'the market' so late in the day and getting integrated into the world market, the global economy of late-capitalism.

As Gorbachev's reform programme – *perestroika and glasnost* – progressed, they steadily revealed their disintegrative, anti-socialist character, opening the road to capitalism in the Soviet Union. May be, this is not what Gorbachev had said or intended. But it was Marx who had insisted that we must judge people or tendencies not by their intentions, but by their acts and the consequence of their acts. Gorbachev's 'new thinking' certainly served to promote the capitalist outcome of his reforms. The 'de-ideologisation' he opted for was only an unilateral ideological disarmament before the capitalist offensive. The abandonment of 'class values' for 'universal human values' only helped the bourgeois values to parade as universal values. Contrary to Gorbachev, class struggle had not become *passé*. What he was participating in, and we witnessed, was very much a class conflict with class victories for one side and the class values of one side triumphant. There was no convergence, systemic or otherwise, to some higher plane of purely or essentially universal values or interests. Only the universalising dynamic of one system, capitalism, progressively defeating and replacing another system, putting an end finally to what was still left of history's first great experiment in socialism.

VII

In responding to the crisis of the system, Gorbachev had, rhetoric apart, chosen the option the Soviet rulers always had, namely, a reform of the system to save it as it was. There was never any question of reforming it in a socialist direction, of 'restoring' socialism in the Soviet Union. All sort of clichéd repetition of socialist principles was there but the so-called 'renewal of socialism' had a meaning, if any, only in the sense that the established system was believed to be socialism, albeit with some unfortunate 'departures' and 'distortions'. Gorbachev had no vision stretching beyond a more efficient and productive economy and a democratised version of the *nomenklatura* rule. His six and a half years in power establish this beyond any doubt or ambiguity. The restoration or institution of producers' power in the economy, or the abolition of the power and privileges of the *nomenklatura* never became the issues in his reforms. The basic issue was rather to modernise and liberalise the system he had inherited from Brezhnev, Andropov and Chernenko, and thus save it. It is another matter that the forces released by his reforms, *perestroika*, and even more *glasnost* – launched with a boastful warning to enemies abroad to 'not rush to toss us on the "ash-heap of history"' – ultimately destroyed the system and country called the Soviet Union that Gorbachev was presiding over. No parallel is intended, but this puts one in mind of what Alexis de Tocqueville wrote way back in 18th-century France on the subject of reforming an oppressive regime:

> For it is not always when things are going from bad to worse that revolutions break out. On the contrary, it oftener happens that when a people which has put up with an oppressive rule over a long period without protest suddenly finds the government

> relaxing its pressure, it takes up arms against it.... and experience teaches us that, generally speaking, the most perilous moment for a bad government is one when it seeks to mend its ways. Only consummate statecraft can enable a king to save his throne when after a long period of oppressive rule he sets to improve the lot of his subjects. Patiently endured so long as it seemed beyond redress, a grievance comes to appear intolerable once the possibility of removing it crosses men's minds. For the mere fact that certain abuses have been remedied draws attention to the others and they now appear more galling; people may suffer less, but their sensibility is exacerbated.

Gorbachev failed to save his system or the Soviet Union itself from destruction. He simply lacked the 'consummate statecraft' the situation demanded. On the contrary, one can have some measure of the man, of the quality of his mind and morals, if one notes that when it was all over for the Soviet Union and it found itself on the 'ash-heap of history', Gorbachev claimed this 'destruction' as *his* achievement and went around the world proclaiming 'I am at peace with myself'!

VIII

Let us go back to take a closer look at what happened for it remains of much theoretical interest and relevant to what has been happening in the former Soviet Union since then.

Far and away from any Marxism, Gorbachev's reformist programme was, if anything, an exercise in conventional *empiricism*, often truly 'barefoot' in its concern with only *appearance* and not the reality of things; and this remained a characteristic feature of his theory and practice throughout. That Gorbachev had no larger vision or conscious plan, or any realisation of the gravity of the situation, can be gauged from his reforms immediately after assumption of power, such as campaigns against alcoholism – which earned him the sobriquet 'Mr. Mineral Water' – and smoking, or against unearned incomes, corruption and speculation, legislation on cooperatives and the independence of enterprises with ambiguous provisions for workers' self-management (the 1987 Law on Cooperation, the Law on Individual Labour Activity, etc.), technical or managerial changes to improve the administrative system in agriculture or the quality of Soviet-made goods (setting up unwieldy new state structures like Agropromsoyuz, Agroprom of the Russian Federation, 'State Committee for the Control of the Quality of Production', 'Gospriyomka', etc. which collapsed or were abolished subsequently), seeking better production through a system of 'mixed enterprises' with international corporations or better economic management through, in the words of one of his chief aides, Abel Aganbegyan, 'economic levers such as market forces, financial credits and other stronger economic stimuli', or through another of his chief aides Shatalin's 'Programme of Five Hundred Days', the period in which to make the transition to the market, etc., etc. All these efforts at 'reform' were poorly thought through and worse implemented and therefore counter-productive, undermining peoples' confidence in Gorbachev and reform of the system.

The inadequacy or failure of these early efforts was soon only too evident. But compelled to undertake more radical or effective reforms, which he believed to be 'structural', Gorbachev had yet no idea that the system was not only at a dead end but had entered a period of decline which was reversible, if at all, only by reforms that were genuinely structural, that is, reaching deep into its economic and political foundations. This was beyond Gorbachev's understanding, and guts as well.

Gorbachev conceded: 'An unbiased and honest approach led us to the only logical conclusion that the country was verging on crisis'. But there was no deep-going analysis, Marxist or any other, no honest and comprehensive assessment of the system, its past and present, which alone could have suggested the reforms necessary for its future. There was talk of 'socialism' and 'renewal of socialism' but not a hint of recognition that the struggle for socialism in the Soviet Union was lost long before with the emergence and consolidation of a class system, that what was built was not socialism as it should be or might have been but, at best, a socialism as it actually emerged, deeply deformed and mutilated from the crucible of history, and which was, despite its undoubted achievements, now in crisis because of its deep-seated structural contradictions, that its repressive violence over the years had served not to resolve but to confirm and perpetuate these contradictions, that, therefore, what was required was not setting some 'departures' or 'distortions' right, or even reclaiming a lost revolutionary achievement – for, despite the early aspirations or successes of Lenin and the Bolsheviks, the Soviet Union had never really built socialism – but a systematic transformation of society that could again set it on the road to socialism, to genuinely democratic empowerment of the working people at all levels of economy and politics so that they indeed become masters of their own destiny, which is what socialism of Karl Marx was about. In other words what was required was not a restructuring called *perestroika* but a revolutionary reconstruction of Soviet society.

But such a *socialist* response to the Soviet crisis was impossible for Gorbachev to even visualise, much less implement. He lacked the theoretical understanding and moral commitment to pose the issue of reform of Soviet society in these terms. The clichéd Marxism of Party's ideological orthodoxies, an economistic-technocratic view of things, combined with the vacuous moralism of 'new thinking' only produced the essentially pragmatic or empiricist response that was *perestroika* and *glasnost*. Socialism was never an issue in Gorbachev's reform programme.

There was no genuine going to the people either in pursuit of this programme – 'a middle path' which was more market, less socialism, indeed a variant of 'market-socialism'. Gorbachev of course spoke a lot about 'the people', 'their patriotic feelings', his own faith in 'the disposition of our people', their ability to 'work wonders', etc., etc. He defined *perestroika* as 'simultaneously a revolution "from above" and "from below"', and wrote: 'The weakness and inconsistencies of all the known "revolutions from above" are explained precisely by the lack of support from below'. But this was, again, only so much conventional rhetoric. Far from unleashing the missing agent of 'the consciousness and voluntary initiative of the workers', which inspired Lenin's definition of Communism, the opening provided by Gorbachev rather was taken up by workers as an opportunity finally to rid themselves of the hated 'Black Saturdays' that voluntary labour of Lenin's *subbotniks* had degenerated into. No doubt there was a certain emergence of an organised self-management current in the labour movement in the late summer of 1990, in the context of the conflict over power in the enterprises and the deepening suspicion among workers that the proposed 'de-statisation' will in practice mean the transformation of their enterprises into the property of the bureaucrats and 'affairistes' of the 'shadow economy'. There were signs in the late Gorbachev era (1989–91) that an independent worker's movement was taking shape in the Soviet Union, particularly as a result of the two great miners' strikes in the summer of 1989 and the spring of 1991. In the event this movement was still-born. The emergent miners' union itself fell under the influence of liberal parliamentarians committed to pro-market policies, and a little later the Soviet working class, depoliticised over the years, acquiesced in the dethronement of Gorbachev and voted Yeltsin into power.

Far more significant than Gorbachev's rhetoric about 'the people' is the fact of a profound hostility that Gorbachev's neo-liberal economic advisers displayed towards the working class which they regarded as indulged and incapacitated by excessive social welfare and whose solidarity and security they sought to destroy – through large wage differentials and, most importantly, mass unemployment – to be able to make 'the market' the central institution of Soviet society. Equally significant is Gorbachev's own admission in 1996. Out-of-job Soviet president turned copy-righted columnist for the bourgeois press writes: 'We could only do it (reform) from above because initiative from below would have meant an explosion of discontent'.

Away from Marxism and away from any genuine faith in the people, or reaching out to them for his reforms, Gorbachev's 'new thinking' and the accompanying practice of *perestroika* and *glasnost*, always had a certain ambiguity about them. There was a lack of clarity as well as stability in strategic approach and a lack of firmness in commitment to any set of fundamentals. Gorbachev, while he lasted, never gave any impression of knowing where he wanted to go. Gorbachev and his advisers had no idea either of what forces they were unleashing or how rapidly events would develop (as the Czech, Vaclav Havel, later told the admiring US Congressmen in Washington). They often gave the impression of people who dive first and discover whether they can swim afterwards. Vacillations, compromises and continued ad hoc manipulation of goals was a characteristic of their reforming practice. There was manoeuvring and temporising, zigzags to the right and left, balancing between the 'conservatives' and 'radicals', and a constant shifting of ground in response to growing social tensions or prevailing public mood or out of Gorbachev's overriding concern to stay in power. All this, in effect, meant a continuous strengthening of the forces of the anti-socialist, pro-west right. Eventually the supposedly 'socialist' content of perestroika, always rather nebulous, disappeared and the 'radical marketeers' took over. Gorbachev himself ended up in the anti-socialist camp and was there when Yeltsin finally decided to dispense with him.

IX

A look at some details of Gorbachev's argument to supplement our account so far will not be out of place.

Gorbachev noted that 'awareness of a need for change actually manifested itself more than once. But the changes did not go all the way and were inconsistent, under the weight of the "legacy of the past" with all its dominant attributes'. For him, 'a major landmark in our history was the 20th CPSU Congress', its movement away from 'the Stalin personality cult', but he rejected 'the subjectivist methods adopted by the leadership under Khrushchev', 'its willful and changing ideas and actions' which kept 'society and the party in fever'. He approved of Khrushchev's ouster by Brezhnev when 'a line towards stabilisation was taken.... it was a well justified plan'. But, 'having produced a substantial though temporary effect', it 'petered out', 'the solutions that were offered then were not radical, they were halfway measures, which not infrequently missed the essence of the matter...' Gorbachev concluded: 'We have come to see that half-hearted measures will not work up here. We must act on a wide front, consistently and energetically, without failing to take the boldest steps.'

Gorbachev noticed it all – 'economic stagnation', 'ossification of social thought', 'gradual erosion of ideological and moral values of our people', 'a breach formed between word and deed', etc., etc. But, while admitting that 'historical experience has shown that socialist society is not insured against major socio-political crises', Gorbachev insisted that 'the difficulties and problems of the 1970s and 1980s did not signify some kind of crisis for socialism as a social and political system'. He saw them only as a result of some 'departures' or 'even distortions' in applying 'the principles of socialism' as they related to 'the methods and forms of social management', and held out the assurance that 'curing economic maladies would close the gap between ideology and reality, restore the authority of the government and Party and ensure the Soviet Union's position as a superpower'. In offering his cure, *perestroika*, Gorbachev asserted: 'we are conducting all our reforms in accordance with the socialist choice. We are looking within socialism, rather than outside it, for the answers to all the questions that arise. We assess our successes and errors alike by socialist standards.'

Again: 'Those who hope that we shall move away from the socialist path will be disappointed. Every part of our programme of *perestroika* – and the programme as a whole, for that matter – is fully based on the principle of more socialism and more democracy'. The outcome of *perestroika*, he emphasised, would be 'to strengthen socialism, not replace it with a different system'.

'More socialism', significantly seen as distinct from 'more democracy', was thus primarily viewed as a matter of economics and not politics, as 'curing of economic maladies' or better, more efficient 'social management'. It was to be secured through *perestroika* (just as 'more democracy' was the aim of *glasnost*). Even more significantly, *perestroika* sought to secure 'more socialism' through more market. It was a programme of revitalisation of the economy by substituting free markets for administrative command system or bureaucratic planning (and in its later phase by substituting 'privatisation' for 'social ownership'). Given the total or near-total erosion of socialist theory and commitment among the Communist Party leadership and the Soviet intelligentsia, especially the Soviet economists, it is easy to understand the enormous attraction 'market' had for Gorbachev and his advisers, confronted as they were by the rigidity, inefficiency, waste, and palpable failures of their own system of central planning and economic management, and bedazzled as they were by the consumerist cornucopia of the market in the West. To the architects of *perestroika* nothing could seem more logical or appealing than substituting the elegant 'magic' of the market for the discredited Stalinist 'laws of socialism'. That the Soviet economists' alienated thinking had located the evil, all the country's problems, in its planning, only reinforced Gorbachev's and his advisers' faith in the market. In his 'famous' October 1990 reform document, as he decided to move fast on the road to 'the market', Gorbachev wrote: 'There are no alternatives to the market. Only the market can ensure the satisfaction of people's needs, the fair distribution of wealth, social rights, and the strengthening of freedom and democracy. The market would permit the Soviet economy to be organically linked with the world's, and give our citizens access to all the achievements of world civilisation.' 'The market' that was yearned for was of course the historically specific capitalist market which carries with it not only its economic priorities and social, moral and cultural values but also preferred property relations. That 'privatisation' soon followed in its tow was inevitable. As Chairman of the Soviet Party's Ideological Commission and a member of Gorbachev's Politburo, Vadim Medvedev, pontificated about 'choice among many other multi-coloured and various forms', that is other than socialism, and the ideologists of the *perestroika* theorised about 'full equality of all types of property' (including, of course, capitalist private property) to be constitutionally secured by the so-called 'law-governed state', socialism, even as a cliché, disappeared from the dominant discourse. The pro-perestroika sociologist Tatyana Zaslavskaya wrote: 'The creation of a business class is plainly part and parcel of a market economy – but which of the existing classes is this new class to be created out of? That is the question.' The answer to Zaslavskaya's rhetorical question was not long in coming. The post-Soviet new 'business class' came, noticeably from the former *nomenklatura*, particularly its top economic wing, the former managerial class including a slice of the so-called 'red directors', from the Soviet underground or 'shadow' economy which in close connection with lower levels of bureaucracy was a part of Soviet economy for a long time, and from a whole army of small business operators who mushroomed in the late Gorbachev years.

It is noteworthy that there was never anything even remotely socialist about the *perestroika* debates. Such fundamental issues as the meaning and purpose of socialism were entirely missing from the agenda of policy makers and their advisers. Possibly, they did not even know what they were. 'Since Mikhail Gorbachev and his collaborators had learned their trade as politicians under Stalinism', Meszaros has suggested', 'they had no contact with the original meaning of the socialist project'. Their discourse was essentially technocratic, concerned with such matters as the optimal mix of plan and market, when and how to decontrol prices, ways to balance the budget, how to shake the economy out of stagnation or raise the long-run growth rate, etc., etc. It never extended to issues of politics, class or ideology, and resembled those of western bourgeois economists insofar as the diagnosis and proposed remedies were simplistically presumed to be value free. Still more to the point, as the Soviet ruling elite opted for all this, there was little to distinguish it from the pro-western technocratic and modernising elites in a majority of so-called 'developing' countries in the third world.

Whatever the original or ostensible intentions, perestroika on the ground was soon a programme of liberal or neo-liberal 'restructuring'. It sought to break the bureaucratic logjams blocking economic growth and to motivate an apathetic workforce by the undemocratic imposition of market mechanisms from above. The main reforms advocated by Gorbachev's advisers from time to time included extensive privatisation, unemployment as a means of labour discipline (that is to make workers work harder), putting them under the 'discipline of material interests' that is increased material incentives coupled with wider income differentials to overcome 'a psychology of levelling', i.e. solidaristic egalitarianism, and reduction in social welfare programmes. Significant in this connection was the issue of 'Ouvrierism', a standard coded allusion to the concern prevalent among the new managerial cadre of profit-oriented technocrats that workers, taking the rather ambiguous self-management provisions in Gorbachev's early enterprise legislation far more seriously than its authors had intended, were becoming a problem and needed to be induced or broken into fully subordinate partners in the emerging market economy. The well-known Italian Marxist Rosanna Rossanda noticed this hostility to the working class, a 'cold and determined anti-ouvrierism' among reform-minded, market-oriented Soviet economists in the late 1980s. Market mechanisms, as we have already noticed, are not necessarily incompatible with a socialist transition, but the key aspects of Gorbachev's reforms involved a decisive shift away from planning to market and an attack on workers' rights and benefits with only a promise that increased growth would duly trickle down. In Marxist terms, it meant increased exploitation of the working class. Gorbachev and his companions virtually reduced socialism to growing inequality and Marxism to the principle: 'from each according to his labour'! This was now described as 'social justice', but whatever relation it had to justice, it was not socialist.

Gorbachev was hyperbolic about his reforms. He described perestroika as 'the beginning of an era of non-violent, bloodless social transformations...this is the world's first and largest peaceful social revolution'. Again: 'The success of perestroika will be the final argument in the historical dispute as to which system is more consistent with the interests of the people...the Soviet Union will gain a new attractiveness and will become the living embodiment of the advantages that are inherent in the socialist system.' But 'social revolution' or 'revolutionary renewal of society' as he described it elsewhere, or 'the final argument in the historical dispute' between socialism and capitalism, perestroika was all decided 'from above', and Gorbachev's professions notwithstanding, it was not, and perhaps could not be, linked with the initiative or short or long-term interests of the people below. He never once appealed to them seeking their involvement and support. In fact, Gorbachev never sought to mobilise any particular constituency to secure social or political basis of his reforms. Perhaps the inherent power of the idea, of Gorbachev's 'new thinking', was deemed an adequate enough substitute. He kept reiterating ad nauseam: 'We proposed the policy of perestroika to which there was no alternative', 'it is an urgent necessity arising from the profound processes of development in our socialist society', as if that resolved automatically the weighty questions regarding the adequacy or viability of perestroika – it stood vindicated, and assured of success, by the self evident authority of necessity itself, as decreed by 'new thinking'!

X

Nevertheless, an active constituency or social basis in favour of perestroika had by now well crystallised in the Soviet society. This was 'the potential *privilegentsia'*, as it has been called, including among others factory managers, economists, high-ranking engineers and doctors, successful writers and journalists, and all sorts of other upcoming professionals, whose numbers had grown over the years and who sought more say in running the economy and the system as a whole. They saw themselves as a dynamic meritocracy and as such wanted bigger income differentials, incentives involving different standards of housing, health, and education for the successful. (Hence, they also wanted 'the market'). It is not that they were seeking introduction of privileges in an otherwise egalitarian society. More specifically, they were for transfer of privileges and power from the *apparatchiks* of the *nomenklatura,* whose main virtue was their faithful obedience to the authorities at the top, to themselves, whose main quality was allegedly their competence. They saw in Gorbachev's reforms the means of such a transfer. They were the most active and articulate supporters of perestroika as Gorbachev and his reformers embarked on a journey towards a market economy without really knowing where it was going to lead.

In turning towards a market economy, the Gorbachevian reformers certainly reflected the values and aspirations of this relatively privileged stratum of Soviet society who were politically now liberals or social democrats and who felt their place in the world was with the better-off, more privileged intelligentsia of the advanced western capitalism which had, whatever its faults and shortcomings, provided a standard of living and a degree of security, with a wide latitude to dissent and criticism, for its more fortunate citizens, far beyond anything available in Soviet society. Though understanding western society in a very narrow and primitive manner, they were attracted by the living styles of its advantaged sections and oriented to their values. Along with reformers, they hoped and wanted their own country to develop along similar lines, and they saw marketisation as a necessary step in that direction. And insofar as they thought about these things, they believed this could be done without their turning away from its established 'socialist' system. The crisis of Soviet socialism together with the absence or failure of the Marxist left had already produced pupils of Hayek and Friedman in the Soviet Union and there were those who sought a quick transition to capitalism, though they were not prepared to put it that bluntly, not yet. But most others, though looking for major transformations sought them within the existing system and saw marketisation primarily as a necessary technocratic turn in their country's path of socialist development. Much like their predecessors in the Khrushchev era, they believed in the possibility of gradual reform from above, and that a liberal market reform – envisaged as a second edition of Lenin's New Economic Policy and implemented under the guidance of Party leaders conscious of their historical responsibility and helped along by the advice and constructive criticism of progressive intelligentsia – would steadily and smoothly lead to 'more socialism' and 'more democracy' promised by Gorbachev. Hence the new turn to marketisation needed no repudiation yet of socialism or of the conventional socialist rhetoric. Even otherwise, ideology having ceased to matter except for rhetorical purposes, the perestroika reformers, as already noted, looked very much like the pro-western, technocratic or modernising elites in the so-called 'developing' countries. That perestroika was also a step towards restoration of capitalism was not recognised. This recognition came later, further along the reform road, though one must add, when it came it was not unwelcome to the reformers, the Soviet ruling elite or to Gorbachev himself. As the *privilegentsia* deserted him to climb on Yeltsin's bandwagon, assuming that it would take them more rapidly towards a capitalist society, Gorbachev went on a worldwide spree claiming Soviet socialism's collapse into capitalism as his own achievement!

Facilitating this collapse were not only the economic and ideological-cultural offensives of global capitalism, but also the fact that looking westward for advice and assistance, the priviligentsia and allied intellectuals encountered a resurgent, self-confident free-market right, and a left which lacked faith in its own solutions and had no convincing alternative to offer. And since to the last it was believed that the Soviet Union was a socialist society guided by the principles of Marxism-Leninism, its collapse involved not just the end of the Stalin to Brezhnev version of socialism but the loss of the earlier, authentic socialist vision as well, and the throwing out of Marxism itself along with the hidebound Marxism of the Soviet Academy.

XI

Perestroika as conceived by Gorbachev never took off. Scholars have written of its different stages or phases, and the details have their importance. But the overall fact, now largely accepted by its friends and foes, is that perestroika never really happened. With its poor conception, inherent ambiguities, contradictions pulling in opposite directions, together with lack of political will to back it and the inevitable resistance of the entrenched bureaucracy, perestroika soon faltered and failed, it certainly lost its original, intended shape or form. The attempt to fuse components of the market with hierarchical command system, to combine market determinants in economy with central state planning led to a situation in which there were no benefits of either the market or planning. And by attributing what is inherently linked to capitalist mode of production to neutral economic 'laws', the Soviet reformers only incorporated new contradictions into their own system, which contradictions were all the more damaging for a system claiming to be socialist. Treading 'the middle path' between market and planning in the economy, and in politics between the stony regressions of the apparatchik Ligachev and the vapidities of the demagogue Yeltsin, Gorbachev simply did not know where he was going. His half-reforms had the consequence of unsettling the old economic structures without putting new ones in their place. Centralised state planning, which was the lynchpin of the command economy increasingly lost its role in the functioning of the economy and the Soviet economy became, in the words of a western observer, 'a centrally planned economy with the centre knocked out'. And no coherent alternative, market or any other, had emerged. There was a steady deterioration of the already poor economic performance, and after stumbling along for the first few years of perestroika, the economy was nearing a final collapse. The worsening economic situation leading to and in turn exacerbated by instability in the country, a political stalemate or crisis and general unrest released by the reform process including *glasnost* itself, the eruption of multiple class, social or ethnic conflicts, political fragmentation and secessionist assertiveness of the republics of the Union, and, most importantly, the struggle for power at the top between the conservatives and the liberals within the Communist Party and outside – all this further undermined the centre's control over both the reform process and the economy. This control was finally lost and the economy began to collapse in 1991 after the pro-capitalist coalition gained enough strength to dismantle the old system of central direction of production and distribution. On 1 July 1991, *Gosplan*, the central planning agency, and *Gosnab*, the supply agency, were abolished, and the system of state orders and economic plans was declared over. With the old economic links of central planning severed and no new ones put in their place, growing chaos developed in the system of production and distribution. The command economy was dead, but the market sought by Gorbachev's reforms was nowhere in sight. Along with a steep fall in production and crippling inflation, the only market that came up was black market, the flourishing of all sorts of 'informal' socio-economic forces, including 'graftocracy' – a coalition of organised crime with corrupt bureaucracy – which was already a distinguishing feature of the Brezhnev era. The situation began to resemble an unplanned disaster.

As this happened, with no political-ideological intervention of socialist nature forthcoming, the elements of marketisation contained in the original concept expanded, grew in influence and eventually came to define the reform. Even the original reform project never really transcended the bourgeois choices. Now with the failure of this project, 'the market' appeared as *the* salvation, the Holy Grail itself. Talk of 'socialism', 'more socialism', 'renewal of socialism', of 'self-management' and 'workers' participation in decision making' – all became a thing of the past. No longer and no more 'solutions within the framework of the socialist system', but the official intention of moving towards a full-scale market economy. In a major shift, new ideological priorities became clear. The initial insistence on maintaining public ownership was dropped and replaced by a commitment to 'privatisation', along with a renewed emphasis on integration into the world economy, that is, global capitalism. Instead of reforming and democratising socialism, the process turned into one aimed at replacing it with capitalism. It was a shift from 'the reform of socialism' to the effort to implant capitalism.

The failure of perestroika and its disastrous economic outcome, whose primary victims were the common people, led to their near-total disenchantment with the prevailing system. But given their passivity, the more significant was a new disaffection with the socialist goals and ideals among the now increasingly active intelligentsia. As the ideology associated with the old system weakened, many intellectuals were attracted to its opposite. If the official media had previously not been telling the whole truth, perhaps the whole truth was the opposite of what they had previously been told. This is how many of them came to believe in an idealised, 19th-century picture of capitalism, which they saw as a system of economic freedom and opportunity for all. Of course this intelligentsia was never socialist, with a solidaristic identification with the working class and belief in a socialist democracy offering a decent life for all citizens, workers and intellectuals alike. Official propaganda which decreed such solidarity had, if anything, the opposite effect. In its social composition it was a middle class – whatever its defects, the system had created a large, educated middle class – with its own class interests, wanting to enjoy the life its counterparts did in the west and hopeful till recently of the Soviet system providing for it. It is not surprising that, losing this hope, they now adopted an ideology that they expected would further their interests and thus turned towards capitalism. They became an important constituency for those who were now mounting an assault for a return to capitalism.

But while perestroika faltered and failed, or ran into rough weather, the other important part of Gorbachev's reform programme, *glasnost*, was a remarkable success, in more ways than one, with at least one entirely unanticipated consequence. Freedoms that *glasnost* provided served to delegitimise the established Soviet system and with it the very idea of socialism, almost beyond repair, and thus fuelled the above-mentioned turn from socialism, of whatever sort, to capitalism – again, of whatever sort.

XII

Glasnost (openness) was Gorbachev's major opening to 'more democracy' in the Soviet Union. It was no 'broad democratisation of all aspects of society' he had promised in *Perestroika*, much less any kind of *socialist* democratisation, or a restoration of 'democracy of the Soviets' that flowered in the immediate aftermath of the October Revolution but had withered away equally immediately soon after. It was essentially a liberal opening, restoring to people certain freedoms born of bourgeois revolutions in our times and generally associated with 'bourgeois democracy', but no less welcome for that reason, for they are even more necessary in any socialist society. A response to the explosive political situation, glasnost, coming from the top of a hierarchical system, was equally an effort to gain legitimacy for the regime as it embarked on its reform programme. It freed the people from long-established coercive controls, from decades of occasionally meaningful but mostly mindless repression which resolved no contradictions, only perpetuated or added to them. The outcome was literally a country awakening from its slumber, recovering its history as well as its voice. There was a vastly increased freedom of speech and opinion and a new, astonishing, openness of political debate and information. With the reduction of censorship people had access to writings which were considered dangerous and subversive only three or four years ago; books were published, plays staged, films shown that had no chance of being produced a few years earlier; newspapers changed their nature and television its coverage and magazines battled with each other, seeking support for their politics. A variety of political positions began to be articulated in the media and groupings began to form of people who believed in the various old or new unsanctioned positions.

Glasnost was an excellent thing, its granting of liberty of political opinion and action was all to the good. The extraordinary resurgence of public discussion revealed the sore spots of Soviet society – choking of free thought, the moral rot, crimes of the past and the waste and inefficiency built into the command economy, etc. – and permitted the people to express their anger and dissatisfaction with the existing state of affairs. But such was the pent-up anger and so intense the dissatisfaction built up over the years that the overall effect of new freedom was not to cause people to express their goodwill, their suggestions, their constructive ideas, but rather to show their animosity. Instead of popular enthusiasm, there was a flood of complaints. Instead of a serious debate about the problems of society and their resolution, only an enormous negative potential rose to the surface. Long years of anti-people repression and denial of political freedoms, coupled with the unbelievable staleness and sterility of official 'socialist' theory and propaganda, had depoliticised the people and created an ideological vacuum in Soviet society. 'Deideologisation' enjoined by Gorbachev's 'new thinking' now ensured that glasnost opened the doors wide for bourgeois ideology to rush in and fill the vacuum. Duly helped by the elite control of the media, official and non-official, a 'quiet counter-revolution' in ideology occurred, which was not only anti-socialist or anti-communist, but blatantly pro-capitalist and pro-west, not only in behalf of the capitalist market economy, but for imitation of everything western, including all the vices and flippancies of the late-capitalist bourgeois social order. Symbolic of this ideological turn around, at one level, was the official *Literaturnaya Gazeta*, rediscovering and sharing with its readers 'the truth of capitalism', or, a little later, the first issue of the Russian version of *Readers' Digest*, published as a joint venture with Progress Publishers, or, similar other pillars of the old regime featuring articles like 'Ten Myths About Homelessness in America', which sought to dispel the impression that America had a significant problem of homelessness. At another level it was the officially sponsored beauty contests, centres with arrays of gambling machines, columns devoted to astrology in Soviet popular journals, the spread of drugs as well as organised crime and prostitution. Freedoms flowing from glasnost, ranged all the way from freedom to vote to freedom for pornography.

The neo-liberal ideology, thus purveyed by millions of newspapers and journals, TV and radio programmes could not but seriously undermine the established system as did glasnost's release of long-repressed, accumulated, tensions of the Soviet society, giving rise to all sorts of disruptive and centrifugal forces which further weakened the control exercised by the regime over the society. The irrationality of the regime having long abetted the forces of unreason in the society at large, along with the breath of fresh air brought by glasnost also came the stench of prejudice, jingoism, anti-semitism, religiosity and 'patriotism' of 'Great Russian Chauvinism' on the one hand, and the atavistic hatreds and medieval passions of the now secessionist smaller nations of the Union, both developed and oppressed by it, on the other.

An important aspect of glasnost was the welcome urge to recover history, a true understanding of the nation's past. But instead of a critical assessment of this past, its achievements as well as errors or failures and far too many crimes, what took over was a denial, distortion and denigration of the entire Soviet history, even extolling of the Czar and the Czarist period. Stalin alone was not under attack, the October Revolution itself was a 'tragic mistake', Lenin 'the source of all repression', Bolsheviks 'fanatic', 'cruel', 'bloodthirsty', and worst of all 'murderers' of the Czar – all of them brought only misery and suffering and death to the Russian people. The slanders more than equalled those of the early days of the October Revolution or the worst period of the Cold War. And not only TV but influential sections of the official print media, such as *Moscow News* or *Komsomolskaya Pravda*, chipped in with their contributions. One could search their columns to find anything of merit in the Bolshevik record or tradition. *Ogonek* and other publications regularly informed their readers of the crimes of the Bolsheviks who among other things, killed the late Russian Czar. Intellectuals, official or other, were not to be left behind in this historical adventure. In a typical case the well-known philosopher, Alexander Tsypko, writing in the journal *Nauka i Zhizn*, traced the sources of Stalinism all the way back in Marxism and the socialist tradition, which lead in a straight line to the Gulag. Tsypko, it is well to remember, worked in the ideological department of the Central Committee of the Communist Party! It is thus that denigrating the entire Soviet past and turning a blind eye to its historical achievements, there occurred a wholesale blackguarding of Soviet history. The critics 'recovered' it as nothing more than a succession of mistakes, a string of crimes, and its culmination, the Soviet system, had no historical or ethical worth at all.

Thanks to glasnost there was a certain welcome recovery of history, but looking at some of the historians or intellectuals involved, one cannot but agree with Vlasov that there is nothing more repulsive than 'collective recovery of sight'. Needless to add, glasnost's 'recovery of history' severely undermined the legitimacy of the Soviet system and challenged the value of socialism even as an ideal.

It is significant that this delegitimisation of the Soviet system and the socialist ideal went simply unchallenged, even by those who were supposed to be their custodians, above all, the leadership in the Soviet State and the Communist Party. Gorbachev himself, having already dispensed with, even if somewhat ambiguously, the revolutionary heritage of the Soviet people – after using it all these years for the ideological justification and political stability of the system – never felt inclined to defend either his system or its revolutionary heritage against the viciously nihilistic attack of the enemy; he simply acquiesced in the ongoing delegtimisation of everything Soviet. As for the Communist Party, degenerate over the years, and 'deideologised' by Gorbachev, it found itself utterly incompetent to respond to the anti-communist critics and their onslaught and wage a political struggle against them. Leave aside the ideals of socialism, even the universally recognised achievements of Soviet history went undefended. And there was no counter-attack against capitalism, no criticism of its rampant consumerism, its aggressive voraciousness and cultural decadence, the values and venality of the affluent societies of late capitalism. Issues were not joined even with those who were extolling the Czar and the Czarist past. As a dissident leader Alexei Prigarin put it, 'our party resembles the warrior who was retreating from direct fighting'. The Party lost the ideological battle simply by default. It did not even dare to join it.

Indicative of the ideological ascendancy of the critics, the pro-market, pro-west right-wingers, was the way they subverted the categories commonly used to describe political positions. In a deft tactical move, they appropriated the designation 'left' or 'radical' for themselves and their own reform project, thus excluding socialism in the classical sense, in fact any genuine socialist alternatives, from a political spectrum where the 'right' are the 'conservatives', all those who defend 'the system' or oppose their 'radical' reforms, independent of whether what they defend is socialism as a source of power and privileges, as did the Soviet leadership, or socialism as a revolutionary project, as Fidel Castro, for example, still does, or whether they oppose the reforms from the standpoint of authentic socialism or from that of the entrenched *nomenklatura*. It is a symptom of the power of propaganda in our times that it is enough to be in favour of unemployment, of private property, of gross inequality to be proclaimed 'leftist' or 'radical', that is progressive. Since 'left' or 'radical', has a certain progressive resonance in popular consciousness, the 'right-wing' reformers perhaps hoped that their politically astute appropriation of this designation, will make it easier for them to sell their essentially inegalitarian programme in a society still steeped in what they deemed a crude levelling culture.

Glasnost's uncontested delegitimisation of the Soviet system and the socialist ideal propelled the perestroika debates on to an entirely bourgeois terrain. It helped establish the hegemony of the bourgeois problematic in the current Soviet discourse. Marketisation with privatisation became the agenda of reforms. But more than any particular consequences, it disarmed the Soviet people, ideologically and morally, causing a deep and historic loss of confidence in their society and its future. More than any socialism, it was pride in socialism and their own historical achievements which had failed. No one, literally no one who ought to have, stood up in defence of these achievements or the ideal behind them.

Jurgen Habermas spoke of 'the Rectifying Revolution' in Eastern Europe and the Soviet Union. Rectification is alright but from a Marxist view of socialism, what was at work in the Soviet Union, or earlier in Eastern Europe, was a dialectics of surrender, a surrender to capitalism, warts and all.

Facilitated by glasnost's' onslaught on the old system and its past, and its dominant preference for the market and the West, perestroika, its professed purpose of 'renewal of socialism' notwithstanding, rapidly moved on to the rails of a free market economy. As this was happening, Gorbachev continued with his characteristic reformist rhetoric about 'Ideology of Renewal for Revolutionary Restructuring' and equally characteristic *apparatchik* rhetoric about the Party which was to carry out this 'revolutionary restructuring'.

Gorbachev in fact throughout – that is till he betrayed it all including the Party – kept mouthing rhetoric about the Party as the organising and guiding force, indeed the guarantor of perestroika viewed as consolidation of socialism in the Soviet Union. Thus: 'It is the Party, equipped with the scientific knowledge of the past and the present, and of the tendencies having real prospects of development, that is to guide the processes of fostering socialist consciousness in society. It is the Party that can and must theoretically elucidate the new stage of socialist construction, taking into account the innovation introduced by perestroika. It is the Party that must choose and put at the service of all of society what really promotes socialism, meets the interests of its development, advances us to socialist, and not some alien "borrowed" aims'. Or: 'The party acts as the initiator and generator of ideas, the organising and guiding force and, I would say, the guarantor of perestroika in the interests of consolidating socialism, in the interests of the working people. The party has assumed a truly historic responsibility. In 1917, Lenin said: "Having started a revolution we must go all the way." The same is true of perestroika: The party will go all the way'. Or: 'the party's goal is ...above all, to theoretically analyse processes, to sense critical points in the development of contradictions in time, to introduce corrections into strategy and tactics, to elaborate policy and define methods and forms for its realisation, to select and place personnel, and to provide for perestroika both organisationally and ideologically. Only the party could do all this.'

This does recall something of Lenin's view of a communist party, but was really a good example of apparatchik's internalisation of Stalinist rhetoric with a vengeance. For the CPSU, though still referred to as 'the Party is the Mind, Conscience and Pride of our Epoch', had now for decades ceased to be a living party, its bureaucratic structure serving as a protective shield against change, and together with corruption within rendering it incapable of fulfilling the leadership role that Gorbachev hoped for. Restoration of the political legitimacy of the Party was in fact a precondition for undertaking any successful reform of the system. For the party had by now become thoroughly discredited with the people and, despite being 19-million strong, was providing every possible evidence of its utter inability either to defend itself or its 'socialist' system, or in any way intervene in what was going on around it in the Soviet society. And even this party such as it was, under pressure from the right-wing politicians and in a bid to save his personal political power, Gorbachev was willing to see dissolved and banned a couple of years later. However regardless of Gorbachev's rhetorically expressed hopes, or the Party's inability to defend itself or Gorbachev's perestroika, perestroika was doomed to frustration and failure and give way to a turn towards capitalism because of the basic contradiction underlying the very conception of perestroika: if its theoretical commitment to 'renewal of socialism' held out possibilities of one kind, its effective reform proposals and practice were pushing it in an opposite direction.

Any 'renewal of socialism' demanded a dismantling of the apparatus of Party-state control over Soviet economy and society and redeeming of the promise of the October Revolution by empowering the working people, establishing their control over the farms and factories through the workers' and peasants' Soviets. For one who had written, even as a rhetorical flourish, that 'people, human beings with all their creative diversity, are the makers of history', Gorbachev could have, at the very least, sought some counter weight against his Party's bureaucratic inertia inhering in the creative potential of the Soviet masses. But given his background and theoretical equipment, rhetorics apart, a move in this direction was impossible for Gorbachev. And this together with another contradiction *within* perestroika itself further undermined the latter's feasibility. For Gorbachev the system was already socialist, and his adherence to socialism of the apparatchik postulated 'the leading role of the Party' and the Party as the repository of this socialist project. What he, in effect, now wanted was to retain it all as a cleaned-up, democratised 'socialist system'. On the other hand, any turn to the market – which is never likely to remain a limited exercise – to be effective demanded not only a retreat from the Party to the State, but a Pinochet-style forcible imposition of market reforms by the State, ruling out any democratisation whatsoever. But given his *apparatchik* adherence to the Party and 'the socialist system' (till he finally abandoned both) and the newly acquired preference for democracy and a democratised 'socialist system', Gorbachev could not countenance this other option either. The contradiction tore his programme apart; Gorbachev and his perestroika, or for that matter *his* glasnost too, just did not know where to go, to socialism or capitalism. But together they released the forces which made capitalism, of whatever sort, the next destination for the people of the Soviet Union.

XIII

As, with the failure of perestroika and the 'success' of glasnost, the crisis in the Soviet society deepened, a Pinochet-style transition to market economy was indeed advocated by some of the 'left' or 'radical' intelligentsia, showing how vulnerable Gorbachev's democratisation was, with the possibility of being only a bridge on the route to capitalism, both despotic and savage. Gorbachev had harked back to Lenin to speak of socialism and democracy being indivisible. Holding that there can be 'no socialism without democracy' and 'no democracy without glasnost', he defined 'the essence' of perestroika as lying in the fact that 'it unites socialism with democracy', via glasnost. But glasnost turned out to be a rather ambiguous exercise in democratisation. There was a certain superficial experimentation in democracy with emasculated 'soviets' within a one-party framework, though the countrywide multi-party elections was a real and positive advance. But, though 'socialist democracy' as a term was regularly invoked, even on a generous interpretation, Gorbachev's democratic reforms, practice or promises, did not go beyond what already existed in the west, that is bourgeois democracy, or the aspirations associated with its more popular version, social democracy of Western Europe, that is, the political arrangement, even when arising in opposition to capitalism, quite compatible with it. Social democracy today, it is well to remember, bears no relation to the pre-1914 variety which for all its commitment to gradual, piecemeal reform was committed to a thoroughgoing transformation or abolition of capitalism; it is now, at best, an attempt at managing and sustaining a 'capitalism with a human face'. Socialist democracy, the third perspective, distinctive from bourgeois or social democracy, which would do away with not only the power and privileges accruing through special political access in a bureaucratic system but also those obtained through money power in a market system, never became an issue in Gorbachev's democratic reforms programme. On the contrary, the all too visible and tragic denial of democracy in the Soviet system made democracy per se so overriding an issue in the ultimate crisis of the system that anything, including capitalism, could now be smuggled in the name or guise of democracy. To put it differently and more precisely, in a paradoxical coincidence, democratic reforms had now arrived in the Soviet Union in tandem with the market reforms. In a situation where people simultaneously sought freedom from the Party's arbitrary and oppressive exercise of political power and freedom from the command economy's arbitrary planning, irrespective of what they desired as consumers, the demand for democracy became almost synonymous with that for the market economy. This coincidence obscured, for some time at least, the essential contradiction between democracy and the market, between political freedoms or democracy and economic 'liberalisation', in as much as the market or economic liberalisation, whatever the benefits it brings, especially for the few at the top, invariably brings poverty and unemployment for the common people and increased inequalities in society.

This contradiction has been a part of the history of democracy in our times, finding expression in popular discontent, disaffection and opposition which has invariably called forth authoritarian response from the powers that be. This is what happened as the contradiction surfaced in the Soviet society. The social costs of marketisation and privatisation soon stirred up widespread popular resentment, if not active resistance, among the people whose basic needs at least were satisfied by the old regime even if mostly at an elementary level and who were unused to the impersonal hardships and precariousness of a capitalist economy. The miners, for example, who had organised themselves into the Independent Miners Union in 1990, had struck in defence of their interests. Sensing the threat, the 'radical' reformers, and even some of their political opponents, began to see democracy as an obstacle to their recapitalisation of Soviet society. There was a sudden surge of liking for 'the Pinochets of the world', and of serious argument about the need for 'inevitable concentration of power and a new curtailment of democracy' – at least for 'the transitional period'. Govriil Popov, the then Yeltsinite mayor of Moscow, a 'radical' and self-styled 'democrat', more honest than most 'radicals' and 'democrats', frankly expressed doubts about whether the social conflicts engendered by economic perestroika could be contained within a democratic framework. In an article entitled 'Dangers of Democracy'(August 1990), suggestive of problems and shape of things to come, and much noticed at home and abroad, he wrote:

> In my opinion, the forms of democracy being established are exceptionally contradictory and in a very short time they will lead to serious internal conflict. That conflict has already started...
>
> I see the main problem in the relationship between, on the one hand, populism and, on the other, the tasks that must be carried out if the economy and society are to be transformed. Clearly, we could not have overthrown the powerful totalitarian system without the active participation of millions of ordinary people. But now we must create a society with a variety of different forms of ownership, including private property; and this will be a society of economic inequality. There will be contradictions between the policies leading to denationalisation, privatisation and inequality on the one hand and, on the other, the populist character of the forces that were set in motion in order to achieve these aims. The masses long for fairness and economic equality. And the further the process of transformation goes, the more acute and the more glaring will be the gap between these aspirations and economic realities ...(therefore) we must seek new mechanisms and institutions of political power that will depend less on populism.

Again:

> the model of complete democracy we have been trying to follow is bound, in my view, to encounter serious difficulties: first through strikes, and then through the consequences of yielding to the demands of left-wing populism, starting at the lower levels of the soviets, and then going higher and higher. Therefore, it seems to me that we must make an intense effort to find new and different political mechanisms to bring about the transformation that must

> take place if we are to move into a new society. It is absolutely obvious to me that the purely democratic model now being pursued is leading to contradictions that can only grow more severe in the future.

Popov's political opponent, the Moscow party chief, Yuri Prokofiev openly advocated what came to be called the 'Pinochet solution' – that is a transition to capitalism and integration into the world market along the harsh authoritarian course of the Pinochet's dictatorial regime in Chile. In a rare Marxist comment on this developing radical version of a free market and a strong authoritarian state, the 'forcible imposition of market relations on unwilling Soviet workers', Boris Kagarlitsky wrote: 'what we are witnessing today is not the formation of a bourgeoisie and capitalist relations in the Western sense of the term, but the appearance of a hideous monster, a kind of *negative convergence* which combines the worst features of both systems: Western and Eastern. We call this *market Stalinism.*'

A consensus had emerged among the 'freedom loving' so-called radical reformers that democracy has to be rejected for the sake of introducing a market economy, that – as argued for by economists Igor Klymakin and Andranak Migranyan – the sole means of implementing a liberal economic reform is the creation of a strong, authoritarian regime capable of effectively suppressing the resistance of the masses. Klymakin explained: 'Democratization doesn't necessarily encourage reform. For instance, a leader decides to introduce a market economy. Will his idea get support from the people? Of course not! 80% will oppose him'. Another 'perestroika-democrat economist', Sergei Kugushev wrote: 'We can only go for market reforms through strong rule – a typical example is Chile. Basically it is a strong government supported by the army, with the aim of ensuring normal economic development. We should take a closer look at this model, because I consider it the most likely in our situation'. While Klymakin, Migranyan and Kugushev thus looked forward to 'an authoritarian transition to democracy', the *Economist* editorialised approvingly that Gorbachev might yet become a Soviet Pinochet: 'It may be that a push from the president, backed where necessary by the army to ensure vital supplies or to break politically motivated strikes, is the only way to get things going. ...It might, just might be the Soviet Union's turn for what could be called "The Pinochet approach to liberal economics"'.

Gorbachev did not survive politically for the distinction. But the much longed-for authoritarian regime indeed soon arrived with Yeltsin and his tanks on the streets of Moscow. However, the even more longed for market the liberal economic reformers were looking for, the one that advanced capitalist west had, proved elusive.

This market remained elusive because, posing a historical problem without any precedent, it was never a realistic practical option, the road to its achievement was simply not marked on any of history's available maps. Scholars have spoken of the market as 'the last utopia' in the Soviet Union, because the idea was indeed hopelessly utopian. It was utopian above all because, on the one hand, no latecomer to capitalism can today hope for *advanced* capitalist economy in a world dominated by global capitalism, which is itself in crisis. On the other hand, one cannot discard one system for another just like that. The Soviet Union had neither the institutional framework nor the human material needed for a well-functioning market system. These requisites cannot reappear on the historical scene overnight. Bringing them into being can only be the work of decades and not 'five hundred days' or even a few years. It needs to be remembered that the conditions for a comprehensive, functioning market economy in the advanced capitalist world took several centuries to evolve and in some parts it is still far from fully developed. What is needed for a market economy is not only suitable property relations and a sophisticated legal system to regulate and enforce them, but also a whole array of complex infrastructural economic institutions to sustain and service it. Even more important is the shaping of a 'human nature', fit to operate such an economy. The possessive individuals of classical political economy did not appear one fine day. It took centuries and generations to create them, to create the classes of bourgeois society as well as the bourgeois ethos of this society. It was impossible for the emerging adventurers in Soviet economy, the black marketeers, speculators, and former *apparatchiks* to just turn into a new bourgeoisie and the Soviet working class to be overnight transformed into a new proletariat, or for the crumbling administrative command system to provide the infrastructure of a proper market economy, or the seventy odd years of Soviet 'socialism' to leave behind in its disintegration the ethos for a bourgeois society. The conditions in the Soviet Union were available only for a *mafiosi* capitalism and *its* market system.

XIV

It speaks volumes for the degeneration of the Soviet intellectual life that despite the massive upheaval or turbulence – economic, political and social – that had occurred and was continuing and the Soviet society was faced with choices unprecedented in history, the debates of the period were peculiarly characterised by a near-total lack of ideas that were either innovative or genuinely oriented towards the future. They reverberated with a golden silence on basic theoretical questions. None of the major factions involved, the rulers, reformers, or their opponents, were distinguished by any ideological or theoretical coherence. They were simply content to do without theory and operated in an essentially pragmatic manner. Most significant in a way, for it was supposedly the ruling ideology of the system, was the absence of Marxism, either in theory or in practice, except for a few, very small and most marginalised groups in the party or the intelligentsia. (Whatever their significance for the future, they were entirely ineffective in the current crisis). Despite talk of 'renewal of socialism', there was hardly any thinking in terms of Marxism on what was happening, what had gone wrong or where the country was going. There was no even remotely comprehensive critique or analysis of the situation. There was no coherent social theory of the reform process, or genuine Marxist-socialist project in opposition to reformer's capitalism, presenting a global alternative and linking it with the concrete down-to-earth proposals affecting the everyday life of the people, that is, a project of genuine social ownership, democratic planning and self-management and socialist democracy with an egalitarian mobilisation of workers, peasant *kolkhozniks*, women and genuinely radical sections of the intelligentsia. Whereas the reformers in command were increasingly clear about where to go, that is, a west-European capitalist society, no socialist vision or strategic alternative emerged to compete with this bourgeois vision and choice as another possible option. Indeed one of the most surprising discoveries by outsiders concerned the inability of a seventy year-old system claiming to be socialist, to throw up men and women imbued with socialist theory and ideology during its hour of crisis.

Of course there was the long-degenerating official Marxism-Leninism, often reduced to a set of organised, hackneyed clichés and Stalinist dogmas to be regularly incanted on high and holy days of the Soviet calendar. This degeneration had long been a concern with revolutionary Marxists, not necessarily members of the official communist parties, abroad. As the Czech Marxist Frantisek Vacek, a member of Czechoslovak Communist Party at the time of (1968) Soviet invasion, put it: 'Marxism itself degenerated. Instead of its method being a tool to integrate and develop all the creative tendencies, it became a book of convenient quotes to support the orthodoxy. Marxism didn't develop, and now as a result of this, some individuals, and even leftist parties, reject Marxism *enbloc*'. This theoretical degeneration and the consequent historical and ideological bankruptcy was quite evident in Gorbachev, when this last official custodian of 'Marxism-Leninism' – before he formally abandoned it, via his 'new thinking', for the still more vacuous formality of 'the idea of socialism' – in the name of 'renewing' socialism, put his country on the road to capitalism and hailed it as a 'moral' victory, *the* achievement of his life! This degeneration was no less evident among his close advisers and cronies in the leadership of the Soviet Communist Party or outside. Alexander Yakovlev was a Politbureau member incharge of Ideology and Propaganda department of the Soviet Communist Party Central Committee, a member of the Presidential Council of the USSR, practically the second person with Gorbachev in the leadership of the Party and the State. In tandem with Gorbachev's shift from 'class values' to 'human values', this is what Alexander Yakovlev said at the time in an interview:

> Now I have on my shelf a 250 page manuscript, an analysis of my understanding of Marxism. ...Everybody says that Marx created a doctrine about man. He did not create such a doctrine and, I believe, did not even try to. He created a doctrine about class struggle, a brilliant doctrine, yet one which we need to renounce.

Here we have a questionable 'reduction' of Marxism to 'a doctrine of class struggle'. Even more questionable is the implication – the basis for renouncing it – that it was this 'doctrine', the pursuit of class interests of the working class, that in general guided the policy of the Soviet Union in the past, when the truth was elsewhere, if not entirely the opposite. What went on in the Soviet Union was not Marx's class struggle, but far more the rulers' class struggle against the Soviet working class. Most amazing, despite 'everybody says', is the ignorance the statement betrays of the fact, we have already noticed, that Marx's 'theory of man', Marx's humanism, has been one of the most discussed themes of recent years in the advanced capitalist world, with so many claiming Marx, the humanist Marx, Marx of *Economic and Philosophic Manuscripts of 1844*, as the West's very own as against the revolutionary Marx of *Communist Manifesto* and *Capital*, appropriated by the poor and oppressed in the East! Another adviser of Gorbachev, Oleg Bogmolov, head of what was then the 'Institute of Socialist Economics', discovered the benign 'convergence' 'under which capitalism and socialism get closer as they progress and will eventually meet as a single system', and saying 'A Farewell to the Primitive View of Socialism' wrote: 'The West is moving towards a better society, which it refers to as "post-industrial" and "information-based". We usually refer to that kind of society as the first stage of communism'! If the economist Shmelev came out with 'Shmelev's law' which stated that 'Everything which is economically efficient is moral', another economist Shatalin, a long-time Party member, asserting that 'humanity has not developed anything more efficient than a market economy (based on) private property and profit', added: 'The concept of a "democratic humane socialism" is an absurdity.' Yet another adviser Vadim Medvedev, Gorbachev's last 'Ideology Chief' (as he was officially called) hailed 'the market' as 'one of the greatest achievements of human civilisation' and saw in it the 'guarantee of the renewal of socialism'! Alexander Tsypko, once of the ideological department of the CPSU Central Committee openly asked, 'Is it worth risking the fate of the country...of perestroika, for a couple of words ("communism" and "socialism") which have long since become absurd?', and spoke up, in the Thatcherite manner, for 'the older, time-tested values' of 'neo-conservatism, neoliberalism, bypassing social democracy'. Tsypko criticised Marx for 'wanting to subject the logic of the economy to morality', which, incidentally, is as nice a statement of the basic impulse behind socialism as there is. Comment on all this is superfluous. It only remains to be added that Yeltsin too was a 'Marxist-Leninist' once, and a top ranking leader of the Soviet Communist Party.

The quickness and completeness of the conversion of one-time Marxists-Leninists to the new faith of the market was indeed amazing. The past was no longer even a distant memory. Myths of the market had taken over and there was little awareness now of the manifold evils that inevitably go with a market system, of what J.K. Galbraith once said while Eastern Europe was still nominally socialist: 'It is a grim but wholly unshakeable fact that no one in search of a better life would move from East Berlin to the South Bronx'. The attractions of consumerism and its culture were purveyed without restraint, precisely when even non-Marxist critics of capitalism were rejecting them, to say nothing of Marx's own critique and rejection one hundred and fifty odd years ago. The thought processes of the converts were the mirror image of their earlier Stalinist days: undifferentiated, non-contradictory, utopias laden with good tidings. Many had only substituted their earlier docile submission to 'the productive forces' of bureaucratic collectivist society for the imitative submission to the consumer forces of 'free market'. There was the simple-minded faith, at once evolutionist and utopian, in the magic of the market, blind eulogies of the West and the naive enthusiasm of the newly converted. An inversion of political formulas had occurred, with loyalties shifting from socialism to capitalism. Stalinist dogmas had been replaced with liberal dogmas, 'theology of Marxism-Leninism' with 'theology of the market'. 'Liberal fundamentalism' was the new creed as Boris Kagarlitsky called it. However the Soviet born-again celebrants of capitalism retained some of their polemical spleen and intolerance from their Stalinist past; only now it was: either capitalism or barbarism.

That these celebrants were only recently 'Marxist-Leninists', or even members of the Communist Party, brings to mind what Isaac Deutscher wrote thirty odd years ago. In his 'The Ex-Communists' Conscience', he had recalled how ex-communists do not just defend the values of the bourgeoisie but defend it with a traditional Stalinist dogmatism and intolerance. The ex-Communist's conscience had become a kind of collective identity for these new converts to 'liberal fundamentalism'.

Scholars have sometimes seen this as a retreat from Marxism. But in most cases the retreat had never occurred because those supposed to be retreating from Marxism were never ever there. They were never Marxists in any meaningful sense. All that had happened was that they, along with Gorbachev as we said earlier, had transited, in Richard Levins' words, from 'bullshit Marxism' to 'bullshit liberalism', the latter being as true a description as possible for the theory that dominated the last years of the Soviet Union.

XV

The absence of political freedom in the Soviet Union had inevitably led to a degeneration of its intellectual life, including its Marxism or Marxism-Leninism as they called it. If the latter's failure contributed to the rise and spread of liberal theory, the former ensured that its intellectual quality was no better than the Marxism-Leninism it was supplanting. The Soviet Union was identified and generally accepted as a socialist society and one guided by the principles of Marxism-Leninism. It is not surprising therefore that in turning away from the

Stalin-to-Brezhnev or now Gorbachev versions of 'socialism', an increasing number among the intelligentsia abandoned the authentic socialist vision, and its ideals and values as well. And in rejecting the hidebound Marxism-Leninism of the Party and the Soviet Academy they were throwing out all Marxism and Marxist analysis too. Instead, in trying to find a way out of the crisis, they were turning to advanced capitalist economy as a model and to the allegedly value-free bourgeois sociology and economics as a guide. But given their long-conditioned thought processes and the overall intellectual decadence, they carried the simple minded and sterile dogmatism of the Marxism-Leninism they had rejected into their newly discovered neo-liberal theory.

Central to the resurgent liberal discourse was its advocacy of the market and a general defence of capitalism. And its most distinguishing feature throughout was the absence of a single original idea. The virtues of the market were recounted and the consumerist capitalism admired, but almost invariably in the manner of parrots who had quickly mastered new words rather than scholars who had undergone a carefully considered change of heart. Not a revolution as the bourgeois media presented it to the world, but a counter-revolution was on in the Soviet Union, which had the rare distinction of not being fuelled by any reactionary ideology. What was acting as its motive force was nothing other than sheer mimicry – blind imitation of everything West! And this when the mimics had no idea of what this West was really like!

The liberals sang panegyrics to capitalism and the market. They wrote of 'a capitalist or, more precisely, a normal, civilised society', of the market's appeal to the 'real living individuals and their natural interests'. They thought of the USA, Germany, or Japan but did not think of Peru or Bolivia or Kenya. Capitalism was identified with democracy, and market with freedom and both were lauded in a manner that led many to observe that Thatcherism and Reaganism were probably more popular in the Soviet Union than these ideologies were in their home countries. Yet the virtues they were gushing over were those of the fairy tale image of capitalism to be found, if at all, in the writings of the bourgeois ideologues of nascent capitalism. Theirs was a romance with capitalism and the market which never existed in real life. The Yugoslav philosopher Mihalo Markovic suggested that they had accepted the simplified picture of 19th-century laissez faire capitalism presented in (old) Soviet propaganda and merely reversed the value signs: they had said it was bad, now they said it was good.

This is what Leo Panitch and Sam Gindin, who visited Soviet Union about this time, reported: 'we encountered remarkable naiveté about markets and capitalism even among very capable economists... .they are naively of the view that capitalism no longer exists in the West ...Such naiveté is a product of wishful thinking, a hope that a transition to market relations will be something less brutal and more democratic than it is likely to be.' That is how the advent of a highly stratified consumer society was being prescribed by the liberal reformers as the only practical means of dynamising a stagnant economy. They were beguiling themselves and their audiences with the imagery of an advanced industrial capitalism, without realising that this 'ideal' was reached after first passing through the historical ante-chamber of 'classical capitalism' with all its miseries and privations for the vast majority of the common people, and that any kind of 'recapitalisation' of the Soviet Union will immediately involve the loss of all the social welfare achievements of the old regime, really a road to disaster.

Taken in by the ideological constructs of neo-classical propaganda, the reformer economists refused to undertake a realistic analysis of the market. Indeed they gave little evidence of having studied the working of a real-existing free market – 'the idea of free market', it seems played less an economic role than an ideological or political one in the struggle against the entrenched *apparatchiks* and for clearing the road to capitalist restoration.

The 'free market', it is well to remember, is not that free. Of course capitalism does in a way advance freedom and equality as against the multiform bondage of a feudal order, its market does represent a certain area of freedom and personal choice – though even here the crucial issues are what freedom or choice and for whom? But to see the market above all – indeed only – as an area of freedom is not merely uncritical or one-sided but grossly misleading. For more than anything else, it is the arena of operation of 'the blind forces' of a capitalist economy and, therefore, in its essential character a system of coercions and compulsions – what with its law of accumulation of capital, generating growing wealth at one pole and deepening poverty at the other (not only within nations, but between rich nations and poor nations as well), its imperatives of competition, profit-maximisation, and the commodification of all social values and relationships. These coercions and compulsions determine the disposition of people and resources in ways which are anti-thetical to freedom, democracy and self determination – the values that are at the heart of socialism as a capitalism-negating project. The capitalist market is indeed an instrument of the invisible coercive power of the capitalist class. In fact, the neo-liberal votaries of 'free market' in the Soviet Union at the time were embracing the market precisely for its coercions. We have already noticed their animus against the Soviet working class. In their view, a major problem for Soviet economy was its overly indulged working class which, because of the system's social welfare achievements, including guaranteed employment, had escaped the precariousness of modern industrial existence, and could no longer be policed and disciplined to work by basic economic deprivations. The Soviet system lacked the arsenal of economic whips needed to stimulate gainful labour because, as the phrase went, 'nobody sleeps under a bridge in this country'. The market, with its inbuilt unemployment, or threat of unemployment, was to provide the requisite 'economic whips'.

If 'free market' was purveyed more as a myth than anything based on serious analysis, so was capitalism as a model working economy free of problems, without any assessment of the performance of any actually existing capitalism. Entirely missing from the neo-liberal discourse was any mention of the various long-term vices and wastes of capitalism, the multiple evils which even its apologists in capitalism's western homelands can no longer ignore and find difficult to defend – periodic crises of overproduction, mass unemployment, exploitation of one part of the world by another, wars, pillage of nature, stupendous wastage in the form of armaments production and expansion of a largely useless tertiary sector, and so much more that has inevitably been a part of history of capitalism. Nor was there even a trace of awareness of its contemporary problems, slowing down of growth, two-digit unemployment, two-digit inflation, rampant corruption, the fact that the capitalist world had been itself in the grip of a severe crisis for more than a decade then and no Keynes had been in sight to show it a way out. Instead, what was most admired about the western capitalism was its consumerism which even its more perceptive peddlers in the west were compelled to recognise and reject as evil. What is more, most often there was the unstated assumption that the capitalist system comprised only its developed, affluent centres in the USA, Western Europe and Japan, as if its underdeveloped peripheries, the third world underside with its capitalism-produced massive poverty, hunger, human misery and debt crises, did not exist. And if its existence did somehow got acknowledged, 'imperialism' was a forbidden word; there were only eulogies for the multi-national corporations, defence of 'economic growth' they promoted in the third world, advocacy of such market-oriented externally-funded economic growth, etc., etc. There was not an iota of awareness that all this only made for intensified imperialist pillage of the third world.

XVI

In the midst of the cacophonous sterility of the dominant discourse representing the major fractions of the Soviet ruling class, including the somewhat muffled conservative *apparatchiks* and the rather loud liberal technocrats, there was the faint but clear voice of the socialist opposition, the voice of Marxism that still survived in the Soviet Union and was being heard through small scattered groups in Soviet towns, research institutes and universities, though generally ignored by the media controlled by the ruling fractions and by western correspondents. The only ones to even attempt a serious analysis of what had gone wrong, this socialist opposition was and is still searching for its own way. On the ambiguous controversy over economic reform, they insisted that the market-plan debate was about mechanisms of regulation that in and of themselves do not determine the nature of a social system, and that the real issue is not economic but social and political, the issue of power in a socialist society, the power of the working people which alone can resolve the problems of economy in the interests of the people. Accordingly they argued for a 'rebirth of social ownership', power to the Soviets, spreading democracy well beyond the bounds conceived by Gorbachev and his reformist critics through self-management on the shop floor leading to self-government on the national scale, a revision of the old socialist model of 'one big factory', defending planning while attacking bureaucracy, admitting the need for incentives yet setting them in an egalitarian perspective, accepting a role for the market but subject to consumer regulation, and so on.

This socialist opposition was weak and scattered, and very much marginalised, yet, optimistically viewed, it was suggestive of a possible socialist movement in the future. Therefore, its voice, though faint, still deserves to be noticed. This is how it expressed itself at the time through Boris Kagarlitsky – before he succumbed to post-collapse 'realism' and friendship with the now financially well-endowed Gorbachev – who, insisting that we cannot do without theory, least of all without Marxism, said:

> Karl Marx's materialism did not at all assume humanity's simple dependence on the economy – this was known a long time before him – but rather a profound connection between the structure of society and the mode of production that formed within it. The task of socialists is precisely to change relations between people in the production process and not to redistribute property mechanically between rich and poor. This principled position has often been forgotten both by social-democrats with their redistributive socialism and by radicals of all kinds, inspired by the beautiful utopia of universal equality.
>
> We must find answers to many questions. Foremost among them is how to combine economic efficiency with the realization of the hopes of the masses for greater social justice. Here, partial measures to correct the 'extremes of the market' are of no use.

The only way that we can see is to include market relations within an overall structure of democratic planning and self-management, thereby using them to serve the interests of society. The market can serve as a guarantor and defender of individual interests, but it can never automatically serve common interests. For just this reason it cannot and must not occupy a central place in the system of values of a society striving to be democratic and humane. Each individual, irrespective of their talents, earnings and luck, must have the right to a dignified life. A society which turns this principle into its everyday practice will be a socialist society. People who have made this principle central to their lives must inevitably become socialists.

Today, as never before, we need a radical system of values. But this is insufficient. We must understand the dialectic of development, move away from past dogmas, overcome the simplified vision of progress as the accumulation of material values. Today, our country and the world need people capable of thinking dialectically; people who are governed by the interests of the masses and who have confidence in the masses; people who can combine theoretical knowledge with activism. Perhaps someone can see another path – although, personally, I cannot imagine that such a world view could develop other than within the Marxist tradition.

Marxism, which includes the heritage of the 'classical authors' and revisionists of all kinds, the neo-Freudian researches of Marcuse and Fromm, the materialist existentialism of Sartre, the refined analysis of Gramsci's *Prison Notebooks* and the contradictory but invariably stimulating revolutionary thought in the works of Trotsky, must, with all this richness, be viewed least of all as an aggregation of definitive and apocryphal texts. We need texts for one purpose only: to assimilate the lessons in critical method held within them, to form our own culture of thought and provide an impulse to a new theoretical analysis which will allow us to answer the questions facing us today.

Again:

Marxism is the path to European civilization, the path to a Western tradition, seen not as the shelves of a supermarket but as the real wealth of political, cultural and social experience in all its contradictoriness. While remaining ourselves we must overcome provincialism. We must open for ourselves a path to the world, which is not just the West. Finally, we must accomplish the historical and, for Russian culture, very difficult transition from 'Europeanism' and 'Westernism' to universalism. And Marxist internationalism can help us in this.

The slogan of a 'common European home', popularized by the Gorbachev regime, today serves as no more than a justification for definitively turning our backs on the majority of humanity, who live, as is well known, beyond the boundaries of Europe. The task is not only to fight for a workers' Europe which must replace the Europe of the translational corporations and bureaucrats, but to make this Europe part of a more just and humane world.

Fashionable talk about universal human values does not, in itself, help matters. In order to realize human rights in practice one must change political and social structures and, consequently, join in the struggle of the oppressed against the oppressors, exploited against exploiters. This is the key principle of Marxist ethics, without which appeals to the common good are suspended in mid-air or become a justification for the very mercenary policy of the ruling social strata in Russia or many Third World countries who dream of becoming integrated into the world ruling class and of thus receiving their share of the global cake.

It is now time to reject the hypnosis of liberal words and make a choice. Either with the ruling elites against the people or with the majority of humanity against everything which prevents them from living as human beings. This question confronts all of us today in various parts of the globe. But it is posed especially sharply in Russia. *Russia will again become part of a single world; the question is what sort of world will it be. The answer to this question depends to a significant degree on us.*

XVII

Gorbachev's perestroika, as we have seen, never really happened. Even otherwise, with its search for salvation in the market, it could never be a programme for 'renewal of socialism'. It was far more an attempt by the Soviet ruling class to save the system and perpetuate its reign by changing the methods of management and the manner of extracting surplus from its working people. In its failure perestroika ensured a most disorderly and ugly transition to capitalism in Russia, but in helping to dismantle the command economy, it also destroyed the foundation of the existing ruling class and thereby opened the way for the reconstitution of the ruling class in Russia. The destruction of the old economic order presented the neo-liberals with a unique historical opportunity to exploit the popular loss of confidence in complex collectivist solutions and large public institutions, to mobilise a sufficiently large bloc of Soviet society against the suddenly very vulnerable traditional egalitarian value-mix of social solidarity and the welfare state that was still surviving among the people in the Soviet Union. They were emboldened by the rapid collapse of the 'socialist' regimes in Eastern Europe and their turn to capitalism. And, ideological, economic and political pressure of global capitalism apart, the worldwide retreat of labour and communist or socialist movements, together with the collapse in Eastern Europe, not only lent credibility to their propaganda – 'the whole world has embraced the market' – but was an important factor in the relative ease with which the neo-liberal forces now hijacked the 'anti-bureaucratic revolution'. Way back in the mid-1930s, writing in the classic Bolshevik tradition, Trotsky had pointed out that the fate of the October Revolution was inextricably tied to the fate of Europe and of the whole world and that if no revolutions were victorious in the developed capitalist countries 'then a bourgeois counter revolution (in the USSR) rather than an uprising of workers against the bureaucracy will most likely be on the agenda'. This counter-revolution had now appeared on the agenda and as the assault for capitalism was mounted from above, there was no intervention from below to resist it.

Of course, throughout this period, there was one group which stood to benefit from democratisation of 'Soviet socialism' – the working class which now constituted an overwhelming majority of the population. But for reasons going deep into Soviet history, some of which we have noticed earlier, this working class lacked the power to take initiative and direct the reform process. It was what Marx calls a 'class-in-itself', as it exists, and not a 'class-for-itself', by which Marx meant a class which is conscious of its existence as a class, knows its immediate and long-term interests, and given the requisite organisation and leadership can carry them through. It is this class consciousness which makes the working class the most important and resolute force for a socialist project. The Soviet working class did not have the requisite class consciousness, organisation and leadership to either effectively intervene in the reform process or to resist the threatened transition back to capitalism. This does not, however, mean that the Soviet workers, or for that matter the Soviet people, were for capitalism. They never were as more than one American study of the subject during the Gorbachev era has documented. Even as late as May 1991, when the Russians were asked what kind of society they wanted, of those expressing an opinion a majority of 54 per cent chose some type of socialism, preferably 'a more democratic type of socialism'. The same poll found an equally strong support among the Russian public for government ownership of business. Only a minority of 20 per cent chose 'a free market form of capitalism such as found in the US and Germany' that the pro-capitalism Soviet leadership was now pushing for. It is clear, therefore, that the push towards capitalism was not a response to popular pressure in that direction but rather it was proceeding in the face of popular opposition. But this popular opposition never came to be mobilised against the turn to capitalism. The people themselves, depoliticised and 'deideologised', and deprived of any independent self-organisation over the years, were much too disenchanted, too alienated from the system for any intervention. Cynical and indifferent towards the turbulence around them, they had, if any, only one passion, a passive hostility to everything that was pro-establishment. They were in no mood to defend the so-called 'socialist system' against any one, in any manner. As for the Communist Party, supposedly the party of the proletariat, indeed its vanguard, it had turned into a den of bureaucracy, authoritarianism, hauteur, nepotisms and corruption. (What people thought of communists is clear from the fact that during the perestroika period, in order to win elections, communists often requested that they not be listed as communist!) Thoroughly discredited and dissociated from the people, and rotten to the core, far from mobilising the people against the capitalist turn, it could not even defend itself when it later came to be banned by Yeltsin.

It may be here noted that the Communist Party even in its degeneration presented a problem. Of course, it did not concern its top leadership which had already decided to be rid of all constraints of the popular classes and opted to be part of the reconstituted ruling class of capitalist Russia. The *nomenklatura* was only too eager to seize the emergent opportunity and turn into individually or collectively autonomous owners or holders of country's major economic assets and exploit the workers in 'normal', capitalist manner, that is extract surplus labour from them not politically but economically, via the market. But it was still problematic. Not only that there was 'conservative' opposition even at the leadership level, or that the lower levels and the ranks, let down and left confused by the leadership, disoriented and demoralised by glasnost, were anything but supportive of Gorbachevian policies, the Party itself still claimed to represent the working class and spoke in its name, and had its organised presence or dominant role in the workplace and institutions such as the army, KGB, etc. Its behaviour, therefore, had a certain unpredictability about it. Party organisations of the workplace could possibly come in the way of the shift from 'market reform' of the system to its replacement by capitalism that was now on the agenda of Gorbachev and his advisers. Gorbachev himself, who was till recently mouthing rhetoric about the Party as 'the guarantor of perestroika', sensed the obstacle the existence of the Party was or could be to this shift, and tried to push it to the sidelines in 1990 and a year later resigned as Party's General Secretary and advised the Party to 'honourably' dissolve itself, leaving the honour of banning it altogether to Yeltsin, with himself watching contentedly from the sidelines.

Be that as it may, with the Communist Party discredited and dissociated from the people and incapable of mobilising them against the capitalist turn, the only choices the working people were able to make were between different factions of the ruling elites. Gorbachev, associated with previous five years of failures at home and surrenders abroad where he allowed his country to be regularly humiliated by the West, receiving little barring advice on the virtues of the 'free market' in return for huge concessions in Afghanistan, Southern Africa, Central America and Eastern Europe, though still president of the Soviet Union, stood isolated and discredited among the people. No one felt sorry for him when Yeltsin and his associates pushed him out most unceremoniously and seized leadership with initial majority support by virtue of their aggressive opposition to the old system, better exploitation of mass sentiments, and their claim to favour democratisation of society. Though, characteristically enough, Yeltsin was to be soon the leader of that part of the old ruling elite that saw authoritarian capitalism as its best option. And he indeed led them to become one of the two most hated men in the ex-Soviet Union. The other was Gorbachev.

Incidentally, collapse of the president's power automatically entailed the liquidation of the Union as well. The feudal structure of power that had arisen and consolidated itself unavoidably linked the fate of the state institutions with the future of the ruler. This is not to deny the part played by Yeltsin's drive for power in the final break-up of the Soviet Union. Having no base of support outside Russia (to displace Gorbachev within the Union), he announced the death of the Union, and to that result, he suddenly arranged a 'Commonwealth' with the two other Slavic republics, Byelorussia and the Ukraine. Such was the inglorious end of the once great country, the other superpower called the Union of Soviet Socialist Republics.

XVIII

As with the effort to reform the system, the initiative *now* for a change to capitalism also came from above, from the ruling class itself. As already noted, the bulk of intelligentsia had by now turned towards capitalism to improve its prospects. Once relatively weak politically, with its majority subservient to the regime and a small minority voicing dissidence, it had acquired a very influential position now, thanks above all to glasnost and democratic reforms. With the system opening up, its members were even more aware and desirous of the living standards of their counterparts in the west. Divorced from the people, disoriented ideologically and disappointed with the old regime, their material interests impelled them to align with those seeking a change to capitalism. Another significant source of active support for the move to capitalism came from the relatively small but growing class of entrepreneurs that had seized the opportunity for small-scale private business provided by perestroika. There had already existed in the Soviet Union a black and grey market and informal economy and along with it, mafia and criminals apart, a class of illegal and semi-legal private business people, coming from the middle ranks of the *nomenklatura* and the new middle class, some of whom were quite wealthy and influential. Perestroika, with its 'marketisation' and 'privatisation' provided them with new avenues to grow further as well as legalise it all and acquire a legitimate standing in society. Their self-interest in a transition to capitalism was obvious. But however important the intelligentsia and the entrepreneurs, or other specific scientific, technocratic or cultural groups attracted by capitalist liberal democracy may have been, they were essentially *supporters* who joined it, they did not have the social and political power to effect the decisive break with the old regime and undertake the transition to capitalism. The decisive factor here was that the major part of the old political and economic elite, in leadership of the major central political and economic institutions – the communist party, state institutions, economic ministries in Moscow, etc. – had chosen to opt for capitalism. Almost all the leading advocates of capitalism came from backgrounds of high level political and economic positions in the old regime. In other words, it was the old ruling class of the Soviet 'socialist system' which had decided to change to capitalism.

Why should the old ruling class (including its non-technocratic, administrative-political fraction), thriving on the power and privileges central to a command economy, opt for capitalism without either any valid theoretical case being made for it or any lessons being drawn from the history of contemporary capitalism? This calls for an explanation and any satisfactory explanation has to be in terms of dynamics of class and class interests. Of course the Soviet rulers no longer had any knowledge of Marxism or genuine belief either in socialist ideology or that the system they were presiding over was a workers' state. Using whatever ideological device was available for the purpose, they operated as cynical pursuers of power and privilege, who however had become aware of how limited were the material privileges they enjoyed compared to the privileges of those who run the systems of the capitalist west. Once the 'socialist' reform project had failed, indeed culminated in the collapse of the economy, and the very sustainability of their system had come into question, rather than be ground down by its growing impossibility, they decided to scuttle it for a new system on terms they had a chance of controlling. As a ruling class, its primary commitment, like that of ruling classes or elites everywhere, was always, in reforming the system or otherwise, to its own survival as a ruling class. This was no longer possible in the 'old' way. That the Soviet ruling class had no *organic* relation with it, made it all the more easy and safe for them to scuttle the old system.

Capitalism offered the 'new' way, with the additional advantage that rather than merely managing the means of production, a capitalist transition would enable them to own them as well and to openly accumulate substantial personal wealth. Gorbachev's reforms had created the conditions or political space in which the *nomenklatura* could seize the means of production and make their 'revolution', that is break up the Soviet order not in the direction of democratic socialism but of a corrupt, upstart capitalism. The *nomenklatura* saw itself in the mirror of a west it had long envied and aspired to emulate. It seized the opportunity and proceeded to use its state power to effect the transition to capitalism. It would be part of the ruling bourgeoisie in a capitalist Russia. Having made this choice it attacked its own system, repeating all the outworn prejudices of the critique of socialism by bourgeois ideologues, but refrained from pointing out that the system it was abandoning had been marvellously effective in making possible its own constitution as a bourgeoisie. This scuttling of their own system by the Soviet rulers may have come as a surprise to western commentators and official Marxists or communists, but it was not really surprising at all. It was the logical terminus of a long evolutionary process not unamenable to Marxist understanding. Trotsky, for example, had long ago argued that, if it was not overthrown in time by the people, the Soviet bureaucracy would try to transform itself into a property-owning class. And Mao, who understood the evolution involved better than any other socialist in the Marxist tradition, had foreseen it even more clearly. This is what he told the cadres of the Chinese Communist Party – and the larger relevance is obvious – way back in 1963: 'You have constructed a bourgeoisie. Never forget that a bourgeoisie does not want socialism, it wants capitalism'.

With the custodians of the old system deciding to ditch it for capitalism, its fate was sealed. There was struggle for power at the top, but the issue of socialism, reformed or any other, simply vanished from the agenda. 'Marketisation' and 'Privatisation', the transition to capitalism, was the only issue left. And this involved which fraction of the ruling elite shall use the state power to effect this transition, how orderly shall be the end of the old regime and how disorderly the transition to capitalism, and what sort of capitalism it would be. In the power struggle, external pressures emanating from the major western governments, the international financial institutions which they control, such as the IMF and the World Bank, and the economic advisers who came with them, certainly played an important role. They added strength to the thrust for a market economy, and their promise of various forms of aid, whose attraction grew with the worsening economic situation, did give advantage in the domestic political struggle to the side favoured to secure it, supposedly favoured because of its commitment to a more rapid transition to a market economy. (Bush certainly took no chances with making his preference for Yeltsin known). But the shift from reform of socialism to capitalist transformation was not only primarily due to internal forces, it had come to be accepted by the major, more influential fractions of the ruling class in the Soviet Union.

In this situation, it hardly mattered if, in the ongoing political alignments or power struggle, Gorbachev lost or Yeltsin won. The clamorous personal rancour accompanying these alignments or struggle for power within the Soviet ruling class must not obscure the fact that all the major contenders, including the neo-liberals, were creatures of the very same *nomenklatura*, sharing the same class umbilical cord and had now the same basic commitment to capitalism. Again, if in the course of this power struggle, the CPSU came to be decreed out of existence and disbanded and thus possibly the only structure capable of holding the crumbling Soviet Union together destroyed, the significant fact was that it had long, even in Stalin's days, ceased to be a *communist* party and, at once powerful and impotent, though 19 million strong, it failed even to defend itself, leave alone its system, and collapsed ignominiously in just a few days, making for comparison with the collapse of Czarist power in February 1917. Of vastly greater significance was the demonstrated show of contempt of the people for the party. There was no protest, no revolt, nothing. The people simply did not care what happened to the party which was once upon a time and still claimed to be 'the Party of Lenin' – a good reminder of Mao's warnings about the dangers of degeneration in the communist movement. Yet again, the August Coup – an obviously amateurish and bungled job, with Yeltsin's as well as Gorbachev's dubious role in it – certainly hastened the demise of the old order. It enabled Yeltsin and his associates through 'an undeclared coup' of their own, to seize the dominant position in the tottering USSR, elbowing aside first the Communist Party and then Gorbachev himself and putting in power a 'new' political leadership that broke radically with October Revolution and everything it produced, and moved boldly ahead with a programme of transition to capitalism. But then the communiqué issued by the coup leaders' so-called 'Emergency Committee' on 19 August had nothing of the October Revolution or its revolutionary tradition either. Resoundingly devoid of any ideological basis or social content, it invoked the 'centuries old' tradition of the Russian nation and empire, but made no reference to socialism, Karl Marx or even Lenin. What is more, the Russians who failed and those who emerged victorious from the coup were both former members of, or advisers to the old *nomenklatura*.

This was indeed a typically significant fact about the denouement in the Soviet Union. No 'capitalists' proper were available in the country to restore capitalism. But while majority of high party or state officials migrated to the new Russian state administration and the lower sections of bureaucracy resisted change – not because of any socialist or Marxist commitment but power and privileges that state ownership and command economy fetched them – the small minority that went on to become a new 'entrepreneurial' class emerged from the *nomenklatura* in 'a shotgun marriage' with a mafia, if not a class, of blackmarketeers, hoarders and speculators. Even in Gorbachev's day, the first millionaires had come from the *nomenklatura*, along with the mafia of the underground economy. But with the President threatening to fight corruption, they were not entirely sure of their future. But the situation radically changed with Yeltsin's 'democratic' victory in August 1991, and we had even his supporters, like Popov, the ex-Mayor of Moscow, complaining that 'the *nomenklatura* of the CPSU without the CPSU have taken complete control in order to promote reform, but above all to profit from it'. *Nomenklatournyi capital* ('nomenklatura capital') had indeed arrived and was recognised as such. After years of pro-capitalist 'ideological bombardment', capitalism was being referred to by its true name and no longer as 'normal society'. But if *nomenklatura* had thus remained on top in the new, post-Soviet dispensation as well, even those sections of the old ruling class which had neither the imagination nor the material interest to envisage or enthusiastically push through alternatives to communist structures, managed to stay in power using national or ethnic chauvinism and other sectarian devices so that many post-Soviet independent republics came to be ruled not so much by anti-communists as by former communists with a new political base. In other words the past that was *nomenklatura* continued to live and thrive in the post-Soviet present. It was a case of 'communists who have overthrown communism', and then reaped the rewards through cooptation of their ideological opponents, the 'liberals' and 'democrats', as they were called. Not only was Yeltsin a former communist, but 75 to 80 per cent of his ruling stratum, and the presidents and ruling structures of the former Soviet republics were communists, with about half of them being from Brezhnev's day, and the other half Gorbachev's very own. Again, honest as ever, Gavriil Popov recognised the seeming paradox. A revolution, he said in substance, finds expression in the overthrow of a ruling class – as in France in 1789 and as in Russia in 1917 – but this time the same class had remained in power!

It was, perhaps, this fact which helps to explain the relatively peaceful character of the overthrow of a political system once notorious for its ruthlessness. But however peaceful this transfer of ruling power at the top, the turmoil below accompanying the collapse of the old order was anything but peaceful for the common people, though the worse was still ahead of them as the *nomenklatura* now in power went on to become the bourgeoisie of tomorrow, directly appropriating the means of production in the form of private property, through illicit transfer of public wealth to private hands and a general 'mafia-ization' of the economy. Instead of modern western capitalism, the former Soviet Union soon acquired '*mafiosi* capitalism', worse even than most capitalisms in the third world.

XIX

The Soviet state was born of the socialist revolution of October 1917. Despite the loss of its revolutionary or socialist character over the years, it progressed and went on to build a much-deformed socialist system and become the second most powerful state in the world, a super-power. In 1985, following a decade of growing social and economic crisis of the system, and in response to it, the Soviet leadership under Gorbachev initiated the reform programme known as perestroika. Six years later the Soviet state along with its 'socialist' system collapsed and Russia and the other states formed out of the disintegrated USSR, moved on to establish capitalist economic systems in their countries.

There is no denying that pressure from world capitalism, direct or otherwise, was a constant factor throughout the life of the Soviet Union. It ranged from armed intervention of the opening years and the later invasion by Hitler's armies, to efforts to strangle it economically in various ways, subversion by radio and television and secret intelligence services, the imposition of the cold war and its burden of military expenditure, and so on. Over these seventy years and more there was a virtual mobilisation of counter-revolution all over the world, in various forms, from fascism to the most refined social democratic reformism, all mobilised in defence of the capitalist social order and to undermine and destroy the Soviet Union. This was a mobilisation by the capitalist world on a permanent footing. There was also the more subtle external pressure emanating from West's economic superiority, its better performance in the systemic competition with the Soviet Union, and its species of capitalism that had sustained and strengthened itself by compromising in various ways with popular interests and energies. It is tempting therefore to attribute the Soviet collapse to the external pressure, to secret or open machinations of the capitalist world. But that would be patently wrong. The Soviet Union had survived all this for more than seventy years to become an industrially developed, economically viable and politically powerful state. It had even achieved military parity with the capitalist world, eliminating the possibility of a military conquest by the time the reform process started in 1985. As has been well pointed out, if capitalist pressure and machinations have not been able to eliminate Fidel Castro right on the US doorstep, they cannot be supposed to have engineered the remarkable collapse of the Soviet super-power.

Therefore, while the external pressure and machinations were a factor in the Soviet process of the Gorbachev period, the process itself was driven primarily by forces internal to the Soviet system. Our argument has constantly drawn attention to these forces and made it abundantly clear that the basic causes of the crisis and its denouement in the collapse of the system must be sought in the historical evolution of class and strata relations in the post-revolutionary Soviet society, in the deeper-lying structural contradictions that came to exist at the material base of this society, which also involved a total lack of internal democracy in the system, at both the party and state levels. It is in this context that the 'external' had also become the internal and sharpened all the economic and political contradictions of the system. And it is in this context too that individuals and personalities, as also accidental factors, played their part in the Soviet process.

Even so, a question remains. From crisis to reform to an amazingly rapid and peaceful collapse of a system that until recently seemed quite stable and relatively successful, and its turn from whatever kind of socialism it had to capitalism – what happened in the Soviet Union was an unusual historical development. Well-established social systems do not normally collapse suddenly in the absence of violent revolution or military defeat. And in the Soviet Union we had neither, nor anything even remotely similar. The Soviet system was indeed facing a crisis, but a comparable situation can well be noticed in this connection. In the 1930s the United States experienced a depression that was, if anything more severe than the Soviet crisis that began in the mid-1970s. There was tremendous dissatisfaction with the established system, that is, capitalism. But the crisis did not lead to any economic or political collapse. Capitalism managed to survive, making changes and adjustments, accepting reforms, none of which altered the basic institutions of the system. (Capitalism also survived in other major capitalist countries hit by the Great Depression). Why did the Soviet crisis of 1975–85, and the reform efforts which followed it, produce a totally different outcome?

An obvious answer is that the capitalist crisis threw up a leader of the calibre of Roosevelt, wise and farsighted enough to work out and impose a set of reforms that served to stabilise and save the capitalist system. The Soviet crisis produced nothing comparable. Gorbachev was simply not equal to the situation – a poor specimen of a human being, as a leader poor both in theoretical understanding and political commitment, and without wisdom in the choice of his advisers. We shall return to this aspect of the matter later. Immediately, beyond the issue of leadership which is indeed most relevant, it is important to note a more basic difference in the two situations. When capitalism faced the crisis of the Great Depression, more than a good or adequate leadership, it had a ruling class of capitalists determined to save the system, if not by reform or concessions (as in the United States and Sweden), then by repression (as in Germany and Italy). The alternative system threatening them from within, socialism, would have meant complete loss of their privileged position in society. In the Soviet Union it was quite different. The leaders of the Russian Revolution and the early Soviet State believed that they were creating a workers' state; they were committed to its defence and development along socialist lines. But as Soviet society grew into a class system, while it had a ruling class, unlike the capitalists, it did not own the means of production. And they had no longer any genuine belief in socialism either; it was only a matter of received ideology and tradition which, of course, had their usefulness for purposes of legitimisation. Thus the Soviet ruling class had no organic, structural ties with the Soviet 'socialist' system, and any genuine democratic reform of this system would have spelled the end of their power and privileges. (And they did not have even formal or 'bourgeois' democracy to smoothen contradictions of their system and better legitimise it). In other words, the Soviet system had singularly failed, all the more because of its undemocratic nature, to develop a ruling class with an abiding interest in protecting and defending the system over which it presided. Rather, as a ruling class which only controlled but did not own the means of production and whose ideology, even at its best, equated socialism with development of productive forces – its members were more susceptible to abandoning the Soviet system, with the hope that they could actually come to own and profit from owning the means of production in a new system. As a consequence, once the system went into serious social and economic crisis, which in the end was even making the existence of the old system or privileges impossible, the bulk of the old ruling elite deserted the system and opted for capitalism, the alternative which, far from threatening their privileges, promised their retention, even enhancement, albeit in a different form. Hence also the rapid and peaceful collapse of what was only recently a stable and relatively successful socio-economic system.

The Soviet collapse and turn to capitalism, was thus a 'revolution from above', really a counter-revolution, made by the ruling class itself, and not 'a people's revolution from below', as anti-Soviet critics sometime make out. The people, themselves alienated from the system and long depoliticised, were simply hustled into acquiescence to the new dispensation offered by their old rulers. In not intervening in defence of *their* interests, the Soviet people lost even what they had in the old system – full employment, generous social security arrangements, subsidised education and health care, stable prices, rationed food in reasonable quantities, ample clothing even though somewhat unimaginative in design and quality, and music and culture organised for the millions. And with all this they also lost their past, the past of a thousand disappointments no doubt, but also of a thousand glories, of achievements unprecedented in history, which won them the love and admiration of the poor and oppressed the world over, and once made them the hope for the future of humankind.

The loss, as we have noticed more than once, was equally grievous for the people elsewhere. Its deformations notwithstanding, socialists everywhere, even as they hoped for rectification, had an interest, indeed a personal and political stake in the existence of the Soviet Union. There is a similarity between what the October Revolution meant for the rest of the world positively and the negative effects of this lost, missed, opportunity to restore that revolution. If the deformed socialism of the Soviet Union was, in one way or another, a determinant of the most basic developments in other countries (including anarchism of rebellion of the 1960s in the West and cultural revolution in China), its final collapse explains the recharged popularity of the rhetoric of the market, widespread disillusionment with revolutionary political praxis and the near universal triumph of what Sloterdijk calls 'cynical reason' in the omnipresent consumerism of the post-modern today.

XX

As the Soviet Union collapsed, a view current even in the United States was that the Soviet people 'self-destructed'. This rather apt description of what happened underlines that in recognising the more basic or objective causes underlying large historical processes we must not only not ignore or obscure the contingent factors but pay due attention to the role of human action, or inaction, which can be, and often is, of decisive importance in determining the outcome. There are no inevitabilities here, no unconditional necessities. This is very much true of what happened in the Soviet Union. Therefore, whatever other contributing causes there were, the main responsibility for the failure of socialism in the Soviet Union must rest on the Soviet leadership and its apologists over a very long period which does not exclude the Stalin era. This is surely clear from our account so far. But decisive for its final collapse was the leadership that Gorbachev provided to the Soviet system in its crisis. We have already noticed the utter poverty of this leadership in matters of theory as well as practice. Put in power to reform and save the system, his perestroika and glasnost released social forces which eventually destroyed the system and produced the subsequent rush towards capitalism. As it happened, the chequered process of attempted reform of the system, whose undemocratic nature, now as before, ruled out any popular course-correcting intervention, led to the development of an alliance of groups and classes that favoured a transition to capitalism. The increasingly chaotic political and economic situation resulting from the reform process only made for still greater alienation of the people, mass desertion of the system by the old ruling elite and the political dominance of those seeking a rapid capitalist transformation. The ignominious collapse of the old Soviet system and the 'shock therapy' turn towards capitalism were only the culminating episodes in the six-year old drama which was the Gorbachevian reforms.

Thus, while the compulsions in the objective situation making for the downfall of the Soviet system must not be overlooked, and nor do we need to doubt at least Gorbachev's initial intention to 'renew socialism' as he understood it, his personal responsibility for collapse of the Soviet system and destruction of the Soviet Union remains. It was the Soviet people's tragedy that, in its hour of crisis, it could throw up only the likes of Gorbachevs or Yeltsins as leaders. And it speaks volumes for the degeneration of the system and its ruling communist party that these men who either cherished no communist belief ever or soon discarded whatever belief they ever had, could climb all the way up the party and state hierarchy – one to become general secretary, no less, of the party of the entire USSR and President of the Union, the other the supreme party boss in Moscow, the nation's central citadel, before he deserted for the more green capitalist pastures. We have said enough about Gorbachev's theory and practice as the leader in command of the reform process. It only needs to be recalled that while in command, from his early pronouncement for socialist reforms, including the historic speech at a small Siberian town in 1986, calling for a 'societal revolution' in the Soviet Union, to the day when he was unceremoniously pushed out of power by Yeltsin at the end of 1991, Gorbachev never had a clear perspective on where he wanted to go. Symbolising both the crisis and its basic contradictions he continued to contribute to both, all the while setting in motion forces that he did not understand and could not control, and whose consequences he could not predict. He dithered all along, somersaulted on every major issue, indulged in ad hoc manipulation of goals, visions and values, zigzagged to the Right and to the Left, and steadily slid downwards in his politics, from the initially high to lower and lower moral, political and constitutional ground until he finally lost out. In the process he moved from reform socialism to market socialism to a panicky full-scale privatisation and restoration of capitalism; from the early 'socialist option' to the soda-pop social democracy he offered as 'Party Programme' during his last days in power; from one-party democratisation to multiparty system to the disbanding and decreeing away the CPSU itself; from the initial rejection to eventual acceptance of the republics' full right to self-determination or the Draft Treaty of Union – where even the words 'Soviet' and 'socialist' disappear from the name of the country Gorbachev was presiding over – to acquiescence in the final disintegration of the Soviet Union; etc., etc. The only constant concern of his theory and practice as a leader, indeed his obsession was, not for defending the values he regularly proclaimed, or 'the socialist system' he was the custodian of, or the integrity of the country whose first citizen he was, but for the preservation of his personal power in the Kremlin. And even this he could not defend. It is not without merit that a commentator, Michael Dobbs, writing in *Washington Post*, later observed:

> With hindsight of course it is now clear that Gorbachev's historical mission was not to succeed but to fail. He was practically illiterate about economics and had no clear strategy for transforming the Soviet Union into a modern country. In attempting unsuccessfully to tinker with the Soviet system he brought it crashing down around him. This was his greatest achievement. Gorbachev's genius was that he fooled himself and great many other clever people into believing there was a master plan.

Hobsbawm saw Gorbachev simply as a 'passionate and sincere communist reformer' whom events turned into a 'tragic figure'. Viewing the chaos and destruction unleashed by his policies, others are more apt to view Gorbachev as criminally naive if not worse. A former editor of *The Times* (London), William Rees-Mogg had this to say of Gorbachev: 'brilliant when measured in days, persuasive in weeks, mediocre in months and disastrous in years'.

No wonder that Gorbachev who was in power for years, six long years in fact, managed to destroy the Soviet 'socialist' system and his country called the Soviet Union. He helped capitalism ensure the demise, without the expenditure of a single shot, of the great Union of the Soviet Socialist Republics, a task at which its adversaries had been working tirelessly for over seven decades without success, which had earlier proved beyond the pale of the Kolchaks and Denikins, of Winston Churchill, of Adolf Hitler, of John Foster Dulles and John Kennedy, and, without him or others like him, would have remained beyond the pale of Reagans and Bushes too. As the American magazine *Newsweek*, summed it up: 'Without Gorbachev, the Soviet Union would still exist'.

The destruction done, Gorbachev claimed it as the achievement of a lifetime, the fulfilment of 'the main purpose of my life, namely elimination of the totalitarian system'. 'Saying all this straight and honest' in his resignation speech, Gorbachev said:

> ....not once have I regretted that I did not take advantage of the post of (CPSU) general secretary only to rule as a Czar for several years. I considered it irresponsible and amoral...I am convinced of the historic correctness of the democratic reforms which were started in the spring of 1985.
>
> ...work of historic significance has been accomplished. The totalitarian system which deprived the country of an opportunity to become successful and prosperous long ago has been eliminated...

Hours before being evicted from the Kremlin by the Yeltsin dispensation in the final act of disintegration of his country, the ex-General Secretary and still the nominal Soviet President, told *Time* magazine: 'My life's work is done. I think that in my place others would have given up long ago.' Gorbachev also told his American interviewers: 'I feel at peace with myself.'

Ousted from power, Gorbachev has since gone round the world with self-congratulations, giving pedestrian interviews and scribbling newspaper columns, defending the 'correctness' of his perestroika, telling all and sundry what a 'moral' person he has always been and invariably insisting: 'I am at peace with myself'. And why not? – with the Nobel Prize through American patronage, being feted and awarded by the likes of Ronald Reagans and the rest, million-dollar foundations in USA. Russia and elsewhere in his name, agents and publishers lining up to sign up the former president for his flabby speeches and ghost-written books, touring day-night circuits with an appearance fee of 12,5000 dollars for one hour speech (which has to be translated from Russian), lucrative offers from casino owners in Las Vegas and university Presidents elsewhere in America, and equally lucrative television and video recordings, etc., etc. As a spokesman for one of the best known agencies in the field said at the time: 'With right sort of marketing Gorbachev could become an extremely hot property'. And Gorbachev has been well-marketed for the services rendered to world capitalism. Of late there is occasional grumbling about West's lack of 'understanding' or 'reciprocity', a let-down and not getting a fair deal, but the marketing goes on with syndicated columns, cameo appearance in arty films, ads for Apple

Computers in Germany and the fast food giant, Pizza Hut, of the US, Gorbachev said he badly needed the pizza largesse for one of his many foundations (*Foundation de la Research Institute*). And 'the last remaining global leader', as an American blurb has it, still no wiser about the market, keeps swinging around the world, hawking his 'new thinking' and the 'highly valued role' of 'my foreign partners of those years', gushing over 'freedom', 'democracy' and 'social justice', and moralising about 'a new value system', about 'Christian and Buddhist values' and 'oneness with each other', about 'virtuous living', 'self-restraint', 'limiting desires' and 'virtue of enoughness', indeed everything which, according to him, 'the ancients knew' – and promising 'a new civilisation' at the end of it all!

And this is not all. Even as he writes self-justificatory memoirs, laments 'a wasted decade' in Russia and admires 'President Putin's realism', Gorbachev keeps improving upon his claims to have destroyed 'the system'. As a report of his recent speech before an appreciative audience in Holland has it: 'he was thinking of destroying the system when he was not yet even a member of the Politburo. He said he intentionally sought General Secretaryship because no other post provided him with the possibility of destroying it from above'. The minion sure knows how to ask for more rewards for the services rendered.

Life has been a prolonged extravaganza for Mikhail Gorbachev since the demise of the Soviet Union – in stark contrast to the growing unemployment and impoverishment, misery and suffering, and humiliations of daily life of the ordinary citizen in his country. No wonder the people have only contempt now for this former President. And they have since missed no opportunity to show this, in elections or otherwise. As the Russian academic Gregory Kotovsky, basing himself on public opinion polls, has told us, Gorbachev is today one of the two most hated persons in Russia; the other is Yeltsin.

What specimen of a man indeed, this Gorbachev – a true representative of the degenerate tribe that the self-proclaimed 'Party of Lenin', the Communist Party of Soviet Union, had become.

XXI

To say all this of Gorbachev is only to suggest that what happened in the Soviet Union was not inevitable. There were other possibilities. The situation as it developed in the Soviet Union, or earlier in Eastern Europe, in the words of a well-known formulation, was that those below were no longer willing and those above were no longer able to go on in the old ways. This objective situation certainly carried within it the theoretical possibility of a leap forward in the direction of genuine socialism. As always in such situations, it is politics which was of decisive importance. But it did not have to be, necessarily, the politics of a reformist turn to the right that soon yielded to a politics which, in a parody of revolution, described itself as 'radical' and ended up in a counter revolution. It could have been, not rhetorically but really a politics of 'renewal of socialism', of finding 'answers within socialism' and not in the market. The policies could have been debated in terms of socialist principles, party shaken out of its bureaucratic inertia and people reached out in a genuinely democratic effort to build up a movement capable of making the necessary reforms and adjustments, confronting bourgeois alternatives and finding a new revolutionary path. An aroused and motivated Soviet people, led properly, surely had the capability to turn things around. With a stronger, better equipped and more committed leadership it was certainly possible to work out, within a broadly socialist framework, an intelligently conceived, competently researched, properly considered and consistently implemented plan of reforms that would have brought steady improvements to the situation in the economy, in politics and ideology, and with regard to the festering national question. At the very least, such a plan, as a modest exercise, could have remedied the most glaring defects in Soviet economy and politics, provided for cautiously planned but effective democratisation in both areas, accommodated market and private production within limits, and reached out to the people to explain things to them and involve them in the reform process, thus sustaining the system, improving its economic and political potential and keeping it intact and open for a genuine 'socialist option' in the future. Or, 'socialist renewal' could be taken more seriously, and with the necessary theoretical as well as ideological-political preparation over a period of time, bringing the mass of working people actively into politics of the reform process, a beginning could right away be made for a decisive turn in behalf of the 'socialist option'. The objective situation, especially the degeneration of the communist party made this highly unlikely, but not impossible for a bold and committed leadership.

Possibilities other than Gorbachev were certainly there just as they are there for the future as well. As Paul Sweezy, in an interview at the time, said:

> To be sure, the collapse that I considered to be quite probable was not the only possible outcome of the crisis of the Soviet system. I do not believe in any sort of infallible linear determinism in history. The contradictions that pervade every society find their resolution in diverse responses according to their class content. That is to say, there was always the possibility that the Soviet regime would fall to the right (which happened) or that it would evolve (or fall) to the left. This last possibility, which is now impossible in the near future, remains nonetheless the order of the day for history, not only because history is endless, but especially because it is doubtful that the solution of the right can stabilize the societies of the East, even in the intermediate term. The struggle for another solution to their tribulations will therefore continue.

EPILOGUE

Your 'order' is built on sand. The revolution will raise its head again and proclaim to the sound of trumpets: 'I was.... I am.... I shall always be'... *Rosa Luxemburg*
the day before her assassination (1919)

They may be able to kill all the flowers, but they will never hold back the spring. *Pablo Neruda*

In the last resort, the whole of Marxism may be summed up in the statement: rebellion is justified. *Mao Tse-tung*

Be practical! Do the impossible! *Rebel students of Paris, 1968*

The art of the possible can only be restrained from engrossing the whole universe if the impossible can find ways of breaking back into politics, again and again. *Edward Thompson*

"Proletarian revolutions... criticise themselves constantly, interrupt themselves continually in their own course, come back to the apparently accomplished in order to begin it afresh, deride with unmerciful thoroughness the inadequacies, weaknesses and paltriness of their first attempts, seem to throw down their adversary only in order that he may draw new strength from the earth and rise again, more gigantic, before them, recoil ever and anon from the indefinite prodigiousness of their own aims, until a situation has been created which makes all turning back impossible, and the conditions themselves cry out: *Hic Rhodus, hic salta*! (Here is the rose, dance here!) *Karl Marx*

Index of Names

Index of Subjects